W9-AOB-544

PROCEEDINGS OF THE THIRD INTERNATIONAL TURFGRASS RESEARCH CONFERENCE

Sponsored by the International Turfgrass Society, July 11–13, 1977, Munich, West Germany

James B. Beard, editor

James B Beard

Published by
The American Society of Agronomy, the Crop Science Society of America,
the Soil Science Society of America, and
the International Turfgrass Society
Madison, Wisconsin, USA

Library of Congress Cataloging in Publication Data

International Turfgrass Research Conference, 3d,
Munich, 1977.
Proceedings of the third International Turfgrass Research Conference.

Bibliography
Includes index.
1. Turfgrasses—Congresses. 2. Turf management—Congresses. I. Beard, James B. II. American Society of Agronomy. III. Title.
SB433.I57 1977 635.9′642 80-15862
ISBN 0-89118-061-3

The American Society of Agronomy, Inc.
677 S. Segoe Road, Madison, Wisconsin, USA 53711

Printed in the United States of America

FOREWORD

It is again our pleasure and professional opportunity to collaborate with the International Turfgrass Society (ITS) in the publication of these proceedings of the Third International Turfgrass Research Conference. Members of the American Society of Agronomy (ASA), the Crop Science Society of America (CSSA), and the Soil Science Society of America (SSSA) have actively participated in the Conference and thus all four collaborating societies share in presenting this written record in the conviction that it will provide useful documentation to the pursuit of turfgrass science in all parts of the world.

ITS is now more than a decade old. It was organized on the occasion of the First International Turfgrass Research Conference in Harrogate, England, in July 1969. The Second Conference, held in Blacksburg, Virginia, 19–21 June 1972, gave strong evidence of the truly international scope of turfgrass science. Not only were there more scientists present from outside the United States than from within, but total attendance for that second conference was double the first.

And now the efforts of 91 scientists from 12 countries as reported during the July 1977 meetings in Munich, Germany, are recorded here. Thus, an expanding breadth and diversity of participants should provide the individual working as a turfgrass researcher, extension specialist, classroom teacher, industry representative, or practicing turfgrass professional manager with insights and perspectives that will strengthen each one's capacity to perform their chosen roles.

And again participation grows—in the 1977 conference there were 266 participants from 19 countries, an increase over the second conference of 74 participants.

We congratulate all those who shared in making this contribution possible, who labored to present this current summary of turfgrass science in a condensed source to assist all who pursue the field.

Roger L. Mitchell, President
American Society of Agronomy

William E. Larson, President
Soil Science Society of America

Billy E. Caldwell, President
Crop Science Society of America

PREFACE

The future quality of life of man on this earth would be bleak without the aesthetic and functional contributions of turfs and ornamental plants. Man has chosen to cultivate turfgrasses for his benefit since the 13th century when turfs, as we know them today, started to evolve in England. The culture of turfs has increased steadily during the past four centuries in the industrialized countries of the world. The continuing effort to seek an improved quality of life is one that people will not readily abandon. In fact, the proper use of plants in environmental manipulation is an important aspect that is receiving greater attention than ever before. The willingness to invest time and money in maintaining turfs in order to provide a more favorable environment for human activities is evidence that turfs are an important aspect in a desirable quality of life.

In the future there will no doubt be changes in the types of turfs and the ways they will be maintained. These changes will be affected by higher energy costs for maintenance and more limited water supplies in many locations. We will need turfgrasses and cultural practices that require less energy and water inputs, but at the same time continue to provide quality, functional turfs to meet the needs of a modern society. These projected changes present us with a challenge and justification for turfgrass research that is greater than it has ever been. As a science, turfgrass culture is just in its infancy compared to most areas of applied plant science.

The first concepts of an International Turfgrass Research Conference evolved during discussions between Bjarne Langvad and myself at East Lansing, Michigan, in the fall of 1966. The initial projection was that if 20 persons attended the first conference it would be judged successful. In fact, the First International Turfgrass Research Conference held in 1969 at Harrogate, England, had 83 registrants representing 13 countries, with 99 papers presented. The second conference, held at the Virginia Polytechnic Institute and State University in the United States in 1973, had 247 registrants from 15 countries, with 80 research papers presented. Most recently, at the third International Turfgrass Research Conference in Munich, West Germany, 229 persons attended from 17 countries, with 95 papers presented. Participation at these conferences is strong evidence of the growing interest and activity in turfgrass research and education.

The *Proceedings* represents a permanent record of the concepts, research results, and descriptive information presented at the conference. It is particularly significant that this is the only publication which brings together a summary of the representative research activities currently being conducted throughout the world. The *Proceedings* facilitates communications among turfgrass researchers and educators.

As editor, I would like to express appreciation for the cooperation and very hard work of the Editorial Board members and Domenic Fuccillo in preparation of the *Proceedings.* The Associate Editors assumed responsibility for conducting the initial review for specific subject matter areas. Each paper was reviewed by a minimum of three turfgrass scientists, with at least one reviewer being from a European country. The cooperation of individual authors during the revision of manuscripts is also appreciated.

Two types of papers were approved for publication. The first portion of the *Proceedings* contains research papers which represent a new contribution to the scientific field and which test hypotheses through replicated treatments that can be analyzed statistically to establish the validity of the investigation. The second group of papers are Observational Notes which make a contribution to the general knowledge in the field through descriptions of turfgrass conditions or problems that are being reported for the first time. Finally, the meeting minutes and official actions of the International Turfgrass Society, a glossary of the turfgrass terms used in the *Proceedings*, and a subject index, are included in the back of the book.

As with its two predecessors, this *Third International Turfgrass Research Conference Proceedings* will serve as a valuable reference for turfgrass researchers, teachers, adult education instructors, research and development specialists with private companies, and students of Turfgrass Science. The ultimate goal is that through the information contained in the *Proceedings* the public will benefit from lower cost, simplified turfgrasses and cultural systems which still retain their important functional and aesthetic benefits and thus enhance the physical, mental, and environmental quality of life for the peoples of this earth.

James B. Beard
Turfgrass Physiologist
Texas A&M University
College Station, Texas

CONTENTS

SECTION III ENVIRONMENT STRESS

SECTION IV SOIL REACTION, FERTILIZATION, AND ROOT ZONE MODIFICATION

SECTION V WEED CONTROL

SECTION VI DISEASES AND NEMATODES

SECTION VII CULTURAL PRACTICES AND SYSTEMS

SECTION VIII SOD PRODUCTION AND ESTABLISHMENT

SECTION IX OBSERVATIONAL NOTES

PARTICIPANTS & CONTRIBUTORS*

W. A. Adams*	Soil Science Unit, University College of Wales, Aberstwyth, United Kingdom
K. Ahti*	Northrup-King & Co., 1500 Jackson St., N.E., Minneapolis, Minnesota 55413
G. L. Akesson	AB Hammenhoks Fro, 270 50, Hammenhok, Sweden
D. E. Aldous*	Environmental Horticulture, Massey University, Palmerston North, New Zealand
Manfred Altenburg-Herfurth	Ringstr. 17, 3302 Cremlingen 1, Germany
Jan Andringa	Cebeco-Handelsraad, Plantage Willem 111, Elst (Utr.), Netherlands
G. Arnal*	Laboratoire Regional de l'Ouest Parisien 12, Rue Leisserenc de Bort BP 108, 78 195 Trappes Cedex, France
Jobst von Arnim	Versuchsstation Christinenthal, 2211 Christinenthal, Germany
J. M. Audy	FNAMS, 9, Rue des Fleures, 49000 Angers, France
Giacomo Barabino	Interachem SA-15, Cendrier-Centre, 1201 Geneva, Switzerland
Hans Baukloh	Kleinwanzlebener Saatzucht AG, Postfach 146, 3352 Einbeck, Germany
J. B. Beard*	Department of Soil & Crop Sciences, Texas A&M University, College Station, Texas 77843
Philipp Berner*	Saatzucht Steinach, D-8441 Steinach uber Straubing, West Germany
J. Beving*	Institute for Land & Water Management Research, P.O. Box 35, 6700 AA Wageningen, The Netherlands
S. W. Bingham*	Plant Pathology & Physiology Department, Virginia Polytechnic institute and State University, Blacksburg, Virginia 24061
G. R. Blake*	Soil Science Department, University of Minnesota, St. Paul, Minnesota 55108
P. Blumberg	S/48 Grunanlagen GmbH, Holzhausenstr. 18, 5020 Frechen 5, Germany
P. P. Boekel*	Lutsborgsweg 68, Haren (Gr.), Netherlands
Peter Boeker	Institut für Pflanzenbau, Katzenburgweg 5, 5300, Bonn, West Germany
Bernard Bonay	Veyret 16, Rue Cortambert, 75016, Paris, France
R. W. Bond	26 Corning Road, Willowdale, Ontario, M2J 2L7, Canada
P. Boskovic	Sport Object Adviser, Dr. Ribara 1, 21000 Novi Sad, Yugoslavia
Bernard Bourgoin*	Station d'Amelioration des Plantes Fourrageres, 86600 Lusignan, France
Peter Bowen	Fisions Ltd., Levington Research Station, Levington, Ipswich, Suffolk, IP10 OLU, United Kingdom
S. E. Brauen*	Western Washington Research and Extension Center, Puyallup, Washington 98371
H. G. Brod*	Justus-Liebig Univ., Bottengasse 12, 6308 Butzbach 8, West Germany
Jurgen Bronner	Im Johannistal 11, 5600 Wuppertal 1, West Germany
Richard Brunner	Sachsenspiegelstr. 11, 8000, Munchen 50, West Germany

* All names followed by an asterisk indicate contributors.

34

Koos de Bruyn	Barenbrug Holland, b.v. Postfach 4, Arnhem, Netherlands
P. J. Bryan*	Estates and Valuation Department, Kent County Council, Springfield, Maidstone, England
Gunther Buchner	Neckarstr. 33, 6146 Alsbach-Bergstr., Germany
Irmfried Burckhardt	Kleinwanzlebener Saatzucht AG, Postfach 146, 3352 Einbeck, Germany
Andreas Burg	Grieselstr. 32c, 8903 Bobingen, Germany
Herbert Burkhart	BayWa AG, Arabellastr. 4, (Sternhaus), 8000 Munchen 81, West Germany
Walter Buring	Compo GmbH, Postfach 2107, 4400 Munster, West Germany
R. E. Burns*	Georgia Experiment Station, Experiment, Georgia 30212
E. O. Burt*	University of Florida, Agricultural Research Center, 3205 SW 70th Avenue, Fort Lauderdale, Florida 33314
Dominique Cairol	Lycee Agricole et Horticole, 78100 St. Germain en Laye, France
R. N. Carrow	Horticulture Department, Kansas State University, Manhattan, Kansas 66506
Any Castaings	Semouest "le chatelier", La chaize le Vicomte, 85310 St. Florent des Bois, France
C. Alberto Cenci	Instituto de Allevamento Vegetale, Facolta di Agraria, Borgo XX Giugno, Perugia, Italy
Amand Chesnel*	Ets Vilmorin-La Menite, 49250 Beaufort en Vallee, France
Claude Chevallier	S.A.D. I.N.R.A., Route de St. Cyr, 78000 Versailles, France
Yann de Chevigny	14, Avenue du General Leclerc, 60500 Chantilly, France
T. W. Cook*	Horticulture Department, Oregon State University, Corvallis, Oregon 97331
Michel Corbet	E.P.A.D.-Tour Fiat, Cedex No. 1, 92080 Paris-La Defense, France
S. W. Cosky*	Agriculture Department, 300 Cedar Road, Chesapeake, Virginia 23320
Georges Coupelon	Rue de Luzais, Sain-Quentin-Fallavier, 38290 La Verpilliere, France
R. Croise*	Ets Vilmorin-La Menite, 49250 Beaufort en Vallee, France
C. J. M. van Cruchten	Zwaan & de Wiljes B. V., Postfach 2, Scheemda (Gr.), Netherlands
Sven-Ove Dahlsson*	Weibulls Rasensektor, Fack, 261, 20, Landskrona, Sweden
W. H. Daniel	Department of Agronomy, Purdue University, West Lafayette, Indiana 47907
J. M. Davidson*	Soil Science Department, University of Florida, Gainesville, Florida 32611
Philipp Deschamps	Rue de Luzais, Saint-Quentin-Fallavier, 38290 La Verpilliere, France
R. W. Duell*	Department of Soils & Crops, Box 231, Cook College, New Brunswick, New Jersey 08903
J. M. Duich	Agronomy Department, 119 Tyson Building, Pennsylvania State University, University Park, Pennsylvania 16802
Jean Dujardin	35, Rue la Tour Maubourg, 77350 Boissise La Bertrand, France
Kaoru Ehara	10-19, I-Chome, Minami-dai, Kami-fukuoka-Shi, Saitama Ken 356, Japan
Gunter Ehrig	Danziger Str. 7, 8080 Furstenfeldbruck, Germany
Christoph Eisele	Friedrich Naumann-Str. 15, 6100 Darmstadt, West Germany
R. E. Engel*	Department of Soils & Crops, Rutgers University, New Brunswick, New Jersey 08903
Hans Erdmann	Leo Savelsberg Samen-GroBhandlung, Lindenstr. 11, 5170 Julich, Germany

S. L. Fales*	Agronomy Department, Purdue University, West Lafayette, Indiana 47907
A. C. Ferguson	Department of Plant Science, University of Manitoba, Winnipeg, Canada
Rosaleen Fisher*	Department of Agricultural Botany, Queen's University of Belfast, Newforge Lane, Belfast BT9 5PX, North Ireland, United Kingdom
C. D. Foy*	SEA, USDA, AEC Greenhouse, Plant Industry Station, Beltsville, Maryland 20705
Heinrich Franken*	Institut fur Pflanzenbau, Katzenburgweg 5, 5300 Bonn, West Germany
Hansheinrich Friedlander	Celamerck GmbH & Co., KG, 6507 Ingelhein, Rhein, West Germany
Huib Ghysen	Barenbrug Holland, b.v. Postfach 4, Arnhem, Netherlands
V. A. Gibeault*	Agriculture Extension Service, University of California at Riverside, Riverside, California 92500
Dean Glas	Koninlijk Kweekbedrijf D.J., v.d. Have B.V., P.O. Box 1, Rilland 3648, Netherlands
R. L. Goss*	Western Washington Research & Extension Center, Puyallup, Washington 98371
Tom Greenaway	Cheverals, Bow Brickhill, Milton Keynes, Buckinghamshire, MK 17 9LA, United Kingdom
Ewald Grundler	August Schmiederstr. 21, 8441 Steinach, West Germany
Thomas Grundler	August Schmiederstr. 21, 8441 Steinach, West Germany
J. P. M. Guerin	Laboratoire Central des Sols Sportifs, Avenue du Tremplay, 75012 Paris, France
Ulrich Gut	Hauenstein Samen AG, 8197 Rass, Germany
Ernst Habegger	Hauenstein Samen AG, 8197 Rass, Germany
J. R. Hall*	Agronomy Department, Virginia Polytechnic Institute and State University, Blacksburg, Virginia 24061
David Hanson*	Farm Advisor-Coop. Ext., P.O. Box 37, Half Moon Bay, California 94019
D. T. Hawes*	United States Golf Association, 17360 Coit Rd., Green Section, Dallas, Texas 75252
Colin Head	Chipman Ltd., Horsham, Sussex RH, 12 2NR, United Kingdom
Richard Heimes*	Landwirtschaftliche Versuchsstation, BASF AG, Kalmitweg 13, 6703 Limburgerhof, West Germany
Bruno Hellstern	Glatt-Weinberghalde 160, 7247 Sulz, West Germany
P. R. Henderlong*	Department of Agronomy, Ohio State University, 1827 Neil Avenue, Columbus, Ohio 43201
Jan Hendrickx	Mommersteeg International, Vlijmen, Netherlands
Pierre Henensal*	Department de Geotechnique, Laboratoire Central des Ponts et Chaussees, 58, Bld Lefebvre, 75015 Paris, France
Diethard Herbst	Unterdettigenstr. 23, 3032 Hinterkappelen, Switzerland
Peter Hermann	Postfach 220, Landwirtschaftliche, Versuchsstation der BASF AG, 6703 Limburgerhof, West Germany
G. A. Hick	40 Northrup King Ltd., 58 Princes St., Southend on Sea, Essex SSI 19F, United Kingdom
Hildegard Hiller	Laubacher Str. 54, 1000 Berlin 33, West Germany
F. L. Himes*	Department of Agronomy, Ohio State University, Columbus, Ohio 43210
Jacques Hintzen	Mommersteeg International B.V., Postbus 1, Vlijmen, Netherlands
Anton Hirschmann	BayWa AG, Arabellastr. 4 (Sternhaus), 8000 Munchen 81, West Germany
M. S. Hodge	128-134 Gilbert Street, Adelaide, South Australia, 5000, Australia
J. P. van der Horst	Oberrechtlaan lb, Ede, Netherlands

Toyoji Hosotsuji	3-13-8, Minamiaoyama, Minato-Ku, Tokyo, Japan
W. W. Huffine	Department of Agronomy, Oklahoma State University, Stillwater, Oklahoma 74014
M. O. Humphreys	Department of Botany, University of Liverpool, P.O. Box 147, Liverpool L69 3BX, United Kingdom
Shinsaku Ideta	1-15-8, Nishishinjuku, Shinjuku-Ku, Tokyo, Japan
Franz Indra	Lonza AG, Basel, Switzerland
K. E. Jackson*	115 Life Science East, Oklahoma State University, Stillwater, Oklahoma 74078
Noel Jackson*	Department of Plant Pathology, 223 Woodward Hall, University of Rhode Island, Kingston, Rhode Island 02881
J. A. Jagschitz*	Plant & Soil Science Department, Rhode Island Agricultural Experiment Station, Kingston, Rhode Island 02881
Dora Joge	Samen-Mauser, Zurichstr. 98, Postfach 8600, Dubendorf, Switzerland
B. J. Johnson*	Department of Agronomy, University of Georgia Experiment Station, Experiment, Georgia 30212
G. V. Johnson*	Department of Agronomy, Oklahoma State University, Stillwater, Oklahoma 74074
H. A. Jonnson	Weibullsholm Plant Breeding Institute, Fack, 261 20, Landskrona, Sweden
H. E. Kaerwer*	Northrup-King & Co., 1500 Jackson St., N.E., Minneapolis, Minnesota 55413
Saburo Kakuda	Hodoagaya Country Club, 1324 Kami-kawai-cho, Asahi-Ku, Yokohama-Shi, Japan
H. A. Kamp	Veldkantweg, Eerbeck, Netherlands
Ir. Kamps	Vijfhoevenlaan 4, Postbox 35, 5250 AA Vlijmen, Netherlands
Alfred Karban	Waldstr. 2, 5307 Wachtberg-Pech, Germany
Ernst Karpf	Fa. Euflor GmbH, Nymphenburger Str. 120, 8000 Munchen, West Germany
J. E. Kaufmann*	Department of Crop & Soil Sciences, Michigan State University, East Lansing, Michigan 48824
Cornelius Kennema	P.O. Box 49, Hoogezand, Netherlands
Klaus Kind	Am Bierkeller 10, 8751 Eschau, Germany
Hiroshi Kizawa	1-15-8, Nishishinjuku, Shinjuku-Ku, Tokyo, Japan
Barbara Klinzmann	2331 Hohenlieth, Post Holtsee, Eckernforde, Germany
W. R. Kneebone*	Department of Plant Sciences, University of Arizona, Tucson, Arizona 85721
Bretislav Koniček*	CSTV/Czechoslovak Association for Physical Culture, Praha-Strahov, Czechoslovakia
Hermann Koppius	Gounopstraat 35, Zevenaar, Netherlands
J. V. Krans*	Department of Agronomy, P.O. Box 5248, Mississippi State, Mississippi 39762
H. U. Krebs	G. R. Vatter AG, Samen, Sagestr. 65, 3098 Konitz, Switzerland
Jutta Kruger	Moosstr. 20, 8050 Freising, Germany
K. W. Kurtz*	California State Polytechnic University, 3801 Temple Avenue, Pomona, California 91768
Claude Lambert	Ste Truffaut, 21, rue des Pepinieres, Les Noels, 41350 Vineuil, France
E. R. Larssen	3560 Tjotta, Norway
Werner Lanz	Landwirtschaftliche Versuchsstation, BASF AG, Postfach 220, 6703 Limburgerhof, West Germany
F. B. Ledeboer	Cloverdale Nursery, 2528 N. Cloverdale, Boise, Idaho 83702
J. Leinauer	Ludwigstr. 11, 8922 Peiting/Obb., Germany
Francis Lenaire	Station d'Agronomie, Rout de St. Clement, Beaucouze, 49000 Angers, France

Francis Lenior	Rue Emile Semal 21, 1310 Gaillemarde-La Hulpe, Belgium
F. Loecher*	Kropsburgstra. 34, 6703 Limburgerhoff, BRD, West Germany
W. Lohmeyer*	Bundesforschungsanstalt fur Naturschutz und Landschaftsokologie, Heerstr. 110, D5300 Bonn 2, West Germany
Roger Loiseau	Los Goderies, 72000 Ruaudin, France
Ernst Lutke Entrup	Landsberger Str. 2, 4780 Lippstadt, West Germany
Yoshisuke Maki	Hokkaido Nat'l. Agricultural Experiment Station, Hitsujigaoka, Toyohira-ku, Sapporo 061-01, Japan
Johannes von Malek	Stattl. Lehr-u. Versuchsanstalt, fur Gartenbau, Diebsweg 2, 6900 Heidelberg, West Germany
Paul Mansat*	S.A.P.F., 86600 Lusignan, France
Horst Mark	Staudinger Str. 72, 8000 Munchen 83, West Germany
D. P. Martin*	ChemLawn Corporation, 1460 South Walton Blvd., Rochester, Michigan 48063
Marc Masson	Societe L. Claus, 91220 Bretigny, sur Orge, France
Volker May	Westendstr. 16, 8016 Feldkirchen, Germany
Clemens Mehnert*	Lehrstuhl fur Grunlandlehr, 8050 Freising-Weihenstephan, Germany
F. B. Mercer*	
Gunther Michelman	Zuchtstation NFG, 2831 Kirchseelte, Germany
J. W. Minderhoud*	Haarweg 33, Wageningen, Netherlands
Osamu Mizutani	2271, Nishikataokushinden, Kuwana-Shi, Mie-ken, Japan
Roland Moesch	Cellsystem AG/SA, Winkelstr. 19, 4665 Oftringen, Switzerland
Uwe Moller	Compo GmbH, Postfach 2107, 4400 Munster, West Germany
Gunter Molzahn	HESA, Bismarck-Str. 59, 6100 Darmstadt, West Germany
W. C. Morgan	73813 Cholame Dr., Diamond Bar, California 91765
Yoshihiro Mori	6-18-5, Shimbashi, Minato-Ku, Tokyo, Japan
Norbert Mott	Landesanstalt fur Okologie, Landwirtschaftsentwicklung u., Forstplanung, Zum Breijpott 15, 4190 Kleve-Kellen, Germany
Adly Moustafa*	Northrup-King & Co. Research Station, Research Road, Eden Prairie, Minnesota 55344
K. G. Muller-Beck	Auf der Buhnhard, 5241 Schutzbach, Germany
J. J. Murray*	SEA, USDA, Field Crops Laboratory, Rm. 333, B-001, BARC-West, Beltsville, Maryland 20705
Roland Muse	M.R.I. Route 113, Souderton, Pennsylvania 18964
Hideo Nabeshima	No. 211, 23, Chihaya 1-chome, Higashi-Ku, Fukuoka-Shi, Fukuoka-Ken, Japan
Shigemasa Nagae	1318-1, Kamiwajiro, Higashi-Ku, Fukuoka-Shi, Fukuoka-Ken, Japan
R. W. Nelson	Jacobsen Manufacturing Company, 1721 Packard Avenue, Racine, Wisconsin 53403
Maria Nejez	Freytaggasse 21/13, 1210 Wien, Austria
Mitsutaka Nishimura	41-411, Higashiashiya-Cho, Ashiya-Shi, Hyogo-Ken, Japan
F. J. Nudge*	Department of Agronomy, University of California, Riverside, California 92502
Yoichi Oohara*	29-1, Nishi 3-jo, Minami, Obihiro-Shi, Hokkaido, Japan
N. D. Olsen	D. L. F. Oestergade 7-9, 4000 Roskilde, Denmark
W. O. von Boberfeld*	Institut fur Pflanzenbau, Katzenburgweg 5, 5300 Bonn, West Germany
Siegfried Orberger	Gesellschaft Grun, Bruggenstr. 22, 4390 Gladbeck, West Germany
S. P. Orton*	Rt. 1, P.O. Box 722, Sumner, Washington 98390
Motonori Otsuka	9-21, Minamikasugaoka 5-chome, Ibaraki-Shi, Osaka-Fu, Japan

Adelmo Panella*	Instituto de Allevamento Vegetale, Facolta di Agraria, Borgo XX Giugno, Perugia, Italy
Don Parsons	25232 Vermont Dr., New Hall, California 91321
Kenyon T. Payne	Department of Crop & Soil Sciences, Michigan State University, East Lansing, Michigan 48824
Rolf Peine	Aubinger Str. 174, 8000 Munchen 60, West Germany
A. Soren Peterson	Post Langballig, 2391 Lundsgaard, West Germany
Martin Peterson	L. Daehnfeldt A/S. Box 185, Odense, Denmark
Rudolf Pietsch	Wolf-Gerate GmbH, Gregor-Wolf-Str., 5240 Betzdorf, West Germany
E. L. Ponzini	Olin Europe S.A., 90, Champs Elysees, 75008 Paris, France
H. L. Portz	Department of Plant & Soil Science, Southern Illinois University, Carbondale, Illinois 62901
Preben Poulsen	Lohe 61, 2000 Hamburg 65, West Germany
H.-U. Preusse*	Justus-Liebig-Univ., Giessen Inst. fur Bodenkunde und Bodenerhaltung, Ludwigstr. 23, 6300 Lahn-Giessen, West Germany
Hans Prun	Landwirtschaftliche Versuchsanstalt, BASF AG, Postfach 220, 6703 Limburgerhof, West Germany
J. Puig*	Laboratorie Regional de Toulouse, 1, Ave. du Colnel Roche, Complexe aerospatial, 31400 Toulouse, France
A. M. Radko*	USGA Green Section, Golf House, Far Hills, New Jersey 07931
W. Reinders	van Cruchten C.J.M., Zwann & de Wiljes B.V., Postfach 2, Scheemda (Gr.), Netherlands
Hermann Richter	2440 Reisenberg 57, Austria
P. E. Rieke	Department of Crop & Soil Science, Michigan State University, East Lansing, Michigan 48824
R. L. Robertson	Department of Entomology, North Carolina State University, Raleigh, North Carolina 27607
M. J. Robey	Athletic Department, Purdue University, West Lafayette, Indiana 47907
Heinz Roediger	Bezirkspflanzenschutzamt, Christoph Str. 4, 5500 Trier, West Germany
Frank Rogers	Ransomes Sims & Jeffries, Ltd., Nacton Works, Ipswich, Suffolk, United Kingdom
Manfred Roither	BASF AG, GPE/Gartenwesen, 6700 Ludwigshafen, West Germany
Erich Roschel	Wolf-Gerate GmbH, Gregor-Wolf, Str., 5240 Betzdorf, West Germany
Mortisuna Sakaguchi	19-10, Daita 3-chome, Setagaya-Ku, Tokyo, Japan
Junnosuke Sasaki	4-5-3, Kichijoji Higashi-Cho, Musashino-Shi, Tokyo, Japan
Gunther Sauer	Bundesanstalt fur Strassenwesen, Bruhler Str. 1, 5000 Koln 51, West Germany
Jochen Schering	Institute fur Angewandte Botanik, Marseiller Str. 7, 2000 Hamburg 36, Germany
R. W. Schery*	1005 W. 5th Street, Marysville, Ohio 43040
H. C. Schmeisser	3332 Forest Hill Blvd., West Palm Beach, Florida 33406
R. E. Schmidt*	Department of Agronomy, Virginia Polytechnic Institute and State University, Blacksburg, Virginia 24061
R. M. Schmit*	167 Middlesex Avenue, Metuchen, New Jersey 08840
G. Schneider	Celamerck GmbH & Co. KG, 6507 Ingelheim/Rhein, West Germany
Karl Schonthaler	Peter Jordanstr. 82, 1190 Wien, Austria
P. E. Schott*	Landwirtschaftliche Versuchsstation, BASF AG, Postfach 220, 6703 Limburgerhof, West Germany
Albert Schroder	Fa. C.F. Spiess & Sohn, Postfach 1260, 6719 Kleinkarlbach/u Grunstadt, Germany
E. W. Schweizer	P.O. Box 360, 3601 Thun, Switzerland

32

R. L. Shaver* — Department of Plant Pathology and Physiology, Virginia Polytechnic Institute and State University, Blacksburg, Virginia 24061

J. P. Shildrick* — Sports Turf Research Institute, Bingley, West Yorkshire, BD 16 1 AU, United Kingdom

J. F. Shoulders* — Agronomy Department, Virginia Polytechnic Institute and State University, Blacksburg, Virginia 24061

T. R. Siviour — Australian Turf Grass Research Institute, 68 Victoria Avenue, Concord, West Australia 2138, Australia

Werner Skirde — Fachgebiet Rasenforschung, Fachberiech Umweltforschung, Schlossgasse 7, 6300 Giessen, West Germany

C. R. Skogley* — Plant & Soil Science Department, University of Rhode Island, Kingston, Rhode Island 02881

J. D. Smith* — Agriculture Canada Research Station, Saskatoon, Saskatchewan, Canada S7N 0X2

M. H. Smithberg* — Department of Horticulture and Landscape Architecture, University of Minnesota, St. Paul, Minnesota 55108

G. H. Snyder* — University of Florida-AREC, Drawer A, Belle Glade, Florida 33430

John Souter — Souter of Stirling, Cunningham Road, Springkerse, Stirling, Scotland, United Kingdom

John Spantidakis — 118 Kifissias Avenue, Athens 607 TT, Greece

E. R. Steininger — Pine Valley Golf Club, Clementon, New Jersey 08021

W. C. Stienstra* — Department of Plant Pathology, University of Minnesota, St. Paul, Minnesota 55101

Rudolf Stossberger — BayWa AB, Arabellastr. 4 (Sternhaus), 8000 Munchen 81, West Germany

J. R. Street* — Department of Horticulture, University of Illinois, Urbana, Illinois 61801

Kathe Strodhoff — Niedersachisische Rasenkulturen, Annen Nr. 2, 2831 Gross Ippener, West Germany

R. V. Sturgeon, Jr.* — Department of Botany & Plant Pathology, Oklahoma State University, Stillwater, Oklahoma 74074

W. M. Sullivan — Plant & Soil Science Department, Hills Building, University of Vermont, Burlington, Vermont 05401

C. M. Switzer — Ontario Agricultural College, University of Guelph, Guelph, Ontario, Canada

Edmond Szymczak — Lycee Agricole et Horticole de Wagonville, 5509 Douai, France

Toru Takagi — 30, Easki 1-chome, Gifu-Shi, Gifu-Ken, Japan

Kencho Takahashi — 782-3, Nukata, Kuwana-Shi, Mie-Ken, Japan

Marc Tanguy — E.N.I.T.A.H., Rue le Notre, 49045 Angers, France

D. K. Taylor — Research Station, Box 1000, Agassiz, British Columbia, Canada

L. H. Taylor* — Department of Agronomy, Virginia Polytechnic Institute and State University, Blacksburg, Virginia 24061

Gut Thiriet — La Maison des Gazons, Bureau d'Etudes, 7 & 9, Rue Perdonnet, 75010 Paris, France

Robert Thomas — Laboratoire Central des Sols Sportifs, Avenue du Tremblay, 75012 Paris, France

W. Trautmann* — Bundesforschungsanstalt fur Naturschutz und Landschaftsokologie, Heerstr. 110, D5300 Bonn 2, West Germany

Werner Trolldenier — Sudetenlandstr. 27, 8752 Goldbach, Germany

J. R. Trout* — Statistics Department, Cook College, Rutgers University, New Brunswick, New Jersey 08903

A. J. Turgeon* — Horticulture Department, University of Illinois, Urbana, Illinois 61801

Yvon Turpaud — I.N.R.A.-S.E.I., Saint Laurent de la Pree, 17450 Fouras, France

A.L.M. van Wijk*	Institute for Land and Water Management Research, P.O. 35, Wageningen, Netherlands
J. M. Vargas, Jr.*	Department of Botany and Plant Pathology, Michigan State University, East Lansing, Michigan 48824
Walter Versteeg	Heidemy Nederland B.V., Postbus 139, Arnhem, Netherlands
Roelot Vijn	Cebeco Handelsraad, Vijfhoevenlaan 4, Vlijmen, Netherlands
Edmond de Vilmorin	42, Avenue Franklin Roosevelt, 72210 Avon, France
Felix Riem Vis	Institute for Soil Fertility, Oosterweg 92, Haren (Gr.), Netherlands
Reimer Vogel	Wolf-Gerate GmbH, Gregor-Wolf-Str., 5240 Betzdorf, West Germany
Gerhard Voigtlander	Lehrstuhl fur Grunlandlehre, 8050 Freising-Weihenstephan, Germany
James Vorst	Department of Agronomy, Purdue University, West Lafayette, Indiana 47907
Harm Vos	Rivro, Postbox 32, Wageningen, Netherlands
Dieter Wagner	Landwirtschaftliche Versuchsstation, BASF AG, Postfach 220, 703 Limburgerhof, West Germany
Helmut Wagner	Krieger Str. 3, 8000 Munchen 90, West Germany
R. C. Wakefield*	Plant & Soil Science Department, University of Rhode Island, Kingston, Rhode Island 02881
Arnold Walker	GRO-Green Product, Inc., 717 Elk Street, Buffalo, New York 14210
P. L. Waller	Fisons, Ltd., Levington Research Station, Levington, Ipswich, Suffolk, IP10 OLU, United Kingdom
J. R. Watson	The Toro Company, One Appletree Square, 8009-34th Avenue South, Minneapolis, Minnesota 55420
Peter Weibull	Saatzuchtanstalt Weibullsholm, Fack, 261 20 Landskrona, Sweden
D. B. White*	Department of Horticulture and Landscape Architecture, University of Minnesota, St. Paul, Minnesota 55108
Hannelore Will*	Landwirtschaftliche Versuchsstation, BASF AG, Postfach 220, 6703 Limburgerhof, West Germany
H. H. Williams*	1128 East 80th Street, Los Angeles, California 90001
C. E. Wright*	Department of Agricultural Biology, Queen's University of Belfast, Newforge Lane, Belfast BT9 5PX, Northern Ireland
Hisashi Yanagi	Toyo Green Co., Ltd., Nr. 4 Taiso, Koami Bldg. I-I-6, Nihonbashi Ningyo-Cho Chuo-Ku, Tokyo 103, Japan
Masayoshi Yoshida	Faculty of Agriculture, Shizuoka University, 836 Ohya, Shinzuoka 422, Japan
Isao Yoshikawa	3-1-5, Kawamo, Takarazuka-Shi, Hyogo-Ken, Japan
V. B. Youngner*	Department of Agronomy, University of California, Riverside, California 92502
F. Xaver Zacherl	Strassen-u. Teerbau Gmbh, Drachenseestr. 10, 8000 Munchen 70, West Germany

CONVERSION FACTORS FOR ENGLISH AND METRIC UNITS

To convert column 1 into column 2, multiply by	Column 1	Column 2	To convert column 2 into column 1, multiply by
		Length	
0.621	kilometer, km	mile, mi	1.609
1.094	meter, m	yard, yd	0.914
0.394	centimeter, cm	inch, in	2.54
		Area	
0.386	kilometer^2, km^2	mile^2, mi^2	2.590
247.1	kilometer^2, km^2	acre, acre	0.00405
2.471	hectare, ha	acre, acre	0.405
1.076	are, a	1,000 ft^2	0.929
		Volume	
0.00973	meter^3, m^3	acre-inch	102.8
3.532	hectoliter, hl	cubic foot, ft^3	0.2832
2.838	hectoliter, hl	bushel, bu	0.352
0.0284	liter	bushel, bu	35.24
1.057	liter	quart (liquid), qt	0.946
		Mass	
1.102	ton (metric)	ton (U.S.)	0.9072
2.205	quintal, q	hundredweight, cwt (short)	0.454
2.205	kilogram, kg	pound, lb	0.454
0.035	gram, g	ounce (avdp), oz	28.35
		Pressure	
14.50	bar	lb/inch^2, psi	0.06895
0.9869	bar	atmosphere, atm	1.013
0.9678	kg (weight)/cm^2	atmosphere, atm	1.033
14.22	kg (weight)/cm^2	lb/inch^2, psi	0.07031
14.70	atmosphere, atm	lb/inch^2, psi	0.06805
		Yield or Rate	
0.446	ton (metric)/hectare	ton (U.S.)/acre	2.24
0.892	kg/ha	lb/acre	1.12
0.892	quintal/hectare	hundredweight/acre	1.12
2.05	kg/are	lb/1,000 ft^2	0.488
		Temperature	
	Celsius	Fahrenheit	
	−17.8C	0F	
$\left(\frac{9}{5}\,°C\right) + 32$	0C	32F	$\frac{5}{9}\,(°F - 32)$
	100C	212F	
	20	68	

Water Measurement

8.108	hectare-meters, ha-m	acre-feet	0.1233
97.29	hectare-meters, ha-m	acre-inches	0.01028
0.08108	hectare-centimeters, ha-cm	acre-feet	12.33
0.973	hectare-centimeters, ha-cm	acre-inches	1.028
0.00973	meters^3, m^3	acre-inches	102.8
0.981	hectare-centimeters/hour, ha-cm/hour	feet^3/sec	1.0194
440.3	hectare-centimeters/hour, ha-cm/hour	U.S. gallons/min	0.00227
0.00981	meters^3/hour, m^3/hour	feet^3/sec	101.94
4.403	meters^3/hour, m^3/hour	U.S. gallons/min	0.227

Plant Nutrition Conversion—P and K

P (phosphorus) × 2.29 = P_2O_5
K (potassium) × 1.20 = K_2O

Section I:

Turfgrass Breeding and Cultivar Evaluation

Chapter 1

Comparisons of Micro-Trials and Spaced Plant Nurseries with Dense Swards as Means for Evaluating Turfgrass Genotypes[1]

B. BOURGOIN
P. MANSAT

ABSTRACT

Three types of test plots—spaced planted nurseries (SP) with plants on a 50-cm grid; micro-trials (MT) with plants on a 10-cm grid; dense swards (DS) broadcast-seeded at standard rates—were compared using 10 well-known cultivars each of red fescue (*Festuca rubra* L.) and Kentucky bluegrass (*Poa pratensis* L.). Ratings were made on all plots for traffic tolerance, seasonal color, disease resistance, leaf color, and leaf texture. Cultivar ranks for each character were determined for each method of planting. Agreement between test methods was then evaluated by Spearman rank correlations. MT plots ranked cultivars in the same way as did DS plots, while SP plot ranks showed little correlation to DS values. Values obtained indicate that MT plots can be effectively used in early testing when seed supplies are too low for normal planting. The use of SP tests should be confined to population studies and evaluation of individual plant characteristics.

INTRODUCTION

In the development of turfgrass cultivars, plant breeders evaluate plant characteristics in spaced plant nurseries and in dense sward plots. Valid assessment of turfgrass characteristics must be in the latter plot type. Typically, because of seed limitations (and for certain characteristics), initial evaluations of selections are made as spaced plants, followed by progeny evaluations in dense swards. When sufficient seed is available, both evaluations can be initiated simultaneously. The basic problem facing most breeders is to economically and efficiently assess turfgrass value as soon and with as little seed as possible.

Many studies with various species, especially cereals and forages, have shown that competition within dense populations alters plant characteristics from those observed in spaced plantings. In breeding forage plants, micro-trials involving dense spacing have been used (1, 2, 3, 4), making assessments under competitive conditions possible with limited

[1] A contribution from the Station d'Amélioration des Plantes Fourragères, Institut National de la Recherche Agronomique, 86600 Lusignan, France.

seed quantities. This study was initiated as a means toward devising more efficient turfgrass breeding procedures by evaluation of interrelationships among assessments at three population densities.

MATERIALS AND METHODS

The following types of test plots were established in the spring of 1972: (i) Spaced plant nursery (SP) with transplants at 50 × 50 cm spacings with 50 plants per basic plot; (ii) Micro-trials (MT) with transplants at 10 × 10 cm spacings with 96 plants per basic plot; (iii) Dense sward (DS) broadcast-seeded at 30 g/m^2 for five Chewings fescue (*Festuca rubra* L.) and 15 g/m^2 for Kentucky bluegrass (*Poa pratensis* L.) into basic plots 2.25 m^2. Twenty cultivars were tested (10 of Chewings fescue and 10 of Kentucky bluegrass).

The SP nursery was laid out with two replicates, the 20 cultivars being allotted at random within each block. For MT and DS treatments the experimental design was a split plot with the sub-units divided into sub-sub units. There were two replicates (randomized blocks), each being split into two plots for height of mowing (2 and 4 cm). Each plot was split into two sub-plots for traffic intensity (two and four passes of a roller each week). Each sub-plot was split orthogonally into 20 sub-sub-plots to which the 20 cultivars were assigned at random. Mowing was once a week during the growing period. The roller, weighing 200 kg, is equipped with studs like those of soccer boots with each stud exerting 8.7 kg/cm^2 of pressure. When two passes were made per week the roller was used continuously from March 1973 to April 1975. For the other traffic intensity (four passes per week) there were three periods from March 1973 to July 1974, August 1974 to December 1974, and January 1975 to April 1975. The spaced plants were mown at 10 cm three times each year, at the end of June, July, and October.

Cultivars used were: 'Bergere' and 'Novorubra' (creeping type); 'Cottage', 'Dawson', and 'Golfrood' (semi-creeping type); 'Famosa', 'Flevo', 'Highlight', 'Koket', and 'Waldorf' (chewings type) for red fescue, 'Baron', 'B.M.', 'Fylking', 'Kenblue', 'Monopoly', 'Prato', 'Primo', 'Silo', 'Sydsport', and 'Troy' for Kentucky bluegrass.

Characteristics assessed in each type of plot are indicated in Table 1. Assessments were made by visual scoring on a 1 through 5 basis, with 5 being allotted at random within each block. For MT and DS treatments gradation, discoloration, diseases, or weeds) would be rated a 5; from 10 to 30% a 4; from 30 to 50% a 3; from 50 to 75% a 2; from 75 to 100% a 1. For each characteristic assessed, the mean score was calculated for each cultivar and then within each species the 10 cultivar means were ranked from 1 to 10.

Well-known cultivars were chosen to provide an accurate reference scale for the characteristics assessed. The only statistical test used was Spearman's rank correlation method.

Table 1. Characters observed and rated in each plot type.

Plot type	Traffic tolerance	Summer behavior	Winter behavior	Disease susceptibility: Rust	Disease susceptibility: Leaf spot
Dense sward (DS)	X	X	X	X	X
Micro-trial (MT)	X	X	X	X	X
Spaced plants (SP)		X	X	X	
	Leaf color	Leaf width	Ground cover	Plant density	Plant spread
Dense sward (DS)	X	X	X		
Micro-trial (MT)	X	X	X		
Spaced plants (SP)	X	X		X	X

RESULTS

Planting and Establishment

Preliminary preparation of land, plot layout, and planting (calculated on the basis of one person) required 25 min for each SP plot, 1 hour for each MT plot, and 15 min for each DS plot. Variabilities in spreading and plant density were obvious between and within the two species when studied in the SP plots. This same variability was evident in the MT plots, where complete sward cover was achieved at intervals varying from 6 months to a year. Once this density was achieved, individual plants were nearly impossible to distinguish. An advantage of the MT plots was that mowing could begin at the same time and proceed at the same intervals as on the DS plots.

Traffic Tolerance

At a 2-cm mowing height, traffic tolerance from DS and MT plots were significantly correlated after the 6th month (Table 2). The relationships were generally closer for the fescue plots than for the Kentucky blue-

Table 2. Rank correlations between dense sward and micro-trial ratings for tolerance to roller-induced traffic stress.

Roller treatment: Months from initiation	Roller treatment: Frequency/ week	Mowed at 2 cm: *F. rubra*	Mowed at 2 cm: *P. pratensis*	Mowed at 4 cm: *F. rubra*	Mowed at 4 cm: *P. pratensis*
6	2	0.82**	0.57*	0.57*	0.52
	4	0.90**	0.61*	0.85**	0.51
9	2	0.77**	0.91**	0.50	0.72*
	4	0.84**	0.82**	0.67*	0.63*
12	2	0.82**	0.61*	0.73*	0.90**
	4	0.85**	0.79**	0.69*	0.71*
18	2	0.78**	0.71*	0.73*	0.30
	4	0.83**	0.83**	0.75**	0.82**
24	2	0.73*	0.80**	0.77**	0.59*
	4	0.80**	0.78**	0.63*	0.76**

*,** Significant at the 0.05 (≥0.57) and 0.01 levels (≥0.75), respectively.

grass plots. At the 4-cm mowing height there was less correlation between plot types, although again the relationships were closer with the fescue.

Summer and Winter Behavior

The summers of 1972 and 1974 were dry, while 1973 was wet. Associations between plot types reflect this difference, with significant correlations between DS and MT plots in all three summers for the fescue, but only in 1973 for the Kentucky bluegrass (Table 3). Correlations between ranks from DS and MT plots and those from SP were generally not significant, exceptions were the Kentucky bluegrass in 1973 and the fescue in 1974. Mowing height on the DS and MT plots had little effect.

Winter behavior ranks on DS and MT plots were significantly correlated for both grasses. In most cases there was little relationship between rankings from DS or MT plots and those from the SP plots (Table 3).

Disease Susceptibility

The diseases observed were rusts (*Puccinia poarum* Niels. and *P. poae nemoralis* Otth. on the Kentucky bluegrass and *P. graminis* Pers. on the fescue) and leaf spots (*Helminthosporium vagans* Drechsl. on Kentucky bluegrass and *H. dictyoides* Drechsl. on the fescue). Leaf spot infestations did not occur in the SP plots. Rusts on the fescue were observed and rated in 1972 only. Rust resistance ranks for fescue from the MT plots were significantly correlated (r = 0.62) with those from the SP plots, but there was no significant correlation between DS plot ranks and those for the other types.

Rust infections on bluegrass were similar for all plot types with significant correlations in most cases (Table 4). Highest correlations were for

Table 3. Rank correlations between plot types using ratings for summer and winter behavior.

		Summer behavior					Winter behavior		
		DS-MT Mowed at 2 cm			DS-MT Mowed at 4 cm		DS-MT Mowed at 2 cm		DS-MT Mowed at 4 cm
Plot types compared	Species	1972	1973	1974	1973	1974	1972–73	1973–74	1973–74
DS vs. MT	*F. rubra*	0.73**	0.95**	0.76**	0.77**	0.75**	0.75**	0.51	0.84**
	P. pratensis	0.33	0.63*	0.33	0.61*	0.21	0.60*	0.65*	0.77**
DS vs. SP	*F. rubra*	0.39	0	0.82	−0.21	0.91**	0.11	0.90	0.39
	P. pratensis	−0.49	0.73*	−0.22	0.66*	−0.30	0.07	0.37	0.65*
MT vs. SP	*F. rubra*	0.41	−0.12	0.56*	−0.30	0.64*	0.55	0.11	0.47
	P. pratensis	−0.30	0.82**	0.36	0.65*	0.11	−0.22	0.18	0.16

*,** Significant at the 0.05 ≥0.57) and 0.01 levels (≥0.75), respectively.

Table 4. Rank correlations between plot types, using ratings for leaf rust and *Helminthosporium* leaf spot susceptibility of *P. pratensis* and *F. rubra*.

Plot types compared	Species	Leaf rust: DS-MT mowed at 2 cm 1972†	1973	1974	DS-MT mowed at 4 cm 1973	1974
DS-MT	*P. pratensis*	0.64* -0.88**	0.73* -0.90**	0.73*	0.82**-0.94*	0.82**
DS-SP	*P. pratensis*	0.34 -0.88**	0.74* -0.89**	0.35	0.69*	0.46
MT-SP	*P. pratensis*	0.28 -0.47	0.69* -0.79**	0.56	0.76**	0.62*
		Helminthosporium leaf spot				
DS-MT	*F. rubra*	0.72* -0.78**	0.88**	0.57*	−0.87**	0.90**
	P. pratensis	0.80**-0.85**	0.75**-0.90**	0.57*	−0.91**	0.65*-0.74**

*,** Significant at the 0.05 (≥0.57) and 0.01 levels (≥0.75), respectively.
† Where there were several assessments, extreme values are recorded.

comparisons of DS and MT and lowest ones when comparing DS or MT ranks with those from SP plots.

Helminthosporium leaf spot ranks were nearly the same from DS and MT plots for both fescue and Kentucky bluegrass cultivars with all correlations significant (Table 4). Mowing height made little difference.

Leaf Color, Leaf Width, and Ground Cover

Cultivars were ranked similarly for leaf color and leaf texture in DS and MT plots for both species with significant correlations in all cases (Table 5). Only a few of the plot type comparisons, primarily those for the Kentucky bluegrass cultivars, were significant in comparisons with SP values. Ground cover ranks on DS and MT plots were significantly correlated for the fescue with values from 0.68 to 0.80, while similar comparisons for the Kentucky bluegrass had lower values of 0.42 to 0.85. Comparisons of ground cover ranks from DS and MT plots and ranks for plant density or plant spread from the SP plots gave generally, low, erratic, and nonsignificant values with coefficients ranging from −0.42 to 0.86.

Table 5. Rank correlations between plot types using ratings for color and leaf texture.

Plot types compared	Species	DS-MT Mowed at 2 cm: Leaf color 1974	Leaf texture 1973	Leaf texture 1974	DS-MT Mowed at 4 cm: Leaf color 1974	Leaf texture 1974
DS-MT	*F. rubra*	0.58*	0.81**	0.92**	0.85**	0.85**
	P. pratensis	0.84**	0.84**	0.87**	0.85**	0.86**
DS-SP	*F. rubra*	0.39	0.60*	--	0.55	--
	P. pratensis	0.87**	−0.20	--	0.80**	--
MT-SP	*F. rubra*	0.35	0.49	--	0.59*	--
	P. pratensis	0.69*	0.23	--	0.86**	--

*,** Significant at the 0.05 (≥0.57) and 0.01 levels (≥0.75), respectively.

DISCUSSION

Correlations between dense sward and micro-trial plots were generally significant for both behavioral and morphological characteristics. All data suggest that MT plots would give valid estimates of potential genotype performance in dense swards. In contrast, spaced planted nursery ranks had few significant correlations with those from dense sward. Even for leaf characteristics, correlations were not very high. Also, it was difficult to estimate density values. Correlations with the micro-trial ranks were not better than those between nursery and dense turf.

With the micro-trial system, it was possible to estimate practically all characteristics under conditions very similar to those of dense turf. Few seeds and relatively small plot areas are required, but the labor requirement for establishment is high. Where seed is limited, they can replace initial DS tests.

The color and texture of the leaves and resistance or susceptibility to rust were most apparent on spaced plants and, when rated for individual plants, provided a basis for calculation of the mean population values. This certainly allows a better discrimination between cultivars or ecotypes than an overall estimation on MT or DS plots.

The spaced planted nursery system cannot be replaced for population studies of earliness, morphological differentiation characteristics, and color homogeneity. Attacks by leaf pests are more visible on red fescue, thus making evaluations more selective. Little seed is required but large areas are necessary. A lot of work is necessary to achieve accurate observations (which are, in fact, the nursery advantage).

In this study, mowing at 2 or 4 cm did not often affect correlation values for the studied characteristics. It would be interesting to estimate the most discriminant height for a given characteristic. Our observations suggested that plots mowed at 2 cm showed differences between cultivars for traffic tolerance earlier and had a wider range of cultivar values for winter behavior and for summer behavior under rainy conditions.

CONCLUSION

Micro-trials using plants spaced at 10 × 10 cm may be extremely useful turfgrass breeding tools. They provide good estimations of performance in densely seeded swards for most population characteristics. They require very little seed, or few vegetative propagules, providing opportunity for early test and progeny test of selections for turfgrass potential. Plots that perform the best can be used as seed sources (by cage isolation) or as sources of propagules for further testing, either in widely spaced plantings for specific characters and population studies or in the ultimate turf test.

LITERATURE CITED

1. Anonymous. 1970. Recherches sur les plantes fourragères. Inst. Natl. Rech. Agron. Lusignan 1962–1969. Fourrages 41.
2. Demarly, Y. 1963. Génétique des tétraploides et amélioration des plantes. Ann. Amélior. Plantes 13:307–400.
3. Jadas-Hécart, J., and G. Génier. 1972. The practical value of micro-trials in connection with grass and lucerne breeding. A 45 /:45–53. *In* M. A. do Valle Ribeiro and Patricia O'Donnel (eds.) Rep. of the Fodder Crops Meet., Eucarpia, Dublin, Ireland. September 1972. An Foras Taluntais, Plant Breeding Dep., Carlow, Republic of Ireland.
4. Rogers, H. H., and A. Lazenby. 1972. The evaluation of grasses in micro-plots. J. Agric. Sci. 66:147–151.

Chapter 2 The Breeding of Lines of *Agrostis tenuis* Sibth. and *Festuca rubra* L. Tolerant of Grass-killing Herbicides[1]

R. FISHER
C. E. WRIGHT

ABSTRACT

Cultivars of amenity grasses which are tolerant of herbicides for weed grasses would facilitate the selective removal of undesirable weed grasses from turf, sod, and seed fields of these cultivars. In an unsuccessful attempt to select 1,1′-dimethyl-4,4′-bipyridinium ion (paraquat)-tolerant red fescue (*Festuca rubra* L. ssp. *rubra*) genotypes, plants of five different ages were sprayed with paraquat. The most tolerant plants were then selected. When paraquat was applied again several months later to these "tolerant" plants, and to unselected plants, there was no significant difference in tolerance between the selected and unselected plants.

The selection of colonial bentgrass (*Agrostis tenuis* Sibth.) and Chewings fescue (*F. rubra* ssp. *commutata* Gaud.) lines tolerant of herbicide IRS resulted in a line of colonial bentgrass which was 2.5 times more tolerant than unselected 'Bardot' colonial bentgrass and a line of Chewings fescue 1.8 times more tolerant than unselected 'Highlight' Chewings fescue. The level of tolerance already obtained in the colonial bentgrass line should permit the selective removal of annual bluegrass (*Poa annua* L.) from swards of this line, but a further increase in tolerance would probably be required before it would be possible to eliminate other undesirable grass species.

Additional index words: Paraquat, Weed control.

INTRODUCTION

Temperate amenity areas sown with *Agrostis* spp., *Festuca* L. spp., perennial ryegrass (*Lolium perenne* L.), and Kentucky bluegrass (*Poa pratensis* L.) in monostands or polystands become invaded with other less desirable grasses as a result of damage caused by wear, disease, improper culture, or weather. The most common and controversial invader in closely mown, intensively used areas such as golf greens is annual bluegrass (*Poa annua* L.). Once established, annual bluegrass plants can displace the sown species because of their prolific seed production and tolerance to close mowing, wear, and soil compaction. Despite these useful qualities, which may cause the species to be regarded as a good amenity grass in cool, wet climates, other characteristics such as susceptibility to

[1] A contribution from the Dep. of Agricultural Botany, The Queen's Univ. of Belfast, Northern Ireland.

drought, extremes of temperature, and various diseases, result in annual bluegrass being regarded as a weed in many circumstances.

Other undesirable grasses include orchardgrass (*Dactylis glomerata* L.), velvetgrass (*Holcus lanatus* L.), and quackgrass (*Agropyron repens* (L.) Beauv), which are unsightly in ornamental turf because of their coarse leaves and rapidity of vertical leaf extension. Amenity species themselves may become undesirable invaders of turf; eg. *Agrostis* spp. in Kentucky bluegrass; and the aggressive warm-season grasses; eg. kikuyu grass (*Pennisetum clandestinum* Hochst. ex Chiov.) and bermudagrass (*Cynodon dactylon* (L.) Pers.), of Australian golf fairways which invade *Agrostis* spp. greens (2, 10). An easy method of removing weed grasses from high quality turf would facilitate the work of gardeners and greenkeepers.

Investigations into the selective control of annual bluegrass and other undesirable grasses by chemical means have been summarized by Woolhouse and Shildrick (12). Soil sterilization using methyl bromide eliminates weed seeds in the seedbed but provides short-term control only. The majority of pre-emergence and post-emergence herbicides investigated have shown insufficient selectivity between certain turfgrasses, especially *Agrostis* spp., and the weed grasses; although *O,O*-diisopropyl phosphorodithioate S-ester with N-[2-mercaptoethyl]benzenesulfonamide (bensulide), arsenates, and 7-oxabicyclo[2.2.1]heptane-2,3-dicarboxylic acid (endothal) have achieved some success. Fisher and Faulkner (6) also found the differences between the tolerances of grass species for a wide range of herbicides to be inadequate for the selective removal of undesirable grasses from amenity areas. These findings indicate that alternative methods to screening existing herbicides to provide selectivity may be more feasible and should be investigated.

One alternative—the control of annual bluegrass seedhead production using growth regulators such as a mixture of 2-chloro-9-hydroxyfluorenecarboxylic acid-9-methyl ester (chlorfluorenol) and 1,2-dihydro-3,6-pyridazinedione (maleic hydrazide)—has resulted in the selective removal of this species from golf fairways and plots of *Agrostis*, fescue, and Kentucky bluegrass in the Pacific northwest of the United States (8).

A second alternative, suggested by several investigators (1, 11, 13), is the development of amenity grass cultivars tolerant to grass-killing herbicides. An area sown with such a cultivar could be maintained free not only of annual bluegrass, but of any other grassy and broad-leaved weeds if the herbicide involved was a broad spectrum herbicide. This would be beneficial not only in amenity areas but also in sod and seed fields where purity is extremely important. The only example of such a cultivar is the 1,1′-dimethyl-4,4′-bipyridinium ion (paraquat)-resistant perennial ryegrass cultivar 'Causeway' which can be maintained free of all undesirable grasses (3). This paper summarizes attempts to breed herbicide-tolerant lines of *F. rubra* L. and colonial bentgrass (*Agrostis tenuis* Sibth).

MATERIALS AND METHODS

Red fescue (*F. rubra* L. ssp. *rubra*) was found to be more tolerant of paraquat than most other grasses, but the level of tolerance was insufficient to give adequate selectivity for weed control purposes (6). In choosing this herbicide for the production of a tolerant line of this species, it was hoped to build on the level of tolerance already available.

Although colonial bentgrass is very susceptible to many herbicides in comparison with other grasses, it was found to be moderately tolerant of one chemical formulation—herbicide IRS. As *F. rubra* is sown in polystands with colonial bentgrass to produce fine turf, lines of both these species tolerant of herbicide IRS would be required. A cycle involving application of herbicide, selection of apparently tolerant lines, and the production of progenies for further selection repeated over several generations was used in an attempt to develop tolerant lines of colonial bentgrass and Chewings fescue (*F. rubra* ssp. *commutata* Gaud.). An assessment of the levels of tolerance achieved by 1976 is presented below.

I. Red Fescue

Five samples of 'Dawson' red fescue of different ages [two-leaf (17 days), 4, 6, 9, and 15 weeks] were sprayed with 0.28 kg ai/ha of paraquat. Each sample consisted of two replicates each of 200 plants. The two-leaf, 4-, and 6-week-old plants were grown in seed trays having internal dimensions of 355 × 215 × 50 mm and containing 3.5 kg of potting compost. The compost consisted of 7 parts loam:3 parts peat:2 parts sand. One kilogram of fertilizer (20 N:13 P:15 K) was mixed with 1,000 kg compost and the mix passed through a 15-mm mesh in order to remove very large particles and produce a homogeneous compost. Seeds were sown in each seed tray at 322, 161, and 84 sites in the two-leaf, 4-, and 6-week-old samples, respectively. The 9- and 15-week-old plants were grown in 60-mm diameter pots for 8 weeks and then transferred to 100-mm pots. Only those seedlings which had two leaves on the 17th day after planting were included in the tests in order to reduce the variation within and among samples. The seed trays and pots were placed in a heated (20 C) glasshouse in irrigated sand beds to which enough water was added at intervals to keep the compost moist. Paraquat was applied using an Oxford Precision Microsprayer with an Allman Jet size 000, at a rate of 562 liters/ha and a pressure of 2.8 kg/cm^2.

The 10 plants which recovered most rapidly were selected from the 200 sprayed plants in each of the two replicates of each age group. These 10 plants, together with 10 unsprayed plants of the same age, were grown in 100-mm pots for several months. Each selected and unselected plant was divided into two ramets each of 50 tillers. One ramet was sprayed with 0.11 kg ai/ha of paraquat several weeks later. The foliage of each part was harvested 7 weeks after spraying when the majority of plants showed signs of recovery (Harvest 1) and 2 weeks after Harvest 1 when shoot regrowth was present (Harvest 2). The tolerance for each selected and unselected plant was calculated at both harvests; ie., DM of the sprayed ramet expressed as a percentage of the DM of the paired unsprayed ramet.

II. Colonial Bentgrass and Chewings Fescue

To assess the levels of IRS tolerance achieved by the summer of 1976, the resistant lines of these species were compared with various cultivars of the same and other species as given in Fig. 1. The assessment was carried out in seed trays, containing 3.5 kg of potting compost. Herbicide IRS was thoroughly mixed with the compost in a seed tray at one of five concentrations (2.25, 4.5, 9, 18, and 36 mg ai/kg compost). Each concentration treatment was replicated three times. Fourteen rows, each of 23 holes at 15-mm spacing, were made in each seed tray using a template. Seeds were sown singly in each hole at a depth of 10 mm. One row of each species was sown in every tray and the two outer guard rows were sown with Dawson red fescue. The procedure used for the seed trays, potting compost, watering, and glasshouse temperatures were as previously described for red fescue. The positions of those seedlings which had germinated 17 days after sowing were noted and seedlings appearing later were ignored. Seedlings surviving the treatments were recorded after a suitable interval.

RESULTS

I. Red Fescue

Approximately 90% of the plants in the two-leaf, 4-, and 6-week samples and approximately 70% of the plants in the 9- and 15-week samples were killed by the rate of paraquat applied prior to selection. There was considerable variation in the apparent tolerances of the plants prior to both Harvest 1 and Harvest 2—some plants had died while others had recovered. However, the apparent tolerances of the selected plants did not appear to be greater than those of unselected plants in any sample. These observations were substantiated by the mean calculated tolerances (Table 1). (At Harvest 1, the tolerance of the selected and unselected plants was very similar and not significantly different at the 5% level of probability.) At Harvest 2, the tolerances of the selected plants were greater than those of unselected plants in the 4-, 6-, and 15-week samples, but again the differences were not significant at the 5% level of probability.

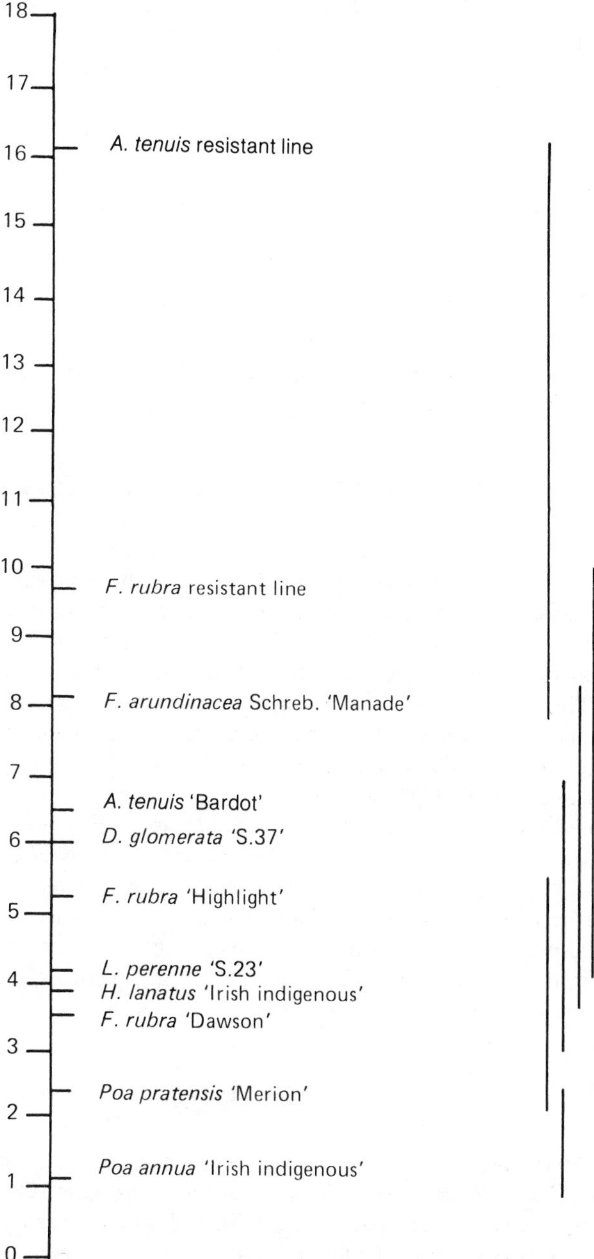

Fig. 1. The tolerances of *A. tenuis* and *F. rubra* resistant lines in comparison with those of other grasses.

Table 1. The mean paraquat tolerance (DM of a sprayed ramet expressed as a percentage of the DM of an equivalent unsprayed ramet) of plants of red fescue selected at five growth stages and of comparable unselected plants determined at two harvest occasions.

	Sample				
	2-leaf	4-week	6-week	9-week	15-week
Harvest 1*					
Selected	69.3	70.5	68.4	61.2	66.8
Unselected	75.0	77.6	71.0	72.6	70.6
SE of Mean	3.6	3.8	4.8	4.4	4.4
Level of significance	NS	NS	NS	NS	NS
Harvest 2					
Selected	16.4	34.3	31.7	9.5	27.7
Unselected	16.0	24.4	22.5	10.1	17.9
SE of mean	4.2	6.2	6.9	2.8	6.2
Level of significance	NS	NS	NS	NS	NS

* At Harvest 1, the tolerance of the selected and unselected plants were very similar and not significantly different at the 5% level of probability.

II. Colonial Bentgrass and Chewings Fescue

The ED50 value (the concentration of herbicide estimated to kill 50% of seedlings) of each species in each of the three replicates was obtained after a Probit Transformation (4) had been carried out on the data. An analysis of variance of Log ED50 values indicated that there were significant differences between the tolerances of the species at the 0.1% level. The mean ED50 value of each species is presented in Fig. 1. Vertical lines embracing various species indicate that there were no significant differences between these species at the 5% level of probability according to Duncan's New Multiple Range Test (9).

Seedlings of the colonial bentgrass IRS-resistant line were approximately 2.5 and 16 times more tolerant than those of 'Bardot' colonial bentgrass and of annual bluegrass, respectively; the resistant line being significantly superior. There was also an increase in the tolerance of the Chewings fescue line which was 1.8 times more tolerant than 'Highlight' Chewings fescue, although this difference was not shown to be significant.

DISCUSSION

The paraquat tolerance of red fescue plants was markedly greater at Harvest 1 than at Harvest 2 because of the large amount of dead material present which contributed to the DM weights at Harvest 1. Although a plant was totally dead it would have a tolerance value greater than 0 at Harvest 1. This was not the case at Harvest 2 where only the regrowth was harvested. For this reason the tolerance values at Harvest 2 are much more meaningful than those at Harvest 1.

In comparison with the colonial bentgrass; Chewings fescue/IRS program, the selection of paraquat-tolerant red fescue was unsuccessful. The increase in tolerance of the selected material at Harvest 2 was nonsignificant. This was unexpected since the selected plants had previously survived a concentration of paraquat which had killed a large proportion of the population and because the selection of paraquat-resistant perennial ryegrass genotypes by Faulkner (3) had been successful.

As with any characteristic, it is essential when selecting for herbicide tolerance that there be adequate genetic variation in tolerance within the sample. Genetic variation in paraquat tolerance within the species *F. rubra* was indicated by the fact that significant differences were found among cultivars of this species with respect to paraquat tolerance (5). However, because a single cultivar was used in this experiment, the available genetic variation in paraquat tolerance may have been limited despite the fact that large variations in the apparent tolerance of the plants were observed. Selection based on a much wider range of genetic material could prove successful.

It is also essential when making selections that environmental effects on tolerance are small in relation to heritable genetic effects. The above results suggest that the ability of plants to survive was largely attributable to characters which altered with environment or plant age. Different selection techniques such as herbicide application to mature plants in the field or in hydroponic media in a controlled environment may be more successful.

Based on this experiment, it was considered that the selection of paraquat-tolerant *F. rubra* plants using the above methods was not likely to be successful. Also, the variables involved, including species, herbicide, and selection technique, require more thorough investigation before selection of tolerant plants can be attempted on a large scale.

The success in selection of colonial bentgrass and Chewings fescue tolerance to herbicide IRS may be partially attributed to the fact that this is a root-absorbed herbicide, in comparison with paraquat which is foliar-absorbed. However, as the results of the IRS herbicide were obtained on seedlings in a glasshouse, field experiments are required to substantiate the findings. Should similar levels of tolerance be found in field experiments, a 16-fold difference between the new lines of colonial bentgrass and annual bentgrass should be sufficient to selectively remove the latter from swards of the *Agrostis* spp. However, the tolerance level of both the colonial bentgrass and *F. rubra* lines would probably have to be increased further to permit selective removal of other undesirable grassy species under a wide range of environmental conditions and herbicide application methods. When using herbicides for the selective removal of undesirable species, it is imperative that the weed species be completely eliminated since it is possible for the weed species to evolve herbicide-tolerant strains over several generations. In conclusion, if the progress in developing herbicide-tolerant lines of turfgrasses is maintained, the selective removal of weedy grasses from amenity areas will no longer be the problem it now is.

ACKNOWLEDGMENTS

The authors are grateful to Germinal Holding Ltd. for the scholarship to Queen's University that enabled this research program to be carried out. We also wish to thank Mrs. M. Moore and Mr. T. Neville for their technical assistance.

LITERATURE CITED

1. Charles, A. H., and J. Lewis. 1962. Observations on the use of herbicides on grassland. p. 75–83. *In* Proc. Br. Weed Control Conf., Brighton, England. November 1962. Br. Weed Control Counc., London.
2. Daniel, W. H. 1972. Midwest current trends in turfgrass weed control. p. 155–159. *In* Richard Schmidt (ed.) Proc. Scotts Turfgrass res. Conf., Maryville, Ohio. July 1970. O. M. Scott & Sons Co., Maryville, Ohio.
3. Faulkner, J. S. 1976. A paraquat resistant variety of *Lolium perenne* under field conditions. p. 485–490. *In* Proc. Br. Weed Control Conf., Brighton, England. November 1974. ARC Weed Res. Organ., Begbroke Hill, Oxford.
4. Finney, D. J. 1971. Probit analysis. Cambridge Univ. Press, Cambridge, England.
5. Fisher, R. 1975. Ph.D. Thesis. Herbicide tolerance in amenity grasses. The Queen's Univ. of Belfast.
6. ————, and J. S. Faulkner. 1975. The tolerance of twelve grass species to a range of foliar-absorbed and root-absorbed grass-killing herbicides. p. 204–215. *In* Proc. Europ. Weed Res. Soc. Symp. Status and Control of Grassweeds in Europe, Paris, France. December 1975. Eur. Weed Res. Soc., Wageningen, Netherlands.
7. Gibeault, V. A. 1974. *Poa annua*. Calif. Turfgrass Culture. 24(2):13–16.
8. Goss, R. L., and F. Zook. 1971. New approach for *Poa annua* control. Golf Superintendent. 39(1):46–48.
9. Harter, H. L. 1960. Critical values for Duncan's New Multiple Range Test. Biometrics 20:671–685.
10. McMaugh, P. 1971. Control of encroachment of *Agrostis* spp. swards by warm season turfgrasses. J. Sports Turf Res. Inst. 47:33–40.
11. Stottlemyer, W. E., and R. Bailey. 1972. Unique approaches to weed control. p. 75–89. *In* Richard Schmidt (ed.). Proc. Scotts Turfgrass Res. Conf., Maryville, Ohio. July 1970. O. M. Scott & Sons, Maryville, Ohio.
12. Woolhouse, A. R., and J. P. Shildrick. 1971. The control of annual meadow grass in fine turf. J. Sports Turf Res. Inst. 47:9–25.
13. Wright, C. E. 1966. Some implications of genotype-herbicide interactions in the breeding of *Lolium perenne*. Euphytica 15:229–238.

Chapter 3

An Approach to Turfgrass Cultivar Evaluation[1]

A. J. TURGEON
J. M. VARGAS, JR.

ABSTRACT

The release of many new turfgrass cultivars and experimental selections for testing by experiment stations and quantity of resources needed to evaluate each candidate has placed a tremendous burden on research personnel. A multiphase system of evaluation is proposed for more efficiently determining the limits of adaptation and obtainable quality levels for cultivars within a region. The system includes: Phase I, evaluation to establish performance characteristics of cultivars sustained under a "moderate intensity" of culture; Phase II, evaluation to determine the mowing, fertilization, and irrigation requirements of the cultivars for best quality, as well as their range of adaptation within a prescribed cultural intensity spectrum; Phase III, evaluation to determine the limits of environmental adaptation for each cultivar and any unique features that affect its potential use.

Results of cultivar evaluations conducted in Urbana, Ill. are reported and some of the problems encountered in reporting data are discussed. Conclusions are based on evaluations conducted with over 40 cultivars of Kentucky bluegrass (*Poa pratensis* L.) and perennial ryegrass (*Lolium perenne* L.)

INTRODUCTION

Variability naturally existing within turfgrass species has allowed development of many cultivars that differ widely in appearance, environmental and cultural adaptation, disease susceptibility, and other characteristics. Until recently, most cultivars resulted from selection and field testing of naturally occurring ecotypes (5). Mutation breeding with ionizing radiation (10) and interspecific and intraspecific hybridization (5, 9) are additional methods employed to modify the turfgrass genotype for developing new cultivars. The number of Kentucky bluegrass (*Poa pratensis* L.) cultivars that have been released for testing and/or commercial distribution has grown from two in 1954 to 38 in 1968 (6), and many additional cultivars have been added and are currently under evaluation.

Before a new turfgrass is released, sufficient testing is necessary to accurately determine the limits of its adaptation and performance under various cultural conditions. Daniel (4) stated that testing was necessary to establish the quality, relative to some standard, of a cultivar under local conditions prior to commercialization. Shildrick (11) suggested that cultivar evaluation should be directed toward determining establishment

[1] A contribution from the Horticulture Dep., Univ. of Illinois, Urbana, IL 61801 and the Dep. of Botany and Plant Pathology, Michigan State Univ., East Lansing, MI 48824 USA.

vigor, persistence under culture, disease resistance, and aesthetic and functional quality. According to Funk (5), the most important attributes of an improved cultivar are dependability, durability, reduced maintenance requirements, and attractive appearance. He emphasized that these attributes are achieved through: improved resistance to diseases, insects, nematodes, and weeds; lower growth habit and better turf-forming properties; increased tolerance to environmental stress, wear, close mowing, and poor soil conditions. Results from extensive evaluation of Kentucky bluegrass cultivars by Beard at Michigan State University were reported by Payne (8); he illustrated wide differences among cultivars in wear tolerance, water-submersion tolerance, water-use rate, low temperature hardiness, shade adaptation, and overall performance.

For a specific cultivar, many of the characteristics listed here may vary depending upon the cultural system imposed on the turf. Turgeon and Meyer (13) showed that the incidence and severity of fusarium blight (*Fusarium roseum* (Lk.) Snyd. & Hans. f. sp. *cerealis* (Cke.) Snyd. & Hans. and *F. tricinotum* (Cda.) Snyd. & Hans. f. sp. *poae* (Pk.) Snyd. & Hans.) and dollar spot (*Sclerotinia homeocarpa* F. T. Bennet) diseases in five Kentucky bluegrass cultivars were significantly affected by mowing and fertilization practices. The prediction of a cultivar's performance based upon test results is thus limited to the cultural intensities employed in the evaluation.

It is apparent from a survey of the existing literature that considerable information from many test sites is needed to properly assess the performance potential of new turfgrass cultivars. The process of accumulating the required information can be simplified, however, by a well-organized system of evaluation in which priorities and a reasonable sequence of investigative activity are clearly established. In the authors' view, such a system would employ three distinct phases of evaluation: Phase I, to provide a general characterization of turfgrass cultivars sustained under a "moderate intensity" of culture; Phase II, to determine the limits of turfgrass cultivar adaptation within a cultural intensity spectrum; Phase III, to evaluate cultivars according to specific criteria.

A. Phase I

The most typical method of cultivar evaluation involves establishing and sustaining replicated plots under lawn conditions to determine seasonal quality levels compared to one or more standard cultivars (perhaps 'Merion' and 'Kenblue' Kentucky bluegrass). Within this context, shoot density, uniformity, leaf texture, growth habit, and color can be measured or estimated. In addition, thatching tendency, seedhead production, diseases, and other easily determined characteristics can be monitored. Phase I testing can serve as a source of plant material for specialized study in Phase III. Data collection should be performed at sufficient frequency to adequately assess the magnitude of variation in quality throughout each growing season. Four to six quality ratings during the growing season, supplemented with ratings of individual diseases and other specific conditions, are usually adequate. It is important that cultural practices be performed uniformly from year to year in order to provide an accumulation of information that is not obscured by cultural variables. The number of years necessary for properly conducting Phase I evaluation is a matter of concern. Too few will obviously not provide information obtainable from a longer evaluation, but very long-term evaluations tie up resources that could be used for other objectives. It is generally believed that 5 to 6 years is minimum for adequately evaluating a new cultivar.

B. Phase II

The purpose of a Phase II evaluation is to determine the performance characteristics of turfgrass cultivars under different cultural intensities. This provides two important areas of information: adaptation of cultivars within the spectrum of cultural intensities imposed and an approximation of cultural requirements of individual cultivars for optimum quality. The time necessary for achieving the objectives of this type of evaluation is debatable, however, the experience of the authors suggests that a shorter period is required for Phase II than for Phase I evaluations.

C. Phase III

Any form of testing that falls outside of Phases I and II can be considered as Phase III evaluation. There are many purposes for conducting specialized investigations; they may reflect the specific interests of the investigator, or they may be related to the conditions existing at a given location. In Illinois, clippings from turfgrass cultivars were analyzed for xanthophyll (12) and crude protein (14) levels to determine the potential use of the leaf material in animal feeds. Investigations have been conducted to determine the shade adaptation and cold hardiness of various turfgrass cultivars (2). In Michigan, Beard (1) and Martin and Beard (7) conducted specialized tests to determine sod strengths and transplant sod rooting of Kentucky bluegrass cultivars. Phase III may involve establishing plots under specific conditions, or simply using plant material from Phase I or II plots for studies conducted in the field, greenhouse, laboratory, or controlled-environment chambers. The duration of Phase III evaluations can vary widely, but may be very short-termed.

The studies reported herein illustrate the use of a multiphase system of turfgrass cultivar evaluation. Results from these investigations are specific to east-central Illinois and may not be representative of other locations.

MATERIALS AND METHODS

A. Phase I

Field plots of 42 cultivars of Kentucky bluegrass were established by seed in April 1972 at the Ornamental Horticulture Research Center in Urbana, Ill. Plots measured 1.8 × 2.4 m and each cultivar or experimental selection was replicated three times in a randomized complete block design. No physical amendments were incorporated into the Flanagan silt loam (Aquic Argiudoll) soil. Phosphorus and K fertilizers were applied at rates based on soil test results. Seeding rate was 30 g/plot. Following planting, each plot was lightly raked and sprayed with an elastomeric polymer emulsion (SOILGARD®) to stabilize the seedbed. Light irrigations were made as needed to encourage germination and seedling growth. After establishment, the plots were irrigated as necessary to prevent wilting. Fertilization was performed four times annually to supply a total of 2 kg N/are using four equal increments of water-soluble 10–2.6–3 (N–P–K) analysis fertilizer applied in April, May, August, and September. The plot area was mowed two or three times per week during the growing season at 3.8 cm with a powered reel mower. Leaf clippings were normally returned during mowing. Visual turfgrass quality ratings were made at least five times each season and disease incidence, thatching tendency, chemical composition of leaf tissue, and other parameters were also evaluated. Most evaluations were made using a rating scale of 1 to 9, with 1 representing best quality and 9 representing poorest quality. For leaf spot (*Helminthosporium vagans* Dreschl.) and fusarium blight diseases the 1 to 9 scale was also used, with 1 representing no visual disease symptoms and 9 representing complete necrosis of the leaves. Stripe smut (*Ustilago striiformis* (West.) Niessl) data were obtained by estimating the percent infected tillers with two 900-cm^2 areas in each plot.

B. Phase II

Organization of Cultural Treatments within Cultivar

Large adjacent blocks of five Kentucky bluegrass cultivars, including 'Nugget', Merion, 'Fylking', 'Pennstar', and Kenblue, measuring 7.8 × 7.8 m, were established in April 1972 as in Phase I (A). In April 1973 each block was divided into 1.8- × 2.4-m plots for different fertilization treatments, then subdivided for 3.8- and 1.9-cm mowing heights. Annual fertilization treatments included 1, 2, 3, and 4 kg N/are applied in four equal increments in April, May, August, and September using a 10–2.6–3.3 (N–P–K) water-soluble fertilizer. Irrigation was performed as needed to prevent wilting. In September 1973 a sixth cultivar block-sodded with 'A-20' Kentucky bluegrass was added to the study.

Organization of cultivars within Cultural Treatments

Twenty-one cultivars of Kentucky bluegrass and one of a perennial ryegrass (*Lolium perenne* L.) were seeded in September 1974. Fifteen plots, measuring 1.5 × 1.8 m each, were planted for each cultivar. In September 1975 five different cultural intensities were initiated, each with three replications. These included: 1.9-cm mowing height with 2 or 4 kg N/are/year; 3.8-cm mowing height with 2 or 4 kg N; 7.5-cm mowing height with 0.5 kg N. Except for plots maintained under the 7.5-cm mowing height, fertilization and irrigation were as above; no irrigation was performed and fertilization was conducted in April for the plots mowed at 7.5 cm.

C. Phase III

Four combinations of two Kentucky bluegrasses (Fylking and 'A-34') and two perennial ryegrasses ('Citation' and 'Pennfine') were seeded in May 1975. The perennial ryegrass component of each cultivar combination was 5, 10, 15, 20, 25, or 50% of the seed mixture by weight. Plots measured 1.5 × 1.8 m and each seed mixture was replicated three times in a randomized complete block design. The seeding rate for all mixtures was 30 g/plot. Establishment and maintenance were as in Phase I (A). After 2 years, two 5- × 5-cm plugs were extracted from all replications of plots planted with 10, 20, and 50% perennial ryegrass for determining the distribution of Kentucky bluegrass and perennial ryegrass by shoot counts.

RESULTS AND DISCUSSION

A. Phase I Evaluation

Cultivars of Kentucky bluegrass varied widely in spring greenup based on data collected in April 1975, with 'Brunswick' ranking best and Nugget ranking poorest (Table 1). In 1975, Touchdown and Park represented the extremes in thatching tendency.

Extensive infestations of stripe smut occurred for the first time in May 1977, however, only Merion and 'Windsor' were consistently high in the percent infected tillers over all replications. Other cultivars varied in the severity of this disease depending upon the proximity of plots to either Merion or Windsor. Helminthosporium leaf spot and fusarium blight disease ratings are averages of 3 and 2 years' data, respectively. Although most cultivars were fairly consistent in the severity of leaf spot from year to year, there were some notable exceptions. Campina had increasingly severe infestations over the 3-year period of observation while the leaf

Table 1. Results from phase I evlauation of Kentucky bluegrass cultivars established in April 1972.†

Cultivar	Spring Greenup 1975	Thatch depth 1975	Leaf spot 1973–75	Stripe smut 1977	Fusarium blight 1974–75	Quality ratings 1973	1974	1975	1976
		cm		%					
A-20	4.0	1.24	1.8	0	1.0	2.8	2.8	2.7	2.2
A-34	3.0	1.11	2.3	0	1.2	2.4	2.3	2.9	2.5
Adelphi	2.7	1.25	2.2	0	1.0	2.5	2.4	2.6	2.9
Baron	5.3	1.37	2.8	2.3	1.2	3.0	2.9	3.3	2.7
Bonnieblue	3.0	1.01	2.0	0	1.3	2.8	2.8	2.9	3.3
Brunswick	2.0	1.54	2.3	0	2.3	2.4	2.7	3.1	2.7
Campina	2.3	1.06	5.8	0	1.0	3.6	3.6	4.7	4.3
Cheri	3.3	1.58	2.8	0	1.5	3.1	2.8	2.9	2.6
Delft	2.3	1.04	3.6	0	4.2	4.3	2.6	4.3	3.1
Enmundi	3.3	1.14	2.6	0	1.0	2.8	2.8	2.9	2.7
Entopper	3.7	1.19	2.1	10.0	1.7	2.9	2.8	3.5	3.2
Enoble	5.7	1.26	2.2	0	1.2	2.8	2.8	3.5	2.7
Fylking	4.3	1.30	2.3	0.3	2.2	2.8	3.0	3.5	3.0
Galaxy	3.7	1.17	1.7	6.7	1.5	2.7	2.4	3.0	2.8
Geronimo	3.0	1.25	2.1	53.3	2.0	3.2	3.0	3.5	3.1
Glade	3.7	1.54	2.7	0	1.0	2.8	2.6	3.1	2.7
Kenblue	3.0	0.96	5.4	0	1.8	4.8	4.3	3.8	3.7
Majestic	2.7	1.41	1.6	0	1.0	2.5	2.4	2.6	3.0
Merion	3.0	1.02	1.7	76.7	1.5	2.8	2.5	2.9	3.1
Monopoly	2.7	1.06	2.4	0	1.0	3.0	2.1	2.5	2.6
Nugget	7.7	1.52	1.4	0	2.2	2.8	3.0	4.7	3.5
Parade	2.3	1.01	2.1	2.0	1.2	2.5	2.6	2.8	2.6
Park	2.3	0.71	6.0	20.3	2.3	5.2	4.4	4.2	3.9
Pennstar	4.0	1.22	1.9	13.3	1.7	2.8	2.8	3.3	2.8
Plush	3.7	1.33	2.6	0	1.8	2.8	2.4	2.9	2.5
RAM #1	4.3	1.68	3.3	0	1.2	3.8	3.3	3.5	3.1
Rugby	2.7	1.21	2.0	25.0	1.2	2.8	2.6	2.9	2.7
Sodco	3.0	1.37	2.9	0.3	1.2	3.0	2.8	2.7	2.5
Sydsport	4.0	1.22	2.1	0	1.3	2.5	2.6	3.1	2.6
Touchdown	3.3	1.91	2.1	0	1.2	2.8	2.3	3.0	2.6
Vantage	3.0	1.02	4.0	0	1.5	3.5	3.2	3.2	3.1
Victa	5.0	1.47	2.4	0	1.0	2.9	2.8	3.4	3.1
Windsor	3.0	1.22	3.2	90.0	1.0	3.0	2.8	2.8	2.8
L.S.D.$_{0.05}$	0.9	0.44	0.6	11.2	1.0	0.7	0.7	0.7	0.6

† Evaluations were made using a scale of 1 to 9 with 1 representing best quality or no disease, and 9 representing poorest quality or complete necrosis from disease activity. Stripe smut is reported as percent infected tillers. Annual quality ratings are an average of five ratings made during each growing season.

spot incidence in RAM #1 was substantially less following the 1st year (Fig. 1). The incidence of fusarium blight disease was quite variable among replications, with only Delft showing consistently high disease ratings (Table 1). However, the occurrence of severely diseased and disease-free conditions in adjacent plots indicated substantial differences among cultivars in their relative susceptibilities to this disease. Thus, any table values above 1.0 should be interpreted as indicating some level of fusarium blight susceptibility even though statistically significant differences may not exist.

Turfgrass quality ratings are typically averaged for each year of observation when reporting several years of data. Cultivars which are consistently good or consistently poor can usually be differentiated by this method of reporting. However, annual quality data do not reflect the variation in quality that may occur during a particular growing season.

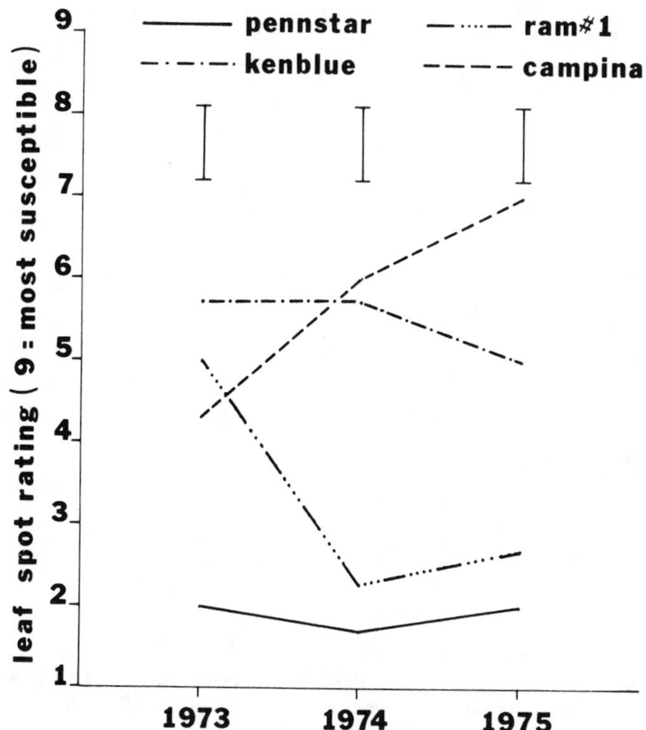

Fig. 1. Variation in helminthosporium leaf spot incidence over 3 years in four Kentucky bluegrass cultivars. Vertical bars indicate significant differences at the 5% level.

For example, Nugget is poor in spring greenup and is susceptible to fusarium blight disease, but its leaf spot resistance is outstanding. Conversely, Park is good in spring greenup, poor in leaf spot resistance, and is also susceptible to fusarium blight. Consequently, these two cultivars may undergo wide variations in quality during the course of a growing season while some others, such as 'P-140', are consistently good throughout the growing season (Fig. 2). The poor heat-stress tolerance of Nugget, irrespective of fusarium blight incidence, also accounts for its poor midsummer quality in central Illinois.

Annual quality ratings reflect the conditions existing during that particular growing season, and the frequency and timing of data collection. Although the annual averages reported in Table 1 are each composed of five quality ratings, 1975 was the only year in which early spring quality was included in the average. Thus, cultivars which are relatively slow to greenup in spring showed somewhat poorer quality for that year. This indicates that quality ratings should be made at approximately the same time each year, otherwise comparisons of the annual averages for a particular cultivar can be misleading.

Information from the Phase I evaluation can provide some direction for proceeding with subsequent evaluations. For example, relatively high thatching tendency may indicate better adaptation to close mowing and

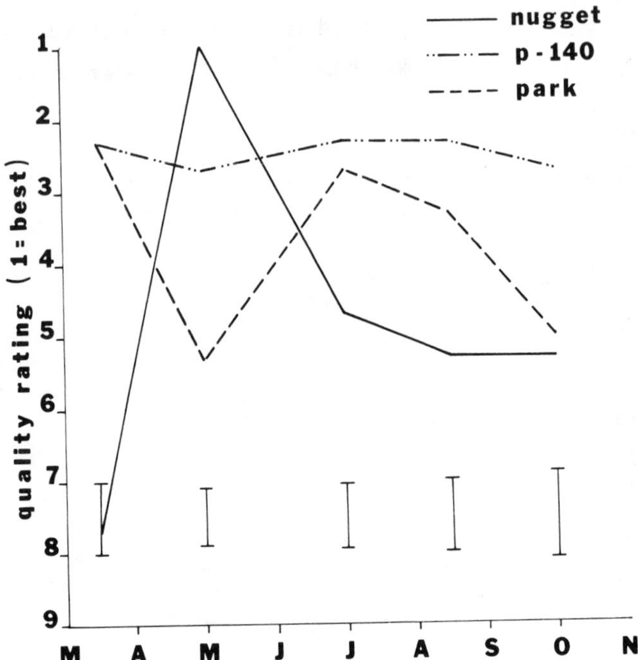

Fig. 2. Variation in turfgrass quality during the growing season in three Kentucky bluegrass cultivars. Vertical bars indicate significant differences at the 5% level.

improved competitive ability against annual bluegrass (*Poa annua* L.) and other weeds.

B. Phase II Evaluation

Different cultural intensities employed in a Phase II evaluation show the cultivars best adapted to different regions of the cultural intensity spectrum. The results, however, depend upon the organizational design used for this test. Where the cultural intensity, including mowing height and fertilization rate, is varied within a cultivar block and irrigation is frequent, annual bluegrass typically develops first in the closely mowed, heavily fertilized plots. With time, adjacent plots may also have more annual bluegrass, especially where the incidence of helminthosporium leaf spot disease and fusarium blight severely reduce the competitive ability of the Kentucky bluegrass (Fig. 3, Table 2). A different organization of cultivars with respect to cultural intensities may yield quite different and, perhaps, more valid results. Where the cultivars were arranged within cultural intensity blocks, the annual bluegrass pressure was most severe in the block sustained under the highest intensity of culture (1.9-cm mowing, 4 kg N/are/year). The cultivars that were quickly invaded by annual bluegrass served as seed sources for adjacent plots to encourage infestation among

Table 2. Statistical analysis of data from phase II evaluation illustrated in Fig. 3.

Source of variation	df	"F" values					
		A-20	Nugget	Merion	Fylking	Pennstar	Kenblue
Mowing height (M)	1	23.9*	19.3*	24.3*	35.3*	497.0**	70.7*
Fertilization (F)	3	0.6	7.9**	8.1**	18.8**	4.3*	10.7**
M × F	3	0.6	5.0*	2.8	7.9**	1.9	0.7

*,** F values significant at the 5 and 1% levels.

all cultivars (Fig. 4). Under these conditions, A-34, Brunswick, 'Sydsport,' and Touchdown were outstanding in their resistance to annual bluegrass invasion. At the same mowing height but under a lower fertilization level of 2 kg N/are/year, annual bluegrass pressure was considerably less so that all but two cultivars had less than 10% infestation. At the higher mowing heights of 3.8 and 7.5 cm, no annual bluegrass invasion was evident.

Under the lowest intensity of culture, differences in turfgrass quality among cultivars were small but usually significant (Table 3). Although

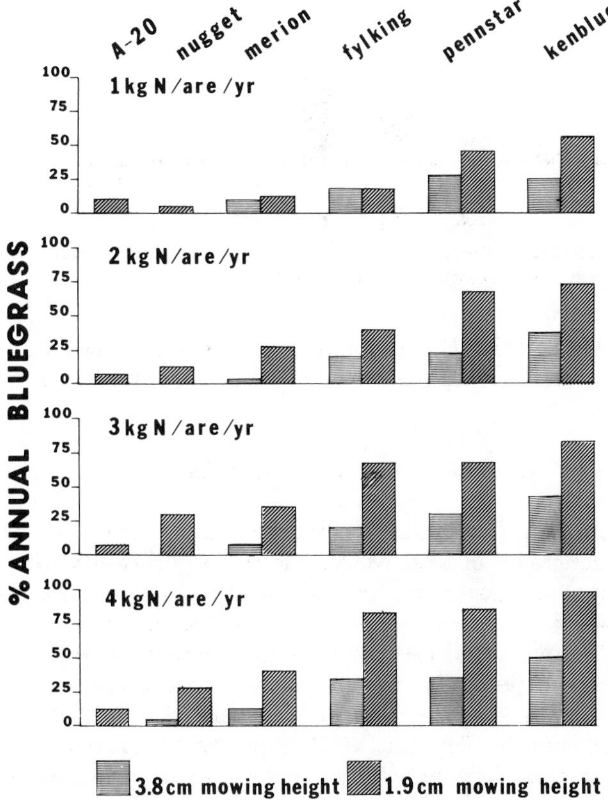

Fig. 3. Effects of mowing height and fertilization rate on the percent annual bluegrass in six Kentucky bluegrass cultivars.

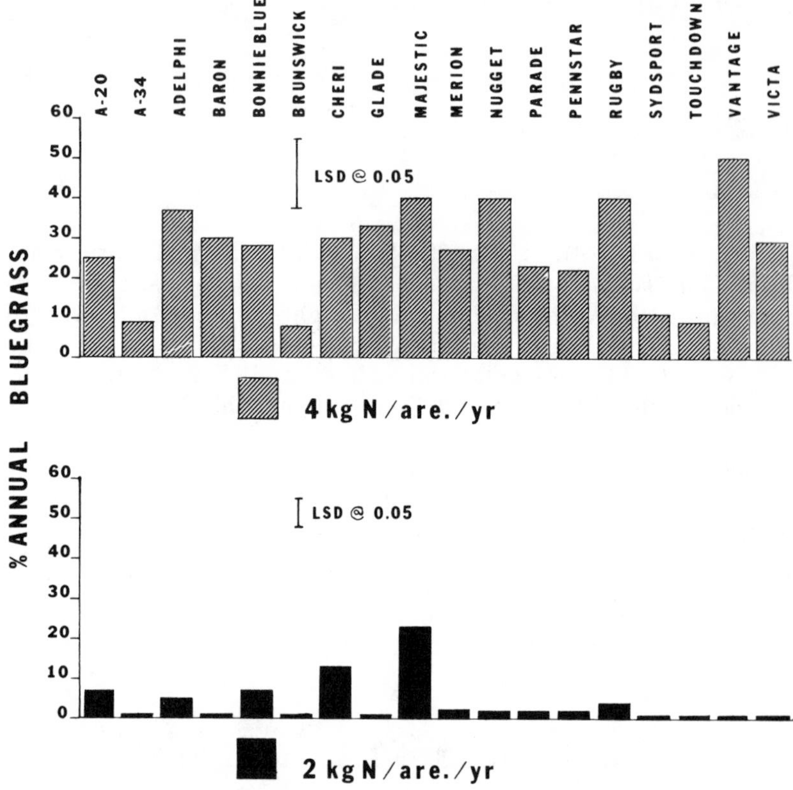

Fig. 4. Comparison of 18 Kentucky bluegrass cultivars in their susceptibility to annual bluegrass invasion at 1.9-cm mowing and two levels of fertilization.

not included in this test, the common Kentucky bluegrasses were observed by Funk (5) to be somewhat better adapted to this cultural regime.

C. Phase III Evaluation

Combinations of Kentucky bluegrass and perennial ryegrass at different percentages of seed weight yielded significantly different proportions of the two species in plots, depending upon the cultivars selected (Fig. 5). A-34 Kentucky bluegrass was more competitive than Fylking, while Pennfine perennial ryegrass was more competitive than Citation. The 20% level of perennial ryegrass in the stand 2 years after planting was exceeded by both perennial ryegrasses at 10% of the seed mixture with Fylking, and by Pennfine at 20% of the seed mixture with A-34. However, less than 20% perennial ryegrass occurred in stands resulting from 50:50 mixtures of A-34 and Citation by seed weight. The rapid germination and vigorous seedling growth of perennial ryegrass makes it desirable in seed mixtures for rapid soil cover, but undesirable where it

Table 3. Performance of Kentucky bluegrass cultivars sustained at 7.5-cm mowing, minimal fertilization, and no irrigation.

Cultivar	Quality ratings†				
	July	Aug.	Oct.	Mar.	May
A-20	4.3	4.7	5.3	8.0	5.7
A-34	4.7	5.0	5.7	8.0	6.3
Adelphi	4.7	4.3	5.7	7.0	7.3
Baron	5.0	4.0	5.0	8.0	6.7
Bonnieblue	4.7	4.0	5.0	7.0	7.3
Brunswick	4.0	4.7	6.3	7.0	6.7
Cheri	5.0	4.7	5.0	8.0	7.3
Glade	4.3	4.3	4.0	7.7	6.7
Majestic	5.3	5.3	5.7	7.0	7.7
Merion	5.0	5.3	6.0	7.7	7.0
Nugget	4.3	4.7	5.3	8.0	7.7
Parade	4.3	5.0	5.0	7.3	5.7
Pennstar	4.7	4.0	4.3	8.0	6.7
Rugby	5.0	5.3	5.0	7.0	6.7
Sydsport	4.3	4.7	5.3	8.0	6.3
Vantage	4.7	4.7	4.7	7.3	6.0
Victa	4.0	4.0	4.7	8.0	6.3
L.S.D.$_{0.05}$	1.0	0.9	1.0	0.4	1.1

† Visual turfgrass quality ratings were made using a scale of 1 through 9 with 1 representing excellent quality and 9 representing poorest quality.

becomes the dominant component of the turf. The selection of appropriate cultivars of these species is important in achieving the seemingly opposing objectives of rapid cover and a predominantly Kentucky bluegrass turf.

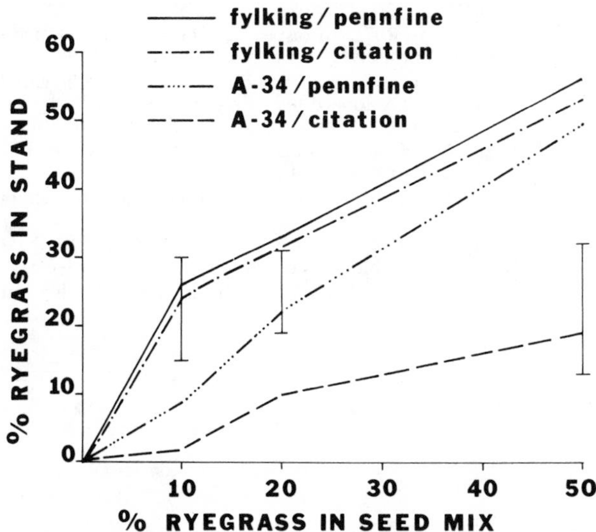

Fig. 5. Effects of two Kentucky bluegrass cultivars (Fylking and A-34) and two perennial ryegrass cultivars (Pennfine and Citation) on the perennial ryegrass composition of turf 2 years after planting with different proportions (by seed weight) of the two species. Vertical bars indicate significant differences at the 5% level.

A comprehensive evaluation of turfgrass cultivars requires much research effort. An organized system of evaluation, however, can be effective in reducing the amount of effort necessary to obtain the answers to questions of cultivar adaptation, culture, and use. It also provides a basis for cooperative efforts among experiment stations, since they can coordinate their Phase I evaluations while dividing responsibility for conducting the various Phase II and III evaluations within their region.

LITERATURE CITED

1. Beard, J. B. 1972. Comparative sod strengths and transplant sod rooting of Kentucky bluegrass cultivars and blends. p. 123–127. *In* Proc. 42nd Annu. Michigan Turfgrass Conf., Michigan State Univ., East Lansing.
2. ————. 1973. Sod production and transplanting for shaded areas. p. 105–111. *In* Proc. 43rd Annual Michigan Turfgrass Conf., Michigan State Univ., East Lansing.
3. ————, W. J. Eaton, and R. L. Yoder. 1973. Physiology research: Chemical growth regulators, water use rates, thatch causes, and low temperature bill. Proc. 43rd Annual Michigan Turfgrass Conf. 2:27–33.
4. Daniel, W. H. 1969. The evaluation of a new turfgrass. p. 57–64. *In* R. R. Davis (ed.) Proc. First Int. Turfgrass Res. Conf., Harrogate, England. July 1969. Sports Turf Res. Inst., Bingley, England.
5. Funk, C. R. 1974. Improving Kentucky bluegrass for turf. Proc. 15th Illinois Turfgrass Conf. p. 94–98.
6. Long, J. A. 1972. Developing superior turf varieties. p. 53–65. *In* V. B. Youngner and C. M. McKell (eds.) The biology and utilization of grasses. Physiological ecology series. Academic Press, Inc., New York.
7. Martin, D. P., and J. B. Beard. 1971. Comparative rooting ability of transplanted sods as affected by the particular variety or blend of Kentucky bluegrass. Michigan State Univ. Turfgrass Field Day Rep.
8. Payne, K. T. 1974. Kentucky bluegrass varietal evaluation results. Proc. 15th Illinois Turfgrass Conf. p. 99–101.
9. Pepin, G. W., and C. R. Funk. 1971. Intraspecific hybridization as a method of breeding Kentucky bluegrass (*Poa pratensis* L.) for turf. Crop Sci. 11:445–448.
10. Powell, J. B. 1974. Induced mutations in turfgrasses as a source of variation for improved cultivars. p. 3–8. *In* E. C. Roberts (ed.) Proc. Second Int. Turfgrass Res. Conf., Blacksburg, Va. June 1973. Am. Soc. Agron. and Crop Sci. Soc. Am., Madison, Wis.
11. Shildrick, J. P. 1969. Turfgrass variety trials in the U.K. p. 88–99. *In* Proc. First Int. Turfgrass Res. Conf., Sports Turf Research Institute, Bingley, England.
12. Turgeon, A. J., and Gene Lester. 1976. Xanthophyll levels in turfgrass clippings. Agron. J. 68:946–948.
13. ————, and W. A. Meyer. 1974. Effects of mowing height and fertilization level on disease incidence in five Kentucky bluegrasses. Plant Dis. Rep. 58:514–516.
14. ————, G. G. Stone, and T. R. Peck. 1979. Crude protein levels in turfgrass clippings. Agron. J. 71:229–232.

Chapter 4

Differences in Sod Strength, Rooting, and Turfgrass Quality of Kentucky Bluegrass Cultivars Resulting from Seasonal and Environmental Conditions[1]

L. H. TAYLOR
R. E. SCHMIDT

ABSTRACT

A field trial of Kentucky bluegrass (*Poa pratensis* L.) cultivars and selections was established at Blacksburg, Va., USA, in 1972 and evaluated for 4 years. Sod samples were removed and various supplementary measurements made to see which might relate to field performance.

Sod was removed in 1974 and 1976 and used to measure sod strength, regrowth from rhizomes (in area where sod was removed), strength of transplant sod rooting in sun and shade, and growth at moderate and high temperatures in growth chambers. Performances in the field and in these supplementary trials are reported and compared for 36 Kentucky bluegrass strains.

Sod strength in April 1974 was not related to turf quality ratings that year but July–August sod strength was. Shoot growth from rhizomes was negatively correlated with 1974 turf quality ratings. High growth chamber temperatures inhibited root and shoot growth. Total root weights and initiation of new roots were not correlated, but both were related to turf quality in the growth chamber and field trial. Rooting in sun and shade was correlated with shoot growth from rhizomes and with turf performance in the field 2 years later.

Additional index words: Sod strength, Transplant sod rooting, Turf quality.

INTRODUCTION

Evaluation of cultivar performance is an important part of turfgrass research programs. It is essential not only for development of improved cultivars but also for making recommendations and, in some countries, for registration. For perennial species, such as Kentucky bluegrass (*Poa pratensis* L.), performance trials must be maintained and observed for a period of years. Results from a particular site, cultural intensity, and years of a trial are assumed to indicate future performance at other sites and cultural regimes. Validity is increased by using performance data from several locations or from more than one trial at a particular location

[1] A contribution from the Dep. of Agronomy, Virginia Polytechnic Inst. and State Univ., Blacksburg, VA 24061 USA.

(8). It may also be desirable to evaluate the effects of cultural variables such as fertility or cutting height upon cultivar performance.

A technique, apparently not widely used, is to attempt other evaluations of a substantial number of Kentucky bluegrass cultivars and selections concurrently with their observation in a conventional performance trial. We report herein such an attempt in which sod pieces were taken from a trial and used to measure sod strength, emergence of shoots from rhizomes, transplant sod rooting, and root production under high and low temperature regimes. Production of tillers, rhizomes, and roots by turfgrasses has been reviewed in detail (2, 6, 12). For Kentucky bluegrass in particular, Etter (3) and Moser et al. (7) have reported on tiller and rhizome development, Hanson and Juska (4) and Watschke et al. (9) on root growth, and a recent study reported on both root and rhizome development for several cultivars and genotypes (10). Beard has evaluated the sod strength and transplant sod rooting for a wide range of Kentucky bluegrass cultivars (1).

MATERIALS AND METHODS

A turfgrass evaluation trial of Kentucky bluegrass cultivars and selections was seeded in Typic Hapludult clayey, kaolinitic mesic soil (Lodi silt loam) at Blacksburg, Va., USA, in May 1972. This trial was part of the northeastern regional (NE-57) turfgrass evaluation effort (8). Seed was obtained from originating stations or other authentic sources and furnished to participating experiment stations. The 66 entries, planted in randomized complete block design with three replications, included 52 Kentucky bluegrass cultivars or selections and 10 Kentucky bluegrass blends and four species mixtures. Plot size was 1.9 × 2.4 m. Annual fertilizer applications consisted of 150 kg/ha of N, 25 kg/ha of P, and 45 kg/ha of K with plots receiving one-third of the N in the fall, one-third in the winter, and one-third of the N and all the P and K in late spring. The grass was mowed at 4 cm and was evaluated periodically for turf quality, percent green cover, and prevalence of diseases.

In April and in July-August of 1974, 1.9- × 0.3-m sod strips 2.5 cm thick were cut from the 52 cultivars or selections in the trial and sod strength was measured by the force needed to pull the strip apart, utilizing the method of Rieke et al. (9). Pieces of April-harvested sod 30 × 45 cm were placed on wood frames with bottoms of hardward cloth and permitted to root on prepared soil in the sun and in the shade of mature oak trees. The amount of force (in kg) required to uproot the sod pieces was measured in June 1974 using the method of King and Beard (5) as modified by Schmidt. Shoots growing from rhizomes in the area from which the sod had been removed were counted in May for April-cut sod and in November for July-August-cut sod.

In March 1976 sod pieces of 36 entries (all of the named Kentucky bluegrass cultivars on that date and several selections of interest) were removed from the first two replications of the trial with a 15-cm cup cutter, trimmed to 2 cm of soil depth, and placed on aluminum mesh over plastic lined 15-cm diam metal cans filled with a complete nutrient solution containing 100 ppm NO_3-N (10). The containers were placed in two growth chambers with light at 32,292 lux for a 12-hour day. After root growth had begun, the cool growth chamber was programmed at 23 to 16 C day-night (T1) and the warm chamber at 34 to 27 C day-night (T2). Sod pieces were clipped weekly to 2 cm for a period of 5 weeks. The experiment was terminated on 21 Apr. 1976 and scored for new root initiation and for turf quality. Total root growth dry weight was determined. While certain measurements were made on all 52 cultivars or selections, data reported herein from all studies are for only the 36 entries in the 1976 growth chamber study.

All data were subjected to analysis of variance. When the F ratio was found to be significant, L.S.D.'s at the 5% level of significance were computed. Simple correlations were calculated using data recorded for individual field plots or for sod pieces taken from those plots.

RESULTS AND DISCUSSION

Turf quality ratings indicate that most entries were still relatively attractive 2 years following establishment (Table 1). Differences among entries for quality were highly significant at each season in 1974. Correlations between quality ratings for the three seasons were significant at the 1% level.

Sod strips cut in the spring averaged 70% greater sod strength than sod strips cut from the same plots in midsummer. Differences in sod strength were significant at the 1% level in April and at the 5% level in July–August. The correlation of sod strength for the two dates was 0.25**. Sod strength in April was not significantly correlated with any of the 1974 quality ratings but sod strength in July–August had correlations of 0.33**, 0.20*, and 0.20* with the quality ratings taken in the spring, summer, and fall, respectively.

When one considers that Moser et al. (7) found that a long photoperiod favored rhizome initiation and growth and Etter (3) found that growth of rhizomes was least in late winter and early spring, the relationships observed seem logical. The July–August sod strength resulted in part from rhizome growth in 1974 while April sod strength should have been related to rhizome growth during 1973.

Counts of shoot regrowth from rhizomes were made in May on the area where sod was cut in April and in November where sod was cut in July–August. Shoot counts among entries were not significant. The shoot counts at the two dates were correlated (r = 0.46**). Shoot regrowth in May was negatively correlated (r = −0.22*) with sod strength in April. This may indicate a tendency for entries with deeper rhizomes to have fewer rhizomes in the sod strip used to measure strength. The May shoot

Table 1. Field turf quality ratings, 1974, sod strength of removed sections, and shoots growing from rhizomes following sod removal.

NE-57 entry no.	Cultivars or strains	Turf quality†			Sod strength		No. of shoots from rhizomes	
		27 Mar.	16 July	24 Oct.	April	July–Aug.	16 May	14 Nov.
					kg			
1	Nugget	4.3	5.3	5.3	38	30	41	11
2	Merion	6.0	5.3	5.3	35	18	15	17
3	Fylking	5.3	4.3	5.0	63	33	21	9
4	Glade	6.0	5.0	6.3	52	29	12	13
5	Touchdown	6.3	5.0	6.3	54	28	28	20
6	Kenblue	5.7	5.7	6.7	31	17	26	8
7	Baron	6.0	5.0	6.0	46	20	19	18
8	Victa	5.7	5.7	6.0	57	19	12	11
11	Vantage	6.3	6.0	5.7	34	19	16	11
12	Park	5.3	6.0	5.7	29	18	28	19
13	Windsor	6.7	6.0	6.0	35	26	13	12
14	Sydsport	6.0	6.3	6.0	47	35	15	15
15	Bonnieblue	6.7	5.7	6.0	52	24	23	13
16	Majestic	6.7	5.7	6.0	46	39	19	18
17	Campina	5.3	4.7	5.7	35	10	19	13
18	Monopoly	6.7	5.0	6.0	46	32	25	20
19	Galaxy	5.7	6.3	6.0	41	24	29	19
20	Geronimo	6.7	5.3	6.0	46	28	28	14
21	Brunswick	7.0	5.7	6.3	61	23	10	12
29	K1-158	6.3	6.3	6.3	38	20	4	10
32	Sodco	7.3	5.3	6.7	44	27	15	14
33	Cheri	6.0	4.7	6.0	53	30	13	9
34	Adelphi	7.3	6.0	6.7	45	30	11	14
35	Parade	6.0	3.7	4.0	45	30	38	19
36	Enmundi	6.3	5.3	6.0	54	35	16	22
39	Enoble	5.7	4.7	6.3	41	22	14	10
40	Pennstar	6.7	4.3	5.7	74	35	15	12
53	Delft	5.3	4.7	5.0	39	17	20	11
54	CEBECO 71-2	7.0	6.0	6.7	38	25	12	8
57	Plush	6.7	6.3	7.0	45	29	10	17
58	PSU 150	6.0	6.0	6.0	36	30	34	22
60	P-154	5.3	5.7	5.3	47	30	28	21
61	P-143	7.0	5.3	5.7	37	34	48	21
64	PSU 197	6.0	4.7	4.7	43	18	9	6
65	PSU 190	7.0	6.0	6.7	56	39	16	16
66	PSU 169	6.0	6.0	6.0	36	27	22	21
Mean		6.18	5.42	5.92	45.1	26.3	20.1	14.6
L.S.D. 0.05		0.43	0.38	0.40	11.3	11.1	n.s.	n.s.

† Turf quality scores from 1 (poorest) to 9 (best).

counts were negatively correlated with spring, summer, and fall quality ratings (r = −0.25**, r = −0.22*, and r = −0.33**, respectively). This relationship might have resulted if plants with fewer rhizomes had more tiller development. Etter (3) reported that strongly tillered plants seldom have many rhizomes.

Turf quality ratings for 1976 reported in Table 2 were much lower than in 1974. The highest average quality ratings were given in July. Difference in quality ratings among cultivars were significant at each season.

Ratings among cultivars for percent green cover were significant at the 1% level at each season. Ratings made at the three dates were correlated with each other and each date was correlated with all 1976 turf quality

Table 2. Field turf quality ratings, 1976, percent green cover, and resistance to red thread.

NE-57 entry no.	Cultivar or strain	Turf quality†			Percent green cover‡			Red thread resistance§
		9 Apr.	19 July	19 Oct.	7 Apr.	19 July	19 Oct.	12 July
1	Nugget	4.0	4.7	5.3	62	63	78	4.0
2	Merion	4.7	5.0	4.7	68	63	72	6.7
3	Fylking	3.3	4.3	3.7	52	60	62	5.7
4	Glade	4.3	4.3	4.3	64	52	70	3.3
5	Touchdown	5.7	5.7	5.3	78	73	78	5.7
6	Kenblue	4.7	4.7	4.0	68	50	70	2.7
7	Baron	4.0	4.3	4.0	57	62	70	3.7
8	Victa	4.0	5.3	5.3	57	70	80	4.7
11	Vantage	5.3	5.0	4.3	73	67	72	6.0
12	Park	4.7	4.7	3.7	65	52	62	4.0
13	Windsor	3.0	4.0	4.3	35	47	72	6.0
14	Sydsport	4.7	4.7	4.7	58	63	75	5.0
15	Bonnieblue	4.3	5.0	4.0	58	63	68	6.3
16	Majestic	4.7	4.7	4.7	70	57	72	6.0
17	Campina	4.0	4.3	4.3	62	57	65	5.3
18	Monopoly	4.7	5.0	4.7	70	63	72	6.0
19	Galaxy	3.3	4.0	3.7	52	50	63	6.0
20	Geronimo	5.7	5.0	4.3	65	62	73	6.3
21	Brunswick	4.3	5.0	4.3	65	62	73	4.3
29	K1-158	5.7	4.7	4.0	71	60	72	5.3
32	Sodco	5.0	5.3	5.0	72	62	77	6.7
33	Cheri	4.7	5.7	5.0	72	68	78	5.0
34	Adelphi	5.0	5.3	5.0	73	65	80	7.3
35	Parade	4.3	4.3	3.0	65	47	53	6.3
36	Enmundi	4.3	5.7	5.0	60	70	78	6.3
39	Enoble	4.3	5.0	4.7	58	60	78	5.0
40	Pennstar	4.3	4.7	4.7	60	57	75	6.0
53	Delft	4.0	4.7	4.0	58	58	65	6.3
54	CEBECO 71-2	5.3	5.3	5.3	82	62	85	6.3
57	Plush	5.0	5.3	5.3	68	65	83	4.7
58	PSU 150	5.0	5.3	4.3	72	65	72	4.3
60	P-154	5.0	5.0	4.0	65	60	72	5.7
61	P-143	5.0	5.0	4.0	73	57	68	5.3
64	PSU 197	5.3	4.7	4.3	72	58	67	4.0
65	PSU 190	5.7	5.3	5.0	73	75	75	6.0
66	PSU 169	4.3	5.7	4.7	65	67	73	5.7
Mean		4.60	4.91	4.47	64.9	60.8	72.2	5.39
L.S.D. 0.05		0.43	0.33	0.35	6.1	3.8	3.9	0.65

† Turf quality scores from 1 (poorest) to 9 (best). ‡ Percentage of plot area that is green tissue of the seeded species. § Red thread disease resistance scores from 1 (entirely diseased) to 9 (no disease).

ratings. As might be expected, the highest correlations were for percent green cover and turf quality ratings made at the same season, the values being 0.80**, 0.75**, and 0.85** for spring, summer, and fall ratings, respectively.

A severe red thread (*Corticium fuciforme* (Berk.) Wakef.) infection was observed during the summer of 1976 and reaction was scored on 12 July. Differences among entries for reaction to this disease were significant at the 1% level. The only significant correlations with the red thread scores were with a quality score of 19 July (r = 0.24*) and with percent green cover on 19 July (r = 0.21*). The disease apparently had only a temporary effect on turf quality.

The 1974 data on transplant sod rooting in sun and shade (Table 3)

Table 3. Strength of transplant sod rooting in sun and shade, 1974, and 21 Apr. 1976, growth chamber total root weights, initiation of new roots, and turf quality at Temperature 1 (T1) and Temperature 2 (T2).

NE-57 entry no.	Cultivar or strain	Transplant sod rooting		Root wt.		New roots†		Turf quality‡	
		Sun	Shade	T1	T2	T1	T2	T1	T2
		——kg——		——g——					
1	Nugget	80	31	0.74	0.14	4.5	2.5	7.0	4.0
2	Merion	59	30	0.52	0.14	5.0	3.5	7.0	4.5
3	Fylking	69	27	0.51	0.16	4.0	2.0	5.5	4.0
4	Glade	64	25	0.53	0.22	4.5	1.5	7.0	5.0
5	Touchdown	59	29	0.44	0.09	5.5	2.0	6.5	4.5
6	Kenblue	46	16	0.10	0.08	4.0	2.5	5.5	2.5
7	Baron	77	27	0.36	0.10	4.0	2.5	6.0	3.5
8	Victa	73	24	0.65	0.22	4.5	2.5	6.5	5.0
11	Vantage	66	27	0.37	0.13	5.5	2.0	7.0	3.0
12	Park	52	18	0.41	0.17	4.0	3.5	5.5	4.5
13	Windsor	63	27	0.12	0.04	4.0	2.0	5.0	3.5
14	Sydsport	80	32	0.54	0.17	5.5	2.5	7.5	5.5
15	Bonnieblue	67	26	0.64	0.35	5.0	3.5	7.5	6.0
16	Majestic	77	27	0.38	0.13	6.0	2.5	7.5	4.0
17	Campina	61	28	0.33	0.24	5.5	2.0	6.5	4.5
18	Monopoly	58	26	0.69	0.26	5.0	3.5	7.5	6.5
19	Galaxy	64	28	0.60	0.14	5.0	2.0	7.5	4.5
20	Geronimo	70	26	0.53	0.12	4.0	2.5	7.0	5.0
21	Brunswick	55	19	0.57	0.22	5.0	2.5	6.5	5.0
29	K1-158	43	21	0.25	0.12	6.0	2.5	6.5	4.5
32	Sodco	60	30	0.29	0.39	5.0	2.0	7.0	5.0
33	Cheri	49	27	0.82	0.22	5.0	2.5	7.0	4.5
34	Adelphi	68	34	0.73	0.22	5.0	2.5	7.5	5.0
35	Parade	65	33	0.22	0.22	4.0	3.0	6.5	5.5
36	Enmundi	91	30	0.73	0.23	4.5	2.5	7.5	5.0
39	Enoble	71	28	0.85	0.07	3.5	2.5	6.0	4.0
40	Pennstar	50	23	0.56	0.04	4.5	2.0	8.0	4.0
53	Delft	55	27	0.33	0.12	5.0	3.0	6.5	4.5
54	CEBECO 71-2	67	38	0.39	0.17	5.5	3.5	7.5	5.5
57	Plush	54	23	0.64	0.09	6.0	2.5	8.0	4.0
58	PSU 150	66	41	0.34	0.18	6.0	3.0	7.0	5.5
60	P-154	76	33	0.51	0.30	5.5	3.0	6.5	4.5
61	P-143	85	32	0.29	0.21	4.5	2.5	6.5	4.5
64	PSU 197	61	26	0.46	0.11	4.5	4.0	7.0	5.5
65	PSU 190	82	35	0.62	0.14	5.5	3.0	6.5	5.0
66	PSU 169	85	32	0.40	0.11	4.5	3.5	7.0	4.5
Mean		65.9	28.1	0.490	0.171	4.86	2.64	6.79	4.60
L.S.D. 0.05		n.s.	4.7	0.158	n.s.	0.59	n.s.	0.60	n.s.

† New root score from 1 (none) to 9 (many). ‡ Turf quality scores from 1 (poorest) to 9 (best).

show that it took more than twice as many kg of force to uproot sod pieces in the sun as to uproot those in the shade. Differences among cultivars and selections for rooting in the sun were not significant, but differences in the shade were significant at the 1% level which suggests that some cultivars were more shade tolerant. The transplant sod rooting data in sun and shade were correlated with each other (r = 0.39**), but neither of the 1974 root pull ratings were correlated with any of the data from the 1976 growth chamber study.

Rooting data in sun and shade reported in Table 3 were available for all three replicates of the field trial and correlations were calculated for the 1974 transplant sod rooting with the items of data reported in Tables 1 and 2. No significant correlations of rooting and sod strength were found.

Table 4. Correlations of total root weight in g (RW), new root initiation score (NR), and turf quality (TQ) on 21 Apr. 1976.

	Temperature 1			Temperature 2	
	NR	TQ		NR	TQ
RW	0.03	0.41**	RW	0.09	0.56**
NR		0.37**	NR		0.47**

** Significant at the 1% level.

Table 5. Correlations of turf quality in 1974 with turf quality and percent green cover in 1976 for spring, summer, and fall.

		1974 Turf quality				
		27 Mar.		16 July		24 Oct.
1976 turf quality	9 Apr.	0.40**	19 July	0.21*	19 Oct.	0.42**
1976 percent green cover	7 Apr.	0.38**	19 July	0.14	19 Oct.	0.50**

*,** Significant at 5 and 1% levels, respectively.

There were significant correlations of rooting in the sun with shoots from rhizome counts on 16 May 1974 (r = 0.33**) and 14 Nov. 1974 (r = 0.24*), and of rooting in the shade with counts on 16 May 1974 (r = 0.21*). Whatever makes for stronger root growth has some relationship to shoots produced from rhizomes, especially in the spring. The rooting data were not significantly correlated with turf quality ratings in 1974 but had some relationship to quality measurements made in 1976. Rooting in the sun was correlated with quality score on 19 July 1976 (r = 0.27**) and with percent green cover on 19 July 1976 (r = 0.24*). Rooting in the shade was correlated with quality score on 19 Oct. 1976 (r = 0.20*) and percent green cover on 19 July 1976 (r = 0.24*) and 19 Oct. 1976 (r = 0.21*). Strong root growth in 1974 was positively related to turf performance in 1976.

The 1976 growth chamber data reported in Table 3 indicate that the more moderate day-night temperatures (T1) were more favorable for total root growth, initiation of new roots, and turf quality than were the higher day-night temperatures (T2). Entries were significantly different at the 1% level for each of these characters at T1. None of the differences were significant at T2. Correlations between temperatures for total root weights and initiation of new roots were not significant. As there were significant strain × temperature interactions for these two characters, it seemed desirable to look at relationships within temperatures for the evaluations made on 21 Apr. 1976. Table 4 reports these correlations. At both temperature regimes, there was no apparent relationship between total root production and number of new roots at the end of the growth chamber trial. At both temperatures there was a relatively close relationship of turf quality with total root production and new roots. Shoot growth is dependent upon root growth and so related to both total roots and new root initiation even when, as in this particular study, these two root characteristics are not closely related to each other.

The data reported are for the 2nd and 4th year following establishment of a trial of cultivars and selections of Kentucky bluegrass. During this period, overall turf quality changed from relatively high in 1974 to below 5 (considered acceptable turf quality) in 1976. The correlations between years of quality measurements reported in Table 5 show that spring and fall quality measurements of these bluegrasses were closely related. Summer measurements made in mid-July were not. Differences in summer precipitation in the 2 years may be related to the poor relationships of turf quality in July. The damage from red thread was also much heavier in 1976 than in 1974. Ratings of turf quality made at successive times on the same plot were correlated within a year and also between years.

The significant correlations reported (although often of low numerical value) indicate when the tendency of two observations to vary together is greater than likely to occur by chance. Relationships observed in these investigations included the following: (i) Spring sod strength was not significantly related to turf quality ratings made that year but summer sod strength was so related. (ii) Shoot regrowth from rhizomes after sod removal was negatively correlated with the strength of the sod strips removed and turf quality ratings made that year. (iii) At the close of a growth chamber study of sod pieces, total root production was not related to new roots being initiated at that time but both were related to turf quality. (iv) Transplant sod rooting of sod pieces measured in 1974 was not significantly correlated with turf quality that year but was significantly correlated with summer and fall turf quality 2 years later.

LITERATURE CITED

1. Beard, J. B. 1972. Comparative sod strengths and transplant sod rooting of Kentucky bluegrass cultivars and blends. p. 123–127. *In* Michigan Turfgrass Conf. Proc., Michigan State Univ., East Lansing.
2. ————. 1973. Turfgrass: Science and culture. Prentice-Hall, Inc. Englewood Cliffs, N.J.
3. Etter, A. G. 1951. How Kentucky bluegrass grows. Ann. Mo. Bot. Gard. 38:293–375.
4. Hanson, A. A., and F. V. Juska. 1961. Winter root activity in Kentucky bluegrass (*Poa pratensis* L.). Agron. J. 53:372–374.
5. King, J. W., and J. B. Beard. 1969. Measuring rooting of sodded turfs. Agron. J. 61: 497–498.
6. Madison, J. H. 1971. Principles of turfgrass culture. Van Nostrand Reinhold Co., New York.
7. Moser, L. E., S. R. Anderson, and R. W. Miller. 1968. Rhizome and tiller development of Kentucky bluegrass (*Poa pratensis* L.) as influenced by photoperiod, cold treatment, and variety. Agron. J. 60:632–635.
8. NE-57 Technical Research Committee. 1977. Northeast regional evaluation of Kentucky bluegrasses (*Poa pratensis* L.) 1968–1973. Pennsylvania Agric. Exp. Stn., University Park, Pa. Bull. 814.
9. Reike, P. E., J. B. Beard, and C. M. Hansen. 1968. A technique to measure sod strength for use in sod production studies. Agron. Abstr. p. 60.
10. Smith, F. E. 1973. Growth of roots, rhizomes and tillers of Kentucky bluegrass (*Poa pratensis* L.) cultivars and genotypes as affected by fertility level, cutting height, and season. M.S. Thesis. Virginia Polytechnic Inst. and State Univ., Blacksburg.
11. Watschke, T. L., R. E. Schmidt, and R. E. Blaser. 1970. Responses of some Kentucky bluegrasses to high temperature and nitrogen fertility. Crop Sci. 10:372–376.
12. Youngner, V. B. 1969. Physiology of growth and development. *In* A. A. Hanson and F. V. Juska (eds.) Turfgrass science. Agronomy 14:187–216. Am. Soc. Agron., Madison, Wis.

Chapter 5

Perennial Ryegrass Mowing Quality and Appearance Response to Three Nitrogen Regimes

V. A. GIBEAULT
D. HANSON

ABSTRACT

Six perennial ryegrass (*Lolium perenne* L.) cultivars established in San Jose, Calif., USA, were subjected to three N fertilization regimes and observed for turfgrass quality and mowing characteristics. Cultivars tested were 'Manhattan', 'S-321', 'Pennfine', 'NK-100', 'Lamora', and 'Linn'. Nitrogen treatments consisted of 73, 146, and 292 kg/ha/year. Average turfgrass quality and mowing quality ratings increased significantly with increased N. Manhattan had the best mowing characteristics followed in ranked order by S-321, Pennfine, NK-100, Lamora, and Linn. Cultivar turfgrass quality ratings largely followed the order expressed for mowing quality. The data indicate that mowing quality is an inherent characteristic of perennial ryegrass cultivars and is difficult to modify except by high N applications. For turfgrass quality ratings, 35% of the variability was due to fertilization and 65% to cultivar. For mowing quality, 4% was due to fertilization and 96% to cultivar.

INTRODUCTION

Perennial ryegrass (*Lolium perenne* L.) is a cool-season species used in the past in areas with mild winters and cool, moist summers. Common, or 'Oregon Certified,' perennial ryegrass was used where quick establishment was needed (1) and a fairly coarse-textured turf with poor shoot density could be tolerated. The resulting turf was generally short lived, had rapid vertical shoot growth rate in the spring and fall, was difficult to mow, and was considered of poor turfgrass quality.

Recent plant selection and breeding within the species have resulted in improved plant types for turf use. The new types are narrow-bladed, dense, of good color, and mow easier and cleaner than common perennial ryegrass (3). These improved turf characteristics have increased species use (6). Turf types are now established in monostands and polystands for quality lawns, golf courses, athletic facilities, and play fields where the species is adapted. Also, warm-season grasses are overseeded with perennial ryegrass for winter color (5).

One of the most important improvements in the "turf types" has been

[1] A contribution from the Agric. Ext. Serv., Univ. of California, Riverside, CA 92500 USA.

 Proceedings of the Third International Turfgrass Research Conference.

the enhanced mowing characteristic (2). This characteristic was emphasized because of the unsightliness of a ragged perennial ryegrass turf following mowing. Leaf blade shredding results from tough, fibrous vascular bundles and is accentuated by plant stress from low nutrition (N), high temperature, and/or low moisture availability. A rotary mower or dull reel mower increases leaf shredding. Mowing quality of some perennial ryegrasses as young stands has also been influenced by the seeding rate (6).

The objective of this study was to examine the mowing characteristics and general turfgrass quality of six perennial ryegrass cultivars as influenced by N fertilization levels.

MATERIALS AND METHODS

The study was conducted at the University of California Deciduous Fruit Field Station in San Jose, Calif., USA. San Jose is characterized by a coastal climate with summer temperatures of 18 to 27 C (low/high average) and moderate temperatures in the winter. The soil type is a Campbell silty clay loam with a pH of 7.3 and low salinity. Phosphorus and K levels are adequate for turf growth.

The seedbed was prepared in a normal manner for turfgrass establishment. The soil was tilled to a depth of 15 cm, rough and final-graded, and surface treatments of 48.6 kg P/ha single superphosphate and 48.6 kg N/ha were applied.

All cultivars (see Table 3) were hand-seeded into 1.5- × 4.6-m plots at the rate of 292 kg/ha in May 1974. There were four replications. Following a four-month establishment period, three N treatments were imposed across the cultivars giving a four-replication split plot design with 1.5- × 1.5-m subplots. The N source was ammonium nitrate. Fertilizer treatment rates were as in Table 1.

Maintenance of the test area consisted of regular mowing at a 3.8-cm height with a reel mower. Irrigation was supplied as needed to maintain adequate soil moisture for desirable turfgrass growth and development.

The ratings consisted of visual scores of mowing and turfgrass quality. Mowing quality ratings were on a 0 to 10 basis with 0 representing poor mowing quality and 10 representing a clean leaf cut. Turfgrass quality ratings considered such factors as shoot density, color, leaf texture, pest activity, and uniformity of stand. A 0 to 10 rating was used with 0 being a completely dead stand and 10 being superior turfgrass quality.

Table 1. Nitrogen treatment rates and frequency

Rate of N/year	Amount of N/application	Frequency of fertilization
kg/ha		
292	24	Monthly
146	24	Every 2 months
73	24	Every 4 months

Twenty-four turfgrass quality ratings (1 year) and 13 mowing quality ratings (7 months) were made.

All data were subjected to an analysis of variance with significant differences being determined by Duncan's Multiple Range Test. Further, data were analyzed to determine the relative importance of two variables, cultivar and fertility level, on turf scores and mowing quality by examining the variability of the two as calculated from the expected values of the mean squares.

RESULTS AND DISCUSSION

Table 2 presents the results of the three N levels with data bulked across six cultivars, 24 observation dates for turfgrass quality, and 13 observations for mowing quality. Both the average turfgrass and mowing quality ratings were increased significantly by increased N rates. However, the increase was not numerically large, which suggests that only minor improvements in average turfgrass quality and mowing quality occurred with increased N rates. Other results from this study, not presented herein, showed greater differences in turfgrass quality among N treatments occurring during late winter/early spring and late summer to mid-fall. High N treatment resulted in higher turfgrass quality ratings at those times. During times of stress, mid-spring (seedhead formation) through summer (temperature), differences in turfgrass quality among N fertility levels were not as great.

Decreased turfgrass quality during mid-spring and through the summer was caused largely by poor mowing characteristics of some cultivars. Seedhead formation in March-April and the resulting stemminess, as well as shredding of leaf blades through the summer, decreased turfgrass quality. The results of differences in mowing and turfgrass quality scores of the cultivars are presented in Table 3.

Cultivars varied widely in mowing performance. 'Manhattan' had the best mowing characteristics and 'Linn' had the poorest. Although a generally close association existed between mowing and turfgrass quality, differences in ranking between 'NK-100' and 'Lamora' were noted. NK-100 had poorer mowing quality than Lamora, but overall had more desirable turfgrass quality characteristics, such as leaf texture, shoot density, and color.

Table 2. The effect of three N fertility levels on turfgrass quality and mowing quality (0 to 10 scale, 10 best).

Fertility level	Visual turfgrass quality ratings	Visual mowing quality rating
kg/ha/year		
73	6.4 Z*	4.4 Z
146	6.5 Y	4.5 Y
292	6.8 X	4.8 X

* Values in the same column having the same letter are not significantly different at the 5% level.

Table 3. The effect of six cultivars on turfgrass quality and mowing quality (0 to 10 scale, 10 best).

Cultivar	Visual turfgrass quality rating	Visual mowing quality rating
Manhattan	7.0 W*	6.0 U
S-321	6.8 X	5.4 V
Pennfine	6.8 X	5.0 W
NK-100	6.5 Y	3.6 Y
Lamora	6.2 Z	4.7 X
Linn	6.2 Z	2.8 Z

* Values in the same column followed by the same letter are not significantly different at the 5% level.

Table 4. The effect of N fertilization on the mowing quality of six perennial ryegrasses (0 to 10 scale, 10 best).

	Fertility level (kg/ha		
Cultivar	292	146	73
Manhattan	6.2 Q*	5.9 R	5.8 R
S-321	5.8 R	5.3 S	4.1 ST
Pennfine	5.3 S	5.0 TU	4.8 UV
Lamora	4.9 TU	4.6 VW	4.5 W
NK-100	3.8 X	3.5 Y	3.3 Y
Linn	3.0 Z	2.7 Z	2.7 Z

* Values followed by the same letter are not significantly different at the 5% level.

Although cultivars ranked the same irrespective of N level, mowing quality of all six cultivars differed significantly within each level (Table 4). Except for Linn, a N fertilization of 292 kg/ha/year was necessary to produce a significantly cleaner mowing turf in comparison to turfs fertilized at the 73- and 146-kg/ha/year rates, which were not significantly different for any cultivar tested. This information strongly suggests that mowing quality is an inherent characteristic of perennial ryegrass cultivars and that it is difficult to modify with N treatments unless high amounts of it are applied.

Table 5 shows that significant increases in turfgrass quality were generally obtained with increases in N fertilization rates. This applied to nearly every cultivar tested regardless of overall ranking. Cultivar ranking remained in order irrespective of N fertilization. With all N fertilizer rates Manhattan had the highest turfgrass quality scores, there was no significant difference between 'S-321' and 'Pennfine', and there was no

Table 5. The effect of N fertilization on the turfgrass quality of six perennial ryegrasses (0 to 10 scale, 10 best).

	Fertility level (kg/ha)		
Cultivar	292	146	73
Manhattan	7.3 S*	6.9 T	6.7 U
S-321	7.0 T	6.7 U	6.5 V
Pennfine	7.0 T	6.7 U	6.5 V
NK-100	6.7 U	6.4 VW	6.3 XY
Lamora	6.4 VW	6.2 YZ	6.1 YZ
Linn	6.4 WX	6.1 YZ	6.0 Z

* Values followed by the same level are not significantly different at the 5% level.

significant difference between Lamora and Linn. The results of this analysis support and expand the comments made relative to Table 2.

When the relative importance of fertilization treatments or cultivars was statistically weighted for turfgrass quality and mowing quality, 35% of the variability for turfgrass quality scores was due to fertilization and 65% to cultivar. For mowing quality, 4% was due to fertilization and 96% to cultivars. For these particular cultivars and fertilization levels, it is clear that variability among cultivars was greater than among fertilization levels. This is especially true regarding the mowing characteristics, which indicate that cultivar selection, not subsequent fertilization treatments, is most important in insuring good mowing quality.

LITERATURE CITED

1. Beard, J. B. 1973. Turfgrass: Science and culture. Prentice Hall, Inc., Englewood Cliffs, N.J.
2. Funk, C. R., and W. K. Dickson. 1975. Breeding perennial ryegrass for improvements in disease resistance and mowing quality. p. 58–65. *In* Ralph Engel (ed.) Rutgers Turfgrass Proc., Cook College, Rutgers Univ., New Brunswick, NJ 68903. January 1975. Rutgers Univ., New Brunswick, N.J.
3. ————, R. E. Engel, and H. H. Indyk. 1966. Ryegrass in New Jersey. N.J. Agric. Exp. Stn. Bull. 816.
4. Gibeault, V. A., E. Johnson, K. Gowans, and D. Donaldson. 1974. An evaluation of perennial ryegrass seeding rates. Calif. Turfgrass Culture 24(2):9–11.
5. ————, and J. Van Dam. 1972. An evaluation of perennial ryegrass varieties for winter overseeding. Calif. Turfgrass Culture 22(2):11–13.
6. ————, V. B.Youngner, R. Baldwin, and J. Breece. 1972. Perennial ryegrass in California. Calif. Turfgrass Culture 22(2):9–11.

Chapter 6 The Principles of Blending Kentucky Bluegrass Cultivars for Disease Resistance[1]

J. M. VARGAS, JR.
A. J. TURGEON

ABSTRACT

Turfgrass blends, which include two or more cultivars of the same species, are frequently recommended over single-cultivar plantings to provide improved disease resistance and turfgrass quality. The purpose of this study was to determine whether specific blends of Kentucky bluegrass (*Poa pratensis* L.) exhibited improved quality and better resistance to melting-out (*Helminthosporium vagans*), stripe smut (*Ustilago striiformis*), and Fusarium blight (*Fusarium roseum* and *F. tricinotum*) diseases, compared to monostands of their component cultivars.

A 1972 planting of Kentucky bluegrass cultivar monostands and blends on Flanagan silt loam (Aquic Arquidoll) was monitored for seasonal quality and disease for 5 years. Results indicate that the melting-out resistance of blends is usually intermediate between that of the component cultivars. The inoculum production by a melting-out-susceptible cultivar usually reduces the generalized resistance of a normally resistant cultivar in a blend. A similar trend was observed for Fusarium blight in blends. The severity of stripe smut was usually, but not always, reduced in polystands in which a cultivar with specific resistance was included. Generally, turfgrass quality of blends was either intermediate between that of the component cultivar monostands, or not significantly different from the components.

Additional index words: Melting-out, Stripe smut, Fusarium blight, Disease resistance.

INTRODUCTION

Turfgrass blends are presumed to provide some advantage over single-cultivar plantings in habitats where disease or insect problems are likely to develop (1). Blends may offer improved disease resistance when no single cultivar is resistant to all of the major diseases, but where component cultivars within the blend each possess resistance to one or more diseases. Thus, no disease should be capable of causing severe deterioration of the turf since at least one cultivar would be capable of compensating for the disease susceptibility of the others (4). Blending is also assumed to improve turfgrass establishment and accelerated sod production when at least one cultivar knits rapidly.

The selection of cultivars for use in blends is based on many considerations. These include: (i) the desired spectrum of adaptation to

[1] Contribution from the Michigan Agric. Exp. Stn., East Lansing, MI 48824 USA. Paper No. 8485.

environmental and cultural conditions; (ii) anticipated pest problems; (iii) sod production schedules; (iv) costs. Madison (4) questioned the advisability of combining "dwarf" and "standard" cultivars of Kentucky bluegrass (*Poa pratensis* L.) since they thrive under different cultural regimes. Yet, reduced cost of "common-type" cultivar seed and potentially improved adaptation of sod to widely varying environments and cultural programs provide incentives for blending common-type and improved cultivars.

In order to provide a uniform-appearing turf, each blend component should be compatible in leaf texture, growth habit, density, and vertical shoot growth rate (1). The relative aggressiveness of cultivars within a blend during establishment and at maturity may substantially influence the characteristics of the resulting turf. Competition between cultivars may involve the physical crowding out of a weaker cultivar by a more vigorous one. Turf that was initially composed of several cultivars may eventually become a monostand due to an imbalance in the competitive aggressiveness of component cultivars. In this instance, the presumed advantages of blending are lost and the future capacity of the turfgrass to adapt to changing conditions is limited to the inherent characteristics of the remaining cultivar or cultivars. 'Touchdown', 'A-34', 'Brunswick', and 'Sydsport' Kentucky bluegrasses are highly resistant to annual bluegrass (*Poa annua* L.) invasion (5). One of these cultivars blended with less aggressive cultivars might dominate the turf and reduce the genetic diversity desired in a blend.

Disease resistance is a primary consideration in selecting cultivars for planting alone or in blends. There are two types of resistance to diseases in plants; specific resistance and generalized resistance (6). Specific (vertical) resistance exists in plants which were bred for resistance to a specific race of a pathogen. In its highest form, specific resistance is synonymous with immunity or complete freedom from infection. It is most effective against pathogens which do not have a sexual stage of reproduction and which undergo only one life cycle per year. Pathogens which reproduce sexually and/or have repeated asexual life cycles during the growing season have the potential to develop new races with the capacity to infect previously resistant plants. Stripe smut, a disease caused by *Ustilago striiformis* (West.) Niessl., is specific to certain cultivars of Kentucky bluegrass (3). Most races of the fungus are specific for 'Merion' and 'Windsor', but new races with the capacity to infect other cultivars can evolve through hybridization. Hence, there is no guarantee that cultivars presently resistant to stripe smut will continue to be resistant. Blends provide some insurance against loss of turf from this disease since some component cultivars may replace a cultivar that becomes susceptible to a new pathogenic race. In selecting components for a blend, however, only presently resistant cultivars should be selected. Other examples of specific resistance include resistance to rusts (*Puccinia* sp.) and powdery mildew (*Erysiphe graminis* DC.).

Generalized (horizontal) resistance is usually less than immunity and is recognized by fewer infections, smaller lesions, longer intervals between infection and sporulation, and the production of fewer spores. Generalized resistance is effective against pathogens with or without a sexual cycle, and with or without repeating cycles. The possible development of new pathogenic races will not affect generalized resistance since it implies resistance to all races. Resistance to melting-out, a disease caused by *Helminthosporium vagans* Dresch., is an example of successful breeding for generalized resistance. Merion was the first Kentucky bluegrass cultivar with generalized resistance to melting-out and its resistance has remained effective since its release in 1947. Today there are many Kentucky bluegrass cultivars with good to excellent melting-out resistance. Resistance to Fusarium blight, a disease caused by *Fusarium roseum* f. sp. *cerealis* (Cke) Synd. and Hans., is also considered generalized resistance. However, isolates of this organism differ in the severity of disease induced in the same cultivar as well as among cultivars (2). Generalized resistance to Fusarium blight has been suggested in various unpublished reports of field test results, but the variability in results creates difficulties in determining if some cultivars are truly resistant.

Certainly, an important basis for blending cultivars of Kentucky bluegrass is to provide improved resistance to diseases that are associated with reduced turfgrass quality. The specific advantages and disadvantages of blending with respect to generalized and specific disease resistance and the resultant overall turfgrass quality will be explored in this paper.

MATERIALS AND METHODS

Field plots of 52 cultivars and experimental selections plus several two-component blends of Kentucky bluegrass were established by seed in April 1972 at the Ornamental Horticulture Research Center in Urbana, Ill., USA. Plots measured 1.8 × 2.4 m and each treatment was replicated three times in a randomized complete block design. The soil at the planting site was a Flanagan silt loam (Aquic Arquidoll) with a pH of 6.6. Phosphorus and K were incorporated into the soil prior to planting based on soil test results. Seeding rate was 30 g/plot. Following seeding, each plot was lightly raked and sprayed with an elastomeric polymer emulsion (SOIL-GARD®) to stabilize the seedbed. The plots were lightly irrigated as needed to encourage germination and seedling growth. After establishment, irrigation was supplied as needed. A total of 2 kg N/are, using equal increments of a water-soluble 10–2.6–3.3 (N–P–K) analysis fertilizer was applied in April, May, August, and September each year. The plot area was mowed two or three times per week during the growing season at 3.8 cm with a powered reel mower. Leaf clippings were normally returned during mowing. Visual turfgrass quality ratings were made at least five times each season and disease ratings were made as infestations developed. Most evaluations were made using a rating scale of 1 to 9, with 1 representing best quality and 9 representing poorest quality. For melting-out and Fusarium blight, the 1 to 9 scale was also used, with 1 representing no visual disease symptoms and 9 representing complete necrosis of the leaves. Stripe smut data were obtained by estimating the percent infected tillers within two 900-cm² areas in each plot.

RESULTS AND DISCUSSION

The three Kentucky bluegrass blends with 'Nugget' differed from the rest in several important respects. The poor spring greenup of Nugget was evident in the 1975 data for April which showed significant differences between this cultivar alone and the Nugget + 'Park' and Nugget + 'Glade' blends (Fig. 1). Park and Glade were apparently sufficiently widespread in the blends to counter the presence of Nugget, while the presence of 'Pennstar' was obscured by Nugget where these two cultivars were combined. The superior melting-out resistance of Nugget was evident in the

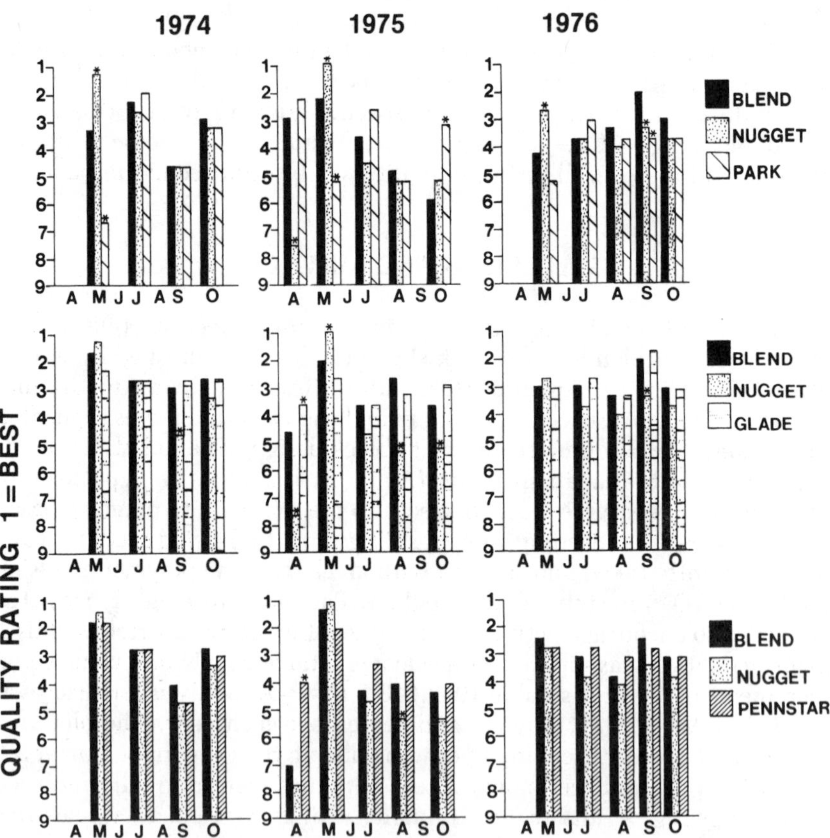

Fig. 1. Seasonal quality variation of single cultivar monostands and blends with Nugget Kentucky bluegrass over 3 years. Significant differences at the 5% level between the individual cultivars and their respective blends are indicated by an asterisk.

Table 1. Disease incidence in single cultivar monostands and in blends with Nugget and Merion Kentucky bluegrasses.

	Melting-out†		Fusarium blight†			Stripe smut‡
Cultivars	1973	1974	1973	1974	1975	1977
Nugget	2.0 a*	1.3 a	1.0 a	1.7 ab	2.7 bc	0 a
Glade	3.0 bc	2.3 abc	2.7 cd	1.0 a	1.0 a	0 a
Nugget + Glade	2.3 ab	1.7 a	2.0 bc	1.0 a	1.3 ab	0 a
Pennstar	2.0 a	1.7 a	2.0 bc	1.3 a	2.0 ab	13.3 bc
Nugget + Pennstar	2.0 a	1.3 a	1.3 ab	1.3 ab	2.0 ab	2.0 a
Park	6.0 d	6.7 d	5.3 e	2.7 b	2.0 ab	20.3 cd
Nugget + Park	2.3 ab	3.3 c	2.3 cd	2.0 ab	3.7 c	0 a
Merion	1.7 a	1.3 bc	2.0 bc	1.3 a	1.7 ab	76.7 f
Kenblue	5.7 d	5.7 e	5.0 e	1.7 ab	2.0 ab	0 a
Merion + Kenblue	3.0 c	3.0 d	3.0 d	2.7 b	1.7 ab	33.3 e
Pennstar	2.0 a	1.7 bc	2.0 bc	1.3 a	2.0 ab	13.3 bc
Merion + Pennstar	2.0 a	1.7 bc	2.0 bc	2.0 ab	1.0 a	73.3 f
Baron	3.3 c	2.3 cd	2.7 cd	1.0 a	1.3 ab	2.3 ab
Merion + Baron	2.0 a	2.0 cd	2.3 cd	1.7 ab	2.0 ab	26.7 de

* Figures in column followed by the same letter do not differ significantly at the 5% level by the Duncans New Multiple Range Test. † Melting out and Fusarium blight disease ratings were made using scale of 1 through 9, with 1 representing no visual disease symptoms and 9 representing complete necrosis of the plot. ‡ Stripe smut data are reported as percent smutted tillers per 900 cm^2.

May quality data for all 3 years of observation, as may be seen in Table 1. The blends were typically intermediate between Nugget and the other cultivars, especially in blends containing the melting-out-susceptible Park. Quality data taken during other periods in the growing season occasionally showed that the blend was intermediate between the component cultivars in quality. At some observation dates, the blends and their component cultivars were so similar in quality that no significant differences are apparent.

The three blends with Merion exhibited relationships similar to those observed in the Nugget blends. The Merion + 'Kenblue' blend was similar to the Nugget + Park blend in that the melting-out-susceptible cultivar, Kenblue, and the melting-out-resistant Merion combined to form a turf of intermediate quality and disease resistance compared to its component cultivars (Fig. 2). However, the differences between Merion and its blends with other cultivars occurred less frequently compared with the Nugget blends because Merion was faster to green up in spring and exhibited better summer quality than did Nugget.

In blends combining cultivars that varied widely in their melting-out susceptibility, it was surprising that the blends remained intermediate in melting-out incidence for the 3 to 4 years following establishment. It would be more reasonable to expect the melting-out-resistant cultivar to dominate each blend because of its superior competitive ability during periods of disease activity. This was not evident in the Nugget + Park blend and was only apparent in the Merion + Kenblue blend 4 years after establishment. A proposed explanation for this is illustrated in Fig. 3. A melting-out-susceptible cultivar is thinned following successive infections from a large buildup of inoculum within the turf. Generalized resistance to this disease is effective in some cultivars because relatively few infec-

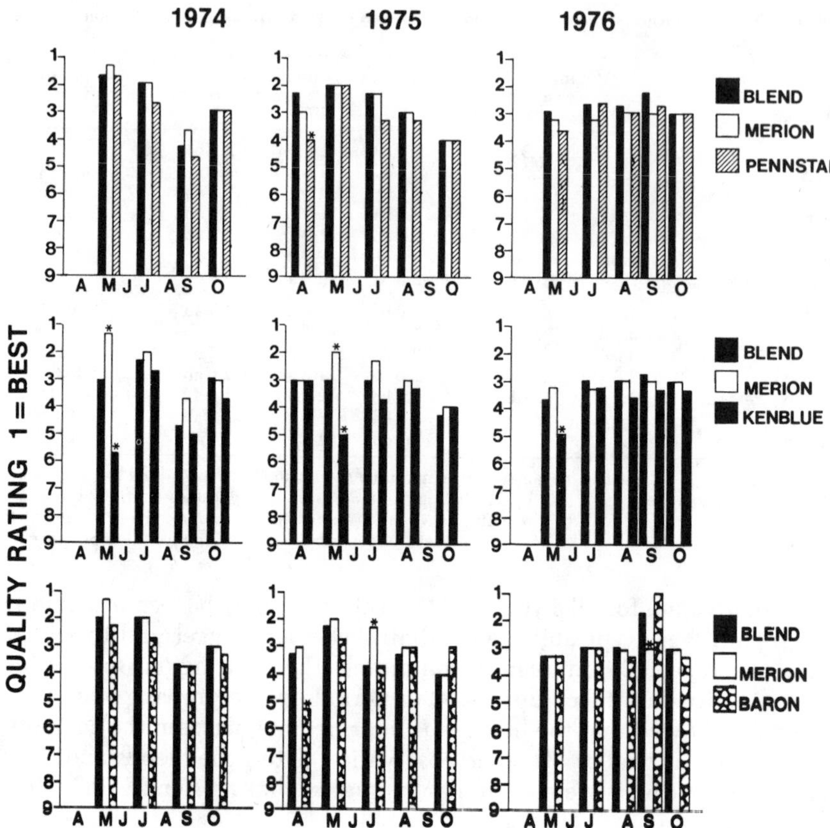

Fig. 2. Seasonal quality variation of single cultivar monostands and blends with Merion Kentucky bluegrass over 3 years. Significant differences at the 5% level between the individual cultivars and their respective blends are indicated by an asterisk.

tions occur, thus the large buildup of inoculum required for massive infections usually does not occur. Where both resistant and susceptible cultivars are combined in a blend, two phenomena occur simultaneously; the susceptible cultivar is diluted by the resistant cultivar so that the buildup of inoculum is not as massive, but the resistant cultivar is still subjected to a more intensive bombardment by inoculum from adjacent shoots of the susceptible cultivar. Therefore, more severe infection is likely to occur on the resistant cultivar in such a blend than if that resistant cultivar were grown alone or blended with other resistant cultivars. The result is that the normally resistant cutlivar cannot rapidly exploit the competitive disadvantage of the susceptible cultivar and, consequently, the blend is more stable than predicted.

Other diseases of some importance in this study were Fusarium blight and stripe smut. Fusarium blight infection was inconsistant among replications. Except for the Merion + Kenblue blend in 1974 and 1975, no significant differences were observed among the Merion blends and their

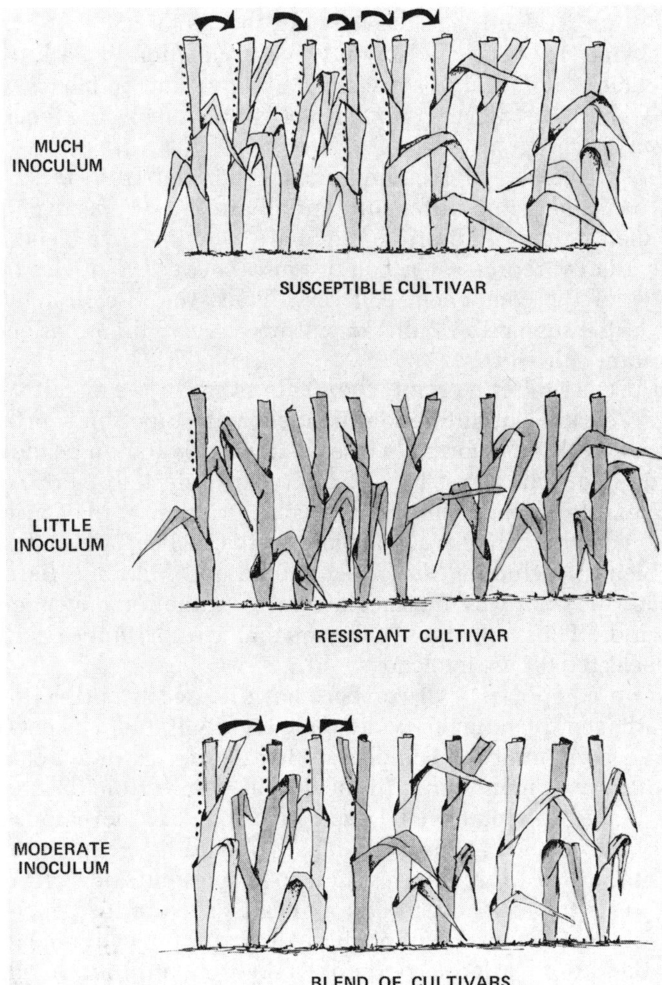

Fig. 3. Hypothetical effect of blending melting-out susceptible and resistant cultivars of Kentucky bluegrass.

component cultivars (Table 1). The Nugget + Park blend was intermediate in Fusarium blight incidence compared to its component cultivars in 1973, otherwise little significant difference was apparent in other combinations. However, in several instances where single cultivars were significantly different, the blends had intermediate values which did not differ significantly from the component cultivars.

Stripe smut was especially severe in Merion. The incidence of this disease in the Merion blends reflected the relative suscepibilities of the component cultivars. Disease severity was not sufficient to cause thinning of the turf in any cultivar or blends. Presumably, with infestations of stripe smut infection severe enough to cause thinning, the susceptible cultivar within a blend would eventually be replaced by the resistant cultivar. Stripe smut occurred in only one replication of Park; this plot was immediately adjacent to a diseased Windsor plot. In blends with the apparently resistant Nugget, Park did not contribute to any incidence of stripe smut.

Several principles of blending can be derived from these results. Where two cultivars that differ substantially in their respective susceptibilities to melting-out or Fusarium blight are combined in a blend, disease incidence usually represents a compromise between that occurring in monostands of the component cultivars. Thus, the disease may be less than that of the susceptible cultivar but more severe than that occurring in the resistant cultivar.

With respect to stripe smut, the relationship between cultivars in a blend is less clear. The differential incidence of stripe smut in the Park plots suggests that some normally disease-free cultivars can be induced to develop disease symptoms by proximity to infected cultivars. The Merion + Pennstar blend exhibited the same stripe smut incidence as the Merion alone, rather than a compromise between Pennstar and Merion. In other blends, including Merion + Kenblue and Merion + 'Baron', the severity of stripe smut was intermediate between the component cultivars in monostands. Thus, only those cultivars that are resistant to stripe smut should be selected for use in blends.

Where a component cultivar becomes disease-susceptible to a race specific pathogen, blending provides some facility for adjustments within the turfgrass community to compensate for the deterioration of a single component cultivar monostand. In conclusion, results from this study suggest that, since new pathogenic races of fungi can develop with the capacity to infect specific cultivars, blends should be composed of cultivars that are, at least initially, resistant to stripe smut, have generalized resistance to melting-out and, insofar as it can be determined, have generalized resistance to Fusarium blight. Along with environmental and cultural adaptation to local conditions and compatibility among component cultivars, properly constituted blends provide the greatest assurance of acceptible turfgrass quality for many years.

LITERATURE CITED

1. Beard, J. B. 1973. Turfgrass: Science and culture. Prentice-Hall, Inc., Englewood Cliffs, N.J. p. 166–172.
2. Cole, H., S. W. Braverman, and J. Duich. 1968. Fusaria and other fungi from seeds and seedlings of Merion and other turf-type bluegrasses. Phytopathology 58:1415–1419.
3. Gaskin, T. A. 1966. Evidence for physiologic races of stripe smut (*Ustilago striiformis*) attacking Kentucky bluegrass. Plant Dis. Rep. 50:430–431.
4. Madison, J. H. 1971. Practical turfgrass management. Van Nostrand Reinhold Co., New York.
5. Turgeon, A. J., and J. M. Vargas, Jr. 1980. An approach to turfgrass cultivar evaluation. p. 19–30. *In* J. B. Beard (ed.) Proc. Third Int. Turfgrass Res. Conf., Munich, West Germany. 11–13 July 1977. Am. Soc. Agron., Madison, Wis.
6. Van der Plank, J. E. 1968. Disease resistance in plants. Academic Press, New York.

Chapter 7 The Performance of *Phleum* and *Cynosurus* Species on Sports Fields[1]

C. MEHNERT

ABSTRACT

In the Federal Republic of Germany the usual winter playing season (September-May) puts traffic tolerance, winter color, shoot growth initiation, cold tolerance, and drought resistance of turfgrasses to a severe test. Because of the climatic conditions, selection of the most appropriate seed mixtures for Bavarian soccer fields is a special problem. Observations of the sports turf fields of the Munich Universities Sports Center (ZHS) over several years have lead to the conclusion that turf timothy (*Phleum bertolonii* DC) behaves very aggressively under limited traffic conditions and provides good winter color due to early shoot growth initiation. However, its drought resistance is only moderate and it cannot tolerate intense traffic. Under intensive culture crested dogtail grass (*Cynosurus cristatus* L.) is not wear tolerant and competitive enough to become a major component of sports turfs.

Additional index words: **Perenniality, Wear tolerance,** *Phleum bertolonii* **DC,** *Cynosurus cristatus* **L.,** *Poa pratensis.*

INTRODUCTION

After improving drainage on soccer fields through standardization of field construction techniques, it was decided in 1970 (3) to recommend only two sports turf seed mixtures for future use in the Federal Republic of Germany. One seed mixture was for maritime and moist inland locations while the second mixture was for dry inland locations. The climatic region of southern Bavaria has considerable rain because of continental influences. Therefore, the "moist" seed mixture was selected for the newly constructed turf fields to be used for the 1972 Olympic Games held in Munich. Later most of the sports turf fields became part of the Munich Universities Sports Center.

The winter playing season in West Germany finds the soccer field turfs in a very disadvantageous condition due to slow growth and unfavorable weather. Except during the growing season, these turfs, particularly those in southern Bavaria, are stressed by frequent, rapid freezing and thawing because they are nearly always on moist soils.

Until 1970, there were no publications discussing the suitability of turf timothy (*Phleum bertolonii* DC) and crested dogtail grass (*Cynosurus cristatus* L.) as soccer turfs for this region. Reports from the Netherlands

[1] Lehrstuhl für Grünlandlehre der TU München, 8050 Freising-Weihenstephan, West Germany.

(4) noted that "*Cynosurus cristatus* withstands wear well, *Phleum bertolonii* only fairly well." These comments were supplemented in 1974 with the finding that "the results with cultivars of *Phleum* spp. under artificial wear were so poor that interest in these species is very low at present (5)." Under conditions in France crested dogtail grass has shown less resistance to heavy wear than turf timothy and Kentucky bluegrass (*Poa pratensis* L.) (1).

The purpose of this research was to determine the adaptation of crested dogtail grass, turf timothy, and Kentucky bluegrass to the actual conditions encountered on soccer fields in southern West Germany.

MATERIALS AND METHODS

Fifteen sports turf fields at the Munich Universities Sports Center (ZHS) were available for the investigation. They were constructed in 1970–71 in accordance with regulation DIN 18 035 B1.4, (1) and were

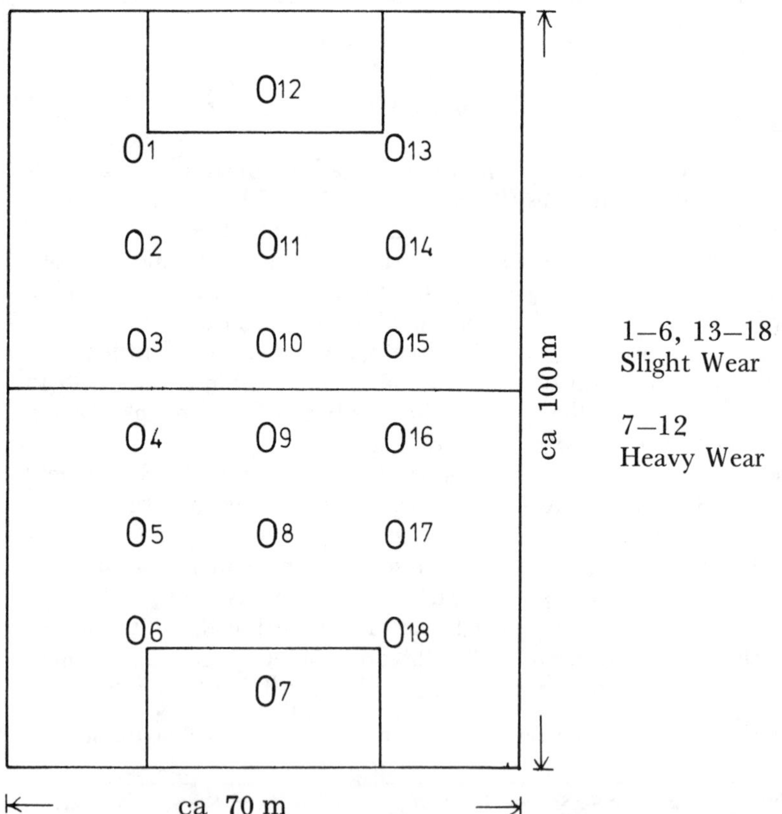

Fig. 1. Position of the plots where botanical composition assessments were done.

seeded with the following mixture: 75% 'Merion' Kentucky bluegrass; 15% 'Credo' crested dogtail grass; 10% 'S 50' turf timothy.

From field 'RA 4', which was representative of all other sports turf fields, the relative proportions of the species in the turf were estimated twice in 1973 and three times yearly from 1974 to 1976 following Klapp (2). Figure 1 shows the position of the 18 plant stands from which the measurements were made during May, July, and October. The locations are ordered in such a way that areas of intense and light traffic could be demonstrated. Traffic stress of field RA 4 was slight in 1973 and 1974, but intense in 1975 and 1976 (2). Fertilization was maintained at an adequate level in accordance to the traffic. The thatch level was between 1 and 2 cm thick in 1976.

RESULTS AND DISCUSSION

One year after the Olympics the stand composition showed a clear dominance of Kentucky bluegrass (Table 1). However, a severe rust infection of *Puccinia poae-nemoralis* in August and September of 1973 weakened the Merion Kentucky bluegrass so much that its proportion of the turf community was reduced. The resultant voids in the light traffic zones were covered relatively quickly by turf timothy. Annual bluegrass (*Poa annua* L.) showed a substantial increase in zones of intense traffic. Crested dogtail grass was unable to compete with Kentucky bluegrass. Essentially, its proportion of the turfgrass community remained at an insignificant level.

In the course of the next 3 years, the differences in turfgrass composition caused by different traffic intensities became even more evident (Table 2). Merion Kentucky bluegrass did not recover from the severe rust infection in 1973 and was continually subjected to rust during the summer months of the following years. Merion did not occupy more than 20% of the turfgrass community without fungicide treatment. The crested dogtail grass stand composition decreased from year to year, regardless of the intensity of traffic stress. In contrast, turf timothy spread into zones of lighter traffic and became a dominant component of the turf. In the intense traffic zones its persistence was minimal and thus annual bluegrass

Table 1. Composition of the sports turf community before and after a rust attack as influenced by two traffic intensities.

	June 1973		October 1973	
Species	Slight traffic	Intense traffic	Slight traffic	Intense traffic
	%			
Poa pratensis	93	96	32	72
P. annua	3	2	9	19
Phleum bertolonii	2	1	56	3
Cynosurus cristatus	2	1	3	6
Ground cover	100	96	88	68

Table 2. Changes in botanical composition of the sports turf community caused by two traffic intensities.

Species	1974 Slight traffic	1974 Intense traffic	1975 Slight traffic	1975 Intense traffic	1976 Slight traffic	1976 Intense traffic
	%					
Poa pratensis	8	19	3	6	8	20
P. annua	26	62	18	81	9	59
P. trivalis	+	0	1	0	2	0
Phleum bertolonii	61	10	76	10	81	6
Cynosurus cristatus	4	4	2	2	+	0
Lolium perenne†	1	5	+	1	+	15
Ground cover	96	73	98	90	98	95

† Overseeded.

replaced it. Turf timothy is much more drought-resistant than annual bluegrass and has the added advantage of earlier shoot growth initiation.

Turf timothy, when mixed with Kentucky bluegrass cultivars appropriate to the locations (e.g. 'Sydsport'), did not show the same aggressiveness on barren substrata. This was attributed to the lack of water which inhibited its development. Improvement of winter color, if any, was therefore according to zones. The color contrasts between zones of intense and light traffic remained throughout the entire year. Because of these characteristics there is no reason to use this species on soccer fields in southern Bavaria.

Crested dogtail grass, in spite of its substantial proportion in the original seeding, never formed a significant component of the turfgrass community. It is therefore difficult to make statements about its traffic tolerance due to its lack of competitiveness under intensive culture. In any event, its use in sports turfs is not to be advised.

Turf timothy and crested dogtail grass have been largely removed from the 1977 mixture recommendations and replaced very successfully by cultivars of perennial ryegrass (*Lolium perenne* L.).

LITERATURE CITED

1. Bourgoin, B. 1974. The behavior of the principal turfgrasses under French climatic conditions. J. Sports Turf Res. Inst. 50:65–80.
2. Klapp, E. 1930. Zum Ausbau der Graslandbestandsaufnahme zu landwirtschaftlichen Zwecken. Pflanzenbau 6:197–210.
3. Skirde, W. 1970. The development, present position and future objectives of turf research in Giessen. J. Sports Turf Res. Inst. 46:33–45.
4. Van der Horst, J. P. 1970. Sports turf research in the Netherlands. J. Sports Turf Res. Inst. 46:46–57.
5. ————, and H. A. Kamp. 1974. Sports turf research in the Netherlands. J. Sports Turf Res. Inst. 50:81–94.

Chapter 8

Turfgrass Seed Mixtures in the United Kingdom[1]

J. P. SHILDRICK

ABSTRACT

The customary United Kingdom turfgrass seed mixtures are reviewed in terms of three elements: perennial ryegrass (*Lolium perenne* L.); *Festuca* and *Agrostis* spp.; "medium grasses" (i.e., species such as *Poa* and *Phleum* spp. which are intermediate in their qualities between the first two types). A seed mixture trial sown at Bingley in 1971 and trials sown at Bingley and two other centers (Bush and Monks Wood, Cambridgeshire) in 1975 were subjected to artificial wear to simulate football games. The 1971-sown trial obtained best results, under football-type wear, from polystands consisting mainly of perennial ryegrass, red fescue (*F. rubra*), and colonial bentgrass (*A. tenuis*) (corresponding in this respect to most of the commercially available seed mixtures). The 1975-sown trials, however, found considerable value in the "medium grasses," timothy (*Phleum pratense*) and Kentucky bluegrass (*Poa pratensis*), in seed mixtures resembling those recommended for sports fields in the Netherlands. This difference may be due to the greater age of the 1971-sown trial when wear started or to the different types of wear treatment.

INTRODUCTION

Perennial ryegrass (*Lolium perenne* L.) is the main United Kingdom turfgrass for areas receiving intense wear and mown to heights above 15 mm. It is quick to establish, wear-tolerant, and recovers from wear quickly. Usually sown alone to renovate football pitches, it may also be used in some turf mown below 15 mm, even though it is not expected to persist; i.e. to renovate the heavily worn parts of cricket pitches. Perennial ryegrass is also frequently included in seed mixtures for "low maintenance" because of its quick establishment, in spite of the cost in more frequent mowing.

Red fescue (*Festuca rubra* L.) and colonial bentgrass (*Agrostis tenuis* Sibth.) are included in most turfgrass seed mixtures. For the most closely mown turf they are the only suitable species. For "low maintenance" seed mixtures they combine an attractive, dense appearance with a relatively low height of growth. They are also used in mixtures likely to receive hard wear, in spite of rather poor wear tolerance, for four reasons: (i) they fill an otherwise open sward, exclude weeds, and cover soil which might turn to mud; (ii) they will persist if an area has to be mown closer than originally intended; (iii) they develop a dense mat of live plant ma-

[1] A contribution from the Sports Turf Research Inst., Bingley, West Yorkshire, BD16 1AU, United Kingdom.

 Proceedings of the Third International Turfgrass Research Conference.

terial, progressively changing to thatch, which cushions players' movements and absorbs some forms of wear, so that a mature colonial bentgrass turf may in fact be very tolerant of some forms of wear; (iv) 'Highland', the colonial bentgrass cultivar almost always used in the United Kingdom, has considerable recuperative potential from rhizomes. [*A. tenuis* is fairly certainly a misnomer for 'Highland', for which the most preferable botanical name appears currently to be *A. castellana* Boiss. et Reut. (6).] All types of *F. rubra*—ssp. *commutata*, ssp. *litoralis*, and ssp. *rubra*— are used in United Kingdom turfgrass seed mixtures, depending on intended purpose, availability, and price. Other fine-leaved fescue species are seldom used except in seed mixtures for "low maintenance" on special soil types. Among *Agrostis* species, Highland is preeminent; apart from limited use of other cultivars of colonial bentgrass, a few cultivars of creeping bentgrass (*A. palustris* Huds.) (e.g. 'Penncross') may be sown occasionally as monostands for golf greens.

Between the two extremes of perennial ryegrass and the fine-leaved species (*Festuca* and *Agrostis* spp.), are several species that can be termed "medium grasses" in respect to plant size and tolerance to wear and relatively close mowing. The principal ones are Kentucky bluegrass (*Poa pratensis* L.), timothy (*Phleum pratense* L.), and turf timothy (*P. bertolonii* DC). Good turfgrass cultivars of these have less leaf bulk and tolerate relatively close mowing better than perennial ryegrass, but are tolerant to wear and have a good recuperative potential (especially Kentucky bluegrass). Crested dogtail grass (*Cynosurus cristatus* L.) and roughstalk bluegrass (*Poa trivialis* L.) can also be called medium grasses, though in recent years various weaknesses have become apparent and they are not used as often. Annual bluegrass (*Poa annua* L.) may also be called a medium grass, though its turfgrass qualities in the United Kingdom—both good and bad—make it unique. It tolerates many forms of wear well, though the dense, shallow-rooting tufts can be kicked out by football players in a way that artificial treatments do not reproduce. It is hardly ever bought as seed or deliberately sown in seed mixtures. If natural spread ever needs encouragement, clippings can be strewn.

Good cultivars of Kentucky bluegrass and *Phleum* spp. are added to perennial ryegrass, red fescue, and colonial bentgrass to form seed mixtures for winter games, golf fairways, or general purposes. These four or five species together give maximum adaptability to varying uses, cultural regimes, and environmental conditions. Alternatively, the medium grasses may be added to *Festuca* and *Agrostis* to improve the wear tolerance of fine turf where perennial ryegrass is not appropriate.

These broad principles of United Kingdom turfgrass seed mixture formulation reflect research at Bingley and elsewhere, and the experience of users and seedsmen. Figure 1 shows the proportions by weight of perennial ryegrass, *Festuca/Agrostis*, and medium grass (most often Kentucky bluegrass) in the turfgrass seed mixtures in a wide cross-section of United Kingdom seedsmen's catalogues in 1975–76. The figure does not show quantities sold, suggested uses, the proportions of *Festuca* and *Agrostis*

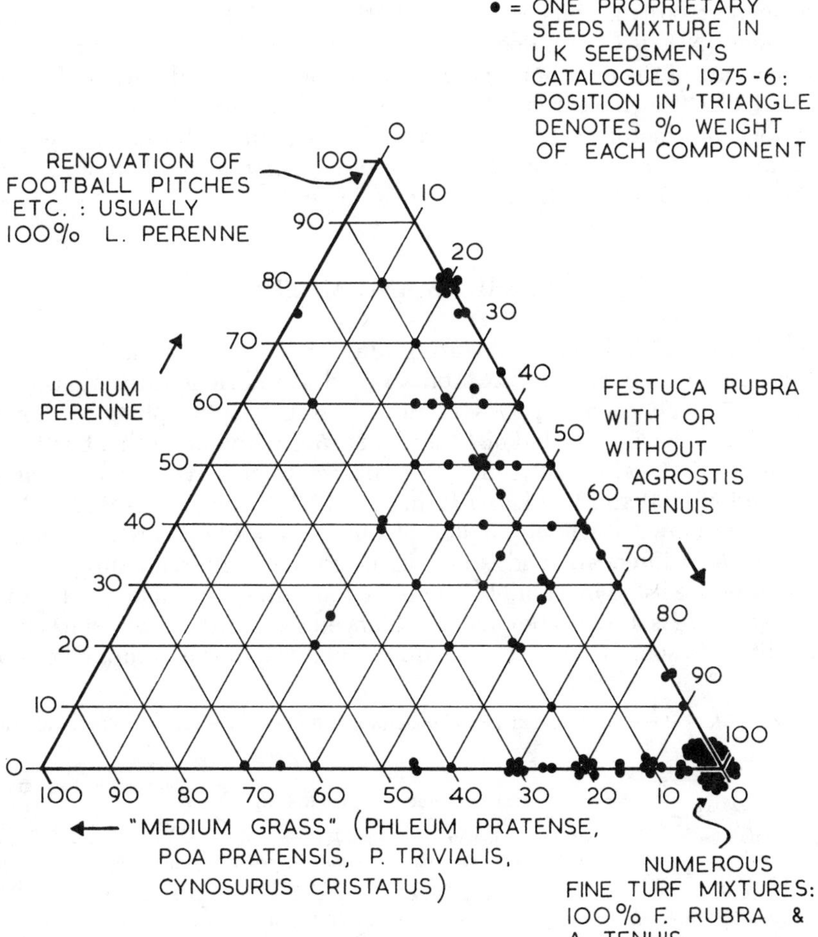

Fig. 1. United Kingdom turfgrass seed mixtures plotted on three axes by percent seed weight to show the relative importance of three constituent elements.

within the combined *Festuca/Agrostis* total, or the use of *Phleum* spp. or crested dogtail grass with or in place of Kentucky bluegrass.

The seed mixtures without perennial ryegrass are on the base line. They form two main groups: (i) those consisting only of *Festuca* and *Agrostis* (right-hand corner of Fig. 1); (ii) those reinforced with medium grasses (along base line of Fig. 1). All the other seed mixtures include perennial ryegrass. Most of them have little or no medium grass, in contrast with, for example, the recommended sports field seed mixtures of the Instituut voor Rassenonderzoek van Landbouwgewassen (I.V.R.O.) (4) which have little or no *Festuca* or *Agrostis*, as shown in Fig. 2.

This paper discusses recent trials of the various turfgrass species in seed mixtures with particular reference to intense winter wear, as on football fields. The 1975-sown trials, of which some preliminary results are given here, are part of a contract with the Natural Environment Research Council (N.E.R.C.) funded by the Department of the Environment. Another part of the contract includes the development and testing of an improved artificial wear machine (D.S.1) as described by Canaway (2), studies on factors affecting wear tolerance in turfgrass species and cultivars (1), and comparison of the effects of real football wear with those of the D.S.1 artificial wear machine (3).

MATERIALS AND METHODS

Three trials were sown during May and June 1975, at Bingley, at Bush near Edinburgh, and at Monks Wood, Cambridgeshire. At each site factorial experiments were laid down using a split split-plot design. Duplicate blocks consisted of 16 seed mixtures with and without artificial wear as the main treatment. The sub-treatments were two levels of applied N (100 and 240 kg/ha from July 1975 through June 1976). Mixtures were sown at 25 g/m^2 in plots of 4 m^2. One seed mixture could not be made up as intended, and is not discussed here: the remaining 15 seed mixtures are listed in Table 1. There are four groups of mixtures. In three groups there is a basic complete or balanced seed mixture which has been modified in some way in the remaining mixtures of the group. The trials

Table 1. Effects of wear in three seed mixture trials sown in 1975 and mown at 25 mm (mean of two N levels).

Description of seed mixture	Proportion in seed mixture at sowing (% weight)			Ranking for % live grass (all species) during month after end of wear stress		
	Lolium perenne	Total medium grass (*Phleum pratense*, *Poa pratensis*† in brackets)	Total *Festuca/Agrostis* (*F. rubra*, *A. tenuis*† in brackets)	Bingley	Bush	Monks Wood
Group 1. Five-species general purpose seed mixture, complete and with each species omitted in turn						
Complete	20	55 (15, 40)	25 (20, 5)	6	13	10
No *Agrostis*	20	60 (15, 45)	20 (20, 0)	5	2	7
No *Festuca*	25	70 (20, 50)	5 (0, 5)	7	4	2
No *Poa*	35	28 (28, 0)	37 (30, 7)	9	12	1
No *Phleum*	25	50 (0, 50)	25 (20, 5)	10	14	5
No *Lolium*	0	68 (20, 48)	32 (25, 7)	11	10 =	11
Group 2. *Lolium*, *Phleum*, and *Poa* seed mixture, balanced and "distorted"						
Balanced	25	75 (20, 55)	0	4	5	9
High *Lolium*	60	40 (10, 30)	0	2	8	4
High *Phleum*	10	90 (55, 35)	0	1	1	8
High *Poa*	10	90 (5, 85)	0	3	3	3
Group 3. *Lolium*, *Festuca*, and *Agrostis* seed mixture, balanced and "distorted"						
Balanced	38	0	62 (50, 12)	13	9	6
High *Lolium*	60	0	40 (32, 8)	12	10 =	14
High *Festuca*	10	0	90 (85, 5)	14	7	12
High *Agrostis*	10	0	90 (55, 35)	15	15	15
Group 4. *Phleum* and *Poa* seed mixture						
	0	100 (10, 90)	0	8	6	13

† *Lolium perenne* 'Aberystwyth S.23': *Phleum pratense* 'Aberystwyth S.48': *Poa pratensis* 'Baron': *Festuca rubra* 'Canadian' and 'Highlight' (50:50): *Agrostis tenuis* 'Highland'.

were mown at 25 mm (cuttings removed). Football-type wear was applied at each location with one of three identical D.S.1 machines (2). Wear treatments were made from January to March 1976 (i.e. starting 7 months after sowing). The machine settings and number of passes were the same at each center, and the timing as similar as possible. Point quadrat assessments (single hit) were made at each center before wear, after wear, and after 3 months of recovery. The three trials were continued during 1976–77 for a second winter of wear.

RESULTS AND DISCUSSION

A. Wear Tolerance of Species

Results from monostands by Shildrick (5) and Canaway (1, unpublished data) give the following groupings of the main United Kingdom turfgrasses (when represented by good cultivars) for tolerance to artificial football-type wear. "Tolerance" in this case implies primarily survival during treatment as opposed to recovery after the cessation of wear stress.

Very good	Annual bluegrass
Good	Perennial ryegrass, timothy, Kentucky bluegrass
Moderate	Colonial bentgrass, red fescue
Poor	Crested dogtail grass, roughstalk bluegrass

There is not yet the same information on other types of wear.

B. Results of Earlier Seed Mixture Trials

In a seed mixture trial at Bingley sown in 1971, 40 mixtures were mown at 25 mm and received football-type artificial wear. The trial has been reported elsewhere by Shildrick (5). Table 2, summarizing some medium grass elements in the polystands, which are arranged in three groups in the table. Table 2 demonstrates the following points: (i) Group A without perennial ryegrass retained appreciably less green leaf cover than Groups B and C containing perennial ryegrass; (ii) Group B, with high proportions and medium grasses, had more bare ground than Group C in which *Festuca/Agrostis* outweighed medium grass; (iii) Group C, therefore, appeared most suitable for turf under intense wear, as in football.

Group C falls within the same general area of Fig. 1 as do most general purpose seed mixtures in commerce, though most of the latter have more perennial ryegrass than Group C. The trial seed mixtures with 35% perennial ryegrass showed very little more green leaf after wear stress than those with 20% perennial ryegrass. This suggests that there was little to be gained from higher percentages of perennial ryegrass in conditions such as those of this trial, with the relatively long period of 15 months to establish before wear stress. This, of course, is not inconsistent

Table 2. Effects of the three seed mixture elements in a mixture trial at Bingley sown in 1971 and mown at 25 mm.

No. of seed mixtures representing each set of proportions	Mixture proportions at sowing (% wt.)			Estimated % cover after wear stress. Mar. 1973	
	Lolium perenne	*Festuca/ Agrostis*	Medium grass†	All green leaf	Bare ground
Group A: No *Lolium perenne*					
4	0	0	100	22	23
6	0	20	80	16	13
2	0	40	60	13	11
6	0	75	25	4	5
Group B: *Lolium perenne*, little *Festuca/Agrostis*, much medium grass					
1	20	0	80	32	29
3	20	15	65	29	19
5	20	20	60	33	21
Group C: *Lolium perenne*, much *Festuca/Agrostis*, little medium grass					
1	20	30	50	27	13
6	20	50	30	29	14
1	25	75	0	28	11
5	35	50	15	33	14

† One of the following—*Phleum pratense, P. bertolonii, Poa pratensis, P. trivialis, Cynosurus cristatus.*

with the value of perennial ryegrass, alone or dominant in the polystand, whenever rapid growth is essential, as in renovating football fields.

The *Festuca* and *Agrostis*, in spite of their relatively poor wear tolerance when tested alone, apparently had value in forming a mat of plant material, anchored by perennial ryegrass, which prevented the playing surface from becoming bare ground and mud. The inclusion of enough medium grass to be noticeable in the sward meant a proportionate reduction in *Festuca/Agrostis,* thus allowing more bare ground. This was most apparent with the most aggressive and persistent medium grass—the *Phleum* spp.—and least with non-persistent roughstalk bluegrass and crested dogtail grass. (Annual bluegrass would probably have been different: seed mixtures containing it in another trial mown at 13 mm showed outstanding wear tolerance.)

C. 1975 Seed Mixture Trials

The trials were sown during May and June instead of the usually preferable late summer or early autumn, and all suffered from drought, especially at Monks Wood. At Monks Wood and Bush, perennial ryegrass was dominant before wear stress (about 55% cover); timothy and red fescue each had 8 to 14%, Kentucky bluegrass 2 to 4%, and colonial bentgrass 1%. At Bingley there was a better balance. Weeds, especially annual bluegrass, were frequent in some polystands at Bush, whereas the polystands at Bingley were almost weed-free (after soil sterilization) and those at Monks Wood only had dicotyledonous weeds. These initial differences were clearly reflected in subsequent performance in tolerance of wear and in recovery.

There was very little difference between the effects of the two N rates, perhaps because a generous seedbed application was common to both treatments in the important pre-wear establishment phase and the recovery assessment may have been too early to see the effects of extra N, especially in the dry summer of 1976.

The most important results concern seed mixture differences. Table 1 shows that at Bingley and Bush the most live grass immediately after wear was given by polystands consisting of perennial ryegrass, timothy, and Kentucky bluegrass with little or no *Festuca/Agrostis*. Bare ground data gave a similar result. The results from Monks Wood did not have the same statistical significance, but in several respects confirmed the results from the other two centers. In so far as the results are unfavorable to *Festuca/Agrostis*, they contradict the conclusions from the 1971 trial, but they can perhaps be explained by the difference in age of turf when wear stress was started. The 1975 trials did not have time to develop the mat of vegetation which seemed advantageous in the 1971 trial. Other differences (in wear

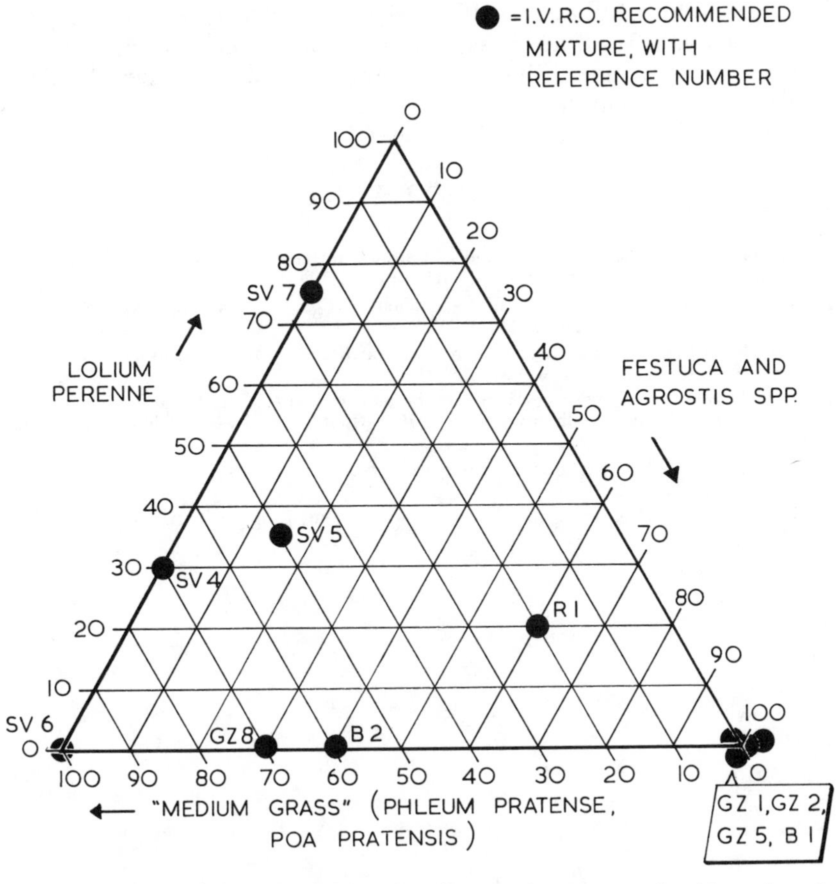

Fig. 2. Dutch turfgrass seed mixtures plotted on three axes by percent seed weight to show the relative importance of three constituent elements.

treatment, method of assessment, or selected cultivars) may also be relevant.

Whereas the 1971 results vindicated the customary United Kingdom seed mixtures, the 1975 trial results support the Dutch recommendations in Fig. 2. Apart from the age of turf when wear starts, cultural factors and the conditions for establishment are very important in practice. They determine the extent to which species other than perennial ryegrass are important and, in particular, the value of the main medium grass, Kentucky bluegrass.

ACKNOWLEDGMENTS

Most of the work has been or is the immediate responsibility of Mr. T. M. Davies (1975 seed mixture trials) and Mr. P. M. Canaway (wear studies), financed by the Department of the Environment through a contract between the Natural Environment Research Council and the Sports Turf Research Institute. The 1975 seed mixture trials have been greatly facilitated by the Institute of Terrestrial Ecology, which has supplied sites and trial maintenance at Bush and Monks Wood and provided statistical assistance throughout the work.

LITERATURE CITED

1. Canaway, P. M. 1975. Fundamental techniques in the study of turfgrass wear: An advance report on research. J. Sports Turf Res. Inst. 51:104–115.
2. ————. 1976. A differential slip wear machine (D.S.1) for the artificial simulation of turfgrass wear. J. Sports Turf Res. Inst. 52:92–99.
3. ————. 1976. The comparison of real and artificial wear: a preliminary study on a soccer field. J. Sports Turf Res. Inst. 52:100–109.
4. Instituut voor Rassenonderzoek van Landbouwgewassen (I.V.R.O.). 1977. 52[e] beschrijvende rassenlijst voor landbouwgewassen, 1977. Leiter-Nypels, Maastricht, The Netherlands.
5. Shildrick, J. P. 1975. Turfgrass mixtures under wear treatments. J. Sports Turf Res. Inst. 51:9–40.
6. ————. 1976. Highland bent: A taxonomic problem. J. Sports Turf Res. Inst. 52:142–150.

Chapter 9 Response of Warm- and Cool-Season Turfgrass Polystands to Nitrogen and Topdressing[1]

D. T. HAWES

ABSTRACT

The growing of high quality, low cut turf in the transition zone is difficult. The following four turf species are commonly used for the above purpose: bermudagrass (*Cynodon dactylon* L.); zoysiagrass (*Zoysia japonica* Steud.); creeping bentgrass (*Agrostis palustris* Huds.); Kentucky bluegrass (*Poa pratensis* L.). A cultural study was conducted using these four species in an attempt to grow polystands of warm- and cool-season grasses which would overcome weaknesses of each individual species. Winter and summer N fertilization programs were compared along with a sand topdressing program on eight grass polystands and monostands of the four species. The summer N fertilization program was unsatisfactory since it encouraged bermudagrass while decreasing the cool-season grass population. The winter N program allowed the cool-season species to dominate in the spring and the bermudagrass to dominate in the summer without loss of either until the bermudagrass was killed in the unusually severe winter of 1976–77. Sand topdressing reduced spring dead spot in bermudagrass and encouraged bentgrass recovery in the fall.

Additional index words: ***Cynodon dactylon*** **L.,** ***Zoysia japonica*** **Steud.,** ***Agrostis palustris*** **L., Transition zone, Competition.**

INTRODUCTION

Growing high quality turf at a height of cut between 1 and 3 cm without a high maintenance input is difficult. If one attempts to grow this type of turf in the transition zone as defined by Keen (8), a well-adapted species is not available. The following turf species have been used for closely mowed turf in the transition zone: the warm-season grasses, bermudagrass (*Cynodon dactylon* L.) and zoysiagrass (*Zoysia japonica* Steud.), and the cool-season grasses, creeping bentgrass (*Agrostis palustris* Huds.) and Kentucky bluegrass (*Poa pratensis* L.).

Their disadvantages in this zone are briefly reviewed here. Bermudagrass goes dormant and turns brown from the first frost until mid-spring. It has a disease complex problem called spring dead spot, and occasionally substantial losses of turf occur in severe winters. Zoysiagrass, the other warm-season grass occasionally used, also has the disadvantage of being brown in winter, but is more winterhardy than bermudagrass. Zoysiagrass is extremely slow growing which results in slow establishment and delayed recovery from injuries. Kentucky bluegrass, the principle cool-

[1] Contribution No. 5353 and Scientific Article No. A-2343 of Maryland Agric. Exp. Stn., Dep. of Agronomy, Univ. of Maryland, College Park, MD 20742 USA.

season turf species used in the northern U.S., deteriorates during the summer stress period if mowed below 5 cm. Recent, more adapted cultivars of this species have resulted in considerable improvement. Creeping bentgrass, another cool-season species, requires frequent irrigation and fungicide applications if high quality summer turf is to be obtained.

Growing perennial warm- and cool-season grasses together to overcome their individual weaknesses has often been suggested (1, 2, 5, 6, 7, 13). Beard (3) has reviewed such polystands and noted that although they have been tried periodically, useage has not been widely adopted.

The purposes of this study were (i) to evaluate the suitability of various warm- and cool-season polystands for the transition zone, and (ii) to study the effects of two N and topdressing programs on these polystands under low mowing.

MATERIALS AND METHODS

The experiment was conducted in the field on a Chillum silt loam (Typic Hapludults) at Fairland, Md., USA. A 2 × 2 × 12 factorial arranged in a split-split plot design with four replications was employed. Sand topdressing applications and a control treatment comprised the whole plots with dimensions of 6 × 18.2 m. The sand used had 22% of its particles larger than 0.5 mm, 75% between 0.1 and 0.5 mm, and 3% less than 0.1 mm in diameter. This topdressing material was applied once in 1975 (May) and thereafter three times a year in May, July, and September at the rate of 0.3 m^3/100 m^2/application.

Subplot treatments were winter and summer N fertilizer programs. Both treatments consisted of four, 0.45-kg/100 m^2 N applications per season using ammonium nitrate as the N source. The summer N program was conducted between early May and early August, with initiation in June 1974. The winter N applications were made after the start of dormancy for the warm-season grasses (usually October) and before mid-March. These applications were initiated in October 1974.

In late August of each year starting in 1974 all plantings received 0.9 kg/100 m^2 of N from ureaformaldehyde. September applications of P and K fertilizer materials were made yearly to maintain adequate levels of these nutrients. When necessary, ground limestone was applied in the fall at rates needed to raise to and maintain a pH of 6.5.

Sub-sub-plots were planted to eight grass polystands and four monostands. These were 1) 'Meyer' zoysiagrass and Kentucky bluegrass, 2) 'Midwest' zoysiagrass and Kentucky bluegrass, 3) 'Tifgreen' bermudagrass and Kentucky bluegrass 4) 'Tufcote' bermudagrass and Kentucky bluegrass, 5) Meyer zoysiagrass and 'Penncross' creeping bentgrass, 6) Midwest zoysiagrass and Penncross creeping bentgrass, 7) Tifgreen bermudagrass and Penncross creeping bentgrass, 8) Tufcote bermudagrass and Penncross creeping bentgrass, 9) Tufcote bermudagrass, 10) Meyer zoysiagrass, 11) Kentucky bluegrass, and 12) Penncross creeping bentgrass. The Kentucky bluegrass was a blend consisting of the following cultivars in equal portions: 'A-34'; 'Adelphi'; 'Fylking'; 'Merion'; 'Pennstar'.

Zoysiagrass and bermudagrass cultivars were established in their appropriate sub-sub-plots using stolons during the summer of 1973. Estimated coverage 30 Aug. 1973 was Tufcote—100%, Tifgreen—95%, Midwest—65%, and Meyer—50%. In early September 1973 the experimental area was heavily vertically cut to prepare a seedbed. Penncross creeping bentgrass and the Kentucky bluegrass blend were then overseeded to obtain the eight grass polystands and four monostands desired.

During establishment of the warm-season grasses the experimental area was sprayed three times for postemergence control of summer annual grasses with monosodium methanearsonate and two times for broadleaf weed control with an amine salt of 2,4-dichlorophenoxyacetic acid (2,4-D). Fungicides and insecticides were not applied to the experimental area.

Irrigation was frequent during the 1973 establishment phase, but, thereafter applied sparingly. All plots were irrigated after fertilizing and topdressing. Summer drought stress was relieved by irrigation only when the majority of the four species showed symptoms.

Grasses were mowed at 2.5 cm from September through May and at 1.9 cm during the remainder of the year. Clippings were removed on days when data were taken and when the height of cut was reduced in May.

The summer N fertilizer program was stopped in July 1976 and these plots were vertically cut and overseeded to perennial ryegrass (*Lolium perenne* L.) in late August 1976. Bermudagrass cultivars in all treatments were killed by the winter of 1976–77.

Visual estimates of the percent cover for each of the four grass species and weeds were taken each May, July, and September and whenever dramatic changes occurred. The percentage of plot area not covered by living material was noted as bare or dead. Verdure samples were taken late each spring, plus three additional dates in 1974 and one additional date in 1975, using methods similar to Madison (9). But, rather than using fresh weight, samples were sorted according to species and weeds with the dry weights of the individual components calculated as a percentage. A 9.7-cm plug was used for verdure samples. The hole remaining was filled with topdressing sand and recuperative rate data were recorded. Recuperative rate was determined at the end of 3 weeks by laying a stiff piece of clean plastic over the holes left by plug removal and tracing onto it the outline of the area not covered by grass. The area in plastic was then cut out and weighed for each hole. These weights were converted to a percentage by dividing their individual weights by the average weight of 10 9.7-cm diameter plastic circles of the same material. The percentage was then subtracted from 100 to give the percentage of the hole covered or the recuperative rate.

RESULTS AND DISCUSSION

The small plot size (1.5 × 1.5 m) and random arrangement of the sub-sub-plots (grass combinations) allowed the introduction of cool-season seed carried by wind and water into neighboring plots. Thus, all plots were contaminated to some extent with scattered plants of creeping bentgrass and Kentucky bluegrass. Also due to the extremely aggressive nature of bermudagrass it invaded all plots to some extent. Due to problems in the establishment and maintenance of the desired combinations, the main emphasis of this paper will be an evaluation of the four grass species in competition with each other under two N fertilizer programs and two topdressing regimes.

The sorted verdure samples showed percentage compositions similar to the visual estimates of percent composition. Thus visual estimates became the preferred method of taking data because a shorter time was required and the average coefficient of variation was one-third smaller.

Grass Polystands

The recuperative rate of holes opened for verdure samples was most rapid for grass polystands containing bermudagrass during the summer months, while polystands containing creeping bentgrass resulted in the fastest recovery in the spring. The slowest recuperative rates regardless of season were the zoysiagrass-Kentucky bluegrass polystands.

The summer N program encouraged bermudagrass to spread and dominate while causing general decline and death of the cool-season grasses present (Table 1). Stoutemyer (14) noted that 'U-3' bermudagrass would dominate polystands with cool-season grasses if the cultural practices did not favor the cool-season component. However, Madison (10) reported no differences in bermudagrass invasion of cool-season grasses under a warm-season fertilization program. The choice of July data for Tables 1 and 2 was a compromise between spring dates when the cool-season grasses tended to dominate and early fall when bermudagrass dominated (Fig. 1, 2, 3).

Table 1. Visual estimates of the percentage grass cover for each of four species during July on those plots receiving summer N. Values are averages over two topdressing treatments and 12 grass polystands.

Grass species	Years 1974	1975	1976
		% cover**	
Bermudagrass	38 C	55 B	78 A
Zoysiagrass	8 B	9 B	12 A
Creeping bentgrass	22 B	28 A	3 C
Kentucky bluegrass	15 A	8 B	5 C

** For each grass species, values followed by the same letter are from the same statistical population at the 1% level of significance according to the Duncan's Multiple Range Test.

Table 2. Visual estimates of the percentage grass cover for each of four species for July on those plots receiving winter N. Values are averages over two topdressing treatments and 12 grass polystands.

Grass species	Years		
	1974	1975	1976
	% cover**		
Bermudagrass	31 A	22 B	29 A
Zoysiagrass	10 A	7 B	7 B
Creeping bentgrass	20 B	45 A	41 A
Kentucky bluegrass	14 C	25 A	21 B

** For each grass species, values followed by the same letter are from the same statistical population at the 1% level of significance according to the Duncan's Multiple Range Test.

The winter N fertilizer program resulted in a more uniform stand of grass species (Table 2 vs. Table 3). Bermudagrass still tended to dominate in the late summer/early fall period (Fig. 2) but the cool-season grasses recovered by early spring each year (Fig. 1, 3). The transition from cool-season grasses to bermudagrass each summer was smoothest under this fertilization program. With zoysiagrass polystands, the transition to warm-season grass was poorest where bentgrass dominated and best where bluegrass was abundant. The Meyer zoysiagrass—Kentucky bluegrass polystand exhibited smooth summer transition to the extent that both of these species were present rather uniformly by midsummer.

The fall-winter transition under the winter N fertilizer program was slow. It generally was not until early spring that a relatively uniform green turf was obtained. This occurred about 2 to 3 months before full greenup of bermudagrass or zoysiagrass.

It is assumed that the extensive weed control program used in establishing the warm-season grasses reduced the seed populations of summer annual weeds to a very low level. Winter annual weeds and some fall-germinating perennials became an increasing problem with time. As

Table 3. Visual estimates of the percent cover by Kentucky bluegrass and creeping bentgrass under winter N fertilization, as influenced by sand topdressing for 2 years. Values are averages over 12 grass polystands.

Months	Kentucky bluegrass		Creeping bentgrass	
	Topdressed	Control	Topdressed	Control
	% cover			
May 1975	39	43	46	45
July 1975	26	24	44	46
Sept. 1975	10	11	21**	10
Nov. 1975	17	18	37**	9
Apr. 1976	36*	46	49**	29
May 1976	39*	50	52*	35
June 1976	30	39	51*	40
July 1976	17	25	45*	36
Sept. 1976	10	13	7	3
Mar. 1977	42*	53	24**	6
Apr. 1977	58	66	20**	7
May 1977	54*	66	27**	9

*,** Within each month and each grass species, means followed by asterisks are statistically different than the control at the 0.05 and 0.1 levels of probability, respectively.

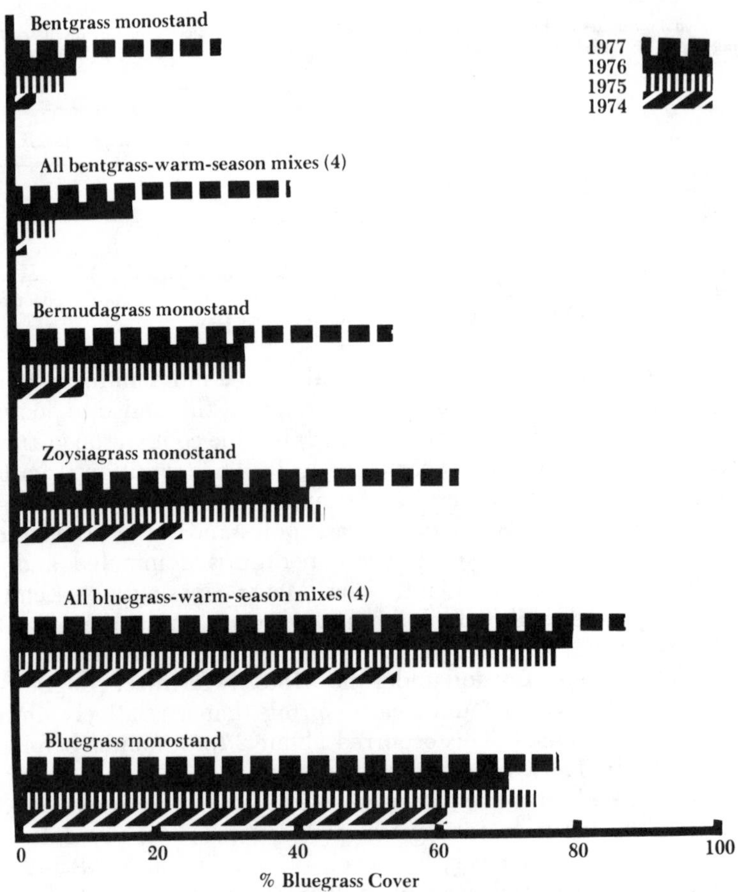

Fig. 1. Percent cover by Kentucky bluegrass in May of monostands and cool-warm season polystands under a winter N program. Values are averages over two topdressing treatments.

might be expected, this problem was more severe under the summer N fertilization which resulted in an almost complete loss of the cool-season grasses. These cool-season grasses could be expected to provide competition for winter annual weeds in a polystand of warm- and cool-season grasses. In May 1975, it was estimated that less than 1% of the cover consisted of weeds on the plots receiving winter N while the summer N plots had 2%. In May of 1976, this had risen to 11 and 30%, respectively. September 1976 data show that the initial fall stand of weeds (Table 4) tended to be lowest on those plots having the more aggressive warm-season grasses.

By the spring of 1977, it was clear that the ability of Kentucky bluegrass to recover from the summer of 1976 (Table 3) resulted in less weeds in those polystands containing this species as compared to those containing creeping bentgrass. The lack of aggressiveness displayed by creeping bentgrass (Table 3) between fall 1976 and summer 1977 was assumed

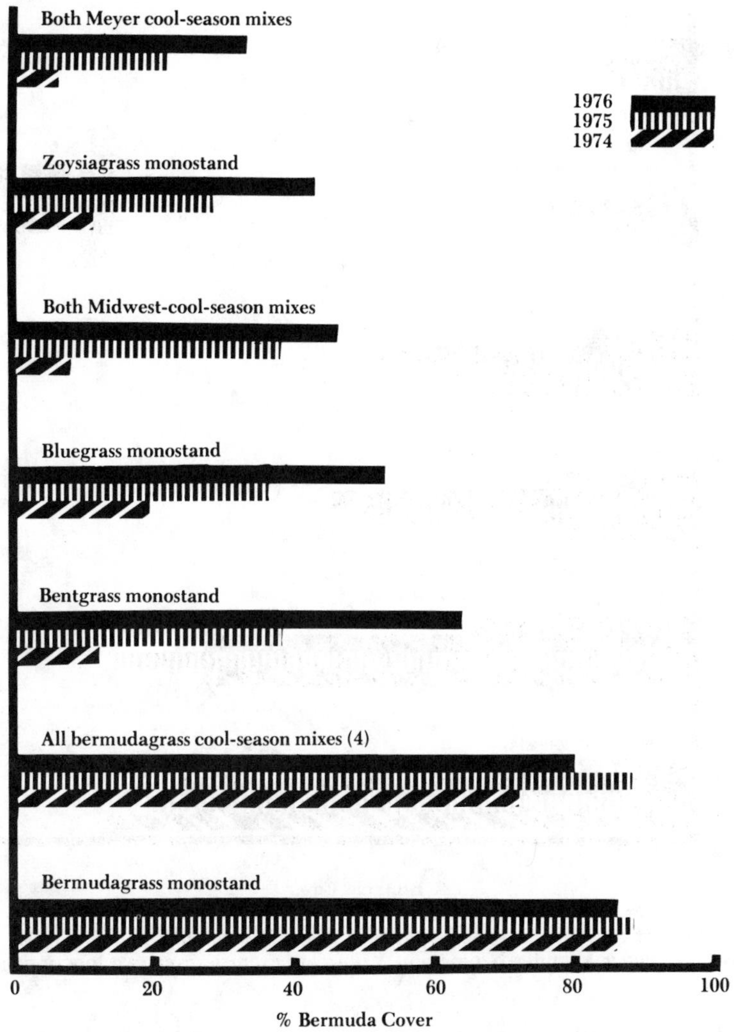

Fig. 2. Percent cover by bermudagrass in September of monostands and cool-warm season polystands under a winter N program. Values are averages over two topdressing treatments.

to be due, in part, to a cold winter and a relatively dry spring. Musser (12) reported that at a 2.5-cm height of cut there was a complete domination of Kentucky bluegrass by bentgrass for two pH levels, two N source treatments, and three levels of P. Davis (4) reported that Kentucky bluegrass was not able to successfully compete against another closely related bentgrass (*Agrostis tenuis* Sibth.) at either a 1.9 or a 5.1-cm height of cut.

Topdressing with sand favored creeping bentgrass and resulted in slightly reduced coverage by Kentucky bluegrass (Table 3). Topdressing appeared to allow creeping bentgrass to recover faster in the fall from summer stress.

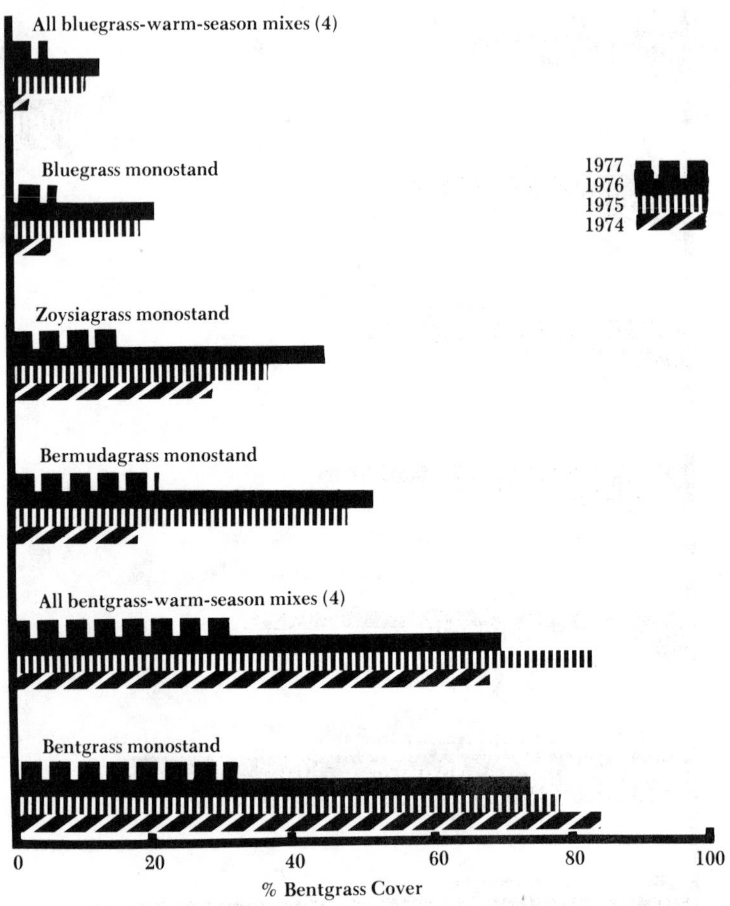

Fig. 3. Percent cover by creeping bentgrass in May of monostands and cool-warm season polystands under a winter N program. Values are averages over two topdressing treatments.

Symptoms like those of spring dead spot were observed in the spring of 1976 under the summer N fertilizer program. The symptoms were significantly less numerous and smaller in size under the sand topdressing subtreatment. No further data are available due to winterkill of all bermudagrass in early 1977.

Overall management of the experiment can be assumed to have strongly influenced the fate of the four grass species in competition with each other (11). Watering only when the majority of the turfgrass showed stress would be expected to favor the more drought-tolerant species (bermudagrass, zoysiagrass, and Kentucky bluegrass) over the least tolerant (creeping bentgrass). Drought duration in Maryland is usually no longer than a month. Large losses of creeping bentgrass in the summers of 1975 and 1976 (Table 3) were probably a result of this irrigation program along with disease and insect damage.

Table 4. Visual estimates of weeds in each grass polystand under winter N fertilization for September 1976 and May 1977. Values are averages over two topdressing treatments.

Grass polystand	Weeds present	
	Sept. 1976	May 1977
	%	
Meyer zoysiagrass + Kentucky bluegrass	7 bc*	6 f
Midwest zoysiagrass + Kentucky bluegrass	13 a	7 ef
Tufcote bermudagrass + Kentucky bluegrass	5 c	8 ef
Tifgreen bermudagrass + Kentucky bluegrass	6 bc	8 ef
Kentucky bluegrass	13 a	13 def
Meyer zoysiagrass	7 bc	14 cdef
Tufcote bermudagrass	4 c	17 bcde
Meyer zoysiagrass + creeping bentgrass	11 ab	20 abcd
Tifgreen bermudagrass + creeping bentgrass	7 bc	24 abc
Tufcote bermudagrass + creeping bentgrass	6 bc	25 ab
Midwest zoysiagrass + creeping bentgrass	11 ab	26 ab
Creeping bentgrass	9 abc	28 a
Avg.	8	16

* Values with the same letter in the same column are from the same statistical population at the 5% level of significance according to Duncan's Multiple Range Test.

The medium to high annual N rate of 2.7 kg/100 m^2 should favor grass species that respond the most to N (bermudagrass and creeping bentgrass) over less responsive species (zoysiagrass). This latter factor and incomplete coverage by zoysiagrass cultivars at the start help explain why the amount of zoysiagrass in the experiment remained low regardless of time of N fertilization (Tables 1, 2).

Mowing height used in this experiment for summer and winter should have favored those grass species adapted to low mowing (creeping bentgrass, bermudagrass, and zoysiagrass) over the least tolerant species (Kentucky bluegrass). This did not appear to have been a major factor, however, since the Kentucky bluegrass was able to increase under the winter N fertilizer program (Fig. 1), once the creeping bentgrass competition was reduced.

As expected N fertilization was a substantial factor in the overall ability to maintain a polystand of cool- and warm-season grasses. Two polystands merit further study under various cultural regimes: bermudagrass—creeping bentgrass for aggressiveness and ability to satisfy the demand for high quality turf under low mowing height and zoysiagrass—Kentucky bluegrass for superior winterhardiness in the northern transition zone, plus ability to persist and provide quality turf under lower maintenance.

LITERATURE CITED

1. Beal, W. J. 1893. Mixtures of grasses for lawns. p. 28–33. *In* W. M. Fear (ed.) Proc. 14th Annu. Meeting of the Soc. for the Promotion of Agric. Sci. Agricultural Science of State College, Pa.
2. ————. 1898. Lawn-grass mixtures as purchased in the markets compared with a few of the best. p. 59–63. *In* Charles S. Plumb (ed.) Proc. of the 19th Annu. Meeting of the Soc. for the Promotion of Agric. Sci. Am. Soc. Agron., Madison, Wis.

3. Beard, J. B. 1973. Turfgrass: Science and culture. Prentice-Hall, Inc., Englewood Cliffs, N.J. 658 p.
4. Davis, R. R. 1958. The effect of other species and mowing height on persistence of lawn grasses. Agron. J. 50:671–673.
5. Engel, R. E., E. Steiniger, and G. H. Ahlgren. 1952. Zoysias as turfgrasses in New Jersey. New York State Turf Assoc. Bull. No. 37:143–144.
6. Forbes, I., Jr., and M. H. Ferguson. 1947. Observations on the zoysia grasses. Greenkeepers Rep. 15(2):7–9.
7. Grau, F. V. 1947. Presenting Meyer (Z-52) zoysia. Greenkeepers Rep. 15(2):4–5.
8. Keen, R. A. 1969. Grasses for the transition zone. p. 84–85. *In* R. R. Davis (ed.) Proc. First Int. Turfgrass Res. Conf., Harrogate, England. 15–18 July 1969.
9. Madison, J. H. 1962. Turfgrass ecology: Effects of mowing, irrigation, and nitrogen treatments of *Agrostis palustris* Huds., 'Seaside' and *Agrostis tenuis* Sibth., 'Highland' on population, yield, rooting, and cover. Agron. J. 54:407–412.
10. ———. 1962. The effect of management practices on invasion of lawn turf by bermudagrass (*Cynodon dactylon* L.). p. 559–564. *In* J. R. Magness (ed.) Proc. of the Am. Soc. Hort. Sci.
11. ———. 1971. Practical turfgrass management. Van Nostrand Reinhold Company, New York.
12. Musser, H. B. 1948. Effects of soil acidity and available phosphorus on population changes in mixed Kentucky bluegrass-bent turf. Am. Soc. Agron. J. 40:614–620.
13. Record, L. 1971. Zoysia—a turf for transition zone fairways. USGA Rec. 9(4):5–6.
14. Stoutemeyer, V. T. 1953. Grass combinations for turf. Calif. Agric. 7(12):9–10.

Chapter 10

Seasonal Performance of Selected Temperate Turfgrasses Overseeded on Bermudagrass Turf for Winter Sports[1]

R. E. SCHMIDT
J. F. SHOULDERS

ABSTRACT

Bermudagrass (*Cynodon* spp.) may be dormant up to 7 months so temperate turfgrasses are overseeded in autumn to provide winter turf. Persistence of the overseeded grass under warm spring temperatures is essential to provide a gradual transition in the spring and is important in the northern limits of bermudagrass adaptation since bermudagrass is often slow to recover because of low temperature injury.

This study was conducted to compare various perennial ryegrasses (*Lolium perenne* L.) alone and in polystands with other temperate grasses for winter turfgrass quality, especially spring persistence, on dormant bermudagrass. Various temperate turfgrasses were overseeded on 'Tifgreen' bermudagrass the 1st or 2nd week in October in southeastern Virginia from 1969 to 1975. The test sites were maintained as a golf putting green through 1973 and as a golf tee or lawn turf thereafter.

When the perennial ryegrass cultivars that had the best overall turfgrass quality as overseeded monostands were included in polystands for golf putting turf, the superior performance in quality was maintained over polystands containing appreciable amounts of Italian ryegrass (*L. multiflorum* Lam.) or inferior perennial ryegrasses. Bentgrass (*Agrostis* spp.) as a component in a polystand generally enhanced turfgrass quality and increased persistence in the summer. Persistence of overseeded temperate grasses in the spring did not necessarily reduce turfgrass quality.

Seed mixtures including 65% perennial ryegrass, 30% fine fescues (*Festuca rubra* L.) and 5% bentgrass and composed of cultivars that performed well in monostands were considered superior for overall golf green turf than the monostands.

Monostands of improved perennial ryegrasses provided excellent overall winter turf on dormant bermudagrass used for turf other than greens. The lower growing cultivars generally had the best turfgrass quality. Higher overseeding rates generally increased winter turfgrass quality. The perennial ryegrasses differed in leaf shredding following mowing in the spring. Manhattan was particularly susceptible to shredding when overseeded heavily. 'Derby', 'Citation', and 'Pennfine' were perennial ryegrass cultivars that provided excellent winter turf and appeared to have good heat tolerance.

Additional index words: *Cynodon* spp., *Lolium* spp., *Agrostis* spp., *Poa* spp., *Festuca* spp., Heat tolerance, Spring persistence, Mower shredding.

[1] A contribution of the Agronomy Dep., Virginia Polytechnic Inst. and State Univ., Blacksburg, VA 24061 USA.

 Proceedings of the Third International Turfgrass Research Conference.

INTRODUCTION

Because of high summer temperatures and high humidity, bermudagrass (*Cynodon* spp.), a semi-tropical species, is an important turfgrass for fairways, athletic fields, and home lawns in the southern U.S. In eastern Virginia, the northern limit of adaptation for semi-tropical species, bermudagrass is dormant up to 7 months from autumn to spring; therefore, temperate turfgrasses are overseeded in the autumn to provide actively growing turf during the winter (6). Success of obtaining good quality turf while the bermudagrass is dormant depends upon the temperate grass species used, time of overseeding, establishment procedures, mowing procedures, thatch control, and fertilization (2, 3, 6, 8, 9).

A desirable turfgrass species used for overseeding must germinate and establish rapidly, provide dense turf for good color throughout the winter, and persist under warm spring and summer temperatures (6, 9). Moderate persistence of the overseeded grasses under warm temperatures is essential to provide a gradual transition from temperate to the semi-tropical species. In the northern limits of bermudagrass adaptation, severe winters often injure bermudagrass, resulting in the necessity to maintain the temperate species until the semi-tropical grass recovers or is reestablished.

Overseeding bermudagrass sports turf with Italian ryegrass (*Lolium multiflorum* Lam.) in autumn has been practiced for many years. However, this species is coarse in texture, lacks cold tolerance, is susceptible to diseases, and does not persist under warm temperatures (5, 9). Roughstalk bluegrass (*Poa trivialis* L.) has been used on dormant bermudagrass turf because it is quick to become established and provides satisfactory turf quality during the winter (8); however, it has been reported by researchers in Virginia (7) to be one of the first overseeded species to become inferior with the approach of higher temperatures. Bentgrass (*Agrostis* spp.) and Kentucky bluegrass (*P. pratensis* L.), are slow to become established and do not provide acceptable turf quality until spring when seeded as monostands (6, 8).

Overseeded monostands of red fescue (*Festuca rubra* L. subsp. *rubra*) do not compete with annual bluegrass (*P. annua*) infestations on putting greens as well as ryegrass (1, 4) and do not provide satisfactory winter turf on areas mowed at 1.2 cm or higher. The new turf type perennial ryegrasses (*L. perenne* L.) have produced excellent winter turf quality on overseeded bermudagrass from autumn to early summer. Ward et al. (9) consistently rated these ryegrasses as having better turf quality than any other overseeded species studied.

The main objectives of this study were to compare various perennial ryegrass cultivars alone and in polystands with other temperate turfgrass species for winter turf quality on dormant bermudagrass. Studies were performed on bermudagrass maintained as golf putting greens and on bermudagrass maintained at a higher clipping height to simulate lawn, fairway, golf tee, and other athletic turf areas.

MATERIALS AND METHODS

Temperate turfgrasses were overseeded on 'Tifgreen' bermudagrass (*Cynodon* spp.) the 1st week of October at the Golden Horseshoe Golf Course, Williamsburg, Va., USA in 1969, 1972, 1973, and 1975 and at the James River Country Club, Newport News, Va. in 1970 and 1973. The Newport News experimental site was established during the summer of 1970 and the Williamsburg site was reestablished in 1971. Both of these areas were modified so that the soil texture consisted of 60% sand between 0.2- and 2-mm particle size.

The areas were mowed at 0.6 cm and maintained as golf putting greens through the spring in 1973. Experiments conducted after this date were mowed at 1.25 cm, similar to bermudagrass golf tees or lawn.

Except for the Newport News 1973 study, the turf was fertilized with natural organic or soluble sources of N at 1 kg/100 m^2 during the summer and with 0.5 kg/100 m^2 applied during October, December, February, and April. Phosphorus and potash were applied to maintain adequate levels based on soil test analyses. In the study initiated at Newport News in October 1973, the overseeded grasses were maintained with N rates ranging from 1 to 3 kg/100 m^2 with and without 0.125 kg of chelated Fe/ 100 m^2 for each 0.5 kg of N from October to the following May.

Cultivars and selections in the tests were as follows: common Italian ryegrass; 'NK100', 'Pelo', 'NK200', 'Manhattan', 'Pennfine', 'Yorktown', 'Citation', 'Derby', 'Game', 'Caprice', 'Eton', 'Ensporta', and 'Epic' perennial ryegrass; 'Biljart' hard fescue (*F. ovina* var. *duriuscula* L.); 'Pennlawn', 'Wintergreen', 'Ruby', and 'Dawson' fescue (*F. rubra* L.); 'Golfrood', 'Jamestown', and common chewings fescue (*F. rubra* var. *commutata* Gaud.); common roughstalk bluegrass; 'Prato' and 'Primo' Kentucky bluegrass; 'Holfior' colonial bentgrass (*A. tenuis* Sibth.); 'Penncross' and 'Seaside' creeping bentgrass (*A. stolnifera* var. *palustris* Huds.). Turfgrass cultivars and amounts used to overseed are listed in the appropriate tables.

Overseedings were made immediately after the bermudagrass turf had been moderately vertically cut in two directions and the debris swept from the experimental sites. After seeding, approximately 0.25 m^3/100 m^2 of soil topdressing was uniformly applied to the turf. The plots were irrigated to keep the soil surface moist until the seedling became well established.

All treatments were arranged in a randomized complete block design except the 1973 Newport News test which was a split plot design. The 1970 Newport News experiment was replicated four times, all other studies were replicated three times.

Visual ratings were taken monthly from autumn to early summer for turfgrass quality (a combined estimate of ground cover, inherent green color, disease, weed encroachment, and uniformity). Botanical composition and fraying or shredding of leaf blades after mowing were estimated at critical times during the year.

RESULTS AND DISCUSSION

Golf Green Turf

Italian ryegrass deteriorated in spring before bermudagrass had begun sustained active growth, therefore, contributing little botanical composition to the bermudagrass turf at a critical period. Whether Italian ryegrass was a monostand or included in a polystand, poor spring turf quality generally resulted with this species (Tables 1, 2, 3).

Most perennial ryegrasses included in these studies were superior in performance and maintained a higher turf quality than the Italian ryegrass on putting greens (Tables 1, 2, 3). Of the grasses studies, Pennfine, Manhattan, Eton, and NK200 performed most satisfactorily. When the perennial ryegrass cultivars that had the best overall turf quality as monostands were included in polystands, the superior performance and quality were maintained over polystands containing appreciable amounts of Italian ryegrass or inferior cultivars of perennial ryegrass.

Bentgrass species used alone were not satisfactory due to slow seedling growth in autumn, but when included in polystands with improved cultivars of perennial ryegrasses, generally resulted in improved turf quality and increased persistence into the summer (Tables 2, 3). Penncross and Holfior were superior to Seaside bentgrass. The persistence provided by the creeping bentgrass component of a polystand is a significant factor in the northern limits of the bermudagrass area of adaptation since this component provides the option of managing greens to retain bentgrass well into or through the summer if bermudagrass is killed or severely injured by low temperatures.

Fine fescues were slower than ryegrass to establish in the autumn, but maintained a high level of turfgrass quality in spring and early summer (Tables 1, 2, 3). Jamestown, Pennlawn, and Dawson established more quickly than Wintergreen or Biljart. Generally, the fescues, when included in polystands, improved texture and provided a smoother surface than a monostand of perennial ryegrass.

Kentucky bluegrass when included in a polystand did not appreciably effect performance of the polystand. Kentucky bluegrass is slow to establish (9) and does not increase persistence as effectively as bentgrass.

Roughstalk bluegrass (Table 3) was less suitable than any other species included in this study because of its lack of persistence in early summer and the rapidity with which this species was lost under the late spring conditions of the area.

Although excessive loss of temperate grass in the spring enhances the percentage of bermudagrass cover, a poor spring transition generally is associated with the rapid fading of the overseeded grass resulting in unacceptable turf quality. A good example of this can be seen in Table 1 by comparing Epic and NK100 with Manhattan for the June quality rating.

Persistence of overseeded temperate grasses in the spring did not

Table 1. Turfgrass quality and spring botanical composition of a Tifgreen bermudagrass putting green overseeded 6 Oct. 1969, at Williamsburg, Va. with various temperate grasses for winter turf.

Grasses overseeded	Amount overseeding	Turfgrass quality rating (1–9 = Best)				Botanical composition (6 Oct. 1970)	
		24 Nov. 1969	29 Jan. 1970	28 Apr. 1970	10 June 1970	Bermudagrass	Temperate grass
	kg/100 m²					%	%
NK100	24.4	7.6	6.3	5.3	3.3	70.0	3.3
Pelo	24.4	8.0	7.3	8.0	4.3	70.0	10.0
Epic	24.4	7.3	6.6	5.6	4.0	65.0	8.3
Eton	24.4	8.3	7.0	6.5	6.0	71.6	10.0
NK200	24.4	7.0	6.6	5.6	5.3	73.3	11.6
Italian ryegrass	24.4	6.3	6.3	4.3	7.0	76.6	5.0
Manhattan	24.4	8.3	8.3	7.6	5.6	52.5	37.5
NK100 50% + Pelo 50%	24.4	8.6	7.3	5.6	5.0	70.0	3.3
Italian ryegrass 50% + NK100 23% + Pelo 22%	24.1	7.6	7.3	6.6	5.6	71.6	13.3
Pennlawn	12.2	6.0	7.0	6.0	7.3	58.3	33.3
Wintergreen	12.2	5.3	5.6	6.6	6.6	56.6	36.3
Biljart	12.2	4.6	4.3	5.3	5.6	46.6	45.0
Pennlawn 33% + NK100 25% + Pelo 25%	18.3	7.3	6.0	7.6	7.0	65.0	21.6
Pennlawn 33% + Italian ryegrass 66%	18.3	6.6	6.3	6.3	6.3	66.6	23.3
Pennlawn 33% + Manhattan 66%	18.3	7.6	6.6	8.0	8.3	71.6	11.6
Pennlawn 92% + Seaside 8%	13.3	4.6	5.6	5.3	6.0	48.3	40.0
NK100 25% + Pelo 25% + Kentucky bluegrass 30% *P. trivialis* 20% + Holfior 10%	12.2	6.3	6.6	7.3	6.3	56.6	26.6
Ruby 25% + Golfrood 20% + Prato 30% + *P. trivialis* 15% + Holfior 10%	12.2	6.3	6.0	3.6	5.3	73.3	10.0
Ruby 25% + Golfrood 25% + Prato 20% + Exp. Kentucky bluegrass 20% + Holfior 10%	12.2	4.6	6.0	6.3	8.3	75.0	21.6
NK100 25% + Pelo 25% + Holfior 5% + Ruby 22.5% + Golfrood 22.5%	12.2	6.0	5.6	6.6	7.6	60.6	31.6
Pennlawn 31% + NK100 31% + Pelo 32% + Seaside 6%	19.4	8.0	6.3	7.3	6.0	56.6	33.3
Pennlawn 31% + Italian ryegrass 63% + Seaside 6%	19.4	6.6	6.6	6.6	6.6	56.6	33.3
Kentucky bluegrass 60% + *P. trivalis* 30% + Holfior 10%	6.1	3.3	5.0	5.3	4.6	57.5	25.0
L.S.D. 0.05		2.08	1.28	2.00	2.41	17.82	17.11

Table 2. Turfgrass quality and spring botanical composition of a Tifgreen bermudagrass golf putting green overseeded 7 Oct. 1970, at Newport News, Va., with temperate grasses for winter turf.

Grasses overseeded	Amount of overseeding	Turfgrass quality ratings (1–9 = Best)				Bermudagrass
		25 Nov. 1970	2 Nov. 1971	29 Apr. 1971	16 June 1971	16 June 1971
	kg/100 m²					%
Italian ryegrass	24.2	7.5	6.8	7.0	4.3	85.0
Manhattan	24.2	8.3	9.0	7.3	6.0	36.3
Pennfine	24.2	8.8	8.5	7.8	6.3	50.0
NK100	24.2	7.3	6.8	7.3	6.0	50.0
Pelo	24.2	7.8	8.0	8.0	6.5	35.0
NK100 50% + Pelo 50%	24.2	7.5	6.5	6.5	6.0	42.5
NK200	24.2	8.3	8.3	8.5	6.3	51.3
Eton	24.2	8.0	7.8	7.8	8.3	42.5
Pennlawn	14.4	7.0	5.8	7.3	7.3	45.0
Biljart	14.4	5.3	5.5	6.3	8.5	42.5
Holfior	0.9	3.8	3.0	6.8	8.3	32.5
Penncross	0.9	3.8	5.3	6.8	8.3	10.0
Chewings 16.7% + Pennlawn 16.7% + Manhattan 66.7%	18.2	8.3	8.3	7.8	6.5	40.0
Chewings 16.7% + Pennlawn 16.7% + Italian 66.7%	18.2	8.0	7.0	7.5	5.3	55.0
Chewings 16.7% + Pennlawn 16.7% + NK100 33.3% + Pelo 33.3%	18.2	7.3	7.5	8.0	7.8	42.5
Chewings 16.7% + Pennlawn 16.7% + Pennfine 66.6%	18.2	8.3	8.0	7.8	7.0	47.5
Pennlawn 33.3% + Italian 33.3% + Pennfine 33.3%	18.2	8.2	7.5	7.5	5.8	45.0
Pennlawn 32.5% + Italian 65% + Penncross 2.5%	18.7	7.8	7.0	7.0	5.0	67.5
Pennlawn 32.5% + Italian 65% + Seaside 2.5%	18.7	8.0	7.3	8.0	5.0	65.0
Pennlawn 32.5% + Pennfine 65% + Penncross 2.5%	18.7	7.8	8.0	8.8	6.3	35.0
Pennlawn 32.5% + Pennfine 65% + Holfior 2.5%	18.7	8.5	8.5	8.0	7.5	33.8
Pennfine 50% + Italian 50%	24.5	8.5	7.3	7.8	6.0	57.5
L.S.D. 0.05		0.91	1.1	1.0	1.6	19.6

Table 3. Turfgrass quality and spring botanical composition of a Tifgreen bermudagrass putting green overseeded 12 Oct. 1972 at Williamsburg, Va. with various temperate grasses for winter turf.

Grasses overseeded	Amount of overseeding	Turfgrass quality rating (1–9 = Best)					Botanical composition: Bermudagrass		Botanical composition: Temperate grasses	
		22 Nov. 1972	3 Dec. 1973	5 Mar. 1973	6 Nov. 1973	28 June 1973	5 Mar. 1973	6 Nov. 1973	2 Jan. 1973	28 June 1973
	kg/100 m²						%			
Italian ryegrass	27.0	5.7	5.0	4.0	3.3	3.0	8	53	78	0
Manhattan	27.0	8.3	7.7	7.3	5.0	6.7	10	28	91	37
NK200	27.0	7.0	7.0	7.3	3.7	4.0	10	27	83	15
Pennfine	27.0	8.3	8.3	7.3	6.7	8.0	12	37	90	23
NK200 50% + Pelo 50%	27.0	7.0	6.7	6.0	5.0	5.7	10	32	89	25
Pennfine 50% + NK200 50%	27.0	7.7	8.0	8.3	5.7	7.0	10	30	87	25
Jamestown	13.5	6.0	6.3	7.3	5.7	8.0	17	25	83	60
Pennlawn	13.5	5.7	6.7	6.7	6.0	7.0	28	30	83	57
Dawson	13.5	6.7	5.7	8.0	5.3	8.7	30	27	80	52
Penncross	1.2	3.3	5.3	6.7	7.0	8.0	10	20	67	70
Seaside	1.2	3.0	5.3	5.7	6.3	6.0	10	23	58	35
Poa trivialis	7.5	5.7	7.0	5.0	1.3	1.7	25	28	90	1
Manhattan 66% + Jamestown 33%	20.3	7.0	8.3	8.3	6.3	7.7	27	30	88	57
Pennlawn 45.9% + Chewings 45.9% + Penncross 8.1%	14.8	6.3	7.7	7.3	6.3	7.3	10	37	87	58
Manhattan 33.25% + Italian 33.25% + Pennlawn 16.7% + Chewings 16.7%	20.3	7.0	6.7	6.0	5.3	6.7	13	30	87	47
Pennfine 28% + NK100 27% + Dawson 40% + Seaside 5%	20.25	8.0	8.3	8.3	6.7	7.0	10	27	88	72
Manhattan 62.8% + Pennlawn 15.8% + Chewings 15.8% + Penncross 5.6%	21.5	7.7	8.7	8.7	6.3	7.7	22	37	92	58
Pennfine 27% + NK200 28% + Dawson 30% + Primo 7.5% + Prato 7.5%	21.6	7.3	8.3	8.3	6.0	8.0	10	30	91	50
Pennfine 32% + NK200 32% + Primo 15% + Prato 15% + Seaside 5%	17.3	7.0	8.0	7.7	6.0	7.7	10	27	88	28
L.S.D. 0.05		1.2	1.4	1.7	1.7	1.5	7.8	11.2	5.3	12

necessarily reduce turfgrass quality. For example, in the spring of 1971 (Table 2), the plot overseeded with Penncross had an excellent turfgrass quality rating on 16 June, but only had 10% bermudagrass coverage; whereas the plot overseeded with Italian ryegrass had the poorest turfgrass quality with 85% bermudagrass turf coverage.

Polystands that included 65% perennial ryegrass, 30% fine fescue, and 5% bentgrass and were composed of cultivars that performed well in monostands were considered superior for overall golf green turf to the monostands. Perennial ryegrass provided quick establishment, was competitive to annual bluegrass, and resisted wear (9). The fine texture and upright growth of the fine fescues provided resilience and a smooth putting surface. Bentgrass insured improved spring turf quality and persistence into hot summer weather.

Golf Tees, Athletic Fields, and Fairways

Bermudagrass used for turf other than green is frequently medium-textured. Grasses with the texture of ryegrass provide more compatible winter turf than those with finer texture. Traditionally, Italian ryegrass has been used for this purpose.

The turfgrass quality of all the perennials in this test were superior to Italian ryegrass during winter and spring when seeded as monostands or in mixtures (Tables 4, 5, 6) and maintained as golf tee turf. Pennfine, Manhattan, and NK200 provides the best overall winter turfgrass quality in 1973. These three cultivars were superior to polystands consisting predominantly of Pelo, NK100, or 'Oregon' perennial ryegrass and Italian ryegrass. A 50–50 seed mixture of Pennfine and NK200 was similar to Pennfine in maintaining turfgrass quality, but was subject to more mower shredding in mid-spring and early summer. In mid-May, differences in shredding following mowing became quite apparent and were more pronounced as the spring progressed. Pennfine had less shredding from mowing than cultivars in monostands or in blends at all seeding rates. Manhattan was particularly susceptible to shredding at the high seeding rate (Table 4). Increasing the amount of temperate grass seed from 2.45 to 7.35 kg/100 m^2 generally increased winter turfgrass quality, however, the shredding in the spring was more noticeable with the higher amount of overseeding, suggesting that a rate of 4.9 kg/100 m^2 (Table 4) is adequate for overseeding tees, athletic fields, and similar turf areas and that a lower rate is adequate for fairways and similar turf areas.

The severity of shredding was also influenced by applications of N and Fe (Fig. 1). Applications of 0.5 kg N and 0.125 kg chelated Fe/100 m^2 in October, December, February, April, and May resulted in an acceptable degree of shredding in most cultivars, while appliction of only the above N fertility in October and December were insufficient to reduce shredding to a desirable level.

Another obvious aspect was that the lower growing cultivars gener-

Table 4. Performance of various ryegrasses overseeded at three rates for winter turf on a Tifgreen bermudagrass tee on 10 Oct. 1973 at Williamsburg, Va.

Grasses overseeded	Turf quality ratings (1–9 = best) Avg. of four dates from 30 Jan. 1974 to 15 Apr. 1974 Amount of overseeding (kg/100 m²)			Shredding rating (1–9 = severe) 15 Apr. 1974 Amount of overseeding (kg/100 m²)			3 days topgrowth 30 Jan. 1974
	2.45	4.9	7.35	2.45	4.9	7.35	Avg. of three amounts
							cm
NK200	5.7	6.3	7.3	1.3	1.0	1.4	1.5
Manhattan	6.3	6.6	8.2	2.0	3.3	5.3	1.2
Pennfine	6.7	7.8	8.5	1.0	1.0	1.3	1.4
Pennfine 50% + NK200 50%	6.0	6.9	7.7	1.0	2.0	2.3	1.2
NK100 50% + Pelo 50%	5.9	6.4	7.3	4.3	3.3	3.7	1.6
NK100 70% + Oregon perennial ryegrass and Italian ryegrass 30%	5.3	5.7	6.6	2.7	4.3	3.7	2.2
Avg.	6.0	6.6	7.6	2.1	2.5	3.0	1.51
		L.S.D. 0.05			L.S.D. 0.05		L.S.D. 0.05
Amount		0.68			NS		NS
Grass		0.50			1.2		0.24

Table 5. Turfgrass quality and shredding ratings of various ryegrasses overseeded for winter turf on a Tifgreen bermudagrass golf tee 10 Oct. 1973 at Newport News, Va. Averaged over four fertility regimes.

Ryegrasses	Overseeding amount	Turfgrass quality rating (1–9 = best) 31 Jan. 1974	1 Mar. 1974	28 Mar. 1974	15 May 1974	Shredding rating (1–9 = severe) 15 May 1974
	kg/100 m²					
NK200	4.9	5.8	4.4	6.3	7.7	1.9
Manhattan	4.9	6.6	5.4	7.3	7.4	2.3
Pennfine	4.9	5.0	4.1	6.1	7.9	1.5
Pennfine 50% + NK100 50%	4.9	5.0	4.6	5.8	7.5	1.9
NK100 50% + Pelo 50%	4.9	6.0	4.5	5.3	6.9	3.0
NK100 70% + (Oregon perennial and Italian ryegrass) 30%	4.9	6.8	4.9	5.7	7.2	3.9
L.S.D. 0.05		1.0	0.81	1.04	0.56	1.03

Table 6. Performance of ryegrasses overseeded at 2.45 kg/100 m² for winter turf on a Tifgreen bermudagrass golf tee on 2 Oct. 1975 at Williamsburg, Va., and subsequent botanical composition.

	Turfgrass quality ratings (1–9 = best)				Bermudagrass		Ryegrass		
Ryegrasses overseeded	2 June 1976	24 Mar. 1976	17 June 1976	22 July 1976	17 June 1976	22 July 1976	17 June 1976	22 July 1976	23 Nov. 1976
					%				
Derby	6.7	6.3	6.0	6.0	49.0	56.7	43.3	41.7	36.7
Citation	6.3	7.0	5.7	5.3	51.7	55.0	41.0	36.7	36.7
Pennfine	7.0	6.0	5.3	5.7	53.3	66.7	36.7	30.0	58.3
Yorktown	7.0	6.0	5.0	6.3	53.3	73.3	35.0	26.7	41.7
Manhattan	7.0	6.3	4.7	5.0	56.7	70.0	31.7	23.3	48.3
NK200	7.0	5.7	4.7	5.0	48.3	71.7	40.0	21.7	10.7
Eton	6.7	5.3	4.0	5.3	53.3	68.3	28.3	28.3	16.7
Game	5.7	5.0	5.0	4.7	50.0	66.7	35.0	25.0	18.3
Caprice	5.7	4.6	4.7	4.7	61.7	70.0	25.0	23.3	11.7
Ensporta	4.7	4.7	4.7	5.7	65.0	70.0	23.3	25.0	11.7
NK100	4.3	4.3	5.0	5.0	53.3	70.0	36.7	21.7	13.3
Epic	4.8	4.8	3.7	4.7	56.7	65.0	30.0	25.0	8.3
Italian	4.3	3.0	2.7	5.3	53.3	80.0	10.0	15.0	0.0
25% Italian + 75% Pennfine	5.8	6.0	6.3	6.3	59.3	75.0	37.7	23.3	56.7
50% Italian + 50% Pennfine	5.3	5.3	4.7	5.3	61.7	68.3	28.3	26.7	45.0
Pennfine 50% + NK200 50%	7.0	6.3	3.7	5.0	55.0	63.3	21.7	28.3	33.3
NK100 70% + Oregon perennial ryegrass & Italian ryegrass 30%	4.3	4.3	4.3	4.3	61.7	71.7	25.0	18.3	21.7
L.S.D. 0.05	1.3	1.1	1.3	NS	NS	12.2	13.7	12.4	17.3

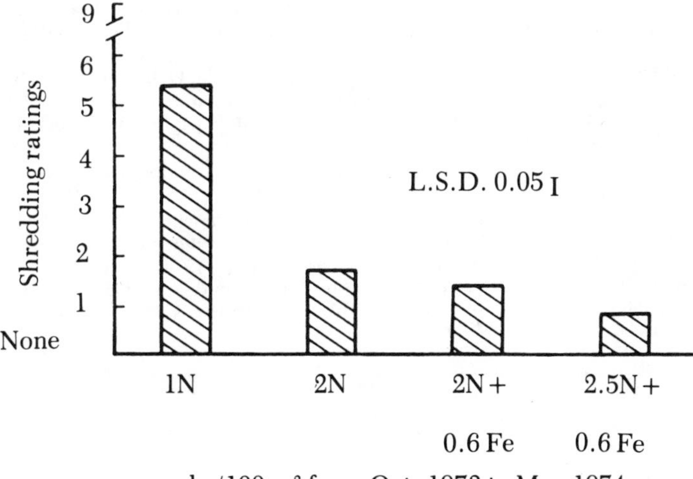

Fig. 1. Nitrogen and Fe fertility influence on shredding 15 May 1974) of perennial ryegrasses overseeded for winter turf on a Tifgreen bermudagrass tee 10 Oct. 1973 at Newport News, Va.

ally had the best turfgrass quality. Possibly, the lower turfgrass quality of the more upright cultivars resulted from removing a larger proportion of leaf area when mowed. It appears desirable to use perennial ryegrasses that have relatively low growth characteristics. This trait would also enhance its compatibility with bermudagrasses.

During the winter of 1975–76, 10 of the 12 perennial ryegrass cultivars performed satisfactorily (Table 6). Derby, Citation, and Pennfine exhibited the most desirable performance throughout the period from October to June. These ryegrasses also appear to have excellent heat tolerance as they produced over 35% ground cover by November following the first summer after establishment, suggesting that less seed would be needed for overseeding after the first year if these cultivars were used.

The turfgrass quality of the 25% Italian ryegrass—75% Pennfine perennial ryegrass seed mixture was not significantly different from a monostand of Pennfine. Possibly because of economic considerations, up to 25% of an inferior species may be used as a seed mixture component without significant quality reduction.

LITERATURE CITED

1. Bingham, S. W., R. E. Schmidt, and C. K. Curry. 1969. Annual bluegrass in overseeded bermudagrass putting green turf. Agron. J. 61:908–911.
2. Kneebone, William R., and G. L. Major. 1969. Differential survival of cool-season turfgrass species overseeded on different selections of bermudagrass. Crop Sci. 9:153–155.
3. McBee, G. C. 1970. Performance of certain cool-season grasses in overseeding studies on a Tifgreen bermudagrass golf green. Prog. Rep. 2457. Texas Agric. Exp. Stn.

4. Menn, W. G., and G. C. McBee. 1971. An evaluation of various cool-season grasses and grass mixtures in overseeding a Tifgreen bermudagrass golf green. Prog. Rep. 2878. Texas Agric. Exp. Stn.
5. Schmidt, R. E. 1962. Overseeding winter greens in Virginia. Golf Course Rep. 30:44–47.
6. ————. 1970. Overseeding cool-season turfgrasses on dormant bermudagrass for winter. p. 124–129. *In* R. R. Davis (ed.) Proc. First Int. Turfgrass Res. Conf., Harrogate, England, 15–18 July 1969.
7. ————, and R. E. Blaser. 1967. Establishing winter bermuda putting turf. U.S. Golf Assoc. J. Turf Management. 15:30.
8. ————, and J. F. Shoulders. 1972. Winter turf development on dormant bermudagrass as influenced by summer cultivation and winter N fertilization. Agron. J. 64:435–437.
9. Ward, C. Y., E. L. McWhirter, and W. R. Thompson, Jr. 1974. Evaluation of cool-season turf species and planting techniques for overseeding bermudagrass golf greens. p. 480–495. *In* E. C. Roberts (ed.) Proc. of the Second Int. Turfgrass Res. Conf., Blacksburg, Va. June 1973. Am. Soc. Agron., Madison, Wis.

Section II:

Turfgrass Growth and Development

Chapter 11

The Effects of Stage of Seedling Development on Selected Physiological and Morphology Parameters in Kentucky Bluegrass and Red Fescue[1]

J. V. KRANS
J. B. BEARD

ABSTRACT

Net photosynthesis, dark respiration, distribution of ^{14}C-photosynthate, and selected morphological parameters were monitored in seedlings of 'Merion' Kentucky bluegrass (*Poa pratensis* L.) and 'Pennlawn' red fescue (*Festuca rubra* L.) at 1-week intervals for a 10-week period in environmentally controlled plant growth chambers. Elucidation of these inherent physiological and morphological changes may lead to improved turfgrass vigor and quality through adjustments in cultural practices (fertilization, irrigation, clipping, pesticide application. . .) which coincide with specific time sequences found to be critical.

Lateral shoot development occurred after the third leaf stage (3 weeks after seedling emergence) in red fescue and after the fifth leaf stage (3 to 4 weeks after seedling emergence) in Kentucky bluegrass. Tillers were initiated in the axils of leaves below fully expanded leaves in both species. Tiller development preceded rhizome initiation in red fescue. Tillers and rhizomes were not initiated preferentially in Kentucky bluegrass. Accelerated dark respiration and high percent leaf dry weights occurred for 2 weeks after seedling emergence in both species. Net photosynthesis was greatest 1 week following seedling emergence in both species. A high percent of the ^{14}C-photosynthate shifted from the leaves to stems between the 2nd and 3rd weeks after seedling emergence in Kentucky bluegrass and the 3rd and 4th weeks after seedling emergence in red fescue. The stem fractions remained the dominant sinks for ^{14}C-photosynthate following the initial ^{14}C-photosynthate shift in both species.

Additional index words: Net photosynthesis, Dark respiration, ^{14}C-photosynthate, Turfgrasses, Establishment, Tillers, Rhizomes, Secondary lateral shoots.

INTRODUCTION

Knowledge of the physiological and morphological parameters associated with turfgrass growth and development will aid in selecting improved turfgrass cultural regimes. Rapid seedling growth is an essential phase of turfgrass culture and is a key attribute for effective erosion control, weed competition, and a rapid turf cover.

Soper and Mitchell (12) reported that a minimum level of maturity

[1] Michigan Agric. Exp. Stn., East Lansing, MI, USA 48821. Journal Article No. 8285.

must be reached prior to tiller initiation in perennial ryegrasses (*Lolium* spp). Beard (3) has indicated that turfgrasses must reach a specific size and leaf area prior to rhizome initiation. Net photosynthesis and dark respiration rates have been reported to change with specific levels of plant maturity (5, 7, 12). Carpenter (4) monitored the distribution pattern of photosynthate in dicotyledons and showed a gradual shift of photosynthate accumulation from leaves to stems and finally to the roots. Enhanced movement of photosynthate into newly initiated rhizomes in developing Kentucky bluegrass plants was reported by Nyahoza (9).

The relative stages of plant maturity have been shown to correlate with physiological and morphological phases of plant growth. However, limited information which specifically describes these inherent changes is available. The objectives of this study were to investigate morphological and physiological changes associated with turfgrass seedling growth and development. Net photosynthesis, dark respiration, and distribution of ^{14}C-photosynthate were monitored as major physiological parameters for describing levels and sites of plant metabolic activity. Leaf stage, leaf position, and initiation and development of secondary lateral shoots were selected as morphological parameters for characterizing stages of plant development. It was anticipated that the reciprocal relations of these morphological and physiological parameters could provide new information concerning seedling growth and development. This knowledge could then be utilized to adjust turfgrass cultural regimes (irrigation, fertilization, mowing, pesticide application. . .) so that growth will improve during these periods of apparent critical change.

MATERIALS AND METHODS

'Merion' Kentucky bluegrass (*Poa pratensis* L.) and 'Pennlawn' red fescue (*Festuca rubra* L.) were selected for this study based on their widespread use as cool-season turfgrasses in temperate regions. Plants of each species were grown from seed in 5-cm diam × 15-cm deep plastic containers with perforated bases for free drainage. The pots were filled with washed silica sand. Each species was seeded at 15 to 20 seeds per pot and the seedlings gradually thinned to one plant per pot by the end of 4 weeks. The high plant density during the first 4 weeks was necessary to obtain adequate plant material for sampling during this time period.

Plants were grown in an environmental growth chamber at 23 C day and 16 C night temperatures. The light radiation level was 600 $\mu E\ M^{-2}\ sec^{-1}$ and the photoperiod was 14 hours. Relative humidity ranged between 65 and 75%. A modified Hoagland (6) nutrient solution drench was applied every 3rd day, while the plants were irrigated with tap water on alternate days. Weekly clipping of the leaves was initiated 4 weeks after seedling emergence at a height of 7.5 cm.

Photosynthesis, dark respiration, and distribution of ^{14}C-photosynthate were measured on separate, individual pots of turf randomly selected from a collectively grown group at 1-week intervals for a 10-week period following seedling emergence. Photosynthetic and dark respiration rates were measured by monitoring the rate of change in CO_2 concentration between 270 and 330 ppm in a closed CO_2 exchange system. This CO_2 exchange system consisted of a Beckman Model 215 infrared gas analyzer, an FMI Model RRP piston pump for air circulation, a Sargent Model SR strip chart recorder, a Drierite column, and a cyclindrical assimilation chamber (internal volume 220 ml). The air flow rate was 500 ml/min and the total volume of the system was 313 ml. The connecting lines were constructed primarily of 0.63-cm diam copper tubing with short lengths of tygon tubing to aid in flexibility. A 400-watt Sylvania mercury vapor lamp was placed above the assimilation chamber. The lamp was suspended above a water bath to reduce the amount of heat in the assimilation chamber. A radiation level of 600 μE M^{-2} sec^{-1} was maintained at the plant surface within the assimilation chamber. The entire system was located in a Puffer Hubbard UNI-THERM refrigerator operated at a constant temperature of 23 $\pm$ 1 C. A bulb thermometer was inserted into the chamber to monitor temperatures. Soil respiration was eliminated by flooding the container with distilled water to a depth of 0.5 to 1.0 cm above the sand surface. Photosynthetic and dark respiration rates were measured 4 hours after initiation of the light period. Dark respiration was monitored first, followed by photosynthetic measurements.

Plants were treated with 1 μCi of $^{14}CO_2$ for photosynthate distribution experiments after the photosynthetic and dark respiration measurements were completed. Labeling was done by diverting the air stream within the closed CO_2 exchange system into a reaction flask containing 0.2 ml (1 μCi) of $Na^{14}HCO_3$ solution ($Na^{14}HCO_3$ and H_2O) plus 5 ml of 45% lactic acid. The $^{14}CO_2$ evolved was continually circulated around the grass leaves for 30 min during which time the plant reached its CO_2 compensation concentration. The plants were returned to the environmental growth chambers for a 24-hour period after labeling. The root system was then washed free of sand, immediately frozen, and stored. Plants were subsequently sectioned into leaf, root, stem, and rhizome fractions and freeze-dried.

The leaf fraction consisted of tissue located above the collar. The crown and leaf sheath were included in the stem fraction. Root segments were removed below and immediately adjacent to the crown. The rhizome fraction consisted of subsurface secondary lateral shoots that developed extravaginally and extended horizontally. Rhizomes which did not reach the soil surface were included in this fraction, while those which had emerged into the light and formed photosynthetically active leaves were separated into leaf and stem fractions.

Each plant segment was weighed and sub-sampled (50 to 100 mg) for the $^{14}CO_2$ incorporation analysis. The amount of radioactivity was measured by combusting plant samples in a sealed 1,000-ml Erlenmeyer flask containing an oxygen-pure atmosphere. The radioactive $^{14}CO_2$ which evolved was captured in 20 ml of ethanol-ethanolamine (2:1). A 5-ml aliquot was combined with 10 ml of scintillation solution [0.3 g of dimethyl POPOP (1,4-bis 2-(4-methyl-5-phenyloxazolyl)-benzene, 5.0 g of PPO (2,5-diphenyloxazole) per liter of toluene] and radioassayed by liquid scintillation spectrometry. Counting efficiency was determined by channel ratios and ranged between 70 and 75%. Net radioactive incorporation was measured as disintegrations per min (dpm).

Leaf area was determined with a LI-Cor, Model LI-3000 portable area meter using a sub-sample of fresh leaf blades (five to 10). A subsample of leaf area was measured for each sampling period. A leaf area: weight ratio was used to estimate the total leaf area.

Three replications were used at each sampling period. The experimental design employed was a completely randomized block. Differences between treatment means were tested statistically using Duncan's Multiple Range Test.

RESULTS AND DISCUSSION

Pennlawn red fescue initiated lateral shoots after the third leaf stage of development (3 weeks after seedling emergence). Merion Kentucky bluegrass initiated lateral shoots after the fifth leaf stage (3 to 4 weeks after seedling emergence). Soper (11) reported tiller initiation in perennial ryegrass (*Lolium perenne* L.) 3 to 4 weeks after plant emergence. These data suggest a specific maturity level is á prerequisite for lateral shoot development and that the time period is species dependent.

Tiller development in both species occurred only in the axils of leaves below fully expanded leaves. Patel and Cooper (9) reported similar leaf positioning in several other grasses undergoing tiller development. Tiller development in red fescue preceded rhizome initiation in all observations. However, in Merion Kentucky bluegrass, neither tillers nor rhizomes were initiated preferentially to one another.

Turfgrass seedling development in both species showed similar dry weight distribution patterns (Table 1). The percent distribution of dry weight in the root fraction tended to increase from the initial sampling to 3 weeks after seedling emergence. The leaf fraction showed a high percent dry weight accumulation during the 1st 2 weeks. These initial levels were followed by lower dry weights. The proportion of dry weight in the stem fractions of Merion Kentucky bluegrass and Pennlawn red fescue showed only slight changes throughout the study.

Net photosynthesis and dark respiration rates were similar for both species (Table 2). High photosynthetic rates occurred 1 week following emergence. Dark respiration was greatest 1 week after emergence and declined to one-half the original level at the second sampling period. Both net photosynthesis and dark respiration remained unchanged following these initial trends. The acceleration in dark respiration and net photosynthesis suggests a time sequence of high energy supply and demand. The period of heightened photosynthetic rates corresponds with high percent

Table 1. The effect of stage of development on the percent distribution of dry weight in Pennlawn red fescue and Merion Kentucky bluegrass.

Species	Plant tissue	Percent distribution of dry weight†								
		Sampling period (week)								
		1	2	3	4	5	6	7	8	10
		%								
Pennlawn red fescue	Roots	19 a*	29 b	36 cd	33 bcd	35 cd	33 bcd	34 bcd	30 bc	32 bcd
	Stems	24 a	18 b	18 b	21 ab	26 a	23 ab	21 ab	25 a	24 a
	Leaves	57 a	53 a	46 b	46 b	38 c	43 bc	44 bc	44 bc	42 bc
	Rhizomes	0 a	0 a	0 a	0 a	1 a	1 a	1 a	1 a	4 b
Merion Kentucky bluegrass	Roots	21 a	27 b	34 c	30 bc	30 bc	35 c	32 bc	30 bc	29 bc
	Stems	20 ab	17 a	20 ab	22 b	27 cd	28 cd	28 cd	30 d	24 bc
	Leaves	59 a	56 a	46 b	47 b	40 c	36 c	37 c	37 c	41 c
	Rhizomes	0 a	0 a	0 a	1 a	2 a	2 a	3 b	3 b	6 c

* Means within rows (across) with common letters are not significantly different at the 5% level by the Duncan's Multiple Range Test.

† Values represent the percent dry weight based on total plant weight.

leaf dry weights and suggests a plant response designed for high photosynthate output.

The percent distribution of ^{14}C-photosynthate varied with time and species (Table 3). A noticeably high level of ^{14}C-photosynthate shifted from the leaf to the stem fractions during the third and fourth sampling periods in Pennlawn red fescue and during the second and third sampling periods in Merion Kentucky bluegrass. The ^{14}C-photosynthate accumulation remained relatively stable in both these fractions following this initial shift.

The percent distribution of ^{14}C-photosynthate in the root fraction remained unchanged until the sixth sampling period in Kentucky bluegrass when it declined. In Pennlawn red fescue, ^{14}C-photosynthate distribution in the root fraction was highest initially and declined slowly thereafter. These trends in ^{14}C-photosynthate accumulation in the root fractions of both species correspond inversely with the percent ^{14}C-photosynthate found in the rhizomes. Crafts and Crisp (5) and Nyahoza (8) have reported rhizomes to be strong sinks within plant systems which alter photo-

Table 2. The effect of stage of development on the net photosynthetic (P_N) and dark respiration (R_D) rates in Merion Kentucky bluegrass and Pennlawn red fescue.

Species	Plant measurement	Net photosynthesis and dark respiration rates*								
		Sampling period (week)								
		1	2	3	4	5	6	7	8	10
		$MgCO_2$ dm^{-2} $hour^{-1}$								
Pennlawn red fescue	P_N	41 a	23 bc	22 bc	26 b	20 bc	21 bc	20 bc	20 bc	17 c
	R_D	13 a	7 b	5 c	4 c	4 c	4 c	5 c	5 c	4 c
Merion Kentucky bluegrass	P_N	34 a	15 b	16 b	b17 b	16 b	18 b	15 b	14 b	14 b
	R_D	16 a	8 b	5 c	5 c	4 c	4 c	5 c	4 c	5 c

* Means within rows (across) with common letters are not significantly different at the 5% level by the Duncan's Multiple Range Test.

Table 3. The effect of stage of development on the percent distribution of ^{14}C-photosynthate in Pennlawn red fescue and Merion Kentucky bluegrass.

Species	Plant tissue	Percent distribution of ^{14}C-photosynthate†								
		Sampling period (week)								
		1	2	3	4	5	6	7	8	10
		%								
Pennlawn red fescue	Roots	27 a*	20 b	21 ab	19 b	16 bcd	17 bc	12 cd	10 d	10 d
	Stems	26 a	25 a	32 ab	49 bc	53 bcd	51 bc	48 bc	55 cd	59 d
	Leaves	47 a	55 b	47 a	32 de	30 de	31 de	40 cd	33 de	40 de
	Rhizomes	0 a	0 a	0 a	0 a	1 a	1 a	1 a	2 a	2 a
Merion Kentucky bluegrass	Roots	18 a	16 a	17 a	14 ab	16 a	9 c	7 c	10 bc	8 c
	Stems	20 a	22 a	50 b	50 b	53 b	51 b	51 b	51 b	47 bc
	Leaves	62 a	62 a	33 de	35 cd	30 e	36 cd	38 cd	37 cd	40 c
	Rhizomes	0 a	0 a	0 a	1 a	1 a	4 b	4 b	3 b	5 c

* Means within rows (across) with common letters are not significantly different at the 5% level by Duncan's Multiple Range test.

† Values represent the percent radioactivity based on total ^{14}C-incorporation per plant.

synthate distribution. This relationship between the rhizome and root fractions suggests rhizomes have priority over roots for photosynthate in these C-3 perennial grasses. The high percent ^{14}C-photosynthate accumulation in the stem fractions of both species agrees with reports showing that stem tissue is a dominant sink for carbohydrates in grasses (1, 2, 10).

These patterns in morphological and physiological parameters measured during seedling growth may reflect critical inherent stages of turfgrass development. The patterns appear to be species dependent and may be related to turfgrass compatibility and/or vigor. Knowledge of these patterns may lead to improved cultural regimes. Proper timing of cultural practices (fertilization, irrigation, mowing, pesticide application. . .) during these periods of high energy supply and demands or changes in photosynthate distribution may lead to improved turfgrass establishment, quality, and vigor.

ACKNOWLEDGMENTS

This investigation was supported by grants from the Michigan Turfgrass Foundation, The Toro Company, and Spartan Distributors of Sparta, Mich.

LITERATURE CITED

1. Adegbola, A. A., and C. M. McKell. 1966. Effect of nitrogen fertilization on the carbohydrate content of coastal bermudagrass (*Cynodon dactylon* L. Pers.). Agron. J. 58:60–64.
2. Alberda, T. 1957. The effects of cutting, light intensity, and night temperature on growth and soluble carbohydrate content of *Lolium perenne* L. Plant Soil 8:199–230.
3. Beard, J. B. 1973. Turfgrass: Science and culture. Prentice-Hall, Inc. Englewood, Cliffs, N.J.

4. Carpenter, S. B. 1971. Developmental changes in assimilation and translocation of photosynthate in black walnut (*Juglans nigra* L.) and honeylocust (*Gleditsia triancanthus* L.) seedlings. Ph.D. Thesis. Michigan State Univ. Univ. Microfilms, Ann Arbor, Mich. (Diss. Abstr. 8995).

5. Crafts, A. S., and C. E. Crisp. 1971. Phloem transport in plants. W. H. Freeman and Co., San Francisco, Calif. p. 127–156.

6. Hoagland, C. R., and D. I. Aron. 1950. The water culture method for growing plants without soil. California Agric. Exp. Stn. Circ. 347.

7. Kortschak, H. P., and A. Forkes. 1969. The effect of shade and age on the photosynthesis rate of sugar cane. p. 383–387. *In* H. Metzner (ed.) Progress in photosynthesis research. Vol. 1. Institute fur Chemisese Pflanzanphyfiologi, Tubingen, Germany.

8. Nyahoza, J. L. 1973. The interrelationship between tillers and rhizomes of *Poa pratensis* L.—An autoradiographic study. Weed Sci. 21:304–309.

9. Patel, A. S., and J. P. Cooper. 1961. The influence of several changes in light energy on leaf and tiller development in ryegrass, timothy and meadow fescue. J. Br. Grassl. Soc. 16:299–308.

10. Smith, D. 1968. Carbohydrates in grasses. IV. Influence of temperature on the sugar and frustosan composition of timothy plant parts at anthesis. Crop Sci. 8:331–334.

11. Soper, K., and K. J. Mitchell. 1956. The developmental anatomy of perennial ryegrass (*Lolium perenne* L.). N.Z. J. Sci. Technol. Sect. A. 37:484–504.

12. Wilson, D., and J. R. Cooper. 1969. Apparent photosynthesis and leaf characters in relation to leaf position and age, among contrasting *Lolium* genotypes. New Phytol. 68: 645–655.

Chapter 12 Tillering and Persistency in Perennial Ryegrass[1]

J. W. MINDERHOUD

ABSTRACT

Two field trials were performed to investigate the regeneration of divergent perennial ryegrass (*Lolium perenne* L.) cultivars in monostands under various treatments. The first trial investigated the effects of simulated traffic and N fertilization on the number of vegetative shoots during the season. It revealed that perennial ryegrass, though considered to be a "tread-species", does not need traffic to thrive. Nitrogen fertilization increased shoot density with close, frequent cutting.

It was found that perennial ryegrass produced vegetative shoots with extended internodes. Therefore, a second experiment studied the incidence of these abnormal tiller types. In addition to the normal, unelongated shoots, two types of abnormal shoots were found in perennial ryegrass: (i) subsidiary shoots on the raised nodes of flowering stems; (ii) partly elongated vegetative shoots. Both types occurred in all the cultivars examined, but not to the same extent. The percentage of shoots of the first type varied little among the different cultivars, but the percentage of elongated shoots of the second type varied greatly in proportion to shoot density. Cultural practices common on sports fields did not seem to influence the incidence of abnormal vegetative shoots.

Raised or elongated shoots in a horizontal position (pseudostolons) enable the plant to spread at rates of 1 to 5 cm per year, at least twice the rate resulting from gradual apex displacement by unelongated internodes. Nevertheless, it may be undesirable to develop new cultivars with even more internode elongation because present-day cultivars already produce many elongated shoots, and cultivars with even more would be rather frost-susceptible and thus persistency would be threatened.

Additional index words: Simulated traffic, Shoot density, Raised subsidiary shoots, Elongated shoots, Pseudostolons, N fertilization.

INTRODUCTION

Shoots or tillers are the unit structures of a grass cover. In studying the effects of various cultural practices on turfgrass, it is useful to follow the number of vegetative shoots per unit area during the season to ascertain whether shoot density increases or decreases with a given treatment. Persistency is closely related to turf regeneration, the process whereby new tillers replace mature or injured shoots. Therefore, the efficacy of a treatment on turf regeneration is important.

Shoots in monostands of two contrasting perennial ryegrass (*Lolium perenne* L.) cultivars were periodically counted to study the effect of simulated wear (Experiment 1). There were three reasons for focussing on perennial ryegrass: (i) it is a very important grass species in the Nether-

[1] A contribution from Wageningen, The Netherlands.

lands, both in sports fields and in pastures; (ii) it is an easy species to investigate because the shoots are usually big enough to be counted in situ; (iii) according to various turfgrass publications (2, 5), it is a non-creeping tufted species that only produces reproductive shoots (flowering stems) and unelongated vegetative tillers (elongated shoots in the form of stolons have not been previously reported).

It was decided to focus on the effects of simulated traffic (turfgrass wear and soil compaction) during the growing season because perennial ryegrass is known as a "tread-species" (7) in western European grasslands where it often dominates the sward. The discussion as to whether or not perennial ryegrass really needs traffic to thrive is revived from time to time, especially in the case of recently sown sports fields.

Unfortunately, Experiment 1 revealed that perennial ryegrass does not solely or mainly produce unelongated vegetative tillers. Many stolon-like vegetative shoots were found that belonged to two distinctly different types. Consequently, the persistency of a perennial ryegrass cultivar does not merely depend upon its capacity to replace vegetative shoots; but equally upon the nature of the new tillers that are formed, i.e. their ability to develop and establish successfully. Therefore, attention was paid to the classification, incidence, and significance of the types of vegetative tillers of this species in a second experiment. This paper summarizes some main findings. The complete results of both experiments will be published later.

MATERIALS AND METHODS

Both experiments were done in Wageningen, Netherlands, on fields each measuring 2.6 × 10 m. The soil was completely modified. The topsoil (30 cm), fumigated in order to prevent weed invasion, consisted of a medium sand containing a high percentage of organic matter. The subsoil was a coarse sand.

Seeding was done by hand at a rate of 10 seeds/dm^2. After emergence, the seedlings were thinned to six primary shoots/dm^2. This procedure resulted in very uniform turfs in both experiments, a necessary condition for neither of them had proper replications. The fields were well fertilized with P and K and were mowed 40 times per year to a height of 3 cm. Clippings were removed. The turfs were watered throughout the summer. Disease problems were not observed.

Experiment 1

Experiment 1 included two cultivars of perennial ryegrass; 'Pelo', a pasture-type also recommended for turfs, and 'Hunsballe', a hay-type. Seeding was done in April 1975. There were two N treatments, 468 and

Table 1. Shoot density of perennial ryegrass in monostands during the 1976 growing season as influenced by cultivar persistency, N supply, and simulated traffic tests.

	Shoots/dm²						
Comparison	Mar.	Apr.	May	June	July	Aug.	Sept.
Persistent cultivar—Pelo	159	189	239	201	217	212	174
Non-persistent cultivar—Hunsballe	88	108	127	84	65	69	59
High N—468 mg N/dm²	173	233	299	246	237	235	178
Low N—234 mg N/dm²	145	145	179	155	197	189	170
Simulated summer traffic	168	191	244	206	227	219	156
No simulated summer traffic	150	187	234	195	206	205	193

234 mg N/dm²/year, and two traffic treatments, 0 and 240 passages using a studded roller from March to October. The treatments were initiated in 1975 and were repeated in 1976.

Once or twice monthly the shoots in an area of 5 × 1 dm² (exactly the same squares every time) were counted in situ for each cultivar and treatment. The size of the area was chosen to obtain a better mean shoot density. Thus Table 1, which summarizes the main results, is based on 53,060 counted shoots. Since shoots were always counted just after mowing, any flowering stems were decapitated, and therefore all shoots present were considered vegetative. A subdivision into types of vegetative tillers was not possible.

Experiment 2

Experiment 2 included four contrasting cultivars of perennial ryegrass: Hunsballe, Cropper, Pelo, and Manhattan. Seeding was done in August 1975. The whole field was treated with a studded roller during 1976 as in Experiment 1. Fertilization was at 468 mg N/dm² annually. Shoots were counted regularly. The numbers shown in Table 2 were obtaned from counting the shoots in an area of 24 × 1 dm² per cultivar at the end of September 1976. Samples for shoot examination were taken from an area of 4 × 1 dm² per cultivar in October 1976.

Table 2. Shoot densities and shoot types of four divergent cultivars of perennial ryegrass in October 1976.

			Vegetative shoots			
					Partly elongated	
Cultivar	Usage and type	Mean no. of shoots/dm²	Un-elongated	At raised nodes of reproductive shoots	1x	≥ 2x
			% of total no. of shoots			
Hunsballe	Non-persistent hay	91	82	15	3	0
Cropper	Persistent hay	156	66	16	15	3
Pelo	Persistent pasture or turf	160	53	14	30	3
Manhattan	Persistent turf	174	41	17	33	9

RESULTS

Effects of Cultural Practices on Shoot Density—Experiment 1

The seasonal trends in shoot density of the two contrasting cultivars are given in Table 1, together with the effects of two cultural practices on the persistent cultivar. The shoot density counts provided a fairly good parameter for measuring turfgrass response to the three factors. These results show that the right cultivar must be chosen to achieve good shoot density. The good cultivar showed a high shoot density at the end of the season, whereas the density of the poor, non-turf cultivar gradually deteriorated. Nitrogen fertilization markedly increased the number of shoots.

Simulating traffic with a studded roller had only a slightly favorable effect on shoot density. Therefore, the conclusion that ryegrass stands summer traffic very well is confirmed. Moreover, Table 1 shows that perennial ryegrass has little or no physiological need of being rolled or trodden, if closely mown, good cultivars of this species "that do not per sist in meadows regularly cut for hay" (8), do persist without being trafficked. In a polystand, however, traffic stress will favor domination by traffic-tolerant because of the decreased competitiveness of non-tolerant plants.

Types of Vegetative Shoots—Experiment 2

The results of the two experiments enabled a classification of vegetative shoots of perennial ryegrass to be made. Most vegetative grass shoots have a stem consisting of a number of closely packed, very short internodes. Each fully grown node bears a leaf and at the top, a few millimeters above soil-level, the apical meristem is found. Axillary meristems develop successively on the nodes from which subsidiary tillers arise. This description also applies to the normal, unelongated perennial ryegrass shoots (Fig. 1). However, it was found that ryegrass also produces two types of vegetative shoots with extended internodes (Fig. 2, 3) concurrently. These stolon-like tillers have specific properties and play a distinct role with regard to persistency. Therefore, they must be distinguished from the normal ones.

Subsidiary Shoots on the Raised Nodes of Flowering Stems

While normal flowering culms only show some subsidiary tillers at their base, reproductive shoots sometimes have subsidiary shoots—as such mostly unelongated—at the first, second, third, fourth and, if present, sometimes even at the fifth raised node. In closely mowed turfs the upper part of the flowering stalk with the ear is soon lost, but the lower sub-

Fig. 1. Five normal, unelongated, vegetative shoots of perennial ryegrass around a former flowering stem. The squares in the grid in the background fill 1, 25, and 100 mm², respectively, according to the thickness of the lines.

Fig. 2. Raised subsidiary shoots at the successive nodes of a more-or-less vertical reproductive culm of perennial ryegrass. The lowest raised node already shows three rooted vegetative shoots. The squares in the grid in the background fill 1, 25, and 100 mm², respectively, according to the thickness of the lines.

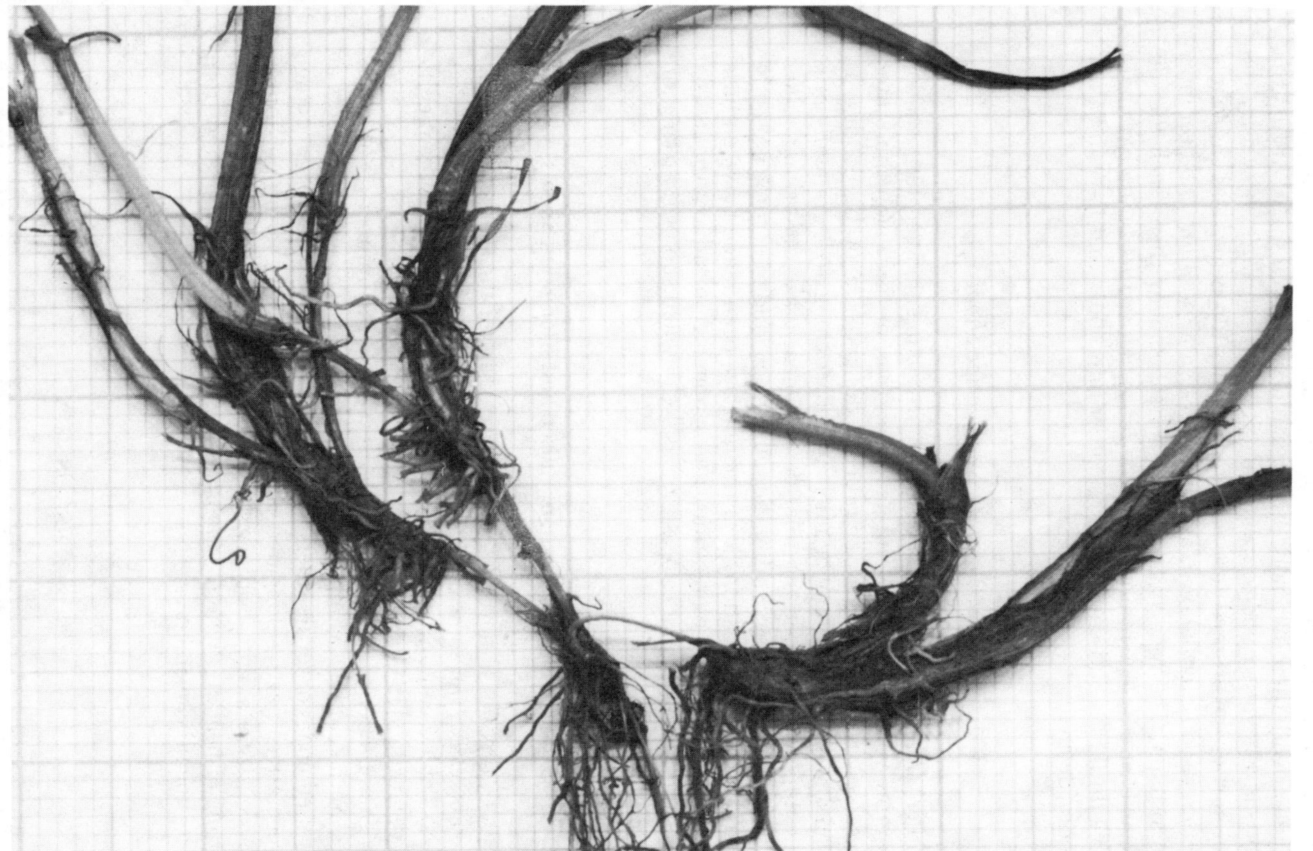

Fig. 3. Partly elongated vegetative shoots of perennial ryegrass; on the left elongated subsidiary shoots that arise from the upper nodes of elongated shoots. The squares in the grid in the background fill 1, 25, and 100 mm^2, respectively, according to the thickness of the lines.

sidiary tillers are either left or only develop soon after decapitation. Under favorable conditions these elevated tillers may grow into complete specimens with their own nodal roots, axillary meristems, etc. At first the shoots on the raised nodes are aerial tillers (6). In turfs, however, the basal part of the original fertile shoot becomes top-heavy and the whole shoot may soon over balance, assume a horizontal position, and become a pseudostolon. The roots of the subsidiary shoots may then reach the soil and penetrate it. The internodes of the reproductive shoot usually remain visible until fall. Subsequently those older internodes that have lost their function decay.

Partly Elongated Vegetative Shoots

Perennial ryegrass is able to form partly elongated vegetative shoots that grow vertically at first and have one, two, or three elongated internodes. New roots develop at the raised nodes under favorable conditions. Subsidiary tillers, that may be unelongated or elongated, gradually arise at the upper node. Root and tiller development make the primary shoot top-heavy, causing it to bend to the soil surface, and to become a pseudostolon. In this classification, a distinction has been made between basal elongated shoots (one elongation) and elongated subsidiary shoots that arise from the upper nodes of these basal elongated shoots (two or more elongations).

Occurrence and Origin of Raised and Elongated Shoots

Both types of abnormal shoots occurred in all the turf and non-turf cultivars tested, but some cultivars had many more abnormal shoots than others. Table 2 contains a survey of the shoot types of four divergent cultivars determined in October 1976.

The number of "abnormal" tillers exceeded the number of "normal" tillers in the cultivar Manhattan. The percentage of vegetative shoots at the raised nodes of fertile tillers was fairly constant, while the percentage of vegetative, partly elongated shoots varied greatly in proportion to shoot density. Raised subsidiary shoots were formed on fertile tillers from the time of heading, whereas elongated vegetative shoots appeared from about June till November.

DISCUSSION

Though the information obtained in these and other experiments is still incomplete, it seems that the incidence of "abnormal" tillers is not influenced by the cultural practices common on sports fields. However, this experiment confirmed that mowing affects the length of the elongated shoots. The higher and less frequent the mowing, the taller the elongated internodes. Therefore, treatments applied in modern grassland culture (delayed cutting, increased mowing height) clearly promote the incidence of elongated shoots. The mowing regime did not affect the number of elongated internodes per shoot.

Many tropical grasses, and also annual bluegrass (*Poa annua* L.), have raised subsidiary shoots on a flowering culm. Partly elongated vegetative shoots also occur in velvetgrass (*Holcus lanatus* L.) and fescue (*Festuca rubra* L. var. *trychophylla* Gaud.). The fully elongated vegetative tillers or culmed vegetative shoots (3) of roughstalk bluegrass (*Poa trivialis* L.), annual bluegrass and colonial bentgrass (*Agrostis tenuis* Sibth.) occupy an intermediate position. Usually, these partly or fully elongated shoots are neither plagiotropic from the outset nor extravaginal. Therefore, they should not be called stolons, nor should the raised and elongated shoots of perennial ryegrass.

Significance of Elongated and Raised Shoots

Normal vegetative shoots of perennial ryegrass may grow out horizontally 1 to 2 cm/year by the formation of approximately 10 internodes. Some cultivars have a strong branching tendency and their stems grow out in different directions (Fig. 4).

The displacement of the stem base by the gradual formation of several short internodes is small; but is, nevertheless, important in filling open areas. As soon as the elongated shoots have become prostrate, the plant can spread at a rate of 1 to 5 cm/year. This rate is more or less determined by the mowing regime. The more severe the cut, the shorter the internode elongation. Thus the smaller the risk of being decapitated but also the smaller the final stem base displacement. If the basal parts of the flowering culm escape the mowing action, a horizontal spread of more than 5 cm/year is possible by raised subsidiary tillers. The greatest elongations have been found in grassland situations.

The ability to fill bare patches is a useful property for a turfgrass species. On the other hand, both "abnormal" tiller types have at least one unfavorable property. As long as the shoots have not yet formed new roots and are still standing on their pedestals, their frost resistance is insufficient (1). Partly elongated shoots formed in the fall that are still upright at the beginning of the winter are particularly vulnerable. Shoots formed in turfs during the summer are usually already lodged and well rooted at the highest node of the upper elongated internode as winter begins. Since their apex is only a few millimeters above the roots they have the same chance as normal shoots for surviving the winter.

In closely mowed turfs the advantages of elongation for persistency may compensate for the disadvantages. However, there seems to be no point in developing cultivars with even more internode elongation, since

Fig. 4. Development of three branched, unelongated vegetative stems in a 14-month-old perennial ryegrass plant. The plant base displacement is due to the formation of many short internodes and not to the elongation of a few of them. The squares in the grid in the background fill 1, 25, and 100 mm^2, respectively, according to the thickness of the lines.

present-day cultivars produce so many elongated shoots that they can fill up bare patches quite successfully.

Finally, the elongated or raised perennial ryegrass shoots may pose a problem in the long run in pastures (4). The internodes are stronger, stiff stubbles from flowering stems prevent the shoots from assuming a horizontal position, the rooting of the upper nodes is delayed, and normal basal tillering is smothered so that the value of aerial shoots in grassland may be quite different from that of these tillers in turfs. Persistency is harmed by shoot elongation in grasslands, whereas in turfs persistency may be fostered if some of the shoots display elongation.

One wonders why so few agrostologists are acquainted with the shoots of such a very important and well studied species as perennial ryegrass. The answer may be that these shoots cannot be observed from above nor from broken individual specimens. It is absolutely necessary to dig out complete shoots with their roots, wash them, and examine them under a binocular microscope with 10 × magnification. Seasonal investigation into the state of the stem apex is indispensable.

ACKNOWLEDGMENT

This paper is based on the results of experiments subsidized by the Commissie van Bijstand inzake Stikstofonderzoek T.N.O.

LITERATURE CITED

1. Baker, H. K. 1967. Note on the influence of previous management on the death of perennial ryegrass during winter. J. Br. Grassl. Soc. 11:235–237.
2. Beard, J. B. 1973. Turfgrass: Science and culture. Prentice-Hall, Inc., Englewood Cliffs, N.J.
3. Hyder, D. M. 1972. Defoliation in relation to vegetative growth. p. 304–317. *In* V. B. Youngner and C. M. McKell (eds.) The biology and utilization of grasses. Academic Press, New York.
4. Jackson, D. K. 1974. Some aspects of production and persistency in relation to height of defoliation of *Lolium perenne* (var. S.23). Int. Grassl. Congr. Proc. 12 (Moscow, USSR) 3(1):202–214.
5. Schery, R. W. 1976. Lawn keeping. Prentice-Hall, Inc., Englewood Cliffs, N.J.
6. Simons, R. G., A. Davies, and A. Troughton. 1974. The effect of cutting height and mulching on aerial tillering in two contrasting genotypes of perennial ryegrass. J. Agric. Sci. Camb. 83:267–273.
7. Walter, H. 1960. Einführung in die Phytologie. Band 3. Grundlagen der Pflanzenverbreitung. Eugen Ulmer, Stuttgart, Germany.
8. Whyte, R. O., T. R.G. Moir, and J. P. Cooper. 1962. Grasses in agriculture. 2nd Ed. FAO Agric. Stud. 42. Roma.

Chapter 13

Variations in the Growth and Development of Annual Bluegrass Populations Selected from Seven Different Sports Turf Areas[1]

W. A. ADAMS
P. J. BRYAN

ABSTRACT

Populations of annual bluegrass (*Poa annua* L.), selected from seven turfgrass sites, and 'Highland' colonial bentgrass (*Agrostis tenuis* Sibth.) were compared under three levels of N and at three heights of cut in a glasshouse experiment. The parameters of growth and development examined were: yield of clippings, tiller production, leaf width, seedhead production, root length, and root weight. All selections showed general variations in performance attributable to N level and cutting height. The differential performance among selections varied with treatment.

The annual bluegrass populations ranged between an erect, prolific seeding type and prostrate, high tillering, nodal rooting types which produced few seedheads. The semi-perennial/perennial types varied in vigor and leaf fineness. The differences among the selections were loosely related to the culture and use of the sports turf from which they were isolated, reflecting selection within a range of genotypes. It is suggested that annual bluegrass types possessing characteristics desirable for sports turfs are present in long established turf and selections from such sites could be made for use in a breeding program.

INTRODUCTION

Annual bluegrass (*Poa annua* L.) occurs throughout the world as a variable species adapted to a wide range of habitats. The species is commonly found as a component of sports turfs; however, its occurrence in this situation is rarely encouraged because the majority of turfgrass managers regard it as a weed. The reasons advanced for this opinion are its characteristic light color, profuse flowering habit, and susceptibility to heat, drought, disease, and low temperatures (2, 5, 7). In areas of high summer temperatures where annual bluegrass behaves as a true annual

[1] A contribution from the Soil Science Unit, Dep. of Biochemistry and Agricultural Biochemistry, Univ. College of Wales, Aberystwyth, United Kingdom.

 Proceedings of the Third International Turfgrass Research Conference.

these criticisms may be valid. However, semi-perennial prostrate types have been recorded (2, 4, 9, 10, 11) which are favored by moist soil conditions, a cool temperate climate, high soil nutrient levels, and frequent, close mowing. Under these conditions annual bluegrass exhibits vegetative propagation through nodal rooting and produces a dense, fine-textured turf. There is also both field and experimental evidence that these types are tolerant of wear (3, 8).

It might be expected that variations in sports turf maintenance would, over a period, bring about the selection of annual bluegrass types suited to particular environmental conditions. The natural variability in the species lends itself to this selection. An investigation was conducted to examine the differences in annual bluegrass behavior selected from various sports turf sites when subjected to a range of nutrient level and cutting height regimes.

MATERIALS AND METHODS

Populations of annual bluegrass were collected at seven localities in the northwest and west of Great Britain (Table 1). The plants were then grown under identical conditions in the glasshouse. After 3 months a single plant representative of each population was selected. Single tillers of the same morphological appearance were detached from the parent plant and used for the experiment. The tillers were planted in 7.5-cm diam plastic pots filled with acid-washed (5 *M* HCl) silica sand and placed in a glasshouse. The experimental period was May through July, no supplementary light was used, and the temperatures were within the range 15 to 25 C. Nutrient solution was applied every 3rd day and had the composition given in Table 2. Three nutrient regimes varying only in N level were used.

Clipping was carried out once per week and begun 1 month after the tillers were transplanted. Clipping heights were 1 cm (LC), 2 cm (MC), and 4 cm (HC). Clippings were collected, dried, weighed, and a running total kept of the yield. The nine clipping height/N treatments were replicated three times. The pots were re-randomized on the glasshouse bench at frequent intervals. In addition to the annual bluegrass selections, Highland colonial bentgrass was included in the experiment. The grass was harvested 2 months after clipping commenced.

Table 1. Origin of annual bluegrass populations.

Sample no.	Location
1	Manchester United F.C. Old Trafford Pitch
2	Blackpool F.C. Pitch
3	Lancashire County Cricket Club, Old Trafford Outfield
4	Royal Lytham St. Anne's Golf Club, 12th Green
5	Jubilee Park, Warrington, Bowling Green
6	Aberystwyth Golf Club, 18th Green
7	U.C.W. Aberystwyth Vicarage Fields Football Pitch

Table 2. Composition of nutrient solutions.

Element	Level†
	mM
N	1, 4, 10
K	2.0
Ca	1.5
P	1.0
S	1.0
Mg	1.0
Fe	0.1
B	0.03
Mn	0.01
Cu	0.001
Zn	0.001
Mo	0.0002

† High N = 10 mM; medium N = 4 mM; low N = 1 mM.

RESULTS AND DISCUSSION

In the following discussion the annual bluegrass selections will be differentiated by type number based on the number allocated to selection site in Table 1. Type 1, which was selected from Manchester United F.C., was infected by *Fusarium nivale* and failed to survive.

Yield of Clippings

The overall mean yield of Type 7 was significantly greater than that of Types 5 and 6 (Table 3). There were no significant differences among the overall mean yields of Types 2, 3, 4, 5, and 6 and colonial bentgrass. The potential growth response or vigor is probably best illustrated by the treatment means at the highest N level and the highest height of cut. Type 7 gave a significantly higher yield with this treatment than all others except Type 2. Types 2, 3, and 7 gave significantly higher yields than Types 4, 5, and 6 and colonial bentgrass. Thus the types selected from less closely mowed turf, that is soccer pitches and a cricket outfield, showed themselves to be potentially more vigorous in terms of vertical shoot

Table 3. Yield (g) of accumulated clippings of Highland colonial bentgrass and six annual bluegrass selections.

Sample no.	High N			Medium N			Low N			Type mean
	HC	MC	LC	HC	MC	LC	HC	MC	LC	
2	1.085	0.407	0.142	0.187	0.261	0.192	0.043	0.101	0.116	0.281
3	0.968	0.411	0.148	0.139	0.209	0.113	0.028	0.092	0.116	0.247
4	0.808	0.505	0.218	0.090	0.171	0.202	0.011	0.097	0.117	0.246
5	0.750	0.410	0.203	0.065	0.160	0.130	0.014	0.083	0.095	0.212
6	0.632	0.415	0.179	0.148	0.186	0.181	0.039	0.103	0.129	0.218
7	1.389	0.539	0.197	0.195	0.231	0.150	0.034	0.088	0.102	0.325
Colonial bentgrass	0.808	0.416	0.247	0.123	0.207	0.144	0.035	0.098	0.104	0.240

L.S.D.$_{(P=0.05)}$ for type means = 0.100 g
L.S.D.$_{(p=0.05)}$ for treatments = 0.140 g

growth rate than those from closely mowed golf and bowling greens. The general trend in shoot yield with treatment follows that described by Adams et al. (1), but there are small differences in detail. In particular, Type 4 shows less sensitivity to close mowing than the other types.

Tiller Production

Type 7 gave a significantly higher general mean for tiller number than all other types and colonial bentgrass (Table 4). Type 2 consistently produced a low number of tillers. There was no significant difference between the general means for Types 3, 4, 5, and 6 and colonial bentgrass. The treatment means indicate a particularly high production of tillers by Types 4 and 7 at the intermediate N level and 2-cm cutting height.

Leaf Width

The vigorous Type 7 had a significantly higher general mean for leaf width than any other selection (Table 5). Type 4 from a golf green is a fine-leafed type having a significantly lower general mean than all annual bluegrass types, except Type 3 and colonial bentgrass. The data indicate

Table 4. Number of tillers of Highland colonial bentgrass and six annual bluegrass selections.

Sample no.	High N			Medium N			Low N			Type mean
	HC	MC	LC	HC	MC	LC	HC	MC	LC	
2	115	52	35	58	47	42	26	28	22	47
3	258	76	45	84	64	37	33	43	33	75
4	171	108	41	106	131	46	31	50	49	81
5	129	73	39	75	81	52	35	52	50	65
6	150	142	99	91	90	61	40	40	37	83
7	207	156	134	179	180	141	16	23	17	117
Colonial bentgrass	105	89	67	61	58	51	42	40	36	61

L.S.D.$_{(P=0.05)}$ for type means = 30
L.S.D.$_{(P=0.05)}$ for treatments = 24

Table 5. Width in mm of leaves of Highland colonial bentgrass and six annual bluegrass selections.

Sample no.	High N			Medium N			Low N			Type mean
	HC	MC	LC	HC	MC	LC	HC	MC	LC	
2	2.8	2.1	2.0	2.3	1.8	1.8	2.5	2.1	1.7	2.1
3	2.1	2.0	1.0	2.2	2.0	1.6	2.4	2.0	1.2	1.8
4	2.5	1.6	1.2	2.2	1.4	1.4	2.1	1.6	1.3	1.6
5	2.6	2.1	1.7	2.0	1.9	1.7	2.4	1.7	1.0	1.9
6	2.5	2.2	1.7	2.5	2.0	1.7	2.2	1.7	1.6	2.0
7	3.0	3.0	3.0	2.7	2.2	2.0	3.0	3.0	1.9	2.5
Colonial bentgrass	2.2	2.0	1.2	2.2	1.8	1.1	2.1	1.2	1.1	1.6

L.S.D.$_{(P=0.05)}$ for type means = 0.3 mm
L.S.D.$_{(P=0.05)}$ for treatments = 0.4 mm

Table 6. Number of seedheads produced by six annual bluegrass selections.

Sample no.	High N			Medium N			Low N			Type mean
	HC	MC	LC	HC	MC	LC	HC	MC	LC	
2	27	2	11	55	0	26	6	3	2	15
3	10	0	0	5	12	0	16	11	0	12
4	20	0	0	62	60	2	10	12	0	18
5	26	49	18	71	44	61	80	120	74	60
6	0	0	0	5	0	0	0	0	0	0.6
7	8	0	0	18	4	0	7	9	1	5

L.S.D.$_{(P=0.05)}$ for type means = 20

that, for a given type, cutting height is much more significant in influencing leaf width than N level.

Seedhead Number

The number of seedheads produced varied within types (Table 6). The data clearly indicate that Type 5 is quite different from the other annual bluegrass selections among which there was no significant difference. Type 5 was selected from a poorly maintained municipal bowling green and the profuse seeding habit particularly under the low N treatments may well reflect a survival characteristic.

Length of Longest Root and Total Root Weight

The general mean for maximum root length of colonial bentgrass was significantly greater than for all annual bluegrass types except Type 5 (Table 7). The general mean for Type 5 was significantly greater than Types 4 and 6. Types 2, 3, and 7 from less closely mown situations behaved similarly in terms of general mean maximum root length and response to treatment; however, some types showed a clear differential influence of treatment on root length. Type 6 produced particularly short roots under the high N treatments and colonial bentgrass gave a signifi-

Table 7. Length of longest root in mm of Highland colonial bentgrass and six annual bluegrass selections.

Sample no.	High N			Medium N			Low N			Type mean
	HC	MC	LC	HC	MC	LC	HC	MC	LC	
2	205	150	158	153	165	158	207	188	185	174
3	166	167	162	182	185	163	188	182	186	176
4	171	174	141	161	172	151	158	182	175	165
5	208	168	180	173	181	181	197	212	205	189
6	150	142	99	179	180	141	180	155	173	155
7	207	151	134	179	180	141	186	190	186	173
Colonial bentgrass	219	211	210	234	210	205	206	192	143	203

L.S.D.$_{(P=0.05)}$ for type means = 24 mm
L.S.D.$_{(P=0.05)}$ for treatments = 23 mm

Table 8. Yield in g dry weight of root growth of Highland colonial bentgrass and six annual bluegrass selections.

Sample no.	High N			Medium N			Low N			Type mean
	HC	MC	LC	HC	MC	LC	HC	MC	LC	
2	0.248	0.069	0.037	0.373	0.137	0.065	0.362	0.198	0.067	0.172
3	0.305	0.096	0.024	0.498	0.162	0.036	0.261	0.190	0.044	0.179
4	0.223	0.093	0.029	0.450	0.230	0.041	0.272	0.132	0.066	0.171
5	0.175	0.092	0.021	0.363	0.208	0.067	0.337	0.174	0.082	0.168
6	0.215	0.095	0.040	0.518	0.263	0.077	0.381	0.171	0.106	0.207
7	0.358	0.099	0.037	0.479	0.234	0.053	0.220	0.148	0.057	0.187
Colonial bentgrass	0.389	0.114	0.043	0.546	0.166	0.052	0.344	0.134	0.051	0.204

$L.S.D._{(P=0.05)}$ for type means = 0.051 g
$L.S.D._{(P=0.05)}$ for treatments = 0.073 g

cantly lower maximum root length under the low N and closest cut than all annual bluegrass types despite its high general mean. Maximum root length was not reflected in total root weights. Indeed, there were no significant differences among the general means (Table 8). However, root weight was greatly influenced by treatment and the different types showed clear differences in response. For example whereas the vigorous Type 7 had a significantly greater root weight than Types 2, 4, 5, and 6 under the high N and 4-cm cut regime, its root weight under the low N regime and at the same height of cut was significantly less than Types 2, 5, and 6.

Of the annual bluegrass types examined 4, 5, and 7 displayed the most widely differing characteristics. Type 5 showed a profuse seeding habit and resembles most closely the annual bluegrass found frequently in agricultural grassland. Type 7, a very vigorous perennial/semi-perennial type, displayed considerable tillering potential and growth response to N. It is very well suited to the soccer pitch requirement from which it was selected. It is very different from the annual bluegrass selection made at Aberystwyth and examined by Ellis et al. (6). Type 4, selected from a green of long standing on the Royal Lytham and St. Anne's golf course is also a perennial type, but with narrow leaves and moderate to low vigor. It also showed a high potential for tiller production. Types 2, 3, and 6 fell within the performance range defined by Types 4, 5, and 7.

The purpose of this work was only to examine some of the variability in annual bluegrass to be found in United Kingdom sports turfs. However, it is of interest that Types 4, 5, and 7 seem to fit fairly well into the subspecies differentiation suggested by Timm (9) as follows:

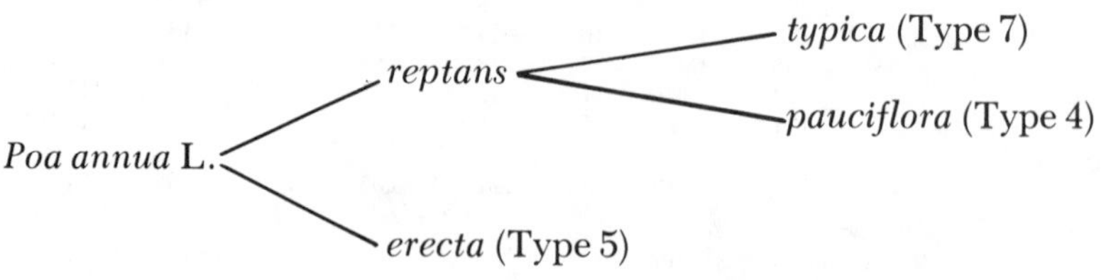

Two further points of particular relevance are illustrated by this work. First is the association between the behavior and characteristics of the annual bluegrass selections and the culture/survival factors of the turf from the different sports turf situations. This indicates both the genetic variability of annual bluegrass in sports turf and the selection within this variability imposed by turfgrass culture and usage. The second point is also relevant to other turfgrass species: it is clear from the data obtained that the parameters of shoot growth and development examined were substantially influenced by treatment, both N supply and cutting height. Not only this but the effects varied among types. It is to be expected that at least some of the parameters measured are involved in turfgrass survival and persistence. Thus, it can be concluded that the performance in terms of success in sports turf of any given ecotype, not merely species, will vary with fertility level and cutting height. This is important to recognize in cultivar assessment.

The annual bluegrass selections made were limited in number and cannot be expected to reflect the complete range in genotypic variation in British sports turfs. Nevertheless they show the presence of widely differing shoot growth and developmental characteristics which could be exploited by the plant breeder. Annual bluegrass is a dominant turfgrass in Britain and deserves much closer scrutiny than it has yet received.

ACKNOWLEDGMENT

P. J. Bryan is grateful for a grant provided by the British Sports Council.

LITERATURE CITED

1. Adams, W. A., P. J. Bryan, and G. E. Walker. 1973. Effects of cutting height and nitrogen nutrition on the growth pattern of turfgrasses. p. 131–144. *In* Eliot C. Roberts (ed.) Proc. 2nd Int. Turfgrass Res. Conf., Blacksburg, Va. June 1973. Am. Soc. Agron., Madison, Wis.
2. Beard, J. B. 1970. The plant characteristics, dissemination, environmental adaptation, and cultural requirements of *Poa annua* L. Razen Turf Gazon. 2:33–35.
3. Bryan, P. J., and W. A. Adams. 1971. Observations on grass species persisting on English League soccer pitches in spring 1970. Razen Turf Gazon. 2:571–577.
4. Cooper, J. P. 1957. Development analysis of populations in the cereals and herbage grasses. 2. Response to low temperature variation. J. Agric. Sci. 49:361–383.
5. Daniel, W. H. 1966. I'm tired of *Poa annua*. Golf Course Rep. 34:16–18.
6. Ellis, W. M., B. T. O. Lee, and D. M. Calder. 1971. A biometric analysis of populations of *Poa annua* L. Evolution 25:29–37.
7. Gibeault, V. A. 1966. Investigations on the control of annual meadow grass. J. Sports Turf Res. Inst. 42:17–41.
8. Shildrick, J. P. 1975. Turfgrass mixtures under wear treatments. J. Sports Turf Res. Inst. 51:9–40.
9. Timm, G. 1965. Beitrage zur Biologie und syztematik von *Poa annua* L. Z. Acker Pflanzenbau 122:267–294.
10. Tutin, T. G. 1957. A contribution to the experimental taxonomy of *Poa annua* Watsonia 4:1–10.
11. Youngrer, V. B. 1959. Ecological studies on *Poa annua* in turf grass. J. Br. Grassl. Soc. 14:233–237.

Chapter 14

Comparisons of Direct and Indirect Determinations of Root Weights of Several Turfgrasses[1]

W. OPITZ VON BOBERFELD

ABSTRACT

Extensive research is being undertaken at the Institute of Plant Cultivation of Bonn University on cultivating root mass of different cultivars of monocotyledon and dicotyledon species in various nutrition substances with regard to the selection of suitable methods for the simplification of root weight determinations for series investigations. As greater differences occurred among the investigated root masses, a homogenization of the variances is necessary to give a statistical interpretation. The log-transformation was considered suitable for eliminating such problems. Among plant material with a homorhized root system and a relatively short growth period, no relationship existed between ashed and non-ashed root mass or it is weak. Between the various sand-free and ash-free root masses and the corresponding C-content or ignition loss in the individual soil strata, no significant positive correlations occurred.

The relatively expensive root mass determinations, involving wide dispersons, cannot be simplified by foregoing either ashing the root mass or ascertaining the soil organic matter content without considerable loss of information.

Additional index words: Festuca pratensis, Lolium perenne, F. rubra, Soil organic matter content, Cultivars.

INTRODUCTION

Methods for measuring grass root mass may be grouped as visual (5, 10, 11), gravimetric (6, 8), radiometric (4, 12), and others (3, 5, 9). For continuing investigations under conditions of outdoor grass cultures, use of the gravimetric method appears to be favored.

The Institute for Plant Cultivation at Bonn Universiy has conducted a considerable amount of research on this subject. Plant material with varying types of root systems are tested in a number of different nutrient regimes. This paper compares the direct and indirect determinations of root weight for series investigations of Gramineae.

[1] A contribution from Institut für Pflanzenbau, Katzenburgweg 5, 1]-5300 Bonn, Federal Republic of Germany.

MATERIALS AND METHODS

In order to assess potential variations within the Gramineae for a methodical investigation, 'Bergamo' and 'Cosmos' meadow fescue (*Festuca pratensis* L.) have been chosen as tall growing grasses (1), perennial ryegrass (*Lolium perenne* L.) cultivars 'Dolewi' and 'NFG,' as the medium range species (1), and as the low growing species red fescue (*Festuca rubra* L.) cultivars 'Oase' and 'Rasengold' were selected (2). In order to avoid increasing genetic variants, all experiments were conducted with seed from a single seed lot.

The experiments were conducted on a grey-brown Podzolic loam soil located at high flood level on the low terrace of the Rhein, 60 m above sea level. The area, fallowed for 1 year, was treated with methyl bromide to prevent weed growth. One thousand seeds/m^2 were sown by broadcasting, resulting in 400 plants/m^2. The cultivars were laid out in the design of a latin square with three blocks. Either two or four soil profiles were taken from each individual plot. The root mass was extracted by a sampling tube of 6-cm^2 diam and a working depth of 30.0 cm. Each sample included two shoots. Samples for organic matter content of soil were taken in the immediate vicinity of those for root mass.

The root material was separated by hand in warm water without additives or technical instruments. In order to ascertain the subjective influence of the person performing the root washing on the results, the entire material from a block was handled by a single person. Wet-burning (7) was employed to determine the organic content. Loss from ignition was determined by dry-burning at 500 C with the addition of a 2% solution of NH_4NO_3.

RESULTS AND DISCUSSION

Ash-Free Root Mass Comparisons Among Species, Cultivars, and Growth Time

An increase in average clearly entails an increase in variance. The homogenization of the variances necessary for variance analytical evaluation was achieved by a logarithmic transformation and separate evaluation of the individual sampling periods. Calculations were made at the Computer Center of Bonn University on an IBM 370/168. With an increase in growth time, the significant differences in root mass also increased (Table 1). On the basis of the cultivars used in this study, there were no significant cultivar differences within any species. But an assessment of the variations in root mass found between the species disclosed significant cultivar specific differences.

Table 1. Logarithmic ashed and non-ashed root dry matter determinations for selected turfgrasses.

	Root weights						
	1975 weekly ratings				1976 weekly ratings		
Species and cultivar	3	6	9	12	6	12	$\bar{x}_{Cultivar}$
	mg/1,000 cm²						
Lolium perenne NFG	3.654†	11.223†	22.228†	28.114†	5.123†	28,984†	
	3.464‡	3.949‡	4.317‡	4.442‡	3.658‡	4.451‡	4.047‡
Lolium perenne Dolewi	4.550†	12.546†	11.288†	24.427†	6.624†	28.100†	
	3.504‡	3.982‡	4.052‡	4.383‡	3.736‡	4.437‡	4.016‡
Festuca pratensis Cosmos	3.644†	13.553†	17.456†	21.460†	4.331†	25.955†	
	3.367‡	4.103‡	4.198‡	4.323‡	3.604‡	4.413‡	4.001‡
Festuca pratensis Bergamo	5.687†	9.394†	18.861†	23.792†	5.630†	28.641†	
	3.551‡	3.857‡	4.263‡	4.355‡	3.746‡	4.444‡	4.036‡
Festuca rubra Oase	4.796†	7.498†	13.583†	14.116†	4.434†	17.834†	
	3.450‡	3.687‡	4.120‡	4.129‡	3.631‡	4.234‡	3.875‡
Festuca rubra Rasengold	5.746†	5.595†	13.974†	15.325†	3.465†	17.778†	
	3.390‡	3.536‡	4.138‡	4.147‡	3.456‡	4.231‡	3.816‡
$\bar{x}_{Time}$	3.454‡	3.853‡	4.181‡	4.297‡	3.639‡	4.368‡	3.965‡
L.S.D. 5% Cultivar	0.4860	0.4044	0.2881	0.2120	0.2758	0.1279	--

† Not ashed. ‡ Ashed.

Table 2. Simple correlation coefficients of the relation between cleaned and uncleaned roots in 1976.

Soil layer	Weeks after seeding	Correlation coefficients
cm		
0–30	6	−0.115
0–30	12	0.885†
0– 5	6	−0.054
0– 5	12	0.909†
25–30	6	0.508*
25–30	12	0.904†

*,† Significant at the 0.05 and 0.001 levels, respectively.

Comparison of Ashed vs. Non-ashed Root Mass Measurement Techniques

When conducting cultivar tests on one location and evaluated by few persons, the question arises whether it is necessary to record non-root components and make allowance for them. For this reason correlation analyses were made with data from the 1976 growth period (Table 2). For plant material with a homorhized root system and a relatively short growth period, there is no or little observable correlation between ashed and non-ashed root mass sampled from a loam soil.

Soil Organic Matter Content Assessment

Since the overwhelming majority of soil microorganisms are C heterotrophic, the soil organic matter formed from root and harvest residues, apart from external sources. The question arises, whether it is possible to ascertain the root mass formed, after a relatively short growth period, from the C content of the upper soil strata.

A correlation analysis was made to determine whether there is a relationship between the sand-free and ash-free root mass on the one hand and the C content of the soil or the ignition loss on the other hand. For this purpose perennial ryegrass and red fescue were considered because their root mass was found to differ throughout the observation period. The analyses were made separately for three strata: 0 to 10, 10 to 20, and 20 to 30 cm.

Results of the correlation analyses show that there is no significant positive relation between the root mass and the C content or ignition loss at any time during the observation period or for any soil stratum. The relatively high C content of the soil and the relatively low C content in the root mass in this one short-term cultivation appears problematic in this context.

ACKNOWLEDGEMENT

The TESTA Company of Hamburg, West Germany, is thanked for its cooperation in the treatment of the experimental area.

LITERATURE CITED

1. Bundessortenamt. 1975a. Beschreibende sortenliste 1975, graser und landwirtschaftliche leguminosen. Verlag Alfred Strothe, Hannover.
2. ————. 1975b. Beschreibende sortenliste 1975, rasengraser. Verlag Alfred Strothe, Hannover.
3. Doss, B. D., D. A. Ashley, and O. L. Bennett. 1960. Effect of soil moisture regime of root distribution of warm season forage species. Agron. J. 52:569–572.
4. Johnen, B. G. 1974. Bildung, menge und umsetzung von pflanzenwurzeln im boden. Ph.D. Diss. Inst. of Agric. Chem. Bonn. Univ. Zentralbiliothek der Landbauwissenschaft, Meckenheimer Allee 172, D-5300 Bonn 1 (Diss. Popp 1635).
5. King, J. W., and J. B. Beard. 1969. Measuring rooting of sodded turfs. Agron. J. 61: 497–498.
6. Kohnlein, J., and H. Vetter. 1953. Ernteruckstande und wurzelbild. Verlag Paul Parey, Hamburg und Berlin.
7. Rauterberg, E., and F. Kremkus. 1951. Bestimmung von gesamthumus und alkalischen humusstoffen. Z. Pflanzenernahr. Dueng. Bodenkd. 54:240–249.
8. Rogers, W. S., and G. A. Booth. 1960. The roots of fruit trees. Sci. Hort. 14:27–34.
9. Sauerlandt, W., and C. Tietjen. 1970. Humuswirtschaft des ackerbaues. Verlag DLG, Frankfurt/Main.
10. Taylor, H. M. 1969. New laboratory gets to the roots. Crops Soils 22(3):20.
11. Thiel, H. 1892. Anleitung zu wurzelstudien. Mitt. DLG. 7:75–76.
12. Troughton, A. 1960. Uptake of phosphorus-32 by the roots of *Lolium perenne*. Nature (London) 188:593.

Section III:

Environment of Turfgrass

Chapter 15 Root Growth and Phosphorus Responses Among Clones of Creeping Bentgrass at Low Temperatures[1]

WILLIAM R. KNEEBONE
GORDON V. JOHNSON

ABSTRACT

Some creeping bentgrasses (*Agrostis palustris* Huds.) often turn reddish-purple and grow slowly while others maintain good color and some growth when night temperatures range from 0 to 5 C. Increasing available P tends to keep the bentgrass turf greener. These studies were initiated to determine if bentgrass genotypes differed in P needs or uptake at low temperatures.

Twenty-seven clones selected from 'Seaside' plus 'Penncross', Seaside, and 'Eldorado' creeping bentgrasses grown in field plots in Tucson, Ariz., USA, were fertilied differentially with P. Foliage color and root length were evaluated periodically from 1973 to 1976.

Selected genotypes grown in cool environmental growth chambers were also differentially fertilized with P. Color and shoot growth were rated and the foliage was analyzed for P. Additional experiments were conducted with selected genotypes under constant root temperatures. Phosphorus uptake was measured with ^{32}P.

Color differences among creeping bentgrass clones at low temperatures were related to P nutrition. There were significant differences among clones in ^{32}P uptake at 5, 15, and 25 C. More ^{32}P was recovered in roots than in shoots, especially at 5 C. Color response differences among clones were not related to ^{32}P uptake rate differences, nor were uptake rate differences associated with significant clonal root length differences. Results indicate that clones subject to P deficiency symptoms at low temperatures have higher P requirement thresholds at those temperatures than clones which remain green.

Additional index words: Genotypic variation, Low temperature color retention, ^{32}P uptake.

INTRODUCTION

Creeping bentgrass (*Agrostis palustris* Huds.) is highly variable and many vegetatively propagated selections have been made for use on golf greens. Irrigated bentgrass greens grow all year at Tucson, Ariz., USA, with two periods of slow growth. One of these is in midsummer with temperatures from 20 to 40 C. The other is in December and January when night temperatures typically range from 0 to 5 C and day temperatures from 15 to 20 C.

During the winter of 1973–74 certain creeping bentgrass selections in

[1]Journal Paper No. 255, Arizona Agric. Exp. Stn., Tucson, Ariz., USA.

 Proceedings of the Third International Turfgrass Research Conference.

field plots at Tucson turned reddish purple and grew slowly while others maintained good color and some growth. Many clones in old 'Seaside' greens differentiate this way in winter. Laboratory studies showed that the red color was temperature dependent. Red color is also a symptom of P deficiency. Preliminary studies indicated that increasing available P would keep bentgrass greener. In addition, genotypes could also differ in P needs or P uptake rates at low temperatures. Studies were initiated in 1974–75 to determine mechanisms involved in the widely varying cool temperature color responses of certain clones.

Intra-specific differences in P and other nutrient element concentrations occur in many species (7). Perhaps the most extensive data on such differences with a grass are those obtained at Pennsylvania State University with maize (*Zea mays* L.) (6). These data are from a plant breeding approach; i.e., screening available genotypes to see if exploitable differences exist. Another approach is ecological; concerned with differences in plant P content related to adaptation in soil sites varying in P availability. Ecotypes taken from such sites have been examined for P content and rates of P uptake. Goodman (5), for example, found that three populations of perennial ryegrass (*Lolium perenne* L.) differed significantly in uptake of ^{32}P under equivalent temperatures and P availability.

Differences among plants in rates of P uptake are obviously most important when P availabilities are low. Low available P can reflect either low total P and/or reduced availability per se. At low pH values, Al reduces P availability. Clark and Brown (3) demonstrated that maize inbreds selected for differential P accumulation differed in their ability to extract P under Al stress.

More important to this study than chemical restrictions are the effects of temperature on P availability. Desorption P isotherms at 5 and 20 C were derived by Gardner and Jones (4) for two Idaho soils. They found much lower equilibrium solution concentrations when P was desorbed at the low temperature. They stated that ". . .the effect of temperature on P level in solution at equilibrium accounts for at least part of the reduced P uptake under lower temperature conditions." Such temperature effects could change adequate levels of available soil P to submarginal levels. The effect of low availability is compounded because lower temperatures also affect the ability of roots to absorb P. Carter and Lathwell (2) used excised maize roots to measure P uptake at 20, 30, and 40 C over a range of P concentrations. Uptake was directly proportional to temperature at all P concentrations.

An example of the ecological approach with a striking demonstration of temperature differentials is a study on ^{32}P uptake by roots of cattail (*Typha latifolia* L.) ecotypes derived from low and high altitudes, respectively, by McNaughton et al. (9). At root temperatures of 3 and 25 C, the relative uptakes (10^3 cpm ^{32}P/5 mg root) were 1.57 and 16.95 for the low altitude and 2.15 and 8.48 for the high altitude ecotypes. These differences illustrate natural selection for root uptake efficiency related to temperatures.

Table 1. Identifications and origins of creeping bentgrass clones or cultivars studied.

Clone or cultivar	Identification or origin
A25	Old Seaside green No. 12, Apache Wells Country Club, Mesa, Ariz.
A53	Evansville from W. Daniel, Purdue University
A54	Old Seaside green No. 15, Apache Wells Country Club, Mesa, Ariz.
A58	Arrowood from R. Keen, Kansas State University
A61	Old Seaside green No. 9, Eldorado Country Club, Palm Springs, Calif.
A66	Washington from Warren's Turf Nursery Inc., Palos Hills, Ill.
Penncross	certified seed from Oregon

MATERIALS AND METHODS

Field studies

Data to be reported were obtained in conjunction with field experiments evaluating creeping bentgrass selections for growth capacity under heat stresses. Selections came from other investigators or were made from old Seaside golf greens in Phoenix, Tucson, and Yuma, Ariz. and at Palm Springs, Calif., during July and August 1971 and 1972. In 1973, the most promising 27 clones plus 'Penncross', Seaside, and 'Eldorado' as checks were established in three randomized complete blocks of 1.2- × 1.4-m plots in a putting green test at Tucson. The selections were sprigged in a sand medium. Screened and washed "mortar sand" (80% of the particles in the range 0.1 to 1.0 mm) was laid 20 cm deep over 8 cm of pea gravel (particles averaging 10 to 15 mm in diam). Mowing height varied from 6 to 10 mm over the duration of the study. Fertilization was at the rate of 1.25 g N/m^2/week as ammonium sulfate during the cool season with no fertilizer applied during June, July, and August. Differential P rates were established in 1974 with 0–46–0 granules applied in early November to opposite plot ends at 0 and 1 g P/m^2. In October 1975 corresponding rates were 1 and 2 g P/m^2 with plot centers unfertilized.

Root lengths were measured in mm from ground surface to the estimated median point as observed on 5-cm diam cores scratched to reveal the root mass. Color was rated on a 1 to 9 scale; 1 indicating dark reddish purple and 9 completely green. Bentgrasses studied in the field and/or the laboratory are identified in Table 1.

Laboratory Studies

A preliminary study (Experiment 1) of temperature and genotype effect on P response was made in a growth chamber with 5-cm plugs of A53, A54, A58, and A61 taken from field plots and transplanted onto pots containing sand. The growth chamber was maintained at a day maximum of 15 C and a night minimum of 5 C with 12-hour day-night intervals. Light intensity was 32 kilolux. Turfs were fertilized at 0, 0.25, 0.50, 1, and 2 g P/m^2. Nitrogen was supplied at 5 g/m^2 to each pot. Prior to placement in the growth chamber and P fertilization, all turfs were clipped back to the rim of the pot (approximately 15 mm). After 4 weeks, the color and degree of shoot growth were rated and all growth above the pot lip was harvested for P analysis. The turfed pots were then kept in a greenhouse at 25 to 30 C for a 4-week recovery period. The experiment was then repeated with the same turfed pots in the same way in the growth chamber.

Observations in Experiments 2 and 3 were made on creeping bentgrass stolons taken from potted greenhouse plants of A25, A53, A54, A58, A61, and A66. Stolons were rooted in 225 ml of tap water in glass milk bottles [413 ml (half pint)] maintained in the greenhouse. After a week the tap water was replaced with an equal amount of 10% Hoagland nutrient solution No. 1 (8). Plants were maintained in the nutrient solution for 6 weeks. Three days prior to the uptake studies, the complete nutrient solution was replaced with one deficient in P. No forced aeration was provided during this period.

Differential root temperatures used in Experiments 2 and 3 were provided by three large water baths aligned side by side in the greenhouse. These were programmed to maintain temperatures of 5, 15, and 25 C (±0.5 C), respectively. In both experiments, the bottles were placed in milk cases and immersed to the neck in the water baths so that water levels outside and within the bottles were equal. Water in each bath was covered with a 2-cm floating layer of 3-mm styrofoam beads. Air temperatures above the styrofoam averaged 25 C (±5 C) during both studies. Forced aeration was provided in each bottle in the tanks through plastic tubing connected to a small aquarium pump. Experiment 2 was conducted in March 1976 and Experiment 3 in January 1977.

Immediately after the complete nutrient solution was replaced with P deficient nutrient solution, all bottles were placed in the 15 C tank for 24 hours. Bottles assigned to 5 and 25 C were then moved to their respective tanks for another 48 hours before changing to ^{32}P enriched complete Hoagland No. 1 solution. Bottles were arranged in the tanks in randomized complete blocks with two replicates in Experiment 2 and three in Experiment 3.

An excess of complete nutrient solution labeled with ^{32}P in phosphoric acid was prepared 36 hours prior to each experiment to assure equilibration. Activities of the prepared solutions were 0.008 and 0.124 mCi/liter in Experiments 2 and 3, respectively. The P deficient nutrient solution was replaced with ^{32}P enriched solution, taking bottles sequentially beginning at 1000 hours. Harvesting was done 24 hours later in the same sequences, providing 24-hour P uptake opportunity. Plants were harvested by removing them from the bottles and clipping the shoots with scissors just above the crown area. The roots and middle portions which had been exposed to the solution were washed three times in non-radioactive isotonic Hoagland solution to remove labile sorbed ^{32}P. After washing, the roots were cut off just below the crown area. Root and shoot tissue samples were placed in Kraft paper bags, air-dried at 60 C for 24 hours, weighed, and then digested over low heat, first with HNO_3 and then with $HClO_4$. The residue was diluted to 10 ml volume with 10% HCl. One milliliter of this solution was transferred to a counting vial, evaporated to near dryness, and 10 ml POPOP phosphorus added (1,4-Bis[2-(5-phenyloxazolyl)]-benzene). The POPOP solution was prepared from 0.3 g phenyl-oxazoly-phenyl-oxazolyl-phenyl in 16.5 g 2.5 diphenyl-oxazide in 1 liter Triton x-100 and 2 liters toluene. Activity was then measured with a Packard Tri-Carb Liquid Scintillation Spectrometer. An aliquot of the remaining solution was used to determine total P content by the standard vanadate-molybdate method. All data were subjected to statistical analysis of variance.

RESULTS AND DISCUSSION

Field Studies

There are three generalized color response modes (purple, variable, and green) to cool temperatures and P fertilization. These are illustrated by clonal data in Table 2. Clone A54 is typically off-color most of the cool season. Clones A25 and A53 tend to turn purple later and to a lesser degree than A54 and may turn green during warm spells. The response of A25 and A53 to added P tends to be proportionately greater than that of A54. Clones A58 and A61 may show some response to added P, but are generally green under all temperatures at Tucson.

Median root length measurements made from 1974–76 showed consistent differences among clones in root length (Table 3). Differences found appeared to have no relationship to color response to cool temperatures. The clone with the poorest color (A54) had the longest roots, while Penncross plots (with equally long roots) were variable in color response. Clones A58 and A61 were consistently green, yet had significantly shorter roots than A54 and Penncross (Table 3). There was a parallel reduction in

Table 2. Color ratings for creeping bentgrass clones showing varying responses to cool temperatures and P applications in the field at Tucson, Ariz.

	Temperatures previous week		Clonal type					
			Purple (A54)		Variable ($\bar{x}$ A25,A53)		Green ($\bar{x}$ A58,A61)	
			P fertilization					
Date	Maximum	Minimum	No P	2 g P/m^2	No P	2 g P/m^2	No P	2g P/m^2
	C							
25 Nov. 1975	21	4	4.0†	4.7	7.2	8.5	8.7	9.0
31 Dec. 1975	16	3	2.0	3.0	5.5	7.5	8.2	8.4
27 Jan. 1976	19	9	4.7	5.7	5.5	6.5	7.4	8.3
Clonal means by type*			3.6	4.5	6.1	7.8	8.1	8.6

* L.S.D.$_{0.05}$ for comparison individual clonal means = 1.09.
† Rating system: 1 = purple; 9 = green.

Table 3. Median root lengths and color ratings for six creeping bentgrasses grown in the field on sand without P fertilization at Tucson, Ariz.

Bentgrass	Root lengths			Visual color ratings‡	
	1973–1976†	20 Nov. 1975	31 Jan. 1976	25 Nov. 1975	27 Jan. 1976
A25	113cd*	147 a	111 c	7.3 ab	6.0 abc
A53	125 c	135 a	102 c	7.0 ab	5.0 bc
A54	141 a	138 a	135 ab	4.0 c	4.7 c
A58	119 cd	127 a	109 c	8.7 a	7.0 ab
A61	125 c	125 a	106 c	8.7 a	7.7 a
Penncross	140 ab	152 a	140 a	6.7 b	6.3 abc

* Means within columns followed by the same letter are not significantly different at the 0.05 level of probability according to Duncan's Multiple Range test. † $\bar{x}$ 15 observations.
‡ Rating system: 1 = purple; 9 = green.

root length and in color from November to January. Both reductions may have been related to lower food reserves in the roots during a period of slow winter growth. Since P uptake requires energy expenditure (1), low root reserves and low respiration rates might well produce a combined effect.

Consistent clonal differences in color response to cool temperatures and effects on that response by added P suggested that clones differed either in P uptake rates or in P requirements for green color. Since root lengths showed no apparent association with color responses, potential differences in uptake rates would be due to differences in efficiency from the root soil interface to the shoot growth rather than differences in capacity to exploit larger volumes of soil.

Laboratory Studies

Experiment 1

Color ratings show that clones differed significantly in color under similar temperature and P levels (Table 4). There was also a significant color response to additions of P. Phosphorus levels in the leaves did not differ significantly between color response types and leaf P levels did not increase appreciably with added soil P, except at the two highest rates (Table 4). The green clones, A58 and A61, were both greener at low P levels and responded better to lower levels of added P than did A53 or A54. At the same time, P levels in leaves at given rates of added P were similar for both types of clones. Results suggest that differences in color response were due to P requirement level rather than P uptake differences at cool temperatures. However, the clones had been growing actively under warm temperaures in the greenhouse before growth chamber tests were conducted. Although shoot growth was clipped back each time, there may have been residual mobilizable P in root or crown tissues from the pre-growth period. Therefore, P uptake differences or differences in P transport rates from root-soil interfaces to leaf at cool temperatures might have been obscured by P already available. Studies were then initiated

Table 4. Color ratings and P contents for leaves of four creeping bentgrasses grown in a growth chamber at low temperatures (5 to 15 C) under various P levels.

Clone	Field response	P levels (g/m^2) 0.0	0.25	0.50	1.0	2.0
				Color rating†		
A54	Purple	1.8	1.8	2.0	2.7	2.7
A53	Variable	2.5	2.2	2.0	3.8	4.8
A58	Green	5.3	5.2	7.8	7.2	7.3
A61	Green	3.8	4.8	4.8	5.7	6.3
				P content [ppm, dry weight]		
$\bar{x}$ A53-54		2,600*	2,400	2,800	3,600	5,000
$\bar{x}$ A58-A61		2,000	2,600	3,000	3,400	4,500
L.S.D.$_{0.05}$ for individual color ratings = 1.9						

* P analyses of combined clippings from two growth chamber tests. F values not significant at the 0.05 level for clones, P levels, clones by P levels. † Rating system: 1 = purple; 9 = green.

with labelled P to determine more conclusively whether P uptake or P transport differences among clones might be involved in leaf color responses to cool temperatures.

Experiments 2 and 3

Although the period of cold stress in the water bath was too short to induce color changes, temperature effects on ^{32}P uptake and total P contents were obvious (Tables 5 and 6). Phosphorus content and ^{32}P uptake were much lower at 5 than at 15 or 25 C. Levels of ^{32}P, including total P in most cases, were significantly higher in roots than in shoots. There were also significant differences among clones in ^{32}P and in total P contents of roots and shoots, although these differences had no relationship to mode of color response observed in the field. Washington (A66) was used in these tests because of its known tendency to turn reddish purple under cool conditions. It had the lowest P values at 5 C, although not significantly lower than those for the green clones A58 and A61. Highest P values were those for A54, the first clone to turn purple under combined cold and P stress in the field.

The combined analysis of variance for ^{32}P values from Experiments 2 and 3 showed no significant interaction between clones and temperatures, all clones responding to the same degree. Relative levels of ^{32}P in shoots and roots, however, differed among clones and among temperatures (significance 1% part by clone, 5% part by clone × temperature). Expressing proportioning by root-shoot ratios, the range among clones was 6.5 to 15.0 at 5 C and 1.5 to 3.3 at 25 C. Ratios were not associated with color response modes.

The data from Experiments 2 and 3 show that low temperatures significantly reduced ^{32}P uptake and transport rates and that the degree of this effect differed among clones. Phosphorus uptake and transport rate differences were not associated with differences in color response to cool

Table 5. Root and foliar ^{32}P contents of six creeping bentgrasses exposed to ^{32}P for 24 hours at three temperatures. Data are combined means from Experiments 2 and 3.

	Clonal types											
	Purple				Variable				Green			
	A54		A66		A25		A53		A58		A61	
Temperature	Roots	Shoots	Roots	Shoots	Roots	Shoots	Roots	Shoots	Roots	Shoots	Roots	Shoots
C	counts/min/cg											
5	737 f*	113 j	456 hi	43 k	538 gh	64 k	594 fg	60 k	534 gh	61 k	544 gh	36 k
15	219 lb	504 hi	1,632 c	381 ij	1,467 cd	466 hi	1,773 c	488 hi	1,249 d	487 hi	1,104 de	311 j
25	3,037 a	928 f	2,688 a	864 f	1,716 c	1,140 e	2,956 a	1,154 e	2,256 b	794 fg	1,523 cd	697 fg
Clonal means	1,988 u*	515 y	1,592 v	429 z	1,240 x	557 y	1,774 u	567 y	1,346 w	447 yz	1,057 x	348 z

* Values which do not have a letter in common (series a-j and u-z) differ at the 0.05 level (DMR) when expressed as square roots in the original analysis.

Table 6. Total root and foliar P contents of six creeping bentgrasses exposed to ^{32}P for 24 hours at three temperatures. Data are combined means from Experiments 2 and 3.

	Clonal types											
	Purple				Variable				Green			
	A54	A66	A25	A53	A58	A61						
Temperature	Roots	Shoots	Roots	Shoots	Roots	Shoots	Roots	Shoots	Roots	Shoots	Roots	Shoots
C	P ppm dry wt.											
5	5,083 d-i*	4,098 g-j	3,422 i-j	3,710 h-j	4,776 e-j	3,513 i-j	5,972 b-d	4,365 e-j	5,345 c-h	4,288 f-j	4,334 e-j	3,723 h-j
15	6,706 a-c	4,202 g-j	5,512 e-g	4,169 g-j	4,704 e-j	3,701 h-j	4,977 d-j	4,760 e-j	6,416 a-d	4,466 e-j	5,727 c-g	3,339 j
25	4,702 e-j	4,702 e-j	7,624 a	4,625 e-j	5,093 d-i	4,182 g-j	7,362 a-b	5,260 c-h	6,345 a-e	5,613 c-g	5,938 b-f	4,905 d-j
Means	6,373 z*	4,333 x-w	5,522 z-y	4,168 x-w	4,858 y-x	3,799 w	6,104 z-y	4,795 y-x	6,035 z-y	4,789 y-x	5,333 y	3,989 x-w

* Values which do not have letters in common (series a-j and z-w), differ at the 0.05 level (DMR).

temperatures and P fertilization in the field. These data support indications from Experiment 1 that color responses of clones are related to minimum P levels required by those clones at given temperatures.

ACKNOWLEDGMENTS

Studies reported here were supported in part by grants from the U.S. Golf Association Green Section Research Fund and from the Penncross Bentgrass Growers Association.

LITERATURE CITED

1. Bieleski, R. L. 1973. Phosphate pools, phosphate transport and phosphate availability. Annu. Rev. Plant Physiol. 24:225–252.
2. Carter, O. G., and D. J. Lathwell. 1967. Effects of temperature on orthophosphate absorption by excised corn roots. Plant Physiol. 42:1407–1412.
3. Clark, R. B., and J. C. Brown. 1974. Differential phosphorus uptake by phosphorus-stressed corn inbreds. Crop Sci. 14:505–508.
4. Gardner, B. R., and J. P. Jones. 1973. Effects of temperature on phosphate sorption isotherms and phosphate desorption. Commun. Soil Sci. Plant Anal. 4:83–93.
5. Goodman, P. J. 1969. Intra-specific variation in mineral nutrition of plants from different habitats. p. 237–253. *In* I. H. Rorison (ed.) Ecological aspects of the mineral nutrition of plants. Blackwell Scientific Publications, Oxford.
6. Gorsline, G. W., W. I. Thomas, and D. E. Baker. 1968. Major gene inheritance of Sr-Ca, Mg, K, P, Zn, Cv, B, Al-Fe and Mn concentration in corn (*Zea mays* L.). Pennsylvania State Univ. Bull. 746.
7. Hill, R. R., and S. B. Guss. 1976. Genetic variability for mineral concentration in plants related to mineral requirements for cattle. Crop Sci. 16:680–685.
8. Hoagland, D. R., and D. I. Arnon. 1950. The water-culture for growing plants without soil. California Agric. Exp. Stn. Circ. 347 (Revised).
9. McNaughton, S. J., R. S. Campbell, R. A. Freyer, J. E. Mylroie, and K. D. Rodland. 1974. Photosynthetic properties and root chilling responses of altitudinal ecotypes of *Typha latifolia* L. Ecology 55:168–172.

Chapter 16

Temperature Influences on Mineral Nutrient Distribution in Two Kentucky Bluegrass Cultivars[1]

J. E. KAUFMANN
D. E. ALDOUS

ABSTRACT

Shoot growth inhibition occurs in cool season turfgrasses at supraoptimal temperatures. To identify possible mechanisms of growth inhibition, temperature influences on the concentration and distribution of nutrients were evaluated.

Kentucky bluegrass (*Poa pratensis* L.) cultivars 'Merion' and 'Nugget' were established from seed on coarse sand in a greenhouse propagation bed for 10 weeks. Sod pieces were then transferred to pots, allowed to acclimate for 2 weeks, and placed in an environmental growth chamber where air temperatures were increased 4 C every 2 weeks from 22 to 38 C. The effects of root temperature maintained at 22 C in half of the pots (controlled root temperatures, CRT) were compared to the other half where root temperatures were allowed to equilibrate with air temperatures (non-controlled root temperatures, (NRT). Shoot growth above 4.0 cm was clipped weekly from plants grown at 22 to 34 C. After the 38 C period, the plants were separated into verdure (live, green tissue), thatch (dead, brown tissue), crowns, and roots. The distribution of dry weight, N, P, K, Ca, Mg, Na, Mn, Fe, Zn, Cu, B, and Al was determined among the four plant fractions.

The N content of leaves was significantly lower at 26, 30, and 34 C compared to 22 C. Significant reductions in Mn, Fe, and Zn content occurred in leaves at 30 C compared to 22 and 26 C. Significant increases in Al, B, and Na content were found at 34 C compared to 22 C. Compared to dry weight distribution, roots were found to accumulate proportionally high levels of P, Fe, Cu, and Al; while K, Ca, Na, Mg, and B were at very low levels in the root. Nitrogen was essentially non-detectable in thatch, but occurred at high levels in leaf and verdure tissue. The thatch accumulated high levels of the other nutrients while leaf and verdure tissue exhibited low levels.

Where growth and high temperature survival of both cultivars was improved at CRT compared to NRT, no major change in the pattern of mineral nutrient concentration or distribution was detected. Thus, even though changes occurred in mineral nutrient levels as temperature increased from 26 to 38 C, changes in these levels do not appear to be involved in high temperature growth inhibition of cool-season turfgrasses.

Additional index words: Heat tolerance, Growth, Nutrient concentration, Turfgrass.

[1] Contribution from the Dep. of Floriculture and Ornamental Horticulture, New York State College of Agriculture and Life Sciences, Cornell Univ., Ithaca, NY 14853 USA.

INTRODUCTION

Environmental factors play an important role in the growth and survival of grasses. In the cool, humid region of the United States, the cool-season grasses are best adapted for roadsides, lawns, and intensively maintained recreational turfs. Environmental extremes in shade, wear, flooding, and drought can often be corrected to maintain superior turfs. However, high temperature is one stress factor controlling the growth of cool-season grasses that is usually not practical to manipulate on extensive turf areas.

High temperature growth inhibition occurs in summer when cool-season grasses are receiving maximum use and abuse. Thus wearability and recuperative potential need to be maximized during these hot periods. Cool-season grasses exhibit these growth inhibition responses at approximately 28 to 30 C (2, 3, 5, 9) and direct high temperatures kill at approximately 40 C. Improving the growth and production temperature range of these grasses 10 C would greatly reduce summer maintenance problems and improve sod production.

The mechanism of high temperature growth inhibition is not known. A theory that has been promoted since the 1930's (8) states that carbohydrates or energy levels are exhausted at high temperatures because respiration exceeds photosynthesis. However, more recent research data indicate that respiration does not exceed photosynthesis and that carbohydrate levels increase as growth decreases under supraoptimal temperatures (3, 5, 6, 9).

A second theory, advanced in the 1960's, suggested that total N levels were reduced during the summer season (4). It was subsequently determined that the N fraction depleted was glutamine, the major supply of reduced N in the cool-season turfgrass plant. This led to immediate speculation that certain critical amino acids were not available for growth. It now appears quite probable that the mechanism of supraoptimal temperature growth inhibition alters a series of biochemical pathways which results in the metabolism of the glutamine pool in the plant.

Many of the mineral nutrients are involved as cofactors of enzymatic reactions in these biochemical pathways. Major concentration changes of a specific nutrient could suggest alteration of the biochemical pathways requiring that nutrient as a cofactor.

It has been shown that P and K levels in Merion Kentucky bluegrass leaves during summer were lower and that Mg, Fe, and Al were higher when compared to spring and fall levels (7). As the season progressed, levels of Ca and Mn decreased while Zn levels increased. Levels of B were highly variable while Cu levels were largely unaltered.

The objectives of this investigation were to determine temperature influences on mineral nutrient concentration and distribution throughout the turfgrass plant and whether these influences would partially identify the location and biochemical pathway of high temperature growth inhibition.

MATERIALS AND METHODS

'Merion' and 'Nugget' Kentucky bluegrass (*Poa pratensis* L.) were established from seed on coarse sand in a greenhouse propagation bed. After 10 weeks the sod was transplanted onto coarse sand in 15-cm diam plastic pots with three replications and acclimated for 2 weeks prior to initiation of the temperature treatments in a growth chamber. The chamber was maintained at a light intensity of 600 $\mu E/m^2/sec$ and a daylength of 16 hours.

Air temperatures in the growth chamber were increased 4 C every two weeks (from 22 to 38 C). Successively incremented temperatures were chosen to simulate field conditions. Root temperature was controlled at 22 C (controlled root temperatures, CRT) in half of the pots while the root zone of the other half was allowed to equilibrate with the ambient temperature of the chamber (non-controlled root temperatures, NRT).

Since several investigations have shown that the level of nutrient application influences nutrient levels in plant tissues (10, 11, 12), it was considered important to insure adequate nutrient availability at all times. Thus, the pots were subirrigated with a full nutrient solution utilizing the method outlined in a previous paper (1). The final solution contained the following nutrients with concentration expressed in $\mu g/ml$: NO_3, 7.5; H_2PO_4, 0.5; K, 3.0; Ca, 5.0; Mg, 2.0; Na, 0.5; SO_4, 2.0; Cl, 0.5; Fe, 2.3; B, 0.25; Mn, 0.25; Zn, 0.025; Cu, 0.01; Mo, 0.005. The nutrient solution was completely changed on a weekly basis to prevent nutrient concentration or pH shifts. The irrigation frequency was at a 4-hour interval at air temperatures of 22, 26, and 30 C, but was reduced to 3 hours for 34 and 38 C to minimize moisture stress.

Shoot growth above 4.0 cm was harvested weekly at the beginning of the photoperiod. Clippings from 2 weeks were combined for each temperature regime. After 10 weeks, plants were divided into four fractions: verdure (living green tissue), thatch (brown shoots and stems), crowns, and roots. All tissue was freeze dried, ground through a 40-mesh sieve, and kept at 0 C until analysis.

All mineral element concentrations were determined with the emission spectrograph operated by the Cornell University Spectrography Laboratory. Nitrogen was determined by the macro-Kjeldahl procedure.

RESULTS AND DISCUSSION

The influence of root and air temperatures on mineral levels of Merion Kentucky bluegrass is shown in Table 1. At NRT ambient temperatures of 34 C resulted in significantly higher levels of N and P, compared to 22 C. Levels of Mn, Fe, and Zn were highest at 22 C, decreased at 26 C and again at 30 C, but showed recovery as growth subsided at 34 C. Levels of K and Cu were largely unaltered. At CRT the

Table 1. The influence of temperature on the mineral composition of various plant parts of Merion Kentucky bluegrass.

Plant fraction	Root temperature†	Ambient temperature	N	P	K	Ca	Mg	Na	Mn	Fe	Zn	Cu	B	Al
		C	% of dry wt.					μg/g						
Leaf	NRT	22	4.43 d*	0.44 c	4.11 a	0.64 a	0.35 b	785 a	442 e	186 b	150 bc	19 ab	34 a	67 b
Leaf		26	3.89 a	0.46 cd	4.23 a	0.71 a	0.35 b	1,523 b	332 d	111 a	88 a	21 ab	36 a	65 ab
Leaf		30	3.48 a	0.36 ab	4.07 a	0.89 ab	0.37 b	2,500 c	228 ab	69 a	86 a	21 ab	44 abc	63 ab
Leaf		34	3.61 b	0.32 a	4.36 a	1.05 b	0.56 c	2,583 c	310 cd	82 a	134 b	15 a	55 bc	93 c
Leaf	CRT	22	4.61 e	0.52 d	4.03 a	0.73 a	0.38 b	995 a	444 e	186 b	143 bc	21 ab	31 a	63 ab
Leaf		26	3.86 c	0.44 c	4.81 b	1.04 b	0.50 c	2,783 c	368 d	111 a	176 c	29 b	31 a	65 ab
Leaf		30	3.84 c	0.42 bc	4.34 a	0.64 a	0.28 a	1,842 b	166 a	66 a	58 a	23 ab	42 ab	55 a
Leaf		34	3.82 c	0.48 cd	4.30 a	0.72 a	0.36 b	1,528 b	238 bc	77 a	68 a	24 ab	56 c	67 b
Verdure	NRT	38	2.74 t	0.32 r	5.64 t	2.52 t	1.10 s	8,033 t	338 r	285 rs	--	41 r	42 t	128 r
Thatch		38	--	0.35 r	5.93 t	3.40 u	1.25 s	8,567 t	839 s	670 t	--	66 rs	64 u	172 rs
Crown		38	1.77 s	0.55 st	2.60 r	1.16 rs	0.27 r	3,200 s	296 r	776 t	--	80 st	28 s	274 st
Root		38	1.18 r	0.63 tu	0.59 r	0.88 r	0.15 r	1,695 r	440 r	1,350 u	--	121 u	18 r	369 tu
Verdure	CRT	38	2.61 t	0.34 r	5.33 t	2.73 s	1.26 s	9,000 tu	418 r	255 r	--	63 rs	46 t	140 rs
Thatch		38	--	0.39 rs	6.69 u	4.31 v	1.53 t	9,817 v	849 s	502 s	--	97 t	66 u	207 rs
Crown		38	1.34 r	0.50 s	1.97 s	1.62 s	0.32 r	2,705 rs	304 r	719 t	--	85 st	26 rs	217 rs
Root		38	1.34 r	0.71 t	0.93 r	1.03 rs	0.15 r	1,795 r	412 r	1,530 u	--	131 u	20 rs	430 u

* Means having the same letter within vertical columns were not significant at the 5% level according to Duncan's Multiple Range Test.

† Non-controlled root temperatures (NRT) were allowed to equilibrate with ambient; controlled root temperatures (CRT) were held at 22 C.

Table 2. The influence of temperature on the mineral composition of various plant parts of Nugget Kentucky bluegrass.

Plant fraction	Root temperature†	Ambient temperature	N	P	K	Ca	Mg	Na	Mn	Fe	Zn	Cu	B	Al
		C	% of dry wt.					μg/g						
Leaf	NRT	22	4.06 c*	0.42 bc	4.01 b	0.55 b	0.26 cd	325 a	308 c	90 b	110 c	22 bc	32 ab	58 a
Leaf		26	3.39 b	0.44 c	4.12 b	0.61 c	0.23 bc	667 abc	237 b	66 b	82 b	22 bc	39 c	57 a
Leaf		30	2.87 a	0.33 a	3.49 a	0.47 a	0.17 a	1,078 bc	134 a	34 a	64 ab	16 a	32 ab	52 a
Leaf		34	2.78 a	0.37 abc	3.52 a	0.60 c	0.20 ab	978 bc	134 a	31 a	50 a	18 ab	44 d	63 a
Leaf	CRT	22	4.14 c	0.40 abc	3.95 ab	0.45 a	0.30 d	590 ab	364 d	143 c	122 c	23 bc	30 a	77 b
Leaf		26	3.46 b	0.39 abc	4.18 b	0.63 c	0.27 cd	1,150 bc	234 b	74 b	83 b	24 c	34 abc	58 a
Leaf		30	2.95 a	0.34 ab	4.12 b	0.50 ab	0.19 ab	1,342 d	122 a	39 a	52 a	20 abc	37 bc	57 a
Leaf		34	2.94 a	0.33 a	3.90 ab	0.51 ab	0.19 ab	1,235 c	96 a	34 a	43 a	20 abc	37 bc	58 a
Verdure	NRT	38	1.90 t	0.37 rs	5.39 s	2.03 st	0.90 st	7,116 t	512 r	339 r	--	40 rs	50 tu	156 r
Thatch		38	--	0.40 rs	5.92 s	3.03 u	1.21 u	8,383 t	952 s	599 rs	--	72 rs	62 u	227 rs
Crown		38	1.80 st	0.63 t	1.75 r	1.42 rst	0.36 r	2,240 rs	344 r	679 rs	--	41 rs	22 r	257 rs
Root		38	1.51 s	0.50 st	0.34 r	0.73 r	0.11 r	1,028 r	416 r	1,300 t	--	81 s	16 r	362 rs
Verdure	CRT	38	2.37 u	0.32 r	6.07 s	2.35 tu	1.05 tu	7,833 t	450 r	197 r	--	46 rs	41 st	170 r
Thatch		38	--	0.33 r	4.13 s	2.10 stu	0.71 s	4,166 s	447 r	293 r	--	47 rs	45 tu	138 r
Crown		38	1.03 r	0.35 rs	1.65 r	1.22 rs	0.24 r	1,752 rs	218 r	952 st	--	29 r	26 rs	283 rs
Root		38	1.07 r	0.51 st	0.43 r	0.71 r	0.14 r	1,418 r	326 r	1,420 t	--	82 s	10 r	530 s

* Means having the same letter within vertical columns were not significant at the 5% level according to Duncan's Multiple Range Test.

† Non-controlled root temperatures (NRT) were allowed to equilibrate with ambient; controlled root temperatures (CRT) were held at 22 C.

Table 3. The influence of temperature on the distribution of dry weight and mineral nutrients in Merion Kentucky bluegrass.

Plant fraction	Root temperature†	Ambient temperature	Dry wt.	N	P	K	Ca	Mg	Na	Mn	Fe	Cu	B	Al
		C	% of total											
Leaf	NRT	22	7.3	21.0	7.9	6.3	2.1	3.0	1.0	5.4	2.4	2.4	5.0	2.9
Leaf		26	10.4	26.2	11.8	9.3	3.3	4.3	2.8	5.7	2.0	3.8	7.6	4.1
Leaf		30	5.2	12.8	4.6	4.4	2.0	2.3	2.3	2.0	0.6	1.9	4.6	2.0
Leaf		34	3.6	12.2	2.9	3.3	1.7	2.4	1.6	1.9	0.5	0.9	4.0	2.0
Verdure		38	5.9	11.0	4.6	7.0	6.5	7.7	8.2	3.3	3.0	4.2	5.0	4.5
Thatch		38	51.2	--	44.4	64.1	77.0	76.2	77.0	71.7	60.9	58.5	66.2	53.0
Crown		38	8.5	10.4	11.5	4.6	4.3	2.7	4.8	4.2	11.7	11.8	4.8	14.0
Root		38	7.9	6.4	12.3	1.0	2.1	1.4	2.3	5.8	18.9	16.5	2.8	17.5
Total			100.0	100.0	100.0	100.0	100.0	100.0	100.0	100.0	100.0	100.0	100.0	100.0
Total wt.‡			9.9	144.1	40.0	470	224	83.3	56.5	5.94	5.59	0.57	0.49	1.65
Leaf	CRT	22	5.5	11.9	6.6	4.7	1.6	2.3	0.9	4.7	2.2	1.6	3.7	2.1
Leaf		26	7.0	16.6	7.1	5.5	2.9	3.8	3.2	4.9	1.7	2.8	4.7	2.7
Leaf		30	5.7	11.0	5.5	5.2	1.4	1.7	1.7	1.8	0.8	1.8	5.1	1.9
Leaf		34	6.0	13.7	6.6	5.5	1.7	2.3	1.5	2.7	1.0	2.0	7.2	2.4
Verdure		38	19.9	30.4	15.5	22.6	21.5	26.9	29.1	15.8	10.8	16.9	19.5	16.5
Thatch		38	35.0	--	31.1	49.7	59.5	57.4	55.7	56.4	37.4	45.8	49.3	42.9
Crown		38	12.6	9.9	14.2	5.2	8.0	4.3	5.5	7.2	19.2	14.4	7.0	16.1
Root		38	8.3	6.5	13.4	1.6	3.4	1.3	2.4	6.5	27.0	14.7	3.5	15.4
Total			100.0	100.0	100.0	100.0	100.0	100.0	100.0	100.0	100.0	100.0	100.0	100.0
Total wt.‡			12.0	204.2	52.3	564	302	111.4	73.7	6.39	5.62	0.88	0.56	2.02

† Non-controlled root temperatures (NRT) were allowed to equilibrate with ambient; controlled root temperatures (CRT) were held at 22 C.
‡ Total weight in g dry wt. and mg nutrients/dm^2.

nutrient levels were similar to NRT with the exception of P and Ca. Phosphorus did not exhibit the lower levels at high air temperature and Ca did not exhibit the significant increase.

With the exception of N in crown tissue, no apparent differences in nutrient concentration occurred in plant parts between NRT and CRT. At NRT and CRT nutrient levels of thatch were highest, except for N, P, Fe, Cu, and Al. Levels of P, Fe, Cu, and Al were statistically higher in roots compared to most other plant parts.

The nutrient levels of Nugget were only slightly different than Merion (Table 2). Where a decline and recovery occurred with increasing temperature increments in Merion for Mn, Fe, and Zn, a continuous decline occurred in leaf tissue of Nugget. Other elements did not appear to be as greatly influenced by temperature in Nugget as compared to Merion. Differences in mineral concentration of leaf tissue between NRT and CRT were not apparent. The relationships between verdure, thatch, crown, and root concentrations at NRT and CRT were the same for Nugget as for Merion, with the exception that the Nugget levels were generally lower.

CRT resulted in greater leaf growth in Merion at 34 C and a higher verdure-thatch ratio of dry weight distribution compared to NRT (Table 3). Total dry weight was 12 g/dm^2 at CRT compared to 9.9 g/dm^2 at NRT. At both CRT and NRT, the roots accumulated proportionally high levels of P, Fe, Cu, and Al. The thatch accumulated high levels of all nutrients except P.

During the period of maximum shoot growth (26 C), only N and P were found in leaves at a proportionally higher level than dry weight. However, at 34 C, N and B were detected at a higher level. A very small portion of K, Ca, Mg, Na, and B was recovered in the roots. This may have been partially due to leaching loss during sample preparation when sand was washed from the roots.

Nugget exhibited a greater verdure-thatch ratio and greater survival to supraoptimal temperatures than Merion (2). However, nutrient shifts (Table 4) were complementary to a dry weight distribution shift. Thus, a high temperature-tolerant cultivar (Nugget) had similar nutrient distribution patterns to the susceptible (Merion) cultivar.

Supraoptimal temperatures resulted in significant changes in nutrient concentration in leaf tissue. Data showing that supraoptimal temperatures for growth resulted in a lower N concentration in leaf tissue (Tables 1 and 2) were consistent with earlier reports by Beard (4). Additionally, high shoot levels of Ca, Mg, and Al, and low levels of P found in Merion at 34 C compared to 22 C (Table 3), were similar to seasonal data reported by Hall (7).

However, when growth inhibition was partially overcome by controlling root temperatures at 22 C, or when a high temperature-tolerant cultivar was evaluated, these same significant differences occurred when air temperatures were increased from 22 to 34 C. Therefore, changes in nutrient concentration or distribution due to supraoptimal temperatures

Table 4. The influence of temperature on the distribution of dry weight and mineral nutrients in Nugget Kentucky bluegrass.

Plant fraction	Root temperature†	Ambient temperature	Dry wt.	N	P	K	Ca	Mg	Na	Mn	Fe	Cu	B	Al
		C	% of total											
Leaf	NRT	22	5.0	10.5	5.0	4.7	1.5	1.9	0.3	2.8	0.9	2.2	3.6	1.6
Leaf		26	7.9	18.7	8.3	7.5	2.7	2.6	1.1	3.5	1.0	3.5	7.0	2.4
Leaf		30	4.7	11.8	3.7	3.8	1.2	1.1	1.0	1.2	0.3	1.5	3.4	1.3
Leaf		34	3.7	8.7	3.3	3.0	1.2	1.0	0.7	0.9	0.2	1.3	3.6	1.2
Verdure		38	32.0	33.2	28.3	39.7	36.3	40.8	45.4	30.1	25.2	26.0	36.1	26.9
Thatch		38	27.4	--	26.1	37.3	46.3	46.9	45.7	47.8	32.3	40.0	38.3	33.4
Crown		38	7.5	7.4	11.3	3.1	6.0	3.9	3.4	4.8	10.1	6.3	3.8	10.4
Root		38	11.7	9.7	14.0	0.9	4.8	1.8	2.4	8.9	30.0	19.2	4.2	22.8
Total			100.0	100.0	100.0	100.0	100.0	100.0	100.0	100.0	100.0	100.0	100.0	100.0
Total wt.‡			10.3	189.2	43.3	449	185	73.0	51.9	5.63	5.23	0.51	0.46	1.92
Leaf	CRT	22	3.8	7.5	4.3	4.0	1.1	2.0	0.60.6	4.0	1.2	2.2	3.3	1.5
Leaf		26	6.2	12.7	6.8	6.8	2.5	3.0	1.9	4.2	1.0	3.7	6.0	1.8
Leaf		30	4.6	12.8	4.4	5.0	1.5	1.6	1.6	1.6	0.4	2.3	4.8	1.3
Leaf		34	4.5	10.0	4.2	4.6	1.5	1.5	1.5	1.3	0.3	2.3	4.7	1.3
Verdure		38	25.2	37.7	22.8	40.8	38.0	47.5	52.5	33.2	10.8	25.4	29.6	21.9
Thatch		38	26.3	--	24.4	28.8	35.4	33.4	29.0	34.2	16.7	31.0	33.8	18.5
Crown		38	20.5	13.3	20.3	9.0	16.0	8.8	9.6	13.1	16.7	14.9	15.3	29.7
Root		38	8.9	6.0	12.8	1.0	4.0	2.2	3.3	8.4	27.3	18.2	2.5	24.0
Total			100.0	100.0	100.0	100.0	100.0	100.0	100.0	100.0	100.0	100.0	100.0	100.0
Total wt.‡			11.8	188.1	41.9	446	185	66.1	44.6	4.06	5.46	0.47	0.41	2.32

† Non-controlled root temperatures (NRT) were allowed to equilibrate with ambient; controlled root temperatures (CRT) were held at 22 C.
‡ Total weight in a g dry wt. and mg nutrients/dm^2 turf.

appeared to be independent of the growth inhibition response of cool-season grasses.

LITERATURE CITED

1. Aldous, D. E., and J. E. Kaufmann. 1977. Method of soil temperature control for turfgrass research. Agron. J. 69:325–326.
2. ————, and ————. 1979. Role of root temperature on shoot growth of two Kentucky bluegrass cultivars. Agron. J. 71:545–547.
3. Beard, J. B. 1973. Turfgrass: Science and culture. Prentice-Hall, Inc., Englewood, N.J.
4. ————, and W. H. Daniel. 1967. Variations in the total, nonprotein, and amide nitrogen fractions of *Agrostis palustris* Huds. leaves in relation to certain environmental factors. Crop Sci. 7:11–115.
5. Duff, D. T., and J. B. Beard. 1974. Supraoptimal temperature effects upon *Agrostis palustris*. Part I. Influence on shoot growth and density, leaf blade width and length, succulence, and chlorophyll content. Physiol. Plant. 32(1):14–17.
6. ————, and ————. 1974. Supraoptimal temperature effects upon *Agrostis palustris*. Part II. Influence on carbohydrate levels, photosynthetic rate, and respiration rate. Physiol. Plant. 32(1):18–22.
7. Hall, J. R. 1971. The effect of phosphorus, season and method of sampling on foliar analysis, mineral depletion, and yield of Merion Kentucky bluegrass. Ph.D. Thesis, Ohio State Univ., Columbus.
8. Harrison, C. M. 1934. Responses of Kentucky bluegrass to variations in temperature, light, cutting, and fertilizing. Plant Physiol. 9:83–106.
9. Martin, D. P. 1972. The influence of temperature, cultural factors and analytical techniques on carbohydrate levels in turfgrass. Ph.D. Thesis. Michigan State Univ., East Lansing.
10. Monroe, C. A., G. D. Goordts, and C. R. Skogley. 1969. Effects of nitrogen-potassium levels on the growth and chemical composition of Kentucky bluegrass. Agron. J. 61:294–296.
11. Pellet, H. M., and E. C. Roberts. 1963. Effects of mineral nutrition on high temperature induced growth retardation of Kentucky bluegrass. Agron. J. 55:473–476.
12. Walker, W. M., and W. J. Pesek. 1963. Chemical composition of Kentucky bluegrass as a function of applied nitrogen, phosphorus, and potassium. Agron. J. 55:247–250.

Chapter 17

Influence of Aeration and Genotype upon Root Growth of Creeping Bentgrass at Supra-Optimal Temperatures[1]

KENT W. KURTZ
W. R. KNEEBONE

ABSTRACT

Creeping bentgrass (*Agrostis palustris* Huds.) is widely used on specialized turfgrass areas such as golf putting greens. When grown where summer temperatures are high for long durations, the resistance of bentgrass to other stresses is lowered and turfgrass quality is reduced. The practices of frequent soil cultivation by mechanical means have been utilized to enhance bentgrass vigor. The objective of this study was to determine the influence of aeration on root development of selected bentgrass clones grown under high temperatures.

The effect of aeration and temperature on rooting ability of nine creeping bentgrass clones was measured by placing cut stolons in bottles of tap water at 36, 38, and 40 C. Rooting over a 2-week period was evaluated in terms of root numbers per stolon node, number of stolon nodes rooted, and total number of roots grown with and without aeration. Bottles were aerated by bubbling air from tubes attached to a small aquarium pump. Differences between bentgrasses were significant only at 36 C and there was no significant clone by aeration interaction. Aeration significantly increased rooting at all temperatures with the most pronounced differences being at 40 C. These data emphasize the advantage of adequate aeration of creeping bentgrass grown under high temperatures.

Additional index words: Heat stress, Stolons.

INTRODUCTION

Creeping bentgrass (*Agrostis palustris* Huds.) is one of the most widely used cool-season species on putting and bowling greens. Its popularity is derived from its fine texture, superior shoot density, uniformity, and adaptation to very close mowing. Most active growth occurs under cool temperatures and a decline in vigor is evident with the onset of increased summer temperatures. Even though the species generally survives midsummer heat stress, shoot growth is frequently impaired and extensive loss of the root system may occur. With increased temperature stress, plant resistance to other stresses is lowered and turfgrass performance is decreased. Sometimes higher levels of culture are required to insure survival.

[1] A contribution from the Dep. of Plant Sciences, Univ. of Arizona, Tucson, AZ 85721 USA.

Optimum temperatures for bentgrass range from 20 to 30 C (1) and are considerably lower than those experienced in the southwestern U.S. during the summer months. Monthly mean maxima in Phoenix and Tucson, Ariz., for example, range from 35 to 40 C from June through September and approach these levels in May (8). Root efficiency and root growth are affected more severely than shoot growth at high temperatures. Schmidt and Blaser (7) measured root and shoot growth of 'Cohansey' bentgrass at 12, 24, and 36 C. Shoot growth actually increased with temperature, but root weights grown at 36 C were only 70% those grown at 24 C and 54% those grown at 12 C. Respiration rates of the shoot growth were 50% higher at 36 C than at 24 C. Since Cohansey is more heat tolerant than many bentgrasses (4), such reduced root growth and increased respiration is a conservative estimate of potential high temperature effects.

Root development varies among grass species and among cultivars within species (2). Recent studies by Kneebone et al. (5) have shown that degree of rooting of bentgrass stolons at temperatures of 36 C and above can be used to differentiate clones known for field heat tolerance from others known to be less tolerant.

Soil cultivation is a well-known cultural tool for encouraging increased root growth. Hansen and Jensen (3) have shown that respiration rates necessary for growth and maintenance of annual ryegrass (*Lolium multiflorum* Lam.) roots are higher than those for shoots. Letey (6) has pointed out that root growth is directly related to oxygen concentrations in the surrounding soil with closest relationships at low oxygen levels. Increased respiration rates and lower solubility of oxygen in water at high temperatures emphasize root stresses during the summer.

MATERIALS AND METHODS

This study was conducted under greenhouse and growth chamber conditions at California State Polytechnic University, Pomona, Calif., USA. Nine creeping bentgrass clones from the University of Arizona collection were used (Table 1). Each clone was maintained in the greenhouse in 25-cm plastic pots containing a mixture of sand and redwood shavings. Stolons possessing six nodes were cut with a razor blade from the

Table 1. Origin of nine creeping bentgrass clones from the University of Arizona collection.

Clone no.	Identification and source
A4	Cohansey, F. Juska, Beltsville, Md.
A7	Toronto, F. Juska, Beltsville, Md.
A12	Kansas, F. Juska, Beltsville, Md.
A22	MCC3, Muskogee C. C., W. Huffine, Okla.
A44	Thunderbird C. C., Green 16, R. Henegan, Phoenix, Ariz.
A49	Legg, G. Kozelnicky, Athens, Ga.
A50	Nimisilla, G. Kozelnicky, Athens, Ga.
A52	ARC 1, A Dudeck, Ft. Lauderdale, Fla.
A90	Penncross propagule, W. Kneebone, Tucson, Ariz.

parent clone and the leaves similarly removed from the lower four nodes. The lower four nodes were then inserted into clear glass milk bottles [237 ml (half-pint size)] containing 237 ml of tap water. Four stolons were placed in each bottle. The bottles were placed in wooden boxes in a growth chamber under constant temperature regimes. Three successive sets of stolons were exposed for 2 weeks each set at temperatures of 36, 38, and 40 C, respectively, with and without aeration. Aerated bottles received air bubbled from tubing attached to a small aquarium pump. A randomized complete block design was used. Treatments were replicated four times with one bottle per treatment per replicate. Plants received approximately 22 klux light for 12 hours each day. Heat tolerance was evaluated after 2 weeks of treatment by counting the roots produced per node, the number of nodes having roots, and the total number of roots.

Table 2. Mean number of roots per stolon node from nine creeping bentgrasses grown for 2 weeks in aerated and non-aerated water at three temperatures.

	Growth chamber temperature					
	36 C		38 C		40 C	
Clone	Air	No air	Air	No air	Air	No air
	Roots/node					
A4	2.8	3.3	2.8	2.0	1.5	0.5
A7	2.8	2.2	2.8	1.8	1.2	1.2
A12	2.2	2.0	2.5	2.3	1.5	0.5
A22	2.2	2.5	1.7	1.0	1.0	0.5
A44	3.5	2.5	2.5	2.0	1.2	0.0
A49	3.0	2.5	2.8	2.0	2.2	0.0
A50	3.2	3.2	2.5	1.0	1.5	0.5
A52	3.0	2.5	1.8	1.7	1.2	0.2
A90	3.2	2.8	2.0	2.1	1.5	0.5
Means	2.8	2.6	2.4	1.8	1.4	0.4
"F" air	N.S.		*		*	
"F" clones	**		N.S.		N.S.	

Table 3. Mean number of stolon nodes rooted from nine creeping bentgrasses grown for 2 weeks in aerated and non-aerated water at three temperatures.

	Growth chamber temperature					
	36 C		38 C		40 C	
Clone	Air	No air	Air	No air	Air	No air
	Nodes rooted					
A4	10.5	6.8	3.5	1.3	2.8	0.8
A7	9.0	7.5	3.2	1.8	2.8	1.8
A12	8.2	6.5	2.8	2.7	1.5	0.8
A22	9.5	7.0	2.0	1.5	1.0	0.2
A44	12.8	8.0	4.0	1.2	3.0	0.0
A49	12.0	8.0	3.5	2.0	2.2	0.0
A50	13.0	9.2	2.0	3.0	4.5	0.8
A52	11.2	8.0	2.2	1.3	2.5	0.2
A90	11.2	8.5	2.0	2.0	4.2	0.5
Means	10.8	8.7	2.7	1.9	2.7	0.6
"F" air	**		*		**	
"F" clones	**		N.S.		N.S.	

Table 4. Mean number of roots from nine creeping bentgrasses grown for 2 weeks in aerated and non-aerated water at three temperatures.

Clone	Temperatures					
	36 C		38 C		40 C	
	Air	No air	Air	No air	Air	No air
	Total roots					
A4	27	15	9	2	4	1
A7	23	17	8	3	4	3
A12	18	13	6	6	4	1
A22	22	16	4	1	2	0
A44	36	18	12	3	5	0
A49	30	18	11	5	6	0
A50	34	26	6	3	9	1
A52	28	20	4	3	5	0
A90	31	20	7	5	8	4
Means	27.7	18.1	7.4	3.4	5.2	1.1
"F" air	**		*		**	
"F" clones	**		N.S.		N.S.	

RESULTS AND DISCUSSION

There were significant differences among clones in degree of rooting at 36 C (Tables 2, 3, 4), but not at 38 or 40 C. In no case was the clone by aeration interaction significant, indicating that the clones were similar in their responses. Root responses to aeration were least at 36 C, and increased with increasing temperatures. Aeration meant the difference, in some cases, between roots and no roots over the 2-week exposure time. Mean root numbers on aerated stolons were 153, 218, and 472% more than those for non-aerated stolons at 36, 38, and 40 C, respectively (Table 4). Similar values for roots per node were 108, 113, and 350% (Table 2); while those for nodes rooted were 124, 142, and 450% (Table 3) more for aerated than for nonaerated stolons.

Since continued effectiveness of turfgrass roots depends upon replacement of senescent tissue by new growth, these data emphasize the importance of aeration in the rooting of creeping bentgrass stolons exposed to high water temperatures.

LITERATURE CITED

1. Beard, J. B. 1973. Turfgrass: Science and culture. Prentice Hall, Inc., Englewood Cliffs, N.J.
2. Boeker, P. 1974. Root development of selected turfgrass species and cultivars. p. 55–61. *In* E. C. Roberts (ed.) Proc. Second Int. Turfgrass Res. Conf., Blacksburg, Va. June 1973. Am. Soc. Agron., Madison, Wis.
3. Hansen, G. K., and C. R. Jensen. 1977. Growth and maintenance respiration in whole plants, tops, and roots of *Lolium multiflorum*. Physiol. Plant. 39:155–164.
4. Kneebone, W. R. 1973. Heat tolerance in creeping bentgrass. Agron. Abstr. p. 60.
5. ————, D. P. T. R. Bhola, and K. W. Kurtz. 1975. Genetic differences in heat tolerance in a cool-season grass demonstrated by differentials in rooting ability at supra-optimal temperature. J. Ariz. Acad. Sci. 11:5 (Proc. Suppl.).
6. Letey, J. 1961. Aeration, compaction and drainage. Calif. Turfgrass Cult. 14:9–12.
7. Schmidt, R. E., and R. E. Blaser. 1967. Effect of temperature, light, and nitrogen on growth and metabolism of 'Cohansey' bentgrass (*Agrostis palustris* Huds.). Crop Sci. 7: 447–451.
8. Smith, H. V. 1956. The climate of Arizona. Ariz. Agric. Exp. Stn. Bull. 279.

Chapter 18

Cold Acclimation and Deacclimation in Cool-Season Grasses[1]

D. B. WHITE
M. H. SMITHBERG

ABSTRACT

Cold acclimation of turfgrasses in Minnesota, U.S.A., precedes normal environmental demand. Acclimation begins in July and August and increases steadily to a peak in January. Loss of hardiness in midwinter is at first slow, followed by a rapid loss in the March-April growth initiation period. 'Penncross' creeping bentgrass (*Agrostis stolonifera* L.) was the hardiest grass followed by Kentucky bluegrass (*Poa pratensis* L.), red fescue (*Festuca rubra* L.), and perennial ryegrass (*Lolium perenne* L.), which often does not tolerate Minnesota winter temperatures. Cultivars within species varied in degree of acclimation and acquisition of cold hardiness. Kentucky bluegrass cultivars ranged from −30 to −48 C, red fescue cultivars from −32 to −45 C, and perennial ryegrass cultivars from −28 to −38 C. Late fall post hardening N application did not adversely affect acquisition of cold tolerance and it enhanced spring quality and growth patterns. Cutting height did not visibly affect hardiness in Kentucky bluegrass or red fescue, but Penncross creeping bentgrass maintained at 5 cm was less hardy than when mowed at 1.5 or 0.5 cm. The critical period in overwintering cool-season grasses appeared to be primarily associated with the dehardening phase in the spring.

INTRODUCTION

Annual acquisition and loss of cold hardiness is important to overwintering turfgrasses in the northern ranges of adaptability for both warm- and cool-season grasses. Investigations into the complex processes associated with this phenomena have been limited and the current state of knowledge is largely based on observation.

In 1943 Carroll (4) indicated that perennial ryegrass (*Lolium perenne* L.) and Italian ryegrass (*L. multiflorum* Lam.) were least tolerant of −25 C temperatures while Kentucky bluegrass (*Poa pratensis* L.), wood bluegrass (*P. nemoralis* L.), and colonial bentgrass (*Agrostis tenuis* Sibth.) were most tolerant. Beard (1) indicated that creeping bentgrass (*A. stolonifera* L.) and roughstalk bluegrass (*P. trivialis* L.) were hardiest; followed by Kentucky bluegrass, annual bluegrass (*P. annua* L.), 'Pennlawn' red fescue (*Festuca rubra* L.), and redtop (*A. alba* L.) which

[1] Scientific Journal No. 9953, Univ. of Minnesota, Agric. Exp. Stn., St. Paul, MN 55108, USA.

were intermediate in hardiness; while tall fescue (*Festuca arundinacea* Schreb) and ryegrass were least hardy. In 1966 Beard (2) noted that grasses peaked in hardiness during December followed by a slight decrease in January and a sharp reduction in April. 'Nugget' and 'Merion' Kentucky bluegrass ceased growth early in the fall, but 'Newport' continued growth into the fall, resulting in a shorter hardening period (3).

Early investigations indicated injury to Kentucky bluegrass from late or high fall applications of N fertilizers (6). Others found that grass populations treated with low rates of N late in the fall withstood winter temperatures as low as the control populations (5). A complete bibliography of cold hardiness research with special emphasis on grasses is available from the authors upon request.

The main objective of this research was to investigate the acclimation-deacclimation phenomena in cool-season grasses grown in a continental climate at 45° N Lat. 93° W Long. (St. Paul, Minn.). It is an appropriate place for such research because minimum winter air temperatures often approach −35 C and turfgrasses are important to the life style of the area. Other objectives relate to determining the role and influence of N-nutrition and cultural practices on the acclimation and deacclimation processes in turfgrasses.

This paper is offered as a review of unpublished data from several different experiments. The purpose for this is to depict a more comprehensive picture of cold acclimation and deacclimation in a northern continental climate than might otherwise be possible.

MATERIALS AND METHODS

Cold Hardiness (General)

Grasses involved in the investigations include: Nugget, 'Pennstar', 'Baron', and 'Kenblue' Kentucky bluegrass; 'Jamestown' chewings fescue (*F. rubra* var. *commutata* Gaud.); "Wintergreen', 'Ruby,' and 'Arctared' red fescue; 'NK-100' and 'NK-200' perennial ryegrass; 'Penncross' creeping bentgrass.

All grasses were field grown as turfs, unless otherwise indicated, for at least one season on a silt loam soil before being evaluated for cold tolerance. Grass populations were irrigated as needed to make up deficits in evapotranspiration, and except for specific nutrient investigations, fertilized according to accepted practice. Kentucky bluegrasses, ryegrasses, and red fescues were fertilized with 2.5 to 3.3 kg N/100 m^2/year with the last fall application between 10 and 15 September (approximately 6 weeks before freeze-up in Minnesota). Creeping bentgrass was fertilized with 0.4 kg N/100 m^2 every 10 to 14 days from May to 10 to 15 September for a total N application of 5 to 6 kg N/100 m^2/season.

Grasses to be investigated were collected from the field as 5-cm diam (29.6 cm^2) plugs with 8 to 9 cm of soil in the root zone. The individual root zones were protected with polyethylene plastic bags throughout the experiments. The 29.6 cm^2 populations to be evaluated during the winter were collected as plugs in November, surrounded by soil in flats, and stored outside until treatment time. Snow cover was allowed to accumulate on the exposed grass on the surface of the plug as in the field and usually was present from mid-December through March.

Each cultivar was subjected to monthly hardiness evaluations from 1972 to 1976 in a freezer (Revco) with a – 118 C capability. Grass plugs were collected for treatment and placed directly into the freezer. Temperatures were monitored by means of thermocouples placed in the crown area of selected plugs and recorded on a Barber-Colman multipoint recorder. Freezer temperatures were then lowered 6 C/hour. Two replications of each grass were removed from the freezer at predetermined temperature intervals (usually 8 C). After grasses were removed from the freezer they were stabilized for 2 days at 5 C, planted in flats, and placed in a greenhouse at 22 C days and 16 C nights.

Grasses were rated on a scale of 1 to 5; with 1 indicating 100% survival, 3 indicating 50% survival, and 5 completely dead. Readings of injury and regrowth were made 14 to 21 days subsequent to cold stress treatment.

Nitrogen Fertilization

'Penncross' creeping bentgrass was maintained at a 0.5-cm cutting height and received an application of 0.4 kg N/100 m^2 on or about 10 September (control). Additional treatments of 0.5 kg N/100 m^2 were applied in early October and mid-November during the study years (1972–76). Annual application dates varied according to weather conditions. Also, the October N application date was determined by the ability of the grass to withstand – 15 C as measured by the monthly freezer test.

Nitrogen treatment dates, at approximately 2-week intervals, included early and mid-October and early November from 1972 to 1976 with three replications. Nitrogen sources included: soluble fertilizer (NH_4NO_3); a natural organic material (processed Milwaukee sewage-6–3–0); a slowly soluble fertilizer (isobutylidene diurea); a resin-coated soluble fertilizer (Osmocote). Grass plugs from all treatments were collected and treated as previously described to ascertain cold tolerance.

Cutting Height

The potential effects of cutting height on cold hardiness were investigated by maintaining Nugget, Kenblue, and Pennstar Kentucky bluegrasses and Jamestown chewings fescue turfs at 1.5 and 5 cm and Penncross creeping bentgrass at 0.5, 1.5, and 5 cm for 3 years. Hardiness determinations of these grasses were conducted as in other experiments.

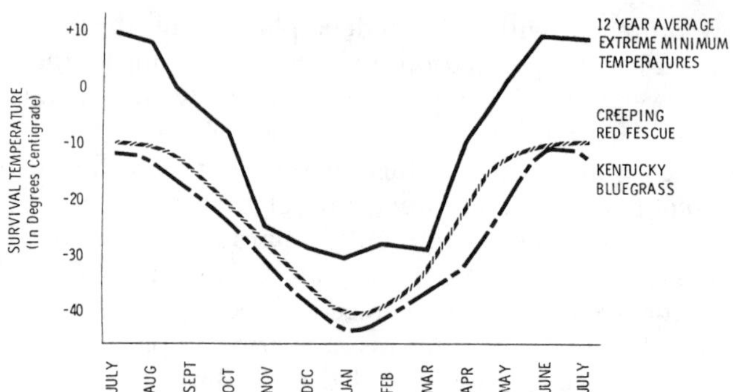

Fig. 1. Cold hardiness curve for typical creeping red fescue and typical Kentucky bluegrass.

RESULTS AND DISCUSSION

General Hardiness

The reader should be cautioned that the temperatures recorded and presented here may or may not be lower than the killing temperatures under normal outdoor conditions. However, under the conditions of the experiments and relating to out-of-doors, we have found that grasses withstanding at least −35 C (measured by our equipment) survive well in Minnesota. Those grasses tolerating −30 to −35 C have been borderline and those that do not survive −30 C in our experiments do not survive in the field over winter. The hardening curves for each species (Fig. 1 and 2), derived by averaging curves of different cultivars of the same species grown under Minnesota conditions, are self explanatory.

In January, the Kentucky bluegrass cultivars (Fig. 1) varied in hardiness from Kenblue (−30 C) to Baron (−48 C). However, the typical curve indicates a gradual acquisition of cold tolerance starting in July and peaking in January. In the spring, early losses of hardiness were gradual until ambient temperatures approached freezing. At that time the ability

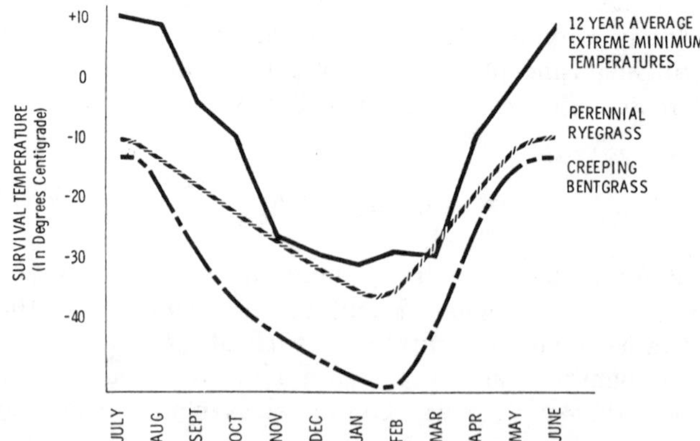

Fig. 2. Cold hardiness curve for typical perennial ryegrass and typical creeping bentgrass.

to tolerate cold temperatures was lost rapidly until June when the cycle was repeated.

The red fescue cultivars varied in hardiness from 'Arctared' at −45 C, the hardiest, to 'Wintergreen' at −32 C, the least hardy, in January. Red fescue began to harden later (August), but hardened more rapidly than Kentucky bluegrass, peaking in hardiness in January. Loss of hardiness proceeded in March and April at a steeper rate and somewhat earlier than with Kentucky bluegrasses.

Perennial ryegrass (Fig. 2), the least hardy of the species studied, acquired hardiness in a relatively linear relationship from July to January, but never acquired the degree of hardiness associated with the other species. Hardiness varied between the cultivars in January from −28 C in NK 100 to −38 C in NK 200. The reader should be aware that these curves (Fig. 1 and 2) were derived by averaging several years data. Annual variance however, was within ± 4 C over the period.

The Penncross creeping bentgrass curve for hardiness (Fig. 2) indicates that initial acclimation started early (July) followed by rapid hardening from September to January. The greatest cold tolerance of the grass species evaluated was associated with Penncross creeping bentgrass with a tolerance of −50 C. It is also important to note that the deacclimation curve of Penncross was the steepest of all species studied. Loss of hardiness was initiated early (February) and proceeded rapidly so that by the end of April Penncross had lost most of its cold tolerance. It is followed closely in this characteristic by red fescue and perennial ryegrass.

All the grasses, under conditions of the freezer-applied cold stress, acquired tolerance to cold substantially greater than could normally be expected throughout the hardening phase in the field. Conversely, hardiness was lost at a more rapid rate in the spring when chances of wide fluctuations in temperature are likely. Therefore, the likelihood of low temperature kill in Minnesota should be much greater in the spring, except for the least hardy species which would not even survive the winter. This means that winter losses with cool-season grasses are more likely to be associated with the deacclimation phase of the annual cycle rather than with direct low temperature kill. This supports the earlier research findings of Beard (2).

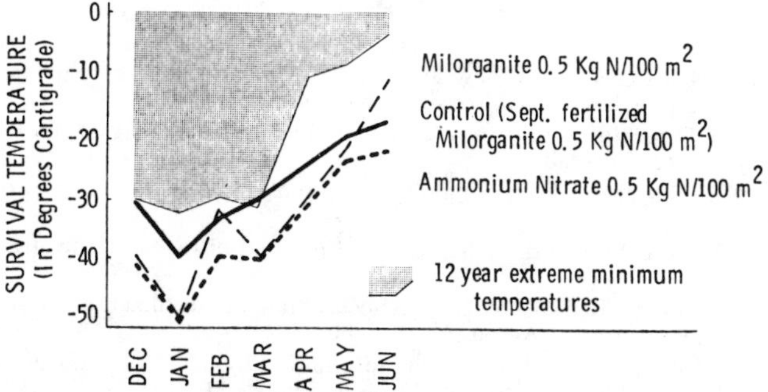

Fig. 3. Relative hardiness of Penncross creeping bentgrass after posthardened (25 October) fertilizer treatments.

Table 1. Effect of cutting height on cold hardiness in Penncross creeping bentgrass.

Cutting height	Survival rating†			
	−3 C	−12 C	−24 C	−35 C
cm				
5	4	5	5	5
1.5	1	1	1	5
0.5	1	1	1	5

† 1 = 100%; 2 = 80%; 3 = 50%; 4 = 30%; 5 = dead.

Nitrogen Fertilization

Cold hardiness was either unaffected or enhanced by late fall post hardening N application (Fig. 3). Post hardening applications of natural organic and soluble N to turf resulted in observed pre-winter shoot and root growth responses. All N fertilizer applications enhanced color, except the soluble N treatment of 2 kg N/100 m^2 and the 0.5-kg natural organic treatment. The 0.5-kg treatment showed little effect while the 2-kg soluble burned the turf to a point that evaluation was not realistic.

Cutting Height

After 3 years there were no differences observed in hardening between the low and high mowing levels in Kentucky bluegrass and red fescue. Penncross creeping bentgrass mowed at 5 cm for 3 years was less hardy than when mowed at 1.5 and 0.5 cm (Table 1). This phenomenon cannot be explained with our current state of knowledge. One could speculate that the stolons and crowns might have been elevated and therefore more exposed during the treatments. However unpublished data with ryegrasses indicated that the same cultivar might survive under mowing that did not overwinter in the unmowed condition. The indication is to continue normal mowing practices on Penncross creeping bentgrass putting greens to the cessation of growth in late fall. However, the reason for kill can only be speculated upon.

LITERATURE CITED

1. Beard, J. B. 1964. Effects of ice, snow and water covers on Kentucky bluegrass, annual bluegrass, and creeping bentgrass. Crop Sci. 4:638–640.
2. ————. 1966. Direct low temperature injury of nineteen turfgrasses. Q. Bull. Michigan Agric. Exp. Stn. 48(3):377–383.
3. ————. 1973. Turfgrass: Science and culture. Prentice-Hall, Inc., Englewood Cliffs, N.J.
4. Carroll, J. C. 1943. Effects of drought, temperature, and nitrogen on turf grasses. Plant Physiol. 18:19–36.
5. Ledeboer, F. B., and C. R. Skogley. 1968. Effects of late fall fertilization on the performance of cool-season turfgrasses. Agron. Abstr. p. 59.
6. Powell, A. J., R. E. Blaser, and R. E. Schmidt. 1967. Physiological and color aspects of turfgrasses with fall and winter nitrogen. Agron. J. 59:303–307.

Chapter 19 Anatomical and Physiological Effects of Air Pollutants on Turfgrasses[1]

V. B. YOUNGNER
F. J. NUDGE

ABSTRACT

Air pollution, found in most urban areas, may be a significant factor in turfgrass culture. A series of studies were conducted at the University of California, Riverside, to determine the effects of air pollutants, primarily ozone and peroxyacetylnitrate (PAN) on various turfgrass species and cultivars.

Distinct differences in susceptibility were noted among species and among cultivars within a species. Anatomical observations showed pronounced internal leaf injury following a single 3-hour exposure to 0.5 ppm ozone or 50 ppb of PAN. Field observations on cultivars of perennial ryegrass (*Lolium perenne* L.) following exposure to natural air pollution correlated well with laboratory observations.

Repeated exposure to low concentrations of ozone reduced tillering and total shoot growth of some species, but did not affect others. Nonstructural carbohydrate levels were also reduced in some cases. No acute toxicity symptoms were noted on any of the plants in this study. Apparent photosynthesis of a susceptible and of a tolerant *Cynodon* hybrid was not reduced in either cultivar during exposure to 0.5 ppm ozone for 2 hours. Thus, differences in stomatal response to ozone could not explain differences in susceptibility. Because genotypes differ in their susceptibility to air pollution, breeding more highly resistant strains should be possible.

Additional index words: Ozone, PAN, Peroxyacetylnitrate, Leaf injury, Shoot growth, Apparent photosynthesis.

INTRODUCTION

Plant injury from photochemical air pollutants (smog) has been recognized for several decades and numerous studies have documented the various effects of specific substances on crop and forest plants (7). However, until recently little attention has been given to the turfgrasses in this respect. Since the use of turf is concentrated in urban areas where air pollution is a common problem, air pollution may be a significant factor in turfgrass culture.

The purpose of this paper is to review the literature on air pollution effects on turfgrasses, discuss recent air pollution studies on turfgrasses at the University of California, Riverside, USA and, where possible, consider their relationship to turfgrass culture.

[1]Contribution from the Dep. of Plant Sciences, Univ. of California, Riverside, CA 92521 USA.

MATERIALS AND METHODS

Grasses in all of the studies at the University of California, Riverside, USA, were started in a greenhouse equipped with activated charcoal filters to remove ambient air pollutants. Treatment fumigations were provided in specially constructed growth chambers or greenhouses through which peroxyacetylnitrate (PAN) or ozone was circulated at the desired concentration. Following fumigation, the plants were kept in the chambers for ½ hour with fans blowing pollutant-free air over them. They were then returned to the filtered-air greenhouses. Plants representing the untreated controls were kept in the filtered-air greenhouses throughout each experimental period.

Symptoms of acute toxicity in the form of necrotic areas on leaf blades were noted over a 10-day period following treatment fumigation. These responses were visually rated on a scale of 1 to 5; no injury to severe injury. Free-hand sections were made from fresh leaf blades for microscopic examination when lesions were clearly visible. No stains were used.

Where applicable, shoot growth was measured as total dry matter and total number of innovations produced per plant during the experimental period. Nonstructural carbohydrate extraction and analysis were by the methods of Smith (10).

Apparent photosynthesis of hybrid bermudagrass [*Cynodon dactylon* (L.) Pers. × *C. transvaalensis* Burt-Davy] cultivars was measured by placing small plastic pots of grass in a plexiglass chamber 12.7 cm in diam and 12.7 cm high. The chamber was closed and compressed air containing 300 ppm CO_2 was passed through the chamber at 550 ml/min. A relative humidity of approximately 40% was maintained by passing the air stream through a water bath. Temperature in the chamber was maintained at 25 C with a circulating water bath and 21 klux of light at plant height was provided by a single mercury vapor lamp. Carbon dioxide exchange rates were determined with a Beckman model 15A infrared gas analyzer. Carbon dioxide exchange was monitored for 1.5 hours; ozone was then introduced at 0.5 ppm for 2 hours after which the ozone was turned off and CO_2 exchange monitored for an additional hour.

Field cultivar test plots were evaluated for injury following severe natural smog episodes. Plants were scored on a scale of 1 to 10; no injury to complete discoloration. Specific experimental treatments will be described in the appropriate places in the discussion to follow.

RESULTS AND DISCUSSION

Acute Toxicity From High Pollution Levels

A summary of results from several experiments with different species and cultivars fumigated with 0.5 ppm ozone for 3 hours or 50 ppb PAN for 3 hours (Table 1) shows distinct differences in species susceptibility.

Table 1. Summary of responses† of various turfgrass species to 0.5 ppm ozone or 50 ppb PAN for 3 hours; means for all cultivars of each species.

Species	Ozone	PAN
Lolium multiflorum Lam.	4.5	4.5
L. perenne L.	4.2	3.6
Agrostis palustris Huds.	4.0	2.8
Festuca rubra L.	3.4	2.6
A. tenuis Sibth.	3.4	2.2
Poa pratensis L.	2.5	2.2
Cynodon transvaalensis Burtt-Davy	2.4	2.2
C. Hyb., 'Tifgreen'	2.3	2.8
F. elatior L.	2.3	1.0
F. arundinacea Schreb.	1.8	2.5
Zoysia Hyb., 'Emerald'	1.8	1.0
C. dactylon (L.) Pers.	1.0	1.0
Stenotaphrum secundatum (Walt.) Kuntze	1.0	1.0
Z. japonica Steud., 'Meyer'	1.0	1.0
C. Hyb., 'Santa Ana'	1.0	1.0

† Visual estimate on a 1 to 5 scale; 1 = no injury, 5 = severe injury.

The warm-season grasses as a group are much more resistant to both air pollutants than are most cool-season grasses. The principal exception is African bermudagrass (*Cynodon transvaalensis* Burtt-Davy) which showed a moderate susceptibility to both ozone and PAN. This susceptibility appears to be imparted to some but not all of its hybrids with common bermudagrass. The high susceptibility of creeping bentgrass (*Agrostis palustris* Huds.) and perennial ryegrass (*Lolium perenne* L.) to ozone is in accord with the work of Brennan and Halisky (2).

Considerable variation in response to specific air pollutants exists among cultivars of several species (12). Although high susceptibility of a cultivar to more than one substance has been demonstrated, many cultivars may show pronounced differences in responses to ozone, PAN, and SO_2. Thus, it is necessary to determine the primary types of pollutants in an area before an attempt is made to select tolerant species or cultivars for that area.

Field plot observations in southern California of perennial ryegrass cultivars following a heavy smog episode showed a wide range in injury (Table 2). Ozone was the primary phytotoxic air pollutant in this area

Table 2. Responses of 12 perennial ryegrass cultivars to a heavy natural air pollution episode.

Cultivar	Smog damage†
Common	6.5
Lamora	5.3
Wendy	5.0
Ensporta	3.7
S-321	3.7
Clipper	3.3
Manhattan	3.0
Yorktown	2.0
Derby	2.0
Diplomat	1.7
Pennfine	1.7
Citation	1.0

† Rating scale of 1 to 10; 1 = no injury, 10 = complete discoloration.

and leaf symptoms were like those observed for ozone in the laboratory. Of those cultivars which had also been tested in the laboratory (12), the injury ranking was the same except for Manhattan which showed less injury in the field. Laboratory tests would thus appear to be a valid basis for selection of ozone-tolerant strains.

Noble (8) and Bobrov (1) described injury from ambient smog on annual bluegrass (*Poa annua* L.) as distinct bands of necrotic tissue across the leaf blade. They related the location of these bands to leaf age, especially to cell age. Since grass leaves mature basipetally, on a fully expanded leaf, leaf blade tip cells will be senescent, midblade cells mature, and basal cells immature. Only mature cells were found to be sensitive to smog. Immature and senescent cells were resistant so the bands of necrotic tissue would be at the tip of an old leaf, through the mid-section of a fully expanded leaf, and at the base of a young leaf; wherever cells had just reached maturity.

In our studies with specific pollutants, the relationship to leaf age

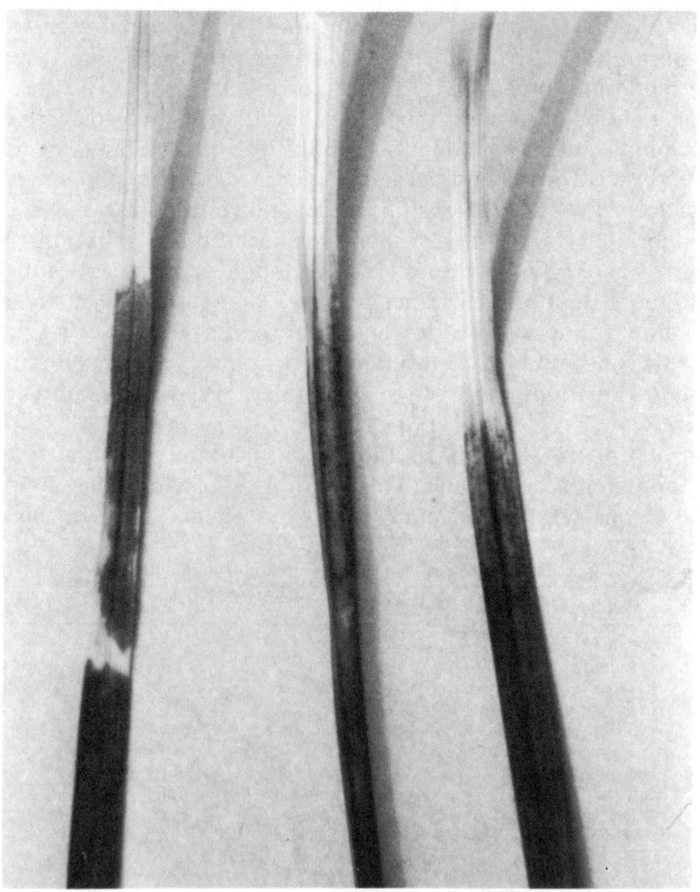

Fig. 1. Typical leaf injury from ozone.

was not as distinct. Ozone injury occurred most frequently towards the blade tip, while PAN injury usually occurred near the mid-section (Fig. 1, 2). PAN injury may occur on younger grass leaf tissue than that from ozone as has been demonstrated for pinto beans (*Phaseolus vulgaris* L.) by Dugger et al. (4). The ozone injury symptom corresponded more closely to those described by Brennan and Halisky (2), except that a general bleaching of damaged tissue was characteristic of all species. A russetting or stippling of the damaged tissue was the early symptom of PAN injury followed by a bleaching of the area.

Microscopic examination of free-hand transverse sections through injured leaves confirmed and extended the observations of Bobrov (1) on annual bluegrass. All injured species examined showed a disintegration of the chloroplasts of the cells surrounding the substomatal chamber. This was followed by plasmolysis and eventually a skeletonization of all the injured cells. This destruction of the mesophyll cells extended from the abaxial to the adaxial epidermis and was not limited to one side of the leaf

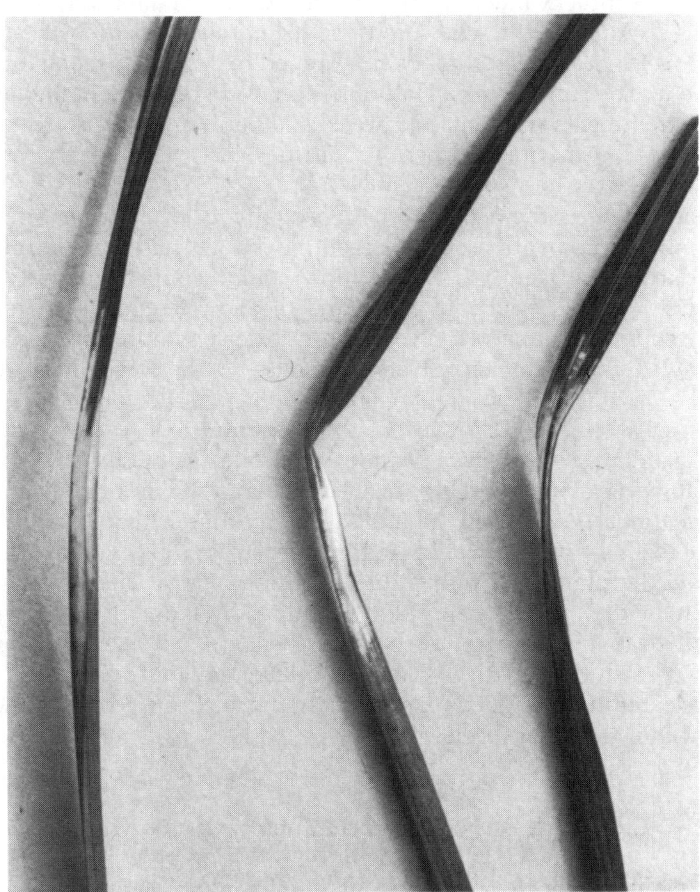

Fig. 2. Typical leaf injury from PAN.

as has been reported for some other plants (6). Leaves of most cool-season grasses do not have a palasade layer but only a loosely arranged spongy mesophyll from three to seven cells deep. Stomata are located on both leaf surfaces, therefore, these mesophyll cells are exposed to the toxic substances from both sides producing areas of complete mesophyll destruction.

Effects of Low Levels of Ozone on Grass Development

Acute toxicity from air pollutants which produces necrotic areas on leaves usually occurs during periods of high pollutant levels which may be of short duration. In many urban areas these episodes may be infrequent with much lower pollutant levels prevailing for longer periods. Exposure to such chronic conditions may have less visible but nevertheless serious effects on the grass plant.

'Newport' Kentucky bluegrass (*Poa pratensis* L.), 'Manhattan' perennial ryegrass, 'Alta' tall fescue (*Festuca arundinacea* Schreb.), and meadow fescue (*Festuca elatior* L.) were exposed to 0.25 ppm ozone for 5 hours, twice weekly, for 8 weeks. Half of the plants in both the fumigated and control treatments were clipped weekly to 5 cm and half were unclipped during the experimental period. Distinct differences in responses were noted among the four species (Table 3).

Newport showed the most pronounced effects from ozone. Dry matter, number of innovations, and percent nonstructural carbohydrates were all reduced significantly in both clipped and unclipped treatments. Lesser effects were observed in the tall and meadow fescues. Perennial ryegrass, although it has shown severe acute toxicity symptoms in other studies, showed essentially no adverse response to the lower levels of ozone.

Dugger et al. (4) have shown that the concentration of soluble and reducing sugars is lowest in pinto bean leaves of the age most susceptible to ozone. However, Ting and Dugger (11) have also shown that keeping tobacco (*Nicotiana tabacum* L.) plants in the dark for 72 hours prior to exposure to ozone—which would reduce nonstructural carbohydrate levels—made the plants less susceptible to ozone injury. There was no conclusive indication in this study that clipping, by reducing nonstructural carbohydrate percentages, affected the response to ozone. Although the reduction in shoot growth of Kentucky bluegrass and tall fescue by ozone was greater in the clipped plants than in the unclipped, this was not clearly shown for the other species.

Effect of Ozone on Apparent Photosynthesis

Ozone cannot enter the plant and no injury can occur if stomata are closed. Many plants respond to high ozone levels by closure of stomata (5). When this occurs ozone injury will be reduced. To test if stomatal

Table 3. Mean foliar dry matter yield, number of innovations, and percent nonstructural carbohydrates (NSC) of four grass species after repeated exposure to 0.25 ppm ozone and weekly clipping for 8 weeks.

Treatment	Kentucky bluegrass			Tall fescue			Meadow fescue			Perennial ryegrass		
	Dry wt.	No. innovations	NSC	Dry wt.	No. innovation	NSC	Dry wt.	No. innovation	NSC	Dry wt.	No. innovation	NSC
	g		%	g		%	g		%	g		%
Unclipped No ozone	6.33 a*	106.6 a	21.9 a	4.36 a	26.5 b	46.7 a	4.93 a	32.3 a	35.7 a	4.81 a	77.9 a	44.4 a
Unclipped Ozone	4.72 b	87.8 b	16.5 b	4.01 a	23.3 b	45.7 a	3.97 b	36.0 a	32.7 a	4.95 a	76.5 a	45.6 a
Clipped No ozone	3.05 c	73.6 c	13.0 c	2.82 b	31.3 a	42.0 a	2.64 c	41.0 a	25.6 b	2.56 b	74.9 a	36.3 c
Clipped Ozone	1.86 d	49.8 d	6.5 d	1.70 c	23.4 b	42.5 a	2.06 d	27.4 a	19.0 c	2.33 b	67.6 a	40.6 b

* Numbers in the same column followed by the same letter do not differ significantly at the 0.05 probability level.

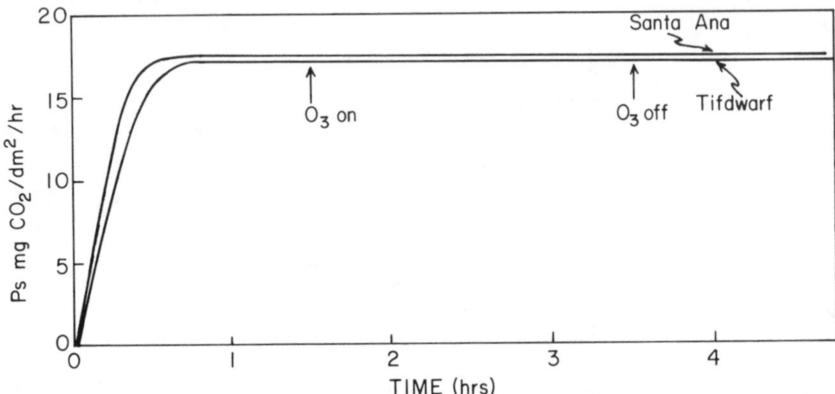

Fig. 3. Apparent photosynthesis of a susceptible (Tifgreen) and a tolerant (Santa Ana) *Cynodon* hybrid during exposure to ozone.

closure might be a mechanism for resistance to ozone injury in some turfgrasses, apparent photosynthesis was measured for an ozone-susceptible *Cynodon* hybrid ('Tifdwarf') and an ozone-resistant *Cynodon* hybrid ('Santa Ana') by the method previously described. Differences in apparent photosynthesis during exposure to ozone would indicate possible differences in stomatal closure. Figure 3 shows that there were no changes in apparent photosynthesis for either cultivar during 2 hours of 0.5-ppm ozone fumigation. Severe leaf injury was observed on Tifdwarf, but not on Santa Ana within 24 hours after fumigation. If Santa Ana's ozone resistance was due to rapid stomatal closure, this would have been indicated by a rapid drop in apparent photosynthesis. Therefore, differences in stomatal response cannot explain the differences in ozone susceptibility. This work also indicates that the internal photosynthetic apparatus of these *Cynodon* cultivars is not immediately damaged by ozone at the concentration used in this study.

Turf Culture to Reduce Injury

High soil moisture levels produce maximum sensitivity to air pollution in many plants (9). As water stress increases, causing stomatal closure, sensitivity to air pollution decreases. Similarly, low relative humidity decreases sensitivity (9). Although this relationship of stomatal closure to ozone resistance was not supported by our studies with *Cynodon* hybrids, it is possible that it may be true for other turfgrass species. Injury to those grasses from air pollution could be minimized by scheduling irrigations to avoid anticipated peak air pollution periods.

Although not conclusive, research indicates that high N levels increase susceptibility to air pollution by promoting plant succulence (3). Other nutrients may decrease sensitivity. By reducing N levels or modifying fertilizer ratios during the season of high air pollution (usually late summer), it may be possible to reduce air pollution injury.

Ozone injury was found to be less severe in unclipped Kentucky bluegrass and tall fescue plants. Therefore, it may be possible to reduce air pollution injury in some grasses by raising the cutting height during the air pollution season.

The most promising approach to reducing air pollution injury to turfgrasses is the selection of tolerant species and cultivars. As the studies discussed herein show, some species are much more tolerant than others. Breeders of turfgrasses may justifiably include tolerance to air pollution as a worthwhile additional objective.

ACKNOWLEDGMENT

The authors gratefully acknowledge the technical assistance provided by O. C. Taylor and R. Oshima of the Statewide Air Pollution Research Center and of R. A. Ackerson, formerly of the Plant Sciences Department, University of California, Riverside.

LITERATURE CITED

1. Bobrov, R. A. 1955. The leaf structure of *Poa annua* with observations on its smog sensitivity in Los Angeles County. Am. J. Bot. 42:467–474.
2. Brennan, E., and P. M. Halisky. 1970. Response of turfgrass cultivars to ozone and sulfur dioxide in the atmosphere. Phytopathology 60:1544–1546.
3. Brewer, R. F., F. B. Guillemet, and R. K. Creveling. 1961. Influence of N–P–K fertilization on incidence and severity of oxidant damage to mangels and spinach. Soil Sci. 92:298–301.
4. Dugger, W. M., Jr., O. C. Taylor, E. Cardiff, and C. R. Thompson. 1962. Relationship between carbohydrate content and susceptibility of pinto bean plants to ozone damage. Proc. Am. Soc. Hort. Sci. 81:304–315.
5. Hill, A. C., and N. Littlefield. 1969. Ozone: Effect on apparent photosynthesis, rate of transpiration and stomatal closure in plants. Environ. Sci. Technol. 3:52–56.
6. Middleton, J. T. 1956. Response of plants to air pollution. J. Air Pollut. Control Assoc. 6:1–4.
7. Mudd, J.B., and T. T. Kozlowski. 1975. Responses of plants to air pollution. Academic Press, New York.
8. Noble, W. M. 1955. The pattern of damage produced on vegetation by smog. Agric. Food Chem. 3:330–332.
9. Rich, S., and N. C. Turner. 1972. Importance of moisture on stomatal behavior of plants subjected to ozone. J. Air Pollut. Control Assoc. 22:718–721.
10. Smith, D. 1969. Removing and analyzing total nonstructural carbohydrates from plant tissue. Wisconsin Agric. Exp. Stn. Res. Rep. 41.
11. Ting, I. P., and W. M. Dugger, Jr. 1971. Ozone resistance in tobacco plants: Possible relationship to water balance. Atmos. Environ. 5:147–150.
12. Youngner, V. B., and F. J. Nudge. 1979. Air pollution oxide effects on cool-season and warm-season turfgrasses. Agron. J. 72:169–170.

Chapter 20 Tolerance of Turfgrass Cultivars to Salt[1]

KEITH AHTI
ADLY MOUSTAFA
HOWARD KAERWER

ABSTRACT

Salt is used on northern U.S. and Canadian highways to reduce ice hazards. Much of this salt washes, splashes, or sprays onto highway shoulders, killing the grass cover. Turfgrasses are also grown extensively in areas where soils are saline or where salt-laden water is used for irrigation.

This study determined the response of turfgrasses to toxic levels of NaCl applied as aqueous solutions. Plants were established in deep, open-bottomed flats. Salt solutions were applied by subirrigation through a compounded sand-clay loam soil mix.

'Fults' weeping alkaligrass (*Puccinellia distans* (L.) Parl.) was highly salt tolerant. Of the grasses tested, the fine-leaved fescues (*Festuca* spp.) had the broadest range of tolerance. 'Dawson' and 'Golfrood' red fescue [*Festuca rubra* (L.) var. trichophylla Gaud.)] were most tolerant of high salt concentrations. The Kentucky bluegrass (*Poa pratensis* (L.) cultivars evaluated did not show an extensive range of salt tolerance. Of the cultivars tested 'Nugget' was the most tolerant.

Additional index words: Turfgrass, Nitrogen nutrition, Winter hardiness.

INTRODUCTION

Turf cover is desirable on areas where excess salts damage or kill the grass. Salt used to deice highways also damages roadside grasses as does saline water if used to irrigate turf in some areas of the world. Salt-tolerant turfgrass species and cultivars are valuable for maintaining grass cover in these saline areas.

Past investigations have indicated that weeping alkaligrass (*Puccinellia distans* (L.) Parl.) possesses a high level of salt tolerance (2, 3). It has been discovered growing along saline roadsides (1). Kentucky bluegrass (*Poa pratensis* L.) is recognized as having a low level of salt tolerance (1, 2, 3). These experiments were undertaken to identify commercially available cultivars of Kentucky bluegrass and red fescue (*Festuca rubra* L.) that possess a suitable level of salt tolerance to be of value in establishment of turfgrass cover on saline soils.

[1] A contribution from the Research-Service Dep., Northrup King Co., Minneapolis, MN 55413 USA.

MATERIALS AND METHODS

A double-walled container constructed of galvanized sheet metal and consisting of an outer water jacket with drain spigot and an inner flat with a screen mesh bottom was used for the study. The inner flat (107 × 78 × 23 cm deep), when filled with soil, was subirrigated by flooding the outer jacket with water or salt solution without disturbing the soil within the inner flat. This method allowed for uniform soil depth and structure and uniform distribution of water, salts, and nutrients.

A drum was used to mix a field soil of high clay content with washed, unsized, coarse masonry sand in the ratio of one part clay soil to three parts sand. The final soil mix was classified as a sandy clay loam with approximately 15% water-holding capacity. Potassium and P were incorporated into the soil mix at the time of blending. A 3-cm layer of 3-mm diam roofing gravel was placed on the bottom of the inner flat and was topped with 15 cm of soil mix. The soil was leveled to a uniform depth. Flats were then subirrigated with fresh water to further settle the soil.

Seed treated with captan fungicide were sown either in rows or in square plots at a rate of approximately 10 seeds/cm^2 for fine fescues and 20 seeds/cm^2 for Kentucky bluegrasses and weeping alkaligrass. Rows and plots were randomized with two to four replications per flat. After planting, the seed was covered with 2 mm of finely ground peat moss and the entire flat was shrouded with clear plastic sheeting. Soil moisture from the initial subirrigation was sufficient for germination and establishment. The plastic was removed following germination. Seedlings were allowed to grow for 3 to 6 weeks prior to the first treatment with saline water. It was not necessary to rewater during this period.

The initial salinization was accomplished by subirrigation with a 0.8% NaCl solution containing soluble N fertilizer (4). Subsequent irrigations were made with 0.8 to 1.25% NaCl solutions applied approximately every 3 to 6 weeks, or as needed to prevent wilting. The salt solution was poured into the outer jacket to a point above the soil level of the inner flat. This procedure allowed solution to move from bottom to top, fully saturating the soil. After 30 to 60 min the excess solution was drained off. No attempt was made to maintain a closed system by recycling drainage water. The concentration of the salt solution, the number of irrigations, and the clay content of the soil controlled the salt level in the soil.

Salt levels were determined by soil tests. Soil samples to a depth of 10 cm were taken with a core sampler 2 to 4 weeks after each salting from relatively dry soil. Eight to 10 cores were taken at random from each flat and combined for analysis by the University of Minnesota Soil Testing Laboratory, St. Paul. Each sample was analyzed for pH, texture, organic matter, total soluble salts, P, and exchangeable K. Primary measure of the salt level was electrical conductivity (EC_e) of a standard saturation extract expressed in mmhos/cm at 25 C. The saturation extract was prepared using demineralized water with an equilibration time of 2 hours. The EC_e was read using a conductivity bridge.

The flats were maintained in a growth chamber or greenhouse for approximately 90 days, or until most entries appeared dead. They were mowed to a height of 5 cm when shoot growth reached 7 to 10 cm. This occurred approximately once a week initially and less frequently as growth decreased. Clippings were removed. Appearance notes were taken four to six times during the experiment on a subjective 1 to 9 rating system where 1 represents ideal appearance and 9 represents death.

Species evaluated included: weeping alkaligrass; red fescue with strong rhizomes (*Festuca rubra* L. var. *rubra*); red fescue with fine rhizomes (*F. rubra* L. var. *trichophylla* Gaud.); chewings fescue (*F. rubra* L. var. *commutata* Gaud.); hard fescue (*F. ovina* spp. *duriuscula* L. Koch); sheep fescue (*F. ovina* L. var. *tenuifolia* Sibth. Dum.); Kentucky bluegrass.

RESULTS

Weeping Alkaligrass

'Fults' weeping alkaligrass was highly salt tolerant in all experiments. This cultivar was planted in each test as a salt-tolerant control against which the fine fescues and Kentucky bluegrasses were compared. It was green, healthy, and vigorous at soil salt levels of $EC_e \times 10^3 = 32$ mmhos/cm after 80 days exposure (see Table 2). High salt levels did not materially injure Fults in any of the experiments. These tests did not identify the maximum salt level or exposure time which Fults can withstand.

Fine Fescues

A series of three experiments were conducted in 1975 and 1976 at Woodland, Calif. and Minneapolis, Minn. in which 19 fine fescue cultivars plus Fults weeping alkaligrass were assessed for relative salt tolerance. The three tests were handled as described in "Materials and Methods" with minor variations in frequency of watering, salt irrigations, mowing, and test duration. The results from all three tests were consistent. results from two of the experiments are included in this report (Tables 1, 2).

Fine rhizome red fescue cultivars 'Dawson' and 'Golfrood' were found to be the most tolerant of high soil salt levels. These cultivars showed very little deterioration in quality when grown for 71 days at salt levels of 32 mmhos/cm (Table 2). These tests did not determine the maximum salt levels or exposure times required to kill or severely damage these cultivars.

A number of the creeping red fescues with strong rhizomes displayed intermediate salt tolerance. 'Ruby', 'Rainier', 'Steinacher', and 'Illahee' all survived the tests to some extent but were judged to have poorer turf quality than Dawson and Golfrood. These cultivars showed 50% or more

Table 1. Appearance† of 18 fescue cultivars grown in saline soil at Woodland, Calif.

Cultivar	27 days from first salt	31 days from first salt	45 days from first salt	Mean
Dawson	3.0†	2.5	2.5	2.7
Golfrood	3.0	3.5	2.0	2.8
Common red fescue	3.5	3.0	4.5	3.7
Durlawn	4.0	4.5	4.5	4.3
Illahee	4.5	4.5	4.5	6.5
Ruby	4.0	5.0	5.0	4.7
Rainier	3.5	5.0	6.0	4.8
Centurion	4.5	4.5	6.0	5.0
Scaldis	4.5	4.5	7.0	5.3
Pennlawn	5.5	6.0	5.0	5.5
Steinacher	5.0	5.0	7.0	5.7
Atlanta	5.0	5.5	7.0	5.8
Jamestown	4.5	5.0	8.5	6.0
Wintergreen	5.0	5.5	7.5	6.0
Barok	5.5	6.0	6.5	6.0
Waldorf	5.5	5.0	8.0	6.2
Durar	6.0	6.5	6.0	6.2
Firmaula	6.5	7.0	7.5	7.0
P. distans—Fults	2.5	2.5	1.5	2.2
F value	2.0	6.3	10.1	
L.S.D.	2.2	1.1	1.9	
C.V. (%)	22.8	16.8	15.5	

† Appearance rating 1 to 9, 1 = ideal and 9 = dead.

dead leaves. The turf quality of these grasses deteriorated as the experiments progressed but at a slower rate than the very salt-sensitive cultivars.

A third group of cultivars, including 'Scaldis' and 'Centurion' hard fescues, 'Pennlawn' and common creeping red fescues, and 'Atlanta' chewings fescue, displayed a low level of tolerance. These cultivars deteriorated in quality at lower salt levels and with shorter exposure times than did the more tolerant cultivars. These fescues generally contained a low percentage of surviving plants (usually 20 to 40% at the termination of the experiments). Except when salt levels were low at the beginning of the experiments, the turf quality of these cultivars was unacceptable.

The least tolerant group of cultivars included 'Wintergreen', 'Waldorf', and 'Jamestown' chewings fescues, 'Firmaula' and 'Barok' sheep fescue, and 'Durar' hard fescue. These cultivars were severely damaged at an early date and no green tissue remained at the termination of the tests.

In the Minneapolis experiment, growth of all cultivars had ceased after 60 days at the $EC_e \times 10^3$ = 32 mmhos/cm. The grass was then clipped to a height of 1 cm and regrowth was observed 80 days following the initial salting. Only Dawson and Golfrood produced new shoot growth.

Kentucky Bluegrass

Two Kentucky bluegrass experiments were conducted at Minneapolis, Minn. in 1976 and 1977. The two tests were handled as described in "Materials and Methods." Relative tolerance rank was approximately the same in the two tests.

Table 2. Appearance† of 18 fescue cultivars grown in saline soil at Minneapolis, Minn.

Cultivar	52 days from first salt	71 days from first salt	Mean
Dawson	2.0†	2.4	2.2
Golfrood	3.0	2.5	2.8
Durlawn	3.5	5.5	6.5
Rainier	5.2	6.0	5.6
Ruby	6.8	6.5	5.7
Steinacher	5.0	6.5	5.8
Illahee	5.2	6.6	5.9
Common red fescue	5.5	7.0	6.3
Scaldis	6.2	7.0	6.6
Pennlawn	5.8	8.0	6.9
Atlanta	6.0	8.4	7.2
Centurion	6.8	8.0	7.4
Barok	7.0	8.3	7.7
Firmaula	7.2	8.3	7.8
Jamestown	6.8	9.0	7.9
Waldorf	6.8	9.0	7.9
Wintergreen	7.5	9.0	8.3
Durar	8.0	9.0	8.5
P. distans—Fults	1.0	2.8	1.9
F value	45.4	47.4	
L.S.D.	0.8	1.0	
C.V. (%)	7.1	9.8	

† Appearance rating 1 to 9, 1 = ideal and 9 = dead.

The most salt-tolerant cultivar of Kentucky bluegrass was 'Nugget' (Tables 3, 4). This cultivar maintained a healthy, dark-green color with good stand density and very little leaf browning throughout the experiments. At a salt level of $EC_e \times 10^3$ = 32 mmhos/cm and 60 days exposure, Nugget began to show considerable damage and deteriorated with time. The other Kentucky bluegrasses were killed or severely damaged at this level of soil salt. Nugget was the only cultivar with an acceptable tolerance level.

One experimental cultivar, 'K1-148', showed a greater level of tolerance than all other cultivars except Nugget (Table 4). Its quality was acceptable. 'Parade' Kentucky bluegrass showed intermediate tolerance in both tests and was significantly better than all cultivars except 'Nugget' and 'K1-148' (Tables 3, 4).

A large group of cultivars and experimental sections were less tolerant and were judged unacceptable. This group included 'Windsor', 'Victa', 'Fylking', 'A-34', 'Newport', 'Majestic', 'Aquila', 'Park', and 'Baron'. At the termination of the experiments, most plants of these cultivars were dead. The least tolerant group of cultivars included 'Merion', 'Adelphi', 'Bonnieblue', 'Vantage', 'Prato', and 'Pennstar'.

DISCUSSION

These experiments indicate salt tolerance differences between species as follows: weeping alkaligrass > red fescue > Kentucky bluegrass > chewings fescue > hard fescue = sheep fescue. Individual cultivars were ranked as follows: Fults weeping alkaligrass > Dawson and Golfrood red

Table 3. Appearance† of 13 Kentucky bluegrass cultivars grown in saline soil.

Cultivar	61 days from first salt	75 days from first salt	Mean
Nugget	3.0	4.3	3.6
Pennstar	4.3	7.0	5.6
Parade	4.8	6.5	5.6
Park	5.0	7.0	6.0
Aquila	5.0	7.5	6.3
Fylking	5.3	7.5	6.4
Victa	5.3	7.5	6.4
Adelphi	5.8	8.0	6.9
Newport	6.0	7.8	6.9
Code 95	5.5	8.3	6.9
Rubgy	6.3	7.8	7.0
Prato	6.8	8.0	7.4
Merion	7.8	8.0	7.9
P. distans (Fults)	3.2	2.8	3.0
Dawson (Red fescue)	3.8	3.0	3.4

S.E. between two cultivars = 0.50
S.E. between two salints = 0.40
S.E. for saltings over cultivars = 0.9
S.E. for cultivars over salting = 1.03

† Appearance rating 1 to 9, 1 = ideal and 9 = dead.

fescues > Nugget Kentucky bluegrass > Parade and K1-148 Kentucky bluegrasses. The more tolerant bluegrass cultivars produced better turf quality than did any of the fine fescues except Dawson and Golfrood.

Table 4. Appearance† of 23 Kentucky bluegrass cultivars grown in saline soil.

Cultivar	87 days from first salt	97 days from first salt	Mean
Nugget	3.0	4.0	3.5
K1-148	3.5	5.5	4.5
Bristol	5.5	6.0	5.3
Parade	4.5	6.5	5.5
Sydsport	5.5	7.0	6.3
Windsor	5.5	7.0	6.3
Cheri	5.5	7.0	6.3
Victa	5.5	7.5	6.5
Touchdown	5.5	7.5	6.5
A-34 (seeded)	5.0	8.0	6.5
Fylking	6.0	7.5	6.8
Newport	6.0	7.5	6.8
Rugby	5.5	8.0	6.8
Park	6.0	8.5	7.3
South Dakota Certified	6.0	9.0	7.5
Aquila	6.0	9.0	7.5
Majestic	6.0	9.0	7.5
Baron	6.5	8.5	7.5
Bonnieblue	6.5	9.0	7.8
Pennstar	7.5	8.5	8.0
Adelphi	7.0	9.0	8.0
Merion	7.0	9.0	8.0
Vantage	7.0	9.0	8.0
P. distans—Fults	3.0	4.0	3.5
Dawson (Red fescue)	3.5	4.0	3.8

S.E. for comparison between two cultivars = 0.59
S.E. for comparison between two salting dates = 0.10
S.E. for saltings at the same cultivar = 0.61
S.E. for cultivars at the same level of salting = 0.60

† Appearance rating 1 to 9, 1 = ideal and 9 = dead.

Both the red fescues and Kentucky bluegrasses displayed a broad range of cultivar differences in salt tolerance. Some of the red fescue cultivars displayed variable salt tolerance; i.e., a small number of surviving plants were noted in cultivars, most of which were killed at high salt levels.

Each species and cultivar had different growth patterns. At the conclusion of one test at Minneapolis, Minn., Fults, Dawson, and Golfrood remained green, but Fults displayed more vigor. In the Woodland, Calif., experiment where high greenhouse temperatures and drought stress were factors, all three cultivars remained green but Dawson displayed the most vigor. Thus, seed mixtures containing different species and more than one cultivar should prove superior to the cover provided by a single cultivar. Also, it should be possible to structure mixtures that would utilize the strengths of various cultivars for specific use situations. Seed mixtures used along roadsides in the northern U.S., where salt hazard tends to be seasonal, may require different formulas than those best suited for the western U.S., where the salt hazard stems from permanent high soil salt levels and where growth is hampered further by using saline irrigation waters, high daytime temperatures, and lower annual precipitation.

These experiments were managed so that the salt hazard developed after the grasses were well established. No attempt was made to establish stands in previously salinized soil.

LITERATURE CITED

1. Butler, J. D., T. D. Hughes, G. D. Sanks, and P. R. Craig. 1971. Salt causes problems along Illinois highways. Ill. Res., Fall p. 3–4.
2. Hughes, T. D., J. D. Butler, and G. D. Sanks. 1975. Salt tolerance and suitability of various grasses for saline roadsides. J. Environ. Qual. 4(1):65–68.
3. Lunt, O. R., V. B. Youngner, and J. J. Oertli. 1961. Salinity tolerance of five turfgrass varieties. Agron. J. 53:247–249.
4. U.S. Salinity Laboratory Staff. 1954. Diagnosis and improvement of saline and alkali soils. Agric. Handb. No. 60, USDA, U.S. Government Printing Office, Washington, D.C.

Section IV:

Soil Reaction, Fertilization, and Root Zone Modification

Chapter 21 Lime Responses of Kentucky Bluegrass and Tall Fescue Cultivars on an Acid, Aluminum-Toxic Soil[1]

J. J. MURRAY
C. D. FOY

ABSTRACT

Kentucky bluegrass (*Poa pratensis* L.) and tall fescue (*Festuca arundinacea* Schreb.) cultivars, chosen to represent acid-tolerant and sensitive extremes, were grown for 6 weeks in greenhouse pots (1 kg) of Al-toxic Tatum soil (clayey, mixed thermic, typic, Hapludults) limed to a pH range of 4.1 to 7.9.

Kentucky bluegrass cultivars differed significantly in tolerance to the acid, Al-toxic soil. 'Fylking', 'Victa,' 'Pennstar', 'Touchdown', and 'Majestic' were among the most tolerant and 'Kenblue', 'Windsor', and 'South Dakota Common' were among the most sensitive at pH 5.0. Relative shoot yields (pH 5.0% /pH 5.7%) varied from 94% for Majestic to only 28% for Kenblue. Among the acid-tolerant group, Fylking and Victa yielded as well at pH 7.3 and 7.6 as at 5.7, but Pennstar declined in yield at the higher pH levels. Acid-tolerant cultivars (pH 4.4 to 5.0) were also most tolerant to alkaline soil (pH 7.3 to 7.6). For example, the relative yields (pH 7.6% /pH 5.7%) for Kenblue and Windsor were only 37 and 42%, respectively, compared with 100% for Fylking and 96% for Victa.

Tall fescue was much more tolerant to acid soil than Kentucky bluegrass; however, cultivars differed significantly in tolerance. For example, the relative shoot yields (pH 4.1% /pH 6.7%) ranged from 46% for 'Kentucky 31' to 20% for 'Kenmont'. Unlike Kentucky bluegrass, acid-tolerant cultivars (pH 4.1) were most sensitive to alkaline soil (pH 7.4 to 7.9). Yields of shoots and roots were highly correlated.

INTRODUCTION

Aluminum toxicity is an important growth-limiting factor in many acid soils (5, 13, 22), especially those below pH 5.0 (10, 13, 23), but it has been reported at soil pH values as high as 5.5 (1, 12). Detrimental effects of strongly acid soils (below pH 5.5) on many turfgrasses include a general decline in shoot and root growth, vigor, and competitive ability. These effects may result from decreased tolerance to environmental stresses, such as mineral element toxicity or unavailability and drought (2).

Optimum soil pH ranges for many turfgrass species have been determined (2). However, on many sites the conventional practice of liming the soil to some optimum level is not economically feasible. Soil acidity

[1] A contribution from the Field Crops Laboratory, Plant Genetics and Germplasm Inst. and the Plant Stress Laboratory, Plant Physiology Inst., Beltsville Agric. Res. Ctr., SEA, USDA, Beltsville, MD 20705 USA.

under turfgrass sod is not always corrected by liming. Lime moves slowly through the soil profile (15) and there is no practical method for cultivating soils under established turfgrass sod.

Several agronomic crop species, and cultivars within species, differ widely in tolerance to soil acidity and excess soluble or exchangeable Al (4, 6, 8, 9, 10, 11, 21, 23). Some of these differences are genetically controlled (3, 14, 19, 22). Murray and Foy (16) reported that Kentucky bluegrass (*Poa pratensis* L.) and tall fescue (*Festuca arundinacea* Schreb.) cultivars vary widely in tolerance to acid, Al-toxic soil. Further, a few plants within several cultivars of tall fescue showed a high level of tolerance. These results indicated a good potential for selecting germplasm of these species with increased tolerance to acid soil conditions. Randall (18) increased the Al tolerance of perennial ryegrass (*Lolium perenne* L.) considerably after two generations of selection. Thus, an alternative or supplementary approach to liming to correct soil acidity problems may be to select or develop cultivars having greater tolerance to strongly acid, Al-toxic soils. The physiological and biochemical mechanisms of plant tolerance to excess Al are not clearly understood. However, it is not absolutely essential that they be understood in breeding for tolerance.

In previous studies, the most sensitive cultivars to acid (pH 4.3 to 4.6), Al-toxic soil conditions produced more root growth than tolerant cultivars when soil was limed to increase its pH (pH 5.7) and eliminate Al toxicity (Murray and Foy, unpublished data). This indicated that acid-tolerant cultivars may have a disadvantage over nontolerant cultivars under nonacid soil conditions. The objectives of the work reported here were to: (i) confirm the previously established relative tolerance of cultivars to acid soil; (ii) determine the relative responses of sensitive and tolerant cultivars to a wide range of soil pH and available Al levels. Our long-range objective is to develop genotypes that are better adapted to acid soil stress conditions that are not economically correctable.

MATERIALS AND METHODS

To determine the relative responses to lime among sensitive and tolerant cultivars within species, 12 Kentucky bluegrass and seven tall fescue cultivars were seeded in greenhouse pots (1.0 kg) of Al-toxic Tatum soil (clayey, mixed thermic, typic, Hapludults) at six pH levels (4.1 to 7.9). Kentucky bluegrass cultivars were selected based on their relative growth on tatum soil at pH 4.6 vs. 5.7 (16). The soil was treated with 0, 250, 1,700, 3,500, 7,000, or 14,000 ppm $CaCO_3$ to establish the pH levels. Previous studies showed that 3,000 ppm $CaCO_3$ prevented Al toxicity on this soil (5, 19). The basic fertilizer treatment was 100, 109, and 137 ppm of N, P, and K, respectively, added as NH_4NO_3 and KH_2PO_4. Treatments were replicated three times for cultivars within each grass species.

Acid Tatum soil (previously described) from near Orange, Va., USA is a reliable growth medium in which to screen plants for Al tolerance (7,

20). Unlike many acid soils, Tatum does not contain levels of Mn that are toxic to grasses studied to date. Before fertilizer and lime were added, this soil had an average pH of 4.17 (1:1 soil:water suspension), contained 7.82 meq of KCl-extractable Al/100 g, and had a cation exchange capacity (1*N* NH_4OAc at pH 7.0) of 11.7 meq/100 g. Other cations per 100 g extracted with 1*N* NH_4OAc were: 0.05 meq of Ca; 0.24 meq of Mg; 0.25 meq of K; 0.005 meq of Mn. Distilled water was used for irrigation throughout the experiment. A predetermined amount of water was added after seeding to wet the soil thoroughly. Thereafter, water was added as necessary to promote active growth without saturating the soil. A temperature of 24 to 26 C was maintained, except for short periods on sunny days when the temperature reached 30 ± 2 C.

Dry matter yields of plant shoots and roots were used as measures of response to lime treatments. Kentucky bluegrass plants were harvested at 46 days and tall fescue plants at 50 days after seeding. Plant shoots were harvested by clipping at approximately 0.5 cm above the soil, dried at 46 C, and weighed. Roots of selected cultivars, varying in response to lime levels, were harvested, washed, dried, and weighed. Aluminum concentrations (1*N* KCl-extract) in the soil were determined for each lime level at the start of the experiment.

RESULTS AND DISCUSSION

Mean yields for all cultivars of Kentucky bluegrass and tall fescue shoots increased and soil Al concentrations decreased with increasing increments of lime up to 3,500 ppm (Table 1). However, the increase in yield of tall fescue between 1,700 and 3,500 ppm $CaCO_3$ was not significant ($P \leq 0.05$). These results agreed with those of our previous studies in which shoot and root yields of these two species were closely related to decreases in Al concentrations of Tatum soil obtained by liming (16). The difference in relative yields between species at 1,700 ppm $CaCO_3$ may be explained by the difference in soil pH (Al concentrations) at harvest. At

Table 1. Effects of lime on yield of tall fescue and Kentucky bluegrass shoots and on pH and KCl-extractable Al in tatum soil.* †

		Tall fescue			Kentucky bluegrass		
$CaCO_3$ added	Soil Al	Yield of shoots	Relative yields	Soil pH	Yield of shoots	Relative yields	Soil pH
ppm	meq/100 g	g/pot			g/pot		
0	7.91	1.11 e	33.2	4.1	0.00 –	0	4.0
250	4.31	2.00 d	59.9	4.6	0.14 d	3.7	4.4
1,700	0.41	3.24 a	97.0	5.5	2.94 c	77.2	5.0
3,500	0.02	3.34 a	100.0	6.7	3.81 a	100.0	5.7
7,000	0.09	3.03 b	90.7	7.4	3.16 b	82.9	7.3
14,000	1.13	2.78 c	83.2	7.9	2.77 c	72.7	7.6

* Within a species any two yields having a letter in common are not significantly different at the 5% level by the Duncan multiple range test. † Soil Al (1*N* KCl-extractable) at planting. Yields are averages of three replications. Soil pH (1:1 soil:water) averages of three replications at harvest.

this lime level, the average soil pH's in pots of tall fescue and Kentucky bluegrass were 5.5 and 5.0, respectively. A small decrease in pH of Tatum soil at 5.5 results in a substantial increase in Al concentration of the soil solution (7).

Yields of plant shoots and roots for both species were maximum for the 3,500 ppm $CaCO_3$ treatment, corresponding to final soil pH levels of 5.7 for Kentucky bluegrass and 6.7 for tall fescue. Within this pH range, Al is not soluble in toxic concentrations for either species. The relative reductions in yields with lime treatments, either above or below the optimum (3,500 ppm) were greater for Kentucky bluegrass than for tall fescue (Table 1). For example, the relative yields with increasing lime levels (3,500 ppm $CaCO_3$ %/14,000 ppm $CaCO_3$ %) were 83.2% for tall fescue and 72.7% for Kentucky bluegrass. Relative yields with decreasing lime levels (3,500 ppm $CaCO_3$ %/250 ppm $CaCO_3$ %) were 59.9% for tall fescue and only 3.7% for Kentucky bluegrass. In Tatum soil with no lime added (pH 4.0 to 4.1), the mean yield of tall fescue was 1.11 g/pot or 33% of that with 3,500 ppm (pH 6.7) $CaCO_3$; with no lime added, Kentucky bluegrass either did not germinate or died. These results generally agree with published reports (2, 17) that tall fescue will tolerate a wider range of soil pH than Kentucky bluegrass.

We did not determine the cause of the yield decline with lime levels above 3,500 ppm. No deficiency or toxicity symptoms were observed. However, in general, a decrease in yield would suggest the unavailability of one or more micronutrients. The increase in Al concentration (1.13 meq/100 g) of the soil solution when the soil was treated with 14,000 ppm $CaCO_3$ could have resulted in Al toxicity (Al soluble as anion rather than cation), but this would not explain the decrease in yield with 7,000 ppm $CaCO_3$ (soil Al = 0.09 meq/100 g).

Correlation coefficients between yields of plant roots and shoots for all lime levels were $r = 0.82$ for tall fescue and $r = 0.79$ for Kentucky bluegrass. Both r-values were highly significant ($P \leq 0.01$). Thus, the response to lime applications can be effectively measured by either the dry weight of roots or shoots. We chose to discuss our results based on yields of shoots. The relationship between root and shoot growth of Kentucky bluegrass is illustrated in Fig. 1.

Shoot yields of the 12 Kentucky bluegrasses on Tatum soil treated with different lime levels are shown in Table 2. The top part of the table shows the absolute yields in g/pot and the r-values between lime treatments and cultivars. The bottom part of the table shows yields expressed as percentages of the maximum yields obtained with lime. The treatment without lime was discarded because germination did not occur or plants died during the experiment. Thus, to test Kentucky bluegrasses it is necessary to add small amounts of lime to permit survival of even the more tolerant genotypes.

Kentucky bluegrass cultivars differed significantly in response to lime levels (Table 2). Although the order of relative tolerance to acid, Al-toxic Tatum soil was somewhat different from that of previous studies

Fig. 1. Shoot and root growth of Fylking (A) and Kenblue (B) Kentucky bluegrass cultivars on acid, Al-toxic Tatum soil limed to pH 4.4 (2), 5.0 (3), 5.7 (4), 7.3 (5), and 7.6 (6), 46 days old.

(unpublished data), the overall grouping of cultivars according to tolerance was about the same. For example, in previous tests 'Fylking' and 'Victa' were the most tolerant and'Windsor' and 'Kenblue' were the most

Table 2. Shoot yields of Kentucky bluegrass cultivars on Tatum soil at different lime levels and correlations between soil pH and yields.

	$CaCO_3$ added (ppm)					
	250	1,700	3,500	7,000	14,000	
	Avg. soil pH					Yield vs. soil pH correlation coefficient (r)
Cultivar	4.4	5.0	5.7	7.3	7.6	
	Yield of plant shoots (g/pot)†					
Fylking	0.56 a	3.21 ab	3.66 cd	3.78 abc	3.92 a	0.73**
Pennstar	0.33 b	3.15 ab	3.78 a-d	2.41 ef	2.69 bc	0.38
Touchdown	0.31 b	3.34 ab	4.04 abc	3.91 ab	2.83 bc	0.59*
Majestic	0.20 bc	2.99 ab	2.83 e	3.17 b-e	2.33 cd	0.51*
Victa	0.19 bc	3.76 a	4.46 a	4.49 a	4.29 a	0.68**
Bonnieblue	0.06 c	3.72 a	4.10 abc	3.42 bcd	3.25 b	0.49
Adelphi	0.00 c	3.41 ab	3.81 a-d	3.60 a-d	2.67 bc	0.49
Vantage	0.00 c	3.18 ab	3.75 bcd	2.75 def	2.75 bc	0.48
Merion	0.00 c	3.10 ab	3.87 a-d	3.31 b-e	2.37 cd	0.48
South Dakota Common	0.00 c	2.65 b	4.42 ab	2.88 c-f	3.04 b	0.53*
Windsor	0.00 c	1.76 c	3.67 cd	2.18 f	1.86 d	0.37
Kenblue	0.00 c	0.96 d	3.32 de	2.01 f	1.23 e	0.39
	Yield of plant shoots (% of maximum)‡					
Fylking	14	82	93	96	100	
Pennstar	9	83	100	64	71	
Touchdown	8	83	100	97	70	
Majestic	6	94	89	100	74	
Victa	4	84	99	100	96	
Bonnieblue	1	91	100	84	79	
Adelphi	0	90	100	94	71	
Vantage	0	85	100	74	73	
Merion	0	81	100	86	62	
South Dakota Common	0	59	100	65	68	
Windsor	0	47	100	59	42	
Kenblue	0	28	100	61	37	

*,** Significant at the 5 and 1% levels of probability, respectively. † Average of three replications. Within a given lime level any two cultivar yields having a letter in common are not significantly different at the 5% level by the Duncan multiple range test. ‡ Yield expressed as a percentage of the maximum yield attained with $CaCO_3$.

sensitive cultivars based on relative (pH 4.6%/pH 5.7%) shoot yields. Generally, the most acid-tolerant cultivars were also the most tolerant to alkaline soil conditions. This disagrees with most reports with other crop species (8). Acid-tolerant cultivars can be divided into two groups based on their response to lime treatments. One group yields near maximum shoot growth over a wide range of soil pH levels. The other group declines in yield more rapidly at higher soil pH levels. Fylking and Victa are examples of the first group and 'Pennstar' exemplifies the second. Cultivars most sensitive to acid soil conditions were also more sensitive to the higher soil pH range than were acid-tolerant cultivars. Windsor and Kenblue are examples of acid-sensitive cultivars within very narrow pH ranges when compared with acid-tolerant cultivars such as Fylking (Table 2; Fig. 1). These results show that Kentucky bluegrasses vary widely in soil pH levels needed for maximum growth and in their tolerance to a range of pH levels above and below their optimum level. Our results suggest that the relative yield of a cultivar under acid soil conditions reflects its tolerance to a range of soil pH levels. Thus, acid-tolerant cultivars should be better adapted than nontolerant cultivars over a wider range of soil pH levels.

On Tatum soil at pH 4.4, only six Kentucky bluegrass cultivars produced measurable amounts of shoots. Liming to pH 5.0 substantially increased yields of all cultivars. However, at pH 5.0 nine cultivars were not significantly different in yields of shoots (Table 2). This indicates that for testing Kentucky bluegrasses for tolerance to acid, Al-toxic conditions the best pH of Tatum soil would be in the range of pH 4.4 to 5.0. Yields of plant shoots for most cultivars were maximum at pH 5.7. However, the pH level needed for maximum yields varied for acid-tolerant cultivars. For example, the maximum yields of Fylking, Victa, and Pennstar were obtained at pH levels 7.6, 7.3, and 5.7, respectively. This indicates that acid-tolerant cultivars would not be at a disadvantage over nontolerant cultivars under nonacid soil conditions, but the optimum soil pH for acid-tolerant cultivars may be different and generally higher than that for nontolerant cultivars. Selecting acid-tolerant genotypes based on relative growth on Tatum soil limed to pH levels 4.4+ and 5.7 is a valid selection method. Although some acid-tolerant cultivars yielded slightly more at pH levels above 5.7, comparing acid soil tolerance at pH 4.4 vs. 5.7 does not change the acid tolerance rankings of the cultivars studied. For example, the relative yield of Fylking at pH 5.7 would have been 16% instead of 15% but the order of tolerance would not have changed.

Tall fescue cultivars also differed in response to lime levels on Al-

Table 3. Shoot yields of tall fescue cultivars on Tatum soil at different lime levels and correlations between yields and soil pH.

	$CaCO_3$ added (ppm)						
	0	250	1,700	3,500	7,000	14,000	
	Avg. soil pH						Yield vs. soil pH correlation coefficient (r)
Cultivar	4.1	4.6	5.5	6.7	7.4	7.9	
	Yield of plant shoot (g/pot)†						
Kentucky 31	1.70 a	2.53 a	3.50 a	3.66 a	3.28 a	2.56 bc	0.39
Kenhy	1.32 b	2.04 bc	3.73 a	3.32 b	2.77 c	2.63 abc	0.38
Alta	1.18 b	1.84 c	3.08 bc	3.25 b	3.11 ab	2.53 c	0.54*
Fawn	0.99 c	1.92 c	3.28 b	3.70 a	3.30 a	2.77 a	0.58*
Goar	0.83 d	2.20 b	3.09 bc	3.13 b	2.82 bc	2.98 a	0.61**
Kenwell	0.73 de	1.95 c	2.94 c	3.06 b	2.96 b	2.69 ab	0.63**
Kenmont	0.66 e	1.50 d	3.03 c	3.29 b	3.24 a	3.00 a	0.71**
	Yield of plant shoots (% of maximum)‡						
Kentucky 31	46	69	96	100	90	69	
Kenhy	38	63	100	98	81	77	
Alta	36	57	95	100	96	78	
Fawn	27	52	88	100	89	75	
Goar	26	70	99	100	90	95	
Kenwell	23	64	96	100	96	87	
Kenmont	20	45	92	100	98	91	

*,** Significant at the 5 and 1% levels of probability, respectively. † Average of three replications. Within a given lime level any two cultivar yields having a letter in common are not significantly different at the 5% level by the Duncan multiple range test. ‡ Yield expressed as a percentage of the maximum yield attained with $CaCO_3$.

toxic Tatum soil (Table 3). Shoot dry weights of all cultivars increased markedly as soil neutrality was approached and then decreased as the soil became alkaline. However, in contrast to Kentucky bluegrass, yield reductions of acid-sensitive cultivars were less than those of acid-tolerant cultivars. For example, 'Kenmont' (acid sensitive) yielded 91% and 'Kentucky 31' (acid tolerant) yielded 69% of their maximum at pH 7.9. The greater tolerance of acid-sensitive cultivars to alkaline conditions is also indicated by the significant positive linear relationship between cultivar yields and soil pH levels (Table 3). Yields of all cultivars except 'Kenhy' were maximum at pH 6.7. Kenhy's maximum yield was obtained at pH 5.5. For all cultivars, yields decreased more drastically on the acid side of their yield plateaus than on the alkaline side.

Cultivar differences in yield were maximum at pH 4.1. Increments of lime to increase the soil pH and eliminate toxic concentrations of Al reduced yield differences between cultivars. For example, 'Fawn', which was among the more acid-sensitive cultivars, yielded as much as the most tolerant cultivars when the soil was limed to pH 6.7. This shows that yield differences between these cultivars on the unlimed soil (pH 4.1) were not due to differences in their natural growth habit. This test confirmed the relative tolerance to acid, Al-toxic Tatum soil established previously among cultivars (unpublished data).

Results of this test substantiate previous work indicating the practicability of selecting and developing tall fescue cultivars for increased tolerance to acid soil conditions (16). The wide variation in tolerance to higher soil pH levels observed among cultivars in this study also suggests a potential for breeding cultivars having greater tolerance to alkaline soil conditions. Maximum separation of genotypes for tolerance to alkaline conditions should probably be done on naturally calcareous soils. We made no attempt to determine the cause of yield decline at the higher soil pH levels. Although no obvious deficiency symptoms occurred, a decrease in yield would suggest the unavailability of one or more micronutrients.

LITERATURE CITED

1. Adams, F., and Z. F. Lund. 1966. Effect of chemical activity of soil solution Al on cotton root penetration of acid subsoils. Soil Sci. 101:193–198.
2. Beard, J. B. 1973. Turfgrass: Science and culture. Prentice-Hall, Inc., Englewood Cliffs, N.J.
3. Devine, T. E., C. D. Foy, A. L. Fleming, C. H. Hanson, T. A. Campbell, J. E. McMurtrey, III, and J. W. Schwartz. 1976. Development of alfalfa strains with differential tolerances to aluminum toxicity. Plant Soil 44:73–79.
4. Fleming, A. L., J. W. Schwartz, and C. D. Foy. 1974. Chemical factors controlling the adaptation of weeping lovegrass and tall fescue to acid mine spoils. Agron. J. 66: 715–719.
5. Foy, C. D. 1974. Effects of aluminum on plant growth. p. 601–642. *In* E. W. Carson (ed.) The plant root and its environment. Univ. Press of Virginia, University Station, Charlottesville.
6. ———. 1975. Differential aluminum and manganese tolerance of plant species and varieties in acid soils. Cien. Cult. 28(2):150–155.

7. ———, W. H. Armiger, L. W. Briggle, and D. A. Reid. 1965. Differential aluminum tolerance of wheat and barley varieties in acid soils. Agron. J. 57:413–417.
8. ———, A. L. Fleming, and G. C. Gerloff. 1972. Differential aluminum tolerance in two snapbean varieties. Agron. J. 64:815–818.
9. ———, R. G. Orellana, J. W. Schwartz, and A. L. Fleming. 1974. Response of sunflower genotypes to aluminum in acid soil and nutrient solution. Agron. J. 66:293–296.
10. Gilbert, B. E., and F. R. Pember. 1935. Tolerance of certain weeds and grasses to aluminum. Soil Sci. 39:425–429.
11. Hardy, F. 1926. The role of aluminum in acid soil infertility and toxicity. J. Agric. Sci. 16:616–631.
12. Hester, J. B. 1935. The amphoteric nature of three coastal plains soils. I. In relation to plant growth. Soil Sci. 39:237–243.
13. Kamprath, E. J., and C. D. Foy. 1971. Lime-fertilizer-plant interactions in acid soils. p. 105–151. *In* R. A. Olson, T. J. Army, J. J. Hanway, and V. J. Kilmer (eds.) Fertilizer technology and use. Second Ed. Soil Sci. Soc. Am., Madison, Wis.
14. Kerridge, P. C., and W. E. Kronstad. 1968. Evidence of genetic resistance to aluminum toxicity in wheat (*Triticum aestivum* Vill, Host). Agron. J. 60:710–711.
15. Longnecker, T. C., and H. B. Sprague. 1940. Rate of penetration of lime in soils under permanent grass. Soil Sci. 50:277–288.
16. Murray, J. J., C. D. Foy, and J. P. Knorr. 1976. Differential lime responses of turfgrass cultivars on an acid soil high in exchangeable aluminum. Agronomy Abstracts. p. 102.
17. Musser, H. B. 1950. Turf management. McGraw-Hill Book Co., Inc., New York.
18. Randall, P. J. 1963. Resistance to aluminum and manganese toxicity. Rep. Welsh Plant Breed. Stn. p. 21–22.
19. Reid, David A. 1975. Genetic control of Al response in barley. Agron. Abstr. p. 63.
20. ———, G. D. Jones, W. H. Armiger, C. D. Foy, E. J. Koch, and T. M. Starling. 1969. Differential aluminum tolerance of winter barley varieties and selections in associated greenhouse and field experiments. Agron. J. 61:218–222.
21. Shoop, G. J., C. R. Brooks, R. E. Blaser, and G. W. Thomas. 1961. Differential responses of grasses and legumes to liming and phosphorus fertilization. Agron. J. 53:111–115.
22. Silva, A. R. 1976. Melhoramento genetica para resistencia a toxidez de aluminio e manganes no Brasil; Antecedentes, necessidade e possibilidades. Topica para discussao e pesquisas. Cien. Cult. 28:147–149.
23. Vose, P. B., and P. J. Randall. 1962. Resistance to aluminum and manganese toxicities in plants related to variety and cation-exchange capacity. Nature 196:85–86.

Chapter 22

Nitrogen Leaching in Bermudagrass Turf: Daily Fertigation vs. Tri-Weekly Conventional Fertilization[1]

G. H. SNYDER
E. O. BURT
J. M. DAVIDSON

ABSTRACT

Nitrogen leaching in bermudagrass turf (*Cynodon* × *Magenissii* Hurcombe) grown on an irrigated sand soil in southern Florida was measured for two methods of application: (i) daily fertilization through the irrigation system (termed "fertigation"); (ii) N fertilization with water-soluble material at 3-week intervals (termed "conventional"). In both cases N was applied at 5 g/m²/month from ammonium nitrate. The soil (Pompano fs) had a volumetric field capacity of only 0.08 cm^3/cm^3, which made the soil very conducive to leaching. Nitrate-N observed at a soil depth of 60 cm generally fluctuated more in the conventional treatment, being greater than in the fertigation treatment shortly after the conventional treatment plots were fertilized, but reaching lower levels several weeks after fertilization. As a result of the low field capacity of the soil and the high amounts of irrigation used in this study, from 35 to 55% of the N applied was lost by leaching, depending on irrigation, rainfall, evapotranspiration, and method of N application. When excessive irrigation water was used, or rainfall occurred shortly after the conventional plots were fertilized, about 50% more N was leached in the conventionally fertilized plots than in those plots receiving N by fertigation. Excessive irrigation promoted N leaching by either method of N application.

Additional index words: *Cynodon*, Irrigation.

INTRODUCTION

Nitrogen, more than any other plant nutrient, is used for promoting and maintaining the growth and appearance of turfgrass. But it is difficult to maintain available N in most soils. The movement of mineral N largely follows that of the soil water, since mineral N usually exists as the nitrate anion which is not adsorbed by most soils.

The literature suggests that only small amounts of N are leached from the root zone of turfgrass, except for irrigated turf on sandy-textured soils (8). For maintaining high quality, intensively trafficked turfgrass, the general trend is towards irrigation and coarse-textured soils (5, 6). The sand soils of southern Florida are unusual because they have very low

[1] Contribution from the Univ. of Florida Inst. of Food and Agric. Sciences. Florida Agric. Exp. Stns. Journal Series No. 596.

field capacities and are highly conducive to leaching. For this reason, they are excellent for studying the principles involved in fertilizer leaching. But actual leaching amounts can be expected to be much greater than would be found in most soils used for turfgrass.

Much of the literature on N leaching in turfgrass deals with N distribution within the soil profile. A quantitative measure of N movement is not generally available. In the cases where such flux measurements are given, laboratory columns or field lysimeters were usually employed. Unless these devices are designed to provide the same soil moisture tensions found in the field, which is not the normal procedure, they will underestimate the actual leaching that occurs in the field.

It is recognized that N efficiency can be improved if soluble N sources are applied frequently, but at low rates per application, as opposed to infrequent high rates of application. However, frequent light application by conventional methods requires considerable labor. Slow-release or water insoluble N sources can be applied at higher rates and less frequently than soluble sources. They were designed to make N available to the plant over an extended period of time. They are generally more expensive. Nitrogen release, being governed by various environmental factors, may or may not match the N requirements of the turf.

Applying small amounts of N through the irrigation system simulates N release from water insoluble fertilizers. A small quantity of N can be metered to the turf with each irrigation. This procedure makes it possible to use the least expensive N sources presently available and gives the turf manager the ability to vary N fertilization on an almost daily basis.

This study was conducted to determine the relative amount of N leached under field conditions from irrigated turfgrass grown on a highly permeable sand soil for two methods of application: (i) conventional fertilization with a soluble source; (ii) daily fertilization through the irrigation system (fertigation).

MATERIALS AND METHODS

Two treatments, replicated four times in a randomized block design, were investigated: (i) daily N fertilization through the irrigation system (fertigation); (ii) N fertilization at 3-week intervals. Prior to February 1975, the plots consisted of an elliptical region irrigated by two, facing half-circle irrigation spray heads. Complete details have been previously discussed (9). After this date, individual plots 4.6 m^2 were irrigated by quarter-circle pop-up type irrigation spray heads (Rain Bird 171 HP-QO, Rain Bird Sprinkler Manufacturing Corp., Glendora, CA 91740) placed on the plot corners and operated at a water pressure of 1.76 kg/cm^2. To fertilize through the irrigation system a water aspirator (SYFONEX, Hydroponic Chemical Co., Copley, OH 44321), modified by increasing the size of the inlet and outlet holes to 4.76 and 5.61 mm, respectively, was inserted in the irrigation water supply line of each plot. Fertilizer solution volumes were adjusted so that all the solution was injected in 6 to 7 days. Plastic flow restricting orifices were placed in the fertilizer solution feed lines so that the stored fertilizer solution volume could be reduced to a convenient quantity (approximately 15 liters). Fertilizer solution storage tanks were cleaned and refilled weekly.

Nitrogen fertilization at 3-week intervals (termed the conventional method) was accomplished with a drop-type spreader (61 cm wide, O.M. Scotts & Sons, Marysville, OH 43040). Ammonium nitrate at the rate of 5 g N/m^2/month was used as the N source for both methods of N fertilization. Both treatments were irrigated daily and always received equal amounts of irrigation, even when the irrigation was only required for one treatment, such as to wash in conventionally applied fertilizer. The quantity of irrigation varied during the study according to evapotranspirational demands and rainfall, and is reported for specific periods in the Results and Discussion. The soil was Pompano fine sand, a member of the siliceous hyperthermic family of Typic Psammaquents of the Entisol order (2). The surface 15 cm contained 96% sand, 1.4% clay, and 3.2% organic matter. The saturated hydraulic conductivity was 35.5 cm/hour. Sand content and hydraulic conductivity increased with depth, while the clay and organic matter content decreased. Field capacity of the surface soil was 0.08 cm^3/cm^3. It was measured as the volumetric water fraction observed in the field after approximately 48 hours of natural drainage following a period of saturation (zero tension). It corresponded to the water content at 7 cb soil water tension. Field capacity decreased somewhat with depth. The 'Tifgreen' bermudagrass (*Cynodon* × *Magenissii* Hurcombe) was managed like a golf course fairway. Plots were mowed at 1.6 cm and clippings were not collected. Pesticide treatments were used as needed for insect, disease, nematode, and weed control. Nutrients other than N were periodically supplied by conventional methods.

The treatments were continued for 3 years. During certain 3-week periods, a series of samples and measurements were taken to determine N leaching. One ceramic cup water sampler (Irrometer Co., Riverside, CA 92502) per plot was placed at a depth of 60 cm, which was well below the root system. Soil water samples, 10 to 20 ml, were generally taken daily and analyzed for nitrate-N with a specific ion electrode (1). Determinations were occasionally confirmed by comparisons with the MgO-Devarda's alloy method (3). Distillation in the presence of MgO was used to check for ammonium-N. Irrigation amounts in each plot were checked frequently by measuring the irrigation water caught in small containers placed on the plots. Rainfall was measured with a standard rain gauge located near the plot site.

Water leaching was calculated as the surplus above field capacity in a 60-cm "column" of soil for the quantity I + R − ET, where the symbols represent irrigation, rainfall, and evapotranspiration, respectively. For example, if the soil was at field capacity at the start of Day 1 and I, R, and ET during the day were 0.1, 0, and 0.2 cm, respectively; there would be no leaching and the 60-cm soil column would be 0.1 cm below field capacity at the end of the day. If I, R, and ET on Day 2 were 0.1, 0.5, and 0.1 cm, respectively, leaching would be 0.4 cm (0.1 + 0.5 − 0.1 = 0.5 cm. Since 0.1 cm is required to bring the soil back to field capacity, there is 0.4 cm of water in excess of field capacity; i.e., there is 0.4 cm of leaching). Evapotranspiration was calculated using McCloud's formula, which was developed for use in Florida (7). By this formula, ET is calculated as a function of the daily mean temperature. The product of water leached times N concentration of the water at the 60-cm soil depth provided the quantity of N leached daily.

RESULTS AND DISCUSSION

Nitrogen leaching was measured in a number of 3-week periods during the course of this study. Three representative examples have been selected for presentation here. Little or no ammonium-N was detected in soil water samples, so only nitrate-N data are considered.

There was little rainfall during the 3-week period beginning 28 Jan. 1976. Irrigation was 0.56 cm/day, except for 3 days discussed below. Evapotranspiration (ET) averaged 0.21 cm/day. Thus, irrigation ex-

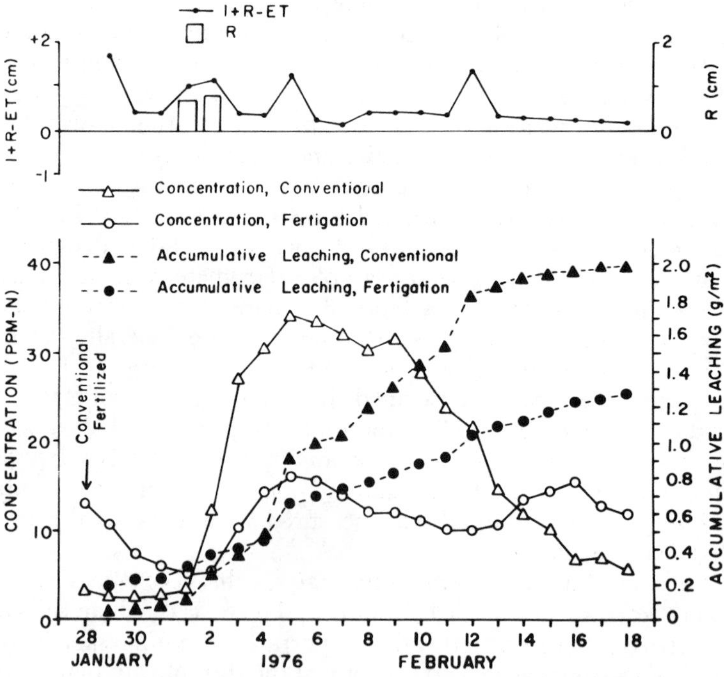

Fig. 1. Nitrate-N at 60 cm, accumulative N leaching, and moisture parameters during a period characterized by moderate evapotranspiration, low rainfall, and excessive irrigation.

ceeded ET (Fig. 1), which brought the soil to field capacity each day. This is the common practice for turfgrass irrigation on sand soils during dry periods. On the day the "conventional" treatment was fertilized, which therefore was 3 weeks since the last fertilization of this treatment, considerably less N was found at 60 cm than was found in the "fertigation" treatment (Fig. 1). Following fertilization of the conventional treatment, N in the soil water increased to twice that of the fertigation treatment. But by the end of the 3-week period N concentration in the soil solution at 60 cm in the conventional treatment had again fallen considerably below that of the fertigation treatment. Thus, N concentrations at 60 cm in the fertigation treatment varied less with time in comparison with the conventional treatment. About 12 of the 16.5 cm of irrigation and rainfall leached during the 3-week period, carrying with it 34 and 54% of the N applied by the fertigation and conventional methods, respectively (Fig. 1). Irrigations above the normally scheduled amounts were applied to "wash in" the conventionally applied fertilizer (1.84 cm on 28 January) and once each week (1.48 cm on 5 February, 1.55 cm on 12 February) to verify proper operation of the irrigation system following mowings. For this research, accurate knowledge of the amount of water applied per scheduled minute of irrigation was essential. This necessitated frequent confirmation of proper operation and calibration of the irrigation system, particularly after mowing, since pop-up sprinkler heads occasionally jammed in the down position after being run over by the mower. These test irrigations produced about 40% of the N leached from each treatment. This illustrates how much N can be leached by a few excessive, though otherwise justifiable, irrigations.

Using data from Fig. 1, it appears that the front of downward moving nitrate (hereafter referred to as the N pulse), resulting from the conventional N fertilization on 28 January, was detected at 60 cm depth in about 6 days (3 February). Irrigation plus rainfall exceeded ET by 5.24 cm during this period. Davidson et al. (4) have shown that the position of the N pulse can be calculated by dividing the amount of water applied in excess of ET by the field capacity of the soil. For these data this calculation becomes:

$$\text{Position of the N pulse in 6 days} = \frac{5.24\ \text{cm}}{0.08\ \text{cm}^3/\text{cm}^3} = 65.5\ \text{cm}.$$

Thus, the data presented in Fig. 1 are very reasonable for the conditions of this study. By contrast, for a silt loam soil with a field capacity of 0.25 cm^3/cm^3, 5.24 cm of water in excess of ET would only move the N pulse 21 cm. Measurements of rooting depth taken during the course of this study show that 80 to 85% of the root system (by weight) was in the upper 10 cm (to be published in detail at a later date). Thus, it only took 0.8 cm of water in excess of ET to move the N pulse below the bulk of the root system. Clearly the high amounts of N leaching observed in this study are reasonable for the conditions of this test, even though they are much greater than would be found in finer textured soils typically used for turf throughout the world.

Nitrate-N was determined in water samples taken during a 3-week period in which ET exceeded irrigation, but which contained considerable rainfall (Fig. 2). Irrigation was 0.38 cm/day except for irrigation following conventional fertilization and two weekly irrigation system checks (1.14 cm in each of the three cases). Evapotranspiration averaged 0.67 cm/day. The nitrate concentration data (Fig. 2) show similar trends to those presented in Fig. 1, being lower in the conventional treatment 3 weeks after fertilization, but much higher than the fertigation treatment 1 week after fertilization. Water samples were taken daily (excluding weekends) in the conventional treatment; but only weekly in the fertigation treatment which requires that some interpolations be made. It became apparent that N movement was so rapid in this irrigated sand soil that daily sampling was necessary for accurate evaluations of leaching. For example, no samples were taken on 27 and 28 July, and N concentrations in the conventional treatment decreased from 29 July on. Thus it cannot be determined whether the peak N concentration actually occurred on 29 July, or whether it occurred over the weekend (27 and 28 July). For this reason, N leached in the conventional treatment may have been somewhat greater than that presented in Fig. 2. Soil moisture occasionally remained below field capacity for several days during this 3-

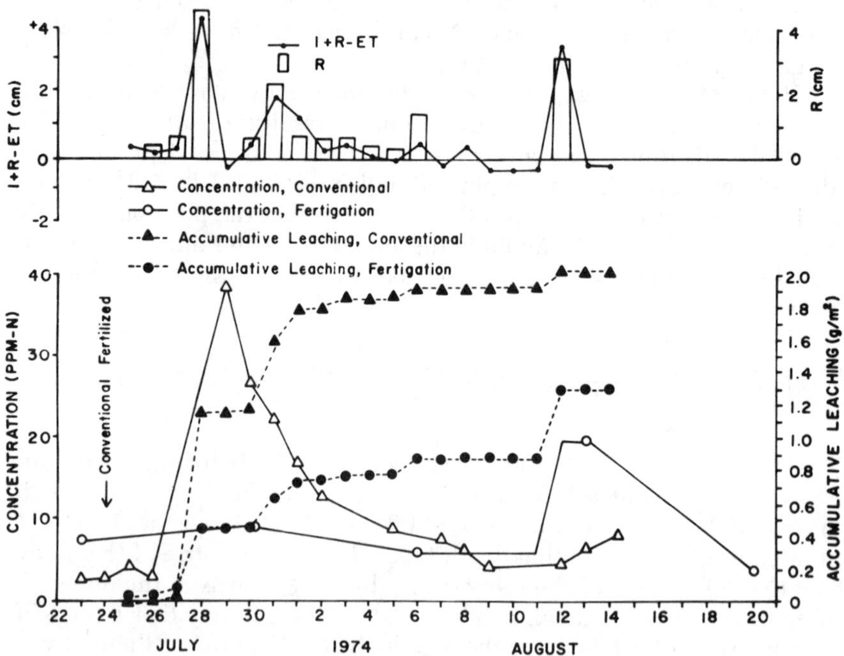

Fig. 2. Nitrate-N at 60 cm, accumulative N leaching, and moisture parameters during a period characterized by high evapotranspiration and high rainfall.

week period, but it was frequently brought back to field capacity by rainfall. Soil moisture calculations were started following a heavy rainfall on 21 July, since field capacity could be assumed, but the conventional treatment was not fertilized until 24 July. About 12 of the 26 cm of rainfall and irrigation leached during this 3-week period, carrying with it 36 and 56% of the N applied by fertigation and conventional treatments, respectively. The irrigation following conventional fertilization and weekly irrigation system checks accounted for 9 to 10% of the total N leached in either treatment. A heavy rain (12 August) following a 5-day dry period leached about 36% of the total N leached in the fertigation treatment and abruptly raised the N concentration in the soil water at 60 cm. Although the ET, irrigation, and rainfall conditions were quite different for the two sampling periods discussed above, the quantity of water leached and the percent N leached were remarkably similar.

Nitrate-N was determined in water samples from the 60-cm soil depth during a 3-week period characterized by irrigations being only slightly greater than ET, and with two intervals of rainfall, one occurring in the middle of the period and one near the end (Fig. 3). Irrigation amounts varied between 0.58 and 0.63 cm/day, with larger amounts following conventional fertilization and two weekly irrigation system checks (1.22, 1.07, and 1.75 cm, respectively). No irrigation was applied on 5

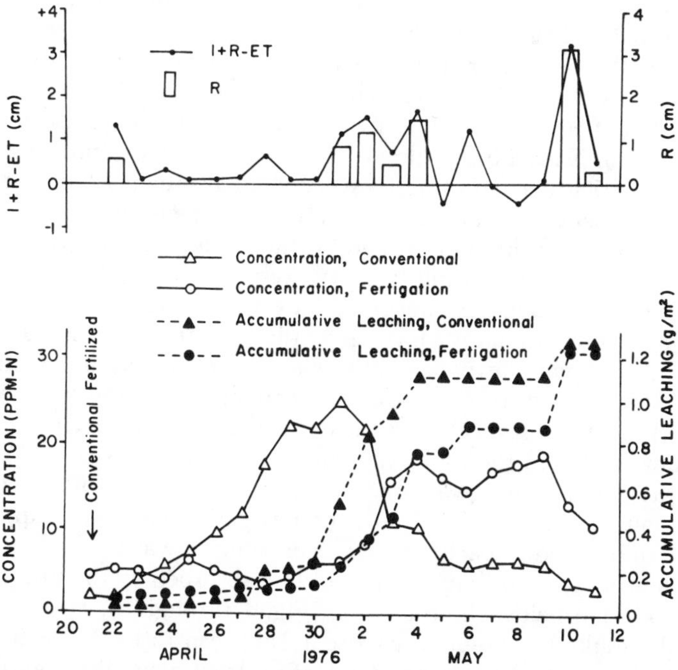

Fig. 3. Nitrate-N at 60 cm, accumulative N leaching, and moisture parameters during a period characterized by high evapotranspiration, moderate irrigation, and several rainy periods.

May, and only 0.13 was applied 8 May. Evapotranspiration averaged 0.49 cm/day. Because ET approached irrigation and there was little rain for 9 days following fertilization of the conventional plots, N leaching in this treatment (Fig. 3) was less than in the examples previously discussed. Nitrogen concentrations in the soil water increased considerably following fertilization, but water leaching during this 9-day period only averaged 0.3 cm/day, as compared to an overall leaching of about 0.6 cm/day in the previous examples. A considerable amount of N probably was taken up by the bermudagrass in the conventional plots during this period, since N concentration in the root zone soil solution should have been relatively high. Rainfall 10 to 13 days after the start of this period resulted in appreciable movement of N in the fertigation plots to 60 cm. Rainfall on 4 and 10 May accounted for over half of the N leached in this treatment. The result of these events was that about the same quantity of N (35%) was leached in both treatments (Fig. 3).

Data collected for other 3-week periods were similar to that presented and will not be discussed in this manuscript. However, in two instances nitrate-N in the leachate from conventionally fertilized plots reached very high levels (80 to 120 ppm), resulting in unreasonably high calculations of total N leached. We were unable to determine the reason for this. Nitrogen leaching in excess of 50% of that applied was observed for both treatments in the fall of 1976 when root systems were severely damaged by nematodes and irrigation exceeded ET by 50%.

The data demonstrate the importance of proper use of irrigation water. In this study, irrigation continued during the rainy periods. Although this clearly is not advisable, it often occurs in actual practice when automatic irrigation equipment is used. With proper use of the irrigation system, N leaching could no doubt have been less than observed in this study. Irrigation and rainfall exceeded ET by about 12 cm in all three examples presented. When the irrigation water continuously exceeded ET, N was leached through the soil profile. When the soil was kept near field capacity, rainfall almost always resulted in significant N losses. Under these conditions, N concentrations in the leachate reached higher levels for conventionally fertilized plots than for the fertigation treatment, but were lower several weeks after fertilization. The fact that N leachate at 60 cm probably reflected conditions in the overlying root zone soil solutions several days earlier indicates that N concentrations were more stable in the root zone when fertigation was used. When excessive irrigation water was used, or rainfall occurred shortly after the conventional plots were fertilized, the fertigation method of application resulted in reduced N leaching. However, some N was applied by fertigation either in excess of that which could be absorbed by the turf each day or to a position below the root zone (Fig. 1 through 3). Heavy rainfalls generally resulted in a temporary rise in N concentration at the 60-cm soil depth and in N leaching in the fertigation treatment. We considered 3-week intervals to be about as often as N might be applied to large turfgrass areas by conventional means. Under most circumstances a longer interval would likely be used. The differences we observed between the two treatments would probably be enhanced if the conventional application interval were longer.

Nitrogen concentration alone did not accurately portray the leaching picture, for at times N concentration was high at 60 cm even though little N was being leached (examples: Fig. 3, conventional treatment, 28 to 30 April or fertigation treatment, 5 to 9 May). Data on both N concentration and water movement are needed to fully understand and illustrate N leaching.

ACKNOWLEDGMENT

The authors wish to express their appreciation to Miss Joan Bergin and to Mr. Richard Graham for their faithful and conscientious assistance in collecting data during this study.

LITERATURE CITED

1. Anon. 1967. Instruction manual nitrate ion electrode. Orion Research Inc., Cambridge, Mass.
2. ————. 1975. Soil taxonomy. USDA, SCS, Agric. Handb. No. 436. U.S. Gov. Print. Off., Washington, D.C.
3. Bremner, J. M. 1965. Inorganic forms of nitrogen. *In* C. A. Black (ed.) Methods of soil analysis. Part 2. Chemical and microbiological properties. Agronomy 9:1179–1237. Am. Soc. Agron., Madison, Wis.
4. Davidson, J. M., D. A. Graetz, P. S. C. Rao, and H. M. Selim. 1978. Simulation of nitrogen movement, transformation, and uptake in plant root zone. EPA-600/3-78-029. EPA, Environ. Res. Lab., Athens, GA 30601. p. 34–45.
5. Davis, W. B. 1973. Sands and their place on the golf course. Calif. Turfgrass Culture 23: 17–20.
6. ————, D. S. Farnham, and K. D. Gowans. 1974. The sand football field. Calif. Turfgrass Culture 24:17–20.
7. McCloud, D. E. 1970. Water requirements for turf. p. 88–90. *In* Proc. Florida Turfgrass Management Conf.
8. Rieke, P. E., and B. G. Ellis. 1974. Effects of nitrogen fertilization on nitrate movements under turfgrass. p. 120–130. *In* Eliot C. Roberts (ed.) Proc. Second Int. Turfgrass Research Conf., Blacksburg, Va. June 1973. Am. Soc. Agron., Madison, Wis.
9. Snyder, G. H., and E. O. Burt. 1976. Nitrogen fertilization of bermudagrass turf through an irrigation system. J. Am. Soc. Hort. Sci. 101:145–148.

Chapter 23

Proposed Standards and Specifications for Quality of Sand for Sand-Soil-Peat Mixes[1]

GEORGE R. BLAKE

ABSTRACT

Two parameters are suggested to define the quality of sand for sand-soil-peat mixes. Fineness modulus is an index of weighted mean particle size. uniformity coefficient is an index of grading, i.e., the range of particle sizes making up the predominant part of a sample. A fineness modulus range of 1.7 to 2.5 and a uniformity coefficient less than 4 are proposed as specifications. The data show that where these standards are met it may be unnecessary to specify limits on the quantity of very coarse or very fine materials, or on the percentage that should fall within specified particle size boundaries.

INTRODUCTION

Sand-soil-peat mixes are currently widely used for turf that is used for field sports such as football, soccer, baseball, golf greens, and tees and also for planting containers and as a base for roof gardens. The U.S. Golf Association Green Section pioneered in the use of sand-soil-peat mixes for supporting golf greens (1). Subsequent evaluations and suggestions for improvement were published (7, 8, 11). Refinements were described by the Green Section Staff in 1973 (2).

While descriptions of sand-soil-peat ingredients used both successfully and unsuccessfully for sports turf installations have been published, there has been no clear effort to develop standards that can be used in specifications for new construction. The purpose of this paper is to bring together various suggestions on sand quality reported in the literature, report other standards not yet published, and suggest a set of criteria for judging sand quality for use in modifying soils.

Typical S-shaped curves showing accumulated weight percentage by particle diameter determined by dry sieving sand samples are shown in

[1] Contribution from the Minnesota Agric. Exp. Stn., Univ. of Minnesota, St. Paul, MN 55108 USA. Scientific Journal Series Paper No. 9956.

Fig. 1 and 2. Names of separates are those used in United States. An advantage of such a particle size distribution is that the quantity of separates in other classification systems can easily be interpolated. Another advantage is that the resulting curve depends only on the use of a reasonable number and distribution of sieve sizes and not on the discrete sieve openings themselves.

PARAMETERS TO DESCRIBE SAND

At least two parameters are needed to describe a sand, namely coarseness and grade. Coarseness refers to the relative size of particles in the sample. Grade refers to the range of particle sizes found in a sample. If the sample consists predominantly of a narrow range of particle sizes, the sample is poorly graded. A wide range of particle sizes is called well graded.

Fineness Modulus

A number of proposals have been made to define a coarseness-fineness index, but the fineness modulus has come to predominate in the U.S. commercial sand industry. Fineness modulus is defined as the sum of the cumulative percentages retained on U.S. standard sieve numbers 4, 8, 16, 30, 50, and 100 divided by 100. An example of the calculation is shown in Fig. 1. Sieve numbers refer to U.S. National Bureau of Standards specifications adopted in 1961 by the American Society for Testing Materials (ATSM), American Standards Association, and the International Standards Association. Sieve openings are 4.76, 2.38, 1.19, 0.595, 0.297, and 0.149 mm, respectively. One can also interpolate weight percentages at these particle diameters from a particle size distribution curve made by use of sieves with other sized openings.

The author has found the fineness modulus to be a most useful index because it is well known to sand suppliers. Its adoption in several industries, particularly in highway and building construction where cement is used, has led to a specification that is readily understood by contractors and suppliers. And it is a standard that they can guarantee and which can readily be controlled.

An alternative coarseness index used, for example, in industrial hygiene dust standards in the United States, is the median particle diameter, i.e., the central diameter (50% accumulation value by weight) of a particle size accumulation diagram. Bingaman and Kohnke (3) used this index for sands for soilless culture. The median particle diameter is highly correlated with the fineness modulus. For the data in Table 1, the relation of the two was found to exceed the 0.005 level of significance, the R^2 value being 0.96 for a quadratic model.

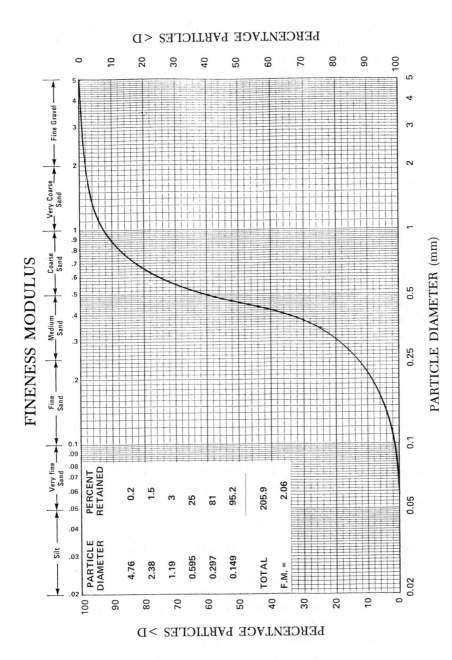

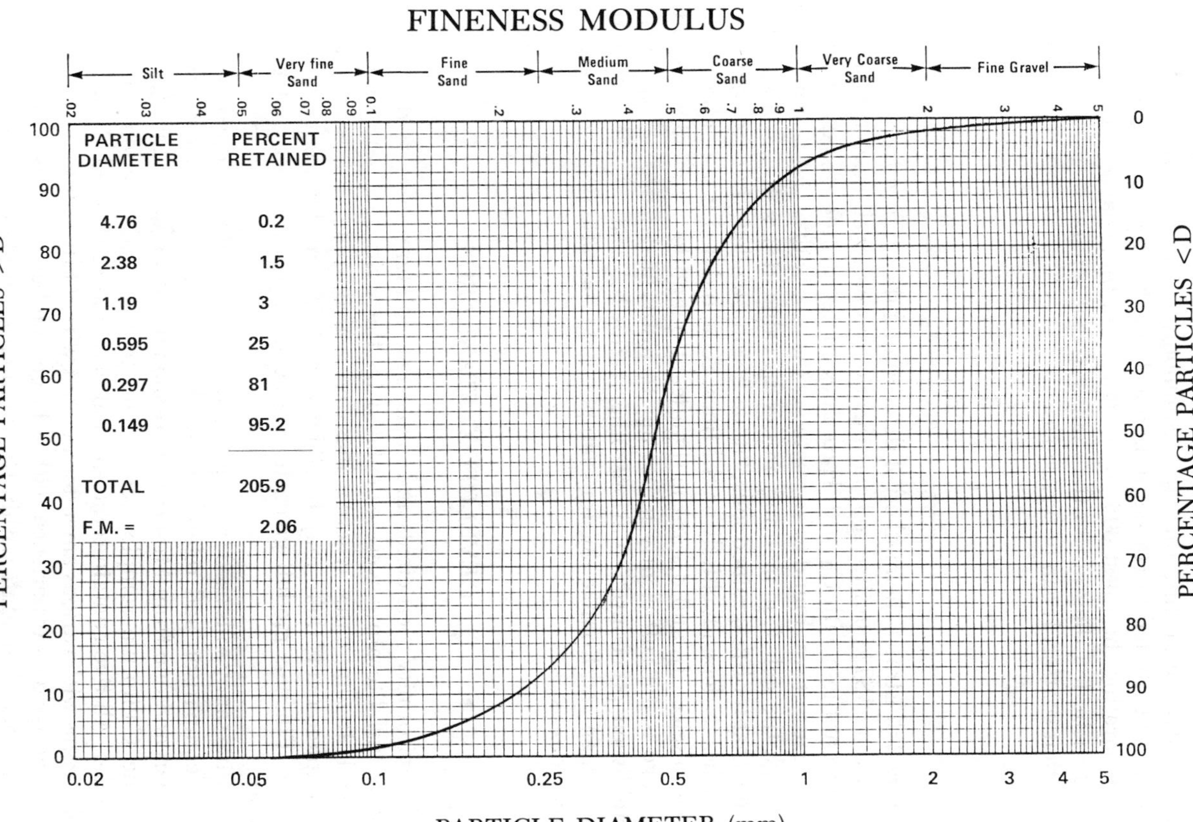
FINENESS MODULUS
Silt
Very fine Sand
Fine Sand
Medium Sand
Coarse Sand
Very Coarse Sand
Fine Gravel
PARTICLE DIAMETER
PERCENT RETAINED
4.76 0.2
2.38 1.5
1.19 3
0.595 25
0.297 81
0.149 95.2
TOTAL 205.9
F.M. = 2.06
PERCENTAGE PARTICLES >D
PERCENTAGE PARTICLES <D
PARTICLE DIAMETER (mm)

Uniformity Coefficient

A second parameter is needed to describe the grading of a sand. The uniformity coefficient, the most commonly used value in the United States, is attributed to Hazen (9) and is defined as the ratio of the diameter separating the finest 60% by weight from that coarser on a particle size distribution diagram to the diameter that separates the finest 10% from that coarser. It can be written as:

$$C_u = \frac{d_{60}}{d_{10}}.$$

Figure 2 illustrates the method of determining the uniformity coefficient.

In the ASTM unified soil classification system, well-graded sands are defined as those with $C_u > 6$. Hazen designated d_{10} the effective particle size because it was found to be related to the ease with which water passed through the soil. Commenting on the d_{10} value, Terzaghi and Peck (15) wrote that for fine-grained soils, "it has become evident that the character of such soils depends chiefly on the finest 20% and that it might be preferable to select d_{20} and d_{70} as the significant quantities. However, the advantage is not sufficiently important to justify a departure from well-established procedure." Various other ratios have also been proposed. Bingaman and Kohnke (3), for example, used the ratio d_{95}/d_5 as a gradation index.

DEVELOPING STANDARDS

Uniformity coefficients and fineness moduli for sands reported in the sports turf literature were calculated by the writer and are shown in Table 1. In some cases, where values were scaled from published curves or incomplete data, there may be slight uncertainty in the accuracy of the values. Fineness moduli given to one decimal place reflect that uncertainty.

Fine sandy soils used from sports turf areas are also included in Table 1 for comparison and reference (two samples each from Germany and Sweden and one from Minnesota). It should also be noted that the data for the California samples refers only to the sand fractions of those samples. All five contain some silt and clay and are intended for use on golf greens with various amendments, but without further soil.

The writer's experience with a large number of sands is that those having fineness moduli within the boundaries of about 1.7 and 2.5 are quality sands for soil modification. From Table 1 it is seen that most of the samples reported in the literature fall within these limits. Let us consider the exceptions.

Of the seven sand samples having a fineness modulus less than 1.7,

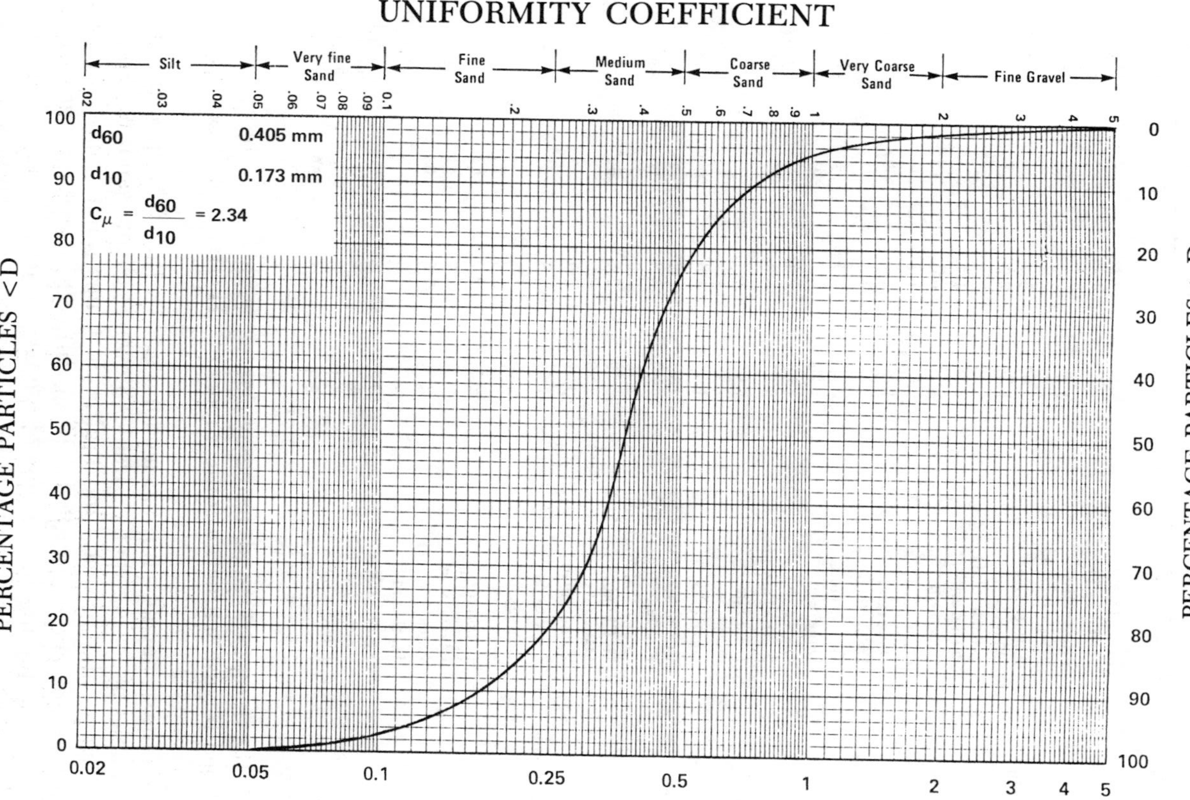

Fig. 2. Particle size accumulation curve showing uniformity coefficient calculation.

Table 1. Indices for some sands described in the turf literature.

Location	Description	Fineness modulus (FM)	Uniformity coefficient (C_u)	Particles 0.25 to 1 mm	Literature cited
				%	
Germany	Fine turf soil	0.7	5.7	20	(13)
	Coarse turf soil	3.3	8.7	34	
Sweden	Fine turf soil	0.5	6.2	14	(10)
	Coarse turf soil	2.5	3.5	59	
California	Antioch river	0.96	2.4	40	(6)
	Dillon beach	1.45	2.2	71	
	Teichert State	2.89	5.1	52	
	Pacific cement	1.78	1.4	94	
	Robertson	2.47	2.0	79	
Illinois	Carni	2.1	1.7	91	(4)
Indiana	Dune sand	1.0	2.0	39	(4)
	Lafayette 3	2.3	3.3	71	
	Mortar sand	2.39	2.6	69	(12)
	Dune sand	1.29	1.6	61	
Iowa	Sioux City	1.86	2.4	73	Author's data
	Prairie Du Chien	2.97	3.0	62	
Kentucky	Louisville	2.0	2.2	81	(4)
	Owensberg	1.7	1.8	74	
	Perry Park	1.7	1.9	88	
Minnesota	Commercial fine	1.74	2.2	66	Author's data
	Fine building sand	2.40	3.8	66	
	Coarse building sand	2.75	3.6	53	
	St. Cloud	2.20	2.4	84	
	Mankato	2.29	2.6	79	
	Zimmerman f. sand soil	0.71	3.0	15	
North Carolina	Purwick use	1.6	2.9	64	(5)
Pennsylvania	Coarse sand	2.95	1.4	85	(17)
	Mortar sand	1.76	2.5	73	
	Concrete sand	2.40	2.7	62	
USA	Client's sand	3.31	3.7	41	(14)
	Expensive sand	2.52	2.6	69	
USA	Ideal sand	2.2	3.9	85	(11)
USA	Fine desirable	0.3	1.3	0	Personal communication, W.H. Daniel
	Coarse desirable	1.7	1.6	89	
	Finest of 60 tested	0.1	1.5	0	
	Coarsest of 60 tested	2.3	1.5	58	

one is the finest in 60 sands tested by Daniel, while four of the others are intended for use without a soil component. The remaining two are reported from California.

Of the six having a fineness modulus greater than 2.5, three are cited as examples of coarser than desirable (Stewart's client's sand, the Minnesota coarse building sand, and Prairie du Chien sand). The California Teichert State sand is described as being difficult to work into the surface when used as topdressing because of the large fraction of large particles. Of the remaining two, one was used successfully in Pennsylvania, while the U.S. expensive sand barely exceeded 2.5.

There is no serious problem in using sand having a fineness modulus greater than 2.5. Indeed, fine turf can be grown on gravelly soil. There are several minor problems. Dilution of soil would certainly require a larger percentage by weight of sand as particle size increases substantially. There is also the problem of separation of large particles on hauling and mixing and at the soil surface of a new planting as rain or water by sprinkler is added. This often prevents as homogenous a soil mix as one would wish for. Since the soil mix used in greens construction is normally also recommended and stored for use as topdressing, particles larger than about 1 mm nick and dull mower blades and are considered undesirable for that reason.

Soils will normally have lower fineness moduli if their sand fractions are calculated as a percentage of the whole sample. It can be seen from Table 1, however, that the fineness moduli of the German and Swedish soils and the Minnesota soil lie between 0.5 and 3.3, ranging smaller and larger than most sands.

Several researchers have indicated a preference for a sand having a narrow range of particle sizes (low uniformity coefficient) because with other factors equal it would have a higher porosity. Only Janson (10) has reported a uniformity coefficient, and then for an optimum turf topsoil rather than for a sand ingredient with soil and peat.

Considering the data in Table 1, it appears that uniformity coefficients of 4 or less may be generally obtainable for sand. Indeed, only four of the sand samples cited in Table 1 exceed 3.5. At the present time, available data do not justify trying to specify a uniformity coefficient closer than 4 or less. Further research to more closely define the upper standard is needed.

Janson (10) indicated that the uniformity coefficient for a turf topsoil should not exceed 10 to 15. However, the writer calculated lower coefficients (3.5 and 6.2 for the lower and upper limits) for what he considered optimum grain size area on a particle size accumulation diagram.

Calculations based on Skirde's data (13) for soils showed uniformity coefficients for the lower and upper limits of what he called vegetation layers of 5.7 and 8.7, respectively. Coefficients for soils would be expected to be greater than for sands. It appears possible, however, that Janson's allowable coefficients of 10 to 15 may give more tolerance than needed for uniformity of turf soils. Admittedly, too few data are available to draw a firm conclusion for all geographic locations.

OTHER STANDARDS

In the past various workers have indicated preference for a preponderance of sand particles within a given set of diameter limits (16, for example). A common statement, for example, is that 60% or more of the sand should lie between the size limits 0.25 to 1.0 mm diam. Data showing this quantity are included in Table 1. When the fineness modulus of sand was within the limits of 1.7 to 2.5, the 0.25 to 1.0 mm fraction exceeded 60%. It appears that this stipulation would commonly be met

Table 2. Proposed sand standards for sand-soil-peat mixes.

Fineness modulus	1.7 to 2.5
Uniformity coefficient	<4
Particles <0.1 mm	<3% wt.
Particles >2 mm	<3% wt.
Particles 0.25 to 1 mm	>60% wt.

with samples within the fineness modulus range of 1.7 to 2.5 and with a uniformity coefficient less than 4.0.

It is also of interest that none of the sand samples in Table 1 having these fineness and uniformity limits contained more than 3% by weight particles greater than 2 mm. Only two contained more than 3% finer than 0.1 mm. Radko's hypothetical "ideal" sand had 6%. It is suspected that this was a quirk that developed from the idealization. The Perry Park sand had 5% of its particles by weight finer than 0.1 mm.

It is quite possible that further data will show that limits on the percent by weight of sample less than 0.1 mm, or greater than 2 mm, or between 0.25 and 1.0 mm are unnecessary if proposed fineness modulus and uniformity coefficients are met. For the time being, however, there seems to be no disadvantage in keeping these criteria.

A particle shape factor is often mentioned by sports turf practitioners by the use of such terms as sharp, angular smooth, or rounded sand. Preferences are expressed that appear to be intuitive rather than objective. This writer knows of no data supporting one or another preference. Perhaps there is need for research that could conceivably lead to a recommendation on particle shape.

In view of the evidence presented, Table 2 presents the standards proposed for sands used in sand-soil-peat mixtures.

LITERATURE CITED

1. Anon. U.S. Golf Association Green Section Staff. 1960. Specifications for a method of putting green consruction. U.S. Golf Assoc. Turf Manage. 13(5):24–28.
2. ————. U.S. Golf Association Green Section Staff. 1973. Refining the green section specifications for putting green construction. U.S. Golf Assoc. Green Section Rec. 11(3): 1–8.
3. Bingaman, David E., and Helmut Kohnke. 1970. Evaluating sands for athletic turf. Agron. J. 62:464–467.
4. Daniel, W. H. 1970. Purr-Wick, rootzone system for turf. Midwest Turf. No. 40.
5. ————, and Devon O. Brouse. 1975. Bringing the Purr-Wick system from talk to green. Golf Super. 43(10):29–31.
6. Davis, W. B., J. L. Paul, J. H. Madison, and L. Y. George. 1970. A guide to evaluating sands and amendments used for high trafficked turfgrass. Univ. of California Agric. Ext. AXT-n113.
7. Duble, R. L. 1974. The U.S. Golf Association green after 15 years. U.S. Golf Assoc. Green Section Rec. 12(2):8–10.
8. Ferguson, Marvin H. 1965. After five years: The Green Section specifications for a putting green. U.S. Golf Assoc. Green Section Rec. 3(4):1–7.
9. Hazen, A. 1892. Physical properties of sands and gravels with reference to their use in filtration. Rep. Mass. State Board of Health.

10. Janson, Lars-Eric. 1969. Adequate soil type for sport turfgrasses. p. 142–148. *In* R. R. Davis (ed.) Proc. First Int. Turfgrass Res. Conf., Harrogate, England. July 1969. Sports Turf Res. Inst., Bingley, England.

11. Radko, A. M. 1974. Refining Green Section specifications for putting green construction. p. 287–297. *In* Eliot C. Roberts (ed.) Proc. Second Int. Turfgrass Res. Conf., Blacksburg, Va. June 1973. Am. Soc. Agron., Madison, Wis.

12. Ralston, D. S., and W. H. Daniel. 1973. Effect of porous rootzone materials underlined with plastic on the growth of creeping bentgrass. Agron. J. 65:229–232.

13. Skirde, W. 1974. Soil modification for athletic fields. p. 261–269. *In* Eliot C. Roberts (ed.) Proc. 2nd Int. Turfgrass Res. Conf., Blacksburg, Va. June 1973. Am. Soc. Agron., Madison, Wis.

14. Stewart, J. 1972. Soil testing: Protect your greens investment. Golfdom 46(9):57–58.

15. Terzaghi, Karl, and Ralph B. Peck. 1967. Soil mechanics in engineering practice. Wiley and Sons, N.Y.

16. Waddington, D. V. 1976. Sands for modifying soils on turfgrass areas. PTC Turfgrass Comments 1(1):1–2.

17. ————, T. L. Zimmerman, G. J. Schoop, L. T. Kardos, and J. M. Duich. 1974. Soil modification for turfgrass areas. Pennsylvania State Univ. Agric. Exp. Stn. Prog. Rep. 337.

Chapter 24

Bentgrass Growth in Relation to Soil Properties of Typic Hapludalfs Soil Variously Modified for a Golf Green[1]

R. E. SCHMIDT

ABSTRACT

This study was initiated to obtain information on the influence of soil physical aspects in relation to turf growth. A 'Penncross' creeping bentgrass (*Agrostis palustris* Huds.) experimental golf putting green was constructed of soil modified with different amounts of coarse river sand and a graded expanded shale. Two compaction levels and two irrigation regimes were imposed on the test site for 9 years. During this time, air porosity, infiltration rates, and shoot growth were measured. Air porosity reduction from 1966 to 1974 was less than the decrease in water infiltration, which was greater for highly modified than for slightly modified mixes. Heavy irrigation and compaction reduced air porosity, but only compaction significantly reduced water infiltration. Although air porosity and infiltration rates were greater with increased amounts of modifying materials, both air porosity and water infiltration were greater in corresponding mixes containing the more uniform expanded shale. After 6 years of heavy compaction and high irrigation, no mix had more than 4.5 cm/hour infiltration.

Yields from the first clipping in the spring were greater on the heavily compacted than lightly compacted plots. The reverse was true during the summer, possibly because of foliar injury imparted by the compactor.

Wilting occurred more frequently and clipping yields were generally less for soil mixes containing the greatest amount of modifying materials. Removal of excess surface water with adequate surface drainage may be more beneficial for bentgrass growth than excess internal drainage.

Additional index words: Porosity, Infiltration, Clipping yields, *Agrostis palustris* Huds.

INTRODUCTION

Modification of soils used to produce turf on sport areas, such as golf greens and athletic fields that are subjected to intense traffic, is considered essential to maintain adequate soil physical condition for desirable turf growth. Sand is the modifying material most used to minimize compaction tendencies of soils high in clay or silt content. Attempts have been

[1] A contribution from the Dep. of Agronomy, Virginia Polytechnic and State Univ., Blacksburg, VA 24061 USA.

made to determine the proper particle size distribution and quantity of modifying materials to obtain the "optimum" soil physical condition for highly used turf areas (3, 4, 5, 10, 11, 12).

The principle soil physical characteristics used to determine properly modified soils are water infiltration rates and soil macropore space percentage. Waddington et al. (12) stated that infiltration rate, in most instances, should be the primary criterion in evaluating soil physical condition of modified turf soils. Skirde (10) reported that an infiltration of more than 5.4 cm/hour was desired for athletic fields in Germany. The U.S. Golf Association (USGA) Green Section recommends that minimum water transmission rates should be 5.0 to 7.6 cm/hour for golf putting greens (9).

Consensus among earlier researchers was that modifying materials should be uniform in particle size and from 0.5 to 2.0 mm (2, 5, 7). In recent years, however, the USGA Green Section has recommended finer texture sand for golf green construction and considers an ideal sand particle size distribution as 65% from 1.0 mm to 0.5 mm, 20% from 0.5 mm to 0.25 mm, 10% from 0.25 to 0.06 mm, and 5% below 0.06 mm (9). This change to finer particle size was apparently to maintain additional moisture holding capacity and to obtain sufficient permeability.

Janson (4) warned that soil modified to obtain excessive permeability may have too little water retention, reduced turf wear resistance, and require larger fertilizer requirements. It has been shown that bentgrass grown on a mix containing a loam topsoil and 90% sand (0.1 to 0.5 mm), had more initial turfgrass wear damage from traffic and a slower recovery than a mix of 50% each of the same sand and soil (1).

A theoretical concept of determining effective sand particle size to provide the desired permeability has been proposed by Janson (4) in which the quantity of modifying materials was dependent upon particle size. Swartz and Kardos (11), using Hagerstown silt loam and a medium quartz sand, found that mixes containing 50% or less total sand had inadequate percolation rates under compaction. Mixes containing 70% total sand maintained adequate percolation rates under compaction but inadequate moisture retention. However, Kuntze et al. (5) reported that 85 to 90% coarse to medium sand was needed to satisfactorily modify a "Houston Black Clay", a soil with expanding lattice clay. Waddington et al. (12), using Hagerstown silt loam, reported that in general, laboratory compacted mixes needed 60% or more coarse amendment to have percolation rates greater than 2.5 mm/hour.

In many locations, ideal modifying materials are not economically obtained. Materials such as concrete sand containing small gravel and very find sand have successfully been used to modify soils for athletic fields and golf greens. An objective of this study was to determine the influence of modifying a "typical" soil, with materials readily available in Virginia, on soil physical criteria and turfgrass growth. Most studies dealing with modified soils for turf have reported on the soil physical aspects and not on turf growth.

MATERIALS AND METHODS

In 1964, the Ap horizon of a fine-loamy, mixed, mesic family of Typic Hapludalfs was removed from a 30.5- × 30.5-m experimental site located at Blacksburg, Va., USA, and stockpiled. The subsoil was graded to a 2% slope, and a 10-cm ceramic tile drainage line was installed in a 10-cm trench following the slope and centered under each of the subsequent eight blocks of soil mix. A 10-cm layer of a 1- to 1.25-cm aggregate was spread over the area followed by a 2-cm layer of coarse sand. The soil was mixed off-site with 5% by volume finely ground pine bark and various quantities of a coarse river sand or a graded lightweight expanded shale, (bulk density 1.0) manufactured by the Weblite Corporation, Roanoke, Va. The particle size distribution of the materials used in blending the soils and the ratios of the soil and modifying materials are listed in Tables 1 and 2.

Wood frames 30.5 cm high, 2.4 m wide, and 3.05 m long (corresponding to the soil mix plot size) were installed on the experimental site and the sides were lined with a heavy reinforced plastic. After the individual mixes were placed into the frames, the wood portion was removed. Irrigation lines to accommodate differential watering regimes were installed in the 1.2-m wide alleys between the blocks of plots. Two blocks constituted one replication. The mixes were seeded with 0.25 kg/100 m^2 of 'Penncross' creeping bentgrass (*Agrostis palustris* Huds.) in May 1965.

The test site was maintained as a golf putting green. It was mowed at 0.64 cm, three times a week during the growing season. Nitrogen was applied at an average of 3.5 kg/100 m^2 each year. Phosphorus and potash were supplied at 1 kg/100 m^2/year. Broad spectrum fungicides, insecticides, and herbicides were applied as needed. The area was irrigated to prevent wilting.

Beginning in 1966, an average of 50 cm additional water was applied each year from late spring to late summer to one block of plots of each replication. A 182-kg lawn roller with golf-spiked shoe soles attached so

Table 1. Particle size of materials used to construct the various putting green soil mixes.

Percent by wt.							
Gravel	Sand					% Silt	% Clay
>2 mm	2–1 mm	1–0.5 mm	0.5–0.25 mm	0.25–0.10 mm	0.10–0.05 mm	0.05–0.002 mm	<0.002 mm
Fine-loamy, mixed mesic family of typic paleudalts soil							
4.6	2.4	3.24	4.49	8.46	7.52	58.61	15.26
Expanded shale							
4.76	33.06	34.9	22.44	3.32	1.16	--	--
River sand							
14.16	29.28	34.50	15.32	4.52	1.18	--	--

Table 2. Air porosity (percent of volume) of nine modified golf putting green soils measured 2, 6, and 10 years after establishment with creeping bentgrass and maintained at two compaction levels and two irrigation regimes.

		Modifying materials									
		Expanded shale				River sand					
		(Soil mix) Ratio—Modifying material: Soil									
Compaction levels	Irrigation regimes	1:3	3:4	4:3	5:2	1:3	3:4	4:3	5:2	19:3	Avg.
					1966						
Light	Low	13.4	21.8	25.4	29.8	12.8	15.7	19.3	22.4	27.3	20.9
Light	High	12.7	21.0	24.7	26.9	11.7	15.5	21.9	18.2	26.5	19.9
Heavy	Low	9.9	16.0	22.9	26.7	9.0	12.2	17.9	19.3	24.6	17.6
Heavy	High	8.1	13.9	18.2	23.6	7.1	13.4	15.9	17.2	22.1	15.5
	Avg.	11.0	18.1	22.8	26.7	10.1	14.2	18.7	19.3	25.1	
					1970						
Light	Low	9.8	19.8	21.6	27.2	12.3	12.2	15.4	19.9	28.1	18.5
Light	High	9.7	14.8	21.9	18.6	11.5	12.0	20.3	21.4	25.7	17.3
Heavy	Low	7.7	16.6	15.2	21.6	7.8	13.1	14.5	13.5	21.6	14.6
Heavy	High	6.0	10.8	13.4	23.3	6.8	10.8	16.8	17.9	19.7	13.9
	Avg.	8.3	15.5	18.0	22.7	9.6	12.0	16.7	18.2	23.8	
					1974						
Ligh	Low	11.5	17.7	21.5	25.2	7.5	14.8	16.2	19.4	25.5	16.7
Light	High	8.6	13.4	18.7	23.5	7.8	11.8	20.0	17.4	26.9	16.4
Heavy	Low	13.2	8.3	15.8	19.8	3.7	11.2	12.2	14.5	21.9	13.4
Heavy	High	6.9	9.3	9.7	17.7	9.3	11.4	15.1	13.9	17.8	12.3
	Avg.	10.0	12.2	16.4	21.5	7.0	12.3	15.9	16.3	23.0	

	L.S.D. 0.05		
	Year		
Source	1966	1970	1974
Irrigation	1.2	1.1	1.3
Compaction	2.8	2.5	1.1
Soil mix	2.7	3.9	3.3

that three soles simultaneously contacted the turf was driven over one-half of each soil mix plot an average of 150 times each summer since 1966. Spikes were removed from the soles after the 2nd year to reduce abrasive effects.

The plots were never cored with a mechanical machine, but the turf was vertically cut and topdressed twice annually with the mix corresponding to that in the plot.

Water infiltration rates were obtained periodically with a double-ring infiltrometer. A 20-cm diam sheet metal cylinder was placed concentrically within a 35.6-cm diam cylinder and both cylinders were driven 5 cm into the soil, leaving 20 cm of the cylinder above the turf. Both cylinders were filled with water and permitted to drain up to 1/2 hour. The cylinders were then refilled to 5 cm of the top of the cylinder.

After 15 cm of water was drained from the inner cylinder, or after 30 min, the loss of water was measured to determine the infiltration rate.

Porosity was determined on undisturbed soil samples obtained by driving a sampling probe that contained removable cylinders (3.7-cm diam × 4.8-cm height) into the soil mix. The thatch was removed from the plug and the soil was trimmed from the bottom of the cylinder to provide a 40.2 cm^3 sample of the top 4.8-cm deep soil mix. Samples were taken to the lab, saturated, and then placed on a 60-cm water tension table (6) for 15 hours. The volume of water and solid material within the cylinder was then determined using a Beckman Model 930 air comparison pycnometer. The samples were dried in a forced air oven for 24 hours at 75 C, and the solid material volume was measured with the pycnometer. Air porosity and total porosity were calculated after the sample was removed from the 60-cm tension table and the oven, respectively, using the formula:

$$f = \frac{Vt - (Vws - Vc)}{Vt} \times 100;$$

where f = percent porosity volume, Vt = total volume within the cylinder, Vws = volume of water and solids, and Vc = volume of cylinder.

Water porosity was determined by subtracting the value for air porosity from total porosity. To determine the precision of the pycnometer reading, the weight of water loss of the samples taken in 1965 was measured and air porosity determination was made with the pycnometer of samples taken from the experimental site 24 hours after a 3.75-cm irrigation and not subjected to 60 cm water tension.

Clipping yields were measured periodically by collecting from 1 m^2 swath cut through the center of the plots. The fresh clippings were immediately transferred to a laboratory and weighed. The statistical design used in this study was a split plot with strips. All treatments were replicated four times and subjected to analysis of variance.

RESULTS AND DISCUSSION

Air Porosity Determinations

Air porosity determinations, using an air comparison pycnometer, of field soil mix samples that were saturated in the laboratory and subsequently placed on the water tension table correlated highly (r = 0.98) with corresponding samples taken from the experimental site 24 hours after a heavy irrigation. Both the pycnometer air porosity of laboratory saturated and irrigated field samples correlated highly (r = 0.97 and r = 0.96, respectively) with water weight loss of laboratory saturated soil samples after 15 hours on the water tension table. These results substantiated the technique used by other workers (11) in which air porosity of putting green soils was determined with an air comparison pycnometer after the sample had been saturated and then subjected to 60 cm water tension. This procedure was adopted for these experiments because the method provided a convenient standard laboratory procedure which closely simulated field conditions.

Air Porosity and Water Infiltration

The average air porosity decreased 21.8% from 1966 to 1974 (Table 2); whereas, infiltration was reduced 45.6% (Table 3). It appears possible that with time the shifting of the mix particles increased tortuosity and impeded water movement through the soil profile more than the particle rearrangement reduced the soil macropore space.

The reduction in air porosity and water infiltration rate between 1966 and 1970 was 13 and 39%, respectively. In 1974, air porosity was further reduced by 8.6% and the infiltration rate was 10.3% less than in 1970. This lower reduction in air porosity and water infiltration rates obtained over the last 4 years of the study indicate that the soil physical factors were stabilizing.

Although both heavy irrigation and heavy compaction reduced air

Table 3. Infiltration rates (cm/hour) of nine modified golf putting green soils measured 2, 6, and 10 years after establishment with creeping bentgrass and maintained at two compaction levels and two irrigation regimes.

		Modifying materials									
		Expanded shale				River sand					
		(Soil mix) Ratio—Modifying material:Soil									
Compaction levels	Irrigation regimes	1:3	3:4	4:3	5:2	1:3	3:4	4:3	5:2	19:3	Avg.
		1966									
Light	Low	15.5	44.0	68.5	109.7	7.9	15.7	22.6	55.9	68.0	45.3
Light	High	14.1	33.4	50.6	94.3	10.5	13.3	33.9	32.1	93.4	41.7
Heavy	Low	9.2	9.9	20.3	24.2	9.5	8.2	13.3	13.1	38.5	16.2
Heavy	High	0.9	10.9	15.8	37.8	1.7	8.3	22.0	16.9	24.9	15.5
Avg.		9.9	24.5	38.8	66.5	7.4	11.4	22.9	29.5	56.2	
		1970									
Light	Low	12.8	27.5	44.9	64.5	15.3	18.0	22.7	29.6	65.1	33.4
Light	High	18.0	23.7	27.9	63.0	8.5	9.9	39.1	23.2	88.8	33.6
Heavy	Low	0.9	2.1	3.0	4.3	1.7	1.1	1.6	3.0	10.1	3.1
Heavy	High	0.3	1.1	1.2	4.1	1.3	1.3	3.9	3.1	4.3	2.3
Avg.		8.0	13.6	19.3	34.0	6.7	7.6	16.8	14.7	42.1	
		1974									
Light	Low	6.7	43.0	74.5	51.1	25.1	8.8	17.5	31.6	27.8	31.8
Light	High	17.5	9.7	20.8	62.5	4.2	4.3	38.0	10.9	41.4	23.2
Heavy	Low	0.3	6.4	16.7	21.8	5.1	13.7	0.4	1.7	3.7	7.7
Heavy	High	4.5	2.6	1.2	0.7	4.5	1.6	0.3	1.5	0.8	1.9
Avg.		7.2	15.4	28.3	34.0	9.7	7.1	14.0	11.4	18.4	

	L.S.D. 0.05		
	Year		
Source	1966	1970	1974
Irrigation	NS	NS	NS
Compaction	8.7	7.4	8.3
Soil mix	16.6	9.1	16.1

porosity, only compaction significantly reduced water infiltration. In 1974, the heavily compacted plots averaged 22% lower air porosity than the lightly compacted plots. Comparatively, the infiltration rate in the heavily compacted plots was 82.5% lower than the lightly compacted plots. Water infiltration possibly was limited by the sealing of the surface as Waddington et al. (12) showed infiltration rates could be increased with mechanical cultivation.

Although air porosity and infiltration rates were greater throughout the experiment with increased amounts of modifying material, the air porosity and water infiltration were greater in mixes with larger amounts of expanded shale than sand. This may be because the expanded shale had a more uniform particle size distribution and provided larger air space within the soil matrix than the sand.

The total water infiltration rate decrease from 1966 to 1974 was greater for highly modified mixes than for slightly modified mixes. The reduced infiltration rates on mixes containing large percentages of coarse particles possibly could be associated with the development of hydrophobic conditions, as has been found by other workers (13). Therefore, addition of excess modifying material to insure high water infiltration in subsequent years does not appear warranted.

When averaged over the compaction levels and irrigation regimes, all mixes in 1974 surpassed the minimum water infiltration rates (5.0 to 7.6 cm/hour) proposed by the USGA Green Section (7). However, no mix met these standards in 1970 or 1974 when subjected to the heavy compaction level and high irrigation regime. Indications are that applications of soil topdressing as a proposed alternative to mechanical cultivation (5) will not maintain the desired soil water infiltration and air porosity after a number of years of traffic. Waddington et al. (12) showed that water infiltration rates were improved with mechanical cultivation illustrating that cultural procedures are an important consideration in evaluating golf putting green soils.

Clipping Yields

Clipping yields were not significantly influenced by the irrigation regimes (Table 4). However, clipping yields differed between compaction levels until 1973. For the first 6 years of the experiment, the largest initial spring yields were obtained from the heavily compacted plots. Thereafter, initial spring yields were not significantly different between the compaction levels.

Air porosity significantly correlated ($r = -0.784$ and $r = -0.762$, respectively) with water porosity and initial spring clipping yields in 1968 and 1970. Therefore, it appears reasonable to assume that the greater amount of moisture in the compacted mixes enhances spring shoot growth more than the lightly compacted mixes. Spring clipping differences between the compacted levels were reduced after 1970 (Table 4), possibly

Table 4. Clipping weights (g/m²) taken three times during 1968, 1970, 1973, and 1974 of nine modified golf putting green soils established in 1964 with creeping bentgrass and maintained at two compaction levels and two irrigation regimes.

Soil mix ratio of			Date			Date			Date			Date		
			1968			1970			1973			1974		
Modifying material : Soil			5 Apr.	8 July	19 Sept.	9 Apr.	15 July	26 Aug.	27 Mar.	3 July	28 Sept.	14 Mar.	10 July	21 Aug.
Expanded shale as modifying material														
1 : 3			189.9	32.9	11.7	42.1	18.5	18.6	78.3	78.1	28.1	55.3	5.7	1.2
3 : 4			183.2	25.0	11.7	42.6	15.9	16.8	80.2	76.7	25.2	49.2	6.0	1.4
4 : 3			160.3	20.4	10.9	38.9	14.8	14.4	82.8	80.9	28.0	42.0	6.4	1.3
5 : 2		44.9	144.9	18.9	9.6	35.9	13.1	13.1	71.0	76.7	26.0	42.3	6.8	1.2
River sand as modifying material														
1 : 3			191.8	29.0	12.6	46.1	17.4	18.5	78.9	78.4	30.2	50.4	5.8	1.5
3 : 4			166.1	32.3	9.6	38.3	15.2	15.4	75.3	73.0	26.1	41.1	6.2	1.3
4 : 3			148.6	28.8	10.0	41.9	15.7	13.5	80.8	76.3	26.3	50.8	6.5	1.4
5 : 2			144.4	26.8	9.9	35.7	13.3	12.6	75.3	80.4	28.0	38.6	6.3	1.5
19 : 3			118.0	21.7	8.3	31.1	13.0	11.3	77.8	76.0	25.9	41.0	7.1	1.3
Compaction levels	Irrigation regimes		Clipping weights averaged over all soil treatments for compaction levels and irrigation regimes											
Light	Low		108.7	25.2	12.9	34.2	19.4	15.0	79.0	63.1	31.7	41.7	6.1	1.2
Light	High		143.5	28.9	11.9	37.2	17.1	15.7	82.2	65.1	27.8	40.1	6.1	1.4
Heavy	Low		200.3	21.1	8.2	43.6	12.4	15.4	77.8	72.7	24.3	50.5	6.6	1.3
Heavy	High		190.7	29.6	8.8	41.8	11.8	13.5	72.1	108.7	24.6	50.3	6.4	1.5
Source			L.S.D. 0.05			L.S.D. 0.05			L.S.D. 0.05			L.S.D. 0.05		
Irrigation			NS	NS	NS	NS	1.6	NS	NS	NS	NS	NS	NS	0.15
Compaction			11.9	NS	2.6	4.51	0.68	NS	NS	19.9	6.38	NS	NS	NS
Soil mix			24.17	8.16	1.97	7.13	2.92	2.9	NS	NS	NS	NS	NS	NS

because the water porosity increased with light compaction and provided more soil moisture during the winter and early spring than in earlier years.

Clipping yields obtained during the summers of 1968, 1970, and 1973 were generally greater from the lightly compacted plots. The only exception was the unexplained increase in yields from the heavily compacted plots on 3 July 1973. The low summer yields for the heavily compacted soil mixes may have resulted partially from foliar injury imparted by the compactor. It does not appear probable that a reduction in gas exchange between soil and atmosphere because of compaction was a factor in reducing turf foliage since mixes with the greatest air porosity had the lowest clipping yields. During late summer, no significant correlations were obtained between clipping yields and water infiltration or air porosity.

Clipping yields for 1968, 1970, and 1973 were greater for the soil mixes containing the least amount of modifying materials (Table 4). Mixes containing the greatest amount of expanded shale or sand were the first to wilt under moisture stress and also had the lowest clipping yields. Apparently, the greater nutrient and moisture holding capacity associated with the mixes containing more soil enhance shoot growth.

Yields were statistically similar for all soil mixes and treatments in 1974, possibly because of thatch buildup and the reduced P and K fertility. Research is underway to determine the influence of mechanical cultivation on these soil mixes.

ACKNOWLEDGMENT

Dr. Marvin Lentner, Department of Statistics, Virginia Polytechnic Institute and State University programmed all statistical analysis.

LITERATURE CITED

1. Custis, S. G. 1976. Growth and net carbon exchange of creeping bentgrass (*Agrostis palustris* Huds.) managed under three moisture regimes in two modified soils. M.S. Thesis. Virginia Polytechnic Inst. and State Univ., Blacksburg.
2. Davis, R. R. 1952. Physical condition of putting green soils and other environmental factors affecting greens. U.S. Golf assoc. J. Turf Manage. 5(1):25–27.
3. Davis, W. B., J. L. Paul, J. H. Madison, and L. Y. George. 1970. A guide to evaluating sands and amendments used for high trafficked turfgrass. Univ. of California Agric. Ext. AXT-n 113. 93 p.
4. Janson, L. E. 1970. Adequate soil type for sport turfgrasses. p. 142–148. *In* R. R. Davis (ed.) Proc. First Int. Turfgrass Res. Conf., Harrogate, England. 15–18 July 1969.
5. Kuntze, R. J., M. H. Ferguson, and J. B. Page. 1957. The effects of compaction on golf green mixtures. U.S. Golf Assoc. Manage. 10(6):24–27.
6. Longwell, T. J., W. L. Parks, and M. E. Springer. 1963. Moisture characteristics of Tennessee soils. Univ. of Tennessee Agric. Exp. Stn., Knoxville. Bull. 376.
7. Lunt, O. R., and C. G. Wyckoff. 1955. A method for minimizing compaction under turfgrasses used for athletic areas. Agron. Abstr. p. 75.

8. Madison, J. H., J. L. Paul, and W. B. Davis. 1973. Alternative method of greens management. p. 431–437. *In* Eliot C. Roberts (ed.) Proc. Second Int. Turfgrass Res. Conf., Virginia Polytechnic Inst. and State Univ., Blacksburg. June 1973. Am. Soc. Agron., Madison, Wis.

9. Radko, A. M. 1973. Refining green section specification for putting green construction. p. 287–297. *In* Eliot C. Roberts (ed.) Proc. Second Int. Turfgrass Res. Conf., Virginia Polytechnic Inst. and State Univ., Blacksburg. June 1973. Am. Soc. Agron., Madison, Wis.

10. Skirde, W. 1973. Soil modification for athletic fields. p. 261–269. *In* Eliot C. Roberts (ed.) Proc. Second Int. Turfgrass Res. Conf. Virginia Polytechnic Inst. and State Univ., Blacksburg, Va. June 1973. Am. Soc.Agron., Madison, Wis.

11. Swartz, W. E., and L. T. Kardos. 1963. Effects of compaction on physical properties of sand-soil-peat mixtures at various moisture contents. Agron. J. 55:7–10.

12. Waddington, D. V., T. L. Zimmerman, G. J. Shoop, L. T. Kardos, and J. M. Duich. 1974. Soil modification for turfgrass areas. I. Physical propeties of physically amended soils. Prog. Rep. 337. Pennsylvania State Univ., College of Agriculture, Agric. Exp. Stn. University Park, Pa.

13. Wilkinson, J. F., and R. H. Miller. 1976. An interpretation of the cause of localized dry spots on sand golf greens. Agron. Abstr. p. 104.

Section V:

Weed Control in Turfs

Chapter 25

Differences in Tolerance of Bermudagrass and Zoysiagrass Cultivars to Herbicides[1]

B. J. JOHNSON

ABSTRACT

Controlling weeds in turfgrasses with herbicides without injuring the desired turf is often a major problem for turfgrass managers. Since repeated annual herbicide treatments are usually required for satisfactory weed control, studies were initiated to determine effects of repeated herbicide treatments on performance of different warm-season turfgrass cultivars. In general, profluralin [N-(cyclopropylmethyl)-α,α,α-trifluoro-2,6-dinitro-*N*-propyl-*p*-toluidine] prosulfalin {*N*-]]4-(dipropylamino)-3,5-dinitrophenyl]sulfonyl]-*S,S*-dimethylsulfilimine} and napropamide [2-(α-naphthoxy)-*N,N*-diethylpropionamide] at the 3× rate reduced the stand of bermudagrass (*Cynodon* spp.) more than DCPA dimethyl tetrachloroterephthalate), butralin [4-(1,1-dimethylethyl)-*N*-(1-methylpropyl)-2,6-dinitrobenzenamine], or oxadiazon [2-*tert*-butyl-4-(2,4-dichloro-5-isopropoxyphenyl)-Δ^2-1,3,4-oxadiazolin-5-one]. 'Tifway' bermudagrass was injured the least, while 'Tifgreen' and 'Tifdwarf' were injured the most from these treatments. The 3× treatments of profluralin, butralin, benefin (*N*-butyl-*N*-ethyl-α,α,α-trifluoro-2,6-dinitro-*p*-toluidine), napropamide, and prosulfalin reduced the stand of 'Meyer' and 'Matrella' zoysiagrass (*Zoysia* spp.) more than 'Emerald' zoysiagrass.

Additional index words: Warm-season grasses, Greenup, Shoot density, Turfgrass quality, *Cynodon* spp., *Zoysia* spp.

INTRODUCTION

When herbicides are used for weed control in turfgrasses, the chemicals must perform satisfactorily in controlling weeds without causing undesirable turfgrass injury. Acceptable weed control has been obtained from a number of preemergence (6, 7) herbicide treatments, but it is usually necessary to repeat these treatments annually for consistent control.

Information on tolerance of turfgrasses to repeated annual herbicide treatments varies. Callahan (2) reported that creeping bentgrass (*Agrostis palustria* Huds. 'Penncross') sod loss was moderate with DCPA (dimethyl tetrachloroterephthalate) and severe with bensulide [*O,O*-diisopropyl phosphorodithioate *S*-ester with *N*-(2-mercaptoethyl)benzenesulfonamide] and benefin (*N*-butyl-*N*-ethyl-α,α,α-trifluoro-2,6-dinitro-*p*-

[1] A contribution from the Dep. of Agronomy, Univ. of Georgia Exp. Stn., Experiment, GA 30212 USA.

 Proceedings of the Third International Turfgrass Research Conference.

toluidine) after three annual treatments. In Michigan (9), the most pronounced effect on turfgrass quality was observed during stress periods associated with midsummer drought and high temperatures. Bensulide temporarily injured Kentucky bluegrass (*Poa pratensis* L. 'Kenblue' and 'Merion') after the third annual bensulide treatment, while red fescue (*Festuca rubra* L. 'Pennlawn') was not injured from any bensulide treatment (9). Repeated DCPA treatments did not injure Kentucky bluegrass, but slight injury occurred on red fescue in Michigan (9) and a mixture of Kentucky bluegrass, bentgrass, and red fescue in Rhode Island (4). After four annual applications of bensulide, there was no measurable accumulation of residue in the soil in Rhode Island (8). Detectable quantities of bensulide were obtained to depths of 13 cm in the soil of a bentgrass putting green in Virginia (1) 11 months after the fourth annual application of a granular formulation, but not after equivalent treatment with an emulsifiable concentrate formulation.

The results from three annual herbicide treatments on 'Tifgreen' bermudagrass [*Cynodon dactylon* (L.) Pers.] in Tennessee (3) showed severe injury occurred when treated with DCPA or benefin and slight to moderate injury resulted when treated with bensulide. In Georgia (5), butralin [4-(1,1-dimethylethyl)-*N*-(1-methylpropyl)-2,6-dinitrobenzenamine] affected the stand of Tifgreen and 'Tifdwarf' bermudagrass more than 'Tifway', 'Ormond', or 'Floraturf' after four annual treatments. DCPA and oxadiazon [2-*tert*-butyl-4-(2,4-dichloro-5-isopropoxyphenyl)-Δ^2-1,3,4-oxadiazolin-5-one] did not result in any permanent injury from similar treatments (5).

Since phytotoxicity data from annual repeated herbicide treatments on responses of different warm-season cultivars maintained for turf are limited, experiments were conducted to evaluate the tolerance of five bermudagrass and three zoysiagrass cultivars to consecutive annual treatments of several preemergence herbicides.

METHODS AND MATERIALS

Repeated annual treatments of DCPA, oxadiazon, and butralin were applied to Tifway, Tifgreen, Tifdwarf, Ormond, and Floraturf bermudagrasses from 1972 through 1976 at Experiment, Ga., U.S.A. Profluralin [*N*-(cyclopropylmethyl)-α,α,α-trifluoro-2,6-dinitro-*N*-propyl-*p*-toluidine], prosulfalin {*N*-[[4-(dipropylamino)-3,5-dinitrophenyl]sulfonyl]-*S*,*S*-dimethylsulfilimine}, and napropamide [2-(α,naphthoxy)-*N*,*N*-diethylpropionamide] were applied to the same bermudagrass during 1975 and 1976. Repeated annual treatments of bensulide, oxadiazon, butralin, profluralin, benefin, and napropamide were applied to 'Emerald' (*Zoysia japonica* Steud. × *Z. tenuifolia* Willd. ex Trin.), 'Meyer' (*Z. japonica* Steud.), and 'Matrella' zoysiagrass [*Z. matrella* (L.) Merr.] from 1974 through 1976. Prosulfalin was applied to the same zoysiagrass cultivars during 1975 and 1976.

All herbicide treatments were applied annually to the same plots in

February or March. Treatments applied to the bermudagrass cultivars were arranged in a split plot design where herbicide treatments were main plots and cultivars were subplots with four replications. The bermudagrasses were included in adjacent 1.5-m strips with individual 1.5- × 1.5-m plots. Treatments applied to the zoysiagrass cultivars were arranged in a randomized block design of 1.5- × 3-m plots with four replications. Each cultivar was included in separate tests but all grasses were included in the same area. DCPA, prosulfalin, and bensulide were applied broadcast as a spray in 376 liters/ha of water. All other chemicals were applied as granules with a spreader.

Turfgrass greenup was visually rated in April 1975 and 1976 based on a scale of 1 = no green color and 10 = complete uniform green color. Turfgrass greenup is a term used to describe the change from a dormant stage to an actively growing stage in the spring. Turfgrass quality and cover ratings were made at monthly intervals from May to August during 1974 through 1976. Turfgrass quality ratings were based on a scale of 1 to 10, with 1 representing total discoloration or plants dead and 10 representing no discoloration with dark green plant color. Percent turfgrass cover ratings were based on a scale of 0 to 100 with 0 representing total loss of turfgrass sod and 100 representing a complete uniform turfgrass cover. All ratings were visually estimated. The bermudagrass cultivars were established on an Applying sandy clay loam soil (Typic Hapludult) with an organic matter content of 1%. The soil composition was 66% sand, 13% silt, and 21% clay. The zoysiagrass cultivars were established on a Cecil sandy clay loam soil (Typic Hapludult) with an organic matter content of 2%. The soil composition was 60% sand, 19% silt, and 21% clay.

The turfgrasses were fertilized with 50–22–42 kg/ha (N:P:K) in April and September and 50 kg/ha N at monthly intervals during the spring and summer of each year. Irrigation was applied as needed to maintain optimum conditions for turfgrass growth. All data were analyzed statistically and treatment means were compared using Duncan's multiple range test.

RESULTS

Bermudagrass Cultivars

Turfgrass Greenup

The rate of greenup of five bermudagrass cultivars was delayed by consecutive annual herbicide treatments during early spring (Table 1). The greenup of Floraturf bermudagrass was later than other cultivars and there was no difference between treated and untreated plots. Oxadiazon at 4.5 kg/ha and napropamide at 3.4 kg/ha were the only herbicides that did not delay greenup of any bermudagrass cultivars in 1975. When chemicals delayed turfgrass greenup, Tifway was affected the least, Ormond was intermediate, and Tifgreen and Tifdwarf were affected the

Table 1. Effects of consecutive annual herbicide treatments on early turfgrass greenup of five bermudagrasses.

Treatments		Bermudagrasses				
Herbicide†	Rate	Tifway	Tifgreen	Tifdwarf	Ormond	Floraturf
	kg/ha			1 to 10 ratings		
				21 Apr. 1975		
Untreated	--	8.4 a*	7.4 a-e	8.0 ab	7.8 a-c	4.0 o-t
DCPA	11.2	7.0 b-g	4.5 n-r	5.3 j-n	6.5 d-i	4.3 n-s
Oxadiazon	4.5	7.5 a-d	6.5 d-i	7.3 d-f	7.3 b-f	4.8 m-q
Butralin	6.7	6.3 f-j	3.8 q-u	3.9 p-t	5.0 k-o	3.8 q-u
Profluralin	3.4	7.6 a-c	4.9 l-p	5.0 k-o	6.3 f-j	3.0 t-v
	10.1	5.6 i-m	2.4 v	2.8 uv	4.3 n-s	3.1 t-v
Prosulfalin	3.4	7.4 a-e	6.3 f-j	6.4 e-i	7.0 b-g	4.0 o-t
	10.1	7.0 b-g	5.3 j-n	5.6 i-m	6.1 g-j	3.5 r-u
Napropamide	3.4	8.0 ab	6.8 c-h	7.5 a-d	7.3 b-f	4.0 o-t
	10.1	6.9 c-h	6.0 g-k	6.9 c-h	5.9 h-l	3.3 s-v
				20 Apr. 1976		
Untreated	--	7.4 ab	6.8 a-e	7.0 a-c	6.5 c-g	4.0 n-q
DCPA	11.2	7.5 a	6.6 b-f	7.0 a-c	6.6 b-f	3.6 o-q
Oxadiazon	4.5	7.3 a-c	5.6 h-k	6.5 c-g	6.9 a-d	3.6 o-q
Butralin	6.7	7.3 a-c	5.4 h-k	5.5 h-k	5.9 f-j	3.6 o-q
Profluralin	3.4	7.3 a-c	5.4 h-k	5.5 h-k	5.9 f-j	3.6 o-q
	10.1	6.1 d-h	4.5 l-n	4.5 l-n	5.3 i-k	3.3 q
Prosulfalin	3.4	7.0 a-c	4.9 k-m	5.8 g-j	6.0 d-i	3.8 o-q
	10.1	7.0 a-c	4.1 n-p	4.4 m-o	5.1 j-l	3.6 o-q
Napropamide	3.4	7.4 ab	6.1 d-h	6.0 d-i	5.6 h-k	3.5 pq
	10.1	6.5 c-g	5.3 i-k	5.8 g-j	5.4 h-k	3.4 pq

* Values with common letters within blocks are not significantly different at the 5% level according to Duncan's multiple range test. Ratings were based on a scale with 1 representing no green color and 10 representing complete uniform green color. † DCPA, oxidiazon, and butralin were applied as 5 annual treatments, while the other chemicals were applied as 2 annual treatments.

most. Profluralin applied at 3.4 kg/ha and prosulfalin at 3.4 kg/ha did not affect greenup of Tifway in 1975, but Tifgreen and Tifdwarf ratings were lower when treated with the same chemicals. Although Tifway treated with DCPA at 11.2 kg/ha, butralin at 6.7 kg/ha, profluralin at 10.1 kg/ha, or prosulfalin at 10.1 kg/ha had lower greenup ratings than untreated Tifway, the delayed greenup was not as serious as with either Tifgreen or Tifdwarf.

The responses of herbicide treatments to different bermudagrass cultivars in 1976 were similar to the previous year (Table 1). However, none of the herbicides except profluralin and prosulfalin applied at the highest rate significantly delayed greenup of Tifway. Rainfall during the first 6 weeks after treatment was higher in 1975 (34 cm) than in 1976 (24 cm). The poorer greenup ratings of Tifway in 1975 may have been associated with the greater amount of rainfall.

Turfgrass Quality

On 19 May 1976 the turfgrass quality of Tifway and Ormond bermudagrass cultivars in the consecutive herbicide-treated plots was as good as the quality in untreated plots (Table 2). However, the quality of Tif-

Table 2. Effects of consecutive annual herbicide treatments on turfgrass quality and cover of five bermudagrasses in 1976.

Herbicide† treatments	Application rate	Turfgrass quality‡					Turfgrass cover§				
		Tifway	Tifgreen	Tifdwarf	Ormond	Floraturf	Tifway	Tifgreen	Tifdwarf	Ormond	Floraturf
	kg/ha	1 to 10 rating					%				
Untreated		9.4 ab*	9.3 ab	9.4 ab	7.6 d-g	7.6 d-g	94 ab	85 b-g	91 a-c	89 a-d	90 a-c
DCPA	11.2	10.0 a	9.3 ab	9.4 ab	7.5 d-h	8.3 cd	94 ab	88 a-d	90 a-c	90 a-c	95 a
Oxadiazon	4.5	9.4 ab	8.1 c-e	8.9 bc	7.6 d-g	7.5 d-h	94 ab	91 a-c	91 ac	88 a-e	90 a-c
Butralin	6.7	9.0 bc	6.8 g-l	7.5 d-h	7.8 d-f	7.5 d-h	86 a-f	79 e-h	84 c-h	86 a-f	85 b-g
Profluralin	3.4	9.3 ab	7.0 f-k	7.4 d-i	7.4 d-i	7.0 f-k	95 a	83 c-h	85 b-g	89 a-d	90 a-c
	10.1	9.0 bc	6.3 kl	6.6 h-l	7.0 f-k	6.5 f-l	90 a-c	70 i	75 hi	78 f-i	85 b-g
Prosulfalin	3.4	9.3 ab	6.6 h-l	7.3 e-j	7.3 e-j	6.6 h-l	94 ab	85 b-g	89 a-d	91 a-c	91 a-c
	10.1	9.3 ab	6.4 j-l	6.6 h-l	6.9 f-l	6.0 l	89 a-d	76 g-i	78 f-i	78 f-i	75 hi
Napropamide	3.4	9.6 ab	7.5 d-h	7.4 d-i	7.3 e-j	6.5 i-l	95 a	85 b-g	90 a-c	91 a-c	90 a-c
	10.1	8.9 bc	6.5 i-l	7.3 e-j	6.9 f-l	6.1 kl	94 ab	80 d-h	84 c-h	86 a-f	90 a-c

* Values with common letters within blocks are not significantly different at the 5% level according to Duncan's multiple range test. † DCPA, oxadiazon, and butralin were applied as five annual treatments, while the other chemicals were applied as two annual treatments. ‡ Ratings made 19 May 1976 and based on a scale of 1 representing total discoloration or plants dead and 10 representing no discoloration with dark green plant color. § Ratings made 24 Aug. 1976 and based on a scale of 0 representing total loss of turfgrass sod and 100 representing a complete uniform turfgrass cover.

green and Tifdwarf was lower than Tifway when treated with butralin, profluralin, prosulfalin, or napropamide. Tifgreen treated with oxadiazon also had a lower quality rating than Tifway. However, the difference between Floraturf treated and untreated was not as great when compared with the respective treatments of Tifgreen and Tifdwarf. In 1973 and 1974, butralin affected the turfgrass quality of bermudagrass more in May or June than DCPA or oxadiazon and there was no differences among cultivars (5). In 1975, quality of Tifgreen and Tifdwarf was lower than Tifway when treated with either butralin or profluralin when compared with the respective untreated checks (data not shown). No other difference occurred in previous years.

The turfgrass quality of all treated turfgrasses was as good as the respective untreated checks by 24 Aug. 1976, except for Tifgreen treated with profluralin at 10.1 kg/ha and Floraturf treated with prosulfalin at 10.1 kg/ha. However, neither turfgrass was affected by the chemicals when each was applied at the 1× rate (3.4 kg/ha).

Turfgrass Cover

None of the consecutive herbicide treatments affected the turfgrass cover of the bermudagrass cultivars when final ratings were made 24 Aug. 1976, except when profluralin and prosulfalin were applied at the highest rate (Table 2). The covers of Tifdwarf and Ormond were lower in plots treated with either chemical. The cover was also low when Tifgreen was treated with profluralin and Floraturf was treated with prosulfalin. Tifway bermudagrass was the only cultivar included in this study whose cover the herbicide treatments did not affect. Similar results occurred from profluralin treatments in 1975 (data not shown).

DISCUSSION

These results indicate that selected herbicides used for preemergence weed control will affect bermudagrass cultivars differently. Most consecutive herbicide treatments either delayed greenup or influenced turfgrass quality or cover sometime during the spring or summer. Therefore, chemicals should be carefully selected on the basis of those treatments causing least injury. In this study, Tifway bermudagrass tolerated the consecutive herbicide treatments better than Tifgreen or Tifdwarf did. However, consecutive oxadiazon, DCPA, and butralin treatments can be used on all these bermudagrasses without causing any severe injury or stand reduction. Caution should be taken with napropamide, profluralin, or prosulfalin. The 3× rate of prosulfalin severely injured all bermudagrass cultivars except Tifway, while similar injury occurred to Tifgreen and Tifdwarf when treated with napropamide and to Tifgreen, Tifdwarf, and Ormond when treated with profluralin.

Table 3. Effects of three annual herbicide treatments on early turfgrass greenup of three zoysiagrass cultivars in 1976.

Treatments		Zoysiagrass cultivars		
Herbicide	Rate	Emerald	Meyer	Matrella
	kg/ha	1 to 10 ratings		
Untreated	--	5.6 a*	6.1 a-c	5.0 ab
Profluralin	3.4	4.8 c	5.6 b-d	3.5 e-g
	10.1	3.5 e	5.1 d	2.8 g
Butralin	6.7	4.1 d	6.0 a-c	3.6 e-g
	20.2	3.0 e	5.8 a-d	3.0 fg
Oxadiazon	4.5	5.1 a-c	6.5 a	4.6 a-d
	13.4	5.1 a-c	6.4 ab	4.4 b-e
Benefin	3.4	5.0 bc	6.3 a-c	4.0 c-e
	10.1	4.9 c	6.0 a-c	4.0 c-e
Napropamide	3.4	5.0 bc	5.8 a-d	4.8 a-c
	10.1	5.0 bc	5.1 d	3.8 d-f
Bensulide	11.2	5.6 a	6.1 a-c	4.6 a-d
	33.6	5.4 ab	6.0 a-c	4.4 b-e
Prosulfalin†	3.4	5.5 ab	5.6 b-d	4.9 a-c
	10.1	5.4 ab	5.5 cd	5.5 a

* Values with common letters within columns are not significantly different at the 5% level according to Duncan's multiple range test. Ratings made 21 Apr. 1976 and based on a scale of 1 to 10 with 1 representing no green color and 10 representing complete uniform green color.
† Applied only as two annual treatments.

Zoysiagrass Cultivars

Turfgrass Greenup

Consecutive annual herbicide treatments delayed the greenup of three zoysiagrass cultivars (Table 3). Meyer zoysiagrass was influenced the least, while greenup of Emerald or Matrella was lower in plots treated with several herbicides. Profluralin and napropamide applied at the highest rate were the only treatments that delayed greenup of Meyer when compared with the untreated check. Profluralin, butralin, benefin, and napropamide, regardless of rate, delayed greenup of Emerald and Matrella. An exception occurred for Matrella treated with napropamide at 3.4 kg/ha. Oxadiazon, bensulide, and prosulfalin were the only herbicides evaluated in 1976 that did not delay greenup of any zoysiagrass cultivars when compared with the respective untreated checks. However, bensulide and prosulfalin treatments delayed the greenup of all zoysiagrass cultivars and oxadiazon delayed greenup of Matrella zoysiagrass in 1975 (data not shown). This occurred from heavier rainfall within a 2-month period after treatment (38 cm in 1975 compared with 24 cm in 1976). Results from the other treatments were similar both years.

Turfgrass Quality

Herbicide treatments influenced the turfgrass quality of zoysiagrass cultivars differently after three consecutive annual treatments (Table 4). The quality of Meyer was not affected by butralin treatments, but the

Table 4. Effects of three annual herbicide treatments on turfgrass quality and cover of three zoysiagrass cultivars in 1976.

Treatments		Turfgrass quality‡			Turfgrass cover§		
Herbicide	Rate	Emerald	Meyer	Matrella	Emerald	Meyer	Matrella
	kg/ha	1 to 10 ratings			%		
Untreated	--	8.1 a*	8.3 ab	7.0 a	100 a	99 a	94 a-c
Profluralin	3.4	6.8 c-e	7.0 c-e	4.8 ef	95 a	91 b	84 de
	10.1	5.5 g	5.9 f	3.3 g	88 b	73 d	65 f
Butralin	6.7	6.6 de	8.5 a	5.6 b-e	100 a	89 b	90 b-d
	20.2	5.8 fg	7.3 b-d	4.0 fg	94 a	81 c	83 de
Oxadiazon	4.5	8.0 ab	7.9 a-c	6.8 ab	98 a	100 a	98 ab
	13.4	8.3 a	7.6 a-c	6.8 ab	95 a	100 a	100 a
Benefin	3.4	7.6 ab	7.8 a-c	5.5 c-e	98 a	90 b	83 de
	10.1	6.4 ef	7.3 b-d	5.3 c-e	98 a	81 c	79 e
Napropamide	3.4	7.3 b-d	7.9 a-c	6.4 a-c	100 a	90 b	96 ab
	10.1	6.4 ef	6.3 ef	4.9 d-f	100 a	69 d	86 c-e
Bensulfide	11.2	8.3 a	7.4 b-d	5.4 c-e	100 a	100 a	89 b-d
	33.6	7.5 a-c	7.4 b-d	5.3 c-e	98 a	100 a	94 a-c
Prosulfalin†	3.4	7.9 ab	7.5 bc	6.4 a-c	98 a	91 b	91 a-d
	10.1	6.8 c-e	6.5 d-f	6.0 a-d	85 b	75 cd	79 e

* Values with common letters within columns are not significantly different at the 5% level according to Duncan's multiple range test. † Applied only as two annual treatments.
‡ Ratings made 10 May 1976 and based on a scale of 1 representing total discoloration or plants dead and 10 representing no discoloration with dark green plant color. § Ratings made 24 Aug. 1976 and based on a scale of 0 representing total loss of turfgrass sod and 100 representing a complete uniform turf cover.

Emerald and Matrella ratings were significantly lower than the respective untreated checks when ratings were made 19 May 1976. Benefin at 3.4 kg/ha did not influence the quality of either Emerald or Meyer, when compared with turfs in the untreated plots. However, when Matrella was treated with benefin at 3.4 kg/ha, the quality was lower than the untreated turf. Emerald treated with 10.1 kg/ha of benefin resulted in lower ratings than in treated Emerald plots, but not in the treated Meyer plots. Bensulide treatments did not influence the quality of either Emerald or Meyer turfs, but it lowered turf quality in Matrella plots. Oxadiazon was the only chemical that did not lower turfgrass quality for any of the zoysiagrass cultivars.

When final ratings were made 24 Aug. 1976 the turfgrass quality of all zoysiagrass cultivars treated with butralin or bensulide had fully recovered. Turfs receiving profluralin or prosulfalin applied at the highest rates did not recover completely.

Turfgrass Cover

The turfgrass cover of Emerald zoysiagrass was affected less than Meyer and Matrella from consecutive annual herbicide treatments (Table 4). Profluralin and prosulfalin applied at the highest rates were the only treatments that reduced the cover of Emerald zoysiagrass. However, the cover was higher in Emerald plots than in Meyer or Matrella. The turfgrass cover of Meyer and Matrella was not as good as Emerald when treated with butralin, benefin, or napropamide. An exception occurred when Matrella was treated with napropamide at 3.4 kg/ha. Oxadiazon and bensulide were the only chemicals that did not affect the cover of any zoysiagrass cultivars when final ratings were made. Results in previous years were similar as the turfgrass cover of Meyer was affected more than either Emerald or Matrella from the treatments.

CONCLUSIONS

These results indicate that oxadiazon was the only herbicide that did not affect turfgrass greenup, quality, or cover of the three zoysiagrass cultivars. In addition, bensulide was safe to apply on any of the cultivars. Benefin did not affect cover of Emerald, but reduced cover of Meyer and Matrella. All chemicals except oxadiazon delayed turfgrass greenup and affected the quality of Emerald and Matrella in early spring more than Meyer zoysiagrass. However, the cover of Emerald zoysiagrass was affected the least when final ratings were made in August following consecutive spring treatments.

LITERATURE CITED

1. Bingham, S. W., and R. E. Schmidt. 1967. Residue of bensulide in turfgrass soil following annual treatments for crabgrass control. Agron. J. 59:327–329.
2. Callahan, L. M. 1972. Phytotoxicity of herbicides to a Penncross bentgrass green. Weed Sci. 20:387–391.
3. ————. 1976. Phytotoxicity of herbicides to Tifgreen bermudagrass green. Weed Sci. 24:92–98.
4. Jagschitz, J. A., and C. R. Skogley. 1965. Turfgrass response to dacthal and nitrogen. Agron. J. 57:35–38.
5. Johnson, B. J. 1976. Bermudagrass tolerance to consecutive butralin and oxadiazon treatments. Weed Sci. 24:302–305.
6. ————. 1976. Herbicides for seasonal weed control in turfgrasses. Agron. J. 68:717–720.
7. ————. 1976. Crabgrass and goosegrass control in bermudagrasses with herbicides. Georgia Agric. Res. Bull. 197:1–29.
8. Mazur, A. R., J. A. Jagschitz, and C. R. Skogley. 1969. Bioassay for bensulide, DCPA, and siduron in turfgrass. Weed Sci. 17:31–34.
9. Turgeon, A. J., J. B. Beard, D. P. Martin, and W. F. Meggitt. 1974. Effects of successive applications of preemergence herbicides on turf. Weed Sci. 22:349–352.

Chapter 26

Development and Rooting of Kentucky Bluegrass Sod as Affected by Herbicides[1]

J. A. JAGSCHITZ

ABSTRACT

Herbicides used for weed control on Kentucky bluegrass (*Poa pratensis* L.) grown for commercial sod may delay its development or interfere with rooting after transplanting. In these studies, herbicides were applied on immature and mature sod for control of annual grasses and on mature sod for control of broadleafed weeds. Sod development was evaluated by sod strength measurements and estimates of grass stand. The herbicide effect on rooting of transplanted sod was determined by measuring the weight of roots grown from sod plugs on sand and by measuring the force required to lift sod plugs from soil.

Mature sod was safely treated with mixtures of 2,4-D [(2,4-dichlorophenoxy) acetic acid] with either dicamba (3,6-dichloro-*o*-anisic acid), mecoprop [2-[(4-chloro-*o*-tolyl)-oxy]propionic acid], or silvex [2-(2,4,5-trichlorophenoxy)propionic acid] at least 4 weeks before or after transplanting in the spring or 4 weeks before transplanting in the fall. Some root inhibition took place when sod was treated earlier or if treated 4 weeks after transplanting in the fall.

Immature sod treated with benefin (*N*-butyl-*N*-ethyl-α,α,α-trifluoro-2,6-dinitro-*p*-toluidine), bensulide [*O,O*-diisopropyl phosphorodithioate *S*-ester with *N*-(2-mercaptoethyl)benzenesulfonamide], butralin [4-(1,1-dimethylethyl)-*N*-(1-methylpropyl)-2,6-dinitrobenzenamine], DCPA (dimethyl tetrachloroterephthalate), oxadiazon [2-*tert*-butyl-4-(2,4-dichloro-5-isopropoxyphenyl)-Δ^2-1,3,4-oxadiazolin-5-one], and prosulfalin [*N*-[[4-(dipropylamino)-3,5-dinitrophenyl]sulfonyl]-*S,S*-dimethylsulfilimine] was less dense and/or exhibited reduced sod strength up to 11 weeks following treatment. Sod treated with bensulide and prosulfalin was weaker up to 25 weeks after treatment. Bensulide and prosulfalin inhibited the rooting of sod transplanted 23 weeks after treatment. Some reduction in rooting was noted with sod treated 15 weeks earlier with benefin and DCPA. Siduron [1-(2-methylcyclohexyl)-3-phenylurea] was safe to use on immature sod. Mature sod treated with benefin, bensulide, and prosulfalin showed some root inhibition when transplanted within 10 weeks. It appeared safe to use butralin, DCPA, oxadiazon, and siduron on mature sod to be transplanted after 5 weeks.

Additional index words: Grass stand, *Poa pratensis* L., Residues, Root inhibition, Root production, Sod transplant, Root strength, Sod strength.

---

[1] A contribution from the Plant and Soil Science Dep., Rhode Island Agric. Exp. Stn., Kingston, RI 02881 USA.

INTRODUCTION

The use of chemical herbicides aids in the production of weed-free turf. Herbicides used in sod production, however, should not delay the development of the crop or interfere with harvesting or successful establishment after harvest. Sod must be strong enough to undergo handling during harvest, and when transplanted should form new roots and knit quickly. Information on how herbicide residues in the sod affect growth and rooting would be valuable to sod growers.

Some information is available on the effect of herbicide residues in the soil, but little information when the residue is in the sod. Research under greenhouse conditions has shown that herbicides may inhibit rhizome production. Juska and Hovin (6) observed that benefin (*N*-butyl-*N*-ethyl-α,α,α-trifluoro-2,6-dinitro-*p*-toluidine), bensulide [*O,O*-diisopropyl phosphorodithioate *S*-ester with *N*-(2-mercaptoethyl)benzenesulfonamide], and DCPA (dimethyl tetrachloroterephthalate) reduced rhizome growth of seedling Kentucky bluegrass (*Poa pratensis* L.). Gaskin (5) observed that Kentucky bluegrass seedlings treated with DCPA produced shorter and fewer rhizomes. Bingham (1) found that bermudagrass (*Cynodon dactylon* L.) stolons did not branch as frequently when root growth at the nodes was inhibited by bensulide, DCPA, or siduron [1-(2-methylcyclohexyl)-3-phenylurea].

Observations of root inhibition caused by these chemicals are common and even used as a bioassay to determine the presence of these herbicides in soil (9). Engel and Callahan (4) reported that bensulide residues remaining in the upper soil layers 8 months after treatment was sufficient to inhibit the rooting of bluegrass sod plugs. Similar studies conducted by Smith and Callahan (11) showed that bensulide, benefin, DCPA, and siduron residues in soil inhibited rooting of sod plugs transplanted up to 10 months after treatment. Bingham (2) found that benefin and bensulide applied to the surface of transplanted Kentucky bluegrass sod reduced its rooting strength.

If root and rhizome inhibition occurs, sod strength may develop more slowly and sod may root poorly when transplanted. The purpose of this investigation was to determine the effects of herbicides used for the control of annual grasses and broadleafed weeds applied to the surface of Kentucky bluegrass sod on its development (sod strength) and its sod transplant rooting.

MATERIALS AND METHODS

During the period from 1970 to 1976, herbicides were applied to Kentucky bluegrass being grown commercially for sod in many separate tests. 'Merion' was the predominant cultivar in the early trials while later the sod was a blend of two or three cultivars. In a few of the earlier trials the sod contained small amounts of red fescue (*Festuca rubra* L.). Sod was treated at either of two stages of development—immature or mature. Sod considered immature was seeded the previous year, had visible seeded rows, lacked complete grass cover (45 to 80%), and was not ready for harvest. Mature sod was about 18 months old, had 100% solid grass cover, and was ready for harvest. The grass was weed-free and maintained at a cutting height of about 3.5 cm.

The herbicides and rates used were as follows: 2,4-D [(2,4-dichlorophenoxy)acetic acid] at 1.1 kg/ha; benefin at 2.1 to 2.8 kg/ha; bensulide at 10.4 to 12.7 kg/ha; butralin [4-(1,1-dimethylethyl)-*N*-(1-methylpropyl)-2,6-dinitrobenzenamine] at 4.5 to 5.6 kg/ha; DCPA at 11.2 to 14.0 kg/ha; dicamba (3,6-dichloro-*o*-anisic acid) at 0.3 kg/ha; mecoprop [2-[(4-chloro-*o*-tolyl)oxy]propionic acid] at 1.1 kg/ha; oxadiazon [2-*tert*-butyl-4-(2,4-dichloro-5-isopropoxyphenyl)-Δ^2-1,3,4-oxadiazolin-5-one] at 3.4 kg/ha; prosulfalin [*N*-[[4-(dipropylamino)-3,5-dinitrophenyl]sulfonyl]-*S*,*S*-dimethylsulfilimine] at 2.2 to 2.8 kg/ha; siduron at 12.7 to 15.5 kg/ha; silvex [2-(2,4,5-trichlorophenoxy)propionic acid] at 0.6 kg/ha. Most spring herbicide treatments were applied from late April to mid-May, while the fall applications were from September to mid-October. Dicamba, 2,4-D, mecoprop, and silvex were applied as sprays while the other herbicides were applied as granulars and/or sprays. Most sprays were at 804 liters/ha. Plot size varied from 1 to 4.3 m^2 and treatments were arranged in a minimum of three randomized complete blocks.

Where herbicides were applied to immature sod, measurement of sod strength and/or visual estimates of grass stand were used to evaluate sod development. Sod strength was measured using an apparatus similar to one developed by Rieke et al. (10). A 30-cm wide sod strip was clamped to a fixed and a movable platform. Thickness of the sod ranged from 1.2 to 2.3 cm but was uniform within each test. Comparisons between tests are probably not valid because sod thickness could influence sod strength. When the apparatus was activated the movable stage was pulled and the maximum force at which the sod broke was measured. A minimum of three breaks were averaged for each sod strip from each plot. Transplant sod rooting strength, which is a measure of the force necessary to uproot sod plugs after transplanting, was measured using a technique developed by King and Beard (7) and modified by Ledeboer et al. (8).

Three to four 10-cm diam plugs were cut in each sod strip. A wire ring with a crossbar was placed beneath each plug. At the end of the rooting period (average of 5 weeks, range of 3 to 7 weeks) a wire was hooked to the crossbar of the ring and a scale with a maximum indicator was used to lift the plug and measure the force necessary to uproot the sod. Root production was measured by transplanting a sod plug from each strip into clay pots filled with mortar sand. Roots that had grown into the sand (average of 5 weeks, range of 4 to 10 weeks) were removed and weighed. Root weights were measured by determining weight loss by ignition at 550C for 12 hours after drying the sample at 105C for 24 hours in all but two treatments (see Table 6). The data from these tests were analyzed at

Table 1. Root strength and root production of mature Kentucky bluegrass sod as influenced by herbicides applied before transplanting.

Herbicide treatment	4 weeks before transplanting			2 weeks before transplanting						
	Spring	Fall		Spring			Fall			
	1975	1971	1975	1972	1973	1975	1970	1971	1972	1975
	strength kg/dm²									
2,4-D	19 a*	14 a	--	12 a	12 a	19 a	--	13 b-f	13 a	--
2,4-D + dicamba	18 a	14 a	14 a	12 a	12 a	19 a	12 a	14 ab	12 a	15 a
2,4-D + mecoprop	18 a	14 a	15 a	12 a	10 a	18 a	12 ab	13 a-f	12 a	13 a
2,4-D + silvex	19 a	15 a	14 a	12 a	10 a	16 a	9 bcd	10 gh	11 a	13 a
Untreated	21 a	15 a	16 a	13 a	12 a	21 a	11 abc	15 ab	13 a	16 a
	root mg/dm²									
2,4-D	479 a	317 a	--	345 a	629 a	409 a	--	256 bcd	180 bc	--
2,4-D + dicamba	495 a	310 a	191 a	270 a	369 b	438 a	285 ab	231 cde	255 ab	190 a
2,4-D + mecoprop	473 a	276 a	193 a	310 a	443 b	450 a	245 b	232 cde	205 abc	206 a
2,4-D + silvex	511 a	270 a	180 a	310 a	371 b	369 a	140 c	136 fgh	160 c	183 a
Untreated	524 a	264 a	238 a	347 a	343 b	524 a	365 a	264 a-d	275 a	238 a

* Means within columns followed by the same letter are not significantly different at the 5% level as determined by Duncan's multiple range test.

the 5% level and means were separated using Duncan's multiple range test (3).

RESULTS AND DISCUSSION

Broadleaf Herbicides

No reduction in grass stand or difficulty in harvesting was noted with the mature sod in any of the tests. Rooting effects from the herbicide treatments to mature Kentucky bluegrass sod before and after transplanting in the spring and fall are shown in Tables 1 and 2. Use of 2,4-D alone or in combination with dicamba, mecoprop, or silvex did not inhibit rooting when applied 4 weeks before transplanting in the fall, 2 or 4 weeks before transplanting in the spring, and 4 weeks after transplanting in the spring. Most herbicides showed evidence of root inhibition when applied to sod 2 weeks after transplanting in the spring and 2 or 4 weeks after transplanting in the fall. Mixtures of 2,4-D with mecoprop and especially silvex applied 2 weeks before transplanting in the fall inhibited sod rooting. Root inhibition was greater from herbicides applied closer to transplanting time, after transplanting time, and in the fall. Based on these results, mature Kentucky bluegrass sod can be safely treated with mixtures of 2,4-D with either dicamba, mecoprop, or silvex if applied at least 4 weeks before or after harvest in the spring or 4 weeks before harvest in the fall. Poor sod rooting may occur if sod is treated sooner or 4 weeks after transplanting in the fall.

Table 2. Root strength and root production of Kentucky bluegrass sod as influenced by herbicides applied after transplanting.

Herbicide treatment	2 weeks after transplanting				4 weeks after transplanting	
	Spring		Fall		Spring	Fall
	1973	1975	1972	1975	1973	1975
	strength kg/dm²					
2,4-D	13 b*	28 ab	10 abc	--	16 a	--
2,4-D + dicamba	11 c	30 ab	10 bc	15 bc	15 a	16 b
2,4-D + mecoprop	11 bc	28 ab	8 c	14 bc	15 a	15 b
2,4-D + silvex	11 bc	26 b	11 ab	13 c	15 a	16 b
Untreated	15 a	33 a	13 a	19 a	16 a	19 a
	root mg/dm²					
2,4-D	442 a	577 ab	165 bc	--	605 a	--
2,4-D + dicamba	475 a	455 bc	205 bc	401 a	596 a	419 a
2,4-D + mecoprop	390 a	353 c	200 bc	390 a	565 a	328 a
2,4-D + silvex	407 a	383 c	220 b	438 a	579 a	405 a
Untreated	536 a	693 a	325 a	402 a	657 a	402 a

* Means within columns followed by the same letter are not significantly different at the 5% level as determined by Duncan's multiple range test.

Table 3. Effect of herbicides on grass stand development when applied in the spring to immature Kentucky bluegrass sod.

	Time after herbicide application			
	1973		1974	1975
Herbicide treatment	9 weeks	11 weeks	7 weeks	7 weeks
	% stand			
Benefin	86 bc*	67 d	62 ab	88 ab
Bensulide	98 a	79 a	65 ab	89 ab
Butralin	69 e	67 d	61 ab	80 de
DCPA	85 bc	72 a-d	63 ab	87 a-d
Oxadiazon	89 b	70 bcd	59 b	78 e
Prosulfalin	68 e	45 e	9 d	38 g
Siduron	96 a	72 a-d	68 a	85 a-d
Untreated	96 a	73 a-d	64 ab	88 ab

* Means within columns followed by the same letter are not significantly different at the 5% level as determined by Duncan's multiple range test.

Annual Grass Herbicides

Immature Sod

Sod Development. The effects of herbicides on grass stand and sod strength are shown in Tables 3 and 4, respectively. Bensulide and siduron did not delay stand development. There was less grass cover in one test with benefin and DCPA, in two tests with butralin and oxadiazon, and in all four tests with prosulfalin. Benefin reduced sod strength 7 and 10 weeks following treatment, while no reduction was evident in sod treated 19 to 25 weeks earlier. Sods treated with bensulide and prosulfalin were weaker up to 25 weeks after treatment. Butralin, DCPA, oxadiazon, and siduron did not alter sod strength.

Based on total plant, tiller and rhizome counts made 12 weeks after treatment (1970), benefin reduced tiller and rhizome production. This could account for the reduced sod strength. There was no reduction in

Table 4. Effect of herbicides on sod strength when applied in the spring to immature Kentucky bluegrass sod.

	Time after herbicide application				
	1970			1974	1975
Herbicide treatment	7 weeks	10 weeks	19 weeks	21 weeks	25 weeks
	kg/dm²				
Benefin	34 b*	23 c	54 a	129 abc	120 bcd
Bensulide	30 b	20 b	44 bc	111 e	112 cd
Butralin	--	--	--	134 ab	129 a-d
DCPA	44 a	31 ab	52 abc	121 b-e	122 bcd
Oxadiazon	--	--	--	132 ab	136 abc
Prosulfalin	--	--	--	56 f	†
Siduron	48 a	32 ab	54 a	140 a	145 ab
Untreated	47 a	37 a	55 a	134 ab	146 ab

* Means within columns followed by the same letter are not significantly different at the 5% level as determined by Duncan's multiple range test. † Sod too weak to harvest.

Table 5. Herbicide effects on root strength and root production when applied in the spring to immature Kentucky bluegrass sod.

Herbicide treatment	Transplanted after herbicide treatment					
	1970	1974	1975	1970	1974	1975
	15 weeks	21 weeks	23 weeks	15 weeks	21 weeks	23 weeks
	strength kg/dm²			root mg/dm²		
Benefin	7 bcd*	14 bc	13 abc	307 a	601 ab	452 a
Bensulide	5 e	6 d	9 d	175 b	206 de	203 b
Butralin	--	15 abc	13 abc	--	644 ab	434 a
DCPA	7 bcd	15 abc	14 ab	314 a	633 ab	386 a
Oxadiazon	--	15 abc	14 ab	--	754 a	433 a
Prosulfalin	--	9 d	†	--	98 e	†
Siduron	9 ab	17 a	16 a	303 a	425 bcd	476 a
Untreated	9 a	15 abc	15 ab	302 a	497 abc	481 a

* Means within columns followed by the same letter are not significantly different at the 5% level as determined by Duncan's multiple range test. † Sod too weak to lift.

tiller or rhizome number with bensulide so it is possible that reduced sod strength was due to restricted root production.

Rooting Effects. Herbicide effects on root strength and production of transplanted sod when treated as immature sod in the spring are shown in Table 5. Bensulide- and prosulfalin-treated sod rooted poorly when transplanted up to 23 weeks after treatment. With prosulfalin this was chiefly due to the reduced grass stand, while with bensulide it was probably caused by root inhibition. Benefin and DCPA showed some reduction in rooting 15 weeks after treatment and none 21 to 25 weeks after treatment. No reduction in rooting was evident from treatment with butralin, oxadiazon, and siduron. On the basis of these trials, it appears safe to use siduron in young, developing stands of certain Kentucky bluegrass cultivars to be used for sod. Use of benefin, butralin, DCPA, and oxadiazon might be satisfactory where slow development can be tolerated and harvesting is not scheduled for 15 to 21 weeks. Bensulide and prosulfalin do not appear suitable for young sod that is to be harvested and transplanted within 23 weeks after treatment.

Mature Sod

Sod Development. The grass stand was unaffected by any of the treatments. Benefin, bensulide, DCPA, and siduron did not affect sod strength in the 1970 test.

Rooting Effects. Butralin, DCPA, oxadiazon, and siduron treatments made to mature sod 5 to 23 weeks before transplanting did not inhibit rooting (Table 6). Sods treated with benefin and prosulfalin showed reduced rooting in some of the tests up to 10 weeks after treatment, while bensulide restricted rooting up to 13 weeks. Root inhibition was not evident 21 to 23 weeks after treatment. Based on these results, it appears safe to use butralin, DCPA, oxadiazon, and siduron on mature sod of certain

Table 6. Root strength and root production of mature Kentucky bluegrass treated in the spring with herbicides.

Herbicide treatment	Transplanted after herbicide treatment								
	1970			1972	1975			1976	
	2 weeks	13 weeks	21 weeks	8 weeks	5 weeks	10 weeks	23 weeks	5 weeks	10 weeks
	strength kg/dm²								
Benefin	14 a*	12 a	7 a	11 bc	11 bc	9 d	15 a	15 a	13 bc
Bensulide	10 bc	8 b	7 a	7 d	9 c	9 cd	12 a	9 b	12 c
Butralin	--	--	--	11 abc	15 a	12 ab	15 a	15 a	14 ab
DCPA	14 a	11 a	9 a	11 ab	15 a	13 a	14 a	16 a	15 ab
Oxadiazon	--	--	--	11 bc	15 a	12 ab	15 a	--	--
Prosulfalin	--	--	--	--	3 de	5 e	16 a	7 b	9 d
Siduron	13 ab	13 a	7 a	11 ab	13 ab	11 bcd	--	17 a	15 ab
Untreated	14 a	12 a	7 a	10 bc	15 a	11 abc	16 a	17 a	16 a
	root mg/dm²								
Benefin	1,920 a†	1,450 a†	430 a	164 a	389 a	313 b-e	332 a	382 a	553 a
Bensulide	2,760 a	800 a	360 a	146 a	171 bc	267 b-e	289 a	293 a	305 a
Butralin	--	--	--	219 a	387 a	409 ab	348 a	422 a	440 a
DCPA	2,940 a	1,480 a	360 a	173 a	356 a	331 bcd	357 a	500 a	527 a
Oxadiazon	--	--	--	159 a	356 a	585 a	393 a	--	--
Prosulfalin	--	--	--	--	4 d	110 e	416 a	76 b	295 a
Siduron	3,510 a	1,910 a	310 a	143 a	268 ab	271 b-e	--	328 a	384 a
Untreated	3,390 a	1,910 a	440 a	138 a	384 a	397 abc	414 a	352 a	575 a

* Means within columns followed by the same letter are not significantly different at the 5% level as determined by Duncan's multiple range test.

† Roots washed, dried, and weighed; others determined by ignition loss.

Kentucky bluegrass cultivars to be harvested after 5 weeks, benefin after 13 weeks, and bensulide and prosulfalin sometime between 13 and 21 weeks.

ACKNOWLEDGMENTS

The author wishes to thank Dr. Barry C. Troutman, presently with ChemLawn Corporation for the 1970 data on benefin, bensulide, DCPA, and siduron and for using portions of his 1971 M.S. thesis research conducted at the University of Rhode Island. Thanks also to Kingston Turf Farms and Tuckahoe Turf Farms in Rhode Island whose donation and maintenance of turf made this research possible.

LITERATURE CITED

1. Bingham, S. W. 1967. Influence of herbicides on root development of bermudagrass. Weeds 15:363–365.
2. ————. 1974. Influence of selected herbicides on rooting of turfgrass sod. p. 372–377. *In* E. C. Roberts (ed.) Proc. 2nd Int. Turfgrass Res. Conf., Blacksburg, Va. June 1973. Am. Soc. Agron., Madison, Wis.
3. Duncan, D. B. 1955. Multiple range and multiple F. tests. Biometrics 11:1–42.
4. Engel, R. E., and L. M. Callahan. 1967. Merion Kentucky bluegrass response to soil residues of preemergence herbicides. Weeds 15:128–130.
5. Gaskin, T. A. 1964. Effect of crabgrass herbicides on rhizome development in Kentucky bluegrass. Agron. J. 56:340–342.
6. Juska, F. V., and A. W. Hovin. Preemergence herbicide effects on the growth of Newport Kentucky bluegrass. Proc. Northeast Weed Control Conf. 24:387–389.
7. King, J. W., and J. B. Beard. 1969. Measuring rooting of sodded turfs. Agron. J. 61: 497–498.
8. Ledeboer, F. B., C. R. Skogley, and C. G. McKiel. 1971. Soil heating studies with cool season turfgrasses. III. Methods for the establishment of turf with seed and sod during the winter. Agron. J. 63:686–689.
9. Mazur, A. R., J. A. Jagschitz, and C. R. Skogley. 1969. Bioassay for bensulide, DCPA, and siduron in turfgrass. Weed Sci. 17:31–35.
10. Rieke, P. E., J. B. Beard, and C. M. Hansen. 1968. A technique to measure sod strength for use in sod production studies. Agron. Abstr. p. 60.
11. Smith, G.S., and L. M. Callahan. 1969. The response of Kentucky bluegrass to soil residues of preemergence herbicides. Weed Sci. 17:13–16.

Chapter 27

Goosegrass Control in Bermudagrasses[1]

S. W. BINGHAM
R. L. SHAVER

ABSTRACT

Preemergence herbicides used for large crabgrass [*Digitaria sanguinalis* (L.) Scop.] and smooth crabgrass [*Digitaria ischaemum* (Schreb.) Muhl.] control also partially controlled goosegrass [*Eleusine indica* (L.) Gaerth.]. However, goosegrass control was more variable from one evaluation to another. Butralin [4-(1,1-dimethylethyl)-*N*-(1-methylpropyl)-2,6-dinitrobenzenamine], benefin (*N*-butyl-*N*-ethyl-α,α,α-trifluoro-2,6-dinitro-*p*-toluidine), and to some extent DCPA (dimethyl tetrachloroterephthalate) gave better results in repeated applications as opposed to single treatments for goosegrass control. Single treatments with oxadiazon [2-*tert*-butyl-4-(2,4-dichloro-5-isopropoxyphenyl)-Δ^2-1,3,4-oxadiazolin-5-one] and prosulfalin [*N*-[[4-(dipropylamino)-3,5-dinitrophenyl]sulfonyl]-*S*,*S*-dimethylsulfilimine] applied early enough for preemergence crabgrass control were also suitable for full-season goosegrass control. Rotation of other preemergence herbicides with oxadiazon during early and late spring gave similar results to repeated treatments. Bensulide [*O*,*O*-diisopropyl phosphorodithioate *S*-ester with *N*-(2-mercaptoethyl)-benzenesulfonamide] failed to adequately control goosegrass and repeated treatments did not improve the program even when oxadiazon was utilized as the late spring treatment following bensulide in April. Satisfactory seedling goosegrass control with DSMA (disodium methanearsonate) required repeated treatments at intervals of 14 days or less. Preemergence herbicides maintained full-season goosegrass control following postemergence control of seedlings with DSMA. During the 3 years of effective goosegrass control, bermudagrass [*Cynodon dactylon* (L.) Pers. 'Common'] cover improved in about the same proportions to the annual grasses controlled.

Additional index words: Herbicides, Oxadiazon, Prosulfalin, Annual grasses, Weed control, DSMA.

INTRODUCTION

Annual grasses continue to require large amounts of resources in maintenance of turfgrasses in the United States (11). Preemergence herbicides are widely used for large crabgrass [*Digitaria sanguinalis* (L.) Scop.] and smooth crabgrass [*D. ischaemum* (Schreb.) Muhl.] control in turfgrasses. Some goosegrass [*Eleusine indica* (L.) Gaerth.] control was obtained when preemergence herbicides were applied for crabgrass control (1, 2, 4, 5, 7, 8, 10). However, goosegrass control with the same herbicide has varied from almost no control at times to complete control, depending on year and location. In bermudagrass turfs there appears to be some relationship between the amount of goosegrass emerging and the density of

[1] Contribution No. 354, Dep. of Plant Pathology and Physiology, Virginia Polytechnic Inst. and State Univ., Blacksburg, VA 24061 USA.

the turfgrass. Any problem that causes thinning in bermudagrass during May or June may allow a serious goosegrass problem. Goosegrass requires light for seed germination (6) and develops in open stands of turfgrass. Goosegrass also reaches a peak in seed germination at a much higher temperature than crabgrass. Thus, if preemergence herbicides are applied for crabgrass control in March, the amount of herbicides present for goosegrass control 2 months later may be too low.

Postemergence crabgrass and goosegrass control has been achieved with arsenical herbicides (3, 9). However, in actual practice many failures are encountered which are related to discoloration of turfgrasses, number and frequency of applications required, and environmental conditions immediately following the treatments. Generally, high temperature results in too much turfgrass damage and rainfall within 24 hours of application reduces the level of control.

The objectives of this research were (i) to determine through repeated applications the influence of a higher herbicide level on goosegrass control at the time of peak seed germination and (ii) to determine the effectiveness of preemergence herbicides in providing continued goosegrass control after seedling control with arsenical herbicide.

METHODS AND MATERIALS

An area heavily infested with goosegrass near Chatham, Va., USA, was selected in the fall of 1971. Soil preparation in the spring of 1972 included plowing about 20-cm deep, disking several times, and hand raking to remove small rock. 'Tifgreen' and 'Tifdwarf' bermudagrass (*Cynodon* × *magennisii* Hurcombe) sprigs were scattered uniformly over separate test areas (460 m^2 each) at 35 liters/100 m^2 and partially incorporated by shallow disking. Irrigation provided 5 cm of water immediately and 2.5 cm daily for the next 6 days. Thereafter, irrigation using 5 cm of water was utilized as needed or at weekly intervals during the summer.

Fertilizer applied just prior to final disking included 1 kg N, 0.44 kg P, and 0.83 kg K/100 m^2. This amount of fertilizer was applied again in April 1973. In addition, ammonium nitrate was applied at 1 kg N/100 m^2 each time at 6- to 8-week intervals during the summer for a total of three applications each year. A reel-type mower was used to cut these bermudagrasses at a 1-cm height once to twice weekly during the peak growing season. a normal fungicide program for maintenance of golf greens was utilized throughout the year.

Plots were 4.18 m^2 and replicated four times in a randomized complete block design. For application of granular herbicides, a turfgrass spreader about 92 cm wide was calibrated to travel over the area in two directions. For the liquid formulations, a bicycle wheel plot sprayer with a boom was calibrated to deliver 421 liters/ha while traveling over the plot twice. Water was used as the carrier of the herbicide on 15 and 22 May 1973.

For the next study, a fairway containing a heavy goosegrass population and approximately 22% common bermudagrass cover was selected during 1973. Mowing was once to twice weekly at a 2-cm height during periods of active growth. Fertilization included 1.2 kg N, 0.53 kg P, and 1.0 kg K/100 m^2 during April of each year. Plots were 13.4 m^2 and replicated four times in a randomized complete block design. Herbicide programs were utilized to continue over a 3-year period and were applied as described above beginning in April 1974. A second application was made in May or June to certain plots to provide a high level of preemergence herbicide near the time that goosegrass began to germinate in fairways. A third date of treatment was included in late August or early in September to prevent winter annual weeds from interfering with bermudagrass growth in fall and early spring. Postemergence treatment with DSMA was superimposed over other herbicide applications to reduce goosegrass populations existing at the time of preemergence treatments. With a few exceptions, the same herbicide program was used each year and each treatment was reapplied to the same plot.

RESULTS AND DISCUSSION

Goosegrass germinates in late spring about 6 weeks after crabgrass begins to emerge from the soil. Herbicides used for crabgrass control are applied too early and are not at the peak level in the soil for goosegrass control. Butralin and DCPA showed considerable promise in preliminary experiments (data not shown) for goosegrass control when these herbicides were applied in split applications with one before seed germination and the second at about the time of normal seedling emergence. There also seemed to be some advantage to including a phenoxy herbicide in mixtures with the butralin. With granular formulations of butralin plus 2,4-D [(2,4-dichlorophenoxy)acetic acid] or 2,4-D and silvex [2-(2,4,5-trichlorophenoxy)propionic acid] followed at goosegrass seedling stage with butralin alone, successful goosegrass responses of 80 to 90% control were obtained (Table 1). Butralin applied alone at 6.7 kg/ha on 22 May 1973 was not sufficient to control emerging goosegrass. Butralin in mixture with phenoxy compounds applied 1 week earlier controlled goosegrass well. An irrigation was made on 16 May and goosegrass germination was initiated. Butralin appeared to give only preemergence responses with goosegrass.

Oxadiazon controlled goosegrass well and was applied after some emergence of the weed. Profluralin [*N*-cyclopropylmethyl)-α,α,α-trifluoro-2,6-dinitro-*N*-propyl-*P*-toluidine] yielded approximately the same level of control. Bensulide provided about 70% goosegrass control; however, with infestations as heavy as encountered, this was an unacceptable level of goosegrass control. With most treatments the control of goosegrass was generally better in Tifgreen than in Tifdwarf bermudagrass. Both bermudagrasses approached complete cover during June 1973, however,

Table 1. Effectiveness of various preemergence herbicides for goosegrass control in Tifgreen and Tifdwarf bermudagrass.

Herbicide	Application rate 1973		Goosegrass control ratings†		Goosegrass	
	15 May	22 May	Tifdwarf	Tifgreen	Tifdwarf	Tifgreen
					Plants/4.18 m²	
Oxadiazon	--	2.2	9 ab*	8 abc	10 a	7 a
Oxadiazon	--	4.5	9 a	9 ab	16 a	4 a
Profluralin	--	2.2	9 ab	8 abcd	20 a	21 ab
Butralin	--	6.7	0 e	0 g	195 c	104 abc
Butralin + 2,4-D + Butralin	4.5+2.2+	2.2	8 ab	9 abc	34 a	18 ab
Butralin + 2,4-D + Butralin	4.5+2.2+	4.5	8 ab	9 ab	16 a	13 ab
Butralin + 2,4-D + silvex + Butralin	2.2+1.1+0.56+	2.2	7 ab	8 abcd	29 a	47 ab
Butralin + 2,4-D + silvex + Butralin	4.5+2.2+1.1+	4.5	8 ab	9 ab	45 a	21 ab
Butralin + 2,4-D + silvex	6.7+3.4+1.7	--	9 ab	10 a	16 a	7 a
Bensulide	14	--	3 cd	5 def	59 a	43 ab
Benefin	3.4	--	8 ab	6 bcde	25 a	103 abc
PPG-139(SL)‡	5.6	--	4 c	2 efg	68 a	54 ab
PPG-139(SL)‡	11.2	--	6 b	6 cdef	54 a	43 ab
PPG-139(FL)‡	5.6	--	1 de	5 def	83 a	53 ab
PPG-139(FL)‡	11.2	--	7 ab	7 abcd	45 a	52 ab
PPG-139(G-CC)‡	5.6	--	0 e	2 fg	180 bc	92 abc
PPG-139(G-CC)‡	11.2	--	0 de	0 g	65 a	116 bc
PPG-139(G-Ver.)‡	5.6	--	2 cd	6 def	103 ab	38 ab
PPG-139(G-Ver.)‡	11.2	--	4 c	4 def	92 a	50 ab
Untreated	--	--	0 e	2 efg	209 c	162 c

* Ratings or number of plants followed by a common letter are not different at 0.05 level according to Duncan's multiple range test. † Goosegrass control ratings, 15 Sept. 1973, were on a 0 to 10 scale where 0 = no control; 1, 2, 3 = slight reduction in density or size of plants; 4, 5, 6 = definite control of the size and/or number of goosegrass shoots; 7, 8, 9 = good control with a few goosegrass plants that survive the treatment; 10 = complete control or not more than two goosegrass plants/m².

‡ The chemistry has not been released for PPG-139 which was furnished by PPG Industries Inc., Pittsburg, Pa. The symbols SL, FL, G-CC, and G-Ver. represent soluble liquid, flowable liquid, corn cob grit granular, and Vermiculite granular formulations, respectively.

Tifdwarf appeared to be a little slower. Goosegrass invaded the slightly more open Tifdwarf during late May. Benefin was an exception and controlled goosegrass better in Tifdwarf than in Tifgreen bermudagrass.

Liquid formulations of PPG-139 (chemistry not released) were better than granular formulations for goosegrass control, however, the 11.2 kg/ha rate provided less than 70% control which was unsatisfactory in bermudagrass. It appeared that the granular carrier held this chemical too tightly.

Since crabgrass and annual bluegrass (*Poa annua* L.) are also problems in most areas in conjunction with goosegrass, several treatment programs were designed (Table 2). It is apparent that fairways heavily infested with annual bluegrass during fall and winter are prone to high goosegrass populations. Annual bluegrass dies in late spring in Virginia

Table 2. Effectiveness of various herbicide treatment programs for goosegrass control on a common bermudagrass fairway during 1974.

Treatment program 1974				Goosegrass control ratings†	Bermudagrass cover‡
16 Apr.		12 June			
	kg/ha		kg/ha		%
Oxadiazon	3.4			10 a*	
Butralin	4.5			5 abcdefgh	
Bensulide	11.2			0 h	
Benefin	3.4			2 fgh	
DCPA	16.8			6 abcdefg	
Oxadiazon	3.4	Oxadiazon	3.4	10 a	
Butralin	4.5	Butralin	4.5	6 abcdefg	
Bensulide	11.2	Bensulide	11.2	2 fgh	
Benefin	3.4	Benefin	3.4	7 abcdef	
DCPA	11.2	DCPA	11.2	9 abcd	
Oxadiazon	3.4§	Butralin	4.5	10 a	
Siduron	11.2	Oxadiazon	3.4	6 abcdefg	
Siduron	11.2	Siduron	11.2	2 fgh	
Oxadiazon	3.4§	DCPA	11.2	6 abcdefg	
Butralin	4.5	Oxadiazon	3.4	9 abcd	
Bensulide	11.2	Oxadiazon	3.4	6 abcdef	
Benefin	3.4	Oxadiazon	3.4	10 a	
DCPA	11.2	Oxadiazon	3.4	10 a	
Oxadiazon	3.4§	Oxadiazon	3.4¶	9 ab	
Butralin	4.5	Butralin	4.5¶	9 abc	
Bensulide	11.2	Bensulide	11.2¶	5 abcdefgh	
Benefin	3.4	Benefin	3.4¶	8 abcde	
DCPA	11.2	DCPA	11.2¶	4 cdefgh	
		Oxadiazon	3.4¶	4 defgh	
		Butralin	4.5¶	4 cdefgh	
		Bensulide	11.2¶	0 h	
		Benefin	3.4¶	4 efgh	
		DCPA	11.2¶	4 bcdefgh	
Untreated	--	Untreated	--	2 fgh	21
Untreated	--	Untreated	--	1 gh	24

* Figures followed by a common letter are not different at the 0.05 level according to Duncan's multiple range test. † Goosegrass control ratings were on a 0 to 10 scale where 0 = no control; 1, 2, 3 = slight reduction in density or size of plants; 4, 5, 6 = definite control of the volume of goosegrass shoots; 7, 8, 9 = good control with a few goosegrass plants that survive the treatment; 10 = complete control or not more than one goosegrass plant/6 m². Estimates were made on 5 Sept. 1974; the untreated plots contained 183 goosegrass plants/m². ‡ Cover was not different at 5% level on 12 June 1974.
§ Oxadiazon in these instances were delayed until 24 May 1974. ¶ DSMA at 3.66 kg/ha was applied on 12 June, 17 July, and 19 Aug. 1974.

leaving the turfgrass open for goosegrass seed germination and establishment.

Single applications in spring were compared with repeated applications in a 3-year study (Tables 2, 3, and 4). Single annual treatments in April with oxadiazon consistently provided complete goosegrass control during the study. Oxadiazon delayed until late May or June was generally not effective for goosegrass. DSMA applied at approximately monthly intervals was unsatisfactory and when used in conjunction with oxadiazon was still unsatisfactory in cases where goosegrass had emerged before treatment (Table 2). At a high rate of DSMA applied at 7- to 14-day intervals for two or three applications, young emerged goosegrass was eliminated and oxadiazon then provided the usual preemergence control for the season (Tables 3 and 4).

Butralin provided intermediate levels of goosegrass control during 1974. Prosulfalin was substituted for butralin during 1975–76. The control of goosegrass was immediately improved with prosulfalin for the remainder of the study (Tables 3 and 4). Prosulfalin was similar to oxadiazon in goosegrass control, but failed to provide complete control in a few instances.

Benefin and DCPA appeared to provide better control when treatments were repeated in June during the 1st year (Table 2). However, annual benefin applications in April were excellent in the 2nd and 3rd years (Tables 3 and 4). DCPA in repeated applications did not consistantly improve effectiveness during the later years. In some cases, supplementing the April treatment with lower DCPA levels in May or June was less effective than the same amount of DCPA applied in one treatment in April.

Bensulide provided little or no goosegrass control during the first 2 years and butralin was substituted for part of the 1976 treatments. These substitutions showed the necessity of repeating the butralin treatment near the time of goosegrass seed germination. Even with adequate DSMA treatments to control seedling goosegrass, bensulide's control for the season was unsatisfactory. Bensulide in April was not sufficient to follow with oxadiazon in late May or June for goosegrass. In bensulide treatments, goosegrass emerged as soon as in untreated plots and oxadiazon failed to control these seedlings.

DCPA, benefin, butralin, and prosulfalin in April provided excellent early goosegrass control, and when followed by oxadiazon in late May or June, adequate full-season control was attained. Since oxadiazon in April provided full-season control, the addition of May or June treatments with the above herbicides was considered excessive for goosegrass control (Tables 3 and 4).

Excessive annual bluegrass populations in spring reduced bermudagrass cover and permitted an open turf for goosegrass germination. Bermudagrass cover in May or June (Tables 3 and 4) was influenced mostly by annual bluegrass competition during spring. September and August treatments were then indirectly affecting the level of goosegrass

Table 3. Effectiveness of various herbicide treatment programs for goosegrass control on a common bermudagrass fairway during 1975.

Treatment program for 1975						Goosegrass control ratings†	Bermudagrass cover
5 Sept.‡		3 Apr.		13 June			22 July
	kg/ha		kg/ha		kg/ha		— % —
Prosulfalin	3.4	Oxadiazon	3.4		--	10 a*	92 ab
Butralin	4.5	Prosulfalin	3.4		--	9 abc	88 abcd
Bensulide	11.2	Bensulide	11.2		--	2 f	55 ef
Benefin	3.4	Benefin	3.4		--	9 abc	88 abcd
DCPA	11.2	DCPA	17.9		--	5 de	72 bcde
	--	Oxadiazon	3.4	Oxadiazon	3.4	10 a	100 a
Butralin	4.5	Prosulfalin	3.4	Prosulfalin	3.4	9 abc	85 abcd
Bensulide	11.2	Bensulide	11.2	Bensulide	11.2	3 ef	65 cdef
Benefin	3.4	Benefin	3.4	Benefin	3.4	9 ab	72 bcde
DCPA	11.2	DCPA	11.2	DCPA	6.7	6 bcde	85 abcd
Butralin	4.5	Oxadiazon	3.4	Prosulfalin	3.4	10 a	90 abc
Prosulfalin	2.2	Oxadiazon	3.4	Bensulide	11.2	10 a	90 ab
Prosulfalin	2.2	Oxadiazon	3.4	Benefin	3.4	9 abc	80 abcde
DCPA	11.2	Oxadiazon	3.4	DCPA	11.2	10 a	92 ab
Butralin	4.5	Prosulfalin	3.4	Oxadiazon	3.4	10 a	90 abc
Bensulide	11.2	Bensulide	11.2	Oxadiazon	3.4	6 cde	82 abcd
	--	Benefin	3.4	Oxadiazon	3.4	10 a	95 ab
DCPA	11.2	DCPA	11.2	Oxadiazon	3.4	8 abcd	90 abc
	--	Oxadiazon	3.4	Oxadiazon§	3.4	10 a	100 a
Butralin	4.5	Prosulfalin	3.4	Prosulfalin§	3.4	10 a	95 ab
Bensulide	11.2	Bensulide	11.2	Bensulide§	11.2	6 bcde	80 abcde
Benefin	3.4	Benefin	3.4	Benefin§	3.4	10 a	90 abc
DCPA	11.2	DCPA	11.2	DCPA	6.7	3 ef	82 abcd
Prosulfalin	3.4		--	Oxadiazon§	3.4	10 a	92 ab
Butralin	4.5		--	Prosulfalin§	3.4	9 abc	85 abcd
Bensulide	11.2		--	Bensulide§	11.2	4 ef	62 def
Benefin	3.4		--	Benefin§	3.4	8 abcd	70 bcde
DCPA	11.2		--	DCPA§	11.2	8 abcd	82 abcd
Untreated	--	Untreated	-- --	Untreated	--	2 f	45 f
Untreated	--	Untreated	--	Untreated	--	2 f	55 ef

* Figures followed by a common letter are not different at the 0.05 level according to Duncan's multiple range test.

† Goosegrass control ratings were on a 0 to 10 scale where 0 = no control; 1, 2, 3, = slight reduction in density or size of plants; 4, 5, 6 = definite control of the volume of goosegrass shoots; 7, 8, 9 = good control with a few goosegrass plants that survive the treatment; 10 = complete control or not more than 1 goosegrass plant per 6 m^2. Estimates were made on July 22, 1975, the untreated plots contained 118 goosegrass plants per m^2.

‡ Treatment applied 5 Sept. 1974.

§ DSMA at 7.32 kg/ha was applied on 13 June and 20 June 1975.

Table 4. Effectiveness of various herbicide treatment programs for goosegrass control on a common bermudagrass fairway during 1976.

Treatment program for 1976						Goosegrass control ratings†	Bermudagrass cover
20 Aug.‡		12 Apr.		24 May			26 Aug.
	kg/ha		kg/ha		kg/ha		— % —
Oxadiazon	3.4	Oxadiazon	3.4	--		10 a*	100 a
Prosulfalin	3.4	Prosulfalin	3.4	--		10 a	99 a
Bensulide	11.2	Burtalin	4.5	--		5 bc	92 ab
Benefin	3.4	Benefin	3.4	--		10 a	100 a
DCPA	11.2	DCPA	17.9	--		7 ab	96 ab
Oxadiazon	3.4	Oxadiazon	3.4	Oxadiazon	3.4	10 a	100 a
Prosulfalin	3.4	Prosulfalin	3.4	Prosulfalin	3.4	10 a	99 a
Bensulide	11.2	Butralin	4.5	Butralin	4.4	9 a	98 ab
Benefin	3.4	Benefin	3.4	Benefin	3.4	10 a	98 ab
DCPA	11.2	DCPA	11.8	DCPA	6.7	9 a	99 a
Prosulfalin	3.4	Oxadiazon	3.4	Prosulfalin	3.4	10 a	98 ab
Bensulide	11.2	Oxadiazon	3.4	Bensulide	11.2	10 a	100 a
Benefin	3.4	Oxadiazon	3.4	Benefin	3.4	10 a	99 a
DCPA	11.2	Oxadiazon	3.4	DCPA	11.2	10 a	100 a
Prosulfalin	3.4	Prosulfalin	3.4	Oxadiazon	3.4	10 a	100 a
Bensulide	11.2	Bensulide	11.2	Oxadiazon	3.4	10 a	100 a
Benefin	3.4	Benefin	3.4	Oxadiazon	3.4	10 a	100 a
DCPA	11.2	DCPA	11.8	Oxadiazon	3.4	10 a	100 a
Oxadiazon	3.4	Oxadiazon	3.4	Oxadiazon§	3.4	10 a	100 a
Prosulfalin	2.2	Prosulfalin	3.4	Prosulfalin§	3.4	10 a	100 a
Bensulide	11.2	Butralin	4.5	Butralin§	4.5	9 a	98 ab
Benefin	3.4	Benefin	3.4	Benefin§	3.4	10 a	98 ab
DCPA	11.2	DCPA	11.8	DCPA	6.7	6 bc	92 ab
Oxadiazon	3.4		--	Oxadiazon§	3.4	10 a	100 a
Prosulfalin	2.2		--	Prosulfalin§	3.4	10 a	99 a
Bensulide	11.2		--	Bensulide§	11.2	3 c	90 bc
Benefin	3.4		--	Benefin§	3.4	10 a	95 ab
DCPA	11.2		--	DCPA§	11.2	8 a	99 a
Untreated	--	Untreated	--	Untreated	--	2 c	84 c
Untreated	--	Untreated	--	Untreated	--	2 c	85 c

* Figures followed by the same letter are not different at 0.05 level according to Duncan's multiple range test.

† Goosegrass control ratings were on a 0 to 10 scale where 0 = no control; 1, 2, 3, = slight reduction in density or size of plants; 4, 5, 6 = definite control of the volume of goosegrass shoots; 7, 8, 9 = good control with a few goosegrass plants that survive the treatment; 10 = complete control or not more than one goosegrass plant/6 m². Estimates were made on 26 Aug. 1976; the untreated plots contained 86 goosegrass plants/m².

‡ Treatment applied 20 Aug. 1975.

§ DSMA at 7.32 kg/ha was applied on 24 May, 7 June, and 14 June 1976.

emergence. The herbicides providing annual bluegrass control permitted earlier covering with bermudagrass. The improved cover was influential toward reduced goosegrass populations. The herbicide programs, which were less effective during the 1st year, did quite well after 3 years. It was apparent that control of annual grasses over a period of years allowed bermudagrasses to improve in texture and cover. The improvement in cover in untreated plots was a partial response to border effects encroaching from treated plots. The centers of untreated plots were still thin and heavily infested with goosegrass after 3 years.

These herbicides are mitotic inhibitors and tend to reduce root growth of turfgrasses, particularly under favorable growth conditions. However, under the program of three herbicide treatments annually for 3 years, winter survival of bermudagrass was as good as or superior to that in untreated plots. Bermudagrass cover in untreated plots reached 85% in 1976, while selected treatment programs allow as much as 100% cover.

ACKNOWLEDGMENTS

The authors appreciate the assistance of John Petty, Agriculture Research Supervisor, Virginia Polytechnic Institute and State University, Chatham, Va., during the 1972–73 study and the cooperation of Bassett Country Club, Bassett, Va. for maintenance of the fairway test during 1974–76.

LITERATURE CITED

1. Barrett, L. H., and J. A. Jagschitz. 1975. Control of crabgrass and goosegrass with preemergence chemicals in turfgrasses. Proc. Northeast. Weed Sci. Soc. 29:359–364.
2. Bingham, S. W. 1975. Goosegrass and annual bluegrass control in golf course turfgrasses. Weed Sci. Soc. Am. (Abstr.) p. 18.
3. ————, and R. E. Schmidt. 1964. Crabgrass control in turf. Proc. South. Weed Conf. 17:113–122.
4. Engel, R. E., C. W. Bussey, and P. Catron. 1975. Crabgrass and goosegrass control in turfgrass with several preemergence herbicides. Proc. Northeast. Weed Sci. Soc. 29:369–394.
5. ————, and K. J. McVeigh. 1971. Crabgrass and goosegrass control with several preemergence herbicides. Proc. Northeast. Weed Sci. Soc. 25:103–108.
6. Fulwider, J. R., and R. E. Engel. 1959. The effect of temperature and light on germination of seed of goosegrass, *Eleusine indica*. Weeds 7:359–361.
7. Jagschitz, J. A. 1972. Preemergence crabgrass and goosegrass control. Proc. Northeast. Weed Sci. Soc. 26:205–210.
8. ————. 1973. Control of crabgrass and goosegrass in turfgrass with herbicides. Proc. Northeast. Weed Sci. Soc. 27:320–323.
9. Johnson, B. J. 1975. Postemergent control of large crabgrass and goosegrass in turf. Weed Sci. 23:404–409.
10. ————. 1976. Dates of herbicide application for summer weed control in turf. Weed Sci. 24:422–424.
11. Virginia Department of Agriculture and Commerce and United States Department of Agriculture Statistical Reporting Service. 1973. 1973 Virginia turfgrass survey. Virginia Coop. Crop Rep. Serv. Bull. No. 38, 203 North Governor St., Richmond, Va.

Chapter 28

Effects of Repeated Applications of Bensulide and Tricalcium Arsenate on the Control of Annual Bluegrass and on Quality of Highland Colonial Bentgrass Putting Green Turf[1]

R. L. GOSS
T. W. COOK
S. E. BRAUEN
S. P. ORTON

ABSTRACT

The effects of bensulide and tricalcium arsenate in combination with fungicides on encroachment of annual bluegrass (*Poa annua* L.) and on color, density, thatch, and root depth of a 'Highland' colonial bentgrass (*Agrostis tenuis* Sibth.) putting green turf were measured. Herbicides tested during the 5-year period were: granular tricalcium arsenate applied the 1st year at 781.2 kg/ha with additional spring and fall applications of 98 kg/ha each in subsequent years; bensulide (EC) (*O,O*-diisopropyl phosphorodithioate *S*-ester with *N*-(2-mercaptoethyl)-benzenesulfonamide) applied at 16.8 kg/ha annually or 13.5 kg/ha applied in September plus 3.4 kg/ha every 3 months for an annual total of 23.7 kg/ha. Fungicides applied were mancozeb (zinc ion and manganese ethylene bisdithiocarbamate) at 25.8 kg, PMA (phenyl mercuric acetate) 1.08 liters/ha of 10% formula, and benomyl (methyl 1-(butylcarbamoyl)-2-benzimidazolecarbamate) at 6.5 kg/ha alone to control *Fusarium* [incited by *Fusarium nivale* (Fr.) S & H]. Significant reductions in annual bluegrass populations were recorded from applications of tricalcium arsenate and repeated applications of bensulide, but not from a single annual application of bensulide nor from the fungicides. Only tricalcium arsenate significantly reduced color and density as compared to the untreated control in some years, but differences were minor and the turf was considered of acceptable quality. Thatch development was reduced in plots treated with bensulide alone as compared to all other treatments. None of the treatments significantly reduced rooting depth.

Additional index words: Preemergent herbicide control, Putting green turf, Rooting, Shoot density, Thatch.

---

[1] Scientific Paper No. 4895. College of Agriculture Res. Ctr., Washington State Univ., Pullman, Project No. 1594.

INTRODUCTION

The control of annual bluegrass *Poa annua* L. in established turfgrasses has been the object of intensive research investigations for many years. Annual bluegrass exists both as an annual under some climatic stress conditions or as a perennial in climatic areas conducive to continuous growth as found in the U.S. Pacific Northwest. Its profuse seeding habit detracts from the appearance and playability of putting greens and provides ample seed for regeneration. Research on the use of preemergence herbicides to control this grass has received major attention.

Jagschitz (6) found that bensulide on a ground corn cob carrier applied at 16.8 kg/ha controlled 33% of the annual bluegrass after 1 year of treatment and with repeated annual applications gave 83% control at the end of 3 years on 'Astoria' colonial bentgrass (*Agrostis tenuis* Sibth.) putting green turf. Tricalcium arsenate, applied in two applications annually of 118 kg/ha each, produced up to 91% control at the end of 3 years. Only slight discoloration of desirable turfgrasses was observed during this test. Bingham et al. (1) reported good control of annual bluegrass with bensulide and DCPA (dimethyl tetrachloroterephthalate) on bermudagrass (*Cynodon* spp.) golf greens overseeded with 'Pennlawn' creeping red fescue (*Festuca rubra* L.) and annual ryegrass (*Lolium multiflorum* L.). Rates of DCPA normally used to control crabgrass (*Digitaria* spp.) were effective in controlling annual bluegrass and allowed establishment of cool-season grasses 1 month after application. Goss (5) reported successful preemergence control of annual bluegrass with bensulide and DCPA. While bensulide continued to be effective throughout the 12-week test period, DCPA dissipated and allowed annual bluegrass to establish. Daniel (4) reported successful pre- and postemergence control of annual bluegrass with a tricalcium arsenate in 1960 on a bentgrass putting green turf at rates up to 1,117 kg/ha. Woolhouse and Shildrick (8) reported effective control of annual bluegrass in a mixed 'Browntop' colonial bentgrass and 'Golfrood' creeping red fescue turf with bensulide at rates of 11.2 and 14.0 kg/ha. They reported severe phytoxicity to red fescue and some to colonial bentgrass and urged caution in continued use of this material. Persistence of bensulide applied to bentgrass putting green turf was reported by Bingham and Schmidt (2). They reported improved turfgrass quality from four annual treatments of 16.8 kg/ha. Granular applications showed strong persistence by milo bioassay 11 months after application, but no persistence from the emulsifiable concentrate formulation. Toxicity was greater in the 0- to 2.5-cm surface layer than from greater depths. Troutman and Jagschitz (7) reported that bensulide at standard and double rates reduced sod strength of immature Kentucky bluegrass (*P. pratensis* L.) sod up to 5 months after treatment, but had no effect on mature sod. Bensulide at these rates did not inhibit sod rooting up to 5 months after treatment. Callahan (3) reported slight foliar injury to a 'Penncross' creeping bentgrass (*A. palustris* Huds.) golf green the 1st treatment year from tricalcium arsenate and none from bensulide. Reduced rates of arsenic resulted in no loss of sod, while continued use of bensulide through the 3rd year resulted in severe sod loss.

The literature review indicates that various preemergence herbicides exhibit extreme variability among turfgrass genera and species and geographic locations. This study was conducted to determine long term effects of some fungicides and preemergence herbicides on the control of annual bluegrass and on 'Highland' colonial bentgrass quality in the Pacific Northwest. It appears that safe use guidelines of these chemicals must be developed at each location to be acceptable in practice.

MATERIALS AND METHODS

A test was initiated at Puyallup, Wash. on a 2-year-old stand of Highland colonial bentgrass putting green turf in 1970 to determine the efficacy of various pesticides on annual bluegrass control and colonial bentgrass quality. The soil was a well drained high river terrace (Sluventic Haploxerolls) derived from alluvial deposits from active glaciers in the Cascade Mountain range. Analysis at the Washington State University Soil Testing Laboratory of the top 7.5 cm showed 5.6 pH, 3.9% organic matter, available P = 16 ppm, exchangeable K = 225 ppm, exchangeable Ca = 10 meq/100 g soil, and exchangeable Mg = 1.5 meq/100 g soil. Plots were mowed at 0.63 cm four times weekly and fertilized in multiple applications with urea for a total annual application of 586 kg N/ha. The plot area was irrigated as needed to maintain optimum soil moisture.

Fungicides were included among the treatments since it is known that *Fusarium* patch disease, caused by the fungus *Fusarium nivale* Fr. S & H, can cause severe turf injury, thus permitting more rapid invasion of annual bluegrass. The fungicides mancozeb at 25.8 kg/ha, PMA at 1.08 liters/ha of 10% formula, and benomyl at 6.5 kg/ha were applied separately every 2 to 3 weeks as required to control this pathogen. When two fungicides were used, they were applied separately on alternate dates. Regular treatments were usually required from September through November and at monthly intervals thereafter.

Bensulide was applied to selected plots in June at 16.8 kg/ha in 371 liters of water once annually and to other plots at 13.5 kg/ha once annually in June plus 3.4 kg/ha every 3 months for an annual total of 23.7 kg/ha to maintain a higher constant residual level. Tricalcium arsenate was applied broadcast as a granular material (48% active ingredient) in the following manner: 195.3 kg/ha product as an initial application on 2 June 1970 followed by three additional 195.3-kg/ha applications at 2 weeks and 2 and 5 months after the initial application for a 1st year total of 781.2 kg/ha. Herbicidal levels were maintained thereafter with applications of 98 kg/ha in spring and fall throughout the 5 year period. Fungicides were included with selected herbicide treatments as shown in the tables. All treatments were applied to plots 3.05 × 3.05 m in a randomized complete block design with four replicates.

Visual evaluations for percent annual bluegrass, color, and density were made prior to treatment initiation and in June of each year thereafter. This coincides with maximum flowering of annual bluegrass plants making them more visible at that time. Annual bluegrass populations were estimated as percent coverage. Color was estimated on a 1 to 10 basis with 1 = brown and 10 = dark green. Density was rated at 1 to 10 with 1 = bare ground and 10 = optimum density.

At the termination of the test in June 1975 all plots were sampled for rooting depth and thatch development. Soil cores, 1.9 × 25 cm, were removed and uniformly cut to 20 cm in length and inspected for root development. Thatch was measured from soil cores in cm from the soil line to the base of the green vegetation. All data were analyzed by analysis of variance. Duncan's new multiple range test and coefficients of variation (CV) are shown in the appropriate tables.

RESULTS AND DISCUSSION

Treatment Effects on Annual Bluegrass

All plots contained near equal amounts of annual bluegrass at the initiation of the test in 1970. Plots receiving split applications of bensulide and tricalcium arsenate contained significantly less annual bluegrass after the 1st year and each year thereafter compared with all other treatments (Table 1). By the end of the 1st year, mature annual bluegrass plants still in existence in these plots had poor vigor. When averaged over 5 years, all treatments, with the exception of benomyl alone, had significantly less annual bluegrass than the check. Annual bluegrass steadily increased in the check plot throughout the 5-year period. This increase is probably related to severe *Fusarium* patch disease attacks and reduction in bentgrass coverage without fungicidal treatment.

Bensulide applied once annually in combination with benomyl had significantly less annual bluegrass than bensulide alone or in combination with mancozeb/PMA in 1973 and 1974, but not in other years. The reasons for this are not clearly understood, although better disease control at that time may have played an important role. A great reduction in annual bluegrass in all bensulide-treated plots the 1st treatment year without regard to the fungicidal treatments suggests some value in single annual treatments of bensulide; but a single treatment is not as effective as several additional, but lighter applications throughout the year.

Treatment Effects on Color

Plots treated with tricalcium arsenate and benomyl had significantly lower color ratings 2 out of 5 years (Table 2). These lower color ratings were due, in part, to plot location in one replication observed to be slower draining than other areas. It is known that the effects of arsenicals are

Table 1. The effects of preemergence herbicides and fungicides on percent annual bluegrass coverage* in Highland colonial bentgrass putting green turf.

Treatment	Annual rate	1970	1971	1972	1973	1974	1975	1971–75 avg.
	kg/ha							
Bensulide	16.8	33.5 a	25.5 cd	26.3 bcd	30.0 cd	32.0 cd	35.3 cd	29.8 cd
Bensulide + mancozeb or PMA	16.8 As required†	29.8 a	21.0 cd	22.5 bc	25.3 c	28.3 c	32.0 bc	25.8 c
Bensulide + benomyl	16.8 As required	31.3 a	14.5 abc	16.8 b	14.8 b	18.0 b	26.8 b	18.2 b
Bensulide + mancozeb or PMA	13.5 + 10.2‡ As required	32.3 a	4.8 ab	1.5 a	11.0 a	1.0 a	1.0 a	1.9 a
Tricalcium arsenate + mancozeb or PMA	196§ As required	29.5 a	2.3 a	1.0 a	1.0 a	1.0 a	1.0 a	1.3 a
Tricalcium arsenate	196§	30.5 a	2.0 a	1.0 a	1.0 a	1.0 a	1.0 a	1.2 a
Tricalcium arsenate + benomyl	196§ As required	29.0 a	2.3 a	1.0 a	1.0 a	1.0 a	1.0 a	1.3 a
Mancozeb or PMA	As required	33.5 a	24.0 cd	26.3 bcd	30.0 cd	35.0 cd	41.3 de	31.3 de
Benomyl	As required	30.3 a	30.8 d	35.0 cd	39.3 ef	40.5 de	45.8 ef	38.3 fg
Untreated	--	34.0 a	29.5 d	32.5 cd	36.8 e	41.8 de	50.3 f	38.2 fg
C.V.		12.2%	49.3%	46.2%	39.2%	29.5%	20.2%	35.8%

* Any mean, within the same column followed by the same letter is not significantly different at the 5% confidence level. † Fungicides were used at rates and time of application as required to control Fusarium patch. ‡ Initial application of 13.5 kg/ha plus 3.4 kg/ha every three months made annually.
§ Four applications of 195 kg/ha made in the 1st year followed by 98 kg/ha in spring and fall annually.

Table 2. The effects of preemergence herbicides and fungicides on color† of Highland colonial bentgrass putting green turf.*

Treatment	Annual rate	1971	1972	1973	1974	1975	1971–75 avg.
	kg/ha						
Bensulide	16.8	8.5 bc	8.5 a	8.8 abc	9.0 cd	9.0 bc	8.8 cd
Bensulide	16.8						
+ mancozeb or PMA	As required‡	9.0 c	9.0 a	9.0 bc	9.0 cd	8.8 abc	9.0 de
Bensulide	16.8						
+ benomyl	As required	8.8 bc	8.8 a	8.5 abc	9.0 cd	9.0 bc	8.8 cd
Bensulide	13.5 + 10.2§						
+ mancozeb or PMA	As required	8.5 bc	8.5 a	8.5 abc	8.8 cd	9.0 bc	8.7 bcd
Tricalcium arsenate	196¶						
+ mancozeb or PMA	As required	8.5 bc	8.5 a	8.3 ab	8.5 ab	8.4 bc	
Tricalcium arsenate	196¶	8.5 bc	8.8 a	8.0 a	8.0 ab	8.3 a	8.3 b
Tricalcium arsenate	196¶						
+ benomyl	As required	7.3 a	8.0 a	8.0 a	7.5 a	8.3 a	7.8 a
Mancozeb or PMA	As required	8.3 c	9.3 a	9.3 d	9.3 c	9.3 c	9.3 e
Benomyl	As required	9.0 c	8.8 a	9.0 bc	9.3 d	9.3 c	9.0 de
Untreated	--	8.5 bc	8.0 a	8.5 abc	8.8 cd	9.0 bc	8.6 bcd

* Any mean, within the same column followed by the same letter is not significantly different at the 5% confidence level. † Rated 1 to 10 (1 = brown, 10 = dark green). ‡ Fungicides were used at rates and time of application as required to control Fusarium patch. § Initial application of 13.5 kg/ha plus 3.4 kg/ha every 3 months made annually. ¶ Four applications of 195 kg/ha made in the 1st year followed by 98 kg/ha in spring and fall annually.

Table 3. The effects of preemergence herbicides and fungicides on shoot density† of Highland colonial bentgrass putting turf.*

Treatment	Annual rate	June 1971	June 1972	June 1973	June 1974	June 1975	1971–75 avg.
	kg/ha						
Bensulide	16.8	9.3 def	9.0 de	9.0 cd	9.0 b	9.0 c	9.1 de
Bensulide	16.8						
+ mancozeb or PMA	As required‡	9.5 ef	9.5 e	9.5 cd	9.3 b	9.3 cd	9.4 ef
Bensulide	16.8						
+ benomyl	As required	9.8 f	9.8 e	9.8 d	9.8 b	9.5 cd	9.7 f
Bensulide	13.5 + 10.2§						
+ mancozeb or PMA	As required	9.5 ef	9.5 e	9.5 cd	9.5 b	9.5 cd	9.5 ef
Tricalcium arsenate	196¶						
+ mancozeb or PMA	As required	7.5 bc	7.5 abc	7.5 ab	7.5 a	8.8 bc	7.8 c
Tricalcium arsenate	196¶	7.0 a	7.3 ab	7.0 a	7.0 a	8.3 b	7.3 b
Tricalcium arsenate	196¶						
+ benomyl	As required	5.8 ab	6.3 a	7.0 a	6.5 a	7.5 a	6.6 a
Mancozeb or PMA	As required	9.8 f	9.8 e	9.8 d	9.8 b	9.8 d	9.8 f
Benomyl	As required	9.5 ef	9.5 e	9.5 cd	9.8 b	9.8 d	9.6 ef
Untreated	--	8.0 bcd	8.0 bcd	9.0 cd	9.0 b	9.0 c	8.6 d
C.V.		10.1%	10.6%	9.0%	7.8%	4.7%	8.61%

* Any mean, within the same column followed by the same letter, is not significantly different at the 5% confidence level. † Rated 1 to 10 (1 = bare ground, 10 = optimum shoot density). ‡Fungicides were used at rates and time of application as required to control Fusarium patch. § Initial application of 13.5 kg/ha plus 3.4 kg/ha every 3 months made annually. ¶ Four applications of 195 kg/ha made in the 1st year followed by 98 kg/ha in spring and fall annually.

more severe in slowly draining soils. Only minor color differences existed among all treatments, indicating that all would be acceptable in good management programs.

Highland colonial bentgrass loses vigor and some color during summer heat stress, especially in July and August, in the Pacific Northwest. It was observed that the bensulide (split applications annually)/mancozeb/PMA treatment had slightly less vigor each year during this time than most other treatments, but vigor and color returned with the onset of cooler weather.

Treatment Effects on Stand Density

Tricalcium arsenate-treated plots, as a group, were significantly less dense than all other treatments (Table 3). This trend remained constant throughout all years. Excessive soil moisture throughout most of the year may have increased toxicity. All treatments except the arsenicals and bensulide alone were significantly more dense than the check. Lack of complete recovery from disease attack in the check may account for this difference; however, bensulide did not adversely affect stand density during this 5-year test.

Effects of Treatments on Thatch

The effects of all treatments on thatch development over 5 years are shown in Table 4. Bensulide alone in annual applications showed significantly less thatch than all other treatments except the check. It is

Table 4. The effects of preemergence herbicides and fungicides on thatch formation in Highland colonial bentgrass putting green turf.

Treatment	Annual rate	Thatch depth*
	kg/ha	cm
Bensulide	16.8	0.76 a
Bensulide	16.8	
+ mancozeb or PMA	As required§	1.67 c
Bensulide	16.8	
+ benomyl	As required	1.76 c
Bensulide	13.5 + 10.2†	
+ mancozeb or PMA	As required	1.51 bc
Tricalcium arsenate	196‡	
+ mancozeb or PMA	As required	1.70 c
Tricalcium arsenate	196‡	1.44 bc
Tricalcium arsenate	196‡	
+ benomyl	As required	1.43 bc
Mancozeb or PMA	As required	1.91 c
Benomyl	As required	1.52 bc
Untreated	--	1.09 ab
C.V.		33.8%

* Any mean within the same column followed by the same letter is not significantly different at the 5% confidence level. † Initial application of 13.5 kg/ha plus 3.4 kg/ha every 3 months made annually. ‡ Four applications of 195 kg/ha made in the 1st year followed by 98 kg/ha in spring and fall annually. § Fungicides were used at rates and time of application as required to control Fusarium patch.

possible that fungicides increased thatch development through partial inhibition of soil inhabiting organisms that normally decompose thatch. Apparently, bensulide alone did not inhibit these organisms if this hypothesis is correct.

Effects of treatments on Root Depth

Core samples were inspected for rooting depth at the termination of the experiment. All treatments in all replications had no effect on this factor. All cores were uniformly cut to 20 cm and all samples had roots extending from the cut. It was assumed that 20 + cm of rooting is evidence of no great treatment effect and was adequate to maintain the plant, even during stress periods. This does not agree with Callahan (3) who reported severe sod loss during the 2nd and 3rd year from bensulide applications. Climatic dissimilarities and a different grass species and cultivar may account for these differences.

LITERATURE CITED

1. Bingham, S. W., R. E. Schmidt, and C. K. Curry. 1969. Annual bluegrass control in overseeded bermudagrass putting green turf. Agron. J. 61:908–911.
2. ————, and R. E. Schmidt. 1967. Residue of bensulide in turfgrass soil following annual treatments for crabgrass control. Agron. J. 59:327–329.
3. Callahan, L. M. 1971. Phytotoxicity of herbicides in a Penncross bent green. Agron. Abstrs. p. 52.
4. Daniel, W. H. 1960. Solving the *Poa annua* problem. Proc. 1960 Midwest Reg. Turf Conf. p. 23–27.
5. Goss, Roy L. 1964. Preemergence control of annual bluegrass (*Poa annua* L.). Agron. J. 56:479–481.
6. Jagschitz, J. A. 1970. Chemical control of *Poa annua* L. in turf and effect of various chemicals on seed production. Proc. Northwest Weed Control Conf. 24:393–400.
7. Troutman, B. C., and J. A. Jagschitz. 1971. Effects of preemergent herbicides on development and rooting of Kentucky bluegrass sod. Agron. Abstr. p. 50.
8. Woolhouse, A. R., and J. P. Shildrick. 1971. The control of annual meadowgrass in fine turf. J. Sports Turf Res. Inst. 47:9–25.

Chapter 29

Glyphosate for Torpedograss and Bermudagrass Control[1]

E. O. BURT

ABSTRACT

Ten experiments were conducted for control of torpedograss (*Panicum repens* L.) and nine experiments were conducted for control of bermudagrass (*Cynodon* × *magenissii* Hurcombe) over a 5-year period. A single application of glyphosate (N-(phosphonomethyl)glycine) at the rate of 2.24 kg/ha controlled these two perennial weeds well. Rototilling within 4 days following the application reduced the effectiveness of the herbicide in controlling torpedograss. No reduction in phytotoxicity occurred when the interval was 7 or more days. Residual phytotoxicity of glyphosate at 4.48 kg/ha dissipated to permit normal germination and growth of perennial ryegrass (*Lolium perenne* L.) on a well-irrigated sandy soil when the interval between application and seeding was 10 or more days. Results from these experiments demonstrate the effectiveness of glyphosate for control of certain hard-to-kill rhizomatous weeds prior to establishing turf.

Additional index words: Establishment, Perennial ryegrass, Rototilling, Soil residual phytotoxicity.

INTRODUCTION

Through the ages, perennial weedy grasses have been among the most competitive and most difficult of all pests for the farmer, the gardener, and the turfgrass manager to control. Of the world's 10 worst weeds, seven are grasses (4). Unlike broadleaf weeds, the populations of some perennial grasses frequently increase in relative abundance following a mechanical operation such as tillage. This is particularly true of weedy grasses that propagate by rhizomes. While mowing and close grazing reduce the vigor of perennial grassy weeds, satisfactory control is usually not attained. Moreover, chemical control is either too expensive or only partially effective. Also, in the past those herbicides that have proved effective usually persisted in the soil for long periods.

The introduction of glyphosate (N-(phosphonomethyl)glycine) in 1971 by Baird et al. (1) was a giant step forward in chemical weed control. A tremendous amount of research has been conducted with this herbicide since 1971 and special interest has been shown in its efficacy for controlling perennial grasses (2, 3, 5). Glyphosate has controlled many weed species that could not be controlled efficiently with previously

[1] Contribution from the Univ. of Florida, Florida Inst. of Food and Agric. Sci., Florida Agric. Exp. Stns. Journal Series No. 650.

available herbicides. In addition, it displays very low mammalian and fish toxicities and has short residual phytotoxicities in soils.

Because of the problems certain perennial weedy grasses cause in the culture of warm-season turfgrasses, a series of experiments were conducted to: (i) determine the efficacy of glyphosate for eliminating two pernicious rhizomatous grassy weeds—torpedograss (*Panicum repens* L.) and bermudagrass (*Cynodon* × *magenissii* Hurcombe); (ii) determine the effects of tillage at varying time intervals on glyphosate efficacy; (iii) determine the residual effects of glyphosate in the soil. Torpedograss and bermudagrass were selected because they are serious pests affecting the establishment of turf in Florida and other areas.

METHODS AND MATERIALS

Naturally occurring stands of weeds near Ft. Lauderdale, Fla., USA, were used in these experiments. Ten experiments were conducted with glyphosate for control of torpedograss and nine experiments were conducted with glyphosate for control of bermudagrass during 1971–76. The weeds were maintained at mowing heights from 0.6 cm for putting-green conditions to 30 cm in some of the torpedograss experiments. Although some of the experiments were conducted during the winter months, the weeds were in an active stage of growth at time of treatment. Maximum daytime temperatures usually ranged between 20 and 25 C during the winters and 26 and 32 C during the summers. The soil in the experiment areas was a Pompano fine sand with an organic matter content varying from less than 1 to 4%. Soil pH varied from 6.5 to 7.5. Experimental areas were fertilized from one to four times annually with N, P, and K at the rates of 49.3, 5.4, and 20.5 kg/ha, respectively, per application. Most of the experimental areas received a minimum of 2.5 cm of water weekly either in the form of rainfall or sprinkler irrigation.

In experiments to determine weed control effectiveness, glyphosate was applied at rates of 0, 0.56, 1.12, 2.24, and 4.48 kg/ha active ingredient in 41.1 liters/ha aqueous spray. Plot size varied from 1.2 × 3 m to 3.7 × 9.1 m. A randomized complete block design with three replications was used.

To determine the effects of tillage intervals on glyphosate efficacy, a split plot experimental design was used. The 3.7- × 3.7-m sub-plots either had no rototilling or were thoroughly rototilled to a depth of approximately 17 cm at 1, 3, 4, 7, or 14 days following glyphosate treatment.

Weed control effectiveness was evaluated by visually estimating the percent control (dead weeds) of selected weed species in the treated plots compared with the same species present in the adjacent untreated plots. Either every other plot or every third plot was not treated. Plots were evaluated approximately 3 months following application of the treatments. Treatments giving more than 90% control were given special attention by determining whether the weeds remaining 3 months after treatment had recovered from the treatment, or were present because of reinvasion from seed or underground parts that had no foliage present at the time of treatment. The presence or absence of phytotoxic symptoms was used to indicate whether the weeds had merely recovered from vegetative organs or reappeared from seed germination.

In studies to determine soil residues of glyphosate, rates of 0, 1.12, 2.24, 4.48, and 8.96 kg/ha were applied to a mixed stand of weeds growing in Pompano fine sand having an organic matter content of less than 1%. A randomized complete block design with four replications was used. A similar experiment using the same procedure was conducted in close proximity on soil that previously had been modified by the addition of 10% (vol./vol.) of peat. Seeds of perennial ryegrass were broadcast at the rate of 1.458 kg/ha at intervals of 1, 5, and 10 days following application of glyphosate. The treated area was not disturbed except to add 0.6 cm of topsoil to cover the seed. Plots were irrigated daily with 0.7 cm of water.

Evaluation of soil residual activity from glyphosate was made by obtaining stand counts of perennial ryegrass from each plot using three circular areas each 7.6 cm in diam. Stand counts are presented as a percent comparison of the untreated plots.

RESULTS AND DISCUSSION

A single application glyphosate applied at 2.24 kg/ha gave excellent (95 to 100%) control of torpedograss during the 5-year study (Table 1). This treatment killed essentially all shoot growth and rhizomes of plants having green foliage at time of treatment. Plots (10 m^2) treated with 2.24 or 4.48 kg/ha had one to three plants to reinfest the area. These torpedograss plants from rhizomes apparently escaped treatment and later produced shoot growth exhibiting no glyphosate toxicity symptoms. In

Table 1. Percent control of torpedograss 3 months after single applications of glyphosate.

Application date	Glyphosate (kg/ha)			
	0.56	1.12	2.24	4.48
	%			
16 Dec. 1971	37 c*	67 b	100 a	100 a
11 Nov. 1972	47 c	67 b	96 a	97 a
28 Dec. 1972	53 c	72 b	94 a	98 a
27 Aug. 1973	88 b	96 a	99 a	98 a
14 July 1974	82 b	88 b	97 a	99 a
16 Sept. 1974	88 b	92 a	99 a	99 a
10 Mar. 1975	64 c	76 b	95 a	98 a
18 July 1975	68 b	72 b	93 a	96 a
14 Apr. 1976	61 c	75 b	96 a	99 a
12 Sept. 1976	58 c	77 b	95 a	98 a

* For each application date, means followed by the same letter are not significantly different at the 0.05 probability level using Duncan's multiple range test.

Table 2. Percent control of bermudagrass with single applications of glyphosate obtained in a series of nine experiments conducted between 1971 and 1976.

Mowing height	Application date	Bermudagrass cultivar	Glyphosate (kg/ha) 0.56	1.12	2.24	4.48
cm			%			
0.6	28 Dec. 1972	Tifgreen	25 c*	63 b	87 ab	89 a
0.6	28 Dec. 1972	Tifway	14 c	47 bc	86 ab	88 a
3.8	27 Aug. 1973	Tifgreen	43 c	78 b	96 a	97 a
3.8	27 Aug. 1973	Tifway	50 bc	84 b	97 a	98 a
5.1	16 Sept. 1974	Tifgreen	69 b	80 b	97 a	98 a
5.1	16 Sept. 1974	Tifway	55 bc	76 b	93 a	100 a
5.1	10 Mar. 1975	Tifway	75 b	90 a	96 a	100 a
5.1	18 July 1975	Tifway	70 b	92 a	94 a	96 a
5.1	14 Apr. 1976	Tifway	64 b	70 b	92 a	99 a

* For each application date, means followed by the same letter are not significantly different at the 0.05 probability level using Duncan's multiple range test.

almost all experiments, the 2.24-kg/ha rate was the critical dosage that consistently controlled torpedograss (Table 1). The 1.12-kg/ha rate gave excellent control (96%) in some experiments and poor control (67%) in others. The 0.56-kg/ha rate gave 37 to 88% kill.

Bermudagrass maintained at putting-green height (0.6 cm) required about twice the amount of glyphosate to give the same degree of kill as bermudagrass maintained at fairway height (3.8 cm) (Table 2). The turf-type bermudagrasses used in these studies appeared to be more tolerant than torpedograss to glyphosate, although the primary factor may have been the limited amount of foliage present on the bermudagrass plants at the time of application. One or more applications of glyphosate to the regrowth appears to be necessary for effective control.

Rototilling within 4 days following application of glyphosate reduced the herbicide's effectiveness in controlling torpedograss (Table 3). Rototilling 1 day following application greatly reduced control, even at the highest rate (4.48 kg/ha) used. No reduction in phytotoxicity occurred when the interval was 7 or more days. Rototilling without application of glyphosate increased torpedograss populations over no rototilling.

Another factor that may be of importance is that almost all nodes on

Table 3. Percent control of torpedograss as affected by tillage following a single application of glyphosate.

Interval between application and tillage (days)	Glyphosate (kg/ha) 0.56	1.12	2.24	4.48
	%			
No tillage	58 bcyz*	86 bxy	99 az	98 az
1	13 cz	23 cz	36 cz	48 cyz
3	48 cyz	81 bx	84 bxy	93 bx
4	60 byz	92 abx	96 ax	96 ax
7	76 bx	97 ax	98 ax	99 ax
14	74 bx	96 ax	99 ax	99 ax

* Means in horizontal rows followed by the same letter (a, b, or c) are not significantly different at 0.05 probability level using Duncan's multiple range test. Means in columns followed by the same letter (x, y or z) are not significantly different at 0.05 probability level using Duncan's multiple range test.

Table 4. Percent stand of ryegrass as affected by glyphosate applied prior to seeding.

Days between application and seeding	Soil organic matter content†	Glyphosate (kg/ha)			
		1.12	2.24	4.48	8.96
		%			
1	Low	99 a*	97 a	73 b	65 b
1	Medium	102 a	98 a	82 ab	76 b
5	Low	98 a	100 a	84 b	81 b
5	Medium	101 a	99 a	88 ab	83 b
10	Low	103 a	98 a	96 a	92 a
10	Medium	99 a	97 a	98 a	96 a

* Means in horizontal rows followed by same letter are not significantly different at 0.05 probability level using Duncan's new multiple range test. † Low organic matter content designates less than 1%, while a medium organic matter content designates approximately 10% content vol./vol. of soil.

the torpedograss rhizomes produced foliage, whereas bermudagrass rhizomes did not. Results from experiments on bermudagrass and torpedograss suggest that a large amount of foliage present at time of treatment may enhance control.

Perennial ryegrass seedling counts showed some residual glyphosate phytotoxicity at the 4.48- and 8.96-kg/ha rates at the 5-day planting interval, but no residual activity at 10 days from any rate used (Table 4). There was no residual activity at the two lower rates (1.12 and 2.24 kg/ha) even at the 1-day intervals. These results indicate that perennial ryegrass seedings can be done safely 10 days after the glyphosate is used to control a perennial weed from a turfgrass area. Sprankle et al. (6) found that clay loam and muck soils rapidly inactivated 56 kg/ha of glyphosate. They postulated that initial inactivation of glyphosate in soil is by reversible adsorption to clay and organic matter through the phosphonic moriety (7).

Glyphosate at 2.24 kg/ha controlled torpedograss and bermudagrass well. Although data are not included in this paper, glyphosate gave excellent control of other perennial weeds as well as annuals. Results from these and other experiments clearly demonstrate the effectiveness and usefulness of glyphosate for weed control prior to establishing turfgrasses. It has also been effective in routine maintenance procedures in southern Florida (Burt, unpublished) as a nonselective spot treatment for many hard-to-kill weeds.

LITERATURE CITED

1. Baird, D. D., R. P. Upchurch, W. B. Homesley, and J. E. Franz. 1971. Introduction of a new broad spectrum postemergence herbicide class with utility for herbaceous perennial weed control. Proc. North Cent. Weed Control Conf. 26:64–68.
2. Cools, W. G., and S. J. Locascio. 1977. Control of purple nutsedge (*Cyperus rotundus* L.) as infuenced by season of application of glyphosate and nitrogen rate. Proc. South Weed Sci. Soc. 30:158–164.
3. McWhorter, C. G. 1977. Weed control in soybeans with glyphosate applied in recirculating sprayer. Weed Sci. 25:135–141.
4. Holm, L. 1969. Weed problems in developing countries. Weed Sci. 17:113–118.

5. Johnson, B. J. 1977. Winter annual weed control in dormant bermudagrass turf. Weed Sci. 25:145–150.
6. Sprankle, P., W. F. Meggitt, and D. Penner. 1975. Rapid inactivation of glyphosate in the soil. Weed Sci. 23:224–228.
7. ————, ————, and ————. 1975. Adsorption, mobility, and microbial degradation of glyphosate in the soil. Weed Sci. 23:229–234.

Section VI:

Turfgrass Diseases and Nematodes

Chapter 30

Yellow Tuft Disease of Turfgrasses: A Review of Recent Studies Conducted in Rhode Island[1]

N. JACKSON

ABSTRACT

Since the early 1920's a disease problem commonly referred to as yellow tuft has been reported on bentgrass (*Agrostis* spp.) turf in the northeast U.S. and also in Europe. Symptoms appear as small yellowed clusters of shoots proliferating from creeping stems and forming a dense tuft 1 to 3 cm in diameter. Individual shoots making up the tuft form few adventitious roots and the tufts are easily detached from the turf.

Recently, similar symptoms occurred on Kentucky bluegrass (*Poa pratensis* L.) in several sod producing areas in the United States. The disease has also appeared on bluegrasses (*Poa* spp.), perennial ryegrass (*Lolium perenne* L.), and red fescue (*Festuca rubra* L.) comprising golf fairway turf.

Investigations at the University of Rhode Island indicate that the downy mildew fungus (*Sclerophthora macrospora*) is consistently associated with yellow tuft symptoms and the causal relationship has been established. Mycelium of this obligate parasite is present in the diseased plants and propagules of the fungus; i.e., zoospore-producing sporangia and oospores occur respectively on and in the leaves given optimum conditions.

In addition to overwintering oospores, resting mycelium survives in the crowns of infected plants and the disease presents a recurring problem in permanent turf. Infected weed grasses on the headlands and volunteer bluegrass plants surviving from the previous crop provide a reservoir of infection on sod farms. Although the disease is unsightly on bentgrass turf, there is usually no permanent injury. However, symptoms on bluegrass sod may be intense enough to render this turf temporarily unsaleable. Cultivar evaluation for resistance and the screening of possible fungicides is underway.

Additional index words: *Scleropthora macrospora*, *Agrostis* spp., *Poa pratensis* L., *Lolium perenne* L., *Festuca rubra* L., Cool-season turfgrasses, Weedy grasses.

INTRODUCTION

The first record of yellow tuft disease on cultivated turf was published in 1932 by Monteith and Dahl (7) without reference to a causal agent. During the ensuing 40 years various causal relationships were suggested (12, 13, 14) but never verified and the incitant of this evanescent and seldom serious disorder of bentgrass (*Agrostis* spp.) golf greens defied elucidation (3). Since 1965 typical symptoms of the disease have been seen intermittently on bentgrass turf in Rhode Island and cursory, unsuccessful

[1] Contribution No. 1749, Agric. Exp. Stn., Kingston, RI 02881, USA.

attempts were made to determine the causal agent. In 1971 yellow tuft symptoms appeared in Kentucky bluegrass (*Poa pratensis* L.) turf on Rhode Island sod farms. Widespread symptoms recurred the following year. Some were so severe that the Kentucky bluegrass sod was temporarily unsaleable. Similar symptoms were observed on sod samples sent to us by growers in New York and in the Midwest. The alarming incidence of the disease in Rhode Island during the early 1970's prompted a more detailed investigation of the problem and culminated in the implication of the fungus *Sclerophthora macrospora* (Saac.) Thirum., Shaw and Naras, as the causal agent (6, 8). Isolation and reinoculation of this obligate parasite has been accomplished recently (5) and the constant presence of this downy mildew fungus in plants with the characteristic symptoms of yellow tuft reaffirms the relationship.

SYMPTOMS

Early symptoms of yellow tuft are often hard to discern. Leaf blades may be thickened or broadened slightly and the infected plants may show some degree of stunting if unmown. In regularly mowed turf this characteristic is masked and even heavily infected plants may appear normal in color and texture for long periods of time.

Advanced symptoms on bentgrasses (*Agrostis* spp.) and red fescue (*Festuca rubra* L.) turfs appear as small yellow spots, 1 to 3 cm in diameter. On Kentucky bluegrass and perennial ryegrass (*Lolium perenne* L.) the spots are 3 to 10 cm in diameter. Each spot is a dense cluster of yellow shoots caused by the proliferation of axillary buds at crowns or at the nodes and terminals of creeping stems. Individual shoots making up the tufts form few adventitious roots and the tufts are easily detached from the turf. Prominent symptoms usually appear in late spring and again in the fall, especially if cool, wet weather conditions prevail. Whole tufts may wither and die during hot, dry periods, but some of the tillers usually survive the stress situation. Further depredation of the tillers may occur due to infection by *Ustilago striiformis* (Westend., Niessl.) and/or *Helminthosporium* spp. Fall seedings may show well-developed yellow tuft symptoms by June of the following year, noticeable first in low lying areas subject to previous flooding. The disease spreads outward from the initial infection sites and once established in a turf, yellow tuft will recur indefinitely with varying severity. Although unsightly, there is seldom permanent injury to the turf.

THE PATHOGEN

Valid name: *Sclerophthora macrospora* (Sacc.) Thirum., Shaw, *Naras*. (15).

Synonyms: *Sclerospora macrospora* Sacc.; *Sclerospora kriegeriana*

Magnus; *Sclerospora oryzae* Brizi; *Nozemia macrospora* (Sacc.) Tasugi; *Phytophthora macrospora* (Sacc.) Tanaka (18).

After clearing and staining the tissues (9, 16) microscopic examination of infected turfgrasses reveals the systemic mycelium of the fungus *Sclerophthora macrospora* within the crowns, stems, and leaves. A few axillary buds may escape the colonizing hyphae emanating from the crown tissue and may produce an occasional healthy tiller free of mycelium. Mycelium has not been observed to progress far in roots.

Mycelium is coenocytic, multinucleate, intercellular, and ranges from 3μ to 60μ in diameter. Narrow diameter hyphae form a complex network within the crown tissue, ramifying leaf and shoot meristems. Narrow "extension" hyphae, closely associated with vascular bundles, carry the fungus up the leaf sheaths. Localized branching and proliferation of these hyphae into tissue between the bundles occurs, increasingly so in the upper sheath. Massive development of multidiameter mycelium occurs in the lamina, again associated initially with the bundles. Hyphae then branch out into the mesophyll tissue and may bridge to adjacent bundles, often via the small transverse bundles. Hyphae reaching the substomatal cavities on upper portions of sheaths, and on both surfaces of the lamina, form distinctive, lobed, irregularly thickened pads from which the sporangiophores eventually develop. These sporangiophoric pads are very numerous in heavily infected leaves.

The intercellular hyphae mould closely to the cell walls, filling all the interstices. Fine hyphae and the many finger-like projections from the lobed and convoluted larger hyphae press between the cells. Minute protuberances occur sparsely on some hyphae, especially those adjacent to the vascular bundles. Although cell walls appear invaginated by these structures, actual penetration of the wall has not yet been observed.

Given optimum conditions, successive initials on the substomatal pads give rise to simple sporangiophores which protrude through the stomates and produce six or more lemon-shaped, apically poroid sporangia. Sporangiophores measure from 4.2 to 25.2 μ long. Sporangia are 37.8 to 60.8 μ wide and 70.0 to 100.8 μ long. In the field, sporangia have been seen in Rhode Island from May to November. Pearly white, turgid sporangia are present in the early morning while leaf surfaces are moist, but they collapse to a dirty white residue as the leaves dry. Sporangial production may be demonstrated readily by placing infected leaves or plants in a moist chamber at 16 to 20 C for 12 to 24 hours. Detached leaves submerged in distilled water or in soil water at 15 C produce copious numbers of sporangia after 4 hours. Sporangia mature rapidly, each releasing 50 or more motile zoospores. Direct germination of sporangia has not been observed but elongation of the apical region frequently occurs, often to form a secondary sporangium. Germination of imperfectly cleaved zoospores or zoospores encysted within the sporangium may result in sporangia with several germ tubes issuing from the apical region.

Zoospores are ovoid to pyriform in shape, 14 to 20 μ long and 5 to 10 μ wide, laterally biflagellate, with one whiplash (anterior) and one tinsel flagellium (posterior). They swim vigorously in a rolling, spiral motion. Temperature inversely affects swimming time; at 5 C spores may remain active more than 24 hours, above 20 C spores encyst within an hour. At encystment the flagella are absorbed and the spores round up, ranging in diameter from 11.2 to 15.3 μ. After a brief resting period, a single germ tube is produced with the spore protoplasm concentrated near the advancing tip.

Zoospores are remarkably chemotactic (1, 4) and respond to low concentrations of sugars (fructose, glucose, maltose, and sucrose) hydrolyzed casein, yeast extract, and several individual amino acids. Guttation fluid and glutamine are very active stimulants. Imbibed seeds and seeds in the early stages of germination are extremely attractive to the zoospores. The latter congregate in large numbers at the region of the mesocotyl and encyst there. Rapid germination of the spores ensues. The first leaf at the region of the ruptured coleoptile is also an area of attraction to the zoospores and a focus for germ tubes. Germ tubes of widely varying (5 to 60 μ) lengths become swollen at the tips (appresoria?) and align with the cell walls. The actual penetration process has not yet been demonstrated, but germinating seed of several grasses exposed to suspensions of *S. macrospora* zoospores produced seedlings containing typical mycelium of the fungus 2 weeks after inoculation. These plants then developed yellow tuft symptoms (5).

Sexual reproduction in *Sclerophthora macrospora* is accomplished by means of oospores. Oogonia, each with an attendent antheridium, are initiated by those hyphae closely associated with the vascular bundles of the lamina. Distortion of the vascular tissue occurs as the globose to roughly spherical oogonia expand to a diameter of 60 to 90 μ delineated by an irregularly pitted wall about 7 μ thick. Oospores measure 50 to 75 μ in diameter with a smooth wall 5 to 8 μ thick. Large numbers of oospores were noted in Kentucky bluegrass leaves obtained from infected sod in May and June 1977. Lesser numbers were seen in bentgrass and bluegrass leaves in the late summer and fall during the previous 2 years. Crabgrass (*Digitaria sanguinalis* (L.) Scop.), a common contaminant of turfgrass areas, may develop enormous numbers of oospores in the fall prior to frost. Germination of these resting spores has been observed in our laboratory, confirming the development of a single sporangium from the oospore and subsequent release of zoospores as reported elsewhere (10).

HOST RANGE AND DISTRIBUTION OF THE PATHOGEN

Sclerophthora macrospora is a well documented, widely distributed pathogen causing "crazy top" in corn (*Zea mays* L.) (16, 18, 19), downy mildew in rice (*Oryza sativa* L.) (2), and "proliferation" diseases in sugarcane (*Saccharium officinarum* L.) (9), sorghum (*Sorghum bicolor* (L.) Moench) (19), small grains, and many grasses (10, 11, 17). This fungus has been found in Rhode Island on the following turfgrasses and associated grass species:

Turfgrasses—velvet bentgrass (*Agrostis canina* L.); creeping bentgrass (*A. stolonifera* L.); colonial bentgrass (*A. tenuis* Sibth.); red fescue; tall fescue (*Festuca arundinacea* Schreb.); perennial ryegrass; Italian ryegrass (*Lolium multiflorum* Lam.); timothy (*Phleum pratense* L.); annual bluegrass (*Poa annua* L.); Kentucky bluegrass; roughstalk bluegrass (*P. trivialis* L.).

Others—quackgrass (*Agropyron repens* L. Beauv.); orchardgrass (*Dactylis glomerata* L.); crabgrass; smooth crabgrass (*Digitaria ischaemum* (Schreb.) Muhl.); velvetgrass (*Holcus lanatus* L.); reed canarygrass (*Phalaris arundinacea* L.); rye (*Secale cereale* L.); corn.

Sporangia have been recorded in the field on leaves of many of the grasses previously listed from early May to November. Sporangia were produced abundantly on the leaves of quackgrass, crabgrass, timothy, annual bluegrass, and rye growing on the headlands and adjacent waste areas of sod fields, providing a reservoir for potential infection. Infected volunteer Kentucky bluegrass plants from the previous crop of sod were often found growing in new seedings.

COMMENTS

If the incidence of yellow tuft in Rhode Island is representative of cool-season turfgrass areas in the United States and elsewhere, then this disease is a particularly common phenomenon. The surprising feature is how the causal agent remained in obscurity for so long. Presumably, the ephemeral nature of the symptoms and consequent superficial damage, the sophisticated, obligate habit of the pathogen, and the shy appearance of any signs of the fungus in closely mown turf, all tended to divert attention from a downy mildew as the causal agent.

The widespread appearance of the disease in Kentucky bluegrass sod-growing areas in Rhode Island and the attendant economic losses place the disease into a more serious category worthy of research. The relationship of *S. macrospora* and yellow tuft disease is now well established, but the infection mechanism needs final confirmation. At the Rhode Island Agricultural Experiment Station, work is progressing on this and other aspects of the etiology of the disease under turf conditions. Possible means of control, both cultural and chemical, are also being studied.

LITERATURE CITED

1. Akai, S., and M. Fukutomi. 1964. Mechanism of the infection of plumules of rice plants by *Sclerophthora macrospora*. Special Res. Rep. on Disease and Insect Forecasting. Studies on the downy mildew of rice plants. II. 17:47–54.
2. ————, and ————. 1966. Change in the external morphology of Gramineous plants attacked by *Sclerophthora macrospora*. Phytomorphology 16:291–301.

3. Beard, J. B. 1973. Turfgrass: Science and culture. Prentice-Hall, Inc. Englewood Cliffs, N.J.
4. Dernoeden, P. H., and N. Jackson. 1978. Zoospore chemotaxin in *Sclerophthora macrospora*. Phytopathol. News 12(10)234 (Abstract).
5. Jackson, N., and P. H. Dernoeden. 1978. *Sclerophthora macrospora* the causal agent of yellow tuft disease in turfgrasses. Phytopathol. News 12(10)236 (Abstract). Maine. July 1978.
6. ———, W. C. Mueller, and J. M. Fenstermacher. 1974. The association of downy mildew with yellow tuft disease of turfgrasses. J. Sports Turf Res. Inst. 50:52–54.
7. Monteith, J., Jr., and A. S. Dahl. 1932. Turf diseases and their control. Bull. U.S. Golf Assoc. Green Sec. 12:87–186.
8. Mueller, W. C., N. Jackson, and J. M. Fenstermacher. 1974. Occurrence of *Sclerophthora macrospora* in turfgrass affected with yellow tuft. Plant Dis. Rep. 58:848–850.
9. Roth, G. 1967. *Sclerophthora macrospora* (Sacc.) Thirum., et al. (Syn.: *Sclerospora macrospora* Sacc.) on sugarcane in South Africa. Z. Pflanzenkr. Pflanzenpathol. Pflanzenschutz 74:83–100.
10. Semeniuk, G., and C. J. Mankin. 1964. Occurrence and development of *Sclerophthora macrospora* on cereals and grasses in South Dakota. Phytopathology 54:409–416.
11. ———, and ———. 1966. Additional hosts of *Sclerophthora macrospora* in South Dakota. Phytopathology 56:351.
12. Tarjan, A. C., and M. H. Ferguson. 1951. Observations of nematodes in yellow tuft of bentgrass. U.S. Golf Assoc. J. Turf Manage. 4:28–30.
13. ———, and ———. 1951. Association of certain nematodes with yellow tuft of bentgrass. (Abstr.) Phytopathology 41:566.
14. ———, and S. W. Hart. 1955. Occurrence of yellow tuft of bentgrass in Rhode Island. Plant Dis. Rep. 39:185.
15. Thirumalachar, M. J., C. G. Shaw, and M. J. Narasimhan. 1958. The sporangial phase of the downy mildew on *Eleusine coracana* with a discussion of the identity of *Sclerospora macrospora* Sacc. Bull. Torrey Bot. Club 80:299–307.
16. Ullstrup, A. J. 1952. Observations on crazy top of corn. Phytopathology 42:675–680.
17. ———. 1955. Crazy top of some wild grasses and the occurrence of the sporangial stage of the pathogen. Plant Dis. Rep. 39:839–841.
18. ———. 1970. Crazy top of maize. Indian Phytopathol. 23:250–261.
19. Whitehead, M. D. 1958. Pathology and pathological histology of downy mildew, *Sclerophthora macrospora*, on six graminicolous hosts. Phytopathology 48:485–493.

Chapter 31 Snow Molds on Minnesota Golf Greens[1]

W. C. STIENSTRA

ABSTRACT

Psychrophilic turfgrass pathogens are of major importance in Minnesota disease control programs. *Typhula* spp. and *Fusarium nivale* are the generally recognized causes of snow mold on golf greens. *Sclerotinia borealis* was found with *T. incarnata* and *T. ishikariensis* on several golf courses in northern Minnesota in 1974, 1975, and 1976. *T. incarnata* is easier to control than *T. ishikariensis*. Fungicides used to control *Typhula* spp. are not as effective against *S. borealis*. Combinations of several snow mold fungicides performed best. Nitrogen fertilizer applications made at the same time as the fungicide treatments did not improve disease control or increase disease damage, but did improve spring turfgrass color and growth responses.

INTRODUCTION

Snow mold is a complex disease in Minnesota. Several psychrophilic pathogens are of major importance in Minnesota disease control programs on golf greens. The snow mold pathogens in Canada (1, 3, 5, 7) are similar to those in Minnesota; however, in certain years one or another pathogen is associated with severe epidemics (1, 2). Surveys conducted in Minnesota since 1971 for snow mold organisms on golf greens have found *Typhula incarnata* Lasch ex. Fr. and *T. ishikariensis* Imai to be the major causal agents. In 1974, 1975, and 1976, Sclerotinia patch, caused by *Sclerotinia borealis* Bubak and Vieugel, was found in several golf greens in northern Minnesota.

The climate in Minnesota is usually favorable for the development of snow mold diseases. Observations in the field and in research plots indicate that *T. incarnata* is easiest to control, while *T. ishikariensis* is harder to control. Further, they indicate that *S. borealis* is not controlled by the fungicides generally used to control *Typhula* species. *Fusarium nivale* (Fr.) Snyd. and Han., which is present in Minnesota, has seldom been a problem in the turfgrass research plots.

The testing of standard and new experimental compounds in Minnesota was begun with the cooperation of the Minnesota Golf Course Superintendents Association to evaluate the performance of presently available alternate fungicides and to improve deficiencies in the present control practices.

These studies support the need for better diagnostic techniques (4, 5) to recognize snow mold fungi and evaluate each low temperature patho-

[1]Paper No. 10,315. Scientific Journal Series, Minnesota Agric. Exp. Stn., Univ. of Minnesota, St. Paul, Minn., USA.

gen alone and in combination against known turfgrass cultivars with and without fungicides.

MATERIALS AND METHODS

Snow mold trials were conducted at 13 locations in Minnesota where winter disease is common and difficult to control. The investigation reported herein was made on a golf green nursery mowed at a 5-mm height. Summer disease treatments were made by the golf course superintendents as required, but no fungicides were used in September or October which might interfere with the snow mold trials. The experimental plot design was a completely randomized block with four replicates. Each fungicide plot measured 1 × 3 m. Fungicides were applied in 0.2 liter H_2O/m^2 using a CO_2-powered, wheel-mounted boom sprayer operated at 2.8 kg/cm^2 pressure. Nitrogen fertilizer was applied at 9.6 g/m^2. Treatments were made in October or November on polystands of 'Penncross' creeping bentgrass (*Agrostis palustris* Huds.) and annual bluegrass (*Poa annua* L.). The data were recorded as percentage of plot area diseased, averaged, and statistically analyzed according to Duncan's new multiple range test.

Table 1. Effect of fungicides on snow mold disease at Duluth, Minn. 5 May 1975.

Fungicide	Application rate	Area of disease†
	$g/93\ m^2$	%
Tersan SP + PCNB	113 + 113	1.5 a*
Tersan SP	255	1.8 a
Tersan SP + Caloclor	113 + 85	4.3 ab
Tersan SP	170	4.7 ab
Tersan SP + Fungo	113 + 57	5.0 abc
Caloclor + PCNB	85 + 113	6.3 abcd
MF 582	255	6.3 abcd
Tersan SP	113	6.7 abcd
tersan SP + Thiram	113 + – 13	6.8 abcd
MF 582	340	10.0 abcd
PCNB	227	10.5 abcd
Actidione RZ	227	12.5 abcd
Actidione RZ	113	15.3 abcd
Caloclor	142	15.5 abcd
MF 582	170	16.0 abcd
PCNB + Fungo	113 + 57	18.0 abcd
PCNB	113	18.5 bcd
Calochlor	85	25.0 bcd
Calogram	3,629	26.3 cd
PCNB + Thiram	113 + 113	32.5 d
RP 26019	227	37.5
Caloclor + Thiram	85 + 113	38.8
Cadminate	113	42.5
Caloclor + Fungo	85 + 57	50.0
Thiram	227	55.8 e
RP 26019	113	57.5 e
Cadminate	170	66.3 e
Untreated	--	60.0 e
Thiram	113	77.5
Fungo	57	78.8
Tersan 1991	57	86.3

* Any two figures followed by the same letter do not differ significantly. P = 0.05, according to Duncan's new multiple range test. The highest four homogeneous subsets and the check subset are presented.
† Values are means of four replicates.

RESULTS AND DISCUSSION

Snow mold severity and distribution of fungi varied with location in the state. In general, *T. incarnata* was present at all locations, *T. ishikariensis* was more common in the north and east, and *S. borealis* occurred only in the far north (6). *T. ishikariensis* occurs more frequently in colder locations and *S. borealis* in areas where snow cover is prolonged in the spring (5).

Successful chemical control depends on which fungus dominates. Field observations indicate that better control occurs when only *T. incarnata* is present and control is poorer when *T. ishikariensis* predominates. It may be that *T. incarnata* is easier to control than *T. ishikariensis;* however, other factors must be tested.

Results from 2 years of chemical treatment at Duluth, Minn., USA, are presented (Tables 1 and 2). Treatment results at Duluth were typical

Table 2. Effect of fungicides on snow mold disease at Duluth, Minn. on 13 Apr. 1976.

Fungicide	Application rate	Area of disease†
	g/93 m²	%
Caloclor + Tersan SP	85 + 113	6.0 ab*
Calogran	4,536	7.5 ab
Caloclor + PCNB	85 + 113	8.0 ab
Tersan SP + PCNB	113 + 112	10.8 ab
Caloclor	142	10.8 ab
Tersan SP + Thiram	113 + 226	13.0 abc
Tersan SP	226	22.5 abcd
Scotts F II	2,728	23.8 abcd
Scotts F II	1,364	26.3 bcd
Caloclor	85	27.5 bcd
Calogran	2,721	33.8 cd
PCNB	226	37.5 d
Tersan SP	113	41.3 d
MF 582	264	42.5 d
PCNB + Thiram	113 + 226	47.5
Actidione RZ	226	47.5
Scotts LDC	2,454	50.0
Scotts FF II	1,455	51.3
Actidione RZ	113	52.5
Tersan SP	57	52.5
Scotts LDC	1,227	53.8
Scotts FF II	2,910	65.0
Turfside	1,814	68.8 o
Turfside	907	70.0 o
MF 582	170	82.5 o
MF 582	240	73.8 o
RR 26019	228	73.8 o
PCNB	113	73.8 o
PCNB	28	82.5 o
RP 26019	113	83.8 o
PCNB	57	83.8 o
Ammon Nitrate	907	85.0 o
Milorganite	907	85.0 o
RP 26019	57	86.3 o
Thiram	228	86.3 o
Untreated	--	89.5 o

* Any two figures followed by the same letter do not differ significantly. P = 0.05, according to Duncan's new multiple range test. The highest four homogeneous subsets and the check subset are presented.

† Values are means of four replicates.

of all other locations. It was clear that fertilizer alone applied at the time of fungicide application did not increase disease or damage from disease. The application of fertilizer with fungicides did not improve snow mold control. However, enhanced turfgrass greenup and the early spring growth response improved the appearance and hastened healing of snow mold damage.

The standard winter disease chemical control of mercurous/mercuric chloride (Caloclor®) and 1,4-dichlor-2-5 dimethoxybenzene (Tersan SP®) did not control *S. borealis* while pentachloronitrobenzene (PCNB) did. Cadmium chloride (Cadminate®) was a more effective control for *S. borealis* than for *Typhula*, but Caloclor® was more effective against *Typhula*. The systemics methyl 1-(butylcarbamoyl)-2-benzimidazole-carbamate (Tersan 1991® or benomyl) and dimethyl 4,4-0-phenylenebis (3-thioallophanate) (Fungo® or Thiophanate methyl)] also controlled *S. borealis*, but did not control *Typhula* sp. The systemics may stimulate the activity of *Typhula* sp. and these fungi may grow better than *S. borealis*.

Because it is not possible to predict which snow mold fungus will dominate, the application of more than one fungicide as a tank mix was tested. The combination of Tersan SP® and PCNB, Tersan SP® and Calochlor®, or PCNB and Calochlor® provided the best disease control. However, mixing of products containing S; i.e., Fungo® or tetramethyl thiuramidisulfide (Thiram®), with Caloclor® is not recommended because the S and Hg react to reduce the effectiveness of Hg (W. A. Small, personal communication). Increasing the concentration of PCNB did not increase disease control.

The success of winter disease control programs in Minnesota depends on which fungi are present and active. The failure of any one fungicide alone must be examined relative to the fungi present. Compounds that may be effective in winter disease control may be discarded because they did not control all fungi active in the winter disease complex.

LITERATURE CITED

1. Lebeau, J. B. 1968. Pink snow mold in southern Alberta. Can. Plant Dis. Surv. 48:130–131.
2. ———, and M. W. Cormack. 1959. Development and nature of snow mold damage in western Canada. IX Int. Bot. Congr. (Montreal) 1:544–549.
3. Platford, R. G., C. C. Bernier, and A. C. Ferguson. 1972. Lawn and turf diseases in the vicinity of Winnipeg, Manitoba. Can. Plant Dis. Surv. 52:108–109.
4. Smith, J. D. 1972. Snow mold on turfgrass in Saskatchewan in 1971. Can. Plant Dis. Surv. 52:25–29.
5. ———. 1973. Snow mold of turfgrasses in Saskatchewan. p. 313–324. *In* E. C. Roberts (ed.) Proc. 2nd Int. Turfgrass Res. Conf., Blacksburg, Va. June 1973. Am. Soc. Agron., Madison, Wis.
6. Stienstra, W. C. 1974. Snow molds on Minnesota golf turf. Proc. Am. Phytopathol. Soc. Vol. 1.
7. Vaartnou, H., and C. R. Elliott. 1969. Snow molds on lawns and lawn grasses in northwest Canada. Plant Dis. Rep. 53:891–894.

Chapter 32

Snow Mold Resistance in Turfgrasses and the Need for Regional Testing[1]

J. D. SMITH

ABSTRACT

In field tests at Saskatoon, Saskatchewan, Canada, plots of mature turf formed from cultivars and strains of Kentucky bluegrass (*Poa pratensis* L.), red fescue (*Festuca rubra* L.), and sheep fescue (*F. ovina* L.) were inoculated with cultures of the nonsclerotial, low temperature-tolerant basidiomycete (LTB). The latter appears to be unique to the low snowfall areas of the Canadian prairies. Inoculum grown on sterile grain was applied each autumn from 1973 to 1975. The severity of the disease was recorded each subsequent spring. Suscepts included several used in other climatic regions where the range of snow molds and other pathogens is different from the northern prairies. No strains completely resistant to the LTB were found, but some new introductions, selections, and established cultivars showed low initial damage and/or recovery. The resistance of 13 lines of *Agrostis* spp. to natural attacks of *Fusarium nivale* is also reported. Cultivars require regional testing for disease resistance, especially snow mold resistance, before being recommended for use. Cultivar descriptions should specify resistance to a particular snow mold pathogen or pathogens and not to "snow mold" only, since the spectrum of these varies greatly from region to region.

Additional index words: Western Canada, Nonsclerotial low temperature-tolerant basidiomycete (LTB), Sclerotial low temperature-tolerant basidiomycete (SLTB), *Typhula ishikariensis* var. *canadensis*, *Sclerotinia borealis*, *Fusarium nivale*, *Poa pratensis*, *Festuca rubra*, *F. ovina*, *F. duriuscula*, *Agrostis* spp.

INTRODUCTION

Winters are long and severe in the prairie region of Canada. However, snowfall is often quite low (3). On domestic lawns and other coarser amenity turfs which are usually composed of Kentucky bluegrass (*Poa pratensis* L.) alone or with red fescue (*Festuca rubra* L.), a nonsclerotial, non-sporulating, low temperature-tolerant basidiomycete (LTB), may cause considerable damage (5, 6, 7; Fig. 1 and 2). When snowfall is heavier and snow cover of longer duration than usual, a sclerotial, non-sporulating, low temperature-tolerant basidiomycete (SLTB), a distinct variety of *Typhula ishikariensis*, var. *canadensis* (Imai) Smith and Årsvoll (1), *Sclerotinia borealis* Bub. & Vleug., and *Fusarium nivale* (Fr.) Ces.

[1] Contribution No. 674, Agriculture Canada Res. Stn., Saskatoon, Saskatchewan, Canada, S7N 0X2.

Fig. 1. Aerial photograph of LTB snow mold tests, 29 Apr. 1974. *P. pratensis* Tests 1, 2, 3, 4, and 5 and *Festuca* spp. Tests 6, 7, and 8.

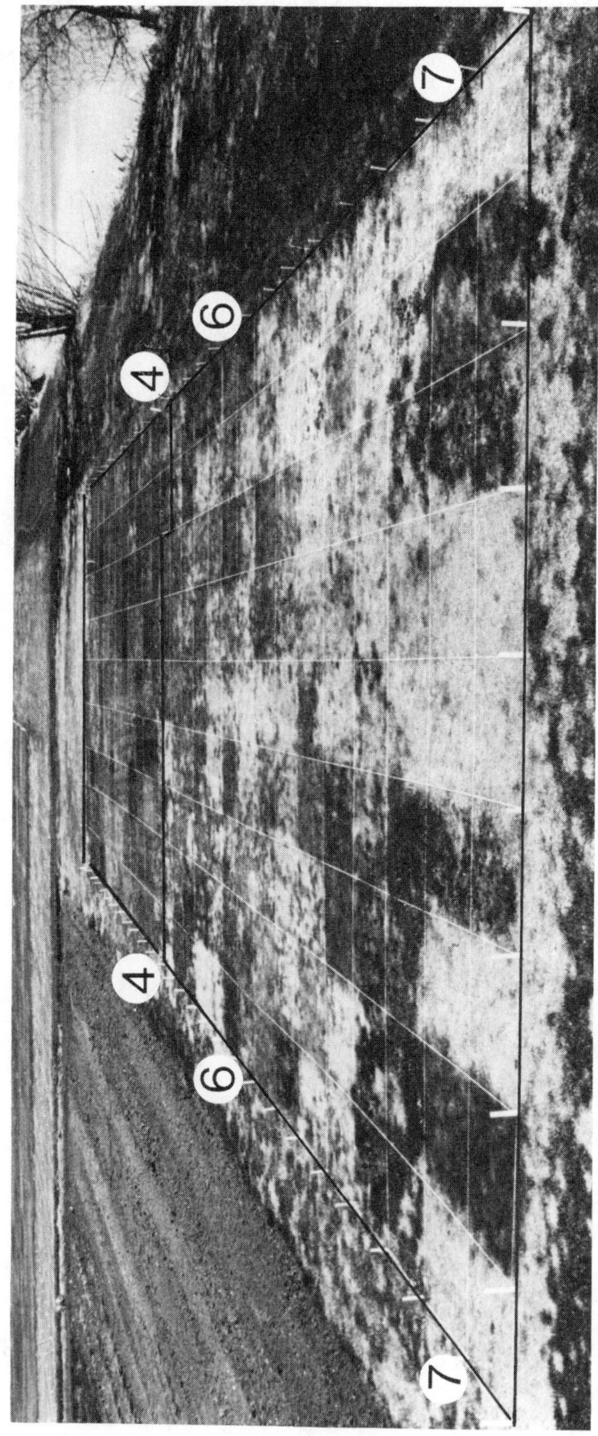

Fig. 2. *F. rubra* and *F. ovina* (tests 6 and 7) in foreground and *P. pratensis* tests (Test 4) in rear, 29 Apr. 1976. Compare severity of same tests in Fig. 1.

may also cause damage, singly and in complexes (6), and attacks of the LTB may be more severe. Finer golf green turf of *Agrostis palustris* Huds. is also subject to attacks by the same pathogens; *F. nivale* is quite common in autumn. Few strains of grasses have been selected specifically for the region, but many introductions and local selections of Kentucky bluegrass and fine-leaved fescues (*Festuca* spp.) have been tested in turf plots since 1971. Resistance and recovery from attacks by the LTB snow mold were the primary consideration. A preliminary report was published on the results of the 1973–74 tests (7).

MATERIALS AND METHODS

Details of the cultural practices, test design, methods of inoculation with cultures grown on sterile grain, rating for resistance and recovery from infection, and data analyses have been reported for the 1973–74 tests (7). Five lawn-type turf tests established in 1971 and 1972 comprised 171 entries, replicated two to six times, of Kentucky bluegrass cultivars and selections (Fig. 1; Tests 1, 2, 3, 4, and 5). There were also 83 entries, replicated two to four times, of fine-leafed fescues in three field tests established in 1971 and 1972 (Fig. 1; Tests 6, 7, and 8). In the spring of 1974 the test entries were scored first for resistance to LTB snow mold and for recovery from the disease on several subsequent dates, but in the 1975 and 1976 tests resistance was rated on a single date in late April or early May. All ratings were made on percent of turf area affected. In addition to the LTB tests, 13 bentgrass cultivars, established in 1972 as putting green turf, were rated for resistance to *F. nivale* in 1975 and 1976 when natural outbreaks of *Fusarium* patch (incited by *F. nivale*) disease developed.

Table 1. Resistance of 20 *P. pratensis* strains to LTB snow mold: average of ratings in 1974, 1975, and 1976. Test 1 (66 entries; six replicates; plots of 3 m²).

Cultivar or strain	Origin	Turf area affected	Cultivar	Origin	Turf area affected
		%			%
Dormie (S-7763)	USSR	8	Adorno	Netherlands	25
S-7766	Canada	14	Arista	Netherlands	29
Park	United States	14	Baron	Netherlands	29
Norma Øtofte	Denmark	15	Newport	United States	29
Delta	Canada	16	Nugget	United States	30
Captan	Netherlands	17	Windsor	United States	31
Skandia II	Sweden	17	Fylking	Sweden	40
Delft	Netherlands	19	Barkenta	Netherlands	40
Kentucky	United States	22	Golf	Sweden	40
Primo	Sweden	24	Sydsport	Sweden	43
Steinacher	Germany	24			
Correlation coefficients between rating			Correlation coefficients between ratings in 1974		
1974/1975 = 0.670**			23 Apr./6 May = 0.798**		
1974/1976 = 0.719**			23 Apr./15 May = 0.699**		
1975/1976 = 0.913**			6 May/15 May = 0.868**		

Table 2. Resistance of 12 *Poa pratensis* cultivars to LTB snow mold: average of ratings in 1974 and 1976.† Test 4 (24 entries; four replicates; plots of 1 m²).

Cultivar	Origin	Turf area affected
		%
Dormie (S-7763)	USSR	15
Delta	United States	22
Park	United States	27
Primo	Sweden	31
Arista	Netherlands	37
Nugget	United States	37
Steinacher	Germany	39
Fylking	Sweden	45
Sydsport	Sweden	47
Baron	Netherlands	47
Barkenta	Netherlands	48
Merion	United States	53
Cougar	United States	58

† No ratings were made on this test in 1975. Correlation coefficients between ratings: 1974/1976 = 0.603**

RESULTS

Data from three of the tests on Kentucky bluegrass cultivars from 1974 to 1976 are given in Tables 1 and 2. Table 3 presents data for the test on bentgrass strains. Severity of LTB damage is indicated in Fig. 1 and 2.

When compared with the mild, short winters of 1975 and 1976, LTB snow mold was more severe in the spring of 1974 after a greater snowfall and longer snow cover than the average for the previous 33 years (7). In the spring of 1974 a few very susceptible Kentucky bluegrass cultivars, including 'Cougar' and 'Line 59', showed more than 80% damage (Fig. 2; Test 4). In several of the fine-leaved fescues 90 to 100% of the foliage was killed (Fig. 1; Tests 6, 7, and 8). No strains of Kentucky bluegrass or fescue were completely resistant to the LTB. Most Kentucky bluegrass

Table 3. Susceptibility of turf of strains of *Agrostis* spp. to *F. nivale*.

		Percent of turf area affected by disease	
		Avg. ratings of four plots	
Cultivar or strain	Species†	7, 17, 24 Oct. 1975	5 May 1976*
		%	%
Penncross	S	5.8	18.8
Kingston	C	1.4	20.0
S-4979	S	3.7	21.3
Emerald	C	7.5	21.3
Seaside	S	12.3	27.5
Boral	T	3.9	36.3
Bore	T	2.9	40.0
Varmland	T	1.9	42.5
Colonial	T	4.2	58.8
Bardot	T	13.5	68.8
Exeter	T	14.6	71.3
Highland	T	2.1	76.3
Astoria	T	14.9	77.5

* Duncan's multiple range test at the 1% level of significance.
† S—*Agrostis palustris* Huds.; C—*A. canina* L.; T—*A. tenuis* Sibth.

lines which showed high or moderate resistance in 1974 also showed little or no disease in 1975 and 1976. Most of the highly susceptible strains in 1974 were moderately susceptible in 1975 and 1976 (Fig. 2). Several Kentucky bluegrass introductions from the USSR, Canada, Italy, and England were superior in resistance to established cultivars; the most notable was S-7763, now registered as 'Dormie' (Tables 1 and 2).

The only red fescue cultivar showing moderate resistance (30% damage) to the LTB was 'Arctared'. Even in 1976 when the disease was generally light some cultivars showed almost complete foliage damage (Fig. 2; Tests 6 and 7). S-1765, introduced from the USSR, was outstanding in resistance, with only 2% damage . In sheep fescue, three introductions from the USSR with 2 to 3% damage were highly resistant, as was the cultivar 'Durar' (7%), but 'Barenza' was susceptible with 65% damage (Fig. 2; Test 8).

The natural infection with *F. nivale* developed in the bentgrass test in October 1975 following cold, rainy weather. Its intensity increased under the snow cover and on some entries it became severe by early May 1976 (Table 3).

DISCUSSION

Although there were considerable differences in resistance to LTB snow mold among strains of Kentucky bluegrass, red fescue, and sheep fescue, highly significant correlations were found between ratings for the 3 test years. In the 1974 tests, when the LTB was most severe, resistance to the disease, as shown by the first rating in the spring, was highly correlated with recovery, as expressed by the last rating. Although the LTB snow mold may cause more disease under lighter and shorter duration snow covers than *T. ishikariensis* var. *canadensis* or *S. borealis*, it was favored by the abundant snowfall and prolonged snow cover of 1974.

Many well-known Kentucky bluegrass cultivars, some of which are marketed for turf use in the prairies, showed poor resistance and/or poor recovery from LTB snow mold in the tests reported herein. They were developed for turf use in climatic regions where the disease spectrum is quite different (2, 4, 5). 'Arista,' Cougar, 'Barkenta,' 'Baron,' 'Fylking,' 'Golf,' 'Merion,' 'Nugget,' 'Primo,' 'Sydsport,' and 'Windsor' performed poorly. 'Park,' although it shows high resistance to LTB (Table 1), suffers from desiccation damage in the spring. Merion is no longer a recommended cultivar in Saskatchewan because of susceptibility to LTB, fusarium patch, and leaf rust (incited by *Puccinia brachypodii*). Cultivars are needed which will not go dormant in mild winter climates, but will remain winter green and thus replace tissues killed or damaged by weather and disease. The situation in the prairies and in regions with similar climates is quite different. Most of the aerial parts of turfgrasses are killed by early winter. Early winter dormancy seems of considerable value in increasing field resistance to LTB snow mold. The S-7763 (Dormie) strain of

Kentucky bluegrass is an example of field resistance to the LTB apparently related to early, deep dormancy. Its rapid recovery in the spring probably results from the early, deep dormancy conserving soil N and storing carbohydrate reserves. Cultivars of Kentucky bluegrass, red fescue, and sheep fescue recommended for use elsewhere than on the Canadian prairies should not be employed for turf formation there without adequate testing in the region. Testing emphasis should be on winter dormancy and reaction to snow molds. Resistance to specific snow molds should be determined because the spectrum of snow molds varies greatly from region to region and cultivars show differential responses to the wide range of pathogens.

Fine-leaved fescues are generally more severely damaged by the LTB and other snow molds (7) and are slower to recover, which may be one reason why these turfgrasses are sometimes omitted from specifications for lawns and golf fairways of the prairies.

In most years *F. nivale* is probably the major snow mold of fine bentgrass and annual bluegrass (*Poa annua* L.) on golf greens in the prairies. Bentgrasses go dormant much earlier than in milder climates, but attacks of *F. nivale* usually start before the onset of dormancy and the pathogen probably does not make as rapid subniveal progress as the LTB since it is not as low temperature-tolerant as the latter (4). Severe damage probably takes place with *F. nivale* in spring at snow melt when temperatures are near 0 C. None of the lines showed complete resistance to the pathogen, but the *A. palustris* and velvet bentgrass (*A. canina* L.) entries showed greater resistance than those of colonial bentgrass (*A. tenuis* L.). Of the two cultivars commonly used on the prairies, 'Penncross' tended to be more resistant than 'Seaside.' S-4979 is a promising new strain for use in the Prairies.

ACKNOWLEDGMENTS

I am indebted to R. L. Goss for presenting this paper at the Third International Turfgrass Research Conference, and to W. W. Reiter, W. Leonard, C. Tennant, and R. E. Underwood for technical and photographic assistance.

LITERATURE CITED

1. Årsvoll, K. A., and J. D. Smith. 1978. *Typhula ishikariensis* and its varieties, var. *idahoensis* comb. nov. and var. *canadensis* var. nov. Can. J. Bot. 56:348–364.
2. de Leew, W. P., and H. Voss. 1970. Krankheiten und schadlinge an räsengräsern in den Niederlanden. Rasen-Turf-Gazon. 1:65–67&84.
3. Potter, J. G. 1965. Snow cover. Climatological studies No. 3. Can. Dep. Trans. Met. Br. Queen's Printer, Ottawa.
4. Smith, J. Drew. 1965. Fungal diseases of turfgrasses. Sports Turf. Res. Inst., Bingley, England.

5. ————. 1974. Winter diseases of turfgrasses. Summary 25th Annu. Turfgrass Conf. R. Can. Golf Assoc., Winnipeg, Manitoba. p. 20–25.

6. ————. 1974. Snow molds of turfgrasses in Saskatchewan. p. 313–324. *In* E. C. Roberts (ed.) Proc. 2nd Int. Turfgrass Res. Conf., Blacksburg, Va. 18–21 June 1973. Am. Soc. Agron., Madison, Wis.

7. ————. 1975. Resistance of turfgrasses to low-temperature basidiomycete snow mold and recovery from damage. Can. Plant Dis. Surv. 55:147–154.

Chapter 33

The Possibility of Controlling Fairy Ring and Rust Diseases in Lawns with Benodanil[1]

R. HEIMES
F. LOËCHER

ABSTRACT

Benodanil was found to suppress growth of the fairy ring fungus (*Marasmius oreades*) when applied to lawns as a drench at 2 to 5 g a.i. in 2 to 5 liters of water/m². Control was obtained both with May and September/October applications. The injured portions of lawn recovered after treatment during the course of the vegetation period.

The same fungicide, sprayed at 1 kg a.i./ha at 14-day intervals also controlled rust diseases (*Puccinia* spp.) of lawngrasses when treatment was made at the beginning of the infection.

INTRODUCTION

The Basidiomycete fungus (*Marasmius oreades*) is the major pathogenic agent of "fairy rings" in West Germany. The name "fairy ring" stems from the time when these rings on grass surfaces were held to be the places where elves or fairies danced. Today we hypothesize that the odd structure of a grass area enclosed by a fungus ring is traceable to the hydrocyanic substances secreted by the fungus. These substances have been located both in the fruiting bodies of the fungi as well as in contaminated soil (2).

Fruiting bodies arranged in the form of a ring emerge in great numbers from the soil. Next to the ring of fruiting bodies, on the inner side of the circle, a zone of distinctly green grass can be seen. This in turn is bordered by a strip where the grass has almost totally died.

Fairy ring infection is becoming increasingly widespread. Since lawns infected by fairy rings have an unpleasant appearance, there is considerable interest, especially in the case of well-tended decorative lawns, sports fields, and golf greens, in the restoration of the infected areas to their original, fungus-free form. Chemical control of the fungi concerned has yielded only limited success in the past.

[1] A contribution from Landwirtschaftliche Versuchsstation, Limburgerhof, West Germany.

 Proceedings of the Third International Turfgrass Research Conference.

Other Basidiomycete fungi that cause rust (*Puccinia* spp., *P. poae-nemoralis*, *P. striiformis*, *P. graminis*, and occasionally *Uromyces dactylidis*) can also negatively effect the appearance of a well-tended lawn. Grasses such as perennial ryegrass (*Lolium perenne* L.), timothy (*Phleum pratense*), and, in particular, Kentucky bluegrass (*Poa pratensis* L.) are severely infected by rust diseases. The fungi spread rapidly under favorable conditions, causing unsightly color canges in well-maintained lawns from early summer until late autumn. The following is a report on several years of experiments concerning fairy ring and rust in West Germany.

MATERIALS AND METHODS

Fairy Rings

Fairy rings have only become a problem in well-tended lawns in Germany in recent years, thus experimental possibilities have been limited. Often only a few examples could be found in a given area. Hence, only replicates of one to three were possible in the years 1974–76 when these preliminary trials were done. A statistical analysis of the results was therefore not possible.

As a result of the recent appearance of fairy rings, no product is as yet registered for *Marasmius* control in Germany and thus no standard comparison was included. The experiments were carried out using various formulations of 2-iodo-benzanilide, a fungicide with the common name of benodanil.

Application rates were 1.5, 2.5, 3.0, and 5.0 g a.i./m^2 (see Fig. 1, 3). A single drench application of 2 to 5 liters/m^2 of ring was made in autumn.

Marasmius oreades forms a dense, solid underground mass of mycelium that is very hydrophobic. Since the chemical must be applied directly into this mycelial mass, it was necessary to loosen or perforate the infected ring area before fungicide treatment and then water it as thoroughly as possible.

Four trials were laid down at the following locations: Limburgerhof, Deidesheim, and Iggelheim (two trials). The effectiveness of benodanil was ascertained by counting the fruiting bodies or by evaluating the infected ring area according to the following scale:

1 = no visible rings;
2 = rings indistinct;
3 = rings more distinct, grass growth suppressed and dark green;
4 = broad rings, grass partially dying;
5 = bare ring area.

In addition, recovery was assessed according to the scale 1 to 9 (1 = fully grown, 9 = fully destroyed). One evaluation was made after 80 days and a second after 360 to 380 days.

Rusts

Trials on rust were carried out in England (two trials) and Germany (four trials). Plot sizes ranged from 2.5 to 5 m^2, according to location, and were replicated three to four times. The wettable powder formulation of benodanil (BAS 317 00 F, Calirus) was applied in comparison with tridemorph (Calixin, 750 gm a.i./liter, EC), carbendazim (Bavistin, 50% WP), metiram (Polyram-Combi, 80% WP) and nickel sulfate + maneb (1:2 mixture). All sprays were applied in 600 to 1,000 liters H_2O/ha (see Fig. 4, 5, and 6 for rates). One or more sprays were applied depending on the infection pressure.

Assessments of trials in Germany were made 7 days after the last treatment, and one trial was further assessed after 27 and 44 days to ascertain the duration of fungicidal effect. One English trial was assessed after 19 and 26 days and the other after 20 days. A 1 to 9 assessment scale was used in which 1 = no disease and 9 = 100% attack.

RESULTS

Fairy Ring Suppression

Figure 1 shows the effect of various application rates; Fig. 2, the effect of a single drench application of BAS 317 00 F on fruiting body formation; Fig. 3, the influence of fungicide application on subsequent turf development.

A single drench of 2.5 g a.i. benodanil/m^2 in autumn (September/October) partially controlled *Marasmius oreades* in all trials to the extent that two months after the application the rings were less distinct (Fig. 1). Approximately 1 year after using benodanil at application rates of 2.5, 3.0, or 5.0 g a.i./m^2, the old rings had practically disappeared and grass from the sides had filled in the bare areas. Results in all four trials were consistent. Fruiting bodies appeared in only one trial (Limburgerhof, Fig. 2). The number decreased markedly with the use of benodanil.

As Fig. 3 shows, benodanil treatment improved the lawn condition in comparison with the untreated control. Phytotoxicity was not observed with any of the formulations (1 = very good stand, 9 = all grasses dead). Subsequent experiments have confirmed that benodanil application in spring is equally effective in controlling the disease.

Rust Control

The percentage effectiveness of the fungicide was calculated according to the formula of Abbott (1):

$$\text{Degree of effectiveness} = \frac{\text{Score for untreated} - \text{Score for treated}}{\text{Score for untreated}} \times 100.$$

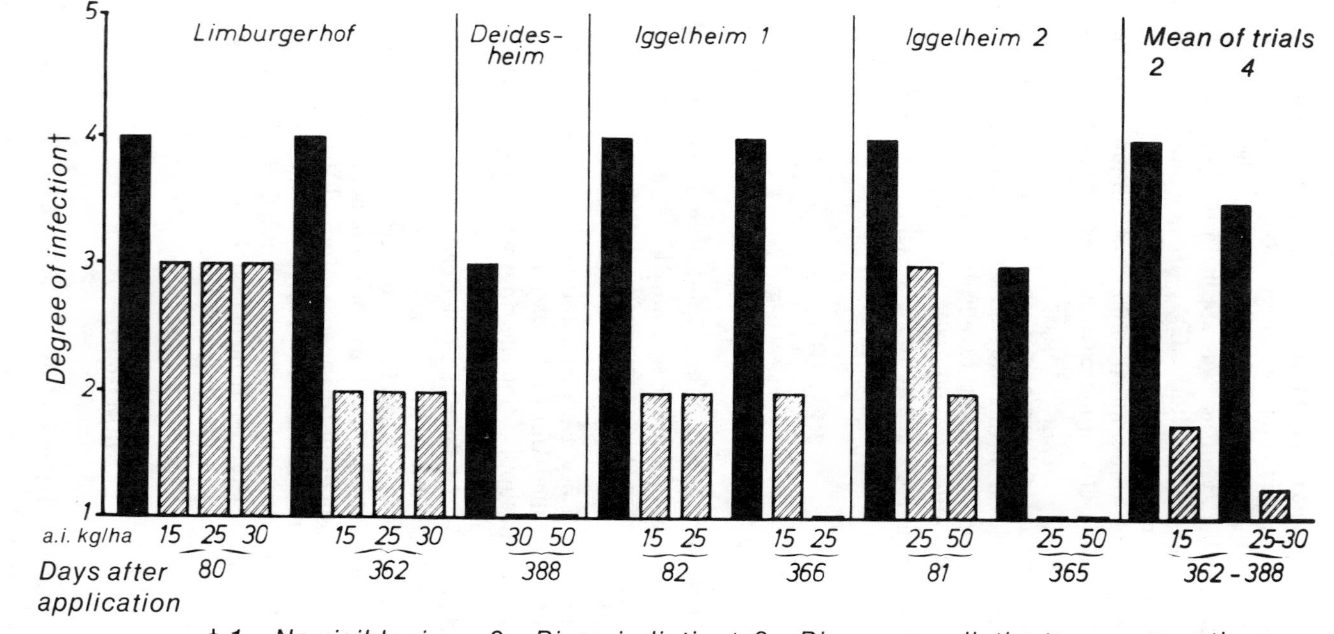

Fig. 1. Controlling fairy ring by means of a single drenching treatment with various benodanil application rates (West Germany, 1974–75 and 1975–76).

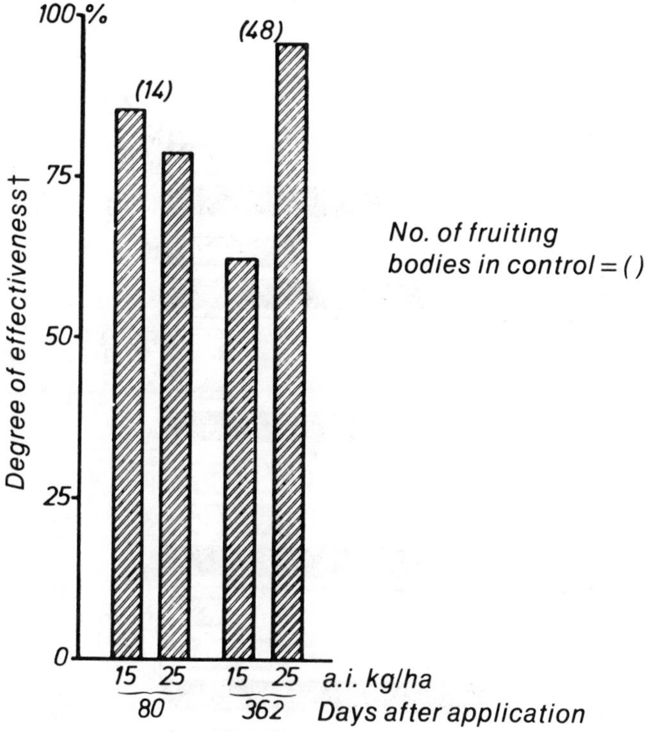

Fig. 2. Reduction of fruiting body formation *Marasmius oreades* after using benodanil in a drenching treatment (West Germany, 1975–76).

The results are shown along side the level of infection in the untreated control (Fig. 4, 5, 6).

Figure 4 shows one or several applications of 1 kg benodanil/ha controls *Puccinia* spp. This reduction in infection remains clearly visible for a longer period of time (6 weeks).

Excellent rust control was obtained in England after a single application of 1 kg/ha benodanil when the disease level was approximately 25% (Fig. 5). On various older bluegrass lawn areas in England, a very low benodanil application rate (0.22 kg/ha) controlled *Puccinia striiformis* completely when applied three times (Fig. 6). The severity of infection was very high. At all application rates (0.22, 0.34, and 0.45 kg a.i./ha), benodanil produced the same or better results than the standard treatment of nickel sulfate plus Maneb at quite high application rates (3.88 + 5.82 kg/ha). No phytotoxicity could be ascertained at any of the rates tested.

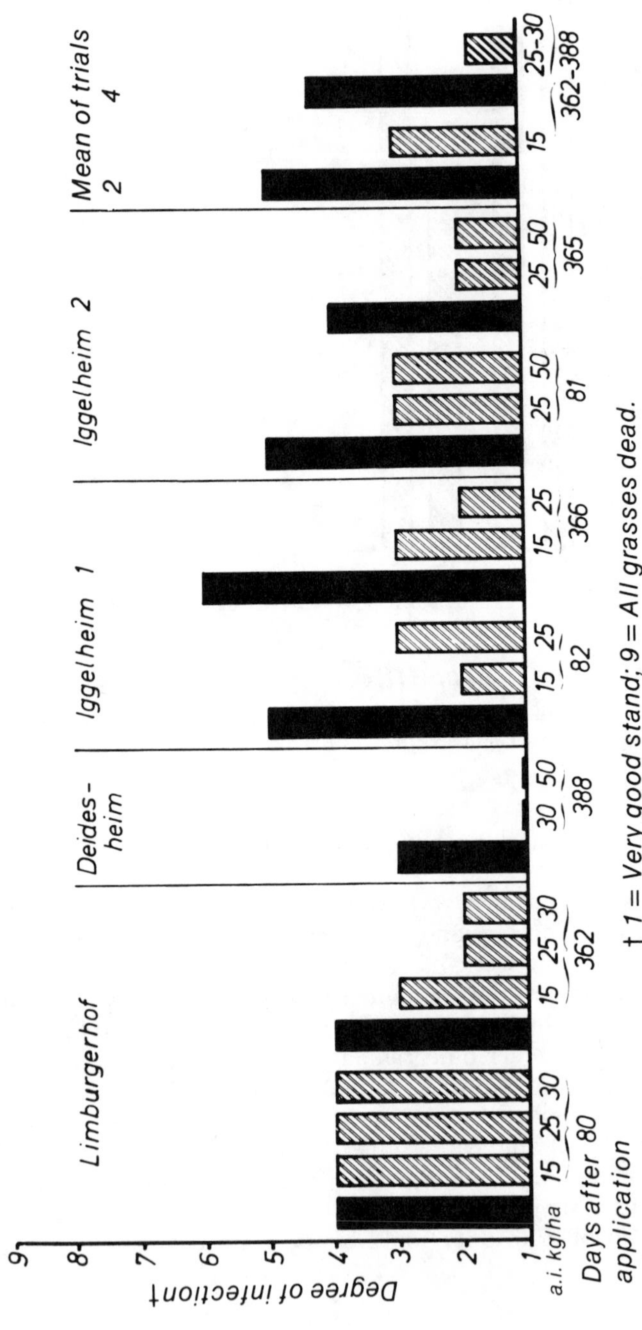

Fig. 3. Influence of a single benodanil drenching treatment at various application rates on the development of the lawn (West Germany, 1974–75 and 1975–76).

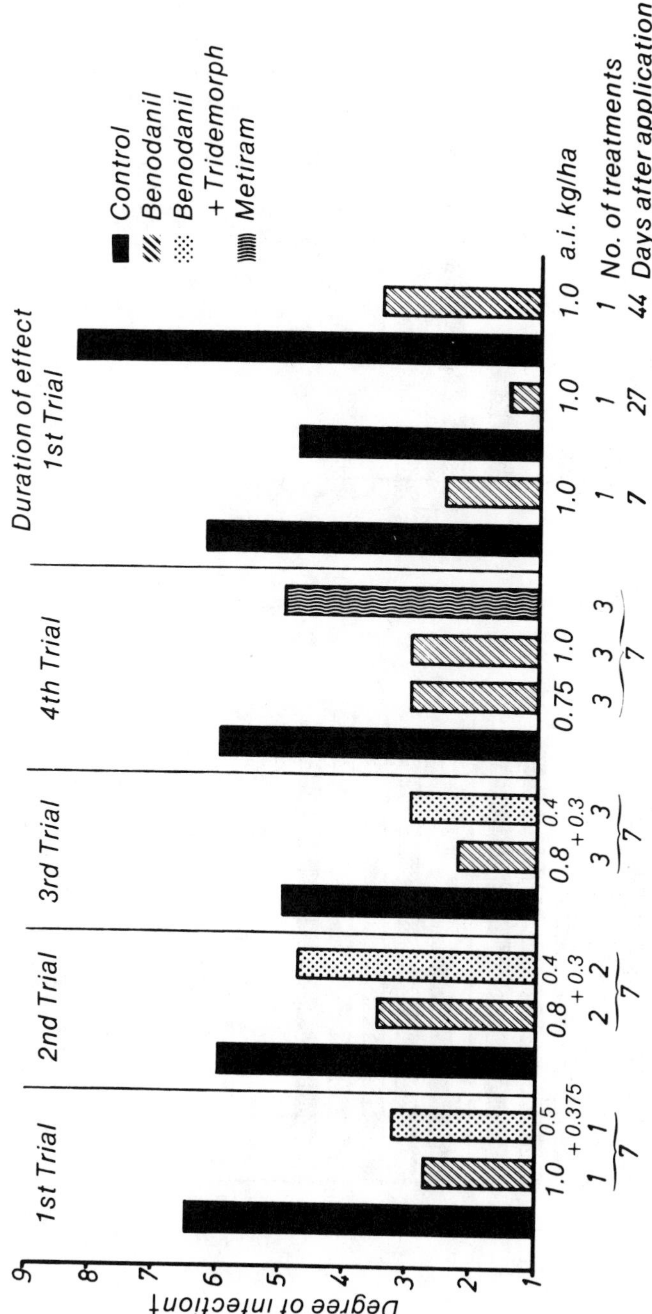

Fig. 4. The effects of three fungicide treatments on *Puccinia* spp. in lawns (West Germany, 1974 and 1975).

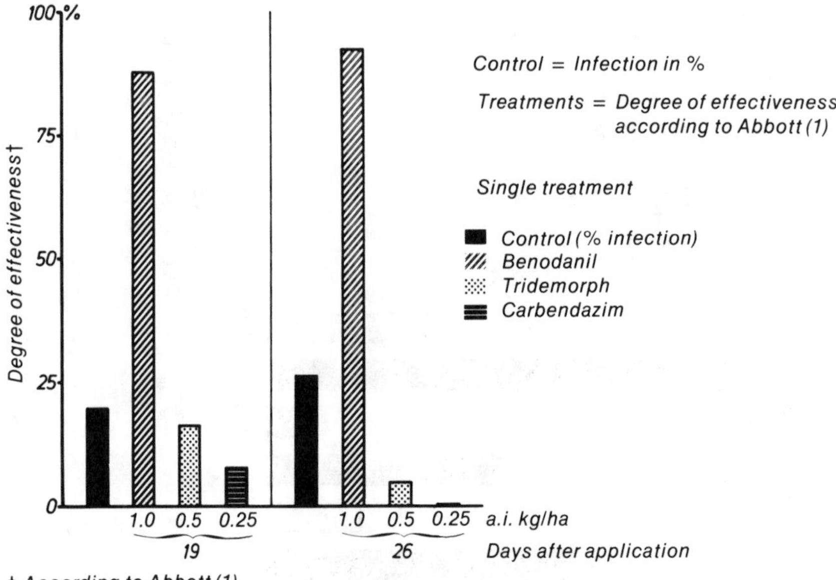

Fig. 5. The effects of three fungicides on *Puccinia* spp. (Great Britain, 1976).

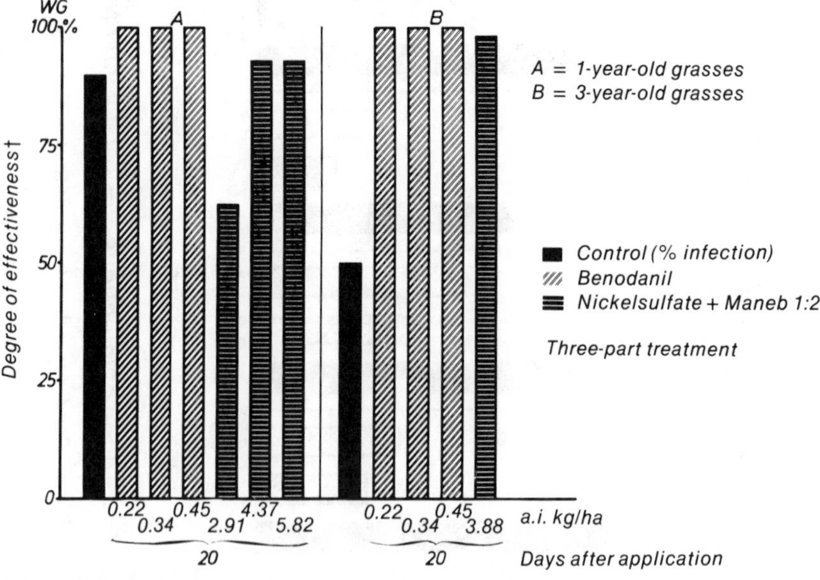

Fig. 6. The effects of two fungicide treatments on *Puccinia striiformis* in Kentucky bluegrass (Great Britain, 1974).

LITERATURE CITED

1. Abbott, W. D. 1925. A method of computing the effectiveness of an insecticide. J. Econ. Entomol. 18:265–267.
2. Leban, S. B., and E. G. Hawn. 1963. Formation of hydrogen cyanide by the mycelial stage of a fairy ring fungus. Phytopathology 53:1395–1396.

Chapter 34

Role of a Soil Fungicide and Two Nematicides in Maintaining Bermudagrass and Creeping Bentgrass Turf[1]

R. V. STURGEON, JR.
K. E. JACKSON

ABSTRACT

Soil-borne pathogens and pests play an important role in the initiation of many turfgrass disease syndromes. Among these, plant parasitic nematodes and fungi damage the plant's root system. A healthy root system is needed to support optimum plant growth, so vital in the plant's ability to recover or withstand environmental stresses. The interaction between plant parasitic nematodes and soil-borne fungal pathogens has not been adequately investigated on turf. Symptoms of root diseases are commonly overlooked and attributed to other causes such as low fertility, drought, or damage from other pests.

Two non-fumigant nematicides, O,O-Diethyl O-[4-(methysulfinyl)phenyl] phosphorothioate (Dasanit®) and O-Ethyl S,S-Dipropyl Phosphorodithioate (Mocap®), and a soil fungicide, pentachloronitrobenzene plus 5 Ethoxy-3-trichloromethyl-1,2,4-thiadiazole (Terraclor Super-X®), were applied alone and in combinations to three cultivars: 'Sunturf,' 'Tifgreen,' and 'U-3', bermudagrass [*Cynodon dactylon* (L.) Pers.]. Plots receiving only Terraclor Super-X® 10–2.5G at 454 g ai (PCNB)/92.9 m^2 when compared to non-treated plots made the greatest improvement in shoot density the 2nd year. Combinations of Dasanit® at 204 g ai/92.9 m^2 and Terraclor Super-X® at 454 g ai (PCNB)/92.9 m^2 were applied to an established creeping bentgrass (*Agrostis palustris* Huds.) nursery composed of a selection from 'Seaside' (HCC-7-2). Following severe moisture stress about 1 September, plots receiving summer (28 July and 22 August) applications of Terraclor Super-X®-Dasanit® combinations showed less than 10% reduction in shoot density as compared to over 60% reduction in non-treated plots. Bermudagrass plots receiving Terraclor Super-X® produced a significant increase in shoot density the second season and typical "Spring Dead Spots" filled in.

INTRODUCTION

Healthy turf is very important to our golf courses, parks, playgrounds, athletic fields, home lawns, and industrial areas. Turf not only provides beauty for our leisure and recreational activities, it plays an important role in maintaining our environment (1). Controlling diseases can be an important factor in maintaining the healthy, vigorous, dense turf. Healthy turfgrass is essential to the operation of our golf courses and is the concern of all professional turfgrass managers. Many superintendents and

[1] A contribution from the Oklahoma State Univ. Ext., Oklahoma State Univ., Stillwater, Okla., USA.

home owners find it difficult to maintain the healthy stand of grass required for a good putting surface or one that can withstand environmental stresses and heavy traffic. A healthy turfgrass root system, vital in the plant's ability to recover or withstand stresses, is needed to support optimum plant growth.

A handful of soil contains a dynamic biological system of hundreds of different kinds of living organisms. Osborne (9) reports that some of these organisms are beneficial and others are plant parasites that can destroy or weaken plant roots. Soil-borne pathogens and pests have played an important role in initiating turfgrass diseases for many years (5, 6, 7, 8, 10). Root disease problems in turf are generally overlooked because the aboveground symptoms are easily confused with low fertility, drought, insects, and other pests. Heald and Perry (7) noted that nematodes feeding on the underground plant parts can cause injury resulting in some mechanical damage when nematodes penetrate roots and individual cells. Most of the damage, however, is due to esophageal secretions. Christie (3) commented that nematode injury can also provide openings for soil fungi and bacteria to enter and increase disease incidence.

Nematode control studies in recent years have shown that the soil fumigants and non-fumigants can reduce nematode populations to a level that will aid growth of the turfgrass (2, 7, 8, 10, 11). Examination of roots and other underground plant parts collected from golf greens, tees, athletic fields, home lawns, and other turfgrass areas not only reveal nematode injury, but often show severe root rot damage associated with increased nematode populations. These findings have stimulated a program in search of a chemical or chemical combinations that will effectively control this soil disease complex and aid in maintaining healthier stands of turfgrass. The objectives of these studies were to evaluate certain nematicides and a soil fungicide for their influence on an established creeping bentgrass (*Agrostis palustris* Huds.) and bermudagrass [*Cynodon dactylon* (L.) Pers.] turf.

MATERIALS AND METHODS

Bermudagrass Studies

Two non-fumigant nematicides, O,O-Diethyl O-[4-(methylsulfinyl) phenyl] phosphorothioate (Dasanit®) and O-Ethyl S, S-dipropyl phosphorodithioate (Mocap®), were evaluated on bermudagrass in 1976 in combination with a soil fungicide, pentachloronitrobenzene plus 5-Ethoxy-3-trichloromethyl-1,2,4-thiadiazole (Terraclor Super-X®), for control of nematodes and soil fungi associated with the soil disease complex. Dasanit®, Mocap®, and Terraclor Super-X® were applied alone and in combinations to 'Tifgreen,' 'Sunturf,' and 'U-3' bermudagrass grown on the Plant Pathology Farm, Stillwater, Okla., USA, in 1976. The bermudagrass plots were irrigated so they received at least 5 cm of water each week, mowed at 2.54 cm, and received 908 g/92.9 m^2 of N fertilizer applied once a month from 1 May to 1 October. N-Butyl-N-ethyl-*a*,*a*,*a*-trifluro-2,6-dinitro-*p*-toluidine (Balan®) at 544.8 g/92.9 m^2 and dimethyl tetrachloroterephthalate (Dacthal®) at 160 ml/92.9 m^2 were applied in the spring and early fall, respectively, to control weedy grasses. Treated areas consisted of 6.25 m^2 replicated three times and randomized in a complete block design. Granular formualtions of each of the chemicals were distributed evenly by a 76-cm wide Gandy Turf Tender on 28 Apr. and 22 Aug. 1976. The treatments were applied to 92.9 m^2 plots as follows: Terraclor Super-X® + Dasanit 10–2.5–5G® (experimental formulation) at 454 g ai; Terraclor Super-X® + Mocap 10–2.5–5G® (experimental formulation) at 454 g ai; Terraclor Super-X® 10–2.5G at 454 g ai; Mocap® at 10G 136 g ai; Dasanit® 15G at 204 g ai; a non-treatment. Following application, 1.27 cm of water was applied to drench in the chemicals. Each plot was sampled for nematodes on 26 Jan. 29 Apr., and 17 Sept. 1976, and a 100-ml subsample of soil was processed by a modification of the Christie-Perry Extraction Technique (4). A rating was given to each treatment based on the amount of dead area in each plot or density of stand. Percentage stand was based on a 0 to 9 rating with 0 = no bermudagrass and 9 = 90% or greater shoot density.

Creeping Bentgrass Studies

To evaluate the effect of a non-fumigant nematicide and soil fungicide on the nematode-soil fungal disease complex, Dasanit® and Terraclor Super-X® were applied alone and in combination during the season to an established creeping bentgrass nursery, a selection from 'Seaside' (HCC-7-2), on the Agronomy Research Farm, Stillwater in 1976. Chemical treatments were applied as granular formulations to 9.3-m^2 plots replicated three times in a randomized block design. The granular formulations were distributed evenly over the plots by a 76-cm wide Gandy Turf Tender and drenched in with approximately 1.27 cm of water. The chemical, rates per 92.9 m^2, and dates of appliction were as follows: Terraclor Super-X® + Dasanit 10–2.5–5G® (experimental formulation) at 454 g ai as one application on 21 April or followed by a second application on 28 July; Terraclor Super-X® 10–2.5G at 454 g ai as one application on 21 April or followed by a second application on 28 July; Dasanit® 15G at 204 g ai as one application on 21 April or followed by a second application on 22 August at 454 g ai. The plots were sampled for nematodes on 21 April prior to treatment, 15 May, 18 July, and 15 September, and 100-ml subsamples of soil were processed by a modification of the Christie-Perry Extraction Technique (4). A disease rating based on percent loss of grass was made 5 September and is given as a 0 to 9 rating where 0 = no loss and 9 = 90% or greater loss of grass (see Table 4). Isolations on water agar and potato dextrose agar were made from diseased roots taken from the various treatments.

RESULTS AND DISCUSSION

Bermudagrass Studies

The greatest response in turfgrass growth and shoot density occurred in plots planted to Sunturf bermudagrass and treated with either a soil fungicide-nematicide combination, Terraclor Super-X® + Dasanit® 10–2.5–5G or Terraclor Super-X® + Mocap 10–2.5–5G® (experimental formulations), or the soil fungicide Terraclor Super-X® (Table 1). Plots receiving only a nematicide treatment were little or no better than no treatment. A significant increase in shoot density was observed following treatment with Terraclor Super-X® + Dasanit 10–2.5–5G®, Terraclor Super-X® + Mocap 10–2.5–5G®, and Terraclor Super-X® when compared to the untreated plots. No significant difference was noted in the plots receiving only the nematicide application when compared to untreated plots. These results suggest that the soil fungicide had a greater influence on the soil disease syndrome than the nematicide. However, the combination of nematicide plus soil fungicide-treated plots produced a more vigorous, dense turfgrass stand. The Terraclor Super-X® treated plots made the greatest improvement in stand ratings during the 2nd year, which indicates a slower response can be expected from the applications of Terraclor Super-X®. *Pythium* spp., *Fusarium* spp., *Helminthosporium* spp., and *Rhizoctonia* spp. were the most commonly found fungal species in the bermudagrass plots. The major plant parasitic nematode populations found in the bermudagrass plots were ring (*Criconemoides* spp.) and spiral (*Helicotylenchus* spp.) nematodes. Light populations of *Tylenchorhynchus* spp. (stunt), root lesion (*Pratylenchus* spp.), dagger (*Xiphinema* spp.), root-knot (*Meloidogyne* spp.), lance (*Hoplolaimus* spp.), stubby root (*Trichodorus* spp.), and sheath (*Hemicycliophora* spp.) were recovered on an inconsistent basis. Because of sample handling problems, no population data are available from the untreated plots or following the 29 April or prior to 23 August chemical applications. However, the

Table 1. Effects of two nematicides and a soil fungicide treatment on shoot density of bermudagrass in 1976.

Treatment†	Application rate	Shoot density rating‡			
		Tifgreen	U-3	Sunturf	Avg.
TSX-Das 10–2.5–5G	g ai/92.9 m²				
TSX-Das 10–2.5–5G	454	8	6	9	7.7
TSX-Mocap 10–2.5–5G	454	7	7	9	7.7
Das 15G	204	5	4	3	4.0
Mocap® 10G	136	6	4	6	5.3
TSX 10–2.5G	454	6	6	9	7.0
No treatment	--	4	4	4	4.0
L.S.D.					1.9

† Chemical treatments applied 29 Apr. and 23 Aug. 1976: TSX = Terraclor Super-X® (Pentachloronitrobenzene plus 5 Ethoxy-3-trichloromethyl-1,2,4-thiadiazole); Das = Dasanit® (0,0-Diethyl 0-[4-methylsulfinyl) phenyl] phosphorothioate); Mocap® = (0-Ethyl S,S-dipropyl phosphorodithioate).

‡ Estimated shoot density rating based on 0 to 9: 0 = no bermudagrass; 9 = 90% or greater shoot density.

Table 2. Effects of two nematicides and a soil fungicide treatment on ring and spiral nematode populations infesting bermudagrass in 1976.

Treatment†	Rate	Date of sample	Plant parasitic nematodes recovered/ 100 ml of soil‡					
			Tifgreen		U-3		Sunturf	
			Ring	Spiral	Ring	Spiral	Ring	Spiral
	ai g/92.9 m²							
TSX-Das 10–2.5–5G	454	21 Jan.	16	64	30	20	44	2
		29 Apr.	48	30	46	4	24	2
		17 Sept.	0	60	20	8	8	0
TSX-Mocap® 10–2.5–5G	454	21 Jan.	2	14	14	8	20	74
	454	29 Apr.	34	18	36	4	30	8
		17 Sept.	44	24	8	0	4	0
Das 15G	204	21 Jan.	10	18	34	12	10	2
		29 Apr.	24	58	50	10	28	0
		17 Sept.	40	8	36	4	52	0
Mocap® 10G	136	21 Jan.	26	36	46	20	32	6
		29 Apr.	20	8	30	28	20	2
		17 Sept.	20	108	4	8	4	4
TSX 10–2.5G	454	21 Jan.	14	14	60	78	20	4
		29 Apr.	74	64	30	10	22	4
		17 Sept.	24	8	56	8	8	4

† Chemical treatments applied 29 Apr. and 23 Aug. 1976: TSX = Terraclor Super-X® (Pentachloronitrobenzene plus 5 Ethoxy-3-trichlormethyl-1,2,4-thiadiazole); Das = Dasanit® (0,0-Diethyl 0-[4-(methylsulfinyl) phenyl] phosphorothioate); Mocap® = (0-Ethyl S, S-dipropyl phosphorodithioate).
‡ Ring = *Criconemoides* spp., spiral = *Helicotylenchus* spp.

sampling data indicate a damaging population occurred within the test during the season (Table 2). The sampling data show that a heavier population of spiral nematodes are found during the season on Tifgreen than Sunturf, for which we have no explanation. The lack of response obtained from the Dasanit® or Mocap® applications with the plant parasitic nematode population could have been overcome by the above-average fertility and watering program carried out during the season. Visual observations indicated no phytotoxicity from any of the chemicals applied to the three bermudagrass cultivars tested. Plots receiving Terraclor Super-X® produced a significantly more dense turf during the second growing season than the untreated or those receiving only Dasanit® or Mocap® and typical "spring dead spot" areas began to rapidly fill in with bermudagrass. The growth response obtained in the dead spots and overall bermudagrass turf from the soil fungicide and nematicide combinations appears to have potential in a turfgrass cultural program.

Creeping Bentgrass Studies

The major plant parasitic nematode populations found in the creeping bentgrass plots were ring, stunt, and pin nematodes (Table 3). Nematode population levels were observed to fluctuate during the summer in untreated plots. However, the populations were considered to be at a high enough level to cause damage throughout the summer. Nematode popula-

Table 3. Effects of two nematicides and a soil fungicide treatment on ring, stunt, and pin nematode populations infesting creeping bentgrass in 1975.

Treatment	Rate	Application	Date of sampling	Plant parasitic‡ nematodes recovered		
				ring	Stunt	Pin
	g ai/92.9 m²					
TSX-Das 10–2.5–5G	454	21 Apr.	21 Apr.	48	16 16	180
		22 Aug.	15 May	128	168	16
			28 July	162	64	128
			5 Sept.	44	152	16
TSX 10–2.5G	454	21 Apr.	21 Apr.	162	72	124
		28 July	15 May	131	174	16
			28 July	151	76	168
			5 Sept.	60	154	12
Das 15G	204	21 Apr.	21 Apr.	56	12	132
		22 Aug.	15 May	62	32	16
			28 July	159	78	178
			5 Sept.	162	124	16
TSX-Das 10–2.5–5G	454	21 Apr.	21 Apr.	64	12	128
			15 May	16	134	12
			28 July	178	124	132
			5 Sept.	88	168	16
Das 15G	204	21 Apr.	21 Apr.	78	16	44
			15 May	56	44	24
			28 July	168	80	64
			5 Sept.	48	48	8
TSX 10–2.5G	454	21 Apr.	21 Apr.	180	8	148
			15 May	72	180	36
			28 July	204	92	136
			5 Sept.	216	208	24
No treatment	--	--	21 Apr.	132	36	148
			15 May	32	188	36
			28 July	174	148	76
			5 Sept.	88	208	8

† TSX = Terraclor Super-X® (Pentachloronitrobenzene plus 5 Ethoxy-3-trichloromethyl-1,2,4-thiadiazole); Das = Dasanit® (0-0-Diethyl 0-[4-methylsulfinyl)phenyl] phosphorothioate); Mocap® = (0-Ethyl S,S-dipropyl phosphorodithioate).

‡ Ring *Criconemoides* spp.; stunt = *Tylenchorhynchus* spp.; pin = *Paratylenchus* spp. Average number of plant parasitic nematodes recovered from 100 ml of soil.

tions in plots receiving Dasanit 15G® applied at 204 g ai/92.9 m² and Terraclor Super-X® + Dasanit® (experimental formulation) 10–2.5–5G applied at 454 g ai (PCNB)/92.9 m² were only slightly lower than plots receiving only Terraclor Super-X® 10–2.5G at 454 g ai/92.9 m². The nematode populations in plots receiving only Terraclor Super-X® were slightly higher on the 15 May and 15 September sampling dates than the untreated plots. The sampling dates are not for the purpose of evaluating chemical control, but are presented to estabilsh the levels of nematode populations during the season. Isolations made from diseased roots taken from the various treatments showed the most commonly occurring fungal species to be: *Pythium* spp., *Fusarium* spp., *Helminthosporium* spp., and *Rhizoctonia* spp. Population levels of these fungi were not determined. However, examination of the root samples taken during the season indicated severe root damage. Following a severe moisture stress on or about 1

Table 4. Response to a nematicide-soil fungicide on creeping bentgrass in 1975.

Treatment†	Rate	Date of application	Disease rating‡
	g ai/92.9 m^2		
TSX-Das 10–2.5–5G	454	21 Apr. 21 Aug.	3.0
TSX 10–2.5G	454	21 Apr. 28 July	0.8
Das 15G	204 454	21 Apr. 22 Aug.	1.0
TSX-Das 10–2.5–5G	454	21 Apr.	4.8
Das 15G	204	21 Apr.	6.7
TSX 10–2.5G	454	21 Apr.	6.8
No treatment			6.7

† Chemical treatments applied: TSX = Terraclor Super-X® (Pentachloronitrobenzene plus 5 Ethoxy-3-trichloromethyl-1,2,4-thiadiazole); Das = Dasanit® (0,0-Diethyl 0-[4(methylsulfinyl)phenyl] phosphorothioate).

‡ Disease rating is based on an average estimated percent turfgrass loss given as a 0 to 9 rating: 0 = no loss; 9 = 90% or greater loss.

September heavy loss of turfgrass occurred in plots not receiving the July or August application of soil fungicide (Terraclor Super-X®) (Table 4). The overall turfgrass vigor and shoot density was better in plots receiving the April and August Dasanit® + Terraclor Super-X® 10–2.5–5G combination. However, the small amount of grass lost in plots receiving only Terraclor Super-X® on these dates indicates the soil fungicide had the greatest influence on maintaining the stand of turfgrass. Plots receiving the spring (21 April) and summer (28 July and 22 August) applications of Terraclor Super-X® 10–2.5G and Terraclor Super-X®+ Dasanit® 10–2.5–5G combination showed less than 10% turfgrass loss as compared to over 60% loss in the untreated plots. This study supports the need for a soil disease control program in some situations. Light yellowing of the creeping bentgrass occurred from the formulations containing PCNB. However, these plots produced a more vigorous, dense stand of grass, and the chlorotic condition remained only for about a 7- to 10-day period following application.

LITERATURE CITED

1. Britton, M. P. 1969. Effects of environmental factors on turf diseases. *In* A. A. Hanson and F. V. Juska (eds.) Turfgrass science. Agronomy 14:290. Am. Soc. Agron., Madison, Wis.
2. Bruton, B. D. 1976. Selected plant pathogens associated with bentgrass production and plant growth response to certain chemical treatments. M.S. Thesis, Okalhoma State Univ. B9125s.
3. Christie, J. R. 1959. Plant nematodes—Their bionomics and control. Agric. Exp. Stn., Univ. of Florida.
4. ————, and V. G. Perry. 1951. Removing nematodes from soil. Proc. Helminthol. Soc. Wash. 18:106–108.
5. Couch, H. B. 1962. Diseases of turfgrasses. Reinhold Publishing Corp., New York.
6. ————. 1973. Diseases of turfgrasses. Robert E. Kreiger Publishing Co., Huntington, New York.

7. Heald, C. M., and V. G. Perry. 1969. Nematodes and other pests. *In* A. A. Hanson and F. V. Juska (eds.) Turfgrass science. Agronomy 14:358–369. Am. Soc. Agron., Madison, Wis.

8. Nutter, G. C. 1956. Nematode investigations in turf. Florida Agric. Exp. Stn. Annu. Rep.

9. Osborne, W. 1973. Root rot disease complex of ornamental plants and turfgrass. Virginia Plant Protection Newsl. no. 8. Virginia Polytechnic Inst. and State Univ., Blacksburg, Va.

10. Powell, W. M. 1964. The occurrence of *Tylenchorhynchus maximus* in Georgia. Plant Dis. Rep. 48:70.

11. Wolfard, D., and R. V. Sturgeon, Jr. 1974. Bentgrass (*Agrostis palustris* ('Penncross') spiral nematode, *Helicotylenchus* spp. and ring nematode, *Criconemoides* spp. control. Fungicide and nematicide test results of 1973. Am. Phytopathol. Soc. 19:158.

Section VII:

Turfgrass Cultural Practices and Systems

Chapter 35

Effects of Growth Retardants on the Shoot and Root Growth of Roadside Turfgrasses

R. C. WAKEFIELD
S. L. FALES

ABSTRACT

Growth retardants were evaluated to determine their effects on shoot and root growth of several turfgrass species under roadside cultural conditions. Growth suppression and phytotoxicity were measured on a typical roadside turfgrass polystand consisting of red fescue (*Festuca rubra* L.), Kentucky bluegrass (*Poa pratensis* L.), and colonial bentgrass (*Agrostis tenuis* Sibth.) and on monostands of Kentucky bluegrass, red fescue, and tall fescue (*Festuca arundinacea* Shreb.). An index of root growth was obtained from treated turfgrass plugs, which were embedded in sand and sampled at 3, 5, 7, and 9 weeks for new growth.

Two growth retardants, fluoridimide (N-[4-methyl-3-[[(1,1,1-trifluoromethyl) sulfonyl]amino]phynyl]acetamide) and mefluidide (N-[2,4-dimethyl-5-]](trifluoromethyl)sulfonyl]amino]phenyl]acetamide) were compared to the standards maleic hydrazide (1,2-dyhydro-3,6-pyridazinedione) and a mixture of maleic hydrazide and chlorflurenol (methyl-2-chloro-9-hydroxyfluorene-9-carboxylate, 8.8%; methyl-9-hydroxy-fluorene-9-carboxylate, 2.1%; methyl-2,7-dichloro-9-carboxylate, 1.6%).

All growth retardants significantly reduced both vegetative and seedhead growth with mefluidide being particularly effective at rates as low as 0.42 kg/ha. Discoloration and loss of shoot density occurred with all growth retardants but was not objectionable with any treatments on the extensively managed highway turf.

Root growth, as measured by root weights from treated turfgrass plugs, was initially reduced by all growth retardants. Reduction in root growth with mefluidide was far less severe, recovery was rapid, and some stimulation of root growth was then measured. Rhizome growth of Kentucky bluegrass was also affected far less with mefluidide than with the other growth retardants.

Additional index words: Red fescue, Kentucky bluegrass, Colonial bentgrass, Tall fescue, Maleic hydrazide, Chlorflurenol, Fluoridimide, Mefluidide.

INTRODUCTION

The use of chemical growth retardants on highway turfgrass to reduce mowing requirements can be a practical method of reducing highway maintenance costs. Chemicals that inhibit growth of turfgrasses have been a subject of much research since the introduction of maleic hydrazide over 30 years ago. This chemical has been used with varying degrees of success (2, 3, 4, 8). Inhibition of shoot growth was achieved but not

[1] Contribution No. 1747, Univ. of Rhode Island Agric. Exp. Stn., Kingston, RI 02881, USA.

without frequent discoloration of turf. Hence, the use of maleic hydrazide was restricted to highways and other areas where appearance of the turf was not a critical factor.

More recent research has shown that chlorflurenol alone and in combination with maleic hydrazide is an effective retardant (6). Two new chemicals, fluoridimide and mefluidide, have also been shown to be successful in retarding growth (6, 7).

Ideally, growth retardation of turfgrass should involve only a slowing of growth rather than a complete inhibition of shoot and root growth so that normal recuperative processes in turfgrasses may proceed (1). The use of fungicides and N fertilizer has been shown to produce excellent turf when used in combination with growth retardants (5, 6).

Growth retardants can inhibit rhizome growth in Kentucky bluegrass (2), resulting in a significant decrease in shoot density of turf. Root growth may also be severely retarded (6, 9) and have a significant effect on the recuperative potential.

The objective of these studies was to determine the effects of growth retarding chemicals on the shoot and root growth of selected cool-season turfgrass species. A technique study was also conducted to assess methods of measuring root growth in treated turfs.

MATERIALS AND METHODS

Field experiments were conducted from 1973 through 1976 at the University of Rhode Island, Kingston, R.I., USA. Growth retardants were applied to a polystand consisting of 'Park' Kentucky bluegrass (*Poa pratensis* L.), 'Pennlawn" red fescue (*Festuca rubra* L.), and colonial bentgrass (*Agrostis tenuis* Sibth.) and monostands of 'Fylking' Kentucky bluegrass, 'Jamestown' red fescue, and 'Kentucky 31' tall fescue (*F. arundinacea* Shreb.). Chemicals used were as follows: Maleic hydrazide (MH) [1,2-dihydro-3,6-pyridazine]; chlorflurenol (CF) [methyl-2-chloro-9-hydroxyfluorene-9-carboxylate-8.8%, methyl-9-hydroxyflourene-9-carboxylate-2.1%, methyl-2,7-dichloro-9-carboxylate-1.6%]; fluoridimide [N-[4-methyl-3-[[(1,1,1-trifluoromethyl)sulfonyl]amino]phenyl] acetamide]; mefluidide [N-[2,4-dimethyl-5-[[(trifluoromethyl)sulfonyl] amino]phenyl]acetamide]. All grasses were mature stands established at least 2 years previously on Enfield silt loam. They were maintained at a low fertility level and at a mowing height of 10 cm to simulate roadside conditions.

Chemical growth retardants were applied during the 1st week of May in all experiments with a 1.8-m boom sprayer delivering 467 liters/ha. Plots were mowed to 10 cm when growth reached approximately 20 cm. Height measurements, color (a visual rating of greenness on the basis of zero to a most desirable 10), and shoot density (also a visual rating on a basis of zero to a most desirable 10, indicating thinness of turf due to injury or suppression of new tillers) were recorded biweekly. Plots were harvested with a rotary mower having a sample bag attached to the chute. Total harvest area for each plot was 4.9 m². A portion of each plot was not mowed in order to investigate the effect of chemicals on seedhead suppression. Seedhead counts were taken for each treatment approximately 2 months after treatment.

Turf plugs were removed from plots immediately after spraying. Forty plugs, each 5 cm in diameter × 5 cm deep, were removed from each treatment and placed in watered sand beds. At the end of 3 weeks, 10 plugs of each treatment were removed from the sand beds, washed, and new root growth beyond the original plug was cut, dried, and weighed. Counts of rhizomes on plugs of Kentucky bluegrass were also recorded.

A variation in the root measurement technique was investigated in order to evaluate an alternative method. Soil was completely removed from one-half of a series of Kentucky bluegrass plugs so that a "disc" of turfgrass was compared to a "plug". Two moisture regimes were maintained in the sand beds in order to provide additional information on each technique.

RESULTS AND DISCUSSION

Shoot growth data for the polystand sprayed with growth retardants in 1973 are shown in Table 1. Clipping weights at 7 weeks revealed that all retardants significantly reduced growth when compared to the untreated plots. Greatest suppression resulted from use of mefluidide and fluoridimide. A combination of maleic hydrazide and chlorflurenol was the least effective. Visual color ratings at 4 weeks showed no significant injury. Reduced shoot density was noted in plots treated with maleic hydrazide and mefluidide. This was attributed to the action of these chemicals in suppressing tiller formation and the generation of new leaves. Clipping weights at 11 weeks showed that all chemicals were no longer effective in retarding growth. In some instances, the growth rate increased. All chemicals were effective in reducing seedhead numbers per unit area by at least 64%.

In general, the 1973 results showed that growth retardants were ef-

Table 1. Effects of growth retardants on a polystand of red fescue, Kentucky bluegrass, and colonial bentgrass.

Chemical(s)	Application rate	Clipping weight—dry		Seedheads	Visual rating at 4 weeks†	
		7 weeks	11 weeks		Color	Density
	kg/ha			no./m²		
MH	5.56	621 cd*	677 cd	222 b	8.0 a	6.7 bc
MH + Chlorflurenol	1.12 + 3.36	832 bc	878 a	176 b	7.7 a	7.3 abc
Fluoridimide	4.48	599 cd	555 cd	129 b	7.7 a	7.3 abc
Mefluidide	0.42	444 de	718 bc	155 b	7.3 a	6.3 c
Untreated	--	1,328 a	507 d	623 a	8.7 a	8.7 a

* Means with a common letter within columns are not significantly different at the 5% level according to Duncan's Multiple Range Test. † A 0 to 10 rating scale was used where 10 = best—dark green color; greatest density or ground cover.

Table 2. Effects of growth retardants on Jamestown red fescue.

Chemical(s)	Application rate	Clipping weight—dry 7 weeks	Clipping weight—dry 14 weeks	Seedheads	Visual rating at 6 weeks† Color	Visual rating at 6 weeks† Density
	kg/ha			no./m²		
MH	5.56	160 bc*	633 ab	2 b	6.1 c	8.0 b
MH + Chlorflurenol	1.12 + 3.36	184 bc	701 a	5 b	7.3 b	7.9 b
Fluoridimide	4.48	329 b	685 a	43 b	7.8 b	7.9 b
Mefluidide	0.56	132 c	476 bc	3 b	7.8 b	7.6 b
Untreated	--	1,509 a	700 a	277 a	9.4 a	9.5 a

* Means with a common letter within columns are not significantly different at the 5% level according to Duncan's Multiple Range Test. † A 0 to 10 rating scale was used where 10 = best—dark green color; greatest density or ground cover.

fective in substantially suppressing vegetative and reproductive growth for several weeks without serious injury to turf, and with only a minor loss of density.

A monostand of red fescue was treated with growth retardants in 1975. The results (Table 2) were essentially the same as in the previous test. Mefluidide was particularly effective in reducing growth as measured by clipping weights at both 7 and 14 weeks. Some discoloration and reduced shoot density was again noted with all chemicals. Seedhead suppression was highly significant in all cases.

A test was conducted in 1976 (Table 3) to further evaluate mefluidide in comparison with standard materials.

Mefluidide significantly reduced clipping weights of Jamestown red fescue at both normal (0.56 kg/ha) and high (1.12 kg/ha) rates. The high rate was particularly effective with no noticeable turfgrass injury compared to the normal rate. Results with Kentucky 31 tall fescue were similar.

These data indicate that mefluidide is a promising new growth retardant for highway-type turfs; i.e., turf that is grown on relatively poor soils and is extensively managed for erosion control along highway rights-of-way. Mefluidide appears to be effective at rates of 0.42 and 0.56 kg/ha and will not cause objectionable injury to red fescue at higher rates up to 1.12 kg/ha.

Table 3. Effects of growth retardants on red fescue and tall fescue 6 weeks after treatment.

Chemical(s)	Application rate	Jamestown red fescue Clipping wt.	Jamestown red fescue Seed-heads	Jamestown red fescue Color†	K-31 tall fescue Clipping wt.	K-31 tall fescue Seed-heads	K-31 tall fescue Color†
	kg/ha	kg/ha	no./m²		kg/ha	no./m²	
MH	5.56	329 bd*	48 b	7.0 b	363 bc*	9 bc	5.8 d
MH + Chlorflurenol	1.12 + 3.36	453 bc	90 b	7.3 b	459 b	11 b	7.3 bc
Mefluidide	0.56	217 de	54 b	7.5 b	306 c	10 bc	8.0 b
Mefluidide	1.12	144 e	11 b	7.5 b	234 c	7 c	7.5 bc
Untreated	--	1,242 a	255 a	9.0 a	1,164 a	33 a	9.0 a

* Means with a common letter within species are not significantly different at the 5% level according to Duncan's Multiple Range Test. † A 0 to 10 rating scale was used where 10 = best—dark green color.

Table 4. Effects of growth retardants on the root growth and number of rhizomes of Fylking Kentucky bluegrass.

Chemical(s)	Application rate	Root growth (g/plug)				Rhizomes (no./plug)			
		3 weeks	5 weeks	7 weeks	9 weeks	3 weeks	5 weeks	7 weeks	9 weeks
	kg/ha								
MH	5.56	0.0 m*	0.0 m	2.3 m	5.5 l	0.9 k	1.2 jk	1.9 ik	3.3 dh
MH + Chlorflurenol	1.12 + 3.36	0.0 m	1.4 m	6.5 kl	14.1 hi	1.2 jk	2.1 hk	3.5 dg	3.5 dg
Fluoridimide	4.48	0.0 m	1.3 m	8.1 jk	12.5 i	3.1 ei	3.3 dh	3.8 cf	4.2 ce
Mefluidide	0.42	2.4 m	6.6 kl	18.5 g	36.1 b	1.8 ik	2.5 fj	3.1 ei	7.4 b
Mefluidide	0.84	1.6 m	9.9 j	19.6 g	43.9 a	1.8 ik	2.1 hk	2.5 fj	5.6 c
Untreated	--	1.8 m	15.0 h	24.6 e	31.0 c	2.5 gi	3.7 cg	4.6 cd	9.1 a

* Means with a common letter within factors are not significantly different at the 5% level according to Duncan's Multiple Range Test.

Table 5. Effects of growth retardants on the root growth of red fescue plugs at four sampling times following treatment.

Chemical(s)	Application rate	Test 1 (1974) (g dry wt.)				Test 2 (1975) (g dry wt.)			
		3 weeks	5 weeks	7 weeks	9 weeks	3 weeks	5 weeks	7 weeks	9 weeks
	kg/ha								
MH	5.56	0.0 n*	0.4 mn	3.8 jm	22.2 fg	0.0 m*	0.9 lm	1.3 km	2.2 km
MH + Chlorflurenol	1.12 + 3.36	0.0 n	1.3 mn	6.4 j	15.4 h	0.0 m	2.1 km	3.5 jm	9.0 gk
Mefluidide	0.42	3.3 jh	9.8 i	37.8 i	43.9 a	6.0 im	18.7 cf	23.4 bc	28.6 ab
Mefluidide	0.56	--	--	--	--	4.2 jm	22.7 bd	23.6 bc	27.7 bc
Mefluidide	0.84	2.3 ln	10.4 i	29.2 e	48.8 a	7.7 lm	19.9 cf	20.3 ce	28.9 ab
Untreated	--	4.3 jl	14.1 h	21.5 fg	38.2 c	14.1 eh	15.9 dg	19.1 cf	35.6 a

* Means with a common letter within years are not significantly different at the 5% level according to Duncan's Multiple range Test.

In an attempt to determine the effects of growth retardants on roots, plugs and discs of turf were evaluated after treatment to determine which technique might provide a better index of root growth. Results were comparable when plugs and discs were compared in sand beds under both moist and dry conditions. Since drying out of discs in the sand beds was a possible problem, plugs were deemed to be the most effective index method of root growth evaluation.

Root growth of Kentucky bluegrass plugs was significantly reduced by the growth retardants maleic hydrazide, maleic hydrazide plus chlorfurenol, and fluoridimide when compared to untreated plugs after 5 weeks (Table 4). Suppression was also noted with two rates of mefluidide, but at a much reduced level. Retarded root growth continued at a severe level with maleic hydrazide up to 9 weeks, the last sampling date. Significant recovery of root growth occurred at 7 weeks with mefluidide-treated turf plugs and at 9 weeks, root growth exceeded that of the untreated plugs.

Rhizome development of Kentucky bluegrass was also reduced by growth retardants. Numbers of rhizomes per plug at 9 weeks ranged from three with maleic hydrazide and maleic hydrazide plus chlorfurenol to seven with mefluidide at 0.42 kg/ha to nine with untreated turf.

Red fescue plugs were taken from treated plots in 1974 and 1975 (Table 5). Suppression of root growth in Test 1 by maleic hydrazide and maleic hydrazide plus chlorfurenol was severe for 5 weeks and recovered only slowly through 7 weeks. Restriction in root growth by mefluidide at 0.42 and 0.84 kg/ha was significant at 3 and 5 weeks, although substantially less so than with the other retardants. At 7 weeks root growth of red fescue sprayed with mefluidide was greater than untreated turf, a trend that continued through 9 weeks.

Results were similar for red fescue plugs in 1975 with maleic hydrazide being particularly severe in retarding root growth. Mefluidide again was far less active in restricting root growth at all sampling dates.

Data on root growth when compared to that of shoot growth revealed that maleic hydrazide and maleic hydrazide plus chlorfurenol effectively retarded both for a period of 7 weeks. While mefluidide effectively controlled shoot growth for a similar period of time, root growth resumed much earlier. This phenomenon appears to be significant for the recuperative processes of turfgrasses following treatment with a growth retardant.

LITERATURE CITED

1. Beard, J. B. 1973. Turfgrass: Science and culture. Prentice-Hall, Inc., Englewood Cliffs, N.J. p. 396–401.
2. Clapham, A. J., R. C. Wakefield, and R. S. Bell. 1969. The effect of maleic hydrazide on the growth of turfgrasses. Univ. of Rhode Island, AES Bull. #399.
3. Elkins, D. M., and D. C. Suttner. 1974. Chemical regulation of grass growth. I. Field and greenhouse studies with tall fescues. Agron. J. 66:487–491.

4. Foote, L. E., and B. F. Himmelman. 1965. Maleic hydrazide as a growth retardant. Minnesota Dep. Highways Invest. 616.

5. Jagschitz, J. A. 1976. Response of Kentucky bluegrass to growth retardant chemicals. NEWSS 30:327–333.

6. Wakefield, R. C., and A. T. Dore. 1974. Growth control for highway turf. p. 569–576. *In* E. C. Roberts (ed.) Proc. 2nd Int. Turfgrass Res. Conf., Blacksburg, Va. 18–21 June 1973. Am. Soc. Agron., Madison, Wis.

7. Watschke, T. L. 1976. Growth regulation of Kentucky bluegrass with several growth retardants. Agron. J. 68:787–791.

8. White, D. B., D. Heng, T. B. Bailey, and C. Foote. 1970. Chemical regulation of growth in turfgrass. p. 481–487. *In* R. R. Davis (ed.) Proc. 1st Int. Turfgrass Res. Conf. July 1969. Sports Turf res. Inst., Bingley, England.

9. Younger, V. G., and F. J. Nudge. 1974. growth retardation effects on various grass tissues and organs. p. 458–462. *In* E. C. Roberts (ed.) Proc. 2nd Int. Turfgrass Res. Conf., Blacksburg, Va. 18–21 June 1973. Am. Soc. Agron., Madison, Wis.

Chapter 36

Growth Retardant Effects on Grasses for Roadsides[1]

R. W. DUELL
R. M. SCHMIT
S. W. COSKY

ABSTRACT

The present report deals with grasses grown under roadside conditions where some discoloration, due to retardants may be acceptable, and the suppression of seedstalks might justify the use of retardants. The cumulative effects of applications of retardants on grass stands treated in consecutive years have not been widely researched.

Twelve grasses, including cultivars within species, were grown without mowing and fertilization in replicated plots in two field trials. Breaking of dormancy and stages of development of these grasses were described relative to times of application of growth retardants that included 1,2-dihydro-3,6-pyridazinedione (MH); N-3-(1,1,1-trifluoromethylsulfonyl)amino-4-methylphenyl acetamide (MBR-6033); and 2,4-dimethyl-5-(trifluoromethylsulfonylamido)acetanilide(mefluidide).

Grasses varied appreciably in their time of seedstalk elongation and hence, response to time of application of retardants with regard to seedstalk control. Loss of stand density was not appreciable after the 1st year of treatment, but after retreatment in the 2nd year grasses were generally thinned by retardants. MH did not significantly reduce the stand of tall fescue (*Festuca arundinacea* Schreb.) in the first trial. MBR 6033 showed no advantage over MH, but mefluidide resulted in good seedhead control of certain species at low rates of application.

Effectiveness of a retardant treatment on a grass polystand partially depends on the species and cultivars in the polystand. The components of compounded seed mixtures, to be sown where retardants will be used, should match in time of seedstalk development. An application time for the growth retardant can then be selected when seedstalks of all the grasses are just beginning to elongate. This will maximize their control.

Additional index words: Maleic hydrazide (MH), MBR-6033, Mefluidide, Seedstalk control, Cultivar interactions, Time of heading.

INTRODUCTION

Most turfgrass researchers conclude that turf discoloration makes chemical retardation unacceptable for intensively managed situations. There is a large potential market, however, for growth retardants on roadsides and comparable extensively managed areas where temporary discoloration is not objectionable, particularly if appreciable savings in cost of mowing is achieved.

Most research on grass retardation has involved single applications

[1] A contribution from the Dep. of Soils and Crops, Cook College, Rutgers Univ., New Brunswick, NJ 08903 USA.

on a particular site. Growing conditions (for such trials) are typically favorable and responses of the relatively uniform turf are generally rather clearcut. Roadsides, however, are typically sown to mixtures of diverse grasses in the hope that some component will survive in each of the varied ecosites encountered.

Billot and Hentgen (1) found that responses to 1,2-dihydro-3,6-pyridazinedione (MH) applied in the spring varied with earliness of heading, which was affected by site and recent weather conditions. Watschke (8) reported that the 'Delta' and 'K-109' Kentucky bluegrass (*Poa pratensis* L.) cultivars were injured more than 'Pennstar' and 'Merion' Kentucky bluegrass by certain growth retardants.

Engel et al. (4) concluded that retardation of turfgrasses resulting from applications of chemicals, as measured by clipping weights, estimates of height control, or seedhead suppression, was related to rates of the retardant materials applied. These factors were also proportional to injury as estimated by leaf curl and loss of green color on Merion Kentucky bluegrass, 'Manhattan' perennial ryegrass (*Lolium perenne* L.), and 'Pennlawn' red fescue (*Festuca rubra* L.). Billot and Hentgen (1) reported that retardants limited the number of seedheads per unit area more markedly than length of stems or leaves. No heading was reported to have resulted from some treatments. Elkins (3) reported that certain treatments resulted in 90 to 95% suppression of seedheads to tall fescue (*F. arundinacea* Schreb.). Foote and Himmelman (5) and Wakefield and Clapham (6) also reported reductions in seedstalk production. Dore et al. (2) and Engel et al. (4) reported that an experimental retardant, 2-ethoxy-2,3-dihydro-3,3-dimethyl-5-benzofluranyl methanesulphonate (NC-8438) prevented seedstalks of Kentucky bluegrass from emerging above the foliar canopy.

A post-retardation stimulation of grasses was noted by Wakefield and Clapham (6) in a polystand dominated by Kentucky bluegrass on a roadside. This same effect was reported by Watschke (8, 9) as occurring with specific Kentucky bluegrass cultivars under more intensive lawn-type culture.

Wakefield and Clapham (7) noted a thinning of tufted grasses including tall oatgrass (*Arrhentherum odoratum* L.) and orchardgrass (*Dactylis glomerata* L.) in roadside turf following treatment with MH plus (2,4-dichlorophenoxy)acetic acid (2,4-D). Fall application of MH caused thinning of tall fescue under these roadside conditions. The authors concluded, therefore, that MH should not be applied to the same grass areas year after year.

The present studies, conducted in central New Jersey, were preceded by trials involving many growth retardants applied to a few turfgrasses under lawn-type culture on productive sites (4). Certain retardants were sufficiently effective to warrant further study in this geographic area. The objective of these trials was to investigate interactions among grass species and cultivars with rates and dates of retardants applied under conditions simulating roadside environments.

MATERIALS AND METHODS

Turfgrasses were established at the Soils and Crops substation of the New Jersey Agricultural Experiment Station at Adelphis, N.J., USA, on a Freehold sandy loam (hapludults belonging to the fine loamy, mixed mesic family), testing pH 6.0 with medium levels of available P and K. Fertilization of well-prepared soil was at 300 kg/ha of 10–8.7–8.3 prior to seeding, and supplemented with 44 kg/ha of N from NH_4NO_3 approximately 6 months later to assure establishment. Grass was mowed infrequently to a height of 10 cm during establishment until, but not including the spring when growth retardants were applied.

Trial I

Grasses sown 16 Sept. 1970 for 1972 and 1973 treatments were randomized in three replicates of plots 2 × 40 m. The Kentucky bluegrass cultivars included Merion, 'Newport', 'Glade', 'Brunswick', Kenblue, and the turf-type selection P-114. The fine fescues included Pennlawn and 'Ruby' spreading fescues (*F. rubra* subsp. *rubra*) as well as 'Highlight' chewings fescue (*F. rubra* subsp. *commutata*). Perennial ryegrasses included Manhattan and 'Linn'. Kentucky 31 tall fescue was also sown in this trial.

Two growth retardants, MH and N-[3-[(1,1,1-trifluoromethylsulfonyl)amino]-4-methylphenyl]acetamide (MBR-6033) were compared at equal rates of 4.5 kg/ha along with MBR-6033 at 9.0 kg/ha applied on three dates during the season. Stages of grass stem elongation were described and ratings of various effects of retardants were made. Treatments were repeated on the same plots the following year. One check plot was mowed at 10 cm on the day of the second spray application and clippings were removed.

Trial II

To the same basic grasses in Trial I, 'Banner' chewings and 'Fortress' red fescues were added. Grasses in this trial, however, were sown in single drill rows 50 cm apart and 45 m long in 5 replicates within a solid seeding of a blend of low growing turf-type Kentucky bluegrass experimental selections. Seeding was done on 19 Sept. 1973.

MH and MBR-6033 were applied at equal rates as in Trial I, and were compared with three rates of 2,4-dimethyl-5-(trifluoromethylsulfonamido)acetanilide (mefluidide): 0.28, 0.56, and 0.84 kg/ha. All retardants were sprayed on the 12 grasses on two dates during internode elongation in each of two successive years on the same plots.

Growth retardants were applied in a randomized block design over the above mentioned grasses at a rate of 374 liters of spray/ha with a CO_2 pressure-regulated boom of two nozzles, producing a 1-m wide swath in Trial I and a single wide angle nozzle producing a 0.9-m wide swath in Trial II. Differential times of spraying and characteristic stages of growth of grasses are given with results of ratings of responses.

RESULTS

Trial I

The 12 grasses established under extensive culture appeared uniform within entries in the spring of 1972, prior to the application of retardants. Marked differences in dormancy were recorded among grass entries on 17 Apr. 1972. On the basis of ratings where 1 = complete dormancy and 9 = essentially complete coverage with new green leaves, the fine turf-type Kentucky bluegrasses all ranged from 2.3 to 4.3; while the fescues and perennial ryegrasses all were within the range of 7.3 to 8.3. Kenblue Kentucky bluegrass was rated 9.

At the time of the first, or early application of retardants on 25 April, apical meristems could be found 2.5 cm above the soil surface in advanced culms of Kenblue Kentucky bluegrass and Linn perennial ryegrass. No evidence of stem elongation was found in the other grasses. The fine turf-type Kentucky bluegrasses appeared to have sufficient actively growing foliage to intercept most of the spray of retardants.

At the time of the second application on 5 May some seedheads of Kenblue had just emerged, those of Linn were still in the culm, and the next most advanced grass, Kentucky 31 tall fescue, had growing points just above the ground in many culms.

By the third application on 12 May seedheads were 10 cm up the culms of Kentucky 31 tall fescue. Kenblue had 50% of its heads fully out of the sheath, but none of the turf-type Kentucky bluegrasses had elongated internodes. Heads of Linn perennial ryegrass were 15 cm up in advanced culms and some were beginning to emerge. Those of Manhattan perennial ryegrass were only 2.4 cm above the soil surface for advanced culms. The fine fescues were elongating seedstalks rapidly at this time. Highlight had more early seedheads in the boot than did Ruby and Pennlawn.

Appreciable leaf-curl injury was detectable on 23 May 1972 on most grasses, particularly among those treated with MBR 6033 on the early date. The perennial ryegrasses were affected more and the fine fescues less. Injury symptoms intensified with time and were better described by color ratings. As Table 1 shows both cultivars of perennial ryegrass were severely discolored on 9 June 1972, particularly by MH applied at the early dates (more time had elapsed). Newport, at the early dates, sustained less discoloration from MH than did the other Kentucky bluegrasses. The fine fescues showed fewer tendencies to interact with re-

Table 1. The influence of time of application of three growth retardants on discoloration of 12 turfgrasses on 9 June 1972.

			Color ratings											
			Kentucky bluegrasses						Fine fescues			Perennial ryegrasses		Tall fescue
Date applied	Treatment	Application rate	Merion	Newport	Kenblue	Glade	Brunswick	P-114	Pennlawn	Ruby	Highlight	Linn	Manhattan	Kentucky-31
		kg/ha												
25 Apr. 1972	MH	4.5	5.7†	8.0	6.0	6.0	6.3	6.3	7.7	7.3	5.7	3.0	2.7	5.7
	MBR 6033	4.5	4.3	5.3	6.0	5.0	6.7	7.3	7.3	6.9	4.7	4.7	5.7	8.7
	MBR 6033	9.0	4.3	5.3	5.7	4.7	5.0	6.3	5.3	6.7	5.0	5.7	6.0	6.7
5 May 1972	MH	4.5	6.3	8.0	5.7	6.7	6.0	6.0	6.3	6.0	4.7	2.3	2.7	4.3
	MBR 6033	4.5	5.0	6.7	4.3	5.0	4.3	5.3	6.7	7.0	5.3	4.0	3.3	6.7
	MBR 6033	9.0	4.3	6.7	4.0	4.0	4.3	4.7	5.3	5.0	5.3	3.7	3.7	6.0
12 May 1972	MH	4.5	7.7	8.7	7.3	7.7	5.0	7.7	6.0	5.3	5.0	3.3	4.3	6.7
	MBR 6033	4.5	5.7	8.3	4.3	5.3	4.7	7.0	7.7	7.3	7.7	4.7	4.3	8.0
	MBR 6033	9.0	4.7	8.3	4.3	3.7	4.7	6.7	5.7	7.0	6.0	4.3	4.0	5.7
	No mow, untreated		9.0	9.0	8.3	8.7	8.7	9.0	9.0	9.0	9.0	9.0	9.0	9.0
	Mow, untreated		7.6	4.0	4.3	8.3	8.7	8.6	5.0	3.7	5.3	2.3	6.0	6.3
	L.S.D. 5%		1.4	1.5	1.6	1.6	1.3	1.6	1.6	2.0	1.5	2.0	2.0	1.5
	1%		1.9	2.0	2.1	2.2	1.8	2.0	2.1	2.8	2.1	2.6	2.6	2.1

† All data are means of three repliates. The rating scale was based on 9 = no browning and 1 = severe browning of the turfgrass foliage.

tardant treatments. Many grasses showed significant discoloration following mowing; this was minimal on the low growing fine turf types.

When seedheads were rated on 14 July 1972 (Table 2), MH was found to be quite effective in controlling seedheads of Kentucky 31 tall fescue, particularly when applied early, or on Manhattan perennial ryegrass when applied at later dates. Response to time of application of retardant appears to generally agree with stages of development at time of treatment. The lower rate of MBR-6033 was particularly ineffective in controlling seedstalks of Kenblue Kentucky bluegrass when applied early. A single timely mowing very effectively removed seedstalks.

Ratings of acceptability were made at a later date. This was a visual integration of factors of discoloration and seedstalk suppression. There is a trend for MBR-6033 to result in lower acceptability values for the fine fescues and Kentucky 31 tall fescue (Table 3). A single mowing usually resulted in a more acceptable appearance for roadside conditions than did any retardant treatment.

Analyses of stand data, taken a year after retardant treatments, indicated no significant effects on most grasses (data not shown); hence identical treatments were reimposed on the same plots. Similar foliar injury, discoloration, and differential control of seedheads resulted. A trend toward lower acceptability at the latest date of application appeared for most grasses (Table 4). The untreated plot that was never mowed usually appeared more acceptable than the plot that was mowed once the previous year.

Stand density ratings taken at the end of the 2nd year of treatment (Table 5) indicate that high rates of MBR-6033 injured the fine fescues. Persistence of turf-type Kentucky bluegrasses and Linn perennial ryegrass was generally poor regardless of treatment, while that of Kentucky 31 tall fescue was generally good.

Two years after the first of two annual applications of growth retardants, the grass stands of most treatments had been severely depleted. Early treatment with MH resuled in stands of Kenblue Kentucky bluegrass, the fine fescues, and Kentucky 31 tall fescue that compared favorably with check treatments. Fine turf-types fared poorest and Kentucky 31 maintained the best stands, but overall stands were too poor to warrant continued treatment.

Trial II

Well established rows of 12 turfgrasses were ready for the first retardant treatment on 10 Apr. 1975. Under the conditions of high rainfall in 1975 and good growing conditions, there were minimal symptoms of discoloration and injury resulting from any of the retardant treatments.

Control of seedstalks was attained (Table 6). MH controlled seedstalks better than MBR-6033 at the same rate of application on the three chewings fescues and Manhattan perennial ryegrass on both dates, except

Table 2. The effectiveness of time of application of three growth retardants on seedhead control of 12 turfgrasses on 14 July 1972.

			Seedstalk ratings											
			Kentucky bluegrasses						Fine fescues			Perennial ryegrasses		Tall fescue
Date applied	Treatment	Application rate	Merion	Newport	Kenblue	Glade	Brunswick	P-114	Pennlawn	Ruby	Highlight	Linn	Manhattan	Kentucky-31
		kg/ha												
25 Apr. 1972	MH	4.5	7.3†	4.7	7.0	7.0	8.0	8.0	7.3	7.7	8.3	7.3	7.7	9.0
	MBR 6033	4.5	7.3	6.7	2.7	7.3	7.0	7.7	5.3	5.7	7.0	3.3	4.7	6.0
	MBR 6033	9.0	8.0	7.0	5.0	8.0	8.3	8.3	7.0	6.3	8.0	5.3	5.0	7.7
5 May 1972	MH	4.5	6.3	4.3	5.0	8.0	5.3	8.0	7.0	7.0	7.6	7.7	9.0	8.7
	MBR 6033	4.5	8.3	4.0	4.6	7.6	8.0	6.7	5.3	5.0	6.3	3.3	4.7	5.0
	MBR 6033	9.0	9.0	5.3	5.3	8.3	8.3	8.0	7.0	6.3	7.0	3.7	5.7	6.7
12 May 1972	MH	4.5	4.3	3.3	4.3	8.0	6.3	7.3	7.6	4.7	8.3	4.7	9.0	6.7
	MBR 6033	4.5	8.0	4.0	5.3	8.0	8.7	7.7	6.0	4.3	6.0	3.3	5.3	3.7
	MBR 6033	9.0	8.7	2.3	6.0	8.0	8.3	8.0	6.3	5.3	6.3	4.7	6.7	6.7
	No mow, untreated		1.0	1.7	1.0	2.0	1.7	2.0	1.0	1.0	1.7	1.0	1.3	1.3
	Mow, untreated		9.0	7.3	8.7	7.0	9.0	8.7	9.0	9.0	9.0	8.6	8.3	9.0
	L.S.D. 5%		1.4	3.2	2.3	2.7	1.6	2.0	1.4	1.8	1.7	1.8	1.8	1.5
	1%		1.9	NS	3.1	3.7	2.2	2.7	1.9	2.4	2.2	2.5	2.4	2.0

† All data are means of three replicates. Seedstalk rating scale was based on 9 = no seedheads and 1 = full complement of seedstalks.

Table 3. The influence of time of application of three growth retardants on the overall acceptability of 12 turfgrasses on 3 Aug. 1972.

Date applied	Treatment	Application rate	Acceptability ratings											
			Kentucky bluegrasses						Fine fescues			Perennial ryegrasses		Tall fescue
			Merion	Newport	Kenblue	Glade	Brunswick	P-114	Pennlawn	Ruby	Highlight	Linn	Manhattan	Kentucky-31
		kg/ha												
25 Apr. 1972	MH	4.5	5.7†	4.7	4.7	6.0	4.7	5.3	4.3	4.3	5.7	3.3	3.7	5.0
	MBR 6033	4.5	5.0	5.0	3.7	4.3	4.7	6.0	2.7	3.3	2.7	2.3	3.0	3.7
	MBR 6033	9.0	4.7	5.0	4.0	4.0	4.0	6.0	2.3	3.0	2.3	2.3	3.0	4.0
5 May 1972	MH	4.5	4.7	4.3	4.0	7.0	4.3	6.0	3.7	4.3	6.3	3.3	4.0	6.0
	MBR 6033	4.5	5.0	4.3	4.0	4.3	4.3	5.7	3.0	3.3	2.3	1.7	2.7	3.3
	MBR 6033	9.0	4.3	4.0	4.0	3.7	4.0	4.7	3.3	3.0	1.7	2.0	3.3	4.3
12 May 1972	MH	4.5	4.3	4.3	3.7	6.3	4.3	5.0	3.7	4.0	5.7	2.3	4.0	3.7
	MBR 6033	4.5	5.0	4.7	4.0	5.3	4.3	6.3	3.0	3.7	2.3	2.0	3.0	3.0
	MBR 6033	9.0	5.7	4.3	3.3	4.7	3.7	4.0	3.0	4.0	2.3	2.3	3.0	3.7
	No mow, untreated		4.0	5.7	4.3	5.7	3.0	5.3	3.7	3.6	3.0	1.3	2.7	2.3
	Mow, untreated		7.7	8.3	6.0	7.3	7.0	6.7	7.0	5.3	8.0	4.3	3.7	6.7
	L.S.D. 5%		1.7	1.1	NS	2.3	1.5	NS	1.8	1.7	1.8	0.9	0.6	1.6
	1%		2.3	1.4	NS	NS	2.0	NS	2.4	2.3	2.5	1.2	0.9	2.2

† All data are means of three replicates. The acceptability rating scale was based on 9 = all green foliage and no seedstalks, 5 = minimum acceptable appearance for roadsides, and 1 = brown foliages and full complement of seedstalks.

Table 4. The influence of two annual applications of three growth retardants at three development stages, on the overall acceptability of 12 turfgrasses on 16 July 1973.

Date applied	Treatment	Application rate	Acceptability ratings											
			Kentucky bluegrasses						Fine fescues			Perennial ryegrasses		Tall fescue
			Merion	Newport	Kenblue	Glade	Brunswick	P-114	Pennlawn	Ruby	Highlight	Linn	Manhattan	Kentucky-31
		kg/ha												
13 Apr. 1973	MH	4.5	5.7†	4.7	5.0	4.7	4.7	4.3	4.3	4.7	3.3	2.7	5.0	4.0
	MBR 6033	4.5	4.0	2.7	4.0	4.0	3.3	4.3	3.7	4.0	4.0	2.0	3.7	4.3
	MBR 6033	9.0	4.0	3.0	4.7	3.0	3.3	4.0	3.3	3.3	3.7	1.7	3.0	4.3
24 Apr. 1973	MH	4.5	5.0	4.3	4.7	3.7	3.0	3.3	4.7	5.0	5.0	2.0	5.0	5.0
	MBR 6033	4.5	4.3	3.0	4.0	4.0	2.7	3.3	4.0	3.3	3.7	2.0	3.7	3.7
	MBR 6033	9.0	3.3	2.3	3.0	3.7	3.0	3.0	3.3	3.7	3.3	2.0	3.3	4.0
10 May 1973	MH	4.5	3.3	2.3	3.3	4.0	2.0	3.7	4.7	4.7	4.0	3.0	4.7	3.0
	MBR 6033	4.5	3.7	1.7	3.0	4.7	2.3	4.0	3.3	3.7	3.3	2.7	3.7	4.0
	MBR 6033	9.0	2.7	1.3	1.7	3.0	2.7	2.7	4.0	3.7	3.0	1.7	3.7	4.0
	No mow, untreated		3.3	2.7	5.0	4.7	3.3	4.3	4.7	5.0	5.3	2.3	3.7	3.7
	Mow, untreated		3.0	1.0	3.3	5.0	3.0	3.7	4.3	4.3	3.7	1.7	3.7	3.3
	L.S.D. 5%		1.6	1.1	1.2	NS	1.0	NS	0.8	1.4	1.2	NS	1.3	1.3
	1%		1.9	1.4	1.6	NS	1.3	NS	1.0	NS	1.6	NS	1.6	1.7

† All data are means of three replicates. The acceptability rating scale was based on 9 = all green foliage and no seedheads, 5 = minimum acceptable appearance for roadsides, and 1 = brown foliage and full complement of seedstalks.

Table 5. The influence of two annual applications of three growth retardants at three developmental stages on the stand density of 12 turfgrasses on 7 Dec. 1973.

			Stand density ratings											
			Kentucky bluegrasses						Fine fescues			Perennial ryegrasses		Tall fescue
Date applied	Treatment	Application rate	Merion	Newport	Kenblue	Glade	Brunswick	P-114	Pennlawn	Ruby	Highlight	Linn	Manhattan	Kentucky-31
		kg/ha												
13 Apr. 1973	MH	4.5	5.0†	5.7	7.3	0.3	1.3	3.0	6.0	3.3	6.0	2.7	6.3	7.0
	MBR 6033	4.5	6.7	4.3	4.7	2.7	2.3	1.7	3.7	6.7	3.3	3.0	5.7	7.7
	MBR 6033	9.0	3.7	4.0	2.3	1.7	1.7	1.7	1.0	0.3	0.7	2.7	4.0	5.7
24 Apr. 1973	MH	4.5	2.3	5.0	6.7	1.0	3.0	2.3	5.0	4.0	6.0	3.0	5.7	6.7
	MBR 6033	4.5	2.0	2.0	5.7	1.0	1.3	1.3	4.7	1.0	5.3	2.3	4.7	7.0
	MBR 6033	9.0	0.7	3.3	5.7	1.7	1.3	1.7	3.7	1.3	2.0	2.0	6.0	7.3
10 May 1973	MH	4.5	4.0	3.3	7.0	1.3	1.7	1.7	6.7	3.0	6.7	3.0	4.0	7.0
	MBR 6033	4.5	1.3	5.7	7.0	3.0	1.7	2.7	5.0	3.0	5.7	3.7	6.7	7.3
	MBR 6033	9.0	4.7	2.7	3.3	1.7	1.7	2.0	3.0	2.7	1.3	2.3	4.3	6.0
	No mow, untreated		1.7	3.7	6.3	1.3	2.0	3.3	6.7	4.7	5.3	2.7	5.7	8.0
	Mow, untreated		6.7	4.0	5.3	2.7	3.0	3.0	6.0	6.7	7.7	1.7	6.0	7.3
	L.S.D. 5%		3.1	NS	2.7	NS	2.1	2.0	2.9	2.7	3.3	NS	NS	NS
	1%		4.2	NS	NS	NS	NS	NS	NS	3.5	4.5	NS	NS	NS

† All data are means of three replicates. Stand density ratings were based on 9 = complete stand of sown grasses and 0 = no survival of sown grasses.

Table 6. The influence of repeated applications of three growth retardants on the seedstalk control of 11 turfgrasses on 5 June 1975.

			Percent seedhead control										
			Chewings fescues			Spreading fescues			Hard fescue	Kentucky bluegrass		Perennial ryegrass	Tall fescue
Date applied	Treatment	Application rate	Banner	Jamestown	Highlight	Pennlawn	Ruby	Fortress	Biljart	Kenblue	Newport	Manhattan	Kentucky-31
		kg/ha	% control										
30 Apr. 1975	MH	4.5	55†	40	85	64	56	57	70	64	65	68	93
	MBR 6033	4.5	20	6	21	24	38	55	67	77	53	14	54
	Mefluidide	0.28	5	28	35	37	44	57	70	42	59	4	62
	Mefluidide	0.56	50	30	61	58	59	80	73	81	74	44	93
	Mefluidide	0.84	47	57	45	68	56	74	82	91	89	64	92
	Untreated		4	8	8	31	21	35	52	46	11	16	32
	L.S.D. 5%		21	NS	24	33	33	NS	28	28	34	33	28
	1%		28	NS	28	NS	NS	NS	NS	37	45	44	38
8 May 1975	MH	4.5	79	87	40	83	71	74	56	63	79	70	88
	MBR 6033	4.5	29	42	36	44	19	36	77	68	70	38	73
	Mefluidide	0.28	33	45	38	49	27	66	62	66	65	44	69
	Mefluidide	0.56	47	63	58	54	57	71	75	79	92	74	80
	Mefluidide	0.84	61	60	62	64	59	72	80	83	96	68	81
	Untreated		4	8	8	31	21	35	52	46	11	16	32
	L.S.D. 5%		18	27	26	29	34	NS	29	27	29	30	25
	1%		24	36	36	39	46	NS	39	36	39	39	33

† All data are means of five replicates.

Table 7. The influence of repeated applications of three growth retardants on seedstalk control of 8 turfgrasses on 8 June 1976.

			Seedhead control							
			Chewings fescues			Spreading fescues		Hard fescue	Tall fescue	Kentucky bluegrass
Date applied	Treatment	Application rate	Banner	Jamestown	Highlight	Pennlawn	Fortress	Biljart	Kentucky-31	Kenblue
		kg/ha	% Control							
29 Apr. 1976	MH	4.5	28†	42	26	28	78	14	70	27
	MBR 6033	4.5	48	54	85	46	72	28	30	56
	Mefluidide	0.28	24	40	25	24	63	20	40	46
	Mefluidide	0.56	48	20	46	18	82	14	47	59
	Mefluidide	0.84	32	40	62	34	66	16	27	64
8 May 1976	MH	4.5	56	24	46	42	63	8	30	35
	MBR 6033	4.5	52	64	79	68	68	40	17	54
	Mefluidide	0.28	28	20	28	18	50	22	10	46
	Mefluidide	0.56	24	22	30	38	47	10	7	48
	Mefluidide	0.84	14	32	10	36	75	8	13	74
	Untreated		14	6	6	6	51	4	0	30
	L.S.D. 5%		28	25	29	30	NS	23	38	38
	1%		37	34	38	39	NS	31	51	NS

† Means of five replicates; three for Kentucky-31 tall fescue.

the early developing Highlight at the second date. The advantage of MH over MBR-6033 in control of the late developing spreading fescues was more prominent from the second date of application. Mefluidide in a lower range of application, compared well in seedstalk control, especially at the highest rate of use on Jamestown, Fortress, and Kentucky 31 at the early date of application, and Biljart, Kenblue, and Newport at either date.

Despite the lack of injury from retardants in 1975, stands of Ruby, Newport, Merion, and Manhattan were too sparse for further evaluation. Following the 2nd year treatment, MBR-6033 was superior to MH in seedhead control in several instances, but notably with Highlight at both dates and Jamestown and Biljart at the later date of application (Table 7). Mefluidide at the highest rate was best in controlling seedheads of Kenblue on both dates of applcation. Seedstalks of Kentucky 31 were not controlled as well as in the previous year. This probably relates to the fact that competition was reducing the numbers of plants in the row and the surviving larger individual plants were producing seedheads over a longer period of time. By 1977 stands of these grasses were too sparse to warrant retreatment.

LITERATURE CITED

1. Billot, C., and A. Hentgen. 1974. Effect of growth regulators on certain turfgrasses. p. 463–466. *In* E. C. Roberts (ed.) Proc. 2nd Int. Turfgrass Res. Conf., Blacksburg, Va. 18–21 June 1973. Am. Soc. Agron., Madison, Wis.
2. Dore, A. T., R. C. Wakefield, and J. A. Jagschitz. 1971. Effect of four growth retardants on Kentucky bluegrass and red fescue used for roadside turf. Proc. Northeast. Weed Sci. Soc. 25:123–130.
3. Elkins, D. M. 1974. Chemical suppression of tall fescue seedhead development and growth. Agron. J. 66:426–429.
4. Engel, R. E., K. J. McVeigh, R. M. Schmit, and R. W. Duell. 1971. The effect of growth regulators on turfgrass species. Proc. Northeast. Weed Sci. Soc. 25:131–140.
5. Foote, L. E., and B. F. Himmelman. 1967. Vegetation control along fence lines with maleic hydrazide. Weed Sci. 15:38–41.
6. Wakefield, R. C., and A. J. Clapham. 1968. Management of turfgrass treated with maleic hydrazide. Highwy. Res. Rec. 246:1–15.
7. ———, and A. T. Dore. 1974. Growth control for highway turf. p. 569–516. *In* E. C. Roberts (ed.) Proc. 2nd Int. Turfgrass Res. Conf., Blacksburg, Va. 18–21 June 1973. Am. Soc. Agron., Madison, Wis.
8. Watschke, T. L. 1974. Growth regulation of Kentucky bluegrasses with commercial and experimental growth regulators. p. 474–479. *In* E. C. Roberts (ed.) Proc. 2nd Int. Turfgrass Res. Conf., Blacksburg, Va. 18–21 June 1973. Am. Soc. Agron., Madison, Wis.
9. ———, J. M. Duich, and D. V. Waddington. 1976. Growth retardation of 'Merion' Kentucky bluegrass. Proc. Northeast. Weed Sci. Soc. 30:321–326.

Chapter 37 Turfgrass Growth Reduction by Means of a New Plant Growth Regulator[1]

P. E. SCHOTT
H. WILL
H.-H. NÖLLE

ABSTRACT

There is a void in registered growth regulators for use on turfs in Germany. This investigation was initiated to study the effects of a new growth regulator, N-[2,4-dimethyl-5-[[(trifluormethyl) sulfonyl]amino]phenyl]acetamide (mefluidide), on turfgrasses grown under conditions in Germany. Initial investigations indicate that turfgrass growth can be retarded in both length and in terms of the number of seedheads formed. A growth depression of approximately 40% can be sustained at 4 weeks after application. The normal mowing interval of about 8 days in Germany could thus be extended up to several weeks. The best results from mefluidide were obtained when the grass was treated about 3 to 4 days after mowing, while the optimum application rate was 240 g/ha.

INTRODUCTION

Temperature, rainfall, nutrient supply, and the intensity of turf culture are the main factors determining the frequency of mowing turfgrasses in Germany. Vigorous shoot growth necessitates frequent mowings. Most turfs need to be mowed every 8 to 10 days during the growing season in Germany. A more restricted growth rate would contribute to less intensity of culture, especially in mowing costs. Thus, the objective of this investigation was to evaluate the potential effectiveness of N-[2,4-dimethyl-5-[[(trifluormethyl)sulfonyl)]amino]phenyl]acetamide (mefluidide) as a growth regulator on turfgrasses, especially in terms of application rate, timing of treatment, and number of applications.

MATERIALS AND METHODS

The growth regulator evaluated in these studies was mefluidide, developed by the 3M Company, St. Paul, Minn., USA. The specific chemical make-up is as follows:

[1] A contribution from Landwirtschaftliche Versuchstation, BASF AG, Postfach 220, D6703 Limburgerhoff, West Germany.

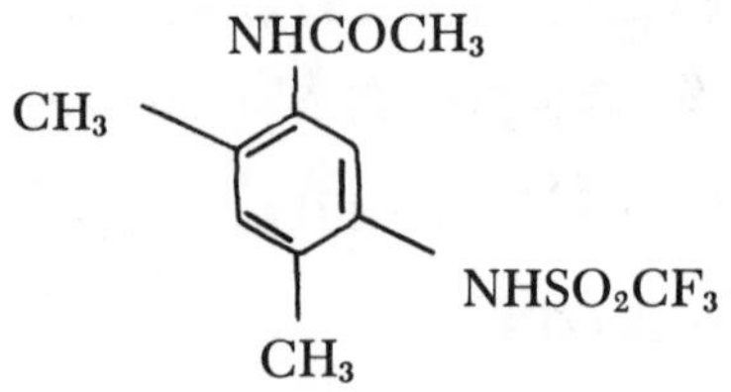

$NHCOCH_3$

CH_3

$NHSO_2CF_3$

CH_3

Mefluidide has a systemic action and is absorbed principally by the leaves. Because no comparable growth regulator is registered for turfgrass use in Germany, it was not possible to include one in the investigations.

The studies were conducted during 1975 and 1976. The specific treatments consisted of: (i) five rates of application—0, 120, 240, 360, and 480 g/ha; (ii) three times of application—spring (12 May 1976), summer (2 Aug. 1976), and autumn (14 Sept. 1976); (iii) three application schedules—spring only, spring and summer, spring, summer and fall. The growth regulator treatments were applied 3 days after mowing at a 3-cm cutting height. The spray solution consisted of mefluidide applied with 1,000 liters/ha of water. The rate of application and time of application studies were conducted on turfgrass polystands containing 55% Kentucky bluegrass (*Poa pratensis* L.), 25% Chewings fescue (*Festuca rubra* var. commutata Gaud.), 10% crested dogtail grass (*Cynosorus cristatus* L.), and 10% perennial ryegrass (*Lolium perenne* L.). In the multiple application study the turfgrass polystand consisted of 55% Kentucky bluegrass and 45% red fescue (*Festuca rubra* L. var. *rubra*). The former two turf experimental areas had been seeded in 1974, while the latter was planted in 1973.

All three studies were conducted with three replications in a randomized block design. Statistical analysis of the data involved a two-way analysis of variance with the L.S.D. calculated by the Tukey test.

RESULTS

Rate of Application Study

The shoot growth inhibition increased as the rate of mefluidide application increased (Table 1). Discoloration occurred where high rates were used under stress conditions. Generally, the discoloration persisted for only a few weeks. Treatment at 240 g/ha of mefluidide produced a significant and adequate shoot growth reduction. The growth inhibition persisted for 4 weeks and sometimes longer, depending on weather conditions. Some evidence of growth repression has occasionally persisted for 2 months. There was no significant difference in the shoot growth inhibition achieved with application rates of 120, 240, and 360 g/ha while a significant increase in growth reduction was achieved at the 480-g/ha rate in

Table 1. The effects of four rates of mefluidide application on shoot growth inhibition, turfgrass color, and seedhead formation.

Treatment 12 May 1976	Application rate	Plant height 10 June 1976		Turf color† 8 June 1976	Seedheads/m² 8 June 1976	
	g/ha	cm	%		No.	%
Untreated	0	16.1 C*	100	1.0	221 D	100
Mefluidide	120	11.3 B	70	1.0	126 C	57
Mefluidide	240	10.1 AB	63	1.0	53 AB	24
Mefluidide	360	9.8 AB	61	1.0	84 B	38
Mefluidide	480	8.9 A	55	1.0	38 A	17
L.S.D. 5.0%		1.7			34.1	

* Means, within a column, followed by the same letter are not significantly different at P = 95%.
† Color: 1 = dark green; 5 = pale green; 9 = brown.

comparison to the 120-g/ha rate. The effect on inhibition of seedhead formation was even more striking than that for shoot growth inhibition (Table 1). In contrast, there is no effect on turfgrass color throughout the investigation.

Time of Application Study

The shoot growth inhibition achieved with mefluidide was comparable regardless of whether it was applied in the spring, summer, or early fall. The degree of inhibition at all three timings was near 35% (Table 2). A slight light green discoloration resulted from the fall applications, while no comparable discoloration was observed from the spring treatment. This discoloration was attributed to extremely dry stress conditions which occurred during the 1976 trial year. Other preliminary trials have also indicated that the use of mefluidide is only slightly effected by seasonal changes in temperature throughout the growing season.

Table 2. Influence of the 1976 growing season on the biological efficacy of mefluidide on turfgrasses.

Application timing treatment	Evaluation date	Plant height 0 vs. 240 g/ha mefluidide		Turf color† 0 vs. 240 g/ha mefluidide		Seedheads/m² 0 vs. 240 g/ha seedheads	
		cm	%			No.	%
Spring—12 May	10 June 1976	16.1 B	63 A*	1.0	1.0	221 B	23 A
Summer—2 Aug.	3 Sept. 1976	10.0 B	60 A	1.0	3.7	--	--
Autumn—14 Sept.	14 Oct. 1976	9.9 B	64 A	1.0	3.0	--	--
L.S.D. 5.0%	10 June 1976	1.7				34.1	
	3 Sept. 1976	1.1				--	
	14 Oct. 1976	1.2				--	

* Means, within a column, followed by the same letter are not significantly different at P = 95%.
† 1 = dark green; 5 = pale green; 9 = brown.

Table 3. Comparison of single with multiple treatment of mefluidide on turfgrasses.

Application no. treatment	Evaluation date	Plant height 0 vs. 240 g/ha mefluidide		Turf color† 0 vs. 240 g/ha mefluidide		Seedheads‡ 0 vs. 240 g/ha mefluidide	
		cm	%				
Spring—10 June 1976	8 July 1976	9.8 B*	68 A	1.0	4.3	9.0	3.7
Spring—10 June 1976 + + Summer—28 July 1976	26 Aug. 1976	10.6 B	61 A	1.0	4.0		
Spring—10 July 1976 + + Summer—28 July 1976 + + Autumn—13 Sept. 1976	14 Oct. 1976	11.3 B	61 A	1.0	4.0		
L.S.D. 5.0%	8 July 1976	0.7					
	26 Aug. 1976	1.6					
	14 Oct. 1976	0.8					

* Means, within a column, followed by the same letter are not significantly different at P = 95%.
† Color: 1 = dark green; 5 = pale green; 9 = brown.
‡ Seedheads: 1 = no seedheads; 9 = dense stand.

Number of Applications Study

The effect of up to three applications of mefluidide per growing season is shown in Table 3. Up to three applications were applied to the same experimental plots within a single growing season without any significant detrimental effect on turfgrass color and appearance. This response was dependent, of course, on the turf receiving normal care, including adequate water and nutrients. With the known period of shoot growth inhibition ranging from 4 to 5 weeks, the treatment interval should not be more frequent than that utilized in this study. By using the latter three-application method shown in Table 3, mefluidide reduced the number of mowings from 12 to three per season under the conditions of this experiment.

Chapter 38

Influence of Silica on Chemical Composition and Decomposition of Turfgrass Tissue[1]

J. R. STREET
P. R. HENDERLONG
F. L. HIMES

ABSTRACT

Two turfgrass species, 'Kentucky-31' tall fescue (*Festuca arundinacea* Schreb.) and 'Pennstar' Kentucky bluegrass (*Poa pratensis* L.), were cultured in hydroponics at silica rates of 0 to 100 ppm SiO_2. Tissue C and N percent decreased with increasing silica supply, but the C–N ratio remained unchanged. Celiulose and lignin content increased slightly with increased silica supply. Dry matter components (stubble:leaf:root ratio of 2:1:1) of the species with established silica gradients (0.35 to 5.5%) from hydroponics were soil incorporated (whole or ground) or layered on the soil surface to determine the effects of silica content and method of incorporation on decomposition. Decomposition (CO_2 release) of tall fescue was decreased 12.1, 12.6, and 13.8% at the highest silica level in the mixed, layered, and ground soil-plant systems, respectively. Decomposition of Pennstar Kentucky bluegrass was reduced 9.1% at the highest silica level in the ground soil-plant system only. Decomposition did not differ between the mixed and layered systems for either species. The silica content of 'Merion' Kentucky bluegrass thatch from field plots ranged from 4.9 to 8.7%.

Additional index words: Kentucky bluegrass, Tall fescue, Thatch, Elemental composition, SiO_2.

INTRODUCTION

Chemical constituents within the turfgrass plant vary in their susceptibility to microbial decay. Simple sugars and proteins are readily decomposed by soil microbes. However, chemical components such as hemicellulose, cellulose, and lignin are more resistant to decay (2, 7). The higher the content of these latter constituents in the turfgrass tissue, the slower the decomposition rate. Lignin content has been reported to be highest in turfgrass roots, followed by stems and then leaves (7). This information correlates with physical observations by Ledeboer and Skogley (6), which showed that sclerified vascular strands, leaf sheaths, nodes, and crown tissue were the most decay resistant, according to amounts found in thatch. Martin (7) and Ledeboer and Skogley (6) reported the lignin content of thatch as high as 16.3 and 23.6%, respectively.

[1]Published with approval of the Director as Ohio Agric. Res. Dev. Ctr. Journal Article No. 118-78, Columbus, Ohio, USA.

Silica is an inorganic constituent of grasses which depresses digestibility (5). Van Soest and Jones (12) indicated that the digestibility depression induced by silica ranged from 3.0 to 3.6 units per unit of silica. Smith et al. (11) also found an inverse relationship between silica content and digestibility of rangeland forages of New Mexico in in vitro systems. The negative relationships between silica content and grass digestibility may be a contributing factor to thatch accumulation.

The nature of the inhibitory effect of silica upon the digestibility of forage grasses is not clearly understood. The encrustation of silica within cell walls is considered the primary factor responsible (12). This theory simply implies that the encrusting silica within the cell wall acts as a physical protectant limiting the availability of organic cell wall components to microbial attack. A second hypothesis is that part of the inhibition may be due to the effects of soluble Si compounds, possibly a soluble cellulolytic inhibitor (12).

The silica content of most grasses has been reported to range from 3 to 10% (5). Blackman (1) stated that the mature and senescent tissue of rye (*Secale cereale* L.) contained two to three times the amount of silica present in young tissue. High levels of silica were noted in dead tissue. Sangster (10) noted that senescent leaves, in contrast to younger mature leaves, typically exhibited extensive extracellular silicification of the mesophyll. Jones and Handreck (5) have noted that total silica in plants increases with plant maturity. These results would suggest that higher levels of silica deposition in dead, sloughed turfgrass components contribute to thatch. Silica deposition in forage grasses occurs in several components observed to be significant contributors of thatch (i.e., leaf sheath, stem, nodes, etc.).

With increased interest in soil mixes of higher silicate content for golf greens and other intensively trafficked areas and the reported effect of silica on lowering the digestibility of grasses, an investigation into the possible role of this element in thatch development was undertaken.

MATERIALS AND METHODS

A. Decomposition Study

'Kentucky-31' tall fescue (*Festuca arundinacea* Shreb.) and 'Pennstar' Kentucky bluegrass (*Poa pratensis* L.) were seeded in 7.5-liter (2-gallon) plastic containers in a controlled environmental chamber on 29 Apr. 1975. The grasses were cultured throughout the 24-week experimental period on a 0.5× dilution of complete Hoagland's solution. Four weeks after seeding, silica treatments of 0, 50, and 100 ppm SiO_2, applied as sodium silicate, were imposed. Each treatment was replicated three times in a complete randomized design.

The environmental chamber was maintained at a day/night temperature regime of 24/18 C and a photoperiod of 14 hours. The nutrient solution was renewed every 5 to 7 days at which time containers were rinsed with distilled water. Polyethylene gas dispersion tubes were used to insure adequate oxygen distribution within the system.

Kentucky bluegrass and tall fescue were maintained at a cutting height of 3.8 and 5.0 cm, respectively. Leaf clippings were collected at 4- to 5-day intervals. Stem and root tissues were obtained at the termination of the study (2 Oct. 1975). After harvesting, the stem and root tissue was subjected to a series of washings with distilled water to insure freedom from external silica contamination. Leaf, stem, and root components were dried at 70 C, portions ground in a micro-Wiley mill to pass a 60-mesh screen, and whole and ground tissue stored over P_2O_5 in a vacuum desiccator for later analysis.

Stubble, leaf, and root components of both species in a 2:1:1 ratio, respectively, were used as a source of decomposition material. The silica content of the samples varied from 0.35 to 5.5% (Table 2). Three soil-plant systems were designed to measure the method of plant incorporation on decomposition: (i) whole plant material mixed with soil; (ii) whole plant material layered on the soil surface in the form of an artificial thatch layer; (iii) ground plant material (20-mesh) mixed with soil.

The decomposition study was conducted in a Seedboro Quality germinator at a constant temperature of 27 C. The CO_2 evolution procedure followed was that outlined by Pramer and Schmidt (9). One hundred 1-g samples of a Miami silt loam soil were wetted to field capacity with distilled water. Two 1-g samples of the turfgrass material were plant-soil incorporated in 0.5-liter (1-pint) Mason jars. A 20-ml beaker containing 15 ml of 0.5*N*NaOH was placed in the center of each jar. The jars were sealed until analysis. When CO_2 analysis was not made daily, the jars were opened every 24 hours for a few seconds to insure an adequate oxygen supply. Each treatment was replicated three times in a completely randomized design.

Analytical determinations for measuring CO_2 evolution were made by titrating the 0.5*N* NaOH with 0.5*N* HCL after adding 2 to 3 drops of phenolphthalein and 2.5 ml of $BaCl_2$ solution. Calculations were made on the mmoles of CO_2 released at each date.

B. Chemical Analyses

Silica determinations were made following the procedures outlined by Jones and Handreck (5). A sub-sample (0.25 g) of ground plant material (60-mesh) was transferred to a 50-ml nickel crucible and ignited in an electric muffle furnace at 550 C. One gram of anhydrous Na_2CO_3 was mixed with the ash and the mixture fused over an airblast Meker burner for 0.5 hour. The cooled cake was dissolved in distilled water and made up to a 100-ml volume; an aliquot was then analyzed for silica.

Silica was estimated by the reduced silicomolybdate method under the following conditions. A 2-ml aliquot was transferred to a 25-ml standard flask. Distilled water was added to bring the volume to approximately 15 ml. Two milliliters of a solution containing 5% (w/v) ammonium molybdate in 1*N* H_2SO_4 was then added. After 10 min, the reaction was stopped by addition of 5 ml of 10*N* H_2SO_4. The silicomolybdic acid was then reduced with 0.5 ml of a solution containing 0.2% 1:2:4 amino-naphtosulphonic acid, 2.4% sodium sulphite, and 12% sodium metabisulphite. Ten minutes after adding the reducing solution, the absorption was determined at 670 μ on a Bausch and Lomb "Spectronic 20" spectrophotometer.

Chemical analyses were made on composite samples of leaf, stubble, and roots used for the decomposition study. Total N was measured following the micro-Kjeldahl procedure of Bremner (3). The dry combustion procedures outlined by Post (8) were used to determine total C. Cellulose and lignin determinations were made following procedures described by Van Soest and Goering (13). Each constituent was expressed as a percentage on a dry weight basis.

C. Field Study

Thatch samples of 'Merion' Kentucky bluegrass were obtained from a mature turfgrass area receiving differential rates of 1.5, 3^a, 3^b, and 6 kg N/are/year. Nitrogen was applied in six equal applications for the 1.5, 3^a, and 6 kg/are treatments in September, October, November, December, April, and July. The 3^b treatment received 1 kg N/are in September and April and 0.5 kg N/are in June and August. The soil textural class was a clay loam with a pH range of 7.3 to 7.5. Twelve cores were randomly collected from each plot using a soil probe.

The thatch cores were initially sectioned into an upper (1.25 cm) and lower (below 1.25 cm) layer. The individual layers were torn apart by hand and washed several times with distilled water. The thatch was dried at 70 C, ground in a micro-Wiley mill to pass a 60-mesh screen, and stored over P_2O_5 in a vacuum desiccator for later analysis.

RESULTS AND DISCUSSION

Carbon dioxide evolution from decomposition experiments for both turfgrass species is reported in Table 1. The silica content of the individual plant components (unreported data) and composite decomposition samples (Table 2) increased almost linearly with increasing silica rates. The silica content of composite samples ranged from 0.35 to 5.5%. The decomposition of Kentucky 31 tall fescue decreased at the highest silica rate or tissue silica content in the mixed and layered plant-soil systems, and at both the 50 and 100 ppm SiO_2 levels in the ground system. At the highest silica rate, the decomposition of tall fescue was reduced 12.1, 12.6, and 13.8% in the mixed, layered, and ground plant-soil systems, respectively.

Table 1. Effects of three silica rates on decomposition of two turfgrass species under various soil-plant systems.

Species	Cumulative CO_2 released in 8 weeks		
	Mixed	Layered	Ground
	mmoles		
Tall fescue			
0 ppm SiO_2	34.1 b*	35.2 b	47.9 d
50	33.2 b	34.3 b	40.8 c
100	29.9 a	30.8 a	41.3 c
Kentucky bluegrass			
0 ppm SiO_2	33.0 a	32.9 a	45.3 c
50	31.8 a	32.5 a	41.2 b
100	31.3 a	31.0 a	41.1 b

* Means not having the same letter within a species are significantly different at the 5% level according to Duncan's Multiple Range test.

The decomposition of Pennstar Kentucky bluegrass was reduced at the 50- and 100-ppm SiO_2 rates in the ground system only. No differences in tissue decomposition were observed among the various silica treatments in the mixed and layered plant-soil systems. At the highest silica rate, tissue decomposition in the ground system was reduced 9.1%.

A comparison of silica content between Kentucky bluegrass and tall fescue would not appear to be responsible for the differential in decomposition since the leaf, stubble, and root components and composite samples of Kentucky bluegrass had consistently higher concentrations of silica (Table 2). It is possible that the metabolism and/or deposition of silica differs between species. In consideration of Van Soest's hypothesis, soluble cellulolytic inhibitors or organo-silicon compounds may be synthesized in one plant system and not another. The supposed inhibitors or organo-silicon compounds may be synthesized in greater concentrations in one plant system than another. The latter may be a possible explanation for the lack of or lower decomposition differences among silica treatments with Kentucky bluegrass. If the role of silica in reducing decomposition of plant tissue involves a soluble cellulolytic inhibitor rather than a physical barrier, grinding may have released the inhibitor more rapidly

Table 2. Effects of three silica rates on the chemical composition and C–N ratio of decomposition tissue of two turfgrass species.

Species	SiO_2	Cellulose	Lignin	N	C	C–N ratio
	% †					
Tall fescue						
0 ppm SiO_2	0.6 a*	29.0 a	3.5 a	2.5 c	38.0 a	15.5
50	2.8 b	31.4 ab	3.7 a	2.4 b	36.1 a	15.0
100	4.3 c	33.7 b	4.1 a	2.3 a	35.4 a	15.0
Kentucky bluegrass						
0 ppm SiO_2	0.4 a	28.7 a	3.5 a	2.5 b	38.6 a	16.0
50	3.5 b	31.1 ab	3.7 a	2.2 a	35.3 a	16.0
100	5.5 c	31.9 b	4.1 a	2.2 a	36.0 a	16.0

* Means within each column of a species not having the same letter differ significantly at the 5% level according to Duncan's Multiple Range test. † All percentages expressed as that of the total sample on a dry weight basis.

or readily to microorganisms, especially if the inhibitor concentration was less in Kentucky bluegrass than in tall fescue.

The highest silica rate used in this experiment was at the maximum level reported for soluble silica in soil solutions. The percentages of silica in turfgrass tissue are, therefore, those that would be anticipated under field conditions. In this regard, the depression in decomposition observed is most likely at the upper limit of the response one could expect at this stage of physiological maturity in the field.

Under edaphic conditions, where the concentration of soluble silica is high, silica would appear to have a depressing effect on decomposition of Kentucky 31 tall fescue. Thatch accumulation in the field resulting from this magnitude of depression may not prove significant since tall fescue is ranked as a low thatch accumulator. It may require a more substantial depression in plant decomposition before a measurable accumulation of surface organic debris would occur under field conditions. However, the reduction in tall fescue decomposition at the highest silica rate suggests silica as a potential causal factor in thatch formation of this species. Other chemical and cultural factors are certainly involved. On the other hand, Pennstar Kentucky bluegrass and many other cultivars are known to be thatch accumulators, and in these turfgrasses silica would appear to play a minor role, if any.

The decomposition rate of both species in the ground system was significantly higher when compared to the mixed and layered systems at 8 weeks (Table 1). This is not surprising since a greater surface area was available for microbial attack and the plant constituents were more readily accessible. However, the decomposition rate did not differ between the mixed and layered systems for either species at 8 weeks. This contradicts the commonly accepted thesis that the physical separation of grass debris from the soil is a major factor responsible for thatch accumulation. The physical separation of thatch from soil is suggested to involve lower microbial populations in the layer. Cole and Turgeon (4), however, indicate comparable, if not higher, microbial populations in thatch compared to underlying soil. Thus, cultural practices that introduce soil into thatch (i.e., topdressing) may improve pH, C–N ratios, and/or moisture relations of thatch more than directly increasing microbial populations.

The age of the composite turfgrass samples used in the decomposition study was 24 weeks. In order to assess the silica content of older, senescent plant material, thatch from a mature stand of Merion Kentucky bluegrass under differential rates of N fertility was measured. The values were quite high when compared to the silica content of leaf tissue from respective plots (i.e., 2 to 3%). The content of the upper and lower thatch layers was significantly different only for the 1.5 and 3[a] kg N/are rates. At both these rates, the silica concentration was higher in the lower thatch layer. This may be explained in part by the more soluble plant constituents being more decomposed in the lower, older thatch layer. Consequently, the silica as a percentage of the thatch remaining would be higher.

Table 3. The silica content of field samples of Merion Kentucky bluegrass thatch expressed as a percentage of the sample dry weight.

N rate	Thatch layer	
	Upper (0–1.25 cm)	Lower (1.25 cm)
kg/are/year	% SiO_2	
1.5	5.3 a*	8.7 c
3 a	5.1 a	6.3 b
3 b	4.9 a	5.0 a
6	5.0 a	5.1 a

* Means not having the same letter are significantly different at the 5% level according to Duncan's Multiple Range test.

In contrast, the silica contents of the thatch at the 3^b and 6 kg N/are rates were not different between layers. With these treatments, a greater amount of N was applied during periods more favorable for microbial decay (spring, summer, and early fall). The amount and time of N fertilization may have favored more rapid decay, resulting in tissue in a more uniform stage of decomposition.

It is worth noting that the silica percentages of the Kentucky bluegrass thatch were similar to silica concentrations of tissue samples in the decomposition study. Thus, silica contents of field samples of Kentucky bluegrass thatch do not appear to be high enough to retard plant decomposition to any greater extent than observed in the incubation studies. This further supports the contention of a minor role of silica in thatch development of Kentucky bluegrass.

Chemical composition was determined for all Kentucky bluegrass and tall fescue decomposition samples to clarify any possible indirect role of silica on turfgrass tissue decomposition (Table 2). Total N and C decreased as silica rates increased for both species, but the magnitudes of these differences do not appear great enough to influence decomposition. In addition, the C–N ratios ranged from 15 to 16 with no differences between silica treatments. The C–N ratios were well within the range considered adequate for microbial decomposition (1). Cellulose content, however, increased with increasing tissue silica levels and may, therefore, be an indirect factor responsible to some extent for the observed reductions in turfgrass decomposition.

In conclusion, the effect of silica on depressing the decomposition of turfgrass tissue appears to be species dependent. Under edaphic conditions in which the concentration of silica in the growing media is high, silica would appear to have a depressing effect on decomposition of Kentucky 31 tall fescue. The magnitude of the depression in enhancing thatch development on tall fescue sites needs to be further assessed, especially since tall fescue is not considered a major thatch accumulator. Silica appears to play a minor role in decomposition and, in turn, thatch accumulation of Kentucky bluegrasses. Other factors are more likely to have an effect on depressing the decomposition of Kentucky bluegrass than soluble silica.

ACKNOWLEDGMENT

This study was partially supported by the Ohio Turfgrass Foundation, Columbus, Ohio.

LITERATURE CITED

1. Blackman, E. 1973. The pattern and sequence of opaline silica deposition of rye (*Secale cereale* L.). Ann. Bot. 32:207–217.
2. Bonner, J., and J. E. Varner. 1965. Plant biochemistry. Academic Press, New York.
3. Bremner, J. M. 1965. Total nitrogen. *In* A. G. Norman (ed.) Methods of soil analysis. Agronomy 9:959–962. Am. Soc. Agron., Madison, Wis.
4. Cole, M. A., and A. J. Turgeon. 1975. Effects of thatch inducing herbicides on soil microflora. 1975 Illinois Turfgrass Res. Summ. p. 14–17.
5. Jones, L. H. P., and K. A. Handreck. 1967. Silica in soils, plants, and animals. Adv. Agron. 19:107–149.
6. Ledeboer, F. B., and C. R. Skogley. 1967. Investigations into the nature of thatch and methods for its decomposition. Agron. J. 59:320–323.
7. Martin, D. P. 1970. The composition of turfgrass thatch and the influence of several materials to increase thatch decomposition. M.S. Thesis. Michigan State Univ., East Lansing.
8. Post, G. J. 1958. A study of three methods for determination of organic carbon in Ohio soils of several great soil groups and the profile distribution of carbon-nitrogen ratios. M.S. Thesis. Ohio State Univ., Columbus.
9. Pramer, P., and E. L. Schmidt. 1964. Carbon dioxide evolution. p. 70–71. *In* Experimental soil microbiology. Burgess Publishing Co., Minneapolis, Minn.
10. Sangster, A. G. 1970. Intracellular silica deposition in mature and senescent leaves of *Seglingia decumbens* (L.) Bernh. Ann. Bot. 34:557–570.
11. Smith, G. S., A. V. Nelson, and Elroy J. A. Boggino. 1971. Digestibility of forages in vitro as affected by content of silica. J. Anim. Sci. 33:466–471.
12. Van Soest, P. J., and L. H. P. Jones. 1968. Effect of silica in forages upon digestibility. J. Dairy Sci. 51:1644–1648.
13. ————, and H. K. Goering. 1970. Forage fiber analysis. p. 1–12. *In* Agric. Handb. 379, USDA.

Chapter 39

Influence of Fertilizer Rate, Mower Type, and Thatch Control on Colonial Bentgrass Lawn Turf[1]

C. R. SKOGLEY

ABSTRACT

With rising cost of fertilizers and other turf maintenance products there is keen interest in finding less expensive methods of establishing and maintaining lawns. An improved cultivar of colonial bentgrass (*Agrostis tenuis* Sibth.), 'Exeter', was sown in the field in 1966 and a study including fertilization, mower type, and mechanical raking was initiated in 1968. A split-split plot design was used with mower type as the main block with one rotary and two types of reel mowers included. Subplot was mechanical raking including treatment in April or in September and no raking. Sub-subplots were fertilizer treatments and included a 10–2.6–3.3 grade material to supply 0.5 kg N/are per treatment applied in April only, September only, April and September, or April, June, and September. Visual quality scores were taken most months during the growing season from 1970 through 1974.

Results showed that mowing with a rotary mower lessened turf quality, while there was no difference between a roller drive or a side-wheel drive reel mower. Mechanical raking for thatch control was not beneficial during the period of this study. Three seasonal applications of fertilizer provided slightly better quality turf while two applications provided much higher quality turf than one.

Additional index words: Agrostis tenuis **Sibth.**

INTRODUCTION

Colonial bentgrass (*Agrostis tenuis* Sibth.) was reportedly introduced into the United States before 1790 (2). It naturalized so thoroughly that during the 19th century it was found growing wild over the northern half of the United States and in many areas of Canada. Early in this century the grass was widely used throughout the northeastern U.S. as an amenity grass. Early trials in Rhode Island (5, 6) showed that, of available turfgrasses, colonial bentgrass was perhaps the most adapted to the climate and soils of the region. Hartwell and Damon (5) particularly noted that when soils were quite acid and if either N, P, or K was deficient productive pasture grasses would "run out" and *Agrostis* species would encroach and persist. In an earlier publication (4) these researchers reported that on very acid soils very few turf or pasture grasses would persist while redtop (*Agrostis alba* L.) and colonial bentgrass grew very well—"Even making their best growth."

[1] Contribution No. 1743, Agric. Exp. Stn., Kingston, RI 02881, USA.

North et al. (6) reported that colonial bentgrass with ordinary care formed an excellent lawn, except in dense shade and in very wet or very droughty soils. They stated that a properly cultivated lawn of colonial bentgrass, when fertilized and cared for, would live indefinitely.

Throughout the northeastern U.S., it is common to find relatively old lawns on village greens, cemeteries, municipal buildings, churches, and homes that have received no routine maintenance aside from mowing. The dominant grass in these old lawns (if not heavily shaded) is generally colonial bentgrass. The quality of many of these old lawns is quite acceptable. This fact might indicate that colonial bentgrass, of all turfgrasses available within the region, is particularly adapted and does not require intense culture. Findings of the early Rhode Island researchers might still be valid.

Throughout much of the northeastern U.S. colonial bentgrass was a usual component of lawn seed mixtures into the 1950's. After that time improved cultivars of Kentucky bluegrass (*Poa pratensis* L.) alone, or in combination with red fescue (*Festuca rubra* L.) and ryegrass (*Lolium* sp.) became the dominant lawn grasses.

There are several reasons why this change away from bentgrass may have occurred. First, improved cultivars of other turfgrass species were released and these improved grasses performed far better than earlier strains within the region. Second, it is known that the period of winter dormancy of colonial bentgrass is longer than for most other lawn grasses. Bentgrass browns earlier in the fall and becomes green later in the spring than Kentucky bluegrass or red fescue. Third, as lawn maintenance intensified and increased amounts of limestone, fertilizer, and water were applied to stands of bentgrass, the weed and disease problems heightened and damaging thatch accumulations occurred. Lastly, poor quality colonial bentgrass seed often contains seed of creeping bentgrass (*A. palustris* Huds.). This grass tends to mat and colonize under lawn culture and is unsightly and difficult to maintain. It is possible that cultural problems caused by over-management may have been the primary reason for the decline in use of colonial bentgrass.

Most research with colonial bentgrass in recent years has apparently involved relatively high levels of maintenance. Current literature relative to its characteristics and cultural requirements differs considerably with earlier literature. Sprague (7) stated that colonial bentgrass prefers moderately fertile soils of good water holding capacity that are not strongly acid. Hanson et al. (3) reported that it grows well on heavy, fertile soils but will persist on acid soils. They noted that it was a competitive grass and may dominate other desirable grasses included in new seedings. Beard (1) wrote similarly about colonial bentgrass adaptation to soils. He stated that the grass had a tendency to form excessive thatch. He wrote that the fertilizer requirement is 0.25 to 0.5 kg/are/growing month.

This study, initiated in 1968, was for the purpose of evaluating cultural requirements and performance of 'Exeter', an improved colonial bentgrass cultivar. Variables included in the study were mower type, mechanical raking for thatch control, and fertilization. It was hoped that this study would help determine whether colonial bentgrass might prove acceptable as a low maintenance lawn species for use in the region.

MATERIAL AND METHODS

A field study for the purpose of evaluating several variables of mowing, thatch removal, and fertilization was initiated in the spring of 1968 on a 2-year-old stand of Exeter colonial bentgrass. Prior to the study the stand was mowed at 1.9 cm and fertilized and watered as required to develop a dense, uniform stand. The study was carried out at the turfgrass research farm of the University of Rhode Island in Kingston. The soil was Bridgehampton silt loam, a member of the coarse-silty, mixed, mesic typic dystrochrepts.

A split-split plot design was used with main plots as mower type, subplots as thatch control, and sub-subplots as fertilizer treatments. Main plots were 4.88 × 12.8 m and included three mower types: a 1967 model ATCO, 50.8 cm wide, six-bladed reel mower with roller drive (M-1); a 1966 model Toro sportlawn, 53.3 cm wide, five-bladed reel mower with side-wheel drive (M-2); a 1967 model Toro, 48.3-cm wide whirlwind rotary mower (M-3). All were adjusted to mow at 1.3 cm. Cutting blades and adjustments were checked routinely to assure sharpness of cut and proper height. Subplot treatments included vertical cutting (thatch control) utilizing a Scott Proturf Aerator. This implement contains a series of blades and flexible tines fixed to a rotating horizontal shaft designed to rake thatch from turf stands. Treatments included no raking (T-1), April raking (T-2), and September raking (T-3). Plot size was 4.27 × 4.88 m. Sub-subplot fertilization treatments included: application in April only (F-1); September only (F-2); April and September (F-3); April, June, and September (F-4). A 10–2.6–3.3 grade fertilizer containing 50% of the N from activated sludge was used at a rate to supply 0.5 kg N/are. All treatments were in triplicate.

Treatments were started in spring of 1968 but data were not taken until the spring of 1970—the 1st year after all treatments had been made. Turf scores (visual quality ratings based on overall attractiveness) were taken early each month from May through October or November. Scoring was done 3 to 4 days after mowing. The scoring system used was based on 9 as ideal or perfect turf to 1 as completely brown or dead grass.

During the years of this study all clippings were removed, the turf was irrigated as necessary to avoid serious drought stress, herbicides were used on occasion to prevent or eliminate annual grass and broadleaved weeds, and insecticides were used when needed. Fungicides were applied on three occasions in 1969 and once in 1972 to combat serious red leaf spot (incited by *Helminthosporium erythrospilum* Drechsler) infection. Soil pH was adjusted to and maintained at 6.0 to 6.5 with ground agricultural limestone through the course of the study. Data were subjected to analysis of variance and means compared using Duncan's multiple range test.

RESULTS AND DISCUSSION

Seasonal turf score averages by treatment, and for the only significant yearly interaction that occurred during the test, are shown in Table 1. Fertilizer treatments provided significant differences in each of the 5 years. During 4 of the years the highest quality turf occurred on plots receiving three yearly applications. During the last year of the study there were no quality differences between turf receiving two and three applications annually. In all 5 of the years two applications provided higher quality turf than did the single spring or fall treatment. When fertilizer was applied only once a year it appeared that spring application benefitted the turf slightly more than did fall application. This was significantly so in 3 out of 5 years, in 1 year there was no difference, and during another year the reverse was true. The difference in turf quality between single annual fertilizer applications, whether spring or fall, was relatively small. Turf quality improved markedly with twice a year fertilization in contrast to single applications. The fertilizer response would be fairly rapid following April application when the grass is resuming growth. Also, leaching losses would not be a factor.

Response to mower type provided significance in only 2 of the 5 years. In both instances, mowing with a rotary mower lowered turf quality. This occurred despite the effort to maintain a sharp cutting edge on

Table 1. Yearly turf score averages for mower type (M), mechanical raking (T), and fertilization (F) for the years 1970 through 1974 and for treatment interactions which occurred in 1973.

	Year				
Treatment	1970	1971	1972	1973	1974
M-1, ATCO reel	5.6 a*	5.7 a	5.5 a	5.9 a	4.0 a
M-2, Toro reel	5.7 a	5.7 a	5.7 a	6.0 a	4.2 a
M-3, Toro rotary	5.2 b	5.7 a	5.4 a	5.3 b	4.0 a
T-1, No raking	5.4 a	5.8 a	5.6 a	5.8 a	4.2 a
T-2, Apr. raking	5.5 a	5.8 a	5.6 a	5.8 a	4.0 a
T-3, Sept. raking	5.6 a	5.7 a	5.4 a	5.5 b	4.0 a
F-1, Apr. fertilization	5.0 d	5.5 c	4.9 c	5.1 c	3.8 b
F-2, Sept. fertilization	5.2 c	4.7 d	4.7 d	5.0 c	3.6 c
F-3, Apr. + Sept. fertilization	5.7 b	6.2 b	6.0 b	6.1 b	4.3 a
F-4, Apr. + June + Sept. fertilization	6.1 a	6.6 a	6.5 a	6.7 a	4.5 a
M-1 × T-1				5.9 bc	
T-2				6.2 a	
T-3				5.6 d	
M-2 × T-1				6.1 a	
T-2				6.0 ab	
T-3				5.7 cd	
M-3 × T-1				5.4 e	
T-2				5.3 e	
T-3				5.2 e	

* Means within each treatment column not followed by the same letter differ at the 5% probability level by Duncan's new multiple range test.

Table 2. List of treatments and interactions which were significant during individual months throughout the study.

Month	Year 1970	1971	1972	1973	1974
May	F†	F	F		F
June	T,F,M‡ × T§	M,F,T × F	F	M,T,F	F
July	M,F,M × F	M,F,M × T	M,F	M,F,M × F	F
August	M,F,T × F		F,T × F	T,F	F
Sept.			M,F	M,F,M × T × F	F
Oct.	M,F	T,F,T × F	T,F	M,T,F,T × F	
Nov.	F		T,F	T,F	T,F

† Fertilizer treatment. ‡ Mower type. § Mechanical raking.

the blade. It was usual to see a slight discoloration of the grass for a day or two following mowing with the rotary mower. For this reason data were taken before mowing. The discoloration was greater during the spring period of seed formation and when the grass was under moisture stress. No differences could be detected in turf quality at any time between grass mowed with a side-wheel or roller-drive reel mower. Both mowers provided excellent cuts even though the frequency of cut per m was greater for the six-bladed ATCO than for the five-bladed Toro.

No objectionable thatch developed on the test plots during the course of this study so raking treatments were not beneficial. Difference in yearly quality attributable to the raking treatments were negligible although turf appearance was always bad for a period immediately following raking. Only during 1 year was significance observed. The September 1973 treatment reduced quality over no treatment, or that performed in April. There appeared to be a trend in this direction. The reason may relate to lack of recovery time following the relatively harsh treatment and the beginning of winter dormancy.

A mower-type-mechanical raking interaction occurred in 1973. Turf quality declined with all three mowers following fall raking. Turf quality was particularly bad with the combination of rotary mower and fall raking treatment.

Table 2 presents a list of all treatments and interactions in which significant differences occurred on various months during each of the 5 years. Treatment differences due to fertilization occurred during 29 months, to mower type during 10 months, raking treatment on 7 months, two-way interactions on nine occasions, and a three-way interaction during only 1 month. Turf quality scores were taken a total of 30 times during the 5-year period.

CONCLUSIONS

At least two applications of fertilizer per year (April and September) are required to promote an acceptible quality of lawn turf with Exeter colonial bentgrass. A third application made in June will provide a slight improvement in seasonal quality. If only single annual applications are to be made, it appears that April is a more favorable time than September.

To obtain the most pleasing appearance on relatively low fertility colonial bentgrass lawn turf, reel mowers are recommended over rotaries. No differences in cutting quality were noted between the two types of reel mowers used in this study.

Mechanical raking treatments for thatch control are not required, at least within the first few years from seeding, for routine maintenance of low fertility Exeter colonial bentgrass lawn turf. If treatments are to be made, April may be a better month to perform the operation than September.

LITERATURE CITED

1. Beard, J. B. 1973. Turfgrass: Science and culture. Prentice-Hall, Inc., Englewood Cliffs, N.J.
2. Dickinson, L. S. 1930. The lawn. Orange Judd Publ. Co., New York.
3. Hanson, A. A., F. V. Juska, and G. W. Burton. 1969. Species and varieties. *In* A. A. Hanson and F. V. Juska (eds.) Turfgrass science. Agronomy 14:370–409. Am. Soc. Agron., Madison, Wis.
4. Hartwell, B. L., and S. C. Damon. 1914. The comparative effect on different kinds of plants of liming on acid soil. Rhode Island Agric. Exp. Stn., Bull. 160.
5. ————, and ————. 1917. The persistence of lawn and other grasses as influenced especially by the effect of manures on the degree of soil acidity. Rhode Island Agric. Exp. Stn., Bull. 1970.
6. North, H. F. A., T. E. Odland, and J. A. DeFrance. 1938. Lawn grasses and their management. Rhode Island Agric. Exp. Stn., Bull. 264.
7. Sprague, H. B. 1970. Turf management handbook. The Interstate Printers and Publishers, Inc., Danville, Ill.

Chapter 40

Effects of Nitrogen Fertilization and Cutting Height on the Shoot Growth, Nutrient Removal, and Turfgrass Composition of an Initially Perennial Ryegrass Dominant Sports Turf[1]

W. A. ADAMS

ABSTRACT

A field experiment was designed to extend observations made in sand culture on the interdependence between cutting height and fertilizer level on the shoot growth of turfgrasses and to examine the ratios of major nutrients removed in clippings over a 22-week experimental period. The factorial experiment included two mowing frequencies, three heights of cut, and three levels of N fertilization.

Clipping yields ranged between 1,670 kg/ha and 6,260 kg/ha. While there was a general trend for cutting height and N fertilizer to be interdependent in their effect on shoot growth, the results were not as clear as those obtained in sand culture. The treatments substantially changed turfgrass composition and different growth responses to the treatment variables by different sward constituents may have affected the shoot growth results.

Percent cover of annual bluegrass (*Poa annua* L.) at the end of the experiment had increased significantly with increases in N and decreases in cutting height. Perennial ryegrass (*Lolium perenne* L.) was not affected by N application, but percent cover was significantly greater at the highest height of cut than at the lowest. Colonial bentgrass (*Agrostis tenuis* Sibth.) showed no significant variation with cutting height, but percent cover was significantly less at the highest N application.

The ratio of major nutrients removed in clippings showed little variation with treatment and was not related to the mean ratio in applied fertilizer. The total N removed in clippings increased by 260%, from 0 to 312 kg/ha of applied N. However, the ratios of N:P and N:K in the clippings changed by only 9 and 2%, respectively.

Additional index words: Dry matter content, *Poa annua*, *Agrostis tenuis*, Cultural weed control, Nutrient ratio, Botanical composition.

INTRODUCTION

In sports turf and in agricultural and natural grassland, N is the plant nutrient which most frequently controls growth. It is generally recognized that the N level in grasses is a dominant factor, controlling not

[1] A contribution from the Dep. of Biochemistry and Agricultural Biochemistry, Univ. of Wales, Aberystwyth, United Kingdom.

only shoot growth, but also the balance between shoot growth and root growth (7, 12). The effect of N supply level on root/shoot ratio is not constant for a single species, but depends upon physiological age and other environmental conditions, including P supply, temperature, light, and aeration state of the root environment (3, 5).

Under sports turf cultural conditions, mowing height affects the shoot growth response of turfgrass species to N (2, 8). Adams et al. (2) demonstrated that the effect of N supply level on shoot growth of perennial ryegrass (*Lolium perenne* L.) and Kentucky bluegrass (*Poa pratensis* L.) could be reversed at different cutting heights. They pointed out that these two cultural variables were interdependent in relation to turfgrass responses. Both Juska et al. (8) and Adams et al. (2) used sand culture under controlled environmental conditions where species composition was also controlled. It is difficult to extrapolate this work to field conditions. First, it is not possible to equate a nutrient solution concentration to a fertilizer application in the field. Second, experiments in which species composition is controlled can neither show changes in turfgrass composition, which may be caused by the imposed treatments on polystands in the field, nor indicate the way changes in turfgrass composition may modify the response to N and mowing height.

It is evident from the literature that cultural treatments alone can, irrespective of wear, influence species composition. Davis (6) and Taylor (11) both recorded increased invasion by bentgrass (*Agrostis* spp.) in turfs containing Kentucky bluegrass and red fescue (*Festuca rubra* L.) at low mowing heights. Bryan and Adams (4) and Shildrick (9) have shown the importance of traffic (turfgrass wear + soil compaction) on the increased invasion of sports turfs by annual bluegrass (*Poa annua* L.). However, it is probable that the status of annual bluegrass as a dominant turfgrass in some less intensively trafficked sports turfs in Britain reflects a competitive ability response to particular aspects of the cultural program (1).

Despite the considerable variations in shoot growth, which changes in N level may cause, published evidence suggests that the ratios of plant nutrients in the clippings remain relatively constant irrespective of species or fertilizer input (10, 13). If this is true, it would appear to have important implications for rationalization of the nutrition of sports turfs on sand-based constructions where mobilization, immobilization, and nutrient turnover processes are generally less significant than in soils of finer texture.

A factorial experiment was designed to examine shoot growth response and major nutrient removal under field conditions when sports turfs are subjected to variations in mowing height and frequency and level of N application. Three turfgrass species were dominant in the initial turf. The imposed culture treatments caused substantial changes in turfgrass composition. These changes provided valuable information complementary to the original objectives of the experiment.

MATERIALS AND METHODS

The experiment was carried out on the sports fields of the University College of Wales, Aberystwyth. The soil was an imperfectly drained silty clay loam with a pH of 6.0 (USDA subgroup: Typic Fragiaquept). The experiment was conducted in 1974, but the site used was sown with 'S23' perennial ryegrass in June 1971 at a seeding rate of 24 g/m^2. During the seeding year the following fertilizer levels were applied (kg/ha) 80 N, 25 P, and 60 K. No fertilizer was applied to the area in 1972 and 1973. During this time the area was used infrequently for sport and was mowed with a gang-mower at a height of approximately 2.5 cm. All clippings were returned to the soil.

Over the period between seeding and initiation the experiment, the initial perennial ryegrass sward had been invaded to an increasing extent by white clover (*Trifolium repens* L.) annual bluegrass, and colonial bentgrass (*Agrostis tenuis* Sibth.). The experimental site was selected for uniformity in botanical composition. No plot differed in mean botanical composition by more than 5%, from the block mean in any of the named species constituents. Botanical compositions of each plot at the beginning and termination of the experiment were recorded as percent cover, assessed visually and independently by two individuals, within eight randomly thrown 25 cm^2 quadrats.

The experiment consisted of 18 treatments randomized in two blocks with 10 m^2 plots (5 × 2 m). The treatments detailed in Table 1 included three fertilizer levels, three cutting heights, and two mowing frequencies. One of the mowing frequencies was related to agricultural management and will only be used for comparison. The experiment was begun on 1 May 1974 and continued for 22 weeks. For 3 weeks prior to the start, plots were mown weekly at their experimental cutting height. Fertilizer was applied in four equal increments to each treatment. The first mowing within the experimental period was carried out 7 days after initial fertilizer application. The remaining fertilizer applications were made 2 days after each 5 weekly mowing. Herbicide treatment (CMPP/2,4-D) at a rate of 28 ml/100 m^2 active ingredient was carried out within 24 hours of the

Table 1. Fertilizer applications made to turfs factorially maintained at 1.25, 2.5, and 7.5 cm heights of cut, each, at 5-day and 5-week intervals.

	Fertilizer†		
	N	P	K
	kg/ha		
N—None	0	22	36
N—Medium	88	34	62
N—High	312	134	250

† Nutrient sources: N—NH_4NO_3; P—$Ca(H_2PO_4)_2\,H_2O$; K—KCl.

initial fertilizer application. Application rates of P and K were raised in the higher N treatments to prevent these nutrients from becoming growth limiting. The grass was cut at the lowest mowing height with a reel mower and with a rotary mower at the two higher heights.

The yield of clippings at each mowing throughout the experiment from a 1- × 4-m strip in the center of each 2- × 5-m plot were dried at 80 C and the percentage of dry matter was calculated and recorded. Subsamples of dry herbage were ground and analyzed for N, P, and K content. Nitrogen and P were determined colorimetrically on a H_2SO_4 × Se catalyst digest. Nitrogen was determined by the indo-phenol blue reaction and P by the molybdenum blue reaction. Potassium was determined by flame photometry. The data were subjected to an analysis of variance.

RESULTS AND DISCUSSION

Dry Matter Content

Mean percentage dry matter values over the whole growth period are given in Table 2. The values show the expected decrease with increases in N and decreases in mowing height. The effect of N on dry matter content was considerably greater than the effect of cutting height although both variables produced significant effects.

Shoot Growth

Mean total yields of dry clippings for the treatments mowed at 5-day intervals are given in Table 3. Yields ranged from 1,670 kg/ha for zero N and a 7.5-cm cutting height to 6,260 kg/ha for the highest N level and a 2.5-cm cutting height. The general effect of fertilizer level on clipping yield was significant for both incremental increases (P = 0.01), while the general effect of raising the cutting height from 2.5 to 7.5 cm brought about a significant decrease in clipping yield (P = 0.01). Nevertheless, the interdependence between cutting height and N level in affecting shoot

Table 2. Mean percent dry matter in clippings over a 22-week period from turfs cut at 5-day intervals and subjected to three heights of cut and three fertilizer regimes.

Fertilizer level	Cutting height (cm) 1.25	2.5	7.5	Fertilizer level means
		%		
N—None	25.3	28.1	29.1	27.6
N—Medium	23.5	25.6	26.3	25.1
N—High	20.2	21.5	21.9	21.2
Cutting height means	23.0	25.0	25.8	
L.S.D. between treatments		2.0*	2.9**	
L.S.D. between fertilizer and cutting height means		1.4*	2.0**	

*,** Significant at the 0.5 and 0.01 levels, respectively.

Table 3. Yield of clippings (dry weight) over a 22-week period from turfs cut every 5 days and subjected to three heights of cut and three fertilizer regimes.

	Cutting height (cm)			
Fertilizer level	1.25	2.5	7.5	Fertilizer level means
		kg/ha		
N—None	2,290	2,250	1,670	2,069
N—Medium	3,010	3,230	2,030	2,755
N—High	6,120	6,260	5,610	6,033
Cutting height means	3,805	3,948	3,103	
L.S.D. between treatments		725*		
L.S.D. between fertilizer and cutting height means		387*	551**	

*,** Significant at the 0.5 and 0.01 levels, respectively.

growth, demonstrated in sand culture with monostands of perennial ryegrass and Kentucky bluegrass by Adams et al. (2), was not obtained in this experiment. A trend of increasing yield with decreasing cutting height was noted at the lowest N level. At the highest N level, the lowest cutting height did not depress yield and the highest cutting height did not produce the greatest growth response. These results, which indicate the difficulty in extrapolating results obtained in sand culture to field conditions, may have been influenced by the following factors: (i) The stand contained several turfgrass species whose response to the cultural variables may have differed. This is supported by observations on changes in turfgrass composition; (ii) Soils, as distinct from sand, modify the N levels available to the plant, both by immobilizing fertilizer N and by mineralizing N from native organic matter.

Turfgrass Composition

Visual examination of the plots at the end of the experiment revealed substantial changes in turfgrass composition (Table 4). Least change from the original composition occurred at the 2.5-cm cutting height and medium N level. Next was the 1.25- and 2.5-cm cutting heights at the zero N level. This is by no means surprising considering the cultural practices utilized prior to the experiment. There were some broadleaved weeds present at the start of the experiment and it can be seen that N level influenced their chemical control. No weeds remained at the end of the experiment in the high N treatment, but they survived in the zero N treatment.

The variation in percentage cover with respect to the grasses were analyzed statistically. In the case of perennial ryegrass there were no significant differences in percentage cover between N treatments. However, percentage cover was significantly greater at the 7.5-cm cutting height compared with the 1.25-cm ($P = 0.05$) height. Colonial bentgrass showed no significant difference in percentage cover between heights of cut, but had a significantly lower percentage cover at the highest N level when

Table 4. Botanical composition of turfs prior to and after a 22-week growing period when mowed at 5-day intervals and subjected to three cutting heights and three fertilizer regimes.

	Cutting height (cm)			
Species	1.25	2.50	7.5	Original
	% of cover			
		N—None		
Perennial ryegrass	40	40	58	45
Colonial bentgrass	30	30	38	35
Annual bluegrass	20	15	0	15
Broadleaf weeds	10	15	4	5
		N—Medium		
Perennial ryegrass	36	45	38	45
Colonial bentgrass	28	40	52	35
Annual bluegrass	34	10	8	15
Broadleaf weeds	2	5	2	5
		N—High		
Perennial ryegrass	32	42	55	45
Colonial bentgrass	20	23	25	35
Annual bluegrass	48	35	20	15
Broadleaf weeds	0	0	0	5

compared with the 88-kg/ha level ($P = 0.05$). The percentage cover of annual bluegrass differed significantly in response to N level and cutting height. Its percentage cover was significantly greater at the highest N level compared with the medium level ($P = 0.05$) and the zero level ($P = 0.01$). It was also significantly greater at the 1.25-cm cutting height compared with the 2.5-cm ($P = 0.05$) and 7.50-cm ($P = 0.01$) heights. The changes in percentage cover of annual bluegrass indicated both increases and decreases from the original composition, but emphasize the strong competitive ability of this turfgrass when subjected to close mowing under high levels of applied N.

Annual bluegrass is more susceptible to moisture stress than the two other turfgrasses present. However, the summer period over which the experiment was conducted contained no long dry period during which high soil moisture deficits could occur.

Cultural control of annual bluegrass in a sward where it is co-dominant with bentgrass (a situation on many golf and bowling greens in Britain) requires an acid soil which is subject to occasional moisture stress and is low in plant nutrients, particularly N. These conditions inevitably lead to a low turfgrass growth rate. While the turf may not show greater initial susceptibility to wear damage, consequences of wear are far more severe because of the slow recovery rate. Thus, the cultural conditions required to control annual bluegrass invasion may restrict the intensity of use to the degree that the use of cultural controls may only be realistic on ornamental lawns.

It is evident that annual bluegrass thrives under close mowing regimes in moist, nutrient rich soils. These same soil conditions are necessary to encourage recovery from wear and provide good verdure throughout the year. Annual bluegrass will probably make an increasing contribution to the future development of sports turf surfaces.

Possibly, the change in turfgrass composition affected the shoot growth yields at the various N levels and cutting heights (Table 3). It could be that the general similarity in shoot growth at the same N level, but different mowing heights, was due to the change in relative productivity of the different sward components at different heights of cut. This experiment indicates the dynamic nature of species composition in sports turf and illustrates the competitive interrelationships among the three grass species in response to variations in fertilizer level and cutting height.

Nutrient Removal

Mean nutrient ratios in the foliage over the experimental period together with those in the applied fertilizer are shown in Table 5. The overall mean ratios for all treatments at the two mowing frequencies are also given. The ratios for all treatments under the 5-day mowing regime are similar and not related to mean fertilizer ratios. The overall effect of reducing mowing frequency was to decrease the N content relative to P and K, although the P:K ratio was similar.

Both Wray (13) and Skirde (10) have quoted data for the N:P:K ratios in turfgrass clippings which make useful comparisons. Skirde's (10) data showed an increase in N:P and K:P ratios with increases in N applications, although the magnitude of the change was less in the present data. The relevant ratios are: Skirde, 0 to 300 kg N/ha, 5.7:1:5.9 to 8.6:1:7.2; compared with 0 to 312 kg N/ha; (means for three cutting treatments) 8.2:1:5.8 to 9.0:1:6.4. Wray (13) quoted nutrient ratio data for four turfgrass species. Again, his data are similar with an overall mean ratio of 7.7:1:5.5.

It is important to recognize the minor nature of variations in internal ratios of major nutrients in clippings with different species and with considerable variations in nutritional levels. This is illustrated by an examination of the data. Taking the mean ratios for the clipping heights from table 5, the ratios N:P and K:P changed by 9 and 2%, respectively, from zero N to high N. Summing the incremental removals of N at each mowing gave mean values for N removal of 73 kg/ha for the zero N treat-

Table 5. The overall ratios (N/P/K) of major nutrients removed in clippings over a 22-week period from turfs mowed at 5-day intervals and subjected to three cutting heights and three fertilizer regimes.

Fertilizer level	Cutting height (cm)			Mean ratio in fertilzier
	1.25	2.5	7.5	
N—None	7.8/1.0/5.5	8.1/1.0/6.3	8.7/1.0/6.3	0.0/1.0/1.7
N—Medium	8.6/1.0/5.6	8.8/1.0/6.1	8.0/1.0/6.2	2.7/1.0/1.9
N—High	8.8/1.0/6.1	9.2/1.0/6.5	9.0/1.0/6.7	2.4/1.0/1.9
	Overall mean for 5-day mowing interval 8.6/1.0/6.1			
	Overall mean for 5-week mowing interval 6.6/1.0/6.4			

ments and 265 kg/ha for the high N treatment. Thus, the removal of N in clippings increased by 260%, moving from zero N to high N levels. This must be noted by turfgrass managers fertilizing turfs on sand-constructed media where much of the nutrient buffering effect of soils is absent. High N input will inevitably lead to a substantial removal of other nutrients in the clippings in almost direct proportion to increases in growth. While the retention of fertilizer P is moderate in sand constructions, the retention of K is quite poor. Super imposed on this seems to be a general underestimate of the K requirement of turfs on such sites. Analyses of sand constructions in Britain frequently show extremely low levels of available K. It must be recognized that proportionate K fertilization is of vital importance in sand construction when all grass clippings are removed.

LITERATURE CITED

1. Adams, W. A. 1975. Some developments in the selection and maintenance of turfgrasses. Sci. Hort. 26:22–27.
2. ————, P. J. Bryan, and G. E. Walker. 1973. Effects of cutting height and nitrogen nutrition on the growth pattern of turfgrasses. p. 131–144. *In* E. C. Roberts (ed.) Proc. 2nd Int. Turfgrass Res. Conf., Blacksburg, Va., 18–21 June 1973. Am. Soc. Agron., Madison, Wis.
3. Brouwer, R. 1966. Root growth of grasses and cereals. p. 153–166. *In* F. L. Milthorpe and J. D. Ivins (eds.) The growth of grasses and legumes. Proc. 12th Easter School in Agricultural Sciences. Univ. of Nottingham, Butterworth, London, England.
4. Bryan, P. J., and W. A. Adams. 1971. Observations on grass species persisting on English league soccer pitches in spring 1970. Razen turf Gazon 2:46–51.
5. Davidson, R. L. 1969. Effects of soil nutrients and moisture on root/shoot ratios in *Lolium perenne* and *Trifolium repens*. Ann. Bot. 33:571–577.
6. Davis, R. R. 1958. The effect of other species and cutting height on persistence of lawn grasses. Agron. J. 50:671–673.
7. Goss, R. L., and A. G. Law. 1967. Performance of bluegrass varieties at two cutting heights and two nitrogen levels. Agron. J. 59:516–518.
8. Juska, F. V., J. Tyson, and C. M. Harrison. 1955. The competitive relationships of Merion bluegrass as influenced by various mixtures, cutting heights and levels of nitrogen. Agron. J. 47:513–518.
9. Shildrick, J. P. 1975. Turfgrass mixtures under wear treatments. J. Sports Turf Res. Inst. 51:9–40.
10. Skirde, W. 1974. Nahrstoffgehalt und Nahrstoffentzug von Rasen bei verschieden hoher Dungung und verschidenem Bodenaufbau. Razen Turf Gazon 5:68–73.
11. Taylor, D. K. 1973. Cultivar response in turfgrass species mixture trials with mowing at two heights. p. 48–54. *In* E. C. Roberts (ed.) Proc. 2nd Int. Turfgrass Res. Conf., Blacksburg, Va. 18–21 June 1973. Am. Soc. Agron., Madison, Wis.
12. Weinmann, H. 1948. Underground development and reserves of grasses. A review. J. Br. Grassl. Soc. 3:111–140.
13. Wray, F. J. 1973. Seasonal growth and major nutrient uptake of turfgrasses under cool wet conditions. p. 79–88. *In* E. C. Roberts (ed.) Proc. 2nd Int. Turfgrass Res. Conf., Blacksburg, Va. 18–21 June 1973. Am. Soc. Agron., Madison, Wis.

Section VIII:

Turfgrass Sod Production and Establishment

Chapter 41

Investigation of Net-Sod Production as a New Technique[1]

J. B. BEARD
D. P. MARTIN
F. B. MERCER

ABSTRACT

The production time of seeded sods needs to be reduced to save on mowing, fertilization, irrigation, and similar production costs. The objective of this study was to determine the feasibility of the net-sod system, including the production techniques and transplanting characteristics. Results over a 3-year period confirmed that a Tuft 5 net-sod production system is feasible and could reduce production time substantially. Studies revealed that the seeding rate and harvesting techniques would be the same as now used in standard Kentucky bluegrass production practices. The depth of net placement in the soil did not affect net-sod production, assuming it was above the projected harvest depth. This was also true when the net was placed on the soil surface. Seasonal studies revealed that production time varied seasonally: shortest in fall; longest in spring, and intermediate for a summer planting under Michigan muck sod production conditions. Observations stress the importance of adequate weed seed control in the seedbed prior to planting. Finally, transplant rooting studies using both field and greenhouse observational techniques showed no differences between Tuft 5 net-sod production and standard production procedures.

Additional index words: Kentucky bluegrass, Net placement depth, Red fescue, Seeding rate, Sod harvesting, Sod strength, Transplant sod rooting, Tuft 5 net-sod.

INTRODUCTION

Commercial sod produced from seeded grasses has not changed fundamentally since the early years. Procedures of seedbed preparation, planting with a cultipacker seeder, mowing, and irrigation have been established for some time and were modifications of establishment procedures utilized on general turf areas. Research on comparative sod strengths, as affected by cultivar selection, mowing, and nutritional programs, has contributed information toward enhancing the rate of sod strength development (1, 4, 8). Still, there have been no major changes in the basic concepts of sod establishment. Production time, from seeding to harvesting of a marketable crop that can be easily lifted, handled, and

[1] Michigan Agric. Exp. Stn. Journal Paper No. 8761. This research partially supported by a grant from Netlon Limited, Blackburn, England.

transplanted, can range from 1 to 2 or more years depending on the irrigation practices and particular turfgrass species being grown (2, 3, 7).

The development of a new concept in sod culture which significantly reduces production time would be very attractive from the perspective of reduced mowing, irrigation, fertilization, labor, and resource cost inputs. A shorter production time would allow greater flexibility in adjusting to unanticipated market demands. Thus, research was initiated at Michigan State University in 1972 concerning the (i) feasibility of net-sod production, (ii) best type of net to utilize, (iii) optimum seeding rate, (iv) net placement depth, (v) mechanical harvesting characteristics, and (vi) transplant rooting. The techniques developed and described in this paper are referred to as the Tuft 5 system of net-sod production.

MATERIALS AND METHODS

The original Tuft 5 net-sod system studies were initiated in 1972 and continued through 1974 at the Michigan Experimental Farm 7 miles northeast of East Lansing, Mich., USA. The soil type was a Houghton muck soil which is predominantly a reed sedge peat having a pH of 6.2. Adequate drainage was provided by a subsurface tile drainage system. The site also had tree windbreaks positioned to minimize wind erosion.

Cultural practices used on the experimental site will be described. Where variations from these norms occur they are indicated under the particular study description. Preplant N fertilization consisted of 45 kg N/ha incorporated into the seedbed along with adequate amounts of P and K based on soil test results. The experimental site was then leveled and tilled to provide a quality seedbed. Next the plot area was staked out and the appropriate planting method accomplished, either with or without a net. Net installation was accomplished manually on the limited plot area because a net-sod installation machine had not yet been developed.

The two primary species utilized were Kentucky bluegrass (*Poa pratensis* L.) and red fescue (*Festuca rubra* L.). Unless otherwise specified, the seeding rate was 45 kg/ha for Kentucky bluegrass and 90 kg/ha for the seed mixture. A solid set main-line irrigation system with portable aluminum laterals was used during these investigations. Irrigation was applied daily during the initial seed germination and seedling establishment period and at 1- to 2-week intervals as needed to prevent wilt during the subsequent sod formation phase. The water table was maintained at approximately 76 cm below the soil surface by means of ditches and a pumping system. The drain tile system consisted of an 18-m spacing with outlets connected to the open ditches. Mowing was accomplished with a 5-gang reel mower at a 5-cm cutting height and a 3-day interval with the clippings returned. Nitrogen was applied at a rate of 45 kg/ha/growing month. The experimental site utilized had been in cultivation for many years and thus was relatively free of weedy perennial grasses. No pre- or post-plant herbicides were applied during the course of these studies. Major weeds occurring were chickweed (*Stellaria* and *Cerastium* spp.), purslane (*Portulaca oleracea* L.), and crabgrass (*Digitaria* spp.). A mechanical sod cutter with a 45-cm wide cutting unit was used to harvest the sod.

The plot size was 1.5 × 3 m unless otherwise specified. A randomized block design of four replications was selected. Data recorded consisted of visual turfgrass quality estimates and percent cover ratings made at 5- to 7-day intervals. Evaluations were also made when weeds or diseases occurred. No insect damage was apparent throughout the course of these investigations.

The rate of sod formation was evaluated during these studies by means of the Michigan Sod Strength Test (6). The test involves placing a harvested sod piece (cut to a uniform soil depth) on a platform, one-half of which is stationary and the other half moveable. A horizontal force is then applied to the moveable platform at a uniform rate. The force required to tear the sod piece loose from that portion secured on the stationary platform is recorded as the sod strength. Values below 84 kg/45-cm sod width harvested at a uniform soil depth of 1.3 cm were considered unacceptable for sod harvesting, handling, and transplanting.

A second evaluation technique involved the transplant sod rooting test developed at Michigan State University (5). It consists of placing a sod piece, harvested to a uniform soil depth of 1.3 cm, in a 25.4-cm^2 wooden frame with a fiberglass screen secured across the bottom. The sod and associated apparatus is then placed on a newly prepared, moist soil and maintained under optimum moisture conditions. The sod is allowed to root into the underlying soil for 21 days. An upward force is then applied to the sod by means of a cable arrangement attached to each of the four corners of the wooden frame. The force is applied in an upward, vertical direction at a uniform rate until the sod is pulled free. The force (weight) required to uproot the sod is measured and recorded as the transplant sod rooting strength.

Feasibility Studies

The two comparative treatments utilized in this study were the Tuft 5 net-sod system and the standard sod production procedure without a net. Plot size for the feasibility studies was 7.6 × 7.6 m. Netlon netting (provided by Netlon Limited of Blackburn, England, in 1.2-m widths) was unrolled across the plot area, 15-cm wire staples placed at the corners, and a shallow 5-mm layer of soil distributed over the surface manually. No net was visible prior to firming with a water ballast roller. These initial plots were seeded to 'Merion' Kentucky bluegrass in August 1972. The rainfall-soil moisture conditions during the fall establishment period were excellent. Thus, no irrigation was required.

Seeding Rate Study

Three comparative seeding rates were utilized: 45, 67.5, and 90 kg/ha of Kentucky bluegrass. The blend consisted of equal parts 'Fylking,' Merion, and 'Nugget' Kentucky bluegrass. The Tuft 5 net-sod system was utilized across all the seeding rate plots. The experimental area was planted 15 May 1973.

Polystand Composition Study

The objective was to determine the effects of combining various percentages of red fescue with Kentucky bluegrass when using the Tuft 5 net-sod system. Three species ratios were utilized: 70:30, 50:50, and 30:70% by weight of (i) the Kentucky bluegrass blend utilized in the previously described seeding rate study and (ii) 'Pennlawn' red fescue. The seeding date was 15 May 1973.

Net Placement Studies

The objective was to determine the effects of soil coverage depth over the net on turfgrass growth and sod formation. The five soil depth treatments were: (i) 0; (ii) 5; (iii) 9; (iv) 13; (v) 19 mm soil coverage over the net. These soil depths were achieved by manual application using a premeasured amount of soil per plot. Following manual application the soil was dragged lightly to level it and firmed with a water ballast roller. A Kentucky bluegrass blend consisting of equal parts 'Baron,' Fylking, and Nugget was used. Plot size was 1.2 × 3 m in a randomized block design of three replications. The experiment was established on 20 Sept. 1973, and was repeated during the spring of 1974.

Seasonal Production Studies

The Tuft 5 net-sod system and the standard sod production procedure used in the Midwest were evaluated by means of three seasonal plantings accomplished in each of 2 consecutive years (1973 and 1974). The seasonal plantings were made on 15 May, 15 July, and 12 Sept. 1973. The 1974 plantings were on approximately the same dates, except for the spring which was 2 weeks earlier. The Kentucky bluegrass blend utilized throughout these studies consisted of equal parts Baron, Fylking, and Nugget. A polystand composed of the Kentucky bluegrass blend (30%) and Pennlawn red fescue (70% by weight) was also included.

Transplant Sod Rooting Studies

The Michigan Sod Transplant Rooting Test described earlier was utilized to evaluate the effects of the Tuft 5 net-sod system on transplant sod rooting. Merion Kentucky bluegrass sods produced from the Tuft 5 net-sod system and by standard production practices used in the Midwest were grown at the Michigan State University Muck Experimental Farm, harvested, and transplanted onto a site at the Michigan State University Turfgrass Field Research Plots in East Lansing, Mich. The soil was a fertile loamy sand having a pH of 6.5. The sods were transplanted on 15 Aug. 1973, with the sod transplant rooting test conducted after 3 weeks of shoot growth and rooting. The transplanted sods were irrigated as needed to prevent visual wilt. Three replications were employed with the study being repeated during the 1974 growing season.

RESULTS

Feasibility Studies

Results of the preliminary late summer tests revealed that acceptable Merion Kentucky bluegrass sod strength could be achieved in 8 weeks by using the Tuft 5 net-sod system. The sod was easily lifted, rolled, and transplanted manually without any signs of tearing. This contrasts with the adjacent sod plots without net which could not be lifted even though the visual estimates of turfgrass quality and percent cover were comparable. Initial harvesting trials with a mechanical sod cutter revealed that the net-sod was readily cut with no apparent problems.

Potential weed problems associated with net-sod production are of concern. A fairly high chickweed population occurred in the fall seeding. The infestation was such that it would certainly impair the market quality and consumer acceptability. One cannot tolerate a significant weed population when attempting to produce sod in a very short time, such as 6 to 14 weeks. This means that the soil site where net-sod production is contemplated should be weed-free or else appropriate steps taken to chemically control the existing weed seeds prior to planting.

Seeding Rate Study

No differences were evident in the comparative sod strengths of a Kentucky bluegrass blend seeded at three rates when produced by the Tuft 5 net-sod system (Table 1). However, as the seeding rate was increased from 45 to 67.5 to 90 kg/ha there was a significant decrease in the weed content, especially purslane and crabgrass. It is evident from these

Table 1. The influence of three seeding rates on the seedling height, weed content, and sod strength of a Kentucky bluegrass blend established on 15 May 1973 using the Tuft 5 net-sod system.

Seeding rate	Seedling height	Weed cover		Sod strength
	6 July 1973	6 July 1973	26 July 1973	28 Aug. 1973
kg/ha	cm	——— % ———		kg to tear
45	3 a	81 a	55 a	82.7 a
67.5	4 a	75 b	40 b	84.0 a
90	3 a	59 c	34 c	90.9 a

data that the preferred seeding rate used in Tuft 5 net-sod production is basically the same as has been widely used in standard Kentucky bluegrass sod production.

Polystand Composition Studies

Increasing the red fescue component in the seed mixture stimulated more rapid establishment and greater seedling height when grown by the Tuft 5 net-sod system (Table 2). These responses also resulted in a decreased weed content. The addition of red fescue produced a more rapid sod formation rate around the net and greater early sod strength than where Kentucky bluegrass was the dominant component of the polystand. The accentuated early sod strength provided by red fescue was due to its more rapid establishment vigor and rooting. This rapid rooting of red fescue around the net was consistent throughout several growing seasons except when a severe *Helminthosporium* leafspot infection occurred.

Some preliminary trials were conducted involving a similar type of polystand study using 'Manhattan' perennial ryegrass (*Lolium perenne* L.). The responses were bascially the same in terms of an accentuated rate of sod formation due to more rapid establishment and rooting around the net.

Net Placement Studies

When comparing five depths of soil coverage utilizing the Tuft 5 net-sod system seeded to a Kentucky bluegrass blend, there were no apparent trends of significance from a practical production standpoint (Table 3). This was true in terms of the shoot density, percent cover, weed content, and sod strength evaluated 7 weeks after planting. This experiment was repeated in the spring of 1974 with comparable results. These studies were conducted under conditions of daily irrigation. Problems with seedling establishment might be more apparent at the shallow soil coverage depths on production sites that are not irrigated.

This research group assumed during the early experiments that net soil coverage was necessary. However, these results indicate that surface net placement presents no problems from a root-net entanglement stand-

Table 2. The influence of adding Pennlawn red fescue to a Kentucky bluegrass blend when established on 15 May 1973 using the Tuft 5 net-sod system and a density of three seeds/cm².

Seed composition by wt.		Seedling height	Weed content	Sod strength
Kentucky bluegrass blend	Pennlawn red fescue	6 July 1973	6 July 1973	28 Aug. 1973
%		cm	%	kg to tear
70	30	11 b	29 a	72.3 b
50	50	13 a	17 b	82.7 a
30	70	13 a	17 b	86.4 a

Table 3. The influence of five soil coverage depths over the net on the shoot density, percent cover, weed content, and sod strength of a Kentucky bluegrass blend seeded on 20 Sept. 1973 at 45 kg/ha using the Tuft 5 net-sod system.

Depth of soil coverage	Shoot† density	Cover†	Weed† content	Spring sod strength
cm	count/25 cm²	%		kg to tear
0	13 a	47 b	3 a	69.0 a
0.5	17 b	61 a	2 a	66.8 a
0.8	12 a	50 b	2 a	71.4 a
1.3	14 a	53 b	0 a	73.6 a
1.9	14 a	67 a	2 a	70.9 a

† On 6 Nov. 1973.

point. Thus, this modified concept of surface net placement can aid in reducing wind erosion problems and offers simpler mechanized procedures for laying the net in production fields. There is the potential for net displacement when placed on the surface in regions where high wind velocities occur. Wind problems were never apparent during these net placement studies over a 3-year period in Michigan.

Seasonal Production Studies

Comparisons across all six planting dates over a 2-year period consistently revealed that the Tuft 5 net-sod system achieved a superior rate of sod strength development compared to standard sod production practices without a net. In all cases, the Tuft 5 net-sod system produced acceptable sod strength at a much faster rate than the standard Midwest procedure. The data shown for the July planting date are typical of the findings throughout the six planting dates (Table 4). Based on 2 year's results under Michigan conditions on a muck soil, a harvestable sod can be produced using the Tuft 5 net-sod system in (i) 13 to 14 weeks from a spring planting, (ii) 10 to 12 weeks from a summer planting, and (iii) 8 to 10 weeks from a late summer planting. These findings suggest that the scheduling of harvest dates relative to the original planting dates vary seasonally and must be taken into account in the long range planning of harvest schedules. Purslane was a problem during the late summer seedings. This reemphasizes the importance of adequate pre-plant weed seed control in reducing production time.

Table 4. The effects of netting on the shoot density and sod strength of a Kentucky bluegrass blend planted on July 17, 1973.

Net treatment	Polystand	Shoot density 2 Aug. 1973	Sod strength 16 Oct. 1973
		count/25 cm^2	kg to tear
No net	Kentucky bluegrass blend†	15 a	27.3 b
	Mixture†	16 a	41.8 b
Tuft 5 net-sod method	Kentucky bluegrass blend†	15 a	60.9 a
	Mixture‡	16 a	72.2 a

† Equal parts Baron, Fylking, and Nugget.
‡ Thirty percent of the Kentucky bluegrass blend† and 70% Pennlawn red fescue (by weight).

Table 5. A comparison of the transplant sod rooting† of Merion Kentucky bluegrass grown with and without a net.

Net treatment	Transplant sod rooting
	kg to lift
Sod without net (14 months old)	27.3 a
Tuft 5 net-sod (12 weeks old)	26.4 a

† Evaluated 21 days after transplanting.

Transplanting Rooting Studies

There were no significant differences in transplant rooting strength between the 12-week-old Tuft 5 net-sod and the 14-month-old sod produced under standard Michigan conditions without a net (Table 5). Apparently there are no potentially negative effects of the net on transplant sod rooting. These results were confirmed in glass-faced root observation box studies conducted under greenhouse conditions where the root growth was followed for 3 months.

LITERATURE CITED

1. Beard, J. B. 1972. Comparative sod strength and transplant sod rooting of Kentucky bluegrass cultivars and blends. 42nd Annu. Michigan Turfgrass Conf. Proc. 1:123–127.
2. ————, and P. E. Rieke. 1966. Sod production in Michigan. Michigan State Univ., Dep. of Crop and Soil Sci. Ext. Memo.
3. ————, and ————. 1969. Producing quality sod. *In* A. A. Hansen and F. V. Juska (eds.) Turfgrass science. Agronomy 14:442–461. Am. Soc. Agron., Madison, Wis.
4. English, K. R., and P. E. Rieke. 1971. Fertilizing for sod strength. Michigan State Univ. Sod Producers Field Day Rep. 1:19–22.
5. King, J. W., and J. B. Beard. 1969. Measuring rooting of sodded turfs. Agron. J. 61:497–498.
6. Rieke, P. E., J. B. Beard, and C. M. Hansen. 1968. A technique to measure sod strength for use in sod production studies. 1968. Agron. Abstr. p. 60.
7. ————, ————, and R. E. Lucas. 1968. Grass sod production on organic soils in Michigan. Proc. 3rd Int. Peat Congr., Quebec City, Canada.
8. Shearman, R. C., and J. B. Beard. 1971. Seeding rate and mowing studies in sod production. Michigan State Univ. Sod Producers Field Day Rep. 1:10–13.

Chapter 42

Techniques for Rapid Sod Production[1]

R. E. BURNS

ABSTRACT

The approximate time when sod is to be used is known several months in advance. Therefore, sod can be preordered and then produced for the specific need. Methods of producing sod in a relatively short time were studied near Atlanta, Ga., USA. 'Tifway' bermudagrass (*Cynodon* sp.) was sprigged in early summer in an 80-mm layer of solid sewage sludge from a secondary treatment plant. Tall fescue (*Festuca arundinacea* Schreb.) was seeded in the fall and winter in a Cecil sandy clay loam, in which 5-mm plastic mesh had been placed approximately 5 mm below the soil surface. Sod strength was measured by applying a slowly increasing force to a 0.3-m wide strip of sod.

The bermudagrass sod had a strength of 12 kg 2 months after sprigging which increased to 17 kg after 5 months. Sod grown on sludge obtained from an industrial area exhibited more environmental stress when transplanted than sod grown on sludge originating from a residential area. After 7 weeks the fall fescue with a single layer of net broke at 45 kg force, a double layer of net required 75 kg, and netting without sod broke at 34 kg. Sod with no net was too weak to remove from the ground. Three-month-old tall fescue sod produced twice as many roots with double the length of those produced on 7-month-old sod. The tall fescue showed no signs of environmental stress when transplanted during winter or early spring months.

Additional index words: Bermudagrass, Tall fescue, *Festuca arundinacea* Schreb., *Cynodon* spp., Lawns, Turf, Sewage sludge, Sod netting.

INTRODUCTION

The demand for sod is increasing in the United States. Developers are specifying sod for quick cover, especially in areas where soil erosion may be a problem. In parts of the Piedmont area of the southeastern U.S. tall fescue (*Festuca arundinacea* Schreb.), a cool-season turfgrass, makes a good turf that stays green throughout the year. Historically, bermudagrass (*Cynodon* sp.), a warm-season turfgrass, has been the predominant lawn grass in this area. Tall fescue around commercial buildings is easier to maintain than bermudagrass.

Sod farms serving this area are in south Georgia on the Coastal Plains and specialize in hybrid bermudagrasses. The nearest source of cool-season turfgrasses is in the midwestern states. Transportation is a problem from both of these areas. Another problem with the cool-season sod is that the ground is often frozen in the northern areas when the sod is needed in Georgia. One of the problems limiting local sod production is the substrate. Few natural soils have the qualities of weight, water retention,

[1]Contribution from the Agronomy Dep., Univ. of Georgia, Georgia Exp. Stn., Experiment, GA 30212, USA.

and texture necessary for good sod (1). There is, however, a ready supply of digested sewage sludge that meets most of the criteria for a good substrate.

This study was initiated to find means of producing both cool- and warm-season sod near the metropolitan areas of the southeastern U.S. piedmont. A method rapid enough to permit growers to plant the sod after a developer had placed his order was needed. Rapid growth is especially important with cool-season turfgrasses since it does not hold quality well through the summer.

MATERIALS AND METHODS

'Tifway' bermudagrass (*Cynodon transvaalensis* Burt-Davy × *C. dactylon* L. Pers.), centipedegrass [*Eremochloa ophiuroides* (Munro) Hack.], and 'Emerald' zoysiagrass (*Zoysia japonica* Steud. × *Z. tenuifolia* Willd. ex Trin) were sprigged to an 8-cm layer of sewage sludge in July of 1974. The sludge came from two secondary disposal plants in Georgia: one serving a residential (R) area in Griffin and one serving an industrial (I) area in Atlanta. The sludges were secondary treated, digested material. The R sludge was dried on a sand bed, while the I sludge was from a vacuum filter cake plant. Except for heavy metals, the sludges were similar in chemical composition (Table 1).

The sludge was spread on the soil to an 8-cm depth and dried to a stage that permitted tilling fine enough to sprig the grasses. Control plots of soil fertilized with 900 kg/ha of a 10–4.4–8.3 N–P–K fertilizer prior to planting and periodically thereafter were used in some tests. The smallest plot size was 1 × 3 m with a minimum of three replicates.

Seeded grasses were used on the plastic netting studies initiated on 7 Oct. 1975. A 5-mm Vexar® plastic netting manufactured by DuPont and a 20- × 25-mm mesh plastic Sodnet® from Conwed Corporation were used. The plots on Cecil sandy clay loam (member of the clayey kaolinitic

Table 1. Characteristics of two sources of municipal sewage sludges.

	Municipality	
Characteristics	Residential	Industrial
Solids (%)	23.2	20.5
pH	5.4	5.6
N (%)	2.5	2.3
P (%)	1.33	0.82
K (%)	0.07	0.12
Ca (%)	1.58	1.12
Mg (%)	0.11	0.12
Cd (ppm)	20	150
Cr (ppm)	360	1,500
Cu (ppm)	350	600
Mn (ppm)	375	1,000
Ni (ppm)	49	200
Pb (ppm)	450	3,000
Zn (ppm)	2,000	10,000

thermic family of Typic Hapludults) were limed according to soil tests, fertilized as above, and tilled with a rotary tiller to produce a fine seedbed. The area was raked and dragged to level the surface. Seed of tall fescue (300 kg/ha) and Kentucky bluegrass (*Poa pratensis* L.) (90 kg/ha) were spread on the surface of the appropriate plots and the netting to be tested was then placed on the soil surface. A layer of soil, approximately 0.5 cm, was spread with a golf green topdressing machine and compacted with a hand-pulled roller. Ten to 25% of the net was still exposed after this treatment. Visual cover estimations were made periodically. Sod was harvested using a 30-cm wide sod cutter, cutting a 2-cm thick sod. Segments approximately 30 cm long, which did not have visible defects, were removed for sod strength and stretch testing.

Sod strength measurements were made using a modification of a procedure developed by Rieke et al. (5). These tests were made by clamping sod pieces securely at both ends with a 14-cm length of sod exposed to the pull. One end of the sod was then retracted at the rate of 10 cm/min on an Instron material tester. The break point was considered to be the point at which a rapid decline in tension was registered (Fig. 1). Stretch was measured from the point at which the sod piece was pulled taut to the

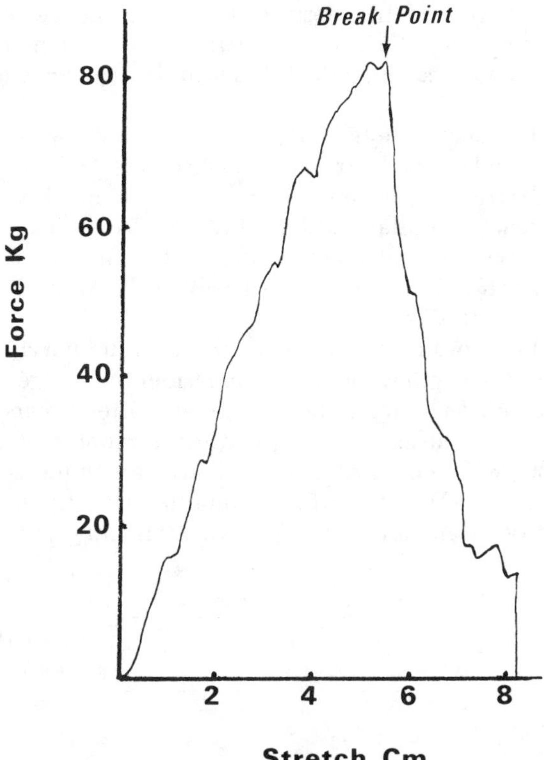

Fig. 1. Recorder graph from Instron Materials Testing Machine showing characteristic of stretch and break of tall fescue sod grown with plastic netting.

point of break. The tension was always exerted in the direction of sod cutting to insure a uniform width and uniform pretreatment of the sod.

Rooting ability was measured by cutting plugs of 5 or 10 cm diam and trimming them to uniform thickness. These plugs were placed on moist sand in the greenhouse or growth chamber. The number and length of the roots in the sand were determined at specific times. The time varied with the species and the environmental conditions.

RESULTS AND DISCUSSION

Warm-Season Turfgrasses.

The three cultivars of warm-season grasses used in this test; Tifway bermudagrass, Emerald zoysiagrass, and centipedegrass, were propagated vegetatively. They were used only with sewage sludge. Zoysiagrass and centipedegrass failed to produce a 50% cover on either sludge in one growing season. A previous study (2) found that the inhibition of root formation on sprigs was much greater in centipedegrass and zoysiagrass than in bermudagrass. This inhibition was apparently too severe to be overcome by any benefits derived from the sludge substrate. The bermudagrass achieved 85% sod cover in 5 weeks when grown on the R sludge, while the sod cover on the I sludge and on the soil was estimated at 50%.

The sod strength, tested after 5 months by the uniform rate of stretching method on the Instron machine, was 18 kg when grown on the R sludge. The strength increased to 29 kg after 10 months. Sod grown on the I sludge reacted similarly at both testing periods (Table 2). In a preliminary study using sand slowly poured into a bucket as the source of force, a 2-month-old sod grown on R sludge broke at 12 kg, but at 5 months increased to 17 kg.

The addition of lime or lime with K and N did not improve the rate of spread or sod strength when grown on residential sludge. No visible difference could be seen between these treatments after 3 years of growth.

The sod had sufficient strength after 2 months of growth to be handled in 30- × 60-cm blocks, which is a common method of handling bermudagrass sod (1). The sod at 5 months was strong enough to be handled by most, if not all, methods used. While it is not good cultural or

Table 2. Sod strength† of Tifway bermudagrass as affected by age.

	June planting	July planting	
Sod age	R-sludge	R sludge	I sludge
	kg		
2 months	12	--	--
5 months	17	18	16
10 months	--	29	32

† Force necessary to break a 30-cm wide strip of sod when stretched at the rate of 10 cm/min.

economic practice to hold sod for a period of years, the sod on the sludge has been growing for over 3 years without any supplemental fertilizer and still has excellent appearance qualities.

Cool-Season Turfgrasses

In a preliminary trial with Kentucky bluegrass planted vegetatively on soil 2 seasons were required to produce a satisfactory cover because the periods of optimum growth were short. Neither Kentucky bluegrass nor tall fescue produced a satisfactory turf when seeded on sewage sludge. Emergence was poor and the plants that did emerge were not vigorous. Some tall fescue seedlings were able to grow on this substrate. This indicates that a strain for use on a sludge could be selected if the demand existed.

Even when planted in well-fertilized soil, the Kentucky bluegrass was too slow in forming a good sod to be considered as a quick sod crop. Tall fescue produced excellent turf in one season, but did not have enough sod strength when harvested to be handled satisfactorily. Hurley (4) noted this same characteristic in red fescue (*Festuca rubra* L.).

When tall fescue was planted on 22 October in plots with 5-mm mesh plastic netting a satisfactory sod was formed in 7 weeks (Table 3). Grass planted in September would be expected to establish more rapidly. The sod without net grown for this period could not be lifted in a 30-cm square to be tested. The plastic net when tested alone broke at 34 kg. The sod grown on a single layer of netting broke at 45 kg of force. A series of samples which had a double layer of netting required 75 kg of force to break. These results show an interaction of roots with the net to produce a strong sod. The strength of the sod alone was essentially 0. Additional root growth yielded a sod on the control plots that could be moved (Table 3), but it still was not satisfactory for handling. Again, the strength of the sod on the net was appreciably greater than that of the sod without net.

Tall fescue was planted in the early spring (12 Feb. 1976) and harvested as sod 12 weeks later (6 May). Much of this period favored tall fescue growth and the sod, when replanted and watered adequately, produced a good turf without undue stress. Sod which was planted on the 5-mm mesh had a break point at 56 kg. The net alone broke at 34 kg. Sod produced on net with a large mesh (20 × 25 mm) with a strength of 42 kg also broke at 56 kg. The sod on the small mesh was 22 kg stronger than the

Table 3. Sod strength† of tall fescue with and without reinforcing net.

	Sod age	
	7 weeks	15 weeks
Sod without net	0	8
Sod with net	45	54
5-cm mesh net without sod	34	34

† Force necessary to break a 30-cm wide strip of sod when stretched at the rate of 10 cm/min.

Table 4. The effect of sod age on the number and length of roots formed on 5-cm plugs of sod transplanted on 1 May.

Date planted	Root characteristics		
	No.	Total length	Avg. length
		cm	
13 Sept.	3.2	5.0	0.8
4 Nov.	6.8	14.4	1.7
2 Feb.	7.6	16.6	2.1

net alone while the increase with large mesh was only 14 kg. This would indicate that the small mesh was more efficient in intertwining with the roots to increase sod strength.

The tall fescue sod at this planting on the small netting had the same strength as that planted in fall (about 4 months earlier) and harvested 1 month earlier. This was attributed to the poor growing conditions in December and January.

The amount of stretch before the sod begins to break is of some interest. Tall fescue sod grown on either net stretched approximately 30% before breaking, while the sod on soil alone stretched only 20%. Both nets also stretched 30% before the major break occurred. These data resulted from slowly stretched sod. In actual handling there probably would be considerable difference due to various rates of pull.

In addition to making the production of sod on order possible, the net method permits younger sod that should have better rooting characteristics than older sod to be used (3). The data in Table 4 indicate that this is true. The period between 4 November and 14 February was much colder than average for this region so that the 4 November planting did not advance beyond the seedling stage by 14 February. The two younger sods produced twice as many roots when transplanted onto a sand substrate and the average root length was double that of the older sod. This difference also showed in lack of stress symptoms when young sod from these studies was transplanted in the field.

The use of netting for production of tall fescue sod will make the production of this sod possible in Georgia and permit production on order. Costs can be reduced by producing for specific needs. With equipment now available, this is perhaps the only feasible method of producing tall fescue sod in the Piedmont area of southeastern U.S.

LITERATURE CITED

1. Beard, James B. 1973. Turfgrass: Science and culture. Prentice-Hall, Inc., Englewood Cliffs, N.J.
2. Burns, R. E., and F. C. Boswell. 1976. Effect of municipal sewage sludge on rooting of grass cuttings. Agron. J. 68:382–384.
3. Dunn, J. H., and R. E. Engel. 1971. Effect of defoliation and root pruning on early root growth from Merion Kentucky bluegrass sod and seedlings. Agron. J. 63:659–663.
4. Hurley, R. H., and C. R. Skogley. 1975. Evaluation of Kentucky bluegrass and red fescue cultivars for sod production. Agron. J. 67:79–82.
5. Rieke, P. E., J. B. Beard, and C. M. Hansen. 1968. A technique to measure sod strength for use in sod production studies. 1968 Agron. Abstr. p. 60.

Chapter 43

Effect of Cultural Factors on Tall Fescue-Kentucky Bluegrass Sod Quality and Botanical Composition[1]

J. R. HALL III

ABSTRACT

Two field experiments were conducted on a Beltsville loam soil (fine loamy mixed mesic typic fragiudult) in Fairland, Md. to study the effect of mowing height, N timing, seeding date, and N level upon botanical composition, sod strength, sod transplant rooting strength, and the number of roots and rhizomes in sod seeded to 90% certified 'Kentucky-31' tall fescue (*Festuca arundinacea* Schreb.)—10% certified common Kentucky bluegrass (*Poa pratensis* L.). The mowing height × N timing study was conducted from 1972 to 1976 and the seeding date × N level study from 1973 to 1976. All plots were harvested as sod at maturity and transplanted on a prepared site to simulate normal harvesting and installation procedures. Plant composition was determined by point quadrant technique.

A 2.5-cm mowing height reduced tall fescue content 15% ($P < 2.5\%$) at harvest when compared with the 7.5-cm mowing height. Mowing height had no effect upon sod strength or sod transplant rooting.

Split N applications applied from February to May, providing a total of 146 kg N/ha, reduced tall fescue populations 21% ($P < 0.5\%$) when compared with equivalent fall applications. Sod strength was not affected by N timing. Nitrogen timing treatments which supplied 73 kg N/ha within 90 days of harvesting significantly increased sod transplant rooting strength. Fall application of N significantly reduced smooth crabgrass [*Digitaria ischaemum* (Schreb) Schreb. ex Muhl.] invasion at the 2.5-cm mowing height when compared with spring fertilization.

August through September and March through April seeding dates increased the tall fescue content of harvested sod an average of 23% when compared with October and November seeding dates ($P < 5\%$). Sod transplant root strength was generally highest in treatments with the greatest tall fescue content. Annual rates of maintenance fertilization, providing 73.2 to 219.6 kg N/ha, did not affect tall fescue content at harvest. High N levels reduced sod strength 21 to 24%, depending on the time of sampling, when compared to low N treatments. High N levels increased sod transplant root strength 17% ($P < 0.5\%$) when compared with low N levels. Sod cutting depths of 1.9 and 3.8 cm did not significantly influence botanical composition.

Additional index words: **Mowing height, N timing, Date of seeding, Sod strength, Sod transplant rooting.**

[1] Approved as Scientific Article No. A2348 and Contribution No. 5358 of the Maryland Agric. Exp. Stn., Dep. of Agronomy, Univ. of Maryland, College Park, MD 20740, USA.

INTRODUCTION

Approximately 680 ha of 90% 'Kentucky-31' tall fescue (*Festuca arundinacea* Schreb.) + 10% common Kentucky bluegrass (*Poa pratensis* L.) sod was grown for sale in Maryland and Virginia during 1973. Tall fescue and tall fescue + Kentucky bluegrass polystands have been popular in the mid-Atlantic region because of their ability to provide medium quality turf over a wide range of biotic, edaphic, and climatic conditions. The Kentucky bluegrass component has been considered essential to provide the sod strength necessary for harvest. In commercial sod production, it has been difficult in certain situations to maintain adequate stands of tall fescue in tall fescue + Kentucky bluegrass polystands at the time of sod harvest. The improved cultivars of Kentucky bluegrass have not performed well with tall fescue because of their tendency to quickly dominate the stand and speed up the clumping of the tall fescue. Observations by Juska et al. (3) indicated that tall fescue in polystands with Kentucky bluegrass tended to clump more than tall fescue alone. This clumping severely reduces the turfgrass quality of a polystand as well as its commercial value.

Very little research has been conducted on tall fescue + Kentucky bluegrass polystands maintained as lawn turf or grown for commercial sod production. Juska et al. (3) indicated that 75 to 25% tall fescue + Kentucky bluegrass seed mixtures (weight basis) grown under mowing heights of 7.5 cm tended to exhibit increased Kentucky bluegrass content and suggested that Kentucky bluegrass might eventually become the main component.

This research was conducted to examine the effects of mowing height, N timing, N rate, and seeding date upon plant composition, sod strength, sod transplant rooting, number of roots and rhizomes, and the turfgrass quality of a polystand seeded to 90% Kentucky-31 tall fescue + 10% common Kentucky bluegrass.

MATERIALS AND METHODS

Mowing Height and Nitrogen Timing Study

The experiment was conducted on a Beltsville loam soil (fine loamy mixed mesic typic fragiudult) (34% sand, 42% silt, 24% clay). The initial soil test indicated a pH of 6.5, Bray P (P_1) of 416 kg P/ha, (1*N* NH_4OAC) exchangeable K of 215 kg K/ha, and exchangeable Mg of 251 kg Mg/ha. The plots were seeded on 3 Oct. 1972 to 244 kg/ha Certified Kentucky-31 tall fescue and 27.1 kg/ha of South Dakota Certified Kentucky bluegrass (90% tall fescue + 10% Kentucky bluegrass). Seventy-three kilograms N/ha from NH_4NO_3, 43 kg P/ha, and 81 kg K/ha were raked into the surface at the time of seeding. The P and K applications were repeated on 31

May 1973 and 28 Oct. 1975. Mowing heights of 2.5, 5.0, and 7.5 cm were imposed on 1 Mar. 1973. Plots were cut with a reel mower. Broadleaf weed control was provided on 27 Mar. 1973 with a combination of 1.1 kg/ha 2,4-dichlorophenoxy acetic acid (2,4-D) plus 0.55 kg/ha 2-(2,4,5-trichlorophenoxy)propionic acid (silvex) and on 19 Oct. 1973 with 1.7 kg/ha 2-(2-methyl-4-chlorophenoxy) propionic acid (MCPP). Nitrogen timing treatments (See Table 2) were initiated on 8 Dec. 1972 and continued throughout the study. Each N timing treatment received 146 kg N/ha annually, one half of this amount was applied in each of the 2 time periods noted.

Plant counts were made with a 10 point 45° angle quadrant and converted to percent. Each unit of data was obtained from averaging a minimum of 60 probe samplings. Tall fescue, Kentucky bluegrass, and weed content was recorded at all times of sampling. Broadleaf weed content never exceeded 3% of the stand in quadrant counts taken in May 1973, 1974, and 1975. The highest broadleaf weed content recorded in any plot was 6.4% in May 1976. Therefore, only tall fescue data are presented since Kentucky bluegrass content can be closely approximated by subtracting the tall fescue percentage from 100.

Sod strength was measured by a modification of the Michigan technique (6) on 22 May 1974 with a 12-volt battery-operated pulling device providing force from a constant torque P-38 Mustang flap motor. A chatillon (50 kg) highest force recording scale measuring in 500-g increments was used to determine sod strength. Sod pieces 0.3 × 0.6 m were harvested at a 1.9 ± 0.6-cm soil depth for sod strength measurement. Two sod pieces were measured per unit of data collected.

Sod transplant rooting was determined by the technique of King and Beard (4) by transplanting the harvested sod pieces into 0.3- × 0.6-m wooden trays with wire mesh bottoms and measuring the force required to lift the flats after they were rooted. Forty-three kilogram P/ha and 81 kg K/ha were disced in prior to transplanting the sod and the sod was tamped and watered as necessary. The harvested sod was transplanted into a Beltsville loam soil on 22 May 1974 and sod transplant rooting measurements were made on 12 June 1974. The remainder of the sod in the experiment was harvested 22 May 1974 and reinstalled on site to simulate field harvesting and transplanting procedures and allow observation of the effect of harvesting upon botanical composition.

Seeding Date and Nitrogen Level Study

This study was also conducted on a Beltsville loam soil, Initial soil tests indicated a pH of 6.7, Bray P (P_1) of 254 kg P/ha, (1*N* NH_4OAC) exchangeable K of 196 kg K/ha, and exchangeable Mg of 310 kg Mg/ha. Plot seeding was initiated on 13 Aug. 1973 and continued (See Table 4). Plots were seeded to 244 kg/ha Certified Kentucky-31 tall fescue and 27.1 kg/ha 'Kenblue' Kentucky bluegrass (90–10%). Forty-three kilograms P/ha and

81 kg K/ha were raked into the surface on the date of seeding. Individual plots were irrigated for 1 month following each seeding date as necessary to insure adequate moisture. Establishment and maintenance N were applied (See Table 5). On 28 Oct. 1975, 49 kg P/ha and 93 kg K/ha were applied. All plots were maintained at a 7.5-cm mowing height with a reel mower.

Plant composition, sod strength, and sod transplant rooting were measured as noted in the previous experiment. Pieces of sod were harvested on 19 May 1975, at a 1.9 ± 0.6-cm cutting depth for sod strength and sod transplant rooting measurements. Sod rooting strength was measured on 5 June 1975. The entire experiment was harvested at 1.9 cm ± 0.6 on 10 Sept. 1975 and reinstalled on site to simulate normal field harvesting and transplanting procedures. In this sod rooting study no P or K fertilizer was utilized at the time of transplanting.

Root counts conducted on 5 June 1975 were made from two 5-cm diam plugs removed at random from sod pieces. White, healthy roots longer than 0.6 cm were counted. Rhizome numbers were determined by counting exposed rhizomes on the bottom of the 0.3- × 0.6-m sod pieces after sod transplant rooting measurements had been made and the sod had been separated from the trays.

Statistical Procedures

The mowing height × N timing study was a split plot design with three replications. The main plot treatment was mowing height and N timing was the subplot treatment randomized within mowing height. Size of individual subplots was 8.3 m^2. The seeding date × N level study was also a split plot design with three replications. The main plot treatment was seeding date and the subplot treatment, randomized within seeding date, was N level. Size of individual subplots was 8.3 m^2. All analyses of variance were conducted with least squares procedures. Nonorthogonal linear contrasts and least significant differences (L.S.D.) were calcualted using standard procedures (7).

RESULTS AND DISCUSSION

Mowing Height and Nitrogen Timing Study

The production of harvestable 90% tall fescue + 10% Kentucky bluegrass sod generally requires a minimum of 18 months when fall seeded. Since all plots were cut as sod and transplanted on site 22 May 1974, the data collected after that date relate to the performance of installed 90–10 tall fescue + Kentucky bluegrass sod.

Table 1. Summary of the effect of mowing height upon tall fescue content and sod strength in sod seeded on 3 Oct. 1972 at 271 kg/ha to 90% Kentucky 31 tall fescue and 10% South Dakota Certified Kentucky bluegrass (w/w). Means are averaged over six times of N application. All plots were harvested and re-installed on site on 22 May 1974.

Mowing height	Tall fescue content				Sod strength
	May 1973	May 1974†	May 1975	May 1976	May 1974
cm	%				kg
2.5	56	37	45	46	23.5
5.0	65	42	48	50	27.6
7.5	66	52	48	50	24.3
$L.S.D._{0.05}$	N.S.	7	N.S.	N.S.	N.S.

† All counts this date were pre-harvest.

Mowing Height

The 2.5-cm mowing height produced a significant reduction (15%) in tall fescue content at harvest time (May 1974) when compared with the 7.5-cm mowing height (Table 1). One year after harvesting and reinstallation, the tall fescue content at 2.5- and 5.0-cm mowing heights increased and was not significantly lower than the 7.5-cm mowing height. Under the conditions of this study, the effect of mowing height was most critical on 18-month-old tall fescue—Kentucky bluegrass. Mowing height did not signfiicantly influence sod strength (Table 1).

Nitrogen Timing

Spring fertilization (February through May) significantly reduced tall fescue content within 18 months of seeding (Table 2). A nonorthogonal linear contrast comparing tall fescue content in fall-applied N treatments (50.8%) with total N applied from February to May (29.8%) indicated a highly significant ($P < 0.5\%$) reduction in tall fescue content with spring fertilization. Similar comparisons of tall fescue content in fall-applied N treatments (50.8%) with N applied from April through July (40.7%) showed less significance ($P < 10\%$). The decrease in tall fescue content, brought about by spring fertilization, was less noticeable at post-harvest sampling dates, however, the effect persisted and was still significant on the May 1976 sampling date. Stand reduction of tall fescue has been previously observed under pasture management where high spring N levels and infrequent mowing occurred (4).

It was suspected that late fall N fertilization would increase winterkill of tall fescue and therefore decrease tall fescue content; however, this did not occur. It appears that in the mid-Atlantic region two 73-kg N/ha applications made between September and mid-December are more effective than equivalent spring applications in maintaining adequate tall fescue populations in 90–10 tall fescue + Kentucky bluegrass sod.

Sod strength in May 1974 was not significantly influenced by N tim-

Table 2. Summary of the effect of N timing upon tall fescue content and sod strength in sod seeded to 90% Kentucky-31 tall fescue and 10% South Dakota Certified Kentucky bluegrass (w/w) at 271 kg/ha on 3 Oct. 1972. Means are averaged over three mowing heights. All plots were harvested and reinstalled on site on 22 May 1974.

	Tall fescue content				Sod strength
Nitrogen timing†	May 1973	May 1974‡	May 1975	May 1976	May 1974§
	%				kg
1–10 Oct. 20 Nov.–10 Dec.	57.2	50.7	47.8	49.4	25.5
1–10 Sept. 20 Nov.–10 Dec.	64.4	49.9	51.6	54.0	26.5
20 Feb.–10 Mar. 20 Nov.–10 Dec.	64.4	40.0	46.9	47.6	24.2
20 Feb.–10 Mar. 20 Apr.–10 May	64.9	29.8	43.0	43.1	23.9
20 Apr.–10 May 5–25 July	60.5	40.7	45.1	42.5	25.6
1–10 Sept. 1–10 oct.	61.6	52.0	47.6	55.7	24.9
L.S.D.$_{0.05}$	N.S.	7.7	N.S.	7.9	N.S.

† N applications of 73 kg N/ha from NH_4NO_3 were made during each indicated time period. A total of 146 kg N/ha was applied annually. ‡ All counts this date were preharvest.
§ A sod strength of 20 kg was considered minimal for conventional harvesting systems.

ing (Table 2). The treatment receiving N in February-March and April-May contained 70% bluegrass and 30% tall fescue and yet it did not provide significantly greater sod strength than the September-October treatment which contained 52% tall fescue and 45% Kentucky bluegrass. Apparently, in May 25% differences in Kentucky bluegrass content do not significantly increase sod strength in 90–10 tall fescue + Kentucky bluegrass sod.

Mowing Height × Nitrogen Timing Interaction

The interaction of mowing height and N timing was significant for crabgrass cover and sod transplant rooting strength (Table 3). Nitrogen timing at the lower mowing heights influenced the competitive ability of smooth crabgrass [*Digitaria ischaemum* (Schreb.) Muhl.] the most. Treatments providing all N in the fall produced considerably less crabgrass than other combinations at the 2.5-cm mowing height. The ability of N timing to reduce crabgrass competition diminished as the mowing height was raised to 7.5 cm, indicating the overriding importance of mowing height in controlling crabgrass.

Sod transplant rooting strength was significantly increased where N timing treatments required applications within 90 days of the harvesting date (Table 3). This observation has been previously made with Kentucky bluegrass sod (2). Excessive N immediately prior to harvest has created sod heating and other management problems (1).

Sod was cut at depths of 1.9 and 3.8 cm on 22 May 1974 to determine

Table 3. Sod transplant rooting and crabgrass cover of 90% Kentucky-31 tall fescue and 10% South Dakota Certified Kentucky bluegrass as effected by N timing and mowing height. Sod was seeded on 3 Oct. 1972 and harvested and transplanted on 22 May 1974.

N timing	Sod transplant rooting strength 12 June 1974				Crabgrass cover Oct. 1975‡			
	Mowing height (cm)				Mowing height (cm)			
	2.5	5.0	7.5	Mean	2.5	5.0	7.5	Mean
	kg/m²†				%			
1–10 Oct. 20 Nov–10 Dec.	606	625	692	642	52	23	0	25
1–10 Sept. 20 Nov.–10 Dec.	664	708	619	663	40	10	0	17
20 Feb.–10 Mar. 20 Nov.–10 Dec.	708	721	696	708	63	23	3	30
20 Feb.–10 Mar. 20 Apr.–10 May	769	691	769	744	67	22	0	29
20 Apr.–10 May 5–25 July	747	745	765	753	60	27	2	29
1–10 Sept. 1–10 oct.	655	635	712	668	35	12	0	15
Mean	692	688	709		53	19	1	

Sod rooting L.S.D.$_{0.05}$
Between mow height N.S.
Between N times 28
Between N times within mow 49
Between N times across mow 168

Crabgrass L.S.D.$_{0.05}$
Between mow height 3
Between N times 8
Between N times within mow 5
Between N times across mow 12

† kg/m² = kg of force required per m² of sod lifted. Sod cut with 1.9 cm soil attached.
‡ Crabgrass cover was determined by visual estimate.

if cutting depth had any effect upon botanical composition. Quadrant counts made from 29 May to 6 June 1975 indicated no significant effect on tall fescue or Kentucky bluegrass content of the sod caused by the sod cutting depth treatment.

Seeding Date and Nitrogen Level Study

The influence of variable seeding dates and N levels upon tall fescue content, sod strength, sod transplant rooting, and root and rhizome number was examined. There were no significant interactions between seeding date and N level for any variable measured in this study.

Seeding Date

Quadrant counts taken approximately 1 year after each seeding date indicated a highly significant effect of seeding date upon tall fescue content (Table 4). Seedings made after 13 Sept. 1973 showed drastic reductions in tall fescue content during the 1st year of growth. By harvest time (May 1975), the tall fescue content had decreased even further. A nonorthogonal linear contrast comparing tall fescue content in April 1975 on

Table 4. Summary of the effect of seeding date upon tall fescue content, sod strength, sod transplant rooting strength, and rhizome and root production. All sod was harvested and reinstalled on site on 10 Sept. 1975. Means are averaged over three levels of N application.

Seeding date	Tall fescue content: 1 year after seeding	Tall fescue content: Apr. 1975	Tall fescue content: June 1976	Sod strength§: Mar. 1975	Sod strength§: May 1975	Sod strength§: July 1975	Sod transplant rooting‡: 2 June 1975	Roots: 5 June 1975	Rhizomes: 5 June 1975
	%			kg			kg/m²†	no./dm²	no./m²
14 Aug. 1973	80	52	47	24.1	31.9	23.8	327	180	33
30 Aug. 1973	71	49	42	22.4	31.4	23.1	315	155	36
13 Sept. 1973	69	48	46	18.8	29.9	20.0	293	119	66
5 Oct. 1973	44	39	36	23.4	28.1	17.6	294	114	55
26 Oct. 1973	30	24	29	21.5	31.1	19.0	271	89	66
15 Nov. 1973	37	21	29	19.6	24.6	18.5	240	102	95
14 Mar. 1974	50	50	38	14.1	22.1	11.4	312	97	67
24 Apr. 1974	54	54	43	12.7	20.7	10.7	327	153	85
L.S.D.$_{0.05}$	7.7	6.5	5.7	5.7	5.0	3.2	22	49	34

† kg/m² = kg of force required per m² of sod lifted. Sod cut with 1.9 cm soil attached.
‡ Sod harvested and transplant in rooting boxes on 19 May 1975.
§ A sod strength of 20 kg was considered minimal for conventional harvesting systems.

plots seeded between 14 Aug. and 13 Sept. 1973 (50%) with those seeded between 5 Oct. and 15 Nov. 1973 (28%) indicated that early seeding caused a highly significant increase in tall fescue content ($P < 0.5\%$). Similar comparisons of tall fescue content in April 1975 between plots seeded in October 1973 (32%) and those seeded in March and April 1974 (52%) indicated a highly significant increase in tall fescue content ($P < 0.5\%$) brought about by waiting to spring seed 90–10 tall fescue + Kentucky bluegrass sod instead of seeding in October. This data suggest that 90–10 tall fescue + Kentucky bluegrass polystands not seeded by mid- to late September can suffer severe decreases in tall fescue content in the mid-Atlantic region. It also suggests that spring seeding, in lieu of October or November seeding, will provide a similar tall fescue content to the August and September seeding dates by the time of harvest.

Sod strength was measured in March, June, and July 1975. The data illustrate the effects of season of harvest and stage of maturity upon sod strength (Table 4). The decrease in sod strength associated with the July sampling date is commonly observed in commercial tall fescue sod production. Nonorthogonal linear contrasts comparing sod strength of August and September 1973 seeded plots with March and April 1974 seeded plots indicated significantly greater sod strength in the August and September seeding dates over all three times of sampling. Since tall fescue contents were similar in these sods, the differences in sod strength are probably due to maturity. The increased sod strengths noted were 3.3 kg in March ($P < 5\%$), 9.7 kg in May ($P < 0.5\%$), and 11.2 kg in July ($P < 0.5\%$). There was no significant difference in sod strength at all three times of sampling between plots seeded from 15 August to 13 September and those seeded from 5 October to 15 November. However, none of the plots seeded between 5 Oct. and 15 Nov. were considered commercially harvestable at the July 1975 harvest date. A sod strength of 20 kg was considered minimal for conventional harvesting systems. Greater sod strength occurred at all three sampling times on plots seeded between 5 October and 26 October when compared with those seeded between 14 March and 25 April. The increase in sod strengths noted were 9.0 kg in March ($P < 5\%$), 8.2 kg in May ($P < 2.5\%$), and 7.2 kg in July ($P < 0.5\%$). This increase in sod strength is likely related to the increased Kentucky bluegrass content associated with the 5 October and 26 October seeding dates.

Seeding before 13 September increased sod transplant rooting strength 17.7 kg/m^2 when compared with seeding later in the fall ($P < 2.5\%$). This apparently resulted from the higher tall fescue content in the early fall seeded sod, since there was a significant positive correlation between tall fescue content in April 1975 and sod transplant rooting strength on 2 June 1975 ($r = 0.416$, $n = 72$). The correlation between sod transplant rooting and Kentucky bluegrass content was negative ($r = -0.390$). Root counts made 5 June 1975 correlated positively ($r = 0.312$) with sod transplant rooting strength, while there was no correlation between rhizomes and sod transplant rooting. The correlation between root count and tall fescue content in April 1975 was positive ($r = 0.366$), whereas this correlation was negative ($r = -0.301$) with Kentucky bluegrass content. This suggests that tall fescue roots made the greatest contribution to sod transplant rooting.

Kentucky bluegrass rhizome counts made on 5 June 1975 correlated negatively with sod strength in March ($r = -0.396$), May ($r = -0.382$), and July ($r = -0.346$), suggesting that rhizomes play a minor role in sod strength.

Nitrogen Level

The N level did not significantly affect the tall fescue content of 90–10 tall fescue + Kentucky bluegrass sod (Table 5). High levels of spring-applied N have led to tall fescue stand reductions under forage management conditions where mowing was infrequent (4).

Sod strength was significantly decreased by the higher N levels at all three times of sampling. This suggests that 73.2 kg N/ha/year (Low N) provided adequate N for 90–10 tall fescue + Kentucky bluegrass sod under the conditions of this experiment (Table 5). Turfgrass quality ratings taken four times during the normal marketing period for this sod (1975 March to October 1975) indicated that the low N treatments did not produce acceptable turf quality and would meet with limited consumer acceptance.

Sod transplant rooting strength was highest at the medium and high N levels (Table 5). It is impossible from this data to discern if the sod transplant rooting strength was primarily derived from the most recent N application or was a result of the total effect of the annual program.

The effect of N level upon root number was not significant, however,

Table 5. The effect of level of N fertilization upon tall fescue content, sod strength, sod transplant rooting strength, and rhizome and root production. Means are averaged over eight dates of seeding.

Level of N†	Tall fescue content			Sod strength§			Sod transplant strength‡	Roots	Rhizomes
	1 year after seeding	Apr. 1975	June 1976	Mar. 1975	June 1975	July 1975	2 June 1975	5 June 1975	5 June 1975
	%			kg			kg/m²¶	no./dm²	no./m²
Low	53	44	38	22.1	30.8	20.5	267	117	48
Medium	54	42	40	19.2	28.6	18.0	302	130	63
High	55	40	38	17.4	23.1	15.6	324	132	78
$L.S.D._{0.05}$	N.S.	N.S.	N.S.	2.2	2.6	1.6	35	N.S.	16

† Low = No N at establishment and 24.4 kg N/ha in Mar., Sept., and Oct. each year; Medium = 73.2 kg N/ha at establishment and 48.8 kg N/ha in Mar., Sept., and Oct. each year; High = 146.5 kg N/ha at establishment and 73.2 kg N/ha in Mar., Sept., and Oct. each year. ‡ Sod harvested and installed in transplant rooting boxes on 19 May 1975. § A sod strength of 20 kg was considered minimal for conventional harvesting systems. ¶ kg/m² = kg of force required/m² of sod lifted. Sod cut with 1.9 cm soil attached.

there was a slight trend toward increasing root numbers with increasing N (Table 5). The high level of N application significantly increased rhizome number over the low N treatment (Table 5).

CONCLUSIONS

These data support the following conclusions relating to the growth of 90% tall fescue + 10% Kentucky bluegrass.

1) Low mowing heights reduced the tall fescue content of this polystand. Mowing height had no significant effect on sod strength.
2) Nitrogen timing significantly affected tall fescue competitiveness. Spring fertilization significantly decreased tall fescue content. Two split applications of 73 kg N/ha provided in the fall increased tall fescue competitiveness the most. Nitrogen timing did not affect sod strength. Nitrogen applications (73 kg N/ha) made within 90 days of harvest appeared to significantly increase sod transplant rooting abiltiy. At the low mowing height, fall fertilization significantly reduced smooth crabgrass competitiveness when compared with spring fertilization.
3) Sod cutting depth had no effect upon tall fescue content of reinstalled sod 1 year after harvest.
4) Late summer seedings (14 August to 15 September) and spring seedings (14 March to 24 April) yielded the highest tall fescue content at sod harvest time and also the greatest sod transplant rooting ability in June. However, the March-April seeding had marginal sod strength at the selected harvest time and would possibly require additional time to mature. The evidence suggests that tall fescue contributes more to sod transplant rooting capability in June than Kentucky bluegrass.

5) Higher N levels decreased sod strength and increased sod transplant rooting ability and rhizome number, however, no effect was observed upon tall fescue content.

LITERATURE CITED

1. Darrah, C. H., III, and A. J. Powell, Jr. 1977. Post-harvest heating and survival of sod as influenced by pre-harvest and harvest management. Agron. J. 69:283–287.
2. Dunn, J. H., and R. E. Engel. 1970. Root response of Merion Kentucky bluegrass sods to various nitrogen applications near the time of transplanting. Agron. J. 62:623–625.
3. Juska, F. V., A. A. Hanson, and A. W. Hovin. 1969. Evaluation of tall fescue, *Festuca arundinacea* Schreb., for turf in the transition zone of the United States. Agron. J. 61: 625–628.
4. King, J. W., and J. B. Beard. 1969. Measuring rooting of sodded turfs. Agron. J. 61:497–498.
5. McKee, W. H., Jr., R. H. Brown, and R. E. Blaser. 1967. Effect of clipping and nitrogen fertilization on yield stands of tall fescue. Crop Sci. 7:567–570.
6. Rieke, P. E., J. B. Beard, and C. M. Hansen. 1968. A technique to measure sod strength for use in sod production studies. Agron. Abstr. p. 60.
7. Steel, G. D., and J. H. Torrie. 1960. Principles and procedures of statistics. McGraw-Hill Book Co. Inc., New York. p. 213–220.

Chapter 44

Seedling Competition of Kentucky Bluegrass, Red Fescue, Colonial Bentgrass, and Temporary Grasses[1]

R. E. ENGEL
J. R. TROUT

ABSTRACT

Competition among turfgrass seedlings was measured in greenhouse tests between three permanent-type grasses: Kentucky bluegrass (*Poa pratensis* L.), red fescue (*Festuca rubra* L.), and colonial bentgrass (*Agrostis tenuis* Sibth.); among plants of the three permanent-type grasses and three temporary types: perennial ryegrass (*Lolium perenne* L.), Italian ryegrass (*L. multiflorum* Lam.), and redtop, (*Agrostis alba* L.); among plants of the three permanent-type grasses and perennial ryegrass at two seedling rates with the latter used as an increasing percent of the mixture by weight. The persistence of seedling competition effects were determined in a field test. In the greenhouse the seedings were made in 12.7-cm diam pots. After 12 weeks, red fescue was consistently more competitive than colonial bentgrass or Kentucky bluegrass. Ryegrass competition severely suppressed size and total shoot weight of the permanent-type turfgrasses. Competition increased with increases in content and seeding rate of the ryegrass in the mixture. Redtop, on an equal number of seed basis, was far less competitive than both ryegrasses. In most comparisons competition severely depressed Kentucky bluegrass, but its development was good when the seeding rate was under 20 seeds/6.5 cm^2. In a field test, the competition of perennial ryegrass delayed Kentucky bluegrass dominance in the turf sward until the fourth season.

Additional index words: Temporary grass, Permanent-type grass, Seed mixture, Kentucky bluegrass, Red fescue, Colonial bentgrass, Ryegrass, Redtop, Seedling competition.

INTRODUCTION

Turfgrass mixtures are formulated to meet the variety of conditions occurring on turfgrass areas that include stress from moisture, fertility, light, heat, erosion, pests, and mowing. Further complication is added because species vary in germination rate and seedling vigor which can interfere with the desired species balance. Growers sow much larger quantities of seed than needed to obtain a grass cover which may change the species content. Also, simpler seed mixtures are desirable if they suffice. Rapid establishment of the turf produced by the seed mixture and cost of the seed mixture have influenced the composition of past mixtures.

---

[1] A contribution from the Soils and Crops Dep. and Statistics and Computer Science, Rutgers Univ., New Brunswick, NJ 08903, USA.

The primary purpose of this study was to determine: (i) seedling competitiveness among the three permanent types of grasses: Kentucky bluegrass (*Poa pratensis* L.), red fescue (*Festuca rubra* L.), and colonial bentgrass (*Agrostis tenuis* Sibth.); (ii) the comparative seedling influence of the temporary species of perennial ryegrass (*Lolium perenne* L.), Italian ryegrass (*L. multiflorum* Lam.), and redtop (*Agrostis alba* Sibth.); (iii) seedling competition of the permanent types vs. temporary grasses. Also, the effect of seeding rate and percentage of temporary grasses on development of mature turf were studied.

Serious competition of seedling turfgrass species has been accepted by many and shown in research studies. Lapp (3) demonstrated that heavy seeding of the temporary species suppressed the permanent-type species. This was followed by a sudden loss of the temporary types and weed invasion as the turf cover thinned. Also, Erdman and Harrison (1) found that domestic ryegrass (*L. perenne* and *L. multiflorum* and redtop in a polystand seriously reduced the total weight of Kentucky bluegrass and chewings fescue (*F. rubra* L. var. *commutata*). Madison (4) showed that high rates of seeding initially produce dense plant populations that decrease in number as the turf matures. Juska and Hanson (2) reported little, if any, advantage for a mixture if a single species can maintain consistently good turf.

Mixtures become more advantageous where two or more individual grass species that have serious deficiencies are complimentary to each other. Despite the value of vigorous seedling growth of temporary grasses, some turfgrass specialists have urged general restrictions on their use. Determining effects of seedling competition on the individual plant will give more understanding to the formulation of seed mixtures.

MATERIALS AND METHODS

Greenhouse tests were used to measure the effects of turfgrass seedling competition in terms of numbers of shoots, largest seedlings, and total weight of shoot growth. The permanent-type grasses in all mixtures were: a common Kentucky bluegrass, 'Pennlawn' red fescue, and a market source of colonial bentgrass. They were included in equal numbers in all combinations of two species and as a group of the three species at seeding rates of 20, 40, and 60 seeds/6.5 cm^2 (1 square inch). These same grasses were seeded in a 3:3:2 ratio by number with one part of a temporary grass, respectively, at rates of 10, 20, 40, and 60 seeds/6.5 cm^2. Perennial ryegrass, Italian ryegrass, and redtop were used as temporary grasses. Also, the same ratio of Kentucky bluegrass, red fescue, and colonial bentgrass seeds was used with an increasing percentage by weight of perennial ryegrass (13, 24, and 39%) at seeding rates of 20 and 40 seeds/6.5 cm^2.

These greenhouse seedings were made in 12.7-cm diam pots that contained a moderately fertile sandy-loam soil that received 48 kg N/ha from a 1:2:1 ratio fertilizer. In both tests, shoot counts were made after 12 weeks on the unclipped cultures. Seedling samples, 6.2 cm^2, were removed from the center of each pot to facilitate determination of the two largest plants of each species and total weight of shoots produced. Figures or tables on greenhouse tests that include Italian ryegrass are based on one test of four replications. All others are based on two separate tests of four and three replications. Low fertility was used to avoid excessive vigor. A few plants had tillered at harvest.

A field test was established with a mixture of Kentucky bluegrass, colonial bentgrass, and perennial ryegrass seeded in a weight ratio of 10:2:3, respectively. It was seeded at five rates from 48 to 242 kg/ha in September. The test area was mowed at 3.8 cm and received 97 kg N/ha from an N–P–K fertilizer per year. Species shoot counts were taken with a point quadrat at the end of the first, second, and fourth seasons.

The data were analyzed by analysis of variance. This procedure was supplemented with the least significant difference procedure to allow for individual comparisons among the means of interest.

RESULTS AND DISCUSSION

Greenhouse Tests

Red fescue was the dominant species after 12 weeks when seeded in equal numbers with Kentucky bluegrass and colonial bentgrass. It was consistently superior in all comparisons for weight of the largest plants, number of shoots, and total weight produced (Fig. 1, 2, 3).

Kentucky bluegrass was the weak competitor of the three species (Fig. 1, 2, 3). It consistently ranked below red fescue in terms of the three size measurements and it ranked below bentgrass except for a tendency to compete with bentgrass in weight of large plants. Weakness of Kentucky bluegrass seedling development jeopardized this species in the presence of red fescue and colonial bentgrass without the competition of the fast growing temporary grasses. These results (i) show that all seedlings compete and (ii) emphasizes the weakness of Kentucky bluegrass seedlings. Both slower germination and slower growth are considered the basis for seedling weakness of Kentucky bluegrass.

The 3:3:2 ratio by number of Kentucky bluegrass, red fescue, and colonial bentgrass used in seed mixtures with equal numbers of perennial ryegrass or redtop seed (24 and 1.2% by weight) and seeded at a rate of 10, 20, 40, and 60 seeds/6.5 cm^2 showed that increased amounts of ryegrass seed severely depressed the permanent-type grasses (Fig. 4, 5, 6, 7). With an increased rate of seeding the mixture, perennial ryegrass decreased large plant size of Kentucky bluegrass, red fescue, and colonial bentgrass. The decreases were 74, 54, and 79%, respectively, for the 60-seed rate, as compared with the 10-seed rate (Fig. 4). With the same comparisons of seed mixtures containing perennial ryegrass, the 10-seed rate decreased total weight of shoot growth from the permanent-type grasses

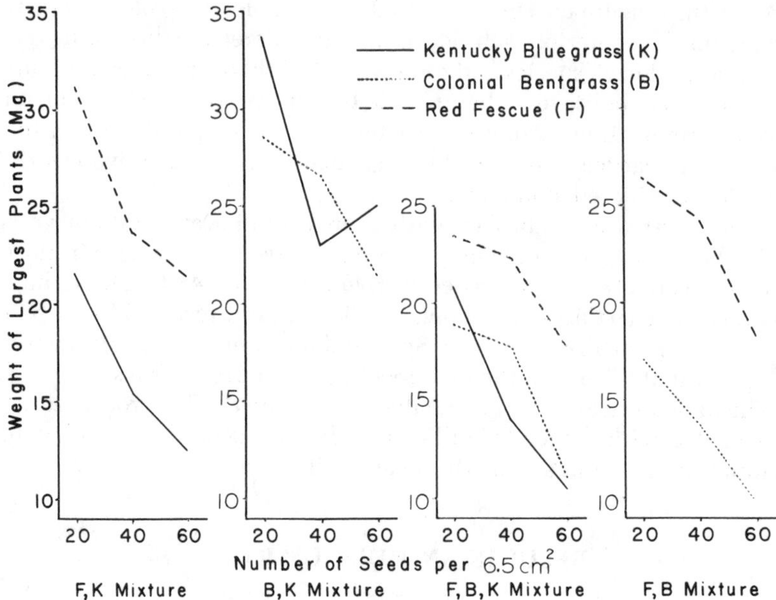

Fig. 1. Weight of largest seedling plants of Kentucky bluegrass, red fescue, and colonial bentgrass when grown in competition in two greenhouse tests for 12 weeks. The L.S.D. values for the respective grasses at 0.05 are: 9; 7; 7.

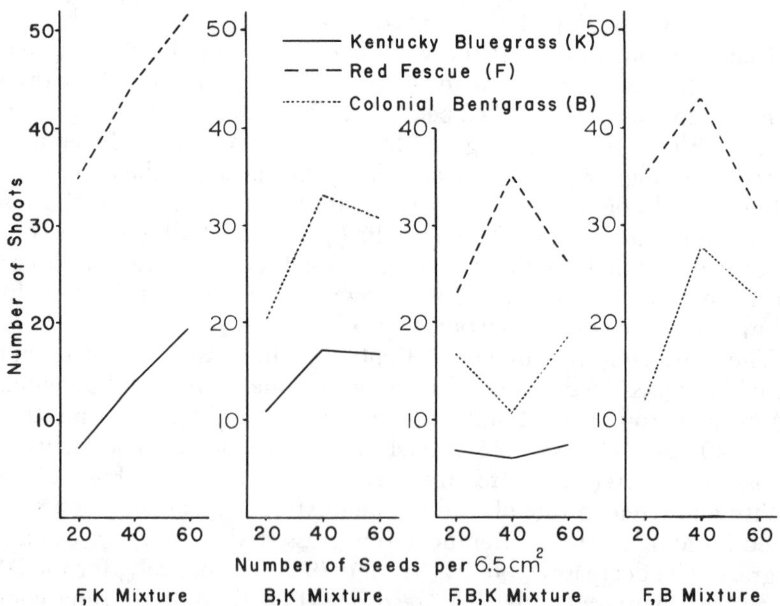

Fig. 2. The number of shoots of seedling plants of Kentucky bluegrass, red fescue, and colonial bentgrass per 6.5 cm^2 when grown in two greenhouse tests for 12 weeks. The L.S.D. values for the respective grasses at 0.05 are: 7; 14; 15.

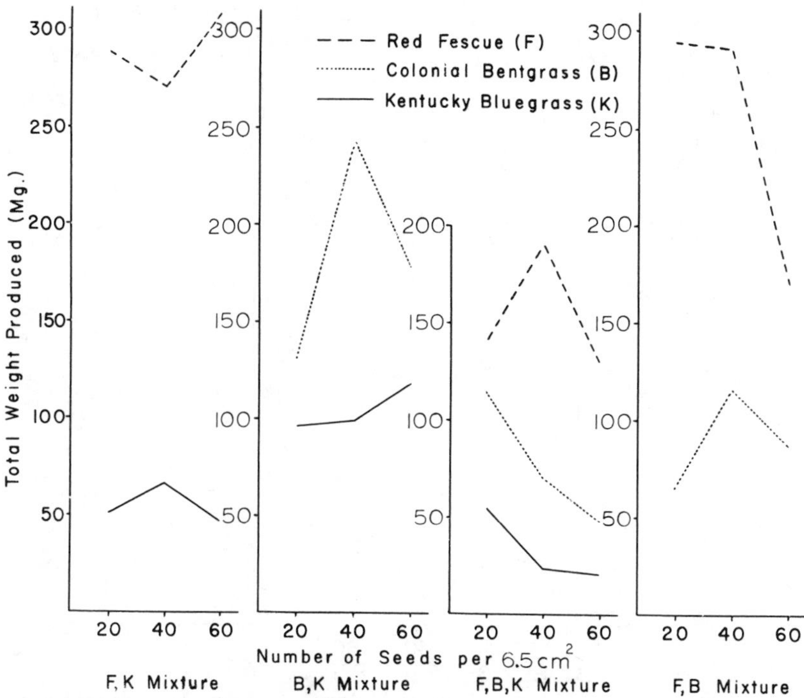

Fig. 3. Total weight of seedling shoots of Kentucky bluegrass, red fescue, and colonial bentgrass per 6.5 cm² when grown in two greenhouse tests for 12 weeks. The L.S.D. values for the respective grasses at 0.05 are: 43; 111; 94.

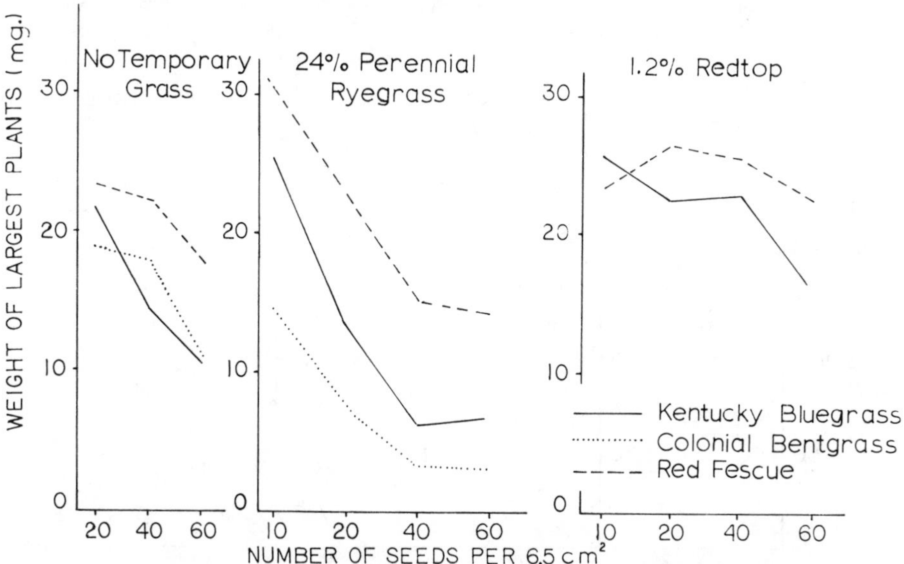

Fig. 4. Weight of largest seedling plants of Kentucky bluegrass, red fescue, and colonial bentgrass when grown in competition with perennial ryegrass or redtop in two greenhouse tests for 12 weeks. The L.S.D. values for the respective grasses at 0.05 are: 8; 14; 5.

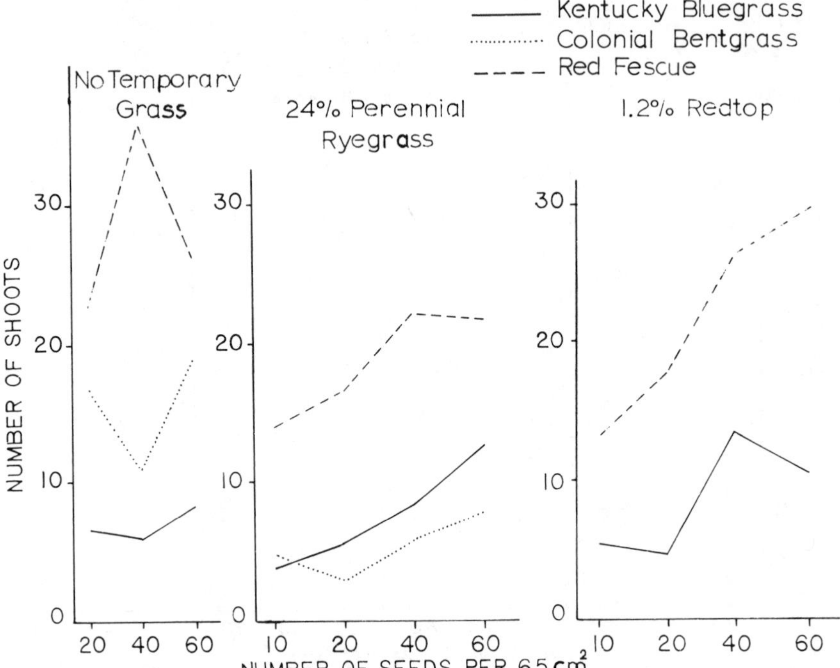

Fig. 5. Number of seedling shoots of Kentucky bluegrass, red fescue, and colonial bentgrass in 6.5 cm² when grown in competition with perennial ryegrass or redtop in two greenhouse tests for 12 weeks. The L.S.D. values for the respective grasses at 0.05 are: 4; 11; 4.

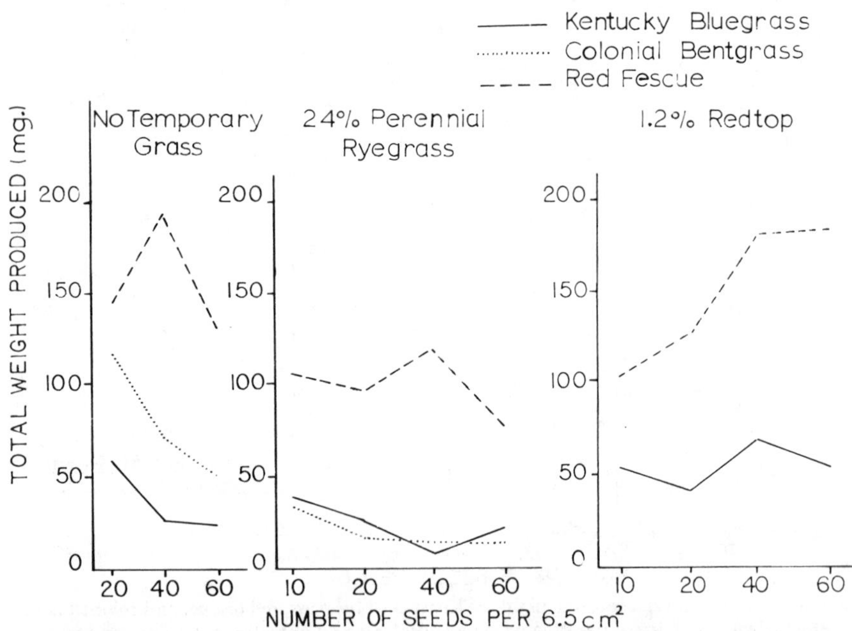

Fig. 6. Total weight of seedling shoots of Kentucky bluegrass, red fescue, and colonial bentgrass per 6.5 cm² grown in competition with perennial ryegrass or redtop in two greenhouse tests for 12 weeks. The L.S.D. values for the respective grasses at 0.05 are: 20; 76; 27.

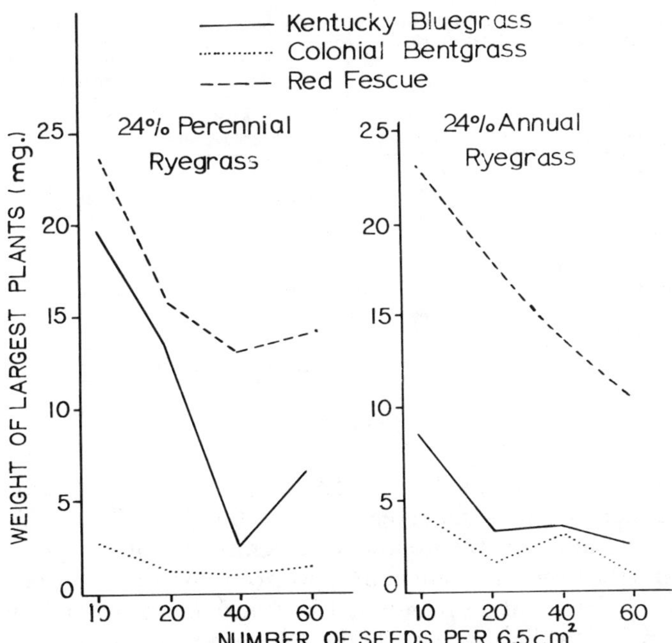

Fig. 7. The effects of perennial and Italian ryegrass competition on the weight of two large plants of Kentucky bluegrass, red fescue, and colonial bentgrass grown from seed in a greenhouse test for 12 weeks. The L.S.D. values for the respective grasses at 0.05 are: 8; 14; 5.

and the 60-seed rate appeared to cause a further decrease (Fig. 6). While there were significant increases in number of shoots with increased rates of seeding, the increases were far below the proportions of seed sown (Fig. 5). Italian ryegrass competition was equally severe, if not greater than that of perennial ryegrass (Fig. 7; Tables 1, 2).

Redtop, when compared with perennial ryegrass on an equal number of seed basis in the mixture, showed little depression of the permanent-type grasses. While this grass has been considered highly competitive in polystands, these data suggest that this concept developed because excessive numbers of this small seed were sown with the commonly used percentages of 10% or more.

Seeding a mixture of Kentucky bluegrass, red fescue, and colonial bentgrass with increasing percentages of perennial ryegrass commonly produced large decreases in plant size with insignificant change in shoot numbers (Fig. 8; Tables 3, 4). Suppression of the permanent-type grasses with increasing percentages of perennial ryegrass is shown at the 20-seed rate. This is less apparent at the 40-seed rate because severe ryegrass competition occurred in polystands with the lowest ryegrass content. Competition from ryegrass in these polystands was a function of the total amount of ryegrass sown per unit area. This suggests that, in practice, the total amount of ryegrass on a given area must be limited to permit optimum development of other species of seedlings.

Table 1. The number of shoots of Kentucky bluegrass, red fescue, and colonial bentgrass developing in polystands with perennial and Italian ryegrass seeded at several rates in the greenhouse.

Temporary grass used	No. of seeds/ 6.5 cm	No. of shoots/6.5 cm² Kentucky bluegrass	Red fescue	Colonial bentgrass
Perennial ryegrass	10	3.5	22	0.3
Italian ryegrass	10	1.5	20	1.8
Perennial ryegrass	20	7.8	21	0.5
Italian ryegrass	20	4.0	18	1.3
Perennial ryegrass	40	2.5	18	0.8
Italian ryegrass	40	8.3	23	3.3
Perennial ryegrass	60	8.8	21	1.5
Italian ryegrass	60	3.3	25	1.0
L.S.D. 0.05		5	NS	3

Field Test

After 1 year in the field test, increasing the seeding rate from 48 to 242 kg/ha increased perennial ryegrass from 33 to 58% (Fig. 9). With this increase in seeding rate, the Kentucky bluegrass content dropped from 22 to 12% and the bentgrass content dropped from 30 to 20%. After 2 years, perennial ryegrass had decreased and Kentucky bluegrass had increased as compared with the 1st year. By the 4th year Kentucky bluegrass was

Table 2. The total shoot weights of Kentucky bluegrass, red fescue and colonial bentgrass in polystands with perennial and Italian ryegrass seeded at several rates in the greenhouse.

Temporary grass used	No. of seed/ 6.5 cm	Total wt. Kentucky bluegrass	Red fescue	Colonial bentgrass
		mg/6.5 cm²		
Perennial ryegrass	10	28	159	1.4
Italian ryegrass	10	11	118	6.3
Perennial ryegrass	20	33	108	0.6
Italian ryegrass	20	7	82	1.5
Perennial ryegrass	40	4	89	1.2
Italian ryegrass	40	9	93	4.2
Perennial ryegrass	60	13	76	1.3
Italian ryegrass	60	3	81	0.7
L.S.D. 0.05		23	NS	NS

Table 3. The number of shoots of Kentucky bluegrass, red fescue, and colonial bentgrass developing from seed mixtures at two seeding rates (SR) with perennial ryegrass at varied percentages of the mixture.

Quantity of ryegrass in mixture	No. of shoots/6.5 cm² Kentucky bluegrass		Red fescue		Colonial bentgrass	
%	SR20	SR40	SR20	SR40	SR20	SR40
0	6	5	32	36	7	3
13	9	6	31	22	3	2
24	8	3	21	18	1	1
39	4	7	15	22	3	2
L.S.D. 0.05	NS		NS		NS	

Table 4. Total weight of shoots of Kentucky bluegrass, red fescue, and colonial bentgrass developing from seed mixtures at two seeding rates (SR) with perennial ryegrass at varied percentages of the mixture.

Quantity of ryegrass in mixtures	Total shoot wt.					
	Kentucky bluegrass		Red fescue		Colonial bentgrass	
%	mg					
	SR20	SR40	SR20	SR40	SR20	SR40
0	36	18	181	211	40	15
13	38	16	169	100	14	4
24	33	4	108	89	1	1
39	11	12	71	87	4	1
L.S.D. 0.05	NS		88		13	

approximately 50% of the sward, while the ryegrass had decreased below 5%. The F values for ryegrass content at differing seeding rates were significant at 0.01 in the 1st year, at 0.05 in the 2nd year, and not significant in the 4th year. This agrees with the work of Niehaus (5) which showed that seedings shifted from common-type perennial ryegrass to Kentucky bluegrass in the 2nd year. Since it took four seasons for Kentucky bluegrass to become dominant in the turf stand, the use of any competing species can seriously delay the major Kentucky bluegrass component for a period of several years. This deterred development of Kentucky bluegrass is easily explained by the suppression in size development of this slow developing grass, as the greenhouse studies show. Increased rates of seeding makes the competition more intense and damaging.

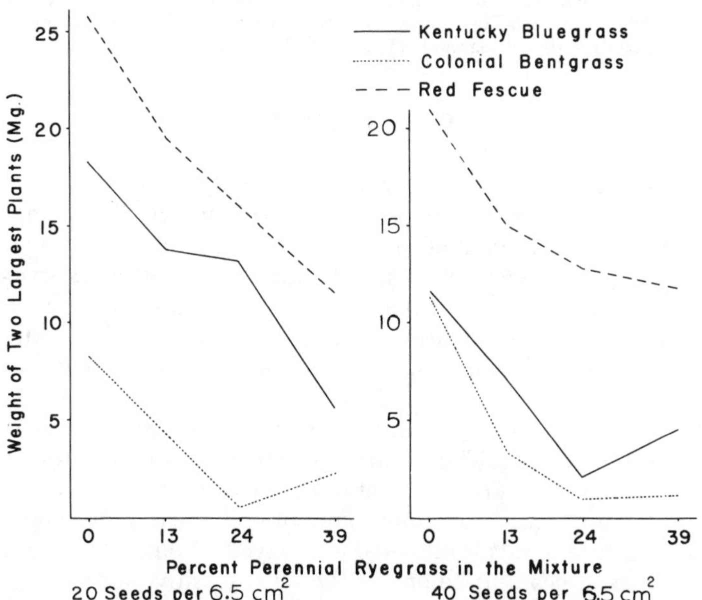

Fig. 8. Weight of the largest plants of Kentucky bluegrass, red fescue, and colonial bentgrass developing from seed mixtures at two seeding rates (SR) with perennial ryegrass at varied percentage of the mixture. The L.S.D. values for the respective grasses at 0.05 are: 10; 9; 5.

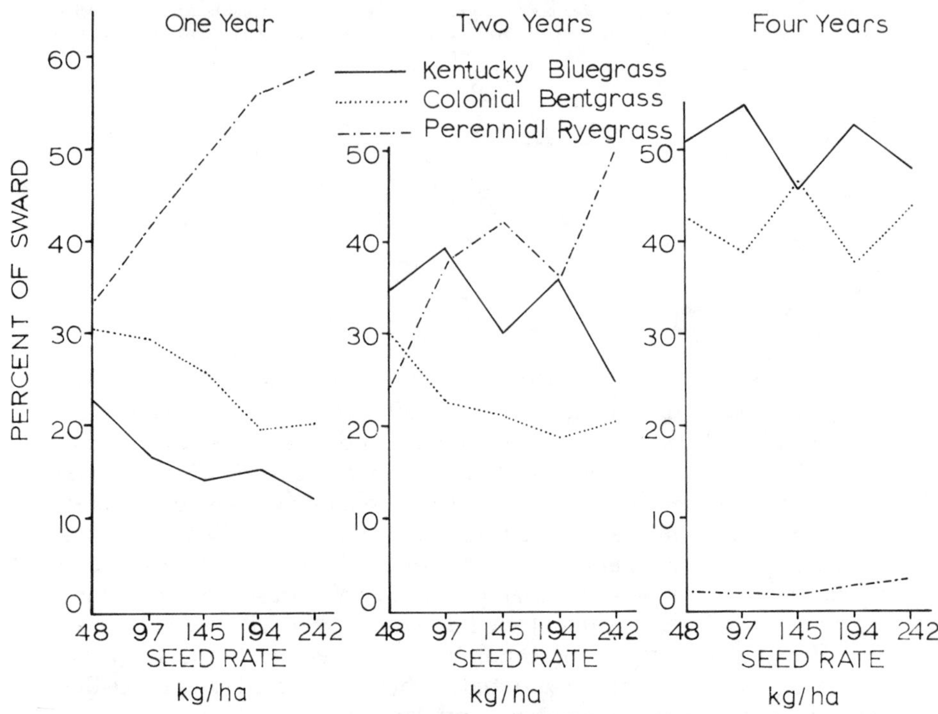

Fig. 9. The effect of perennial ryegrass on Kentucky bluegrass and colonial bentgrass in a seed mixture at five seeding rates ranging from 48 to 242 kg/ha in field grown turf at 3.8 cm mowing height for 4 years. The F values for ryegrass content at different seeding rates were significant at 0.01 in the 1st year and at 0.05 in the 2nd year.

CONCLUSIONS

Seedlings of Kentucky bluegrass, red fescue, and colonial bentgrass compete with themselves during seedling development. This competition was shown by measurement of the largest plants, total shoot growth, and number of shoots for each species. Both Italian and perennial ryegrasses were very competitive to the three permanent-type grasses. Perennial ryegrass was slightly less competitive than Italian ryegrass, while redtop was a weak competitor when compared with ryegrasses on an equal number of seed basis.

The ryegrasses suppressed the slower growing grasses more when rate of seeding was increased. This occurred whether the source of the increase came from a higher ryegrass content of the mixture or an increased seeding rate of the mixture. As seedling competition increases, development of larger and mature plants is hindered or delayed. Prompt development of large seedlings appears to be one of the most sensitive measurements of competition.

Total shoot growth and the number of shoots developing for each species, especially of the slower growing types, showed marked reduction when seedling competition increased. The study shows the futility of high rates of seeding for the attempted purpose of better establishment.

LITERATURE CITED

1. Erdman, M. H., and C. M. Harrison. 1947. The influence of domestic ryegrass and redtop upon the growth of Kentucky bluegrass and chewings fescue in lawn turf mixtures. J. Am. Soc. Agron. 39:682–689.
2. Juska, F. V., and A. A. Hanson. 1959. Evaluation of cool-season turfgrasses alone and in mixtures. Agron. J. 51:597–600.
3. Lapp, W. S. 1943. A study of factors affecting the growth of lawn grasses. Proc. Penn. Acad. Sci. 17:117–148.
4. Madison, J. H. 1966. Optimum rates of seeding turfgrass. Agron. J. 58:441–443.
5. Niehaus, Merle H. 1976. Effect of cultivar, seeding rate and nitrogen fertilization on Kentucky bluegrass-perennial ryegrass mixtures. Agron. J. 68:955–957.

Chapter 45

Research into the Establishment of Roadside Embankments[1]

P. HENENSAL
G. ARNAL
J. PUIG

ABSTRACT

Three years of research by the Laboratories des Ponts et Chaussees in France on turfing roadside embankments indicated that the most suitable grasses for this purpose were *Festuca ovina* var. *duriuscula* A. Gray ex Port. and Coult., *F. pseudovina*, and chewings fescue (*F. rubra* var. *commutata* Gaud.). Two years after the initial fescue seeding (*F. arundinacea* Schreb.) was added to this list because it was found to be drought resistant. Perennial ryegrass (*Lolium perenne* L.), comprising more than 10% of the polystand, greatly interfered with associated species, resulting in a poor appearance of the relevant test plots. The best polystand consisted of chewings fescue, *F. ovina* var. *duriuscula*, and colonial bentgrass (*Agrostis tenuis* Sibth.).

In the fertilizer evaluation during the 1st year of the experiment, a 10-10-10 formulation proved superior to the 10-20-10, 10-10-20, and 10-20-20 fertilizers. The percentage cover (Y, in all formulations) depended on the amount of fertilizer applied. This was positively related as $Y = a \operatorname{Log} X + b$.

It appears that there is an incremental relation between shoot growth rate and the plasticity index, clay content, and "methylene-blue number;" at least up to a plasticity index of ≤25, a clay content of ≤38%, and a methylene-blue value of ≤5 g.

Additional index words: Monostands, Seed mixtures, Polystands, Fertilization, Protracted drought, Plasticity index of soils, Percentage of clay particles, Methylene-blue value.

INTRODUCTION

The Administration des Ponts et Chaussees in France (Civil Engineering Department) has one main laboratory and 16 others scattered throughout the country. Appropriations have been made to six of these 17 laboratories since 1974 in order to research the turfing of roadsides. The laboratories selected were representative of the main types of climates prevailing in France (Fig. 1).

The primary research objectives currently include the following: (i) comparison of the performance of species and cultivars seeded as monostands onto roadside embankments; (ii) comparison of herbage polystands on roadside embankments with and without topsoil; (iii) influence of fertilization (application rate and types of fertilizer) on the shoot growth

[1] A contribution of the Laboratorie des Ponts et Chaussees, 58, Bld Lefebvre, 75015, Paris, France.

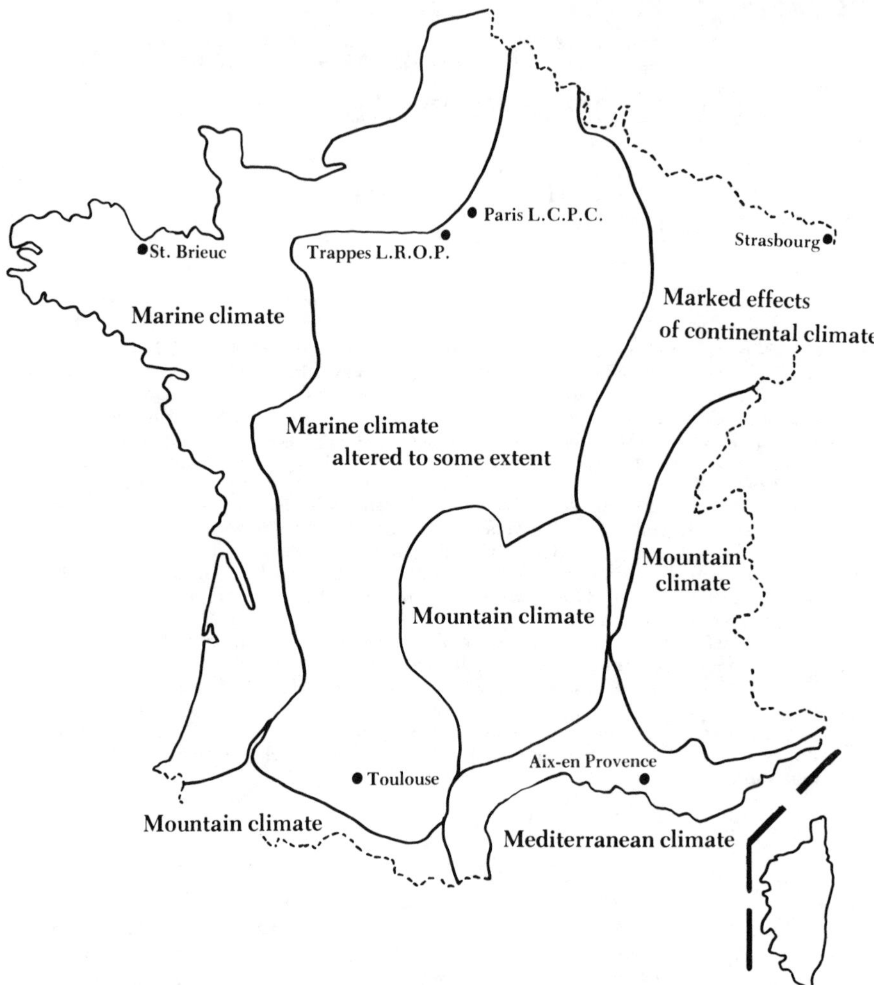

Fig. 1. Location in France, of the Laboratoires des Ponts et Chaussees (Laboratories of the Civil Engineering Department), currently researching the turfing of roadside along improved highways.

and grass cover of a mixture seeded on roadside embankments of clayey soils; (iv) turfing suitability of roadside soils.

MATERIALS AND METHODS

The experimental procedures consisted of: (i) monitoring the growth on test plots located on roadside embankments and comprising a certain number of adjacent plots; (ii) experiments performed in pots; (iii) a survey of actual turfing conditions that includes botanical composition. Details of the research procedure are described at the start of each of the five studies discussed.

RESULTS AND DISCUSSION

Performance of Monostands

Monostands were seeded on a clayey soil roadside in the Paris area along motorway A.86. Twenty-one grass species and seven legumes, involving 41 cultivars, were evaluated at three experimental sites in the Paris area and at Toulouse.

The initial test sites were established along a motorway in the Paris area in July 1974 on a clayey soil and on a fine clayey sand (1). The results presented relate to the clay site only since they were virtually the same as those on the sandy location.

The grasses used and their ratings over a 30-month period, from 1974 through 1976, are shown in Table 1. It appears that the rating derived in late 1975 differed slightly from those recorded in late 1976.

Generally speaking, the grasses that performed the best were the cultivars of *Festuca ovina* var. *duriuscula* A. Gray ex Port. and Coult., *F. pseudovina*, and chewings fescue (*F. rubra* var. *commutata* Gaud.). In 1976, tall fescue (*Festuca arundinacea* Schreb.) was added because it withstood the 1976 drought very well. Conversely, bentgrass (*Agrostis* spp.) species did not do well in 1976, crested dogtail grass (*Cynosurus cristatus* L.) disappeared at the outset of the summer drought, and meadow fescue (*Festuca pratensis* Huds.) proved ill-suited for roadside embankments under the conditions of this study.

Performance of Herbage Polystands on Roadside Embankments

The Laboratories des Ponts et Chaussees are currently investigating 41 polystands composed of from two to eight constituents, 22 of which include perennial ryegrass (*Lolium perenne* L.) or Italian ryegrass (*L. italicum*) while seven include a legume.

This study was conducted in the Paris area along motorway A.86 (1). Seventeen herbage polystands were investigated. Fifteen included perennial ryegrass with proportions ranging from 5 to 50%; plus a polystand of grasses with no perennial ryegrass that consisted chiefly of narrow-leaved fescue; and a polystand of legumes. The rating criteria for these polystands were the same as those previously used for the monostand study.

It appeared that perennial ryegrass (seeded 30 g/m^2, not cut for the first 9 months, and originally comprising more than 10% of the seed mixture) greatly hampered the growth of the associated species. In 1976, the performance of polystands that included perennial ryegrass was usually poor. Under such conditions, the polystand consisting of 'Highlight' and

Table 1. Typical ratings of 14 grasses grown on a roadside embankment on a clayey soil.

	1974–75									Total 1974–75	Class 1974–75	1976			Total 1976	Class 1976	Grand total Gene	Class Gene.
	A‡	B	C	D	E	F	G	H	I			J	K	L				
Tracenta Colonial bentgrass	1†	2	3	3	3	2	2	3	1	20	4e	1	2	2	5	6e	25	5e
'Penncross' Creeping bentgrass (*A. palustris* Huds.)	1	2	3	3	3	2	2	1	1	18	7e	1	1	2	4	9e	22	7e
Smooth brome (*Bromus inermis* Leyss.)	2	2	2	1	2	1	1	2	1	14	11e	1	2	1	4	9e	18	11e
Crested dogtail grass	2	2	2	2	0	1	2	1	1	13	13e	0	0	0	0	14e	13	14e
'Sequana' Meadow fescue	1	1	2	1	1	1	3	1	1	12	14e	1	1	1	3	11e	15	13e
'Ludion' Tall fescue	1	2	1	1	1	1	2	3	2	14	11e	3	3	2	8	4e	22	7e
Biljart *Festuca ovina* Hacked	2	2	3	2	3	3	2	3	2	22	1er	3	3	3	9	1er	31	1er
Vendome *Festuca pseudovina* Hackel	2	2	3	3	2	3	2	2	2	21	2e	3	3	3	9	1er	30	2e
Dawson Chewings fescue	2	2	3	2	2	2	2	2	2	19	5e	2	2	1	5	6e	24	6e
Highlight Chewings fescue	2	2	3	2	2	2	3	2	3	21	2e	3	3	3	9	1er	30	2e
'Pecora' Timothy (*Phleum pratense* L.)	1	2	2	2	1	1	3	2	1	15	9e	2	2	1	5	6e	20	9e
'Sport' Diploid timothy (*P. bertolonii* DC.)	1	1	2	3	3	1	3	1	1	16	8e	1	1	1	3	11e	19	10e
'Fylking' Kentucky bluegrass (*Poa pratensis* L.)	1	2	3	2	1	3	2	3	2	19	5e	3	3	1	7	5e	26	4e
'Perma' Perennial ryegrass	3	3	1	2	2	1	1	1	1	15	9e	1	1	1	3	11e	18	11e

† 0 = no Growth; 1 = Poor; 2 = Average; 3 = Fair. ‡ A = Spring green-up; B = Rate of shoot growth; C = Height of leaves prior to initial mowing; D = Height of flower stems; E = Height of leaves 4 months after mowing; F = Appearance after a late mowing; G = Winter color; H = Summer color; I = Autumnal color; J = Performance during protracted drought; K = Autumnal color; L = Quality of the vegetative cover.

'Dawson' chewings fescue, 'Biljart' *F. ovina* var. *duriuscula* and 'Tracenta' colonial bentgrass was the best, although the lengthy 1976 drought affected the fescue and bentgrass species adversely.

Under the conditions that existed during this study the use of perennial ryegrass on roadside embankments should be restricted to specific instances, such as late seeding and sites having a serious erosion potential. Otherwise the preferred seed mixture would be one with no perennial ryegrass. Such mixtures should be based on chewings fescue and *F. ovina* var. *duriuscula* with special attention given to proper fertilization and getting proper adhesion of the seeds to the soil.

Investigating the Fertilization of Roadside Embankments Consisting of Clayey Soils

A fertilization study was conducted on roadside embankments characterized by clayey soils devoid of organic matter. A seed mixture without perennial ryegrass and based on chewings fescue and *F. ovina* var. *duriuscula* was selected for this study.

The fertilization programs investigated included: (i) four types of fertilizer formulations (10–10–10, 10–20–10, 10–10–20, and 10–20–20); (ii) six application rates (30, 60, 100, 150, 200, and 300 g/m^2); (iii) two application procedures (all fertilizer applied to the seedbed in May 1976, and one-half the fertilizer applied to the seedbed in May 1976 and the other half applied 11 months later in April 1977.

Therefore, the fertilization study included $4 \times 6 \times 2 = 48$ treatments concentrated into $4 \times 2 = 8$ sections (Fig. 2). The six application rates mentioned above were investigated throughout the initial tests which took place from May 1976 to April 1977. These rates were also halved, creating nine different rates: 15, 30, 50, 60, 75, 100, 150, 200, and 300 g/m^2. The vegetative cover results in terms of the application rate for each formulation 9 months after establishment; i.e. February 1977) have been transferred to Fig. 3.

It has also been found that for an equivalent weight of fertilizer applied, the 10–10–10 and 10–20–20 formulations proved to be best during the first test. With all fertilizer formulations, the vegetative cover (Y) was an incremental function of the application rate (X) and takes the following logarithmic form:

$$Y = a \operatorname{Log} X + b.$$

Figure 4 shows this relation at various dates.

Nevertheless, the optimal and most economical application rate was sought. It should be remembered that 10–20–20 contained 50 fertilizing units while 10–10–10 contained only 30 units. The curves matching those on Fig. 3 have been plotted on Fig. 5. These express the total amounts of fertilizing units applied per ha.

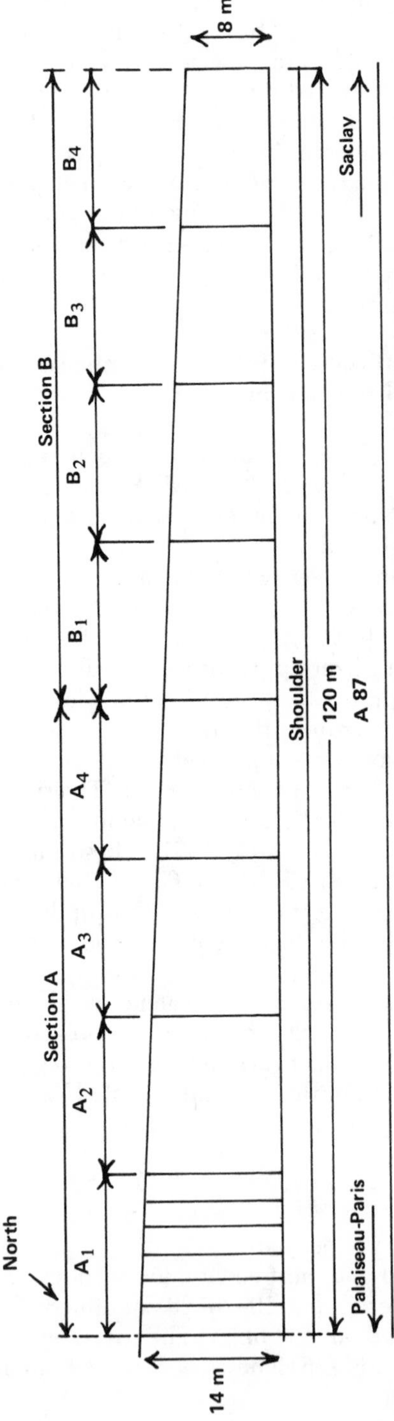

Fig. 2. General view of the fertilization test site. The eight sections in which four different fertilizers were applied at two different times (11 months after seeding) are visible.

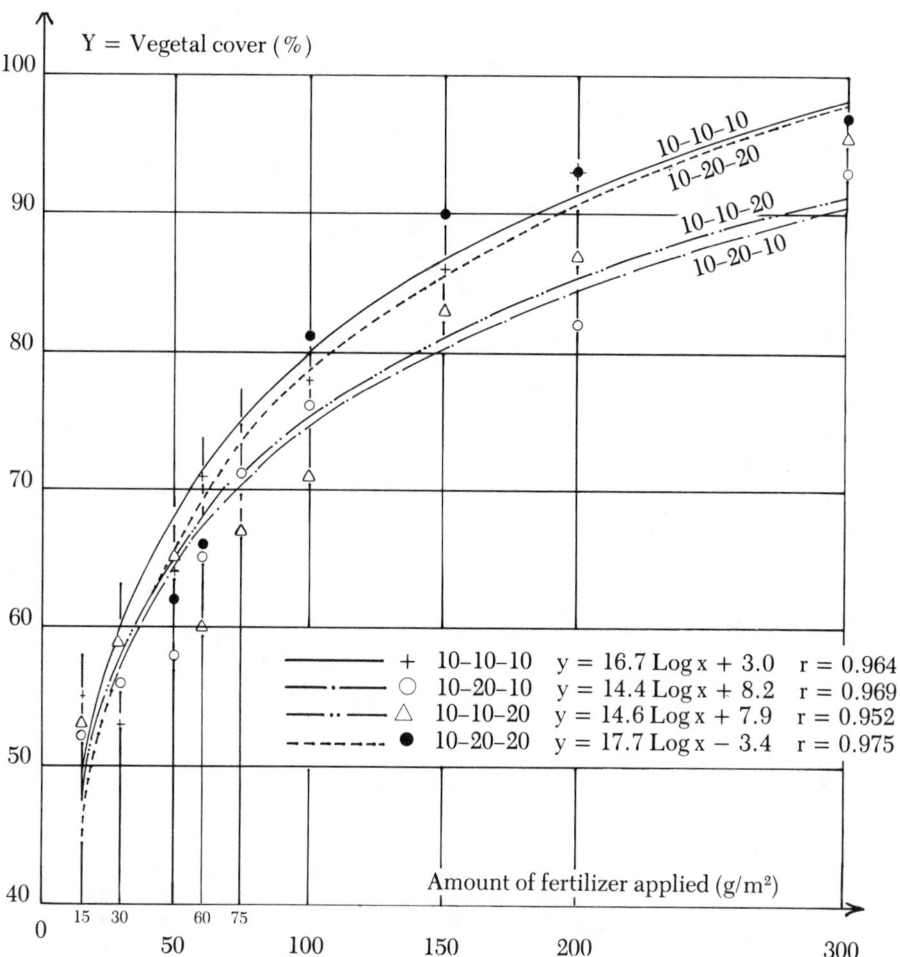

Fig. 3. Vegetative cover percentages in terms of the fertilizer, amount X for four fertilizer types in February 1977, 6 months after actual emergence. Y is a logarithmic function of X in the form Y − a Log X + b.

It was realized that for the initial test (1st year), the 10–10–10 fertilizer is definitely preferred to the three other formulations. This is especially true for 10–20–20 which (Fig. 3) appeared to be much the same.

Turfing Suitability of Roadside Soils

To ascertain their turfing suitability, 13 soils in the Toulouse area were investigated using pots with a water reservoir that contained 18 liters of soil. All soils were initially compacted in the same way, and their surface was seeded with 'Highlight' chewings fescue at 30 g/m^2. Twelve

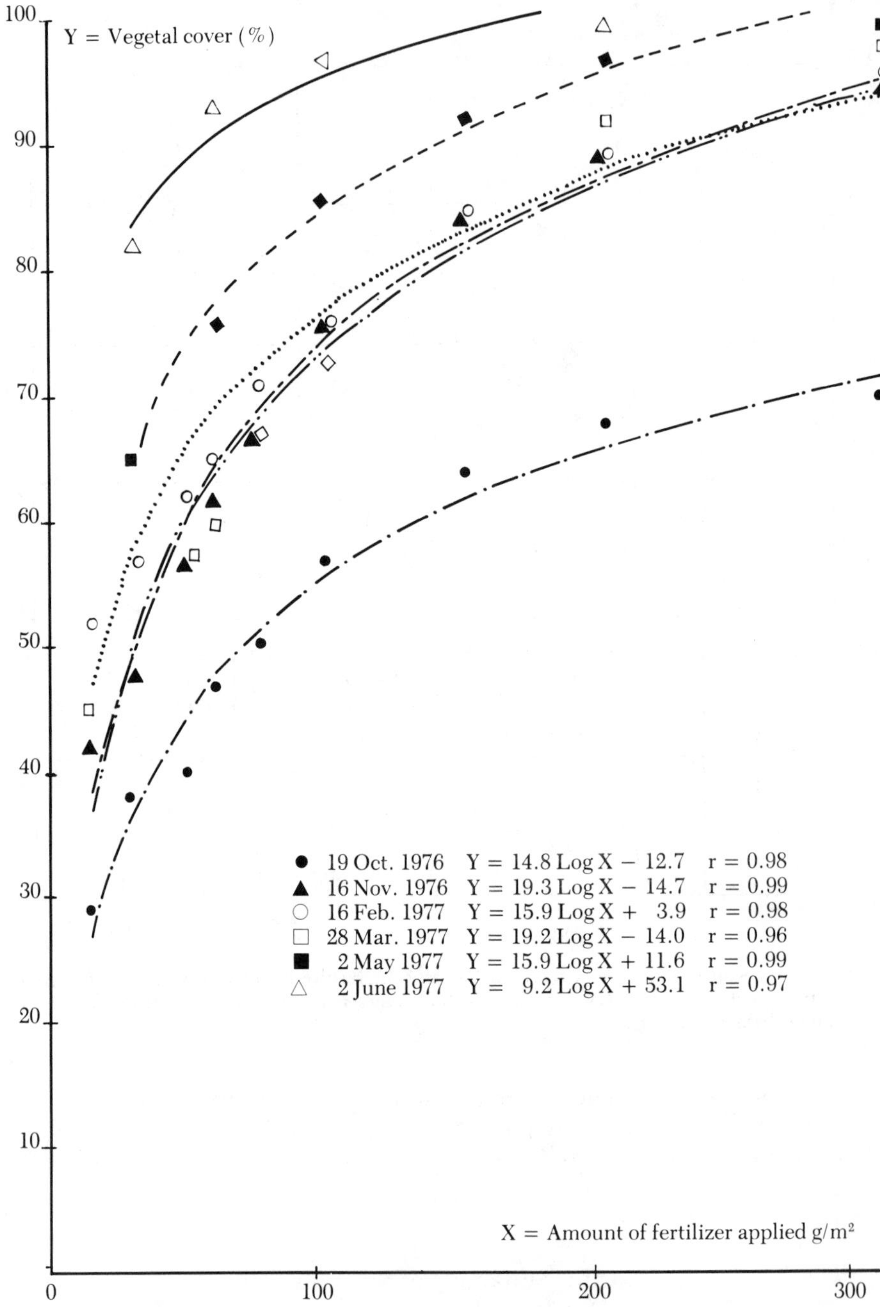

Fig. 4. Evolvement of the vegetative cover, in terms of the amount of fertilizer used as a whole, on successive dates from 19 Oct. 1976 to 2 June 1977.

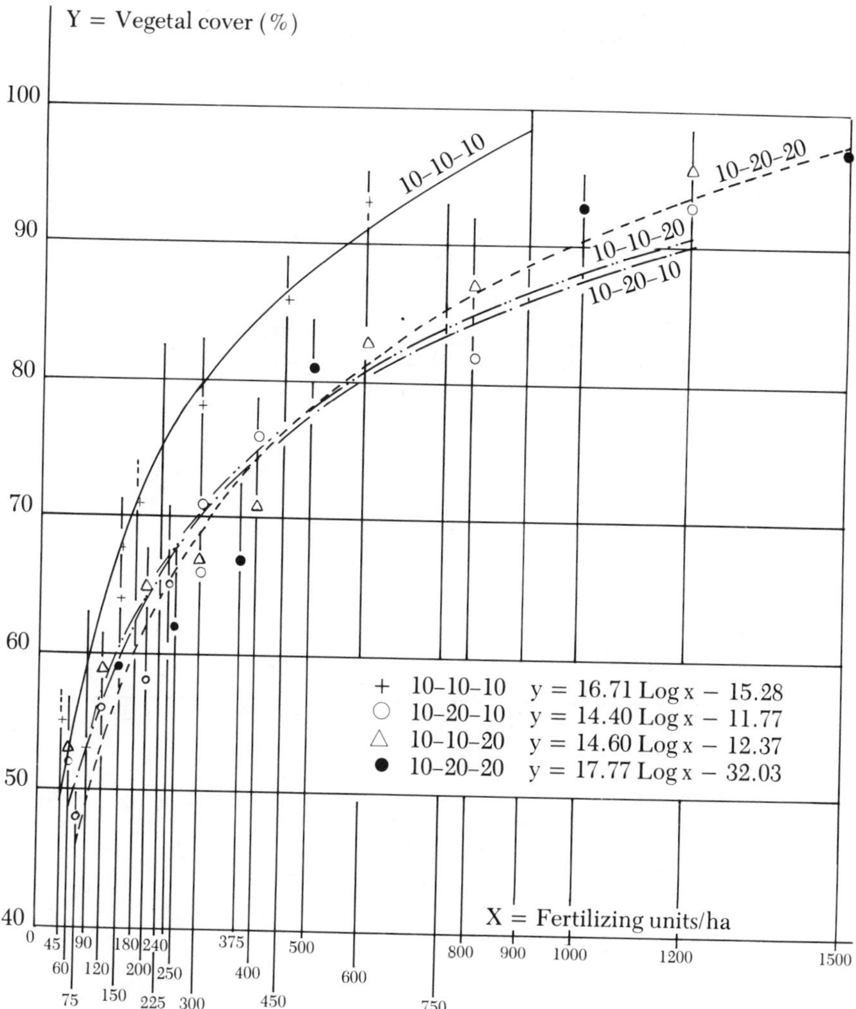

Fig. 5. Percentage of vegetative cover in terms of the total fertilizing units used per ha (four types of fertilizers) in February 1977; i.e., 6 months after actual emergence.

months later the leaf heights were measured at different dates, and an attempt made to correlate these values with various geotechnical characteristics of the 13 soils was investigated.

No correlation was found with either the limestone content or the screen undersize from 80 to 20 μ. However, there was a relation between leaf height and the plasticity index, the percentage of clay particles (<2 μ), and the methylene-blue value (a characteristic which related to the overall surface area of the soil's particles) (2) of the soils used elsewhere (Fig. 6). The number of soils investigated, however, was too limited to draw definite conclusions.

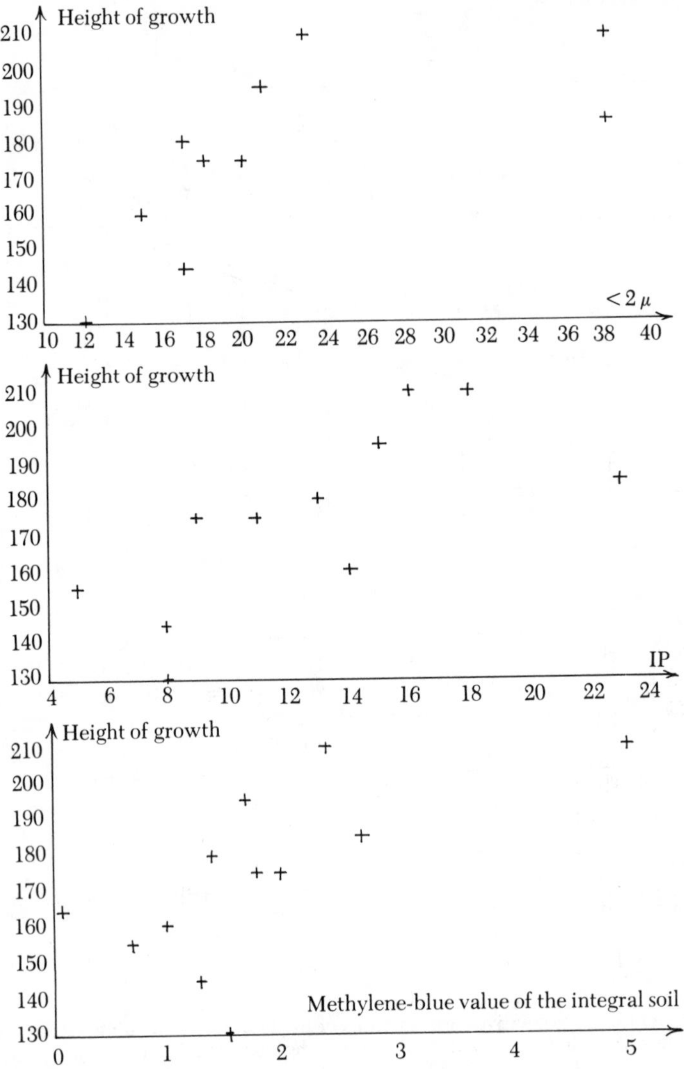

Fig. 6. Cumulative height of leaf growth over a 12-month period on 13 different soils described in terms of clay content, plasticity index, and methylene-blue value.

LITERATURE CITED

1. Arnal, G. 1977. Planches experimentales d'engazonnement sur talus routiers-Premier bilan. Bull. Liaison Lab. Ponts Chaussees. No. 88. p. 45–60.
2. Tran, N. L. 1977. Un nouvel essai d'identification des sols: l'essai au bleu de methylene. Bull. Liaison Lab. Ponts Chaussees. No. 88. p. 136–137.

Chapter 46 Studies on the Development of Turfgrass Seedings on Roadsides in the Federal Republic of Germany[1]

W. TRAUTMANN
W. LOHMEYER

ABSTRACT

Red fescue (*Festuca rubra* L.) was the most important and enduring turf developer on sandy loam soils of the Rheinische Schiefergebirge. This finding applied to at least one third of the roadsides in the Federal Republic of Germany. Sheep fescue (*F. ovina* L.) replaces red fescue on flat, rocky and sandy soils. These results from the Darmstadt area, however, can only be applied to other regions to a limited extent. Thus, in northern Germany, *Festuca rubra* can also be used on loamy sand soils.

The importance of colonial bentgrass (*Agrostis tenuis* Sibth.) and Kentucky bluegrass (*Poa pratensis* L.) as components of seed mixtures for roadside turfs was more minor than expected. The use of perennial ryegrass (*Lolium perenne* L.) as a temporary cover along roadside motorways of the Rheinische Schiefergebirge did not lead to a suppression of the slower emerging grasses. Instead, it assumed the role of the first slope stabilizer on such unfertilized sites, subsequently gave way to species adopted to maintenance conditions, and disappeared some years later. Rough bluegrass (*P. trivialis* L.), annual bluegrass (*P. annua* L.), redtop (*A. alba* L.), and wavy hairgrass [*Deschampsia flexuosa* (L.) Trin.] were unsuited for turfs along the roadsides studied.

Additional index words: Agrostis tenuis, Dactylis glomerata, Festuca ovina, F. rubra, Lolium perenne, Poa pratensis, Sandy soils.

INTRODUCTION

The construction or extension of motorways gives rise to large areas without vegetation which must be quickly planted to prevent erosion damage. Turfgrasses are used for establishing a permanent vegetation cover along with woody plants. Such turfs should be low growing and require minimal culture in order to keep maintenance costs low. For this reason the more productive, hay-type species found in permanent grasslands, such as tall oatgrass [*Arrhenatherum elatius* (L.) Beauv. ex J. & C. Presl.], meadow fescue (*Festuca pratensis* Huds.), and orchardgrass (*Dactylis glomerata* L.), are not suitable for polystands along motorways. Grass species suited to roadsides are more likely to be found in rough grazing and semi-natural grasslands (1).

Until recently, only a few long-term studies on the development of

[1]A contribution from Bundesforschungsanstalt fur Naturschutz und Landschaftsokologie, Konstantinstr. 110, 5300 Bonn 2, West Germany.

turfgrass seedings had been available in Germany. Thus, 28 experimental plots were established on the roadsides of different West German motorways in 1970 (2). The botanical composition of the stands was examined annually between 1970 and 1976. The objective of this study was to follow the botanical changes occurring in the turfs from seeding to the development of a grass sward and to determine which of the grass species would be able to persist. The ultimate goal was to provide information about the suitability of grass species for turfs along roadsides in Germany.

METHODS AND MATERIALS

The size of all experimental plots was 2 × 2 m. They were selected so as to be representative of the larger roadside area. Preference was given to sites with young seedings so that turf development could be followed from the beginning (Fig. 1). Areas selected were those that could be assumed to be most safe from being destroyed by vehicles driving over them, future woody plantings, new installations, etc. Thus, the plots were usually established along the lower parts of slopes underneath the areas planted with shrubs and trees and several meters away from the highway. Areas close to the highway, which are nearly always treated with growth regulators, were not utilized. Nevertheless, one-quarter of the experimental plots were destroyed in the course of the study and only 21 of the 28 plots established in 1970 were still intact in 1976.

Site Details

The plots were situated along three different motorways: 10 on the A 45 between Dortmund and Ludenscheid; 13 on the A 3 Cologne-Frankfurt; and 5 on A 60 and A 5 in the region of Darmstadt. The two sites through the Rheinische Schiefergebirge were characterized by rather acidic sandy loam soils, frequently stony, and a relatively wet climate. Coarse-textured sandy soils and sparse rainfall characterized the Darmstadt site. In determining the annual plant inventories, both the occurrence of species and the quantitative proportions (in percent or according to the Braun-Blanquet scale) were recorded.

According to information obtained from the Motorway Authorities, a total of 12 seed mixtures containing 15 grass species and 10 herb species were seeded on the sites studied. In this study, however, only the behavior of the grasses within the polystands were investigated.

RESULTS

A simplified tabular form was chosen for presenting the results. With the exception of tall oatgrass, meadow fescue, Canada bluegrass (*Poa compressa* L.), and chess (*Bromus secalinus* L.), which were only seeded

Federal Motorway		A 45 Dortmund-Lüdenscheid									
No. of the experimental plot		1	2	3	4	5	6	7	8	9	10
Year of seeding		67	67	67	68	68	67	68	63	63	67
Soil		sandy loam									
Festuca rubra	percentage by weight	20	20	20	20	20	20	20	25	25	24
	70	●	●	●	○	●	◐	●	●	●	●
	76	●	●	●	◐	●	◐	●	▨	●	▨
Festuca ovina	p.b.w.	15	15	15	15	15	15	15			13
	70	◐	●	◐	○	●	○	●	+	+	○
	76	◐	◐	◐	○	●	○	●	▨		▨
Dactylis glomerata	p.b.w.	5	5	5	5	5	5	5			
	70	●	◐	●	●	●	◐	◐	+		+
	76	◐	○	●	◐	○	◐	◐	▨		▨
Agrostis tenuis	p.b.w.	12	12	12	12	12	12	12	18	18	14
	70	◐	●	◐	◐	◐	◐	●	○	●	◐
	76	○	○	◐	○	○	○	○	▨	●	▨
Lolium perenne	p.b.w.	10	10	10	10	10	10	10	23	23	15
	70	●	◐	●	◐	◐	◐	○	○	◐	●
	76	○	○	○	○	○	○	○	▨	○	▨
Phleum pratense	p.b.w.										
	70										
	76										
Poa pratensis	p.b.w.	4	4	4	4	4	4	4	12	12	5
	70	○	○	◐	○	○	○	○	○	○	○
	76	○	○	○	◐	○	○	○	○	○	▨
Poa trivialis	p.b.w.	5	5	5	5	5	5	5			
	70	○	○	◐	○	○	●	○			+
	76	○	○	○	○	○	○	○			▨
Agrostis alba	p.b.w.	8	8	8	8	8	8	8			10
	70	◐	○	○	○	○	◐	○			○
	76	○	○	○	○	○	○	○			▨
Poa annua	p.b.w.	7	7	7	7	7	7	7			8
	70	○	○	○	○	○	○	○			◐
	76	○	○	○	○	○	○	○			▨
Deschampsia flexuosa	p.b.w.	5	5	5	5	5	5	5			
	70	○	○	○	○	○	○	○			
	76	○	●	○	○	○	○	○			

Federal Motorway		A 3 Cologne-Frankfurt												
No. of the experimental plot		11	12	13	14	15	16	17	18	19	20	21	22	23
Year of seeding		68	68	69	69	68	69	69	69	69	69	69	68	69
Soil		sandy loam												
Festuca rubra	percentage by weight	30	30	25	25	15	15	15	15	15	15	15	30	25
	70	●	●	●	●	◐	●	●	◐	◐	◐	◐	●	●
	76	●	◐	◐	●	●	◐	▨	●	▨	▨	▨	▨	●
Festuca ovina	p.b.w.	25	25	30	30									30
	70	○	●	○	○							+		◐
	76	◐	◐	●	◐	+						▨		◐
Dactylis glomerata	p.b.w.												10	
	70						+					+	○	
	76								+			▨	▨	
Agrostis tenuis	p.b.w.	15	15	5	5	8	8	8	8	8	8	8		5
	70	◐	○	◐	●	●	●	○	●	●	◐	●		●
	76	◐	○	○	○	○	○	▨	◐	▨	▨	▨		○
Lolium perenne	p.b.w.			10	10	15	15	15	15	15	15	15		10
	70		+	●	●	◐	●	●	●	●	●	●		●
	76			○	○	○	○	▨	○	▨	▨	▨		○
Phleum pratense	p.b.w.					10	10	10	10	10	10	10		
	70					○	●	●	●	○	○	○		
	76					○	○	▨	○	○	○	○		
Poa pratensis	p.b.w.	15	15	30	30	15	15	15	15	15	15	15	15	30
	70	○	○	○	○	○	○	○	○	○	○	◐	◐	○
	76	◐	○	○	○	●	○	▨	○	▨	▨	▨	▨	○
Poa trivialis	p.b.w.					15	15	15	15	15	15	15		
	70					◐	●	○	○	○	●	○		
	76					○	○	▨	○	▨	▨	▨		
Agrostis alba	p.b.w.					8	8	8	8	8	8	8		
	70					○	○	○	○	○	○	○		
	76					◐	○	▨	○	▨	▨	▨		
Poa annua	p.b.w.													
	70									+				
	76									▨				

Federal Motorway		A 60/A 5 Rüsselsheim-Jugenheim				
No. of the experimental plot		24	25	26	27	28
Year of seeding		66	66	68	67	67
Soil		sand				
Festuca rubra	percentage by weight	20	20	20	15	15
	70	○	○	◐	○	○
	76	○	○	◐	○	○
Festuca ovina	p.b.w.	26	26	35	35	35
	70	●	●	●	●	●
	76	●	◐	●	◐	◐
Agrostis tenuis	p.b.w.	13	13	10	12	12
	70	●	●	●	○	○
	76	○	◐	○	○	○
Poa pratensis	70	+				

● well represented
◐ underrepresented
○ not represented despite seeding
\+ represented without seeding
▨ Experimental plot destroyed in 1976

Fig. 1. Occurrence of sown grass species in experimental plots on roadsides in 1970 and 1976.

in a few scattered places, the table contains the grass species used in terms of percentage by weight of the seed mixture and for comparison, those species found in the plots in 1970 and 1976. We attempted to consider the quantities of species present and establish a relationship between the seeding rate and the actual quantitative proportions of the emerging grasses by using a multi-stage scale.

Every plot had its special perculiarities as to site, so that the individual species would not be expected to show the same behavior in all plots. Nevertheless, it was possible to assign the grass species into three groups, each of different behavior, by using a rough measure as a basis. It must be emphasized, however, that the grasses belonging to a certain group did not correspond with each other regarding their ecology.

Group 1 species were grasses which, according to their seeding rates, were well represented in most plots in 1970 and which occurred at a similar frequency in 1976. Among them were red fescue (*Festuca rubra* L.) (except on sandy soils), sheep fescue (*F. ovina* L.), and orchardgrass (*Dactylis glomerata* L.). Group 2 species, well represented in 1970, but clearly in decline by 1976 were colonial bentgrass (*Agrostis tenuis* Sibth.) perennial ryegrass (*Lolium perenne* L.), and timothy (*Phleum pratense* L.). Group 3 species, poorly represented in most plots, were Kentucky bluegrass (*Poa pratensis* L.), rough bluegrass (*P. trivialis* L.), redtop (*Agrostis alba* L.), annual bluegrass (*Poa annua* L.), and wavy hairgrass [*Deschampsia flexuosa* (L.). Trin.].

The following observations were also of importance. In spite of the high percentage of red fescue seeded it did not succeed in becoming established in roadside turfs of the Darmstadt area. Even sheep fescue distinctly decreased on these permeable sandy soils from 1970 to 1976, probably as a consequence of several extremely dry periods. At a low seeding rate, orchardgrass occurred only sparsely in most of the experimental plots and could, in this respect, not be compared with the two turf developers. In contrast to perennial ryegrass, colonial bentgrass was still represented in one-fourth of the experimental plots in 1976. However, the stand was limited so that it formed a turf in only one plot. Although Kentucky bluegrass had increased a little in 1976, in contrast to the first time the inventory was taken, it had not reached the expected stand proportion.

DISCUSSION

Red fescue was the most important and enduring turf former on sandy loam soils of the Rheinische Schiefergebirge. With respect to roadside areas, this finding applies to at least one-third of the motorway roadsides in the Federal Republic of Germany. Sheep fescue replaces red fescue on flat, rocky, and sandy roadside soils. Results from the Darmstadt area, however, can be applied to other regions only to a limited extent. Thus, red fescue can also be used on the loamy sand soils in northern Germany.

The importance of colonial bentgrass and Kentucky bluegrass as components of polystands for German roadside turfs is much less than expected. Why the colonial bentgrass performed poorly is not known. Perhaps the native wild form (instead of imported seed material) would give better results. Regarding Kentucky bluegrass, the supply of nutrients from the roadside soils was probably insufficient.

The use of perennial ryegrass as a temporary cover on roadsides of the Rheinische Schiefergebirge did not lead to a suppression of the slower emerging grasses (*Festuca* spp.) Rather, it functioned as the first slope stabilizer on unfertilized sites. Subsequently it yielded to the low maintenance species, and disappeared some years later. Species like rough bluegrass, annual bluegrass, redtop, and wavy hairgrass are unsuited for turfs along the roadside studied.

These studies confirmed the observation that, depending upon the soil and time of seeding, different botanical compositions develop even though the same seed mixture was used. The more extreme the site, the higher the rate of loss among the seeded species (3). It is therefore possible, in the long run, for turfs to evolve which no longer contain a single species of the original seed mixture, depending on the seed mixture originally selected.

On moderate sites, however, the seed mixtures and the turf derived from them corresponded best. This applies, above all, to annually mowed red fescue turfs on loamy soils where herbs do not have a chance to spread.

LITERATURE CITED

1. Boeker, P. 1970. Turfgrasses for roadsides. p. 576–579. *In* Proc. 1st Int. Turfgrass Res. Conf., Harrogate, England. July 1969. Am. Soc. Agron., Madison, Wis.
2. Trautmann, W. 1972. Erste ergebnisse von rasenuntersuchungen an dauerflachen der bundesautobahnen. Rasen-Turf-Gazon 1:6–11.
3. ————, and W. Lohmeyer. 1975. Zur entwicklung von rasenansaaten an autobahnen. Nat. Land. 50:45–48.

Section IX:

Observational Notes

Note

1

Characteristics, Breeding Methods, and Seed Production of *Poa supina* Schrad.[1]

P. BERNER

ABSTRACT

Poa supina Schrad. has only recently been recognized for its turfgrass potential. Favorable characteristics include rapid dense stoloniferous spread, short internodes, disease resistance, good wear tolerance, and a reduced mowing requirement. It lacks drought resistance and is a poor seed producer. A breeding and selection program at Steinach, West Germany involves selection of ecotypes, followed by their evaluation for turf characteristics. The most promising types are then tested for seed production. Studies also continue on cultural means for improving seed production. Data indicate that new stands must be well established before winter to initiate seed heads and that excessive thatching of older stands seriously reduces seed production.

SPECIES DESCRIPTION

Grass experts and breeders became interested in *Poa supina* Schrad. only recently when its favorable characteristics were discovered. The more important ones are as follows. Numerous surface stolons with short internodes of 1 to 5 cm form a dense turf since new lateral shoots and roots will develop at each node. *P. supina* thus has a pronounced competitive ability which, under favorable conditions, will not permit the growth of other encroaching plants after the stand has been formed (2). On sports grounds in the Alpine region, *P. supina* has reached nearly 100% coverage through natural invasion (1). Its wear tolerance is good, better than that of perennial ryegrass (*Lolium perenne* L.). The species has a low shoot growth rate in lawns which makes a reduced mowing frequency possible. Although it has poor low temperature color retention, the spring green-up rate is quite early. Even a few balmy days in January will bring forth young leaves. The color is a light green. Resistance to disease is fairly good (2). Shortcomings include a lack of resistance to continued drought as well as considerable difficulties with seed production.

[1] Saatzucht Steinach, D-8441 Steinach über Straubing, West Germany.

RANGE OF USES

Based on these favorable characteristics, *P. supina* was incorporated into a turf breeding program. Accordingly the turf usability was investigated first. A lawn site selected for growing an ornamental turf was plugged with *P. supina* in June at spacings of approximately 12 × 12 cm. Six weeks later *P. supina* covered 97% of the lawn. The turf appearance was good and this level of performance has continued even though 7 years have elapsed since it was planted. The most promising use of *P. supina*, however, would be to take advantage of its durability in recreational and sports turfs. Unfortunately, until the seed production problem is solved, the planting of lawns must be by sod, chopped stolons, or young plants grown from stolons or seed. Monostands may be achieved in this way, while overseeding with other species will provide a polystand equivalent to that from a seed mixture. Planting into old turfs, especially sports grounds, has been successful. If used in polystands, 5 to 10% *P. supina* produces a stand of nearly 100% *P. supina* in 1 to 2 years if other components in the polystand are suitable and both the soil and climate are satisfactory. A test started in 1975 with 3% *P. supina* in a polystand of 60% 'Loretta' perennial ryegrass, 25% Kentucky bluegrass (*P. pratensis* L.), and 12% red fescue (*Festuca rubra* L.) already follows this trend.

BREEDING METHOD

A particularly promising method of breeding *P. supina* might be to collect ecotypes and promising individual plants. This will utilize the variability associated with the species (2). The approach used here is to collect promising ecotypes with the sod pieces further divided and individually planted in plots of 1 m^2. The seed is harvested from the high yielding plots after the second winter of evaluation. From this seed, single plants are selected, divided into nine cuttings, and replanted in a 0.7- × 0.7-m plot, isolated by strips planted with turf timothy (*Phleum bertolonii* DC.). The speed of turf coverage by stolon development and the degree of encroachment into the turf timothy strips are clues to the vitality and competitive ability of the individual plant selections. Evaluations of all the essential criteria associated with grass breeding are based on these plots. Special attention, however, is directed to the adverse characteristics. These are poor resistance to drought, light green leaf color, poor low temperature color retention, and thus, bad winter color. (The latter may be influenced to a degree by fall fertilization.) Conditions were particularly favorable in 1976–77 for observations on drought resistance and winter color. Drought totally destroyed some plots while others remained quite green. How effective a selection program based upon these observations will be remains to be proven. Currently, however, the main goal is to improve seed yield during the 1st and subsequent years. This is illustrated in Table 1.

Table 1. Number of seedheads and seed yields from selected single plants of *Poa supina*.

Selection	Seedheads/m²		Seed yields	
	1976	1977	1976	1977
			g/m²	
Su. 3	--	2,900	34.2	24.2
Su. 8	10,700	2,800	46.5	22.3
Su. 14	4,800	2,500	22.1	5.6
Su. 18	4,300	3,100	20.7	23.0
Su. 19	--	4,300	36.9	39.5
Su. 23	--	5,400	22.1	20.5
Su. 25	--	2,700	52.1	15.6
Su. 27	9,200	2,400	38.2	10.4

Breeding was begun simultaneously with investigations into possible uses. The first cultivar was entered for the official tests in 1971. It received cultivar protection in 1974 under the name 'Supra'.

SEED PRODUCTION

Various tests for the production of *P. supina* seed have been conducted at Steinach, West Germany for several years. A test was completed in Bonn, West Germany in 1974 by Dr. Lutke Entrup (unpublished report in August 1975). Trial plots for seed production were established in 1976 in the Alpine region at different altitudes, in Finland (67° N Lat), and in various North American latitudes and altitudes using uniform clone material of the Supra cultivar. The possibility of such varying environmental conditions exercising a differentiated influence on shoot development cannot be ruled out, but final trial results are not yet available.

Lutke Entrup (unpublished report in August 1975) tested the effects of three seeding dates, two drilling widths, and two N sources on seed production. His data suggest that seeding before mid-August was essential for best seed yields and that row spacings and N sources have little effect. Seeding and planting tests conducted by the author in 1975–76 confirm these results, although the planting date may be somewhat later. Experience has also shown that the standing crop is subject to excessive thatching which tends to reduce flowering.

Establishment of a *P. supina* seed production capability has been difficult. With the above results in mind, there remains the problem of encouraging this grass to develop sufficient seedheads in the 2nd and subsequent years following establishment. The three-factor test outlined in Table 2 was conducted at Steinach in 1976. Results obtained from these trials cover only 1 year and were influenced by extreme drought conditions during the autumn. Thus, only the extremes will be given. The poorest plot yielded 1.5 g/m² from 130 seedheads while the best plot produced 41.5 g/m² from 4,300 seedheads.

Data from the trials to date suggest that certain major factors must be considered. Vegetative growing points, for example, will produce

Table 2. Treatments used in the *Poa supina* seed production test at Steinach, West Germany, in 1976. (All plots treated like turf trials until early August).

Factor 1	Factor 2	Factor 3
Fertility	Mowing	Vertical mowing
1. As in turf trials	1. Regular cut ending in late Oct.	1. None
2. As in turf trials + 20 kg N/ha in spring	2. Regular cut ending in early Sept.	2. Early Aug.
3. 50 kg N/ha in early Aug.	3. Regular cut ending in early Aug.	3. Early Sept.
4. 100 kg N/ha in early Aug.	4. Cut early Aug., mid-Sept., and mid-Oct.	4. Early Oct.
5. 50 kg N/ha in early Sept.	5. Cut early Aug. and late Oct.	
6. 100 kg N/ha in early Sept.		
7. 50 kg N/ha in mid-Oct.		
8. 100 kg N/ha in mid-Oct.		

flowering shoots only if a certain maturity stage is reached in autumn before the onset of winter dormancy. Vernalization takes place during the winter. The more young shoots prepared for vernalization, the better the flowering density and seed production will be. Prior observations that plots entering the winter in a heavily overgrown condition tend to develop few seedheads have been confirmed. The treatment trials outlined in Table 2 were chosen because of their potential effects on the number of young shoots. Preliminary observations indicate that spring fertilization makes seed harvest more difficult with little effect on seed yield, while later October vertical mowing and fertilization were probably too late.

LITERATURE CITED

1. Koeck, L., and A. Walch. 1977. Naturliches vorkommen von *Poa supina* auf Sportplatzrasen in Tirol. Rasen-Turf-Gazon 8:44–46.
2. Skirde, W. 1971. Beobachtungen an *Poa supina* Schrad. Rasen-Turf-Gazon 2:58–62.

Note 2

Observations on Differently Adapted Grasses for Turf in Central Italy[1]

A. PANELLA

ABSTRACT

Turfgrass breeding work in Italy began only a few years ago with a survey of available germplasm derived from domestic and imported sources used mainly for soccer field turfs. Observation trials carried out at the Plant Breeding Department of the University of Perugia, Italy, demonstrate that over a period of 7 years the persistence of the local types of Kentucky bluegrass (*Poa pratensis* L.), bentgrass (*Agrostis* spp.), and red fescue (*Festuca rubra* L.) was superior to that of imported cultivars. The turf persistence estimated as ground cover percentage was related to the resistance to local diseases (especially leaf rust and root diseases) and tolerance to the high temperatures and high light levels of the Mediterranean climate. 'Merion' Kentucky bluegrass from an American seed source performed well, although commercial seed of Merion imported from northern European countries showed poor adaptability. Among the bentgrasses, 'Penncross' and 'Highland' performed well, while among the red fescues 'Pennlawn' was the best. A program for improving the quality of Italian turfgrass ecotypes is on course, along with a study of the physiological mechanisms which are the basis of adaptation to the local environment. Particular interest centers on tall fescue (*F. arundinacea* Schreb.) as having potential for soccer field usage.

INTRODUCTION

Turfgrass research in Italy is receiving very little attention because the general opinion has been that to achieve a quality turf it is sufficient to have a good, honest seedsman. The main purpose of this paper is to demonstrate that species and seed quality are less important in obtaining a good turf than are cultivar and seed source under the conditions peculiar to central Italy.

DISCUSSION

Climatic Conditions

Temperatures are coldest in January and hottest in July. Rainfall shows differing distribution; Italy has very dry summers and a rainy spring and fall. The Italian peninsula is located in the middle of the Mediterranean basin, thus the Alps are an efficient defense from the cold winds from the north.

[1] Istituto di Allevamento Vegetale, Univ. di Perugia, Italy.

All of the important turfgrass species are found in the Mediterranean region, but a botanical composition typifying the turf is neither commonplace nor natural. This also happens frequently in other regions of the world located at the same latitude. The Italian peninsula could be considered subtropical. In central Italy bermudagrass [*Cynodon dactylon* (L.) Pers.] turns deep brown after the first frost. Italy extends from 35° to 47° N Lat; only Sicily and a small portion of southern Italy correspond to regions where irrigated warm-season grasses might be recommended. For most of Italy the same turfgrass species as grown in the cold and temperate regions of the world are more appropriate. These are colonial bentgrass (*Agrostis tenuis* Sibth.), Kentucky bluegrass (*Poa pratensis* L.), and red fescue (*Festuca rubra* L.). In Italy the problem is not so much to select the right species, as to choose in each species the right cultivars; i.e., the cultivars best adapted to the local environmental conditions. The most important turf use in Italy is for soccer fields where a strong sod of a finer texture than that required for American football fields is necessary. Public city parks and gardens are also quite important. A less important use is for golf courses (there are no municipal golf courses). Lawns have little importance, for the Italian family generally prefers patches of flowers and ornamental shrubs or trees in front of the house with vegetables and fruits in the backyard.

Turfgrass Development

All the seed for turf use in Italy has been imported. Each year an average of 2,000 quintals of Kentucky bluegrass, 4,000 quintals of red fescue, and 1,000 quintals of bentgrass are imported from foreign countries. This is mainly because breeding work on turf species in Italy began only recently and, up until now, was studied in very few institutions. One of these is the Forage Breeding Center of the Italian Research Council operating at the Plant Breeding Institute of the University of Perugia. Ten years ago we made a collection of Italian ecotypes of the most important grass species for forage and turf uses. This collection included colonial bentgrass, creeping bentgrass (*A. stolonifera* L.), *A. palustris* Huds., red fescue, tall fescue (*F. arundinacea* Schreb.), perennial ryegrass (*Lolium perenne* L.), and Kentucky bluegrass. Since 1970 we have made observations comparing Italian ecotypes with foreign cultivars.

Only the most important characteristics are referred to herein. Disease resistance was rated in the spring and summer of 1972 in terms of leaf rust infection and leaf browning present. Leaf browning relates to a complex infection of roots by different species of fungi. It is favored by high temperatures and over-watering. Stand persistance was estimated as a percentage of ground cover of the grass under observation. The results of these observations are reported in Table 1. It is evident that the Italian ecotypes of Kentucky bluegrass and 'Merion' Kentucky bluegrass from an American seed source tolerate local leaf rust strains and leaf browning better than the northern European commercial seeds. The percentage of

Table 1. Leaf rust infection, leaf browning, and stand persistence in Italian ecotypes and foreign cultivars of the most important turfgrass species (Perugia, Italy 1971–77).

Species	Ecotypes or cultivars	Seed source	Visual rating† 1972		Ground cover‡ Ground cover‡		
			Leaf rust	Leaf browning	1972	1976	1977
					%		
Kentucky bluegrass	Avg. of four ecotypes	Italy	1	1	100	90	80
	Merion	Holland	4	4	90	40	20
	Merion	Denmark	4	3	100	40	30
	Merion	United States	2	2	95	50	65
Creeping bentgrass	One ecotype	Italy	--	1	95	85	80
Agrostis palustris	Common	Poland	--	5	95	60	40
	Penncross	United States	--	3	100	60	80
	Seaside	Holland	--	2	95	50	40
Colonial bentgrass	One ecotype	Italy	--	2	85	75	85
	Astoria	United States	--	3	95	50	50
	Highland	United States	--	3	100	80	80
Red fescue	Avg. of four ecotypes	Italy	--	2	95	85	80
	Illahee	United States	--	3	60	30	45
	Pennlawn	United States	--	3	95	65	80
	Oase	Holland	--	3	95	20	30
	Topie	Holland	--	4	60	15	20

† Score: 1 = Minimum; 5 = Maximum. ‡ The percentage of ground cover refers to the bluegrass, bentgrass, and red fescue present in the plot.

ground cover data for the imported grasses show a lack of persistance. Severe infection by leaf rust in the spring and root diseases in the summer caused the short persistence observed with many seed sources. After 6 years from seeding time more than 50% of foreign stands had disappeared.

Leaf rust infection was not a problem with the bentgrasses and red fescue, but the root diseases were evident during the summer (high ratings for leaf browning). After 6 years, the best stands were those from domestic seed sources followed by materials coming from the United States. Northern European seed sources performed very poorly. Among the bentgrasses from foreign sources, 'Penncross' and 'Highland' persisted well, while among the red fescue cultivars only 'Pennlawn' from an American source performed well. Local grass populations reflect adaptation to the conditions of our experimental fields, with collections from high elevations performing no better than the northern European seed sources. The ecotypes in Table 1, against which the foreign cultivars were compared, were from natural populations found near Perugia.

Breeding Program

The main objective of a turfgrass breeding program in Italy must consider the need for dense, wear-resistant sods for athletic fields. This could be achieved by: (i) selection from the natural Italian populations which are rich in genetic variation; (ii) backcrossing some good foreign

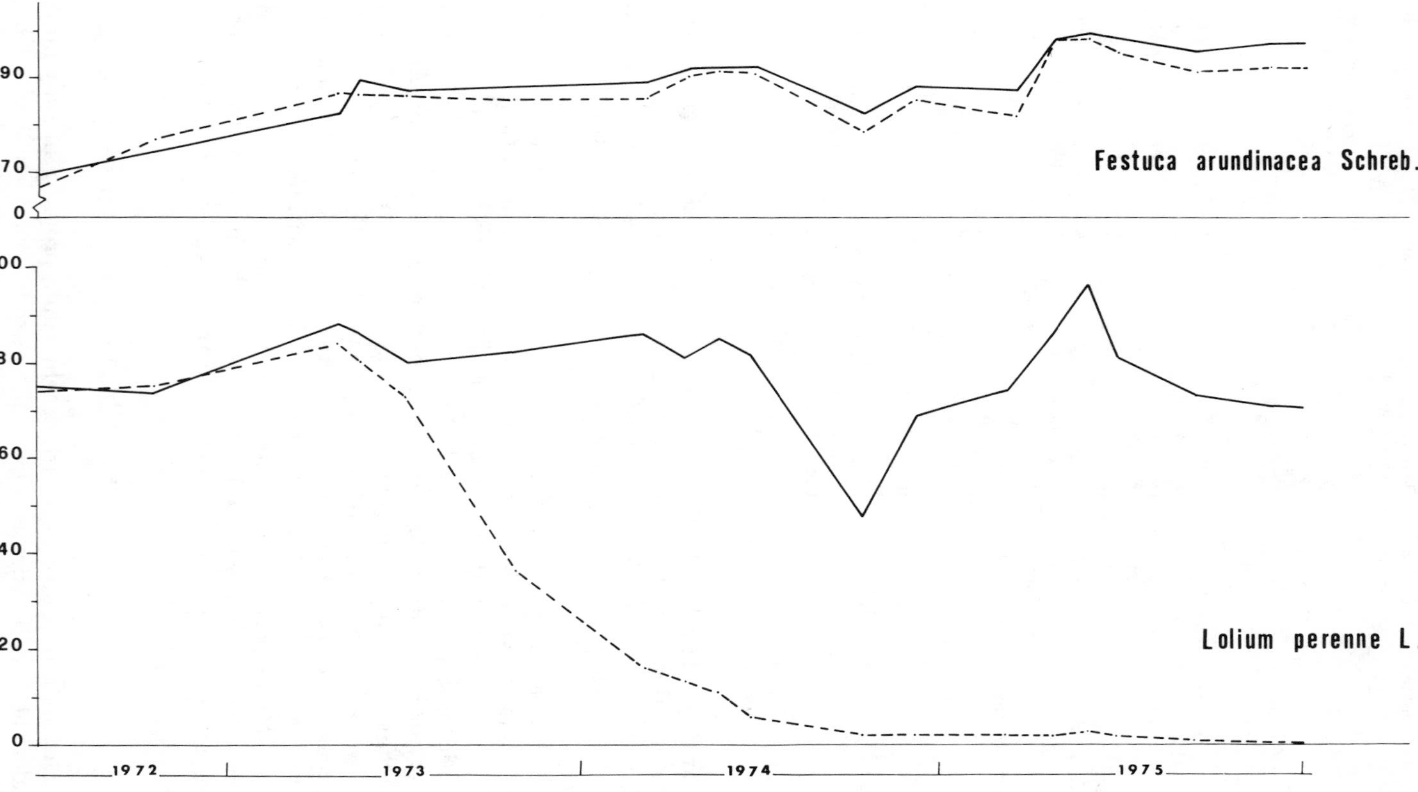

Fig. 1. Ground cover (%) of Italian (——) and foreign (-----) cultivars of two grass species.

cultivars with specific Italian lines for disease resistance and tolerance to high temperature and high light intensity. Some tall fescue cultivars may be adapted for use on soccer fields. This species is supposed to be too coarse-textured for soccer use, but it can be improved by breeding. In Fig. 1 it is evident how well the foreign cultivars of tall fescue, 'Kentucky 31' and 'Alta,' have adapted to Italian conditions and performed similar to the Italian ecotypes. The same figure shows that foreign perennial ryegrass cultivars declined drastically in the end year after seeding. The differential persistence of Italian and foreign perennial ryegrass cultivars is currently being investigated on a physiological level with carbohydrate root reserves being evaluated.

SUMMARY

Although breeding work with turfgrass species is just beginning in Italy, the possibilities for future success are good. Tremendous sources of germplasm exist, but are still unexplored. Our grass populations should certainly have the genes necessary for adaptation to the most important turf uses in Italy.

Note 3

Some Ecological Observations on Turf Establishment and Culture of Turfgrasses in Cool Regions of Japan

Y. OOHARA

ABSTRACT

Turf areas such as golf courses, roadsides, sports grounds, home lawns, and public parks are becoming more important each year in Japan. Interest in turf has stimulated a series of ecological and physiological investigations of turf establishment on golf courses, roadsides, and banks along rivers by the Turf Science Laboratory of Obihiro University of Agriculture and Veterinary Medicine, located in the northern part of Japan.

Among the 10 cultivars tested, 'Penncross' and 'Seaside' creeping bentgrass (*Agrostis palustris* Huds.) were best adapted for golf course greens. 'Fylking,' 'Baron,' and 'Nugget' Kentucky bluegrass (*Poa pratensis* L.), 'Pennlawn' red fescue (*Festuca rubra* var. *rubra* L.), and 'Jamestown' chewings fescue (*Festuca rubra* var. *commutata* Gaud.) were selected from the tests for fairways. Legumes such as New Zealand white clover (*Trifolium repens* L.), 'Emerald' crown vetch (*Coronilla varia* L.), and some birdsfoot trefoil (*Lotus corniculatus* L.) cultivars were adaptable as turf for damsites, roadsides, and river banks.

As for cultural practices, attention should be directed to the preparation of the seedbed, mulching, fertilization, reseeding to get uniform stand density, proper mowing, and the application of herbicides or fungicides where necessary. From these experimental results, the author was able to obtain some favorable information on turf cultivars adaptable to the cool regions of Japan and to identify cultural practices for the establishment and maintenance of cool-season turfgrasses.

INTRODUCTION

Turf has a significant place, both functional and aesthetic, in areas such as golf courses, sports grounds, lawns in public parks and home gardens, roadsides, riverbanks, etc. Although the importance of turf is increasing each year in Japan, little information is available on the adaptation of cultivars to the cool regions of Japan. This report summarizes ecological research being carried out at the Turf Science Laboratory of Obihiro University of Agriculture and Veterinary Medicine, Hokkaido, Japan, on the establishment and maintenance of turfs on golf courses, roadsides, and riverbanks.

[1]Turf Science Laboratory, Obihiro Univ. of Agriculture and Veterinary Medicine, Hokkaido, Japan.

Environmental Conditions in Hokkaido

The environment in Hokkaido, located in the northern part of Japan, varies considerably by location. The climate is of the temperate zone, being generally warm and humid in the summer and severe in the winter. The average annual temperature is about 5 to 9 C, ranging between −30 and 30 C. The yearly rainfall averages about 1,000 mm, generally ranging between 6,000 and 2,000 mm. Normally, the growing season of turfgrass begins in late April and extends to early November, embracing the best season for golf play. Soil conditions vary with location. Soils of light volcanic ash or heavy clay are common with peat soils in some areas, and are relatively acid and infertile. Therefore, soil pH must usually be corrected by liming, and soils must be fertilized before turf establishment.

ESTABLISHMENT OF TURF

Adaptability of Turfgrasses to Turf Utilization

Winterhardiness and resistance to diseases and insects are required to obtain a good turf. Most bentgrass (*Agrostis* spp.), Kentucky bluegrass (*Poa pratensis* L.), and red fescue (*Festuca rubra* L.) cultivars are adaptable to the varying conditions in Hokkaido. The following species or cultivars showed advantages in the experimental screening.

'Penncross' and 'Seaside' creeping bentgrass (*A. palustris* Huds.) were best adapted for golf course greens. These cultivars desired particularly for their winterhardiness and good putting quality. 'Astoria' colonial bentgrass (*A. tenuis* Sibth.) has not been used for golf greens during the last 5 years because of poor putting quality. 'Highland' colonial bentgrass is suitable for golf course tees.

Turf legumes such as New Zealand white clover (*Trifolium repens*

Table 1. Species, cultivars, and seeding rates suitable for golf courses in the cool regions of Japan.

Seed composition	Type of use	Species	Cultivars	Seeding rate
				g/m^2
Single cultivar	Green	Bentgrass	Penncross	8
			Seaside	10
			Astoria	10
	Fairway	Kentucky bluegrass	Fylking	9
			Baron	9
			Nugget	10
		Creeping red fescue	Pennlawn	10
		Chewings fescue	Jamestown	10
Mixture	Fairway	Kentucky bluegrass	Fylking	4
			Baron	4
		Perennial ryegrass	Manhattan	4
	Tee	Bentgrass	Astoria	4
		Kentucky bluegrass	Nugget	8

L.), 'Emerald' crown vetch (*Coronilla varia* L.), and some birdsfoot trefoil (*Lotus corniculata* L.) cultivars ('Viking,' 'Empire,' and 'Mansfield') seem adaptable as vegetation for damsites, roadsides, and riverbanks because they have a high capacity for conserving soil and water.

Cultural Practices

The preparation of the seedbed, mulching, basic fertilization with Ca, P, Mg, N, K, etc., and seeding with the proper seeder are necessary for effective turf establishment. Bark manure and peat moss rich in humus also help establish a good turf.

TURF CULTURE

Reseeding and Topdressing with Chemical Fertilizers

Once a turf is established, reseeding with small amounts of the same cultivars in spring and over winter is effective in helping keep up a good turf density.

The proper application of chemical fertilizer is necessary for the normal and rapid growth of turf. Fertilization after the frequent cutting of young leaves rich in nutrients is particularly important for the persistence of vegetation. Commonly with cool-season turfs, complete chemical fertilizer (10–10–10, 15–15–15, 16–4–8, etc.) and humus-containing fertilizer are applied at 6 g/m^2 on golf courses. Fertilizers are applied seasonally at the rate of 50% in April, 20% in May–June, and 30% from September through November.

Mowing

Although mowing is fundamental in maintaining good shoot density, the cutting height and frequency must be adjusted to the vegetative condition and the utilization of the turf. Since photosynthesis takes place actively in the leaf tissues of turfgrass, removal of the leaves by mowing has a significant influence on the regrowth of turfgrasses, the carbohydrate reserve, and the turf persistence.

Irrigation

Irrigation to provide proper soil moisture needed for the growth of turf is conventional, particularly when the soil becomes too dry. Sprinkler systems operating about 15 min/day are most popular on golf courses.

Weed Control

Many native and naturalized plants grow vigorously as weeds in the cool climatic regions of Japan. Thus, spraying with herbicides such as 2,4-D, MCPP, and gramoxone, reglone, etc., is utilized. Most weeds are broad leaved (*Dicotyledonae*), both annual and perennial. The main weeds appearing on golf courses are *Artemisia* spp. (mainly *A. japonica* Thunb.), plantain species [mainly Asiatic plantain (*Plantago asiatica* L.) and buckhorn plantain (*P. lanceolata* L.)], hawkweeds [mainly narrow-leaf hawkweed (*Hieracium umbellatum* L.)], curly dock (*Rumex crispus* L.), red sorrel (*R. acetosella* L.), California burclover (*Medicago hispida*), and dwarfbamboos (*Sasa* spp.).

Prevention of Diseases and Insect Control

Diseases such as snow mold [mainly *Fusarium nivale* (Fr) Cas.], brown patch (*Rhizoctonia solani* Kohn), and dollarspot (*Sclerotinia homoeocarpa* F. T. Bennett) appear frequently on turfs in the cool climatic regions. They can be controlled by spraying with the proper fungicides such as a mixture of tetrachlor-iso-phthalonitrile and bis-disulfide, etc. Species or cultivars resistant to diseases should be selected for turf.

The main insects which appear on turf are armyworm (*Leucania separata* Walker), striated chafer (*Anomala testaceipes* M.), and redworm (*Limnodrilus socialis* S.). They can be controlled by spraying with diazinon or chlordane.

As stated above, the author could confirm that most turf species or cultivars introduced from foreign countries, mainly the United States, can adapt to the environmental conditions in Hokkaido, which is located in a cooler portion of Japan. However, location causes them to respond differently to fertilization, competition between native plants, invading weeds, and other turfgrasses introduced from abroad. Proper cultural practices, including fertilization and mowing, should be given proper attention, along with the introduction of the most adaptable cultivars.

LITERATURE CITED

1. Beard, J. B. 1973. Turfgrass: Science and culture. Prentice-Hall, Inc., Englewood Cliffs, N.J.
2. Oohara, Y. 1975. Studies on the establishment, management and utilization of northern type turfgrass. J. Jpn. Turfgrass Res. Assoc. 4(2):1–6.

Note 4

Evolution of Improved Lawngrasses in America: A Review of Major Events Leading to the Kentucky Bluegrass Cultivar Revolution[1]

R. W. SCHERY

ABSTRACT

Cool-season lawngrasses from Europe spread widely in America to yield many ecotypes [as with Kentucky bluegrass (*Poa pratensis* L.)] that were quite adaptable. Discovery and market development of 'Merion' Kentucky bluegrass showed that isolates from this huge gene pool could yield superior cultivars finding public acceptance at a premium. Hybridization work in several sections of the country proved the advantage of crossing select parental lines. Development of new cultivars first received serious commercial attention in Europe and then, upon passage of "breeder's rights" legislation, in the United States. Now sophisticated breeding techniques join selection from adventive stands to produce a plethora of fine cultivars. Fortunately, the breeding of ever-better lawngrasses is not seriously threatened by extinction of landraces, as is occurring with many major agricultural species.

INTRODUCTION

Kentucky bluegrass (*Poa pratensis* L.) is probably the leading elite turfgrass species in the United States, measured either by seed usage or total acreage. It will serve as the major example characterizing evolvement of improved lawngrass cultivars. The species was apparently not indigenous to North America, but rather introduced by the early colonists from Europe (1). For more than a century it was known by a number of common names, among which junegrass and Englishgrass were common. Englishgrass usually signified polystand with white clover (*Trifolium repens* L.). It became identified with Kentucky early in the 19th century. As the forests were cleared and the ground opened to cultivation Kentucky bluegrass volunteered and grew superlatively on the phosphatic soils of north central Kentucky.

Few records were kept of Kentucky bluegrass dispersal during the early days of American settlement, but even well into the 20th century the

[1] A contribution from the Better Lawn and Turf Inst., Marysville, Ohio, USA.

species was spreading westward and northward in the eastern Great Plains into areas where it previously was unknown. By the mid-1900's Kentucky bluegrass had established many ecotypes and biotypes. Most of these don't seem to have been genetically isolated other than to the extent that apomixis prevails within the species (Kentucky bluegrass is for the most part highly apomictic, a polyploid marked by aneuploidy, facile genome absorption, and chromosomal variability) (4, 5).

The remainder of this paper reviews the sequence of events leading to the modern era of fine turf cultivars characterized by Kentucky bluegrass, this polymorphic, widely spread, highly plastic, adventive species. Kentucky bluegrass, more than any other entity, has played a leading role in the maturation of the lawnseed industry and in bringing a rapidly expanding, sophisticated lawn technology to suburbanizing America.

HISTORICAL DEVELOPMENT

The status of the lawnseed industry in the United States shortly after World War II, built mostly around Kentucky bluegrass, is reviewed in some detail by Schery (3). The chief distinction between pasture bluegrass and lawn bluegrass seed was the greater care in harvesting, cleaning, handling, and merchandizing of the latter. Since all seed was harvested from naturalizing stands in fields used much of the year for grazing or meadowing, genetic differences were not isolated nor distinguishable (although some ecotypic differences may have prevailed since seed destined for sale as lawnseed tended to be stripped from pastures having richer soil and denser, more vigorous stands). In any event natural selection had evolved a hardy, recuperative, tenacious series of ecotypes that adapted well to a variety of uses in all parts of the bluegrass range (most of the northeastern U.S.) when blended as commercial seed.

These are not bad credentials for a lawn grass. Scatter diagrams (Fig. 1) show some geographical distinctiveness, with perhaps lesser variability towards the periphery of the species' spread from a hypothetical center in Kentucky. When seed collections from differing parts of the Kentucky bluegrass range were planted side-by-side at the Lawn Institute, Marysville, Ohio, USA, however, no phenotypic differences could be noted. All accessions molded to the local environment much like the mimicry Harlan and de Wet describe for wild oats (*Avena fatua* L.) (2). There was no evidence of phenological discrepancies, as a number of prairie grasses show (4). This is the base that has supported the sophisticated selection and breeding of superior Kentucky bluegrass cultivars since World War II (7).

Shortly before World War II Dr. John Monteith, Bureau of Plant Industry, USDA, established a turfgrass testing and selection facility in Arlington, Va., USA. The research, supported by the U.S. Golf association (USGA) emphasized vegetative strains of creeping bentgrass (*Agrostis stolonifera* L.) for golf course greens, but a number of distinctive Kentucky bluegrass selections had also been collected and were being evalu-

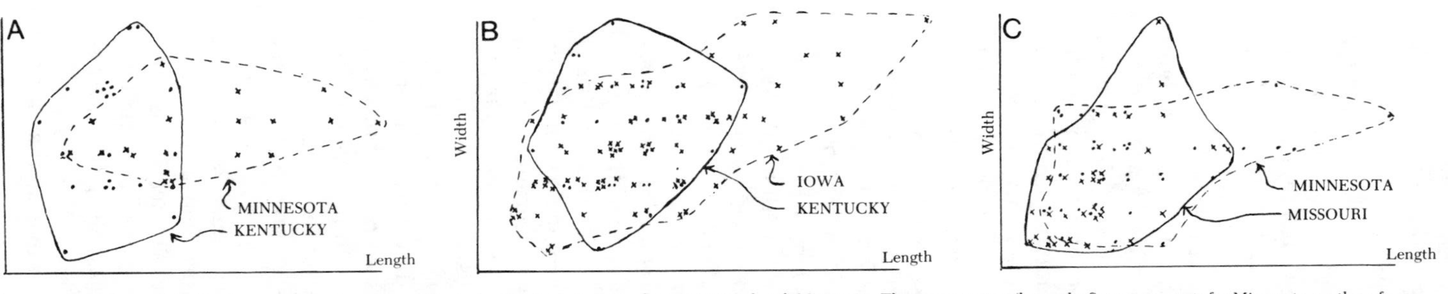

A. Comparison of the no. 1 (tip) leaf on non-flowering culms of Kentucky bluegrass, in Kentucky as contrasted with Minnesota. The more extreme (longer leaf) measurements for Minnesota are those from the northern part of the state; those nearer like Kentucky are from the southern part. B. Comparisons of the no. 2 leaf (second from tip) of non-flowering culms of Kentucky bluegrass, from Kentucky and Iowa. There's a great deal of overlap, but a tendency in Iowa for leaves to become longer, and then show less variability in width. C. Comparison of leaf 3 (third from tip), on non-flowering culms, of Kentucky bluegrass from Missouri and Minnesota. The width/length spread for Missouri is not a whole lot unlike that noted for Kentucky in previous charts, and seems to differ from more northerly populations in the same general way (if not to the extent) that was the case when comparing Kentucky grass (A).

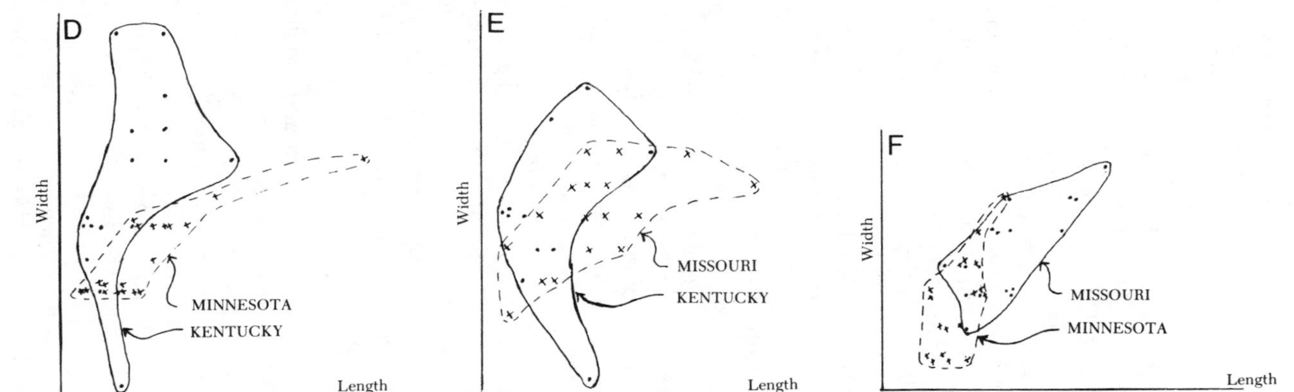

D. Comparison of the second panicle leaf, on Kentucky bluegrass from Kentucky and from Minnesota. Again, the extremes in length for Minnesota are from the northern part of the state (viz. A). E. Comparison of the second panicle leaf of Kentucky bluegrass from Kentucky and from Missouri. It appears that the trend manifest for Minnesota in D is already indicated in Missouri. F. Comparison of the tip (flag) leaf on young panicles of Kentucky bluegrass from Missouri and Minnesota. Although Minnesota flags average shorter, there is perhaps greater genetic restriction.

Fig. 1. Scatter diagram of natural (adventive) Kentucky bluegrass in the midwestern U.S.

ated at Arlington. One of these, B-27, from the Philadelphia, Pa. area (Merion Golf Club), was to become cultivar 'Merion'. Monteith had sent vegetative materials, including the yet unnamed Merion, around the country for testing. When the grounds were taken over for construction of the Pentagon, test selections were transferred to the USDA research facility at Beltsville, Md. In the subsequent confusion some research plantings were plowed out, including that of B-27.

Fortunately, a thimbleful of B-27 seed had been saved and was sent to Pennsylvania State University where it was grown out as spaced plantings. Dr. Joe Duich, assigned to research Merion in 1952 revisited the Merion Golf Club but was unable to find any remnant of the original patch of Merion from which the initial clonal collection had been made. Off-types were common in the spaced plantings made from B-27 seed. A lengthy series of rogueings eventually yielded the standard B-27 which was then named Merion. This led to modern cultivar development. Slightly later a parallel situation involving hybridizations, evaluation, and selection by Dr. Glenn Burton at the USDA Coastal Plains Experiment Station resulted in the Tifton series of bermudagrass [*Cynodon dactylon* (L.) Pers.] cultivars ('Tifgreen,' 'Tifway,' etc.) that did as much for vegetatively planted southern turf as Merion did for northern turf.

Although agronomists could clearly see the wisdom of breeding turfgrasses specifically for fine turf qualities (e.g. lower growth habit, resistance to disease, greater attractiveness, etc.), the advantages were not so apparent to the lawnseed industry. Seedsmen questioned whether Kentucky bluegrass could be successfully grown solely for lawnseed (i.e. be unsubsidized by seasonal grazing) and whether it could compete with less expensive natural Kentucky bluegrass seed then flooding the market. Merion, a notoriously low yielding selection, produces about 300 kg/ha of seed compared to as much as 1,500 kg/ha for a high yielding common type such as 'Newport'. Even though natural Kentucky bluegrass, grown in untended pastures, was not highly productive, it was certainly far less costly per pound than Merion. To prevent sexual crossing, Merion had to be grown in isolation even though it was reported to be highly apomictic. The basic question to be faced was whether the lawnseed consuming public, accustomed to natural Kentucky bluegrass seed of good mechanical quality at less than 50¢/pound, could be induced to pay appreciably more for a genetically superior "star performer" like Merion.

Credit for proving the point goes to Arden Jacklin, president of what was then a rather small and newly organized seed production firm near Spokane, Wash. Although most top quality lawnseed now comes from Washington, Idaho, and Oregon, Kentucky bluegrass was at that time something of a novelty in the Pacific Northwest. This was helpful because pure line plantings were able to remain free from volunteer contamination. This was a problem in the East where Kentucky bluegrass had become an ubiquitous component of the ecosystem.

Mr. Jacklin felt that Merion represented the wave of the future, especially if carefully grown specifically for lawns, with meticulous attention to seed purity, cleanliness, and germination. He accepted the risk that his company could coax relatively high yields from Merion by improved agronomic technology. It was hoped that a sizable minority of seed consumers would pay far more than customary prices for this superior lawnseed. This was quickly proven to be true. By the mid-1950's limited Merion seed supplies could hardly meet demand, even at 10-fold the price of common bluegrass. The efforts extended not only to advanced agricultural techniques for the production of Merion seed, but embraced an articulate promotional program as well. The Merion Bluegrass Association helped achieve widespread recognition for Merion as a superior cultivar.

DISCUSSION AND PROGNOSIS

With Merion having proved the potentiality, expansion of the industry into the breeding of new cultivars has been phenomenal (6, 8, 9). The movement has been particularly strong in the United States where an abundance of space and available transportation permitted dramatic change from the urbanized living conditions characteristic of the early 20th century to the spacious suburban homesites characterizing the mid-20th century. A demand for lawns and lawn products was inevitable, especially when encouraged by promotional programs. Lawns are easily established and maintained when supported by an industry that furnishes convenience products of all sorts [e.g. select cultivars, effective pesticides and other aids, and mechanized equipment (such as mowers, spreaders, thatch removers, etc.)].

Research at the universities can boast of many accomplishments. Farm population has dwindled to about 5%, while the single dwelling suburban population has increased enormously. Thus many academic institutions, such as the University of Rhode Island (in a state having little agricultural activity), have drifted away from traditional farm crop research in favor of servicing the home and the urbanized environmental needs. Rhode Island sensed this trend early and initiated a turfgrass research program in 1890. In recent decades almost all states have experienced appreciable suburbanization and have established or increased turfgrass research staffs.

A noteworthy example is Rutgers, The State University, New Jersey. The first full-time turfgrass breeding position, for which Dr. Reed Funk was hired, was created here. Dr. Funk and his students, utilizing new Kentucky bluegrass bloodlines and breeding techniques, have provided many of today's most highly regarded lawngrass cultivars. Among the Kentucky bluegrasses are 'Adelphi,' 'Bonnieblue,' 'Galaxy,' 'Glade,'

'Majestic,' 'Plush,' 'Ram-I,' and 'Touchdown.' Rutgers was also one of the first academic institutions to grant exclusive proprietary rights to commercial firms on a royalty basis. This has created incentive to promote the cultivars and improve the seed quality (public cultivars are available to everyone and promotional efforts reward the competitors.) This is a practical way to make an improved lawn cultivar available to the public which has supported the program through tax money.

European seedsmen sensed the proprietary possibilities for lawn cultivars early and were active in the decade before "breeders rights" legislation for the United States became effective in 1970. The United States is still indebted to European breeders for many cultivars important to America. 'Baron,' 'Birka,' 'Enmundi,' 'Fylking,' and 'Sydsport' are among the notables. Although Kentucky bluegrass has led the way, similar progress is being made with perennial ryegrass (*Lolium perenne* L.), red fescue (*Festuca rubra* L.), and other species.

For an audience from many countries, it seems appropriate to have reviewed the events that have featured rapid expansion of the turfgrass industry in the United States. One of the more important of these events is the transformation affected by the large array of specially bred cultivars that today provide superior turf quality in wide selection. Almost all modern cultivars have been bred (or selected) for better disease tolerance and a lower growing habit. A low growth habit helps prevent damage from low mowing. Insect resistance, vigorous germination, compatibility in polystands, tolerance to herbicides, and adaptation to low maintenance are also stirring interest in the turfgrass industry.

Much refinement remains to be accomplished, but the events of the last few decades have opened the door to many opportunities and have vastly improved turfgrasses. Fortunately, sources of genetic variability for turfgrasses are not as greatly endangered as for agricultural crops. Landraces of many crop species are threatened with extinction as modern cultivars swamp the ecosystem. Persistent, locally adapted clones and races of Kentucky bluegrass and other species abound in the "hedgerows" of suburbia.

Looking back, several key events stand out. Especially noteworthy in America has been suburbanization and the inevitable recognition of lawn esthetics and functional benefits. Seedsmen accepted the challenge, calling for special cultivars of improved quality and greater attractiveness following the Merion breakthrough. Jacklin and other prominent seed companies provided promotional leadership that created public awareness of lawn values. European establishments were perceptive in recognizing the market for special cultivars and catered to it early. Public research and commercial interests have cooperated to make improved products widely available. It is not surprising that with all of this, turfgrass research has gained recognition and become a worthwhile endeavor with reasonable budgeting in both academic and commercial circles.

LITERATURE CITED

1. Carrier, L., and K. S. Bort. 1916. The history of Kentucky bluegrass and white clover in the United States. J. Am. Soc. Agron. 8:256–266.
2. Harlan, J. R., and J. M. de Wet. 1965. Some thoughts about weeds. Econ. Bot. 19:16–24.
3. Schery, R. W. 1959. Bluegrass' grassroots empire. Econ. Bot. 13:75–84.
4. ———. 1965. This remarkable Kentucky bluegrass. Ann. Mo. Bot. Gard. 52:444–451.
5. ———. 1965. The migration of a plant. Nat. Hist. 74:40–45.
6. ———. 1966. The lawn seed industry comes of age. Crops Soils 19(3):8–11.
7. ———. 1972. Turfgrass cultivars. Am. Hort. 51(2):9–14.
8. ———. 1972. New challenges, opportunities face the lawnseed industry. Crops Soils 25(8):8–11.
9. ———. 1975. Lawns come into their own. Gard. Supply Merch. 26(8):45–50.

Note 5

Tree Shade Adaptation of Turfgrass Species and Cultivars in France[1]

A. CHESNEL
R. CROISE
B. BOURGOIN

ABSTRACT

The comparative shade adaptation of the principle cool-season turfgrass species was investigated under a natural tree shade environment in 1974 and 1975. Two trials were conducted. One was established at Ets Vilmorin at Beaufort en Valleé near Angers, France on an acidic sandy soil under the shade of leafy, coniferous trees and the second site was established by the Institut National de la Recherche Agronomique (INRA) at Poitiers, France on a clay soil with a very dense tree canopy. Comparative adaptation of the various cool-season turfgrass species varied between the two sites in 1974 and 1975. The bentgrass (*Agrostis* spp.) species were best at the Beaufort en Valleé site while shade (*Festuca heterophylla* Lam.) and red (*F. rubra* L.) fescues and roughstalk bluegrass (*Poa trivialis* L.) were the most promising at Poitiers. Most of the cool-season species and cultivars evaluated in the test had almost completely disappeared in both shade sites by late 1975. The rate of disappearance was greater at Poitiers which was attributed to the greater shade canopy density and lower cultural intensity.

INTRODUCTION

The adaptation of turfgrasses to tree and artificial shade environments has been studied by many scientists (1, 2, 3, 4, 5, 6, 7, 8). Shade adaptation is achieved through alterations in plant morphology and physiological mechanisms as Wilkinson and Beard (5, 6) have shown. Research by Beard (2, 3), Wood (8), and Bakker and Vos (1) show that red fescue (*Festuca rubra* L.) and roughstalk bluegrass (*Poa trivialis* L.) have consistently exhibited the best shade adaptation. The bentgrass (*Agrostis* spp.) species, tall fescue (*F. arundinacea* Schreb.), perennial ryegrass (*Lolium perenne* L.), and wood bluegrass (*P. nemoralis* L.) are less adapted. Similar investigations were needed regarding shade adaptation under the environmental and soil conditions in France. The objective of this study was to evaluate the comparative shade adaptation of the common cool-season turfgrass species under two shaded sites within France.

[1] A contribution from Ets Vilmorin, La Ménitré, 49250 Beaufort en Vallée, France and from INDRA-86600 Lusignan, France.

MATERIALS AND METHODS

The investigation was conducted at two distinctly different sites. The rainfall on both sites for 1974 and 1975 was recorded and is shown in Table 1. The precipitation was distinctly greater in 1974 which was more important at Poitiers, France than at Beaufort en Vallée, France. Assessments at both shade experimental sites were made on a 5 to 1 scale in relation to percent cover; 5 = 90 to 100% cover on the plot, 4 = 70 to 90%, 3 = 50 to 70%, 2 = 25 to 50%, and 1 = traces to 25%. A '0' was given to plots where the original grass stand had completely disappeared. The two experimental sites are described as follows.

Vilmorin Site

This site was established on 7 Mar. 1974 at Beaufort en Vallée under the shade of a tree canopy composed of chestnut (*Castanea sativa* Scop.), oak (*Quercus* spp.), and maritime pine (*Pinus pinaster* Soland). Midsummer light intensities were 1,000 to 5,000 lux. The soil was composed of 85% sand with a slightly acidic pH of 6.5 and a low nutrient content, especially P_2O_5 and K_2O. Each of 20 sets of species and cultivars of cool-season turfgrasses were established in 3-m^2 plots with two replications. The cutting height was a relatively high 7 cm along with a minimal mowing frequency of approximately six times per year. The fertilization program consisted of 120 kg/ha N/year in four applications. One application of P_2O_5 and K_2O at a rate of 100 kg each/ha was made. Fallen tree leaves and branches were removed every autumn. Irrigation consisted of two 10-mm applications in August 1974 only during the establishment period.

INRA Site

This experimental site was established on 8 Apr. 1974 in the Poitiers Public Garden with the cooperation of the local park department. The tree-shaded canopy was formed by a stand of lime (*Tilia platyphylla* Scop.) trees which resulted in a midsummer light intensity of 1,000 lux. The soil on the site was a sandy clay with approximately 32% clay and a near-neutral pH of 7.5. The soil was relatively high in organic matter, P_2O_5, and K_2O. This trial consisted of 50 species and cultivars, each planted in 1-m^2 plots. Mowing was accomplished at 2- to 3-week intervals at a 5-cm height. Fertilization consisted of 120 kg/ha N applied in three applications during 1974 and 1975. One application of 100 kg/ha each of P_2O_5 and K_2O was also made each year. The irrigation program at this site consisted of 15 mm of water applied at 2-week inter-

Table 1. Rainfall patterns (mm) in 1974 and 1975 in Beaufort en Vallee and Poitiers, France.

Location	Year	Month						
		Jan.	Feb.	Mar.	Apr.	May	June	
Beaufort en Vallee	1974	58	42	44	23	42	27	
	1975	88	19	61	46	65	12	
Poitiers	1974	72	51	44	40	48	36	
	1975	57	6	87	45	91	10	
		July	Aug.	Sept.	Oct.	Nov.	Dec.	Total
Beaufort en Vallee	1974	3	28	72	45	76	20	480
	1975	29	16	68	18	78	30	530
Poitiers	1974	13	42	80	59	88	22	595
	1975	34	42	118	30	94	47	651

vals throughout the summer. Fallen leaves and branches were removed every fall.

RESULTS

Beaufort en Valleé Study

Results from this 2-year study are summarized as follows. Velvet bentgrass (*A. canina* L.) was slow to establish but eventually formed a good quality turf during 1974. It maintained a very acceptable level of turfgrass quality throughout 1975. Creeping bentgrass (*A. stolonifera* L.) established the most rapidly of all species evaluated in this test. The long-term turfgrass performance under the shaded conditions was also top ranked through the 1974–75 growing season and was still performing quite well in 1976. Colonial bentgrass (*A. tenuis* Sibth.) established slowly but did form a good quality turf. By early 1976 it was ranked among the best.

Orchardgrass (*Dactylis glomerata* L.) a rather vigorous, coarse-textured species, exhibited a very rapid establishment rate. It provided satisfactory cover throughout 1974 and 1975.

Tall fescue had a very good establishment rate in comparison to orchardgrass. Subsequently, a satisfactory green color was maintained throughout both years. Shade fescue (*F. heterophylla* L.) had a very slow establishment rate which impaired the overall performance of this species during 1974 and 1975. However, by January 1976 this species ranked with creeping bentgrass and colonial bentgrass in terms of a satisfactory cover. Hard fescue [*F. ovina* var. *duriuscula* (L.) Koch.] had a rapid initial establishment rate that declined rather rapidly. Meadow fescue (*F. pratensis* Huds.) established poorly under the shade conditions and thus never did form a satisfactory turf. Red fescue had a moderately slow establishment rate. It eventually produced an acceptable quality turf in both 1974 and 1975. The subspecies *F. rubra* var. *litoralis* performed superior to chewings fescue (*Festuca rubra* var. *commutata* Gaud.) and *F. rubra* var. *rubra* established well and had good performance throughout 1974 and 1975, but was severely thinned in 1976. Turf timothy (*Phleum bertolonii* DC.) established quite slowly. Nearly 1 full year was required before a satisfactory cover was achieved. Subsequently the stand was completely destroyed by a midsummer drought in 1975. Timothy (*P. pratense* L.) established somewhat better than turf timothy, but this coarse-textured species never produced an acceptable turf stand, except during the fall and winter of 1974–75.

Wood bluegrass initially exhibited a good establishment rate, but subsequently thinned out quite rapidly. The stand had practically disappeared by late 1975. Kentucky bluegrass (*Poa pratensis* L.) had a relatively slow establishment rate and never produced an acceptable turf stand. From mid-spring in 1975 onwards the density tended to decline and the turf exhibited serious problems with powdery mildew. The initial establishment rate of roughstalk bluegrass was slow, but a satisfactory stand was eventually achieved by the autumn of 1974. However, the drought during 1975 severely damaged this species.

Summary

The overall turfgrass quality ratings for 1974 and 1975 are summarized as follows. 1974: creeping bentgrass, hard fescue, perennial ryegrass > Kentucky bluegrass, tall fescue, wood bluegrass = orchardgrass, red fescue, velvet bentgrass, colonial bentgrass, timothy, roughstalk bluegrass, shade fescue > turf timothy, meadow fescue. 1975: creeping bentgrass, colonial bentgrass, velvet bentgrass, perennial ryegrass > red fescue, hard fescue, orchardgrass, shade fescue, tall fescue, turf timothy, timothy, roughstalk bluegrass > Kentucky bluegrass, wood bluegrass, meadow fescue.

A general decline in turfgrass quality continued following the drought of 1976, and subsequently permitted the extensive invasion of annual bluegrass (*Poa annua* L.). Thus, by January 1977 the only species that still maintained acceptable dominance under the shaded environment were velvet bentgrass, creeping bentgrass, and colonial bentgrass.

Poitiers Study

Velvet bentgrass exhibited the poorest establishment and had completely disappeared within 6 months. Creeping bentgrass had a very poor initial establishment with some plants persisting after 2 years. Colonial bentgrass exhibited very poor establishment in comparison to velvet bentgrass, but eventually formed a modest cover and ranked better than the other two bentgrass species.

Tall fescue ranked best in turfgrass establishment and provided the best overall turfgrass quality in 1974. Distinct decline in overall performance occurred in 1975 and by January 1976 had almost completely disappeared. Shade fescue established at a rapid rate and produced an acceptable turfgrass stand throughout 1974. The overall turfgrass quality declined in 1975, but recovered so that by January 1976 it ranked with roughstalk bluegrass as the best species in overall turfgrass quality and cover. Hard fescue had a good establishment rate but subsequently declined in density and had disappeared within 6 months. A few hair fescue (*F. ovina* var. *tenuifolia* Sibth.) plants persisted for only 3 months. Red fescue had the best establishment when compared to tall fescue and provided one of the best overall turfgrass covers during both 1974 and 1975. Chewings fescue and *F. rubra* var. *litoralis* performed superior to red fescue in this particular shade environment.

Perennial ryegrass established well initially but was adversely affected so that the overall turfgrass cover and performance was quite poor in 1974. The stand had completely disappeared by the summer of 1975.

Turf timothy had a good initial establishment rate, but declined rapidly and had practically disappeared by late 1974.

Wood bluegrass had a very poor initial establishment and within 6 months had almost completely disappeared. Some scattered tufts did manage to persist through the summer of 1975. Kentucky bluegrass established well initially, but declined rapidly and never formed an acceptable turf. By 1975 it was practically nonexistent. Roughstalk bluegrass ranked with tall fescue and red fescue in terms of best overall establishment. The overall turfgrass quality and cover was good in 1974 and satisfactory in 1975. The performance was very good by January 1976.

Summary

The overall comparative rankings for the species evaluated in this study are summarized as follows: 1974: tall fescue, *F. rubra* var. *litoralis*, chewings fescue, roughstalk bluegrass > *F. rubra* var. *rubra*, shade fescue, perennial ryegrass > Kentucky bluegrass, turf timothy > hard fescue > velvet bentgrass, wood bluegrass, hair fescue, creeping bentgrass = colonial bentgrass. 1975: *F. rubra* var. *litoralis*, chewings fescue, roughstalk bluegrass, tall fescue > *F. rubra* var. *rubra*, shade fescue > perennial ryegrass, colonial bentgrass > creeping bentgrass, Kentucky bluegrass, turf timothy > wood bluegrass > velvet bentgrass > hard fescue = hair fescue.

A severe decline in overall turfgrass quality occurred with most species during 1976 which eventually led to invasion by roughstalk bluegrass and to a lesser extent by annual bluegrass. Thus by January 1977 the major species persisting was roughstalk bluegrass. Both shade fescue and red fescue had a modest stand of turfgrass plants persisting. The severe drought was a strong influencing factor on this site in spite of the fact that some irrigation was practiced.

LITERATURE CITED

1. Bakker, J. J., and H. Vos. 1976. Reaktion von grasen auf Schatten einwirkung. Rasen-Turf-Gazon 4:88–91.
2. Beard, J. B. 1965. Factors in the adaptation of turfgrasses to shade. Agron. J. 57:457–459.
3. ————. 1969. Turfgrass shade adaptation. p. 273–282. *In* R. R. Davis (ed.) Proc. 1st Int. Turfgrass Res. Conf., Harrogate, England. 18–21 July 1969.
4. McVey, G. R., E. W. Mayer, and J. A. Simmons. 1969. Responses of various turfgrasses to certain light spectra modifications. p. 264–272. *In* R. R. Davis (ed.) Proc. 1st Int. Turfgrass Res. Conf., Harrogate, England. 18–21 July 1969.
5. Wilkinson, J. F., and J. B. Beard. 1973. Morphological responses of *Poa pratensis* and *Festuca rubra* to reduced light intensity. p. 231–240. *In* E. C. Roberts (ed.) Proc. 2nd Int. Turfgrass Res. Conf., Blacksburg, Va. June 1973. Am. Soc. Agron., Madison, Wis.
6. ————, and ————. 1975. Anatomical response of 'Merion' Kentucky bluegrass and 'Pennlawn' red fescue at reduced light intensities. Crop Sci. 15:189–194.
7. Winstead, C. W., and C. Y. Ward. 1973. Persistence of southern turfgrass in a shade environment. p. 221–230. *In* E. C. Roberts (ed.) Proc. 2nd Int. Turfgrass Res. Conf., Blacksburg, Va. June 1973. Am. Soc. Agron., Madison, Wis.
8. Wood, G. M. 1969. Shade tolerant turfgrasses of the United States and Southern Canada. p. 283–288. *In* R. R. Davis (ed.) Proc. 1st Int. Turfgrass Res. Conf., Harrogate, England. 18–21 July 1969.

Note 6

Some Physical Aspects of Sports Turfs[1]

P. BOEKEL

ABSTRACT

The playability of turf for football and field hockey in autumn is a very important property. This is especially true in countries like The Netherlands where rainfall exceeds evapotranspiration, resulting in a wet, unstable top layer. To find how such situations can be improved, turfs around Groningen, The Netherlands, were investigated for topsoil stability, groundwater table, soil humus, clay content, and bulk density.

By graphical and numerical analyses of the results it was found that the stability increased as the bulk density and depth of the groundwater increased. An interaction between the effects of these two factors was found, indicating that the effect of bulk density became smaller as the groundwater depth increased. For maintenance it is important to know how to control the bulk density. This can be done by changing the content of humus, clay, and sand or by changing the arrangement of soil particles through compaction. An indication of the acceptable humus content in combination with the density of the topsoil for situations varying in depth of the groundwater table is given.

INTRODUCTION

Turf playability in fall or winter is a very important property of turf use for football and field hockey. In climates where rainfall exceeds evaporation during the fall and winter, as in The Netherlands, wet, weak surface layers often result unless an acceptable balance is maintained between groundwater level and soil physical condition without reducing grass growth. To avoid such situations, the topsoil of the turf must be brought or held in such a condition that even in a wet period stability can tolerate intensive use. At the same time the physical condition of the soil should be favorable for turf growth.

To attain and maintain good playability of turf the factors affecting surface layer stability must be known and, if possible be quantified. To more clearly define the relationship of factors affecting surface layer stability, observations and measurements were made from 1970 to 1975 on a number of sports turfs around the City of Groningen in The Netherlands.

[1] A contribution from the Inst. for Soil Fertility, Haren, Groningen, The Netherlands.

MATERIALS AND METHODS

Topsoil stability was estimated from 1 to 9 by pushing the heel of a shoe into the sod (4). A rating of 1 indicated an unstable surface and 9 indicated a stable surface. A rating of 7 corresponds to ideal stability, while 6.5 was barely acceptable, and above 7 was unacceptability hard. This so called "heel method" works very quickly, but requires some experience.

The following factors that were expected to affect soil stability were assessed: (i) groundwater table depth was determined in the autumn and winter by observing the water level in perforated plastic tubes placed in the soil (these observations were made at the time of soil stability estimates); (ii) soil composition of the top 5 cm was determined for humus, clay, and sand particle size; (iii) soil density was determined from soil cores sampled from the top 5 cm.

RESULTS

Groundwater table and soil stability influenced by rainfall and surface evaporation, varied greatly with time. For further interpretation of the results, mean values for both properties in rather wet periods were calculated.

A positive correlation was found between the stability and the depth of the groundwater and the bulk density. Furthermore, there was a negative correlation between the stability and both the humus and clay contents (Table 1).

Table 1 shows strong mutual correlations between the factors of humus and clay content and bulk density. This makes conclusions concerning the real effect of the individual factors very difficult.

Interactions were also found among factors affecting topsoil stability. For example, the effect of the groundwater table increases as the organic matter increases. A graphical procedure was used to determine the effect of groundwater table depth and bulk density of topsoil stability (Fig. 1).

Soil bulk density had little effect on topsoil stability in soils with a deep groundwater table, but soils with shallow drainage were greatly affected by soil bulk density. Thus, a high water table was acceptable if bulk density was high, while a low bulk density was acceptable if the water table was deep. A combination of high water table and low bulk

Table 1. Correlations between different soil factors.

	Groundwater table	Humus content	Clay content	Bulk density
Humus content	−0.15			
Clay content	−0.16	+0.62		
Bulk density	+0.11	−0.77	−0.68	
Stability topsoil	+0.44	−0.42	−0.44	+0.52

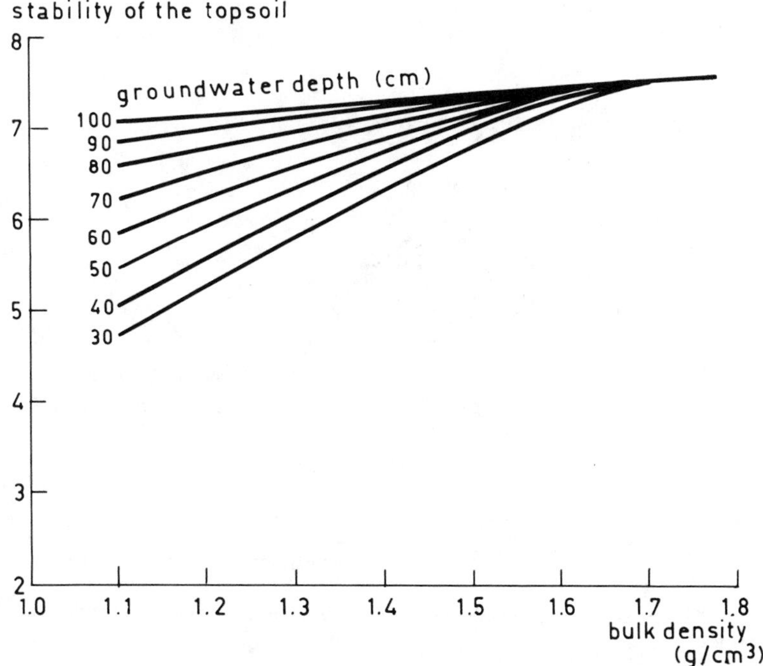

Fig. 1. Topsoil stability in relation to groundwater depth and bulk density.

density does not provide sufficient stability. This condition is graphically presented in Fig. 2 where, for two groups of turfs with a good and poor topsoil stability, the bulk density and the groundwater depth are given. Conditions required for an acceptable topsoil stability can be deduced from Fig. 1 and 2.

DISCUSSION

The results mentioned would indicate that good topsoil stability can be obtained by deep drainage or by producing a rather high bulk density. Generally, a deep groundwater table is preferred to the second possibility because it is somewhat easier and is cheaper in the long run. Also, many systems of drainage are available (1, 3).

However, conditions do exist where a high groundwater table or poor drainage must be accepted. These can sometimes be solved by optimizing the bulk density of the soil. Bulk density depends mainly on the humus and clay composition of the soil and on the arrangement of soil particles which is influenced by the intensity of compaction. Figure 3, gives the relation between bulk density and humus content for soils with a low clay content. This gives an impression of the decrease in bulk density with increasing humus content and of the divergence of the points due to

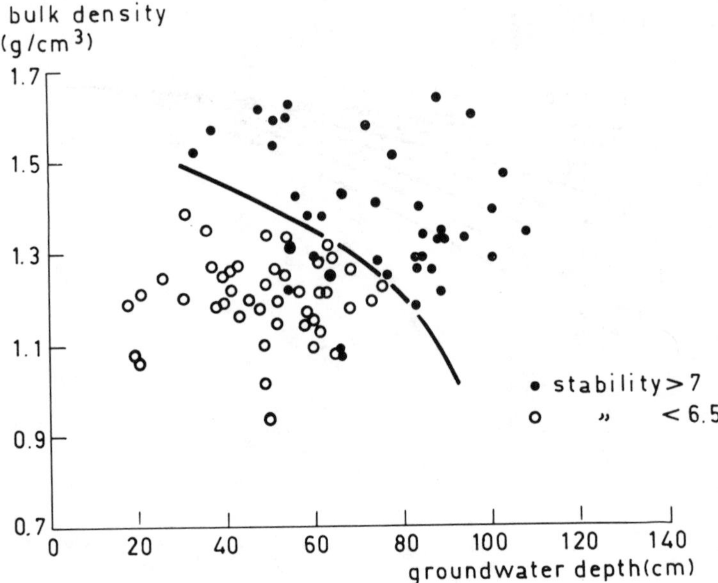

Fig. 2. Topsoil stability in combination with different groundwater depths and bulk densities.

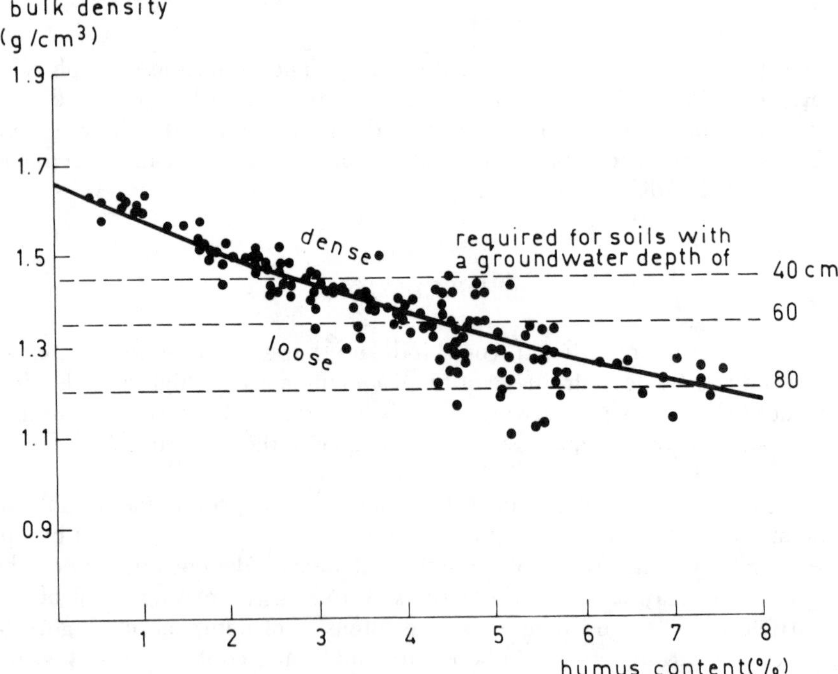

Fig. 3. Bulk density in relation to humus content and the required situation for a good topsoil stability.

the arrangement soil particles (above the curve equal to dense, under the curve equal to loose). Furthermore, three horizontal lines have been drawn which present the desired bulk density for soils with different groundwater tables.

It can be concluded from Fig. 3 that for soils with a high water table at a depth of about 40 cm under wet conditions, the humus content should not exceed 3% and only 2% if the soil particles should be loosely arranged.

In the presence of a water table at 80 cm, the acceptable humus content is 4.5% on rather loose soils and 7.5 to 8.0% on dense soils. The results indicate that maintaining a high relative density is important because a somewhat higher water table or humus content is then acceptable. A high relative density can be realized by a sufficient intensity of play. Many main fields are not used very often and as a result have a loose unstable top layer. The risk that the soil becomes too dense for good growth of the grass is minor since grass suffers more often from a shortage of water than from a shortage of air (2).

LITERATURE CITED

1. Adams, W. A., V. I. Stewart, and D. J. Thornton. 1971. The construction and drainage of sports fields for wintergames in Britain. Univ. Coll. Wales, Welsh Soils Discuss. Group Rep. 12:85–95.
2. Boekel, P. 1975. Het fysisch milieu van grasvelden voor recreatief gebruik en de doeleinden van grondverbetering. p. 71–92. *In* M. Hoogerkamp and J. W. Minderhoud (eds.) Grasveldkunde; aanleg en onderhoud van grasvelden voor gebruiks- en sierveldoeleinden. Centrum Landbouwpubl. Landbouwdoc., Wageningen.
3. Dierickx, W. 1976. Drainage en afwatering van grassportvelden. Landbouwtijdschrift 29:607–623.
4. Pieters, J. H. 1961. Gevoeligheid van grasland voor vertrapping. Landbouwvoorlichting 18:377–383.

Note 7

Soil Conditioning by Synthetic Media[1]

H. FRANKEN

ABSTRACT

Playing surfaces of sports fields are modified by incorporating peat, sand, and other chemically inert materials. In this study, incorporating peat produced a more favorable response than Hygromull, Hygropor, or Agrosil. Hygropor reduced water conductivity in sand soils and had no impact on water movement in silt and clay soils. Agrosil produced a favorable response only when added to a lava/sand mix low in humus.

INTRODUCTION

Turf performance depends not only upon the physical characteristics of the soil, but is also greatly influenced by the root development of the turfgrasses. Between soil and plant there is a close relationship. This is particularly important to sports turf.

In addition to peat, synthetic substances of different efficiencies are being used in increasing amounts in Europe to improve unfavorable soil and growth conditions. Two groups of products are described. They are: (i) plastic foams such as Hygromull, Hygropor 73, and Styromull; (ii) the silicate colloid Agrosil LR. This latter substance is recommended for improving substrates which are rich in sand and poor in humus. The plastic foams, however, are mainly used to regulate the air and water content of the soil. Methods of application and efficiencies of these synthetic soil conditioning substances are detailed in the literature (3, 4, 6, 9, 12, 15, 18, 19).

MATERIALS AND METHODS

The effects of the soil conditioning substances on the root zones, as well as on the root development of turfgrasses, were studied on mixes of lava/sand and soil/sand (Table 1). The lava/sand relation is about 1:1 and the soil/sand relation is about 1:6. In part, however, the addition of sand was abandoned. With the exception of the soil, grain size distribution of the constructing materials is mostly running within the DIN-norm area (Fig. 1).

[1] A contribution from Inst. für Pflanzenbau, Katzenburgweg 5, 5300 Bonn, West Germany.

The research project was started in the spring of 1976. The tests were made 1 year later at the end of March 1977. Methods used are common today (5, 14). The construction materials (soil, sand, and lava) were blended in a mixer (7). Water-holding materials such as peat, Hygromull, and Hygropor were added by a repeated resetting of the substrates. This was done to preserve the structure of these materials (8).

The root mass and the infiltration rate (sec), as a characteristic for the water permeability, were transformed logarithmically before interpretation.

RESULTS AND DISCUSSION

The addition of peat or peat plus Hygromull significantly increased the water holding capacity of the lava/sand mix (Table 2). This effect was not observed when only Hygromull was used. The relatively lower pressure stability of Hygromull probably caused this (13).

With respect to water availability, the higher water holding capacity of the peat sample is not equaled by a slightly higher wilting point. However, the slower and more constant water availability of Hygromull, in opposition to peat, should also be considered (11). These results (Table 2) confirm those of earlier research (6, 10, 17).

The infiltration time of 10 mm water is at a very low level for the lava/sand mix. These substrates have a very high water permeability. The addition of 31% by volume Hygropor (ca. 22% by volume of Hygromull and substituting of ca. 9% by volume Styromull for a portion of the sand) to the soil/sand mix reduced water conductivity. This result could not be obtained by adding 22% by volume Hygromull alone.

The same amount (31% by volume Hygropor) does not improve the water transmission of a soil high in clay and silt. The Hygropor plots showed a strong elasticity when loaded. In this regard, the factor "Agrosil LR" is of no importance or advantage.

Table 1. Composition of the mixes (volume %)

Mix no.	Soil	Sand 0/2	Lava 0/5	Hygromull (Hm)	Peat (P)	Hygropor (Hp)	Agrosil LR
51	–	40	40	20	–	–	–
52	–	40	40	–	20	–	–
53	–	40	40	10	10	–	–
54	–	40	40	10	10	–	+
55	–	50	50	–	–	–	+
56	–	50	50	–	–	–	–
21	11	67	–	22	–	–	–
22	11	67	–	22	–	–	+
23	11	67	–	11	11	–	–
24	11	67	–	11	11	–	+
25	11	58	–	–	–	31	+
26	100	–	–	–	–	–	–
27	69	–	–	–	–	31	–
28	69	–	–	–	–	31	+

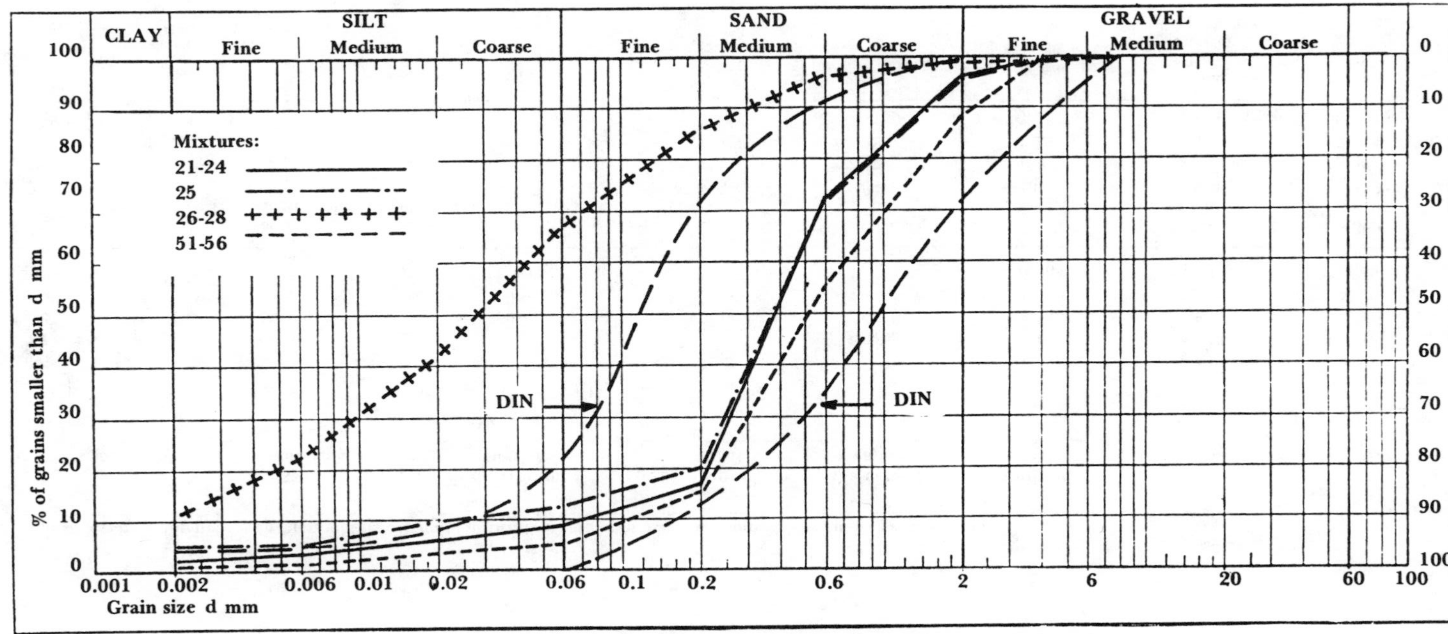

Fig. 1. Grain size distribution (%) for the root zone mixes investigated.

Table 2. Relationship between water holding capacity, infiltration rate, root mass, and some water holding amendments.

Mix no.	Construction material	Water holding material			Agrosil LR	Water holding capacity	Infiltration rate	Root mass	
								0–5 cm	5–10 cm
		Vol. %				Vol. %	log (sec)	log (g/1,000 cm^2•10^3)	
		Hm	P	Hp					
56		–	–	–	–	36.2	1,739	4,529	3,291
51	Lava/	20	–	–	–	38.2	1,626	4,503	3,228
52	Sand	–	20	–	–	43.6	1,815	4,659	3,801
53		10	10	–	–	40.8	1,719	4,658	3,742
L.S.D. 5%						2.43	0.2047	0.2385	0.3888
21	Soil/	22	–	–	–	34.2	2,445	4,658	3,350
23	Sand	11	11	–	–	35.0	2,431	4,774	3,610
25		–	–	31	+	34.1	2,960	4,604	3,483
28	Soil	–	–	31	+	37.2	4,303	4,587	3,472
26		–	–	–	–	35.8	4,257	4,579	3,564
L.S.D. 5%						1.48	0.4137	0.1052	0.2447

Table 3. Relationship between water holding capacity, infiltration rate, root mass, and Agrosil LR.

Mix no.	Construction material	Water holding material			Agrosil LR	Water holding capacity	Infiltration rate	Root mass	
								0–5 cm	5–10 cm
		Vol. %				Vol. %	log (sec)	log (g/1,000 cm²•10³)	
		Hm	P	Hp					
56		–	–	–	–	36.2	1,739	4,529	3,291
55	Lava/	–	–	–	+	39.0	1,730	4,657	3,713
53	Sand	10	10	–	–	40.8	1,719	4,658	3,742
54		10	10	–	+	41.0	1,691	4,518	3,476
L.S.D. 5%						2.43	0.2047	0.2385	0.3888
23		11	11	–	–	35.0	2,431	4,774	3,610
24	Soil/	11	11	–	+	34.4	2,569	4,766	3,438
21	Sand	22	–	–	–	34.2	2,445	4,658	3,350
22		22	–	–	+	35.5	2,331	4,645	3,433
27	Soil	–	–	31	–	38.7	4,122	4,612	3,484
28		–	–	31	+	37.2	4,303	4,587	3,472
L.S.D. 5%						1.48	0.4137	0.1052	0.2447

In contrast to the Hygromull mix, higher amounts of root mass were found in the peat and peat + Hygromull root zones. A marked increase was seen in the 5- to 10-cm layer. In this connection we would emphasize the problems which occur when washing out grass roots from substrates containing peat.

The increases in water holding capacity and root development caused by the addition of water holding amendments have to be weighed against the disadvantages associated with water conductivity (8).

The use of Agrosil LR improved the water holding capacity and an intensity of root growth only in the mix of lava/sand, which was high in sand and low in humus. The effects mostly occurred in the 5- to 10-cm layer (16). This increase of dry root mass was noticed in the time between early January and late March 1977 (Table 3).

When peat and Hygromull (mixes 53, 54, 23, and 24) were added, the trend seemed to be a decrease in dry root mass. A specified Agrosil effect on root development in the time between early January and late March 1977 could not be seen in this study.

The importance of Agrosil, with respect to the water holding capacity of sandy soils and substrates, has already been discussed in several publications (1, 2, 9).

SUMMARY

The effects of some soil conditioning substances on certain root zone characteristics and the root growth of turfgrasses were studied. The results are summarized as follows.

1. Peat showed a greater efficiency than Hygromull as measured by the water holding capacity of the mix and the root development of turfgrasses.
2. High amounts of Hygropor in the mix (ca. 1/3) severely reduced the water conductivity of a sandy substrate. On the other hand, the poor water transmission of a soil rich in clay and silt could not be altered.
3. A specified effect on Agrosil on improved water holding capacity and root development could only be noticed in a mix of lava/sand which was high in sand and low in humus. When peat, Hygromull, or Hygropor were added this response was not observed.

LITERATURE CITED

1. Bartels, R. 1972. Synthetische Bodenverbesserungsmittel auf tiefgepflügten Heidepodsolen. Mitt. Dtsch. Bodenkundl. Gesellsch. 15:247–251.
2. Bohle, H., and P. Holst. 1973. Standorts- und Ertragsbeeinflussung durch den Einsatz von Agrosil auf Heidepodsolen Schleswig-Holsteins. Landwirtsch. Forsch. 28:1. Sonderheft, 347–352.
3. Büring, W. 1969. Wirkungsweise und Anwendungsmöglichkeit von Agrosil. Rasen Rasengräser 6:78–83.

4. ————. 1974. Moglichkeiten der chemischen und physikalischen Bodenverbesserung. Gartenamt., 278–281.

5. DNA. 1974. Sportplätze-Rasenflächen, DIN 18035, Bl. 4. Beuth-Verlag GmbH, Berlin und Köln.

6. Eggelsmann, R. 1972. Versuche mit Torf und Hygromull bei der Begrünung steriler Sandböden. Mitt. Dtsch. Bodenkundl. Gesellsch. 15:171–180.

7. Franken, H. 1975. Bisherige Erfahrungen mit dem Alimix-Zwangsmischer im Sportplatzbau. Neue Landschaft 20:554–566.

8. ————. 1977. Untersuchungen über den Einfluβ der Mischtechnik auf einige Baustoff- und Tragschichteigenschaften. Neue Landschaft 22:443–446.

9. Gebhardt, H. 1972. Physikalische und chemische Wirkung von Bodenverbesserungsmittel auf Kieselsäurebasis (Agrosil). Mitt. Dtsch. Bodenkundl. Gesellsch. 15:225–245.

10. Liesecke, H. J., and U. Schmidt. 1975. Zur Bestimmung der Wasserbindung und Wasserdurchlässigkeit in Rasentragschichten. Rasen-Turf-Gazon 6:111–117.

11. Maier, S. 1969. Über das physikalische Verhalten von Hygromull. Landwirtsch. Forsch. 25:1. Sonderheft, 14–20.

12. Prün, H. 1971. Bodenverbesserung mit Hygromull. Berichtsheft des 11. Seminars des BDGA, Callwey-Verlag, München, 96–101.

13. Rasp, H. 1972. Der Einfluβ von Bodenverbesserungsmitteln auf Struktur und Ertragswirkung von gärtnerischen Böden und Substraten. Z. Pflanzenernähr. Bodenkd. 133: 111–123.

14. Richards, L. A., and M. Fireman. 1943. Pressure-plate apparatus for measuring moisture sorption and transmission by soil. Soil Sci. 56:395–404.

15. Seifert, E. 1970. Zur Technologie einer kolloidchemischen Ergänzung extremer Bodensysteme. Mitt. Leichtweiss-Inst. für Wasser- und Grundbau, TU Braunschweig. 25.

16. Skirde, W. 1971. Bewurzelung der Rasendecke mit Beispielen für Abhängigkeit und Beeinflussung. Rasen-Turf-Gazon. 2:112–115.

17. ————. 1973. Bodenmodifikation für Rasensportflächen. Rasen-Turf-Gazon 4:21–24.

18. Ullmann. 1975. Enzyklopädie der technischen Chemie, Band. 10: Kap. 7. Verlag Chemie, Weinheim/Bergstraβe.

19. Wiede, K. 1976. Der Einfluβ synthetischer Bodenverbesserungsmittel und meliorativer Maβnahmen auf die bodenphysikalischen Werte und die Erträge eines Graulehm-Pseudogleys unter Gras. Ph.D. Diss. Inst. für Pflanzenbau der Univ., Bonn, Germany.

Note 8 | Playing Conditions of Grass Sports Fields: A Soil Technical Approach[1]

A. L. M. VAN WIJK
J. BEUVING

ABSTRACT

The top layer of soil must be strong if grass sports fields are to maintain good playing conditions under the forces exerted when soccer is played. Changes in soil strength, resulting from changing bulk density and soil moisture conditions, can be registered by measuring the penetration resistance. From field investigations the penetration resistance was found to be a measurable and reproduceable criterion of the playing conditions.

In laboratory experiments we investigated the response of medium-fine sand with increasing organic matter content to compactive loadings and soil moisture conditions similar to those that occur under field conditions. A more exact examination in the laboratory of the effect of soil water pressure heads on penetration resistance at different bulk densities of the same sand was made over the range of heads existing during the most vulnerable period of the playing season.

It appeared that the contribution of grass to soil strength depends upon the type of root zone material. The more essential the contribution of the grass to the soil strength, the more the playing frequency must be limited. Finally, a short outline of the method conceived to establish the playing conditions at a certain bulk density of the top layer resulting from a number of physical factors is given.

INTRODUCTION

In the Netherlands the playing season for soccer coincides with a period of surplus precipitation. The soil moisture conditions of the top layer of grass sports fields, therefore, will be continuously high and the soil strength or bearing capacity will be low. The forces exerted from play are determined by the surface over which they are acting. The players' studded footwear reduces contact surface and gives rise to very high values of the exerted pressure (5, 2). For good playing conditions the top layer must be able to receive the forces exerted on it without deforming. If play is adversely affected a repair or modification of the playing surface becomes necessary. Play causes compaction of the top layer and the denser packing of the soil particles increases soil strength. Hence, a greater energy input is now required for distortion. However, compaction occurs at the expense of water and air permeability.

[1] A contribution from Inst. for Land and Water Management Research, Wageningen, The Netherlands.

MATERIALS AND METHODS

To correlate the soil strength, measured as penetration resistance of a cone with a base of 1 cm^2 and top angle of 60°, with playability the following procedure was adopted. Two observers judged the quality of the fields under different conditions by testing the bearing strength with their heels and considering the damage done to the turf. This quality was scaled from 1 to 10. A score of 7 indicated that the quality of the turf was just sufficient for intensive play. Simultaneously the penetration resistance of the upper 2 to 3 cm of the turf was measured. It appeared that a good correlation of soil strength and quality score existed. From this it could be derived that the top layer withstands intensive play without failure or serious deformation if the penetration resistance of the upper centimeters of the top layer is about 13 to 14 kg cm^{-2}. Areas outside the most intensively played middle field must have a penetration resistance of at least 10 kg cm^{-2} (6).

The penetration resistance or playability, as shown by field measurements, is not constant but changes with changes in bulk density and soil moisture (Fig. 1). Under the same soil moisture conditions the penetration resistance of a soil material increases with increasing bulk density. When maintaining the same bulk density the penetration resistance is strongly related to the soil moisture conditions.

RESULTS

Soil Strength—Soil Water Pressure Head—Bulk Density

Concurrent with a reduction of the soil water pressure head and an increase of the bulk density of the top layer there is an increase in soil strength and a reduction in chance injury to the top layer from play. To bring the sandy top layer of sports fields to a desired density and to maintain it one needs more information on the behavior of sand at compactive loadings and moisture contents. Therefore, an investigation was performed on the compactability of sand at different levels of pressure and soil moisture conditions.

In a drained compression test samples with an increasing soil moisture content were compressed with pressures of 2, 4, 8, and 12 kg cm^{-2}. The soil material was a medium-fine sand, as is generally applied on sports fields in the Netherlands, with five organic matter levels ranging between 0.4 and 8.6% (Table 1).

Some results of the experiment are presented in Fig. 2. At equal compactive loading, the compactability of the material increases as soil moisture increases. This effect is associated with the action of water as a lubricant, enabling particles to pack more closely (4). At a low moisture content the rate of compaction is low because of a high shear resistance which

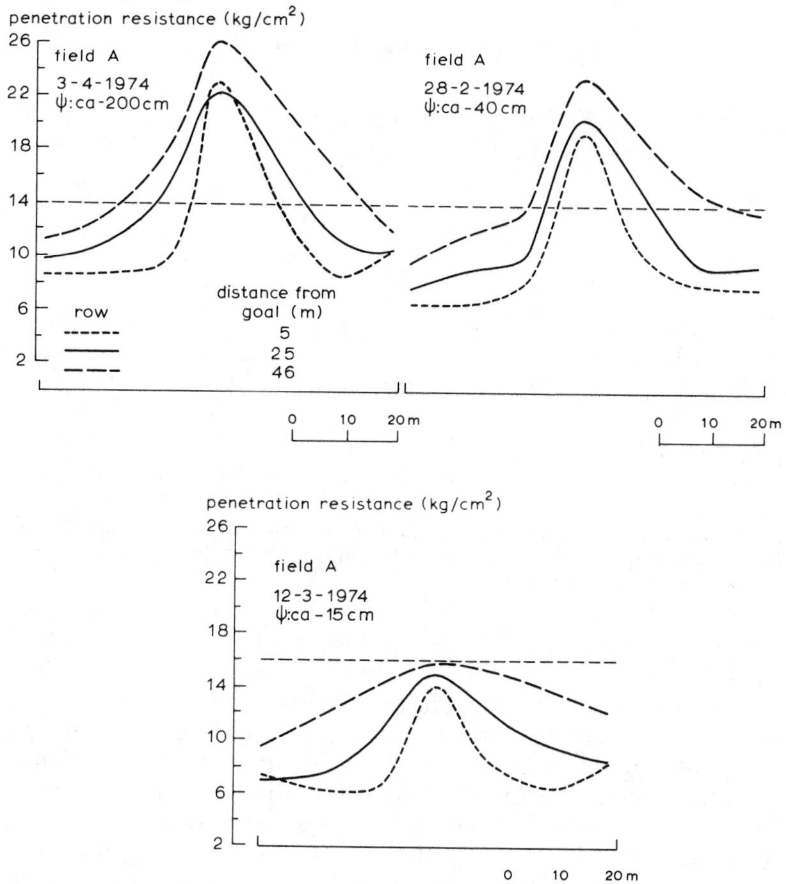

Fig. 1. Distribution of the penetration resistance (14 kg cm^{-2} as criterion for intensive playing) on a grass sports field in relation to soil water pressure head (ψ) in the top layer.

decreases with increasing soil moisture content. When the shear resistance decreases at a continuing equal compaction effort, the bulk density increases up to a maximum. Compaction above this maximum is not possible at equal compression duration and loading.

The susceptibility to compaction increases as the organic matter content of the soil increases. With soil water content at 15%, an increase in

Table 1. Grain size distribution (%) and mid-particle diameter (M50) of the used medium-fine sands.

Organic matter	μm	<2	2–16	16–50	50–105	105–150	150–210	210–420	>420	M50 (μm)
0.4		2.0	0.3	0.2	12.3	27.3	30.9	24.1	2.9	168
2.3		2.5	0.7	1.8	13.3	26.3	30.4	22.4	2.6	166
4.3		3.1	1.2	3.7	14.8	25.1	29.6	20.3	2.2	163
6.6		3.8	1.7	5.8	16.1	23.7	28.9	18.1	1.9	159
8.6		4.4	2.2	7.7	17.4	22.5	28.2	16.1	1.5	156

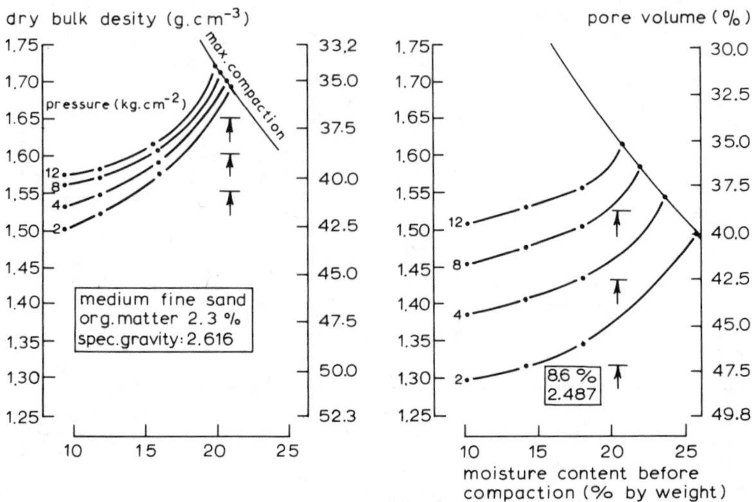

Fig. 2. Relation between bulk density and moisture content before compaction for medium-fine sand at 2.3 and 8.6% organic matter at four pressure levels. The arrows indicate the dry bulk density levels as given in Fig. 3.

pressure from 2 to 12 kg cm^{-2} caused a loss of soil volume of 2 and 9% when the soil contained 2.3 and 8.6% organic matter, respectively. Sand with a low organic matter content has a rather high bulk density even at a low energy input. Increasing the energy input to 12 kg cm^{-2} at an equal soil moisture content will increase the bulk density only a little. At an organic matter content of 8.6% the bulk density increases much more per pressure increment and covers a wider range, but at a lower level.

This means that between lightly and intensively played areas under field conditions the variation in the bulk density and penetration resistance of the top layer will vary within a wider range as the top layer contains more organic matter. This is in full agreement with field measurements. In practice bulk density and penetration resistance of the top layer affected by root growth and loosening activities of soil organisms is often reduced, especially during the period of summer rest. Because this reduction in bulk density will be greater where organic matter content is higher, efforts to maintain a high bulk density favorable for play will be more necessary and effective as organic matter content increases. These fields will require more maintenance.

The extent to which the playing conditions can be improved by compaction depends on how much penetration resistance or soil strength increases as bulk density increases. For sands differing in organic matter content this does not need to be to the same extent. Therefore, an investigation was conducted to determine the relationship between penetration resistance, as measured with a cone having a base of 1 cm^2 and soil water pressure head at different bulk densities, which are indicated by the arrows in Fig. 2. The medium-fine sand used was the same as that used in the compaction test. The range of the soil water pressure heads, from 0 to

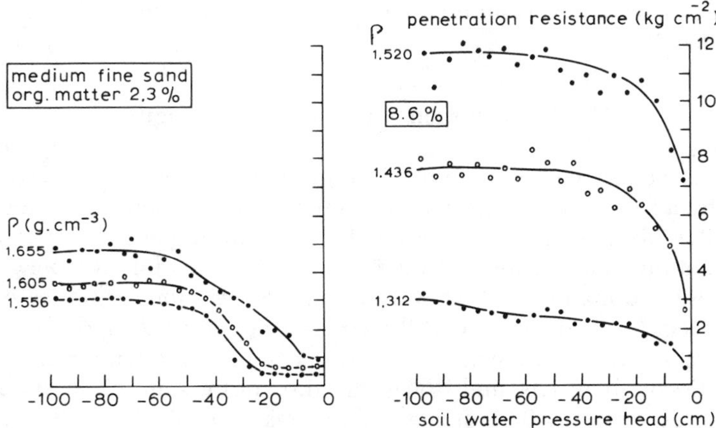

Fig. 3. Relation between penetration resistance and soil water pressure head for medium-fine sand with 2.3 and 8.6% organic matter at three density levels (ρ).

−100 cm water column, was chosen in accordance with field conditions prevailing during the playing season.

Some of the results are shown in Fig. 3. At an organic matter content of 2.3 and 8.6%, the bulk densities represent a less, moderately, and a very compacted state such as is found on a regularly played sports field in accordance with intensity of play. The bulk density levels are obtained at about equal compaction conditions for both sands. Despite lower density levels, the increase of bulk density at 8.6% organic matter was attended with a larger increase of the penetration resistance than occurred at 2.3%. An increase of 0.1 g cm^{-3} from 1.556 to 1.655 g cm^{-3} at 2.3% was accompanied by an increase of the penetration resistance of about 2 kg cm^{-2}. At 8.6% a smaller increase from 1.436 to 1.520 g cm^{-3} was accompanied by 4 kg cm^{-2}. It therefore can be concluded that compaction to increase soil strength is more effective at a higher organic matter content, at least within the investigated range.

The type of relation between penetration resistance and soil water pressure head at 2.3% is different from that at 8.6% organic matter. These differences in strength behavior depend on differences in soil moisture characteristics of both sands at various bulk densities. For the three density levels at 2.3% organic matter, a leveling off of the penetration resistance is measured from pressure heads below about −50 cm. At 8.6% this leveling begins at wetter soil conditions occurring below about −30 cm. The change in strength before leveling off is greater at higher bulk densities. This change in strength behavior within a narrow range of pressure heads agrees with the field measurements as presented in Fig. 1.

Improvement of the playing conditions by drainage must include not only the prevention of surface ponding, but also a reduction of the frequency with which soil water pressure heads occur within this critical range. Outside the investigated range of pressure heads a considerable increase of the penetration resistance is possible at decreasing pressure heads, as evidenced from field measurements in periods with a precipitation deficit.

Contribution of Grass to Soil Strength

As mentioned before, a penetration resistance of 13 to 14 kg cm^{-2} indicates a soil strength adequate for intensive play. Despite the high bulk densities obtained in the experiment, the required penetration resistance was not met and the measured values deviated the more the bulk density and organic matter content were lower. Penetration resistance of 13 to 14 kg cm^{-2} was measured in the correspondingly textured top layer of grass sports fields at mean soil moisture conditions in winter and at bulk densities of about 1.60 and 1.50 g cm^{-3}; i.e., of the same order as obtained in the experiment. This suggests that grass contributes to the in place measured penetration resistance of the top layer at 2.3 and 8.6% organic matter with about 10 and 2 kg cm^{-2}, respectively. Despite that it may concern the same sward and root density in both cases, the strength that the grass contributes is quite different (Fig. 4).

An explanation for this discrepancy can be found in the different basic mechanical behavior of the two soil materials with regard to the penetration resistance measurement. When the cone is inserted into the soil, the soil material surrounding the cone is displaced upwards and in a lateral direction along certain shear planes (Fig. 5 inset). In this investigation the penetration resistance was measured over the upper 2.5 cm of the samples without loading the surface area. If the penetration resistance of a soil sample is determined at increasing surcharge, a linear relationship between penetration resistance and surcharge occurs (Fig. 5). This

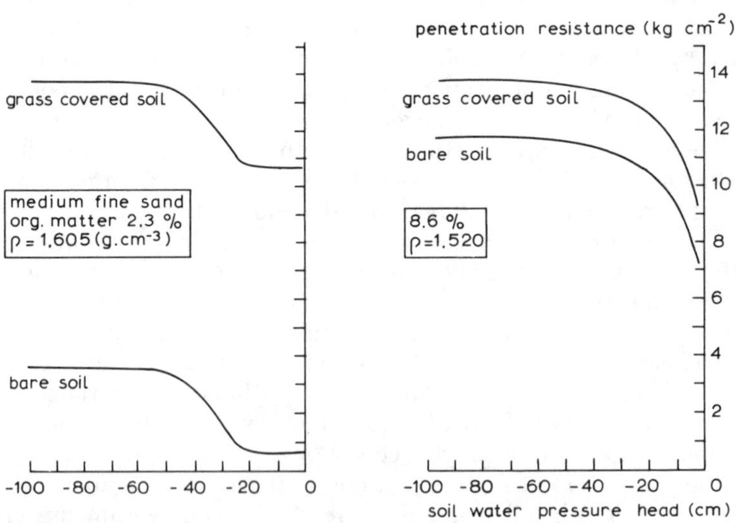

Fig. 4. Contribution of grass to the penetration resistance of medium-fine sand at 2.3 and 8.6% organic matter.

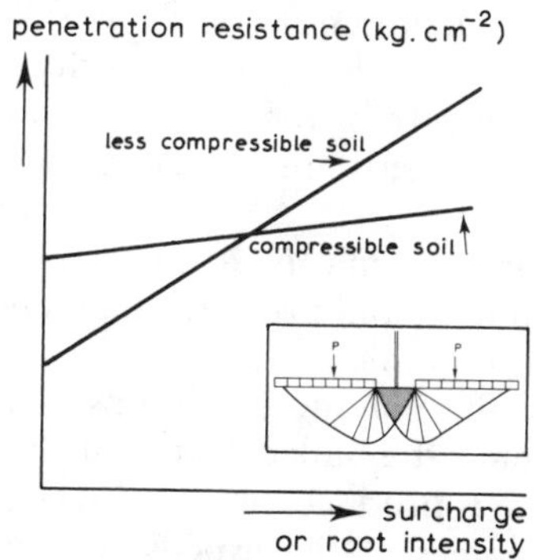

Fig. 5. Relation between penetration resistance and surcharge or root intensity for a compressible and less compressible soil. Inset: shearing around a penetrating cone at surcharge P.

relation strongly depends on the bulk density of the soil (3). The more the surcharge is increased the more the lateral displacement of material at penetration of the cone is hindered, so that the penetration force will increase as the compressibility of the soil decreases. If the rate of penetration of the cone is rather high, the penetration resistance of compressible soils behaves practically independent of the surcharge. Before the penetration resistance can increase, the soil around the cone must first be compacted.

As the measurement of the penetration resistance of a top layer is regarded, grass roots function similarly to a surcharge. About 90% of the total root mass is concentrated in the upper 5 cm of the top layer (1). When the cone penetrates the upper centimeters of this root zone the intensive root system will hinder lateral displacement of the soil. Thus an increase in the penetration resistance will be measured as the root zone material becomes less compressible. Medium-fine sand with 2.3% organic matter is much less compressible at constant soil moisture conditions than that containing 8.6% organic matter (see Fig. 2). Therefore, the contribution of the grass roots to the measured penetration resistance must also be greater at 2.3 than at 8.6% organic matter.

DISCUSSION

Sand low in organic matter is hardly compressible at a given soil moisture content. Further, as the soil moisture content increases there is very little increase in soil compactability. At a dense and a loose state of the material rather low penetration resistances are measured. Compaction to improve the soil strength, thereby improving playability, has little effect. However, thanks to the presence of grass roots combined with low compressibility of the material itself, a soil strength sufficient for intensive playing can be obtained.

Frequent and intensive playing of grass sports fields is attended with a strong reduction of the shoot density on the middle field (6). Reduction of the shoot density results in a lower root density. The latter is coupled with a decrease in soil strength of root zones low in organic matter. The playing frequency on these fields must be kept low to prevent too great a reduction in root intensity.

Sand with 8.6% organic matter is much more compressible at increasing soil moisture content and pressure. An increase of the bulk density is coupled with a considerable increase in soil strength. Compaction is effective for improving the playing conditions. To have a required soil strength of 13 to 14 kg cm^{-2} the bulk density must be rather high. Because the required soil strength is produced mainly by the soil material, playing can be allowed. This comes at the expense of shoot density, but does permit a higher frequency of play.

When a high playing frequency is desired, the root zone mix must have a rather high organic matter content. However, when the organic matter content and bulk density are high, the permeability to water (Fig. 6) and air is generally low. The extent to which high bulk densities conflict with soil aeration and its relation to grass growth was investigated by Van Wijk et al. (7).

Reduction in hydraulic conductivity with increasing organic matter content and bulk density can be accepted only when this does not result in soil moisture conditions that limit play. For example, surface ponding and soil water pressure heads within the critical range for penetration resistance. This requires information on the effect of the increase of dry bulk density on hydraulic conductivity, especially in the range of pressure heads of 0 to − 100 cm that often prevail during the playing season.

If the relation between hydraulic conductivity and soil water pressure head is known, the vertical flow of water in soil can be simulated with a model. Wind (8) describes some of these. This may make it possible to simulate the soil moisture conditions in a top layer at a certain bulk

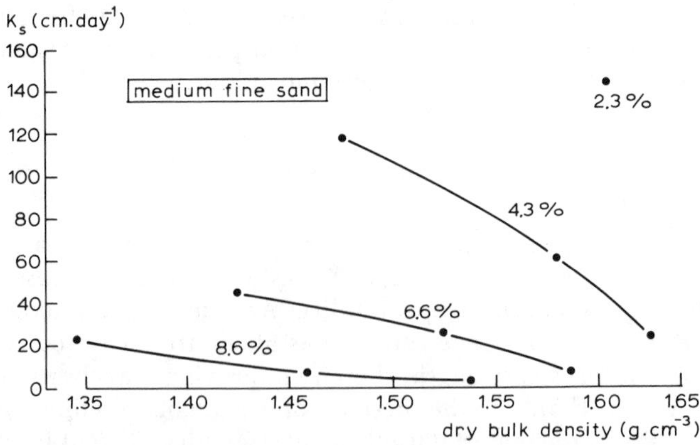

Fig. 6. Relation between hydraulic conductivity at saturation (K_s) and bulk density at various organic matter contents of medium-fine sands.

density as influenced by actual rainfall distribution, underlying profile, and drainage conditions. On the basis of limiting soil moisture conditions (Fig. 3), the playing conditions at a certain bulk density of the top layer can be derived from the simulated soil moisture conditions. This latter aspect of the investigation, which may give insight into the relations between a number of soil physical properties and their significance for the playing conditions, is not yet complete.

LITERATURE CITED

1. Boeker, P. 1974. Die Wurzelentwicklung unter Rasengrserarten und -sorten. Rasen Turf Gazon 5, 1:1–3; 5, 2:44–47; 5, 4:100–105.
2. Canaway, P. M. 1975. Turf wear: A literature review. J. Sports Turf Res. Inst. 51:92–103.
3. Huizinga, T. K. 1969. Grondmechanica (Dutch). Agon. Elsevier, Amsterdam/Brussels. 291 p.
4. Soane, B. D. 1970. The effects of traffic and implements on soil compaction. J. Proc. Inst. Br. Agric. Eng. 25:115–126.
5. Thornton, M. B. 1973. A field trial of sportsfield construction materials extremely high in sand content. J. Sports Turf Res. Inst. 49:29–44.
6. van Wijk, A. L. M., and J. Beuving. 1975. Relation between playability and some soil physical aspects of the toplayer of grass sportsfields. Rasen Turf Gazon 6, 3:77–83. Misc. Reprints ICW 177.
7. ————, W. B. Verhaegh, and J. Beuving. 1977. Grass sportsfields: toplayer compaction and soil aeration. Rasen Turf Gazon 2:47–52.
8. Wind, G. P. 1976. Application of analog and numerical models to investigate the influence of drainage on workability in spring. Neth. J. Agric. Sci. 24, 3:155–172. Tech. Bull. ICW 101.

Note 9

The Influence of Deicing Salts on Soil and Turf Cover[1]

H. G. BROD
H. -U. PREUSSE

ABSTRACT

The increasing use of deicing salts in the last 2 decades of this century has had a great impact on the ecosystem along traffic routes. One result is the injury to plants due to the uptake of salt from the soil and the direct effect of salt spray on plant tissues.

These investigations show the consequences of salting on the soil and turf cover. Experiments with species and cultivars were carried out in pot cultures in the greenhouse as well as outdoors in order to determine the salt tolerance of potential grasses for roadside vegetation. With increased salt application both the average shoot density and the shoot growth decreased. The field trial included investigations on soluble salts as well as sorption ratios. The application of salt led to increasing salinity in the soil, depending upon the total amount of salts applied and upon the weather conditions. There was also a clear correlation between the concentration of soluble sodium and the exchangeable sodium percentage of the soil colloids.

INTRODUCTION

With increasing use of deicing salts on highways during the past 2 decades, there has been a cumulative strain on the ecosystem. The injury done to plants by salt spray on vegetation and the adverse effect on soil structure is evidence of this. This indirectly results in additional drought stress on plants because as soil structure deteriorates soil water decreases. The end result is a natural selection of salt-tolerant grass species and cultivars (1).

MATERIALS AND METHODS

The investigations presented here include studies that test the salt tolerance of grass species and cultivars. Experiments were conducted with grasses grown in pots in a greenhouse (cold house) as well as outdoors so that the suitability of various soil substrates could also be determined. In addition, a 60-plot field study at the Research Station in Giessen, West Germany was conducted to test the tolerance of 12 different grass species and cultivars and three polystands of grass for roadside vegetation to different amounts of deicing salts and distribution periods. The deicing salts were applied two to three times per week from 1 Nov. 1975 to 31 Mar.

[1] A contribution from Justus-Liebig-Univ. Giessen, Inst. fur Bodenkunde und Bodenerhaltung, Ludwigstr. 23, 6300 Giessen, West Germany.

1976 and from 1 Nov. 1976 to 31 Mar. 1977 at rates of 0, 0.5, 1, and 2 kg/m^2. Sodium and chloride concentrations were measured in 1:5 water extract in mixed samples taken monthly from 0- to 15- and 15- to 30-cm depths. Sorption ratios were also analyzed.

RESULTS AND DISCUSSION

Effect on Vegetation

Figure 1 shows results of evaluations made on 1 Nov. 1976. Results are identical to those of the evaluation made at the end of the salt application period (1975-76). At that time there had been no regeneration of the

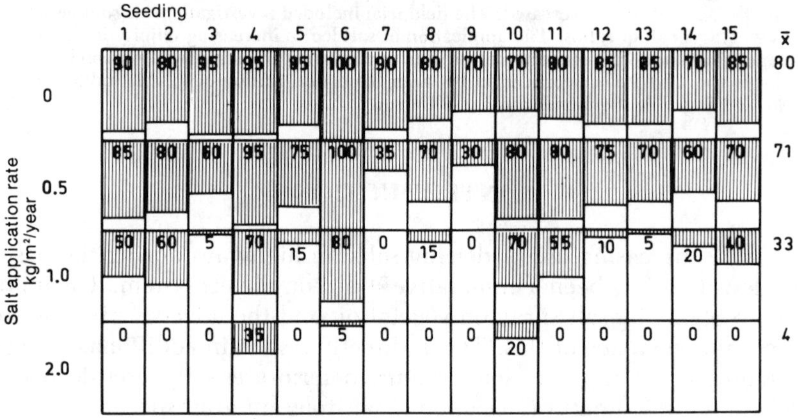

Salt application rate kg/m²/year \ Seeding	1	2	3	4	5	6	7	8	9	10	11	12	13	14	15	$\bar{x}$
0	90	80	95	95	95	100	90	80	70	70	80	85	85	70	85	80
0.5	85	80	60	95	75	100	35	70	30	80	80	75	70	60	70	71
1.0	50	60	5	70	15	80	0	15	0	70	55	10	5	20	40	33
2.0	0	0	0	35	0	5	0	0	0	20	0	0	0	0	0	4

Seedings

1 Lolium perenne — Loretta
2 Lolium perenne — Pelo
3 Festuca rubra — topie
4 Festuca rubra — Dawson
5 Festuca rubra — Ensylva
6 Festuca vallesiaca — Gruber
7 Agrostis tenuis — Bardot
8 Agrostis palustris — Penncross
9 Agrostis canina — Novobent
10 Poa pratensis — Skofti
11 Poa pratensis — Tournier
12 Poa pratensis — Merion
13 15% A. tenuis — Bardot
25% F. ovina — Biljart
60% F. rubra — Topie
14 15% A. palustris — Penncross
25% P. pratensis — Skofti
60% F. rubra — Ensylva
15 20% L. perenne — Loretta
10% A. palustris — Penncross
25% P. pratensis — Tournier
45% F. rubra — Ensylva

Fig. 1. Sward density (% green matter).

surviving, but damaged plants because of the extremely dry weather from February to October 1976. The average density of the control was about 80%. In comparison, shoot density of plots treated with 0.5 kg/m^2 deicing salt decreased only slightly, while an application of 1 kg/m^2 road salt destroyed two-thirds of the remaining stand.

The most salt-tolerant grasses were 'Gruber' *Festuca vallesiaca*; 'Dawson' red fescue (*F. rubra* L.); 'Skofti' Kentucky bluegrass (*Poa pratensis* L.). The dry matter production (Fig. 2), determined in the summer of 1976, showed similar results with respect to species salt tolerance. Skofti was very low in shoot growth but consistently high in shoot density. Also, dry matter production increased for seven of the 15 seedings at the 0.5-kg/m^2 salt level. The question here concerns the relatively salt-tolerant species and cultivars as well as grasses originating from locations rich in salt, which find their ecological optimum in soils of low salt content.

The results of the plot studies compare favorably with the pot trials in the greenhouse and outdoor areas which received NaCl in watering solutions. Some important differences were noted. Among them, 'Penncross' creeping bentgrass (*Agrostis palustris* Huds.) was salt tolerant in the pot test and only moderately salt tolerant in the plot study.

The reason for this may be related to the distribution techniques of the salt application. As the solution dries salt accumulates on the more dense grass stands leading to further plant injury. Such injury does not take place under normal rainfall conditions.

Effect on Soil

The field study consisted of investigations of the turfgrasses and the soil. The Na concentration, expressed in meq/kg, increased in the topsoil (0 to 15 cm) as application rates increased. During the summer of 1976

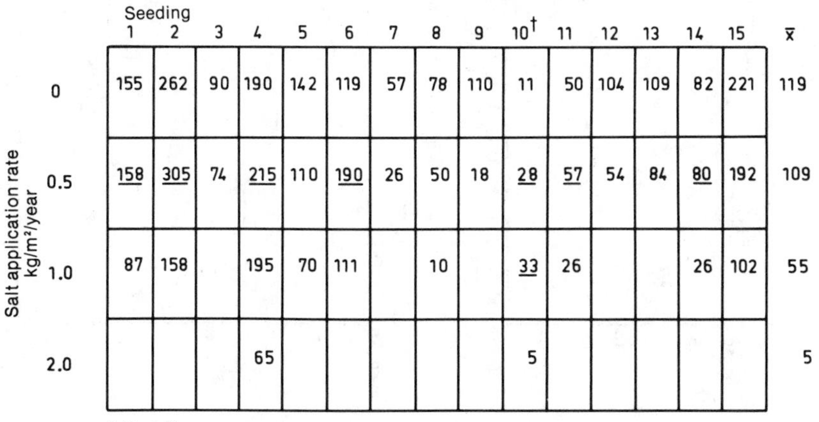

Salt application rate kg/m²/year	Seeding 1	2	3	4	5	6	7	8	9	10†	11	12	13	14	15	x̄
0	155	262	90	190	142	119	57	78	110	11	50	104	109	82	221	119
0.5	158	305	74	215	110	190	26	50	18	28	57	54	84	80	192	109
1.0	87	158		195	70	111		10		33	26			26	102	55
2.0				65						5						5

† Dwarf type.

Fig. 2. Dry matter yield (g/m^2).

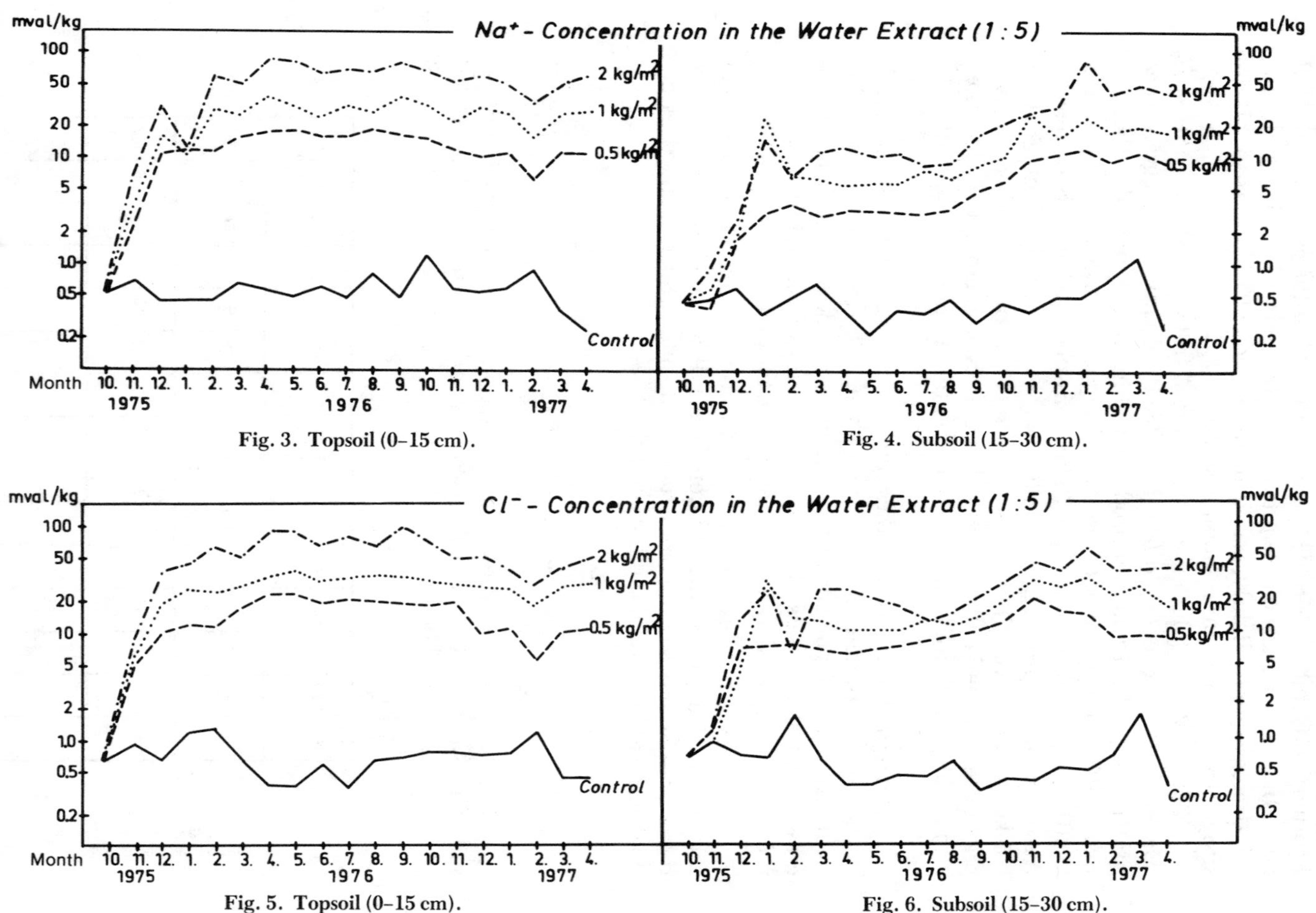

Fig. 3. Topsoil (0–15 cm).

Fig. 4. Subsoil (15–30 cm).

Fig. 5. Topsoil (0–15 cm).

Fig. 6. Subsoil (15–30 cm).

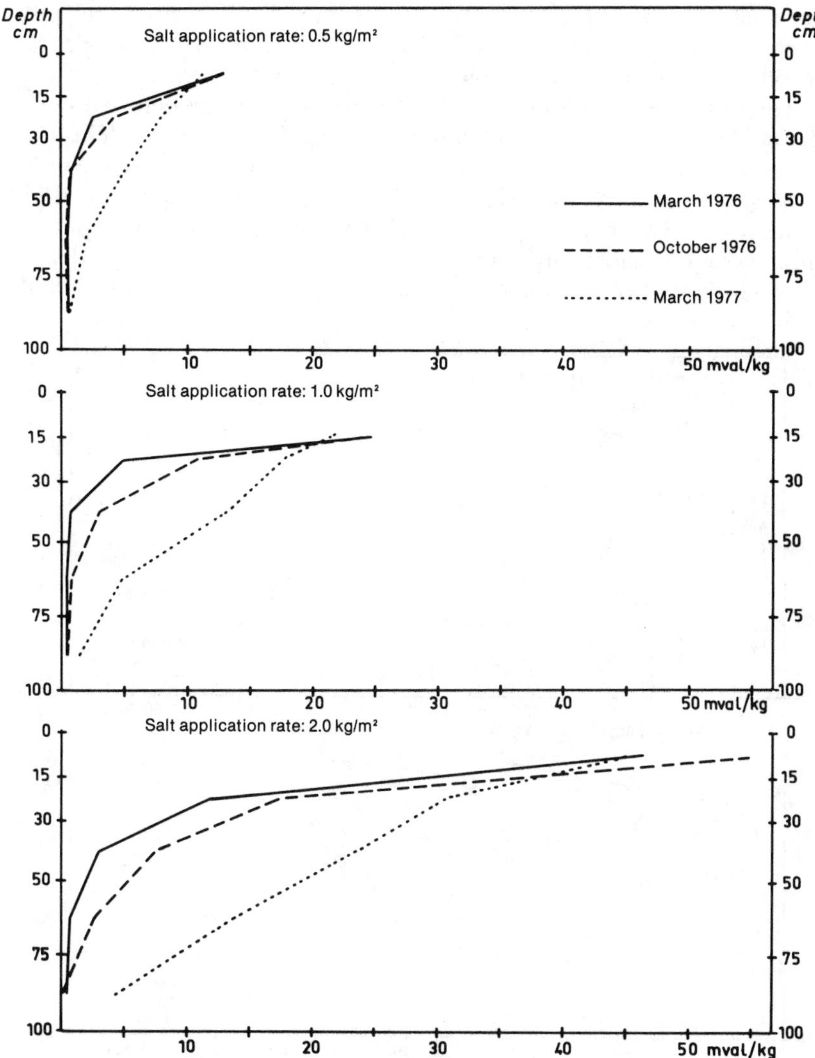

Fig. 7. Soluble Na^+ in the saturation extract (meq/kg soil).

concentrations stayed at approximately the same level as in springtime (Fig. 3). This was due to the warm, dry weather which prevented leaching of the salt and led to a capillary rise. A concentration increase is shown at a salt level of 2 kg/m² in September 1976. Salt was also applied in November 1976. In autumn and winter, however, as a consequence of more rainfall and little evaporation, the Na concentration in the topsoil declined. The Na concentration increased only slightly in March and April 1977.

A similar trend occurred until August 1976 in the 15- to 30-cm layer (Fig. 4), even though the level was slightly less due to the lack of salt displacement from the topsoil as a result of low rainfall. Increased precipitation caused this process to reverse itself and concentration increased as salt leached into the subsoil from September to January 1977.

Chloride concentration curves (Fig. 5 and 6) were comparable to those of Na; but were two times higher in the subsoil than Na. This may be a result of the mobility of Cl relative to Na in the soil and a stronger Na sorption and Ca reception through the plants. Apart from the slight deviation, the concentration curves of the salt levels follow a pattern similar to, but considerably above the values of the control. From this we can conclude that the application of deicing salts leads to a considerable

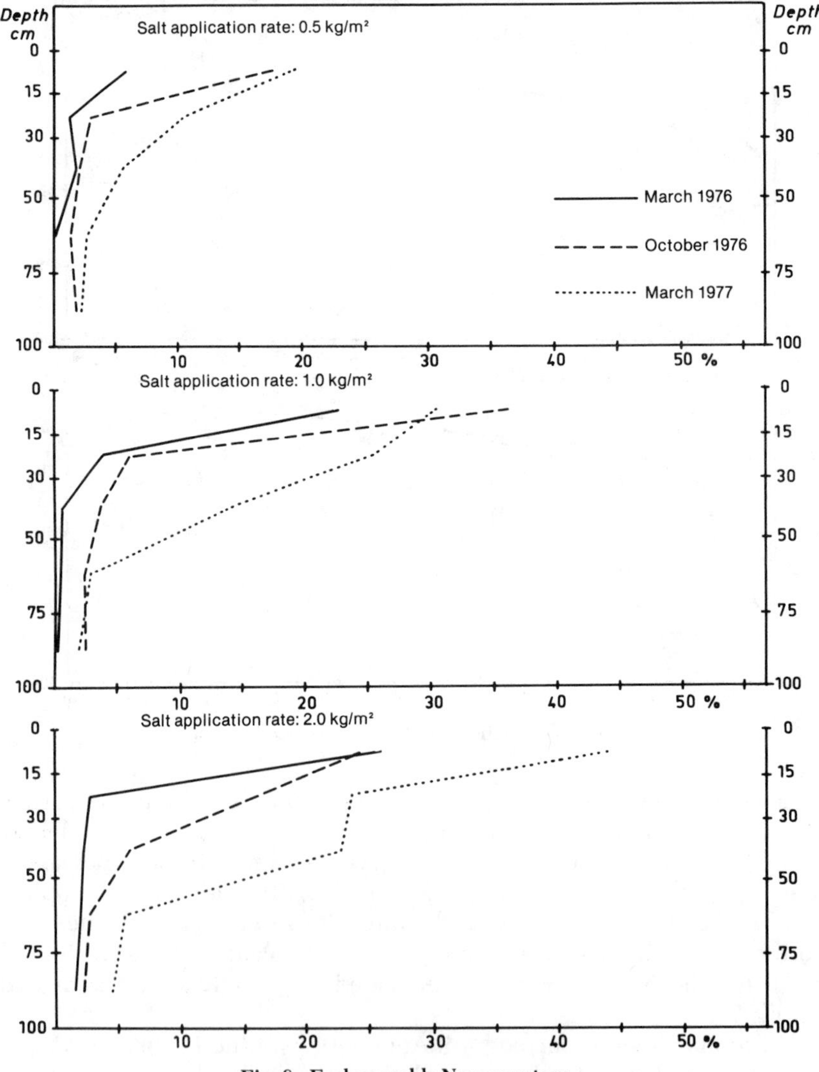

Fig. 8. Exchangeable Na percentage.

accumulation of salt in the soil. The actual amounts depend upon the amount of salt applied and the weather conditions.

In addition to the preceding measurements of concentrations, a measurement of the Na and Cl concentrations in the saturation extract were determined to a depth of 1 m before and after the salt application. Concentrations were most closely related to those of the soil water.

Figure 7 shows the concentrations of soluble Na, expressed in meq/kg, determined at various times and depths. These investigations indicate that continued application of the deicing salts brought about increased soil salinity and that there was a leaching of salt into deeper soil levels in the winter of 1976-77.

The increase of an ion in the form of soluble salts influences sorption depending upon exchange reactions. With a rise of Na concentration in the soil solution, the exchangeable Na percentage increases (Fig. 8). This reached more than 40% in the topsoil of the plots treated with 2 kg/m² of salts. There is a close relationship between the Na concentration in the saturation extract and the Na sorption. Application of deicing salts in-

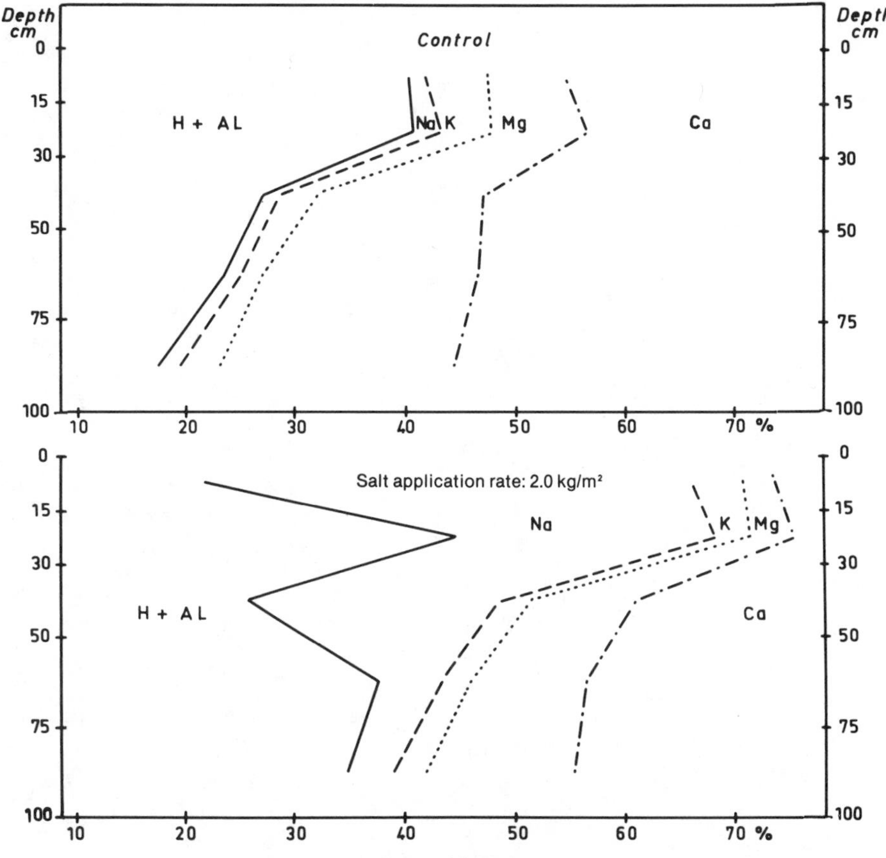

Fig. 9. Exchangeable cation percentage.

creased exchangeable Na, which takes the place of exchangeable Ca, H, and Al. Figure 9 compares the cation content of the control, expressed in percent, and that of the 2 kg/m^2 salt level as analyzed in March 1977.

Finally, it can be stated that an increase in the application of deicing salts leads to a natural selection of grasses and to an increased soil salinity. Without sufficient rainfall to affect leaching, salts may lead to alkalinization, as increases in exchangeable Na percentage indicate.

LITERATURE CITED

1. H. G. Brod and H.-U. Preusse. 1976. Einfluss von Auftausalzen auf Boden, wasser und vegetation. Z. Rasen-Turf-Gazon 6, H. 1 and 2; 21–27, 46–54.

Note 10

Observations of *Fusarium roseum* f. sp. *cerealis* (Snyd. & Hans.) on Turfgrasses in Sweden[1]

S-O. DAHLSSON

ABSTRACT

During 1975 and 1976 turfgrass damage was reported which could have been caused by *Fusarium roseum* f. sp. *cerealis* (Snyd. & Hans.). Putting greens composed of creeping bentgrass (*Agrostis stolonifera* L.) and annual bluegrass (*Poa annua* L.) showed frog-eye (caused by *F. roseum* f. sp. *cerealis* Snyd. & Hans.) symptoms similar to those described in the American literature from which *F. roseum* is frequently isolated. It is not clear to what extent *F. roseum* damages turf in Sweden.

INTRODUCTION

Fusarium nivale is the most common *Fusarium* species in the northern European countries. Reference is also made to *F. roseum*-*F. culmorum*. Comments will be restricted to the two latter species. There is disagreement among authors concerning *Fusarium* classification. Couch (4) considers *F. roseum* f. sp. *cerealis* (CKe.) Snyd. & Hans. to be the same species as *F. culmorum* (W.G.Sm) Sacc. Frequently the fungus is simply referred to as *F. roseum* (2, 3, 10).

Symptoms

According to Couch and Bedford (5) and Couch (4) Fusarium blight is caused by either *F. roseum* f. sp. *cerealis* (Cke) Snyd. & Hans./*F. culmorum* (W.G. Sm) Sacc./ or *F. tricinctum* f. sp. *poae* (Pk) Snyd. & Hans./ Syn. *F. poae* (Pk) Wr/. Both species cause damping off in newly seeded stands (4). In established turf they cause a foliar blight followed by crown and root rot (4). It is suggested that clearer separations should be made between pre-emergence blight (seed rot), post-emergence damping off (seedling disease), and fusarium leaf blight (damage in older turf) (9). In the later stages of disease development, circular patches of blighted turfgrass can be seen in which the centers often contain unaffected grass. This gives the frog-eye symptom (4, 5, 9).

[1] A contribution from Weibulls Rasensektor, Fack, 261 20 Landskrona, Sweden.

 Proceedings of the Third International Turfgrass Research Conference.

TURFGRASS DAMAGE DURING 1975–76 IN SWEDEN

Symptoms were observed in Sweden during 1976 and 1976 which were similar to those described by Couch (4, 5) as being caused by *F. roseum*. *F. roseum* was isolated in each instance (1). Still the question remains if *F. roseum* is the primary cause of damage, since *F. roseum* can be found throughout the soil flora. In some cases *F. roseum* probably has been the main causal agent, but this has not been proven (7).

Severe frog-eye symptoms were observed in mid-July on an old golf green composed of 70% creeping bentgrass (*Agrostis stolonifera* L.) and 30% annual bluegrass (*Poa annua* L.). *F. roseum* was isolated along with *Rhizoctonia solani* which has occasionally damaged turfs in Sweden (6).

The possibility that *F. roseum* might cause damping off or Fusarium leaf blight under Swedish conditions has not been considered. So far there are no confirmed reports in Sweden. Fusarium damping off was observed in Denmark in 1965 and 1966 on newly sown golf greens (8). Not until 1976 was damage again reported, again on a golf green. On the other hand, there are no reports of damage to established turfs in Sweden and Denmark (8, 11).

DISCUSSION

The specific weather conditions during 1974–76 might have influenced development of the fungal flora. Low precipitation combined with high temperatures and intensive sunlight might have increased the possibilities of damage from *F. roseum* in established turf. Modern intensive turfgrass culture (e.g. high N and frequent, close mowing) might also have increased the risk of damage. The disease might also have been overlooked earlier.

From all our observations, some indicate damage from *F. roseum/culmorum* in established turf and several newly seeded stands. A leading plant pathologist in Scandinavia finds it difficult to judge these observations (11). Therefore, caution should be exercised in assessing damage from this pathogen in the Scandinavian countries.

LITERATURE CITED

1. Akesson, I. 1976–77. Swedish Institute for Plant Protection. Personal communication.
2. Bean, G. A. 1966. Observations on Fusarium blight of turfgrasses. Plant Dis. Rep. 50(12):942–945.
3. ————. 1966. Fusarium blight of turfgrasses. Golf Superintendent 34(10):32, 34.
4. Couch, H. B. 1973. Diseases of turfgrasses (2nd Ed.) Robert E. Krieger Publishing Co., Huntington, New York.
5. ————, and E. R. Bedford. 1966. Fusarium blight of turfgrasses. Phytopathology 56(7):781–786.

6. Dahlsson, S-O. 1975. *Rhizoctonia solani* (Kuhn) på svenska golfgreener (Rhizoctonia brown patch on Swedish golf greens). Weibulls Gras-Tips p. 19–23.
7. ————. 1976. Skadar *Fusarium roseum* gronytegras i Sverige? (Does *Fusarium roseum* cause damage to turfgrasses in Sweden?) Weibulls Gras-Tips. p. 33–34.
8. Hansen, K. W. 1976. Danish Golf Union. Personal communication.
9. Smith, J. D. 1965. Fungal diseases of turf grasses (2nd Ed.) Leeds & London, England.
10. Vargas, J. M., C. W. Laughlin, and J. B. Beard. 1973. Fusarium blight. 43rd Annu. Mich. Turfgrass Conf. Proc. 2:112–114.
11. Welling, B. 1977. Danish Institute for Plant Protection. Personal communication.

Note 11

The USGA Stimpmeter for Measuring the Speed of Putting Greens[1]

A. M. RADKO

ABSTRACT

Prior to 1976, standards for measuring the speed and uniformity of putting greens were unavailable. In 1976 the USGA developed the Stimpmeter, a simple device which quickly measures the speed of putting greens. During 1976 and 1977 the USGA Green Section's agronomic staff tested and reported on more than 1,500 greens in 36 states. As a result of these tests, tables were developed which provide green speed test comparison information for (a) membership play and (b) greens in tournament condition.

INTRODUCTION

In 1976 and 1977 the Green Section staff (in cooperation with golf course superintendents in 36 states) tested the speed of more than 1,500 putting greens throughout the United States using the USGA's new Stimpmeter (Fig. 1). The new instrument was designed by Frank Thomas, Technical Director, USGA, based on a variation originated by Edward S. Stimpson (1). It provides a quick, representative reading of green speed that is simple to use.

MATERIALS AND PROCEDURE

All that is required are three regular small-dimpled golf balls, a measuring tape, and the USGA Stimpmeter. The following procedure has proven the most reliable.

1. Select a level area on the putting surface and approximately 3.0 m^2 which is representative of the green's quality.
2. Roll three balls in one direction from the same starting point.
3. Measure and calculate the average distance.
4. Reverse the direction 180° over the same line and repeat steps 2 and 3 from the center point of where the first three balls stopped.
5. Calculate the average speed for each direction.

It is advisable to repeat steps 1 through 5 over a new area on the same green (i) if the difference between the averages measured is greater than

[1] USGA Green Section, Golf House, Far Hills, NJ 07931 USA.

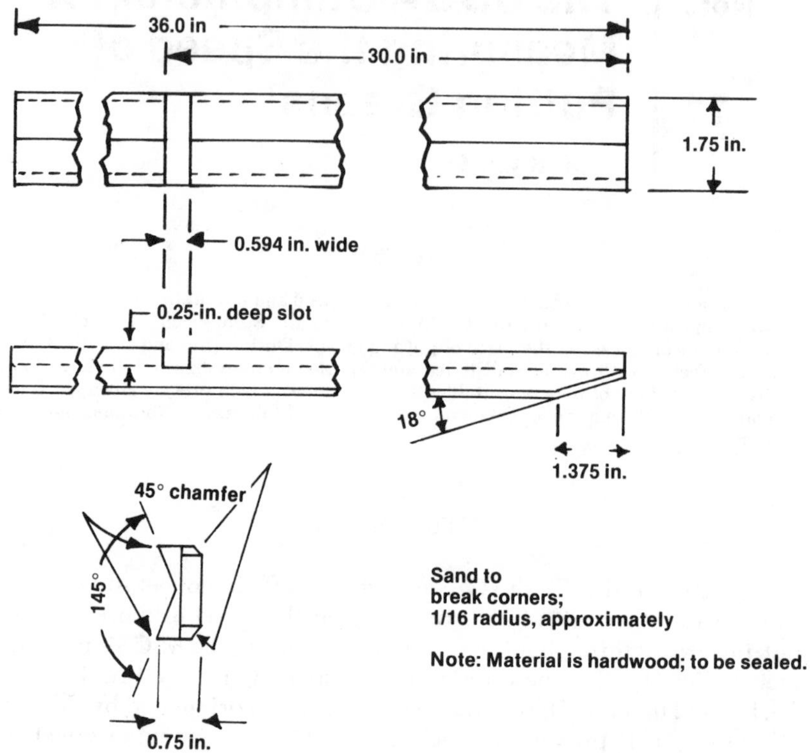

Fig. 1. Diagramatic representation of the stimpmeter design. (USGA Stimpmeter designed by Frank Thomas, Technical Director, USGA, 25 Feb. 1976, revised 30 Mar. 1976.)

20% of the shortest distance or (ii) if the balls had a curving path prior to coming to rest. Measure on a bias or across the slope on sloping greens. This test should be performed on each green of the golf course including the practice green. Accurate records should be kept using the data sheet shown in Table 1.

DATA INTERPRETATION

Analysis of this data has resulted in the development of a USGA Speed Test Comparison Chart of greens maintained for regular membership play conditions as shown in Table 2.

A provisional chart has also been developed for courses in tournament condition (Table 3). This chart may require revision at a future date because the data used to develop it are limited and insufficient to be totally reliable. However, it is being presented as the best available information.

It should be emphasized that this instrument and test procedure is for

Table 1. USGA green speed data sheet.

Course: ____________________
City: ____________________ State: ____________________
Time: ____________________ Date: ____________________

Green Data:

Predominant grass: __________ Annual topdressing program: __________
Type mowing unit: Triplex ______ Single ______ Make __________
Bench setting: __________ Cuts/week: __________
Ever double cut: Yes ______ No ______ How often __________
Approximate hours since last cut: ______ Double cut: ______ Single cut: ______
Soil moisture: Wet __________ Medium __________ Dry __________
Surface moisture (Dew): Heavy ______ Light ______ None ______

Speed data:

Green # ______ "A" ______ "B" ______ Avg. ______
Comments: ____________________
Green # ______ "A" ______ "B" ______ Avg. ______
Comments: ____________________
Green # ______ "A" ______ "B" ______ Avg. ______
Comments: ____________________
Green # ______ "A" ______ "B" ______ Avg. ______
Comments: ____________________

Tests performed by: ____________________
Observed by: ____________________

use by the golf course superintendent to assist in maintaining consistency among the greens on the course and provide a quantitative basis to compare and measure the greens. Each club may choose a different speed for regular membership play which is best suited to their membership. Through the Stimpmeter, the USGA is simply providing a speedometer with which green speed can be set.

The Stimpmeter also serves the following purposes:

1. It indicates whether a cup placement is fair. This is especially important on sloping greens. If the ball cannot be stopped within a reasonable distance from the hole, then it is an unfair placement.

Table 2. USGA green speed test comparison chart for regular membership play.

Speed	Avg. distance
	m
Fast	2.55
Medium fast	2.25
Medium	1.95
Medium slow	1.65
Slow	1.35

Table 3. USGA green speed test comparison chart for tournament conditions.

Speed	Avg. distance
	m
Fast	3.15
Medium fast	2.85
Medium	2.55
Medium slow	2.25
Slow	1.95

2. It establishes whether all greens are uniform on a given course.
3. The variance in speed from the time greens are first cut through any hour of the day can be determined.
4. Seasonal changes may be observed.
5. The effects of various cultural programs upon speed can be measured.

STIMPMETER DESCRIPTION

The Stimpmeter is an extruded aluminum bar (the original Stimpmeter was made of wood, but the process described here was adopted to keep costs minimal) with a V-shaped shoot down its length. It is 0.9 m long with a precisely milled ball release groove cut 0.75 m from the lower "tip" end. The underside of the lower end is cut away at the proper angle so as to reduce bounce when the ball first makes contact with the green. The V-shaped shoot on the bar has an included angle of 145° such that the ball rolls straight down the shoot, supported at two points 12.7 mm apart. The ball thus has a slight overspin of only 5% when first making contact with the green surface. The ball release groove is designed so that a ball will always be released and start to roll when the Stimpmeter is raised to an angle of 20°.

LITERATURE CITED

1. Stimpson, E. S. 1974. Putting greens—how fast? USGA. Golf J. 27(2):28–29.

Note 12

Structuring Courses in Turfgrass Science to Stimulate Improved Management Practices[1]

H. H. WILLIAMS

ABSTRACT

A concept that increased the comprehension of basic science principles (i.e., chemistry, physics, etc.) by all levels of turfgrass management personnel was examined. An experimental syllabus, designed to simplify basic chemistry as related to soils, water, and mineral nutrients, was developed and presented in a 3-hour workshop session to diverse groups of municipal and private industrial employees throughout the greater Los Angeles, Calif., area. Subsequent surveys were conducted to determine any resulting increase in ability to solve common problems in fertilizer selection and use. Questionnaires completed by participants indicated that 78% considered the 3-hour session sufficient to establish a perceived level of understanding rated "reasonable" or higher. Previous study of chemistry appeared to be of only slight advantage (by a factor of 1.2:1). Simple mathematical calculations required to complete the syllabus worksheets posed a serious problem for many participants. The use of electronic calculators alleviated this difficulty. Complete tabulation of the questionnaires indicated encouraging increases in interest and ability to use basic science principles in cultural practices.

INTRODUCTION

A disparity continues between the high quality turf theoretically possible and that more commonly sustained in actual practice. This difference can be characterized as unfortunate, unnecessary, and counterproductive. The educational effort to communicate the scientific information generated at the research facilities of colleges, universities and industry is recognized and the tremendous progress that has upgraded the efficiency, productivity, and prestige of practical turfgrass management is acknowledged. However, current pressures of global economics and unrest mandate the upgrading of our industry in all of its many facets.

Overgrowth in world population generates increasing demands for food, the production of which competes with turf production for natural resources. Depletion of these resources, including fossil fuels, water, minerals, and arable land, constitute increasing restrictions under which we must operate. Environmental pollution concern demands exacting efficiency in the use of all agricultural chemicals. Concomitantly, there is

[1] Los Angeles Trade-Technical College, Los Angeles, CA 90015 and Pasadena City College, Pasadena, CA 91106, USA.

an increased demand for turf areas to be used for utilitarian as well as aesthetic purposes.

Justification for the coexistance of these two agricultural pursuits must be publicized continuously. These efforts must include an upgrading and recognition of the turf profession by both the general public and the industry itself. Success will depend upon attaining ultimate efficiency and economy in field practices.

In 1965 Nutter (2) estimated the annual cost of turfgrass maintenance in the United States at $4 billion. Currently, about $5 billion is spent on turfgrass maintenance. Buetel and Roewekamp (1) listed an annual expenditure of over $90 million for turf care in California, 70% of which was attributed to the cost of labor.

Robert Scofield (personal communication) reported that "Environmental Care," a rigidly structured and managed landscape maintenance firm located in Southern California, grossed in excess of $2 million in 1976. This company successfully reduced operating labor costs 15 to 20% below those of competing businesses and civil service departments of local cities. This reduction is attributed to the employment of a greater proportion of higher salaried, college-trained personnel who can relate to more advanced and efficient management practices, equipment, and materials more easily.

Projecting 15% in labor savings envisions a potential reduction of $13 million annually in California alone. Nationally this projection registers an annual economy in excess of $645 million! These savings suggest that even modest efforts to upgrade employee education and understanding could certainly be economically feasible.

A gap has inadvertently been generated between scientific integrity and popularly accepted methodology. This can be attributed to the contrived threat that highly motivated and better trained individuals now moving into the industry appear to pose to the old established order, especially to those in civil service where seniority is the dominant factor. Researchers and educators must seek more effective methods of overcoming this inertia of status quo and apathy within our industry. It is important to translate the knowledge obtained from scientific technology into actual practice. Effective two-way lines of communication must be established between researchers, educators, and supervisors and field personnel. This presentation deals with one approach to this end.

EXPERIMENTAL PROCEDURES

A concept was developed and examined that increased comprehension of basic science principles (i.e., chemistry, physics, mathematics, etc.) by all levels of turfgrass management personnel and should stimulate the implementation of improved cultural practices. An experimental syllabus was designed that includes a glossary of selected technical terms common to chemistry and basic to understanding plant-soil-water rela-

Table 1. Worksheet #1: Basic chemistry of soils and fertilizers.

Atomic no.	Name of element	Symbol	Atomic wt.	Structure of atom	Structure of ion	Valence(s)
1	Hydrogen†	H				
2	Helium	He				
3	Lithium	Li				
4	Beryllium	Be				
5	Boron	B				
6	Carbon†	C				
7	Nitrogen†	N				
8	Oxygen†	O				
9	Fluorine	F				
10	Neon	Ne				
11	Sodium (Natrium)	Na				
12	Magnesium†	Mg				
13	Aluminum	Al				
14	Silicon	Si				
15	Phosphorus†	P				
16	Sulphur†	S				
17	Chlorine†	Cl				
18	Argon	Ar				
19	Potassium (Kalium)†	K				
20	Calcium†	Ca				

† An essential element for plant growth.

tions, two worksheets, and a set of detailed instructions for completing the worksheets. Workshop sessions of 3 hours each were conducted with diverse groups of municipal and private industry employees throughout the greater Los Angeles, Calif., area.

During the workshop technical terms were explained and further clarified with visual aids and models and the worksheets, which represented the ultimate goal, were completed.

Worksheet #1 (Table 1) was designed to extensively use the atomic number of the first 20 elements. Approximate atomic weights, structures, ionizations, and valences of these elements were determined with simple mathematical calculations. Thus, these complex chemical principles can be simplified for a more easily accepted approach and a greater comprehension (Tables 2, 3, and 4).

Table 2. Determining atomic weights of elements.

		Atomic wt. each
Atomic No. (X)	= No. of protons	1
	= No. (approximate) of neutrons†	1
	= No. of electrons	Insignificant
	Total atomic wt.	2
Thus 2 X	= Approximate atomic wt.	

Example:

Atomic No.	Element	Atomic wt. (approximate)
6	C	12
13	Al	26

† No neutrons present in atoms of ordinary H; no. of neutrons variant in atomic isotopes.

Table 3. Determining structure of the atom (planetary model).

1. Draw ◯ to represent the nucleus
2. Enter atomic no. to represent no. of protons (+) followed by letter "P"
3. Draw successive arcs to right of nucleus to represent appropriate no. of electron (−) shells as follows:
   (a) First (K) shell can accommodate only up to two electrons.
   (b) through first 20 elements, successive shells (L, M, and N) can accommodate only up to eight electrons.

Example:	Element no. 8; O	(8 P)	) 2	) 6		
	Element no. 19; K	(19 P)	) 2	) 8	) 8	) 1

4. Add no. of positive charges (protons) and negative charges (electrons) and note cancellation, indicating no overall atomic charge.

		Charge	
Example:	Element no. 20; Ca	20+	(protons)
		20−	(Electrons)
		0	Neutral

Note: Outside shell determines valence; is referred to as the valence shell.

Worksheet #2 (Table 5) utilizes information generated on Worksheet #1. Given the chemical formula of various fertilizer materials, the formula weight is easily determined by totalling component atomic weights. The elemental analysis as percentage can then be calculated by simple mathematics (division) (Table 6). Strangely, few literature sources reveal how these analyses are derived. Fertilizer ionization is determined

Table 4. Determining structure of the ion (planetary model) and valence.

1. When first (K) shell contains <2 electrons, it tends to lose its single electron (or gain up to its maximum of 2 as in covalent bonding) (non-ionic).

	Element	Atom	Ion		Valence charge
Example: No. 1	H	(1P) 1	(1P) 0		1+
					0−
				Total	1+

2. When successive outer (valence) shells contain <8 electrons, they tend† to lose or gain electrons as follows:

No. electrons in valence shell	Tendency
1–3	Lose to zero
4	Assume charge of 4*
5–7	Gain to 8
8	Inert

Example:	Element	Atom	Ion		Valence charge
No. 5	B	(5P)) 2) 3	(5P)) 2) 0		5+
					2−
				Total	3+
No. 6	C	(6P)) 2) 4	-----	Total	4+
No. 7	N†	(7P)) 2) 5	(7P)) 2) 8		7+
					10−
				Total	3−
		(7P)) 2) 5	(7P)) 2) 0		7+
					2−
				Total	5+
No. 10	Ne	(10P)) 2) 8	-----		Inert

† Note: N (also P and S) can both lose and gain.

Table 5. Worksheet #2: Basic chemistry of soils and fertilizers.

Name of fertilizer	Type‡	Chemical formula	Analysis	Lbs. AI/ton	Cost/ ton†	Cost, lb. AI
Ammonium sulphate		$(NH_4)_2SO_4$			156	
Ammonium nitrate		NH_4NO_3			262	
Ammonium phosphate sulphate (Ammo-phos)		40% $NH_4H_2PO_4$ 60% $(NH_4)_2SO_4$	16–20–0		195	
Calcium nitrate		$Ca(NO_3)_2$			164	
Urea		$CO(NH_2)_2$			273	
Nitroform Ureaform		--	38–0–0		600	
IBDU		--	31–0–0		467	
Potassium sulphate		K_2SO_4	0–0–53		184	
Potassium chloride		KCl			116	
Superphosphate (single)		50% $CaSO_4$ 30% $CaH\ (PO_4)_2$	0–20–0		150	
Nitrohumus (bags)		--	1.5–0–0		43	
Milorganite		--	6–3–0		181	

† Note: Costs per ton based on quotes from commercial sources in March 1977. It is important to recognize that selection of a particular fertilizer should not be based solely on the comparative cost per ton nor the cost per pound of active ingredient (nutrient). The value of the many other factors involved must be considered in relation to the individual situation and circumstances. ‡ I = Inorganic; O = Organic; SO = Synthetic organic; NO = Natural organic; AI = Active ingredient (nutrient). Nitrogen = elemental N, Phosphorus = P_2O_5, Potassium = K_2O.

by adding together the valence values and charges of its component ions (Table 7). This information enhances comprehension of the complex biochemical interactions between soils and plants following fertilizer appli-

Table 6. Determining fertilizer analysis from its formula.

1. Calculate formula wt. by totaling component atomic wts.

Example:

	No. component atoms	Atomic wt.
$(NH_4)_2\ SO_4$ =	2 N	2 × 14 = 28
	8 H	8 × 1 = 8
	1 S	= 32
	4 O	4 × 16 = 64
	Total formula wt.	= 132

2. Divide elemental (atomic) wt. by formula wt.

Example: $\frac{\text{Elemental (N) wt.}}{28} \div \frac{\text{Formula wt.}}{132} = \frac{28}{132} = 0.21 \text{ or } 21\%$

Table 7. Determining fertilizer ionization.

1. Separate fertilizer compound into its component ions.

Example:

$(NH_4)_2\ SO_4$ (Ammonium sulphate) → Cation (+) 2 NH_4 (Ammonium); Anion (−) SO_4 (Sulphate)

2. Calculate ionic charge

Example:	Element		Valence charge	
NH_4 –	N =		3−	
	4 H =		4+	Thus NH_4^+ (Ammonium)
		Total	1+	
SO_4 –	S =		6+	
	4 O =		8−	Thus SO_4^{2-} (Sulphate)
		Total	2−	

[Establishes basis for understanding why sulphate ion $(SO_4)^{2-}$ must be chemically bonded to two ammonium ions $(NH_4)^+$.)

Table 8. Workshop evaluation by participants.

• Sample size over 100	
• Background of participants	
• Professional experience	
Gardening	51.5%
Farm	17.6%
Sales	1.4%
Supervisory	29.5%
	100.0%
• Educational experience	
Incomplete high school	10.8%
High school	32.5%
Junior college level	41.6%
College level	10.1%
College graduate	5.0%
	100.0%
• Participant's exposure to chemistry	41.2%
• Participant's occupations	
Students	
School district employees	
Landscape service company employees	
Fertilizer and chemical company employees	
Parks and recreation employees	
College professors	
Hospital lawn maintenance employees	
• Information was presented	
Much too fast	8.6%
Acceptably fast	78.5%
Too slowly	2.1%
No opinion	10.8%
	100.0%
• Information was	
Very understandable	23.2%
Reasonably understandable	55.8%
Not very understandable	9.5%
Very confusing	7.4%
No opinion	4.1%
	100.0%
• Information as presented	
Inspired interest in further study	80.6%
Discouraged interest in further study	2.2%
No opinion	17.2%
	100.0%
• The information presented appears to have practical application in my work	
Very extensively	11.9%
Extensively	31.1%
Only to a limited extent	53.7%
Not at all	3.3%
	100.0%
• The information presented appears to provide answers to questions I previously had about agricultural chemicals (fertilizers, pesticides, etc.)	
Many	33.0%
Several	37.2%
Few	22.3%
None	3.2%
No opinion	4.3%
	100.0%
• I would be interested in learning more about the practical chemistry of soils, plant nutrition (fertilizers, etc.), and pesticides in	
Home study	16.9%
Night school	9.7%
College	12.3%
Special workshops	22.1%
On-the-job training	39.0%
	100.0%

cation. Worksheet #2 involves subsequent calculations related to unit costs of elemental nutrients, useful as a guide in fertilizer selection.

DISCUSSION AND CONCLUSIONS

An evaluation of the impact of the workshops on the 100 participants was determined by questionnaires. The results are tabulated in Table 8. A significant 78% indicated that these 3-hour presentations were adequate in length to cover the material included in the syllabus. Only 2% considered the presentation too slow, while 8% indicated that more time should have been allowed. Compared to the 7% who considered the presentation very confusing, 79% rated it as reasonably understandable or better. Eighty percent were inspired to continue study of basic chemistry, but 2% were discouraged. The on-the-job approach to training seems to be the preferred approach to learning. This might be attributed to the idea of "earn-while-you-learn."

Many of the participants experienced difficulty with simple math during the completion of the worksheets. This problem was easily circumvented by use of the new, inexpensive electronic calculators.

Basic scientific principles related to turfgrass production and maintenance can be translated into simplified language and presented innovatively to members of the turfgrass industry. This expanded knowledge is imperative to the understanding of higher level information and conducive to the implementation of improved cultural practices. The resulting upgrade in turf quality and the reduced operational costs justifies the training and education of personnel.

ACKNOWLEDGMENTS

The author expresses appreciation to Mr. Thomas Stevens, President, Los Angeles Trade-Technical College; Mr. Robert Scofield, President, Environmental Care; Mr. Arnold Parnell, Director, Affirmative Action Program, TRW, Defense & Space Systems Group; Dr. Irving Bengelsdorff, Professor of Chemical Technology, California Institute of Technology, Pasadena; Dr. W. H. Daniel, Professor, Purdue University. Without their valuable assistance this work would not have been possible.

LITERATURE CITED

1. Buetel, J. and F. Roewekamp. 1954. Turfgrass survey of Los Angeles County. Bull. South. Calif. Golf Assoc.
2. Nutter, G. C. 1965. Turfgrass is a $4 billion industry. Turfgrass Times 1(1):1.

Note 13

The Problems and Present State of Public Green Spaces, Parks, and Sports Grounds in Prague, Czechoslovakia[1]

B. KONIČEK

Environmental improvement is an inseparable part of raising the standard of living and green spaces are an important part of the environment in Czechoslovakia, both in qualitative and quantitative aspects. In Prague, Czechoslovakia, these green spaces can be divided into (i) historical gardens, (ii) parks and housing estate spaces, and (iii) park-forests in the vicinity of the city.

A large part of public green spaces, especially in parks and housing estates, consists of lawns which according to Czechoslovakian territorial planning should account for about 70% of the overall area of green spaces in humid and higher elevation areas with an average rainfall of 800 to 900 mm, 50% in lower elevation beet growing areas with an average annual rainfall of 550 to 600 mm, and 30% in arid maize growing areas with an average annual rainfall of less than 550 mm. These directive figures are often not adhered to and the ratio of lawn area to shrub and tree areas is reversed. That is, larger areas are devoted to trees in the higher elevation regions while lawns are more prevalent in the lower elevations and drier regions.

One single criterion often used to plan for the optimum area of city green space is green space area per inhabitant. In the capital of Prague, there is roughly 11 m^2 of green space per inhabitant. According to available information from 1974–75 there are 17.5 m^2 in Munich, Germany, 23 m^2 in Vienna, Austria, and 13.3 m^2 in Budapest, Hungary.

On the other hand, it must be kept in mind that these figures include only the public green spaces consisting of public parks and housing estate spaces. These values are higher if park-forests in the vicinity of the cities are included. For example, in Prague there were 1,240 ha of park and housing estate spaces and about 2,590 ha of recreational forests by December 1975. Thus, at a population of 1,100,000 there are 11 m^2 per inhabitant devoted to public parks and housing estate spaces and an additional 35 m^2 per inhabitant available in recreational forests.

Enclosed green spaces, which consist of gardens of dwelling houses and areas belonging to sports organizations, are also present. Although

[1] Czechoslovak Assoc. for Physical Culture, Praha-Strahov, Czechoslovakia.

these green spaces are not included in the statistics of public green spaces, they nevertheless play an important part in filling the need for green space. Moreover, they will play an increasingly important part as society increases its demand for physical culture and sport as a necessary means for the harmonic and all-around development of man.

Prague, which has a rich and long tradition of physical culture, now has 855 sports grounds and stadiums which include 101 football fields. The useful area of these sports facilities amounts to 1,352,176 m^2 or 135 ha. The urban norm in Czechoslovakia envisages roughly 5 m^2 of useful area per inhabitant. Since only 25% of this norm is available at the present time, year by year increases will be needed to meet this expectation.

An improvement of this situation can be expected as Czechoslovakia prepares to host the XII European Athletics Championships to be held next year. This event will be held in Czechoslovakia on the 80th anniversary of organized athletics in Czechoslovakia and has given a general imputus to the reconstruction of Strahov Central Sports Stadium in Prague, the venue of the championships. Strahov Station has become the largest sports construction project in Czechoslovakia in the past 30 years. Work is being carried out by more than 50 Czechoslovakian firms and enterprises and many Czechoslovakian athletes, students, and young people are devoting voluntary work.

The project includes the complete reconstruction of the central E. Rosicky Stadium while preserving and maintaining the existing turf area. A new training stadium is being built nearby that will be connected to the old stadium by two road overpasses. Sod will be laid in the new stadium this year. The particle size of the root zone will not exceed 8% by weight of clay fractions below 0.01 mm. This is almost identical to DIN Specification No. 18035.

Adjoining the central sports stadium is the famous Spartakiad Stadium with a useful turf area of 60,000 m^2 and a capacity of 200,000 spectators. It is the largest of its kind in the world. There, too, construction adjustments will take place and an artificial playing surface will be installed.

According to 31 Dec. 1975 estimates the overall area of lawns in Czechoslovakia amounts to 205,000 ha. This includes 22,000 ha of turfs in parks and sports grounds as well as 120,000 ha established for land improvement, recreation, and roadway beautification.

The availability of adequate quantities of grass seed of improved cultivars is a problem in Czechoslovakia. This is especially true of grass species and cultivars suitable for lawn use. The research, breeding, and growing of grass seed has a long tradition in this country. In the course of time, grass breeding has changed gradually from the development of universal cultivars, especially during the pre-war years, to special purpose cultivars which includes the development of cultivars for non-agricultural purposes.

Today in Czechoslovakia there are 19 grass species and 38 cultivars available, seven of which are lawn-type cultivars. They include 'Roznovska' crested dogtail grass (*Cynosurus cristatus* L.), which is the oldest of our lawngrass cultivars. Others include 'Roznovska' wood bluegrass (*Poa nemoralis* L.); 'Entenza' and 'Valaska' chewings fescue (*Festuca rubra* ssp. *commutata* Gaud.); 'Golf' and 'Teno' colonial bentgrass (*Agrostis tenuis* Sibth.); and 'Baca' perennial ryegrass (*Lolium perenne* L.). The two new colonial bentgrass cultivars are in use. Golf is suitable for the best types of golf use and Teno is suitable for lower quality lawns in housing estates.

The problem of developing grass seed cultivars for special use in Czechoslovakia is being satisfactorily solved and the production of this grass seed is now a task of the breeding stations. On the other hand, the large-scale production of these cultivars has not been achieved and we still await the complex solution of producing sufficient high quality seed for the needs of society.

Section X:

Appendixes

Research Conference Program

Organizing Committee

P. Boeker, Chairman
R. Brunner
Chr. Eisele
E. Grundler
R. Hansen
J. P. van der Horst
P. Mansat
C. Mehnert
W. Opitz von Boberfeld
R. Pietsch
W. Skirde
G. Voigtländer
W. Weber

Sunday, July 10, 1977

11.00 h Registration of Participants
20.00 h Reception in the Penta Hotel

Monday, July 11, 1977

9.00 h Opening of the Conference and Welcoming Addresses

SESSION 1: ESTABLISHMENT OF TURF INCLUDING RENOVATION

Chairman: Chr. Eisele

10.15 h Turfgrass seed mixtures in the United Kingdom—*J. P. Shildrick*
10.25 h Observations on differently adapted grasses for turf in Central Italy—*A. Panella*
10.35 h Some ecological observations on turf establishment and culture of turfgrasses in cool regions of Japan—*H. Oohara*
10.45 h Seedling competition of Kentucky bluegrass, red fescue, colonial bentgrass, and temporary grasses—*R. E. Engel*
10.55 h Turfgrass response to competition during seedling establishment—*J. J. Vorst*
10.05 h Discussion
11.15 h The use of perforated, clear plastic tarps in turfgrass establishment and renovation—*W. C. Morgan*
11.25 h The use of new cultivars of *Lolium perenne* in seed mixtures for new lawns and for the regeneration of turf—*R. Pietsch*
11.35 h The development of turf with less management on dry unpaved roads—*H. Hiller*
11.45 h The principles of blending Kentucky bluegrass cultivars for disease resistance —*J. M. Vargas*
11.55 h Establishment and persistence of Kentucky bluegrass (*Poa pratensis* L.) and ryegrass (*Lolium* sp.) in turfgrass mixtures—1968 to 1976—*J. M. Duich**, *B. W. Keckley, and D. V. Waddington*
12.05 h Discussion

---

* Author who reads the paper.

SESSION 2: BREEDING OF TURFGRASSES

Chairman: P. Mansat

14.00 h The turfgrass breeding potential of British ecotypes—*M. O. Humphreys*

14.10 h Evolution of improved lawngrasses in America: a review of major events leading to the Kentucky bluegrass cultivar revolution—*R. W. Schery*

14.20 h Tillering and persistency in *Lolium perenne* L.—*J. M. Minderhoud*

14.30 h Perennial ryegrass mowing quality and appearance response to three nitrogen regimes—*V. A. Gibeault*

14.40 h Discussion

14.50 h Characteristics, breeding methods, and seed production of *Poa supina* Schrad. —*P. Berner*

15.00 h Variations in the growth and development of *Poa annua* L. populations selected from seven different sports turf areas—*W. A. Adams and P. J. Bryan**

15.10 h Lime responses of Kentucky bluegrass and tall fescue cultivars on an acid, aluminum-toxic soil—*J. J. Murray* and C. D. Foy*

15.20 h Differences in sod strength, rooting, and turfgrass quality of Kentucky bluegrass (*Poa pratensis* L.) cultivars resulting from seasonal and environmental conditions—*L. H. Taylor* and R. E. Schmidt*

15.30 h Discussion

SESSION 3: EVALUATION OF TURFGRASS CULTIVARS

Chairman: H. Vos

16.00 h Combined methods for the evaluation of turfgrasses for various purposes—*E. Lütke Entrup*

16.10 h Comparisons of micro-trials and spaced plant nurseries and dense swards as means for evaluating turfgrass genotypes—*B. Bourgoin and P. Mansat**

16.20 h An approach to turfgrass cultivar evaluation—*A. J. Turgeon* and J. M. Vargas, Jr.*

16.30 h The influence of the distance of the vars and nitrogen fertilization on the seed yield of red fescue and sheep fescue—*J. M. Audy*

16.40 h Discussion

17.00 h First ITS Business Meeting

Tuesday, July 12, 1977

SESSION 4: PROBLEMS OF PLANT PHYSIOLOGY AND MORPHOLOGY OF TURFGRASSES

Chairman: J. B. Beard

8.00 h The effects of stages of seedling development on selected physiological and morphology parameters in Kentucky bluegrass and red fescue—*J. V. Krans and J. B. Beard**

8.10 h Tree shade adaptation of turfgrass species and cultivars in France—*A. Chesnel, R. Crosie, and B. Bourgoin**

8.20 h Anatomical and physiological effects of air pollutants on turfgrasses—*V. B. Youngner* and F. J. Nudge*

8.30 h Temperature influences on mineral nutrient distribution in two Kentucky bluegrass cultivars—*J. E. Kaufmann* and D. E. Aldous*

8.40 h Discussion

8.50 h Cold acclimation and deacclimation in cool season grasses—*D. B. White* and M. H. Smithberg*

9.00 h Short term evaluations of turfgrasses for cold hardiness—*G. Wood* and W. M. Sullivan*

9.10 h A method for the selection of salt tolerance in turfgrasses during practical breeding work—*G. Michelman*

9.20 h Tolerance of turfgrass cultivars to salt—*K. Ahti, A. Moustafa, and H. Kaerwer**

9.30 h The influence of deicing salts on soil and turf cover—*H. G. Brod and H.-U. Preusse**

9.40 h Discussion

SESSION 5: ROOT GROWTH OF TURFGRASSES

Chairman: W. Skirde

10.15 h Comparisons of direct and indirect determinations of root weights of several turfgrasses—*W. Opitz von Boberfeld*

10.25 h The root development of turfgrass species and cultivars in the course of three years—*P. Boeker*

10.35 h Root growth and phosphorus responses among clones of creeping bentgrass (*Agrostis palustris* Huds.) at low temperatures—*W. R. Kneebone* and G. V. Johnson*

10.45 h Influence of aeration and genotype upon root growth of creeping bentgrass (*Agrostis palustris* Huds.) at supra-optimal temperatures—*K. W. Kurtz* and W. R. Kneebone*

10.55 h Effects of various sandy media on the root development of the principal turfgrass species—*E. W. Schweizer*

11.05 h Discussion

SESSION 6: SOIL PROBLEMS

Chairman: S.-O. Dahlsson

11.15 h Proposed standards and specifications for quality of sand for sand-soil-peat mixes—*G. R. Blake*

11.25 h Playing conditions of grass sports fields: a soil technical approach—*A. L. M. van Wijk* and J. Beuving*

11.35 h Soil conditioning for turf—plastic barriers under compacted sand—*W. H. Daniel* and R. P. Freeborg*

11.45 h Discussion of prescription athletic turf (PAT)—*M. J. Robey*

11.55 h Trials for sport field construction with Enkamat—*K. Kind*

12.05 h The effect and after-effect of the deposits from the clarification plants on soil preparation and soil construction for sports fields—*W. Skirde*

12.15 h Discussion

14.00 h Soil conditioning by synthetic media—*H. Franken*

14.10 h *Agrostis palustris* Huds. responses and some physical and chemical aspects of a Ultiso soil variously modified for a golf green—*R. E. Schmidt* and R. F. Haynes*

14.20 h Discussion

SESSION 7: TURFGRASS CULTURE

Chairman: W. H. Daniel

14.25 h The problems and present state of public green spaces, parks, and sports of grounds in the Czechoslovak capital-Prague—*B. Konicek*

14.35 h Some physical aspects of sports turfs—*P. Boekel*

14.45 h New possibilities for modern turf management—*W. Lanz*

14.55 h Turfgrass growth reduction by means of a new plant growth regulator—*P. E. Schott*, H. H. Nölle, and H. Will*

15.05 h Structuring courses in turfgrass science to stimulate improved management practices—*H. H. Williams*

15.15 h Thatch accumulation in cool season turfgrasses with variable rates and times of nitrogen applications—*P. R. Henderlong*

15.25 h Influence of fertilizer rate, mower type, and thatch control in colonial bentgrass lawn turf—*C. R. Skogley*

15.35 h Effects of nitrogen fertilization and cutting height on the shoot growth, nutrient removal, and turfgrass composition of an initially perennial ryegrass dominant sports turf—*W. A. Adams*

15.45 h Discussion

16.15 h The performance of *Phleum* and *Cynosurus* on sports fields—*C. Mehnert*

16.25 h The USGA stimpmeter for measuring the speed of putting greens—*A. M. Radko*

16.35 h Practical research and results on spiking with knives on football pitches—*H. A. Kamp*

16.45 h Discussion

16.55 h Response of warm and cool season turfgrass polystands to nitrogen and topdressing—*D. T. Hawes*

17.05 h Utilization of warm season turfgrasses in the transition zone (cooler regions)—*L. H. Portz*, J. Manka, and R. Ridenour*

17.15 h Seasonal performance of selected temperate turfgrasses overseeded on bermudagrass turf for winter sports—*R. E. Schmidt and J. F. Shoulder**

17.25 h Discussion

Wednesday, July 13, 1977

SESSION 8: FERTILIZATION OF TURF

Chairman: J. P. Shildrick

8.00 h Distribution and utilization of different nitrogen carriers in simulated "USGA golf green" laboratory soil columns—*P. R. Henderlong*, K. R. English, and R. H. Miller*

8.10 h Influence of silica on chemical composition and decomposition of turfgrass tissue—*J. R. Street, P. R. Henderlong*, and F. L. Himes*

8.20 h Effects of various nitrogen application regimes on root behavior of mature Manhattan perennial ryegrass and Baron Kentucky bluegrass turfs—*F. B. Ledeboer*

8.30 h Nitrogen leaching in bermudagrass turf: daily fertigation vs. tri-weekly conventional fertilization—*G. H. Snyder*, E. O. Burt, and J. M. Davidson*

8.40 h Some aspects of nitrogen fertilization on sports turf—*F. Riem Vis*

8.50 h Discussion

11.10 h Studies on the development of turfgrass seedlings on roadsides in the Federal Republic of Germany—*W. Trautman* and W. Lohmeyer*

11.20 h Discussion

SESSION 11: GROWTH REGULATORS

Chairman: R. E. Engel

11.30 h Growth regulants on turfgrasses. *P. Bowen*

11.40 h The use of growth regulating chemicals in turf—*C. M. Switzer*

11.50 h Effects of growth retardants on the shoot growth and root growth of roadside turfgrasses—*R. C. Wakefield* and S. L. Fales*

12.00 h Growth retardant effects on grasses for roadsides—*R. W. Duell*, R. M. Schmidt, and S. W. Cosky*

12.10 h Discussion

SESSION 12: WEED PROBLEMS

Chairman: G. Voigtländer

14.00 h Glyphosate for torpedograss and bermudagrass control—*E. O. Burt*

14.10 h Goosegrass control in bermudagrass—*S. W. Bingham* and R. L. Shaver*

14.20 h The effects of repeated applications of bensulide and tricalcium arsenate on the control of annual bluegrass and on quality of Highland colonial bentgrass putting green turf—*R. L. Goss*, T. W. Cook, S. E. Brauen, and S. P. Orton*

14.30 h Development and rooting of Kentucky bluegrass sod as affected by herbicides —*J. A. Jagschitz*

14.40 h Differences in tolerance of bermudagrass and zoysiagrass cultivars to herbicides—*B. J. Johnson*

9.00 h Some results from trials with long term fertilizers including Isodur on turf—*H. Will*

9.10 h A new form of turf fertilization with URA 9595—*J. von Arnim*

9.20 h Discussion

SESSION 9: SODDING

Chairman: J. P. van der Horst

9.30 h The effects of substratum with different sand content per sod number and mechanical root properties of *Poa pratensis*-Merion—*P. Bŏsković* and B. Mišković*

9.40 h Techniques for rapid sod production—*R. E. Burns*

9.50 h Discussion

10.15 h Investigation of net sod production as a new technique—*J. B. Beard*, D. P. Martin, and F. B. Mercer*

10.25 h Effect of cultural factors on tall fescue-Kentucky bluegrass sod quality and botanical composition—*J. R. Hall, III*

10.35 h Discussion

SESSION 10: ROADSIDE TURF

Chairman: E. W. Schweizer

10.40 h Establishing persistent vegetation on steep slopes during highway construction —*R. E. Blaser*, D. L. Wright, and H. D. Perry*

10.50 h Effect of different cultural practices on the establishment of grasses from seed for roadside erosion control—*W. W. Huffine*

11.00 h Research into the establishment of roadside embankments carried out in France by the Laboratoiries des Ponts et Chaussees—*P. Henensal*, G. Arnal, and J. Puig*

14.50 h The breeding of lines of *Agrostis tenius* Sibth. and *Festuca rubra* L. tolerant of grass-killing herbicides—*R. Fisher and C. E. Wright**

15.00 h Discussion

SESSION 13: DISEASES AND INSECTS OF TURF

Chairman: R. L. Morris

15.10 h Observations on *Fusarium roseum* f. sp. *cerealis*—*S.-O. Dahlsson*

15.20 h Snow mold resistance in turfgrasses: the need for regional testing—*J. D. Smith*

15.30 h Snow molds on Minnesota golf greens—*W. C. Stienstra*

15.40 h Yellow tuft disease of turfgrasses: a review of recent studies conducted in Rhode Island—*N. Jackson*

15.50 h Role of a soil fungicide and two nematicides in maintaining bermudagrass (*Cynodon dactylon* (L.) Pers.) and creeping bentgrass (*Agrostis palustris* Huds.) turf—*R. V. Sturgeon, Jr.* and K. E. Jackson*

16.00 h Discussion

16.10 h The possibility of controlling fairy ring and rust diseases in lawns with benodanil—*R. Heimes* and F. Loecher*

16.20 h On the effect of fungicides on fairy rings (*Marasmius* sp.)—*H. Roediger*

16.30 h Insecticidal control of some turfgrass insect pests in North Carolina—*R. L. Robertson*

16.40 h The occurrence of bibionid flies in a sport ground in Münich—*J. Kruger*

16.50 h Discussion

17.00 h Final ITS Business Meeting

Constitution & Bylaws

ARTICLE I

Name

The name of this Society shall be the International Turfgrass Society, hereinafter referred to as the Society.

ARTICLE II

Objects

The objects of the Society shall be:

(a) To encourage research and education in the field of turfgrass science and to further the dissemination of technical information related to turfgrasses and to accept and administer funds for these purposes.
(b) To provide an opportunity for the presentation of research studies before a critical and competent audience.
(c) To strive toward uniform terminology and standard research evaluation techniques.
(d) To maintain liaison with other scientific or educational organizations whose programs are allied to turfgrass science.

ARTICLE III

Membership

Section 1: Membership shall be on an individual basis. Members shall pay such dues or fees as the Executive Committee shall decide.

Section 2: Members shall be those who have attended the regular quadrennial business meeting at least once of the previous two meetings, or who have requested membership by writing to the Executive Committee outlining reasons for being unable to fulfill the above requirement.

Section 3: Membership shall be classified as (a) charter member; (b) regular member; (c) student member; (d) sustaining member:

(a) Charter members are those persons who attended the First International Turfgrass Research Conference held in Harrogate, England, 15–18 July 1969.
(b) Regular members are persons who are qualified research or extension workers or teachers in the field of turfgrass science.
(c) Student members are graduate students in any country. No student members shall remain in this category for a period exceeding 4 years.
(d) A sustaining member is any company or organization interested in the objectives of the Society.

ARTICLE IV

Officers

Section 1: The elected officers of the Society shall be a president, a vice president, a secretary, and five directors. These officers, with the past-president, the appointed treasurer, and the appointed historian, shall constitute the Executive Committee.

Section 2: A minimum of four countries shall be represented on the Executive Committee, and a maximum of four members of the Executive Committee shall come from any one country.

Section 3: All elected officers shall serve for 4 years, but the same incumbents may be reelected. The positions of treasurer and historian shall be filled by appointment by the Executive Committee who may also reappoint them. The treasurer and historian shall not be voting members of the Executive Committee.

ARTICLE V

Election of Officers

Section 1: The Executive Committee shall appoint a nominating committee which shall nominate eligible candidate(s) for each office. As part of the procedure of nominations, the nominating committee will canvass the membership for suggestions for each office. Nominations can be made from the floor.

Section 2: The nominating committee shall consist of the president and the two most recent past presidents plus one member each from three countries not represented by the foregoing. The most recent past president shall be chairman. This committee shall provide an opportunity for the members of the Society to submit names, providing the consent of the nominee and an indication of his willingness to attend general meetings, has been obtained.

Section 3: The nominating committee shall mail the names of the nominees to each member of the Society not less than 4 weeks in advance of the meeting of the Society. Officers will be elected at the regular quadrennial business meeting by those attending.

Section 4: In the event of the death or resignation of any officer of the Society, the Executive Committee shall designate a successor to serve for the unexpired term.

Section 5: If the office of president becomes vacant, the vice president shall fill that position until the time of the next meeting. If both of the above positions are vacant at the same time, the Executive Committee shall appoint a director to act as president for the balance of the 4-year term.

ARTICLE VI

Meetings

Section 1: Meetings of the Society will be held at 4-year intervals unless it is otherwise agreed, and will not normally be held consecutively on the same continent. The time and place will be determined not less than 2 years in advance by the Executive Committee.

Section 2: Special general meetings may be held at the discretion of the Executive Committee. Written notice stating the purpose of such a meeting should be given to all members of the Society at least 6 months in advance.

Section 3: At all meetings of the Society every question shall be determined by a majority voice vote of the members present.

ARTICLE VII

Quorum

Section 1: At any meeting of the Executive Committee a simple majority of the voting members of that committee shall constitute a quorum.

Section 2: At any general meeting of the Society thirty (30) regular members in good standng shall constitute a quorum.

Section 3: In transacting business of the Society by letter ballot, the ballots shall constitute a quorum.

ARTICLE VIII

Amendments

Section 1: The Constitution of the Society may be repealed or amended by a two-thirds majority voice vote of those members attending any regular quadrennial business meeting, provided that the proposed amendment has been mailed to the membership at least 60 days prior to the meeting.

Section 2: Bylaws of the Society may be enacted, repealed, or amended at any regular quadrennial business meeting by a majority vote of the voting members present.

BYLAWS

Duties of the Officers:

(a) The Executive Committee shall have general charge of the affairs of the Society and, subject to the constitutional resolutions and Bylaws, may appoint, at any time, committees or individual members for specific purposes, and exercise governing authority in the administration of the Society, including finances and matters of policy.

(b) The president shall preside at all meetings of this Society and of the Executive Committee. He shall authorize meetings of the Society and of the Executive Committee when necessary and perform all the necessary functions of his office.

(c) The past president shall advise the president on matters pertaining to the activities of the Society and shall act as chairman of the nominating committee.

(d) The vice president shall exercise the rights and powers of the president in the absence of the latter.

(e) The secretary shall keep a record of all proceedings of this Society, of the Executive Committee, and of all committees, and shall deliver such records to his successor in office.

(f) The treasurer shall keep a record of all receipts and disbursements and shall present a financial statement at meetings of the Society.

(g) The historian shall maintain the historical record of the activities of the Society and shall present a written report at each quadrennial meeting.

Dues for the different classes of membership shall be as determined from time to time by resolution of the Executive Committee and approved by a meeting of the Society.

The auditors to audit the account of the Society for the next meeting will be recommended by the Executive Committee and approved by the membership at the meeting.

Minutes

ITRC Planning Meeting of the ITS Executive Committee

9 July 1977
Penta Hotel, Munich, West Germany

Present: President P. Boeker, J. B. Beard (non-voting for R. R. Davis), K. Ehara, R. E. Engel, A. C. Ferguson, F. Ledeboer, R. E. Schmidt, W. Skirde, J. E. van der Horst
Absent: R. L. Morris

Meeting called to order by President P. Boeker

1. Initiation of Membership Dues

R. E. Schmidt proposed membership dues for ITS members in the future of $5.00 (U.S.) annually to cover costs for correspondence and to underwrite publication of the ITRC Proceedings. P. Boeker suggested $10.00 (U.S.) annual dues and commented that this would be in line with other internationally based societies. J. B. Beard asked that, in order to justify dues, a budget for the next 4 years be established first. It would better ensure that the dues amount selected will meet the expenses. P. Boeker stated that he would be in favor of R. E. Schmidt's proposal that annual dues be charged. R. E. Engel made the suggestion to formulate a recommendation to that effect to present to the full membership meeting.

R. E. Engel then made a motion to charge $10.00 (U.S.) annual dues, which includes a copy of the proceedings, and a total of $40.00 (U.S.) for four years. The total fee will be reduced to $30.00 (U.S.) for those who pay this sum within a year of the start of the past conference. The motion was seconded by J. E. van der Horst. Motion carried.

2. Recording of Discussion Questions

J. B. Beard requested, as had been earlier requested in writing, that discussion questions and answers be written down by the individual asking the question and that these papers be collected by each session chairman and then be turned in to the editor for inclusion in the published proceedings. This was done at both the First and Second ITRC. P. Boeker objected to this request as being too late, too cumbersome to enforce and carry through on a multi-lingual basis. He then agreed to a suggestion that participation be on a voluntary basis.

3. Selection of Next ITRC Host Site

P. Boeker announced that official invitations to host the Fourth ITRC had been received from Japan, Canada, and the United States (California).

K. Ehara again extended a cordial invitation to host the conference in Japan, but would not want to actively compete with another country for the site. Comments were made that the high travel cost to Japan may force many people to skip the Japan Conference.

P. Boeker then stated that two choices, Japan and Canada, would be presented at the full membership meeting.

4. Election of the 1977–1981 ITS Executive Committee

P. Boeker stated that the election of the next Executive Committee would be handled at the full membership meeting after the next ITRC host country had been decided. The Nominating Committee would offer two slates, one for each of the two countries (Japan and Canada) which were contending for the next ITRC.

5. Historian Selection

P. Boeker proposed that J. B. Beard serve as historian if he were to accept. J. B. Beard accepted and P. Boeker appointed him to that post.

6. Treasurer Selection

P. Boeker proposed that R. E. Schmidt continue as treasurer of ITS if he were to accept. R. E. Schmidt accepted and B. Boeker appointed him to continue serving as treasurer.

7. ITS Fellows Program

It was suggested in earlier conversation and correspondence from J. B. Beard to P. Boeker and F. Ledeboer that a fellows program be initiated for ITS similar to those now in effect in other scientific societies. Considerable discussion ensued both pro and con, but in the end it was decided to table the proposal until the next meeting at the Fourth ITRC.

Meeting adjourned at 18:22.

Respectfully submitted by Fred B. Ledeboer, ITS Secretary.

Minutes

Executive Committee Meeting

12 July 1977, 15:00
Penta Hotel, Munich, West Germany

Present: President P. Boeker, J. B. Beard (non-voting for R. R. Davis), K. Ehara, F. B. Ledeboer, R. E. Schmidt, W. Skirde, J. E. van der Horst
Absent: R. E. Engel, A. C. Ferguson, R. L. Morris

Meeting called to order by President P. Boeker

Fellows & Awards Program for ITS

P. Boeker opposed the proposal made by J. B. Beard earlier because it could lead to misunderstandings among members from countries where such programs are not known. The proposal was tabled after considerable discussion both pro and con.

Proposal for 1981 Nominating Committee

President Elect	C. M. Switzer, Canada
Immediate Past President	P. Boeker, West Germany
Past Past President	R. R. Davis, USA

plus three members from countries other than the above:

M. Peterson, Denmark
B. Konicek, Czechoslovakia
J. P. Shildrick, United Kingdom
J. E. van der Horst, Netherlands (alternate)

Paper Quality

A lengthy discussion ensued on paper quality. An effort should be made to keep non-research papers out of the program. This would save time, and thus could allow more time for the presentation of research work.

The Executive Committee recommended the following guidelines for the next ITRC:

1. Two to three invitational papers should be presented.
2. Ten minutes should be allowed for minor research papers.
3. 15 to 20 minutes should be schedules for major work.
4. Parallel sessions should be held on separate interest areas.

Meeting adjourned at 16:15.

Respectfully submitted by F. B. Ledeboer, ITS Secretary.

Summary of Executive Committee Members serving the International Turfgrass Society.

Executive committee	First 1969	Second 1973	Third 1977	Fourth 1981
President	J. B. Beard	R. R. Davis	P. Boeker	C. M. Switzer
Vice President	B. Langvad	B. Langvad	J. P. van der Horst	H. Vos
Secretary	J. R. Escritt	J. R. Escritt	F. B. Ledeboer	F. B. Ledeboer
Past President		J. B. Beard	R. R. Davis	P. Boeker
Directors:		W. H. Daniel	R. E. Engel	W. A. Adams
		C. M. Switzer	K. Ehara	K. Ehara
		J. P. van der Horst	A. C. Ferguson	W. W. Huffine
			R. L. Morris	P. Mansat
			W. Skirde	D. K. Taylor
Treasurer	J. R. Watson	R. E. Schmidt	R. E. Schmidt	R. E. Schmidt
Historian	--	--	J. B. Beard	J. B. Beard

Full Membership Meeting

President P. Boeker called the full membership meeting to order at 17:07 on 12 July 1977, at the Penta Hotel, Munich, West Germany, after the conclusion of the formal program of paper presentations. He sincerely thanked all participating members for their fine efforts in making the Third ITRC successful. He also paid particular tribute to those who helped smooth the technical ways for translation of all presented papers into two other languages. Special words of gratitude also were directed at those who assisted in all other areas, in particular during field trips and pre- as well as post-conference tours.

1. Site Selection for the 1981 International Turfgrass Research Conference

Invitations for the 1981 conference were received from Japan and Canada. A vote was conducted by secret ballot. A count of the votes revealed that the 1981 conference will be held at the University of Guelph, Ontario, Canada.

2. ITS Membership Fee

It was proposed by the Executive Committee that a $10.00 (U.S.) annual membership fee should be charged to cover proceedings printing costs and other ITRC operating expenses.

R. E. Engel made a motion, seconded by J. F. Shoulders, that the total fee for the 4-year period be reduced to $30.00 (U.S.) if it is paid before 12 July 1978. The motion carried.

The proposal to levy a membership fee also carried by a majority voice vote.

3. Election of 1977–1981 Executive Committee

The Nominating Committee proposed a new slate of officers consisting of the following:

President:	C. M. Switzer, Canada
Vice President:	H. Vos, Netherlands
Secretary:	F. B. Ledeboer, USA
Past President:	P. Boeker, West Germany
Directors:	W. A. Adams, United Kingdom
	K. Ehara, Japan
	W. W. Huffine, USA
	P. Mansat, France
	D. K. Taylor, Canada

The new slate of officers was elected by majority voice vote for each individual office and as a group for the directors.

4. Proposed 1981 Nominating Committee

The Executive Committee proposed the following new Nominating Committee:

President Elect	C. M. Switzer, Canada
Immediate Past President	P. Boeker, West Germany
Past Past President	R. R. Davis, USA
Members for Other Countries	M. Peterson, Denmark
	B. Konicek, Czechoslovakia
	J. P. Shildrick, United Kingdom

The new Nominating Committee was elected by acclamation.

5. Induction of the New President

P. Boeker then asked for the new president to step forward. President-Elect C. M. Switzer thanked the membership for the confidence expressed by the positive vote for Canada. He assured everybody that he would work hard to make the 1981 ITRC in Canada as rewarding and successful as the one in Munich.

After the conclusion of the business meeting, C. M. Switzer asked to meet with the new Executive Committee to make plans for preliminary meetings in preparation for the 1981 ITRC.

6. Resolution to the Organizers of the 1977 Conference

It was moved by J. F. Shoulders, and seconded by A. C. Ferguson, that the participants of the Third ITRC express their sincere appreciation to Peter Boeker and his associates for their excellent preparations and arrangements for the conference and that an appropriate certificate be prepared expressing this gratitude and be presented to P. Boeker.

The motion carried by acclamation.

With closing words by P. Boeker expressing hope that all would again attend the 1981 meetings, he bid everyone a hearty farewell and enjoyable post-conference tour.

The meeting was adjourned at 17:40.

Respectfully submitted by Fred B. Ledeboer, ITS Secretary.

Treasurer's Reports

I. International Turfgrass Society Financial Statement as of July 1977

Saving Certificate (mature date 9/10/77) @ 6½ % interest	$1,000.00
Saving Certificate (mature date 12/7/77) @ 7¼ % interest	$5,000.00
Passbook Savings @ 5¼ % interest	$1,705.59
Total	$7,705.59

Respectfully submitted,

Richard E. Schmidt
ITS Treasurer
Agronomy Department
VPI and SU
Blacksburg, VA 24061 USA

II. Several attempts to obtain a Financial Statement for the Third International Turfgrass Research Conference were unsuccessful.

Glossary of Turfgrass Terms

Aeration, mechanical (*see* Cultivation, turf)

Aerify (*see* Cultivation, turf)

Amendment, physical—Any substance, such as sand, calcined clay, peat, and sawdust, added to soil for the purpose of altering physical conditions.

Artificial turf—A synthetic surface, simulating turf.

Ball mark—A depression and/or tear in the surface of a turf, usually a green, made by the impact of a ball.

Ball roll—The distance a ball moves (i) after striking the ground upon termination of its air flight, (ii) as the result of a putting stroke, or (iii) as a result of hand-imparted motion as in lawn bowling.

Bed knife—Stationary bottom blade of a reel mower against which the reel blades turn to produce a shearing cut. The bed knife is carried in the mower frame at a fixed distance from the reel axis and an adjustable fixed distance above the plane of travel.

Bench setting—Height the cutting plane (bed knife or rotating blade tip) of a mower is set above a hard, level surface.

Blend, seed—A combination of two or more cultivars of a single species.

Broadcast sprigging—Vegetative turf establishment by broadcasting stolons, rhizomes, or tillers and covering with soil.

Brushing—The practice of moving a brush against the surface of a turf to lift non-vertical stolons and/or leaves before mowing to produce a uniform surface of erect leaves.

Bunchgrass (*see* Bunch-type growth)

Bunch-type growth—Plant development by intravaginal tillering at or near the soil surface without the formation of rhizomes or stolons.

Calcined clay—Clay minerals, such as montmorillonite and attapulgite, that have been fired at high temperatures to obtain absorbant, stable, granular particles; used as amendments in soil modification.

Castings, earthworm (wormcasts)—Soil and plant remains excreted and deposited by earthworms in or on the turf surface or in their burrows; form relatively stable soil granules that can be objectionable on closely mowed turf by producing an uneven surface.

Catcher—A detachable enclosure on a mower used to collect clippings; also called basket, bag, or box.

Centrifugal spreader—An applicator from which dry, particulate material is broadcast as it drops onto a spinning disc or blade beneath the hopper.

Chemical trimming—Using herbicides or chemical growth regulators to limit turfgrass growth around trees, borders, monuments, walks, etc.

Cleavage plane, sod—A zone of potential separation at the interface between the underlying soil and an upper soil layer adhering to transplanted sod. Such separation is most commonly a problem when soils of different textures are placed one over another.

Clipping removal—Collecting leaves cut by mowing and removing them from the turf.

Clippings—Leaves and, in some cases, stems cut off by mowing.

Clonal planting—Vegetative establishment using plants of a single genotype placed at a spacing of 1 m or more.

Cold water insoluble nitrogen (WIN)—A form of fertilizer N not soluble in cold water (25°C).

Cold water soluble nitrogen (WSN)—A form of fertilizer N soluble in cold water (25°C).

Colorant—A dye, pigment, or paint-like material applied to turf to create a favorable green color when the grass is discolored or damaged.

Combing—Using a comb, with metal teeth or flexible tines, fastened immediately in front of a reel mower to lift stolons and procumbant shoots so they can be cut by the mower.

Controlled released fertilizer (*see* Slow release fertilizer).

Cool season turfgrass—Turfgrass species best adapted to growth during cool, moist periods of the year; commonly having temperature optimums of 15 to 24°C (60 to 75°F); e.g. bentgrasses, bluegrasses, fescues, and ryegrasses.

Coring—A method of turf cultivation in which soil cores are removed by hollow tines or spoons.

Cover, winter protection (*see* Winter protection cover).

Creeping growth habit—Plant development by extravaginal stem growth at or near the soil surface with lateral spreading by rhizomes and/or stolons.

Cultipacker seeder—A mechanical seeder designed to place turfgrass seeds in a prepared seedbed at a shallow soil depth followed by firming of the soil around the seed. It usually consists of a pull-type tractor rear-mounted unit having a seed box positioned between the larger front, ridged roller and an offset, smaller rear roller.

Cultivation, turf—Applied to turf, refers to working of the soil without destruction of the turf, e.g., coring, slicing, grooving, forking, shattering, spiking, or other means.

Cup cutter—A hollow cylinder with a sharpened lower edge used to cut the hole for a cup in a green or to replace small spots of damaged turf.

Cushion (*see* Resiliency).

Cutting height—Of a mower, the distance between the plane of travel (base of wheel, roller or skid) and the parallel plane of cut.

Density, shoot (*see* Shoot density).

Dethatch—The procedure of removing an excessive thatch accumulation either (i) mechanically as by vertical cutting or (ii) biologically as by topdressing with soil.

Divot—A small piece of turf severed from the soil by a golf club or the twisting-turning action of a cleated shoe.

Dormant seeding—Planting seed during late fall or early winter after temperatures become too low for seed germination to occur until the following spring.

Dormant sodding—Transplanting sod during late fall or early winter after temperatures become too low for shoot growth and rapid rooting.

Dormant turf—Turfs which have temporarily ceased shoot growth as a result of extended drought, heat, or cold stress.

Dry spot (*see* Localized dry spot).

Effective cutting height—The height of the cutting plane above the soil surface at which the turf is mowed.

Establishment, turf—Root and shoot growth following seed germination or vegetative planting needed to form a mature, stable turf.

Fertigation—The application of fertilizer through an irrigation system.

Fertilizer burn (*see* Foliar burn).

Flail mower—A mower that cuts turf by impact of free swinging blades rotating in a vertical cutting plane relative to the turf surface (*see also* Impact mowing).

Foliar burn—Injury to shoot tissue caused by dehydration due to contact with high concentrations of chemicals; e.g., certain fertilizers and pesticides.

Footprinting, frost—Discolored areas of dead leaf tissue in the shape of foot impressions that develop after walking on live, frosted turfgrass leaves.

Footprinting, wilt—Temporary foot impressions left in a turf when flaccid leaves of grass plants suffer incipient wilt and have insufficient turgor to spring back after treading.

Forking—A method of turf cultivation in which a spading fork or similar solid tine device is used to make holes in the soil.

French drain (*see* Slit trench drain).

Frequency of clip—Distance of forward travel between successive cuts of mower blades.

Grading—Establishing surface soil elevations and contours prior to planting.

Grain, turf—The undesirable, procumbently oriented growth of grass leaves, shoots, and stolons on greens; a rolling ball tends to be deflected from a true course in the direction of orientation.

Grooving—A method of turf cultivation in which vertical, rotating blades cut continuous slits through the turf and into the soil; with soil, thatch, and green plant material being displaced.

Hole punching (*see* Cultivation).

Hot water insoluble nitrogen (HWIN)—A form of fertilizer nitrogen not soluble in hot water (100°C); used to determine the activity index of ureaforms (*see* Nitrogen activity index).

Hydraulic seeding (*see* Hydroseeding).

Hydroplanting—Planting vegetative propagules (e.g. stolons) in a water mixture by pumping through a nozzle which sprays the mixture onto the plant bed. The water-propagule mixture may also contain fertilizer and a mulch.

Hydroseeding—Planting seed in a water mixture by pumping through a nozzle which sprays the mixture onto a seedbed. The water mixture may also contain fertilizer and a mulch.

Impact mowing—Mowing in which the inertia of the grass blade resists the impact of rapidly moving blade and is cut; this is characteristic of rotary and vertical mowers and in contrast to the shearing cut of reel and sickle bar mowers.

Interseeding—Seeding between sod plugs, sod strips, rows of sprigs, or stolons.

Irrigation, automatic—A water application system in which valves are automatically activated, either hydraulically or electrically, at times preset on a controller. The system may or may not be integrated with an automatic sensing unit.

Irrigation, manual—Water application using hand set and hand valved equipment.

Irrigation, semiautomatic—A water application system in which valves respond directly to a manually operated remote-control switch.

Irrigation, subsurface—Application of water below the soil surface by injection or by manipulation of the water table.

Knitting (*see* Sod knitting).

Land rolling (*see* Rolling).

Lapping, mower (backlapping)—Backward turning of the reel against the bed knife while a fluid dispersed grinding compound is applied. Lapping hones the cutting faces and mates the reel and bed knife to a precise fit for quality mowing.

Lateral shoot—Shoots originating from vegetative buds in the axils of leaves or from the nodes of stems, rhizomes, or stolons.

Lawn—Ground covered with a closely mowed vegetation, usually grass.

Lawngrass (*see* Turfgrass).

Layering, soil—Stratification within a soil profile, which may affect conductivity and retention of water, soil aeration, and rooting; can be due to construction design, topdressing with different textured amendments, inadequate on-site mixing of soil amendments, or blowing and washing of sand or soil.

Leaf mulcher—A machine that lifts leaves from a turf and shreds them small enough to fall down within the turfgrass canopy.

Liquid fertilization—A method of fluid nutrient application in which dissolved fertilizer is applied as a solution.

Localized dry spot—A dry spot of turf and soil surrounded by more moist conditions, which resists rewetting by normal irrigation or rainfall; is often associated with thatch, fungal activity, shallow soil over buried material, compacted soil, or elevated sites in the terrain.

Low temperature discoloration—The loss of chlorophyll and associated green color which occurs in turfgrasses under low temperature stress.

Maintenance, turf (*see* Turfgrass culture).

Mat—Thatch which has been intermixed with mineral matter that develops between the zone of green vegetation and the original soil surface; commonly associated with greens that have been topdressed.

Matting—Dragging steel door matting over the turf surface to work-in topdressing and smooth the surface; also used to break-up and work-in soil cores lifted out by coring or grooving.

Mixture, seed—A combination of two or more species.

Monostand—A turfgrass community composed of one cultivar.

Mowing frequency—The number of mowings per unit of time, expressed as mowings per week; or the interval in days between one mowing and the next.

Mowing height (*see* Cutting height).

Mowing pattern—The orientations of travel while mowing turf. Patterns may be regularly changed to distribute wear and compaction, to aid in grain control, and to create visually aesthetic striping effects.

Mulch blower—A machine using forced air to distribute particles of mulch over newly seeded sites.

Nitrogen activity index (AI)—Applied to ureaformadehyde compounds and mixtures containing such compounds; the AI is the percentage of cold water insoluble N that is soluble in hot water. $AI = (\%\ WIN - \%\ HWIN \times 100)/\%\ WIN$.

Nursegrass (*see* Temporary grass).

Nursery, stolon (*see* Stolon nursery).

Nursery, turfgrass—An area where turfgrasses are propagated for vegetative increase to provide a source of stolons, sprigs, or sod for vegetative planting.

Off-site mixing—Mixing soil and amendments for soil modification at a place other than the planting site.

Overseeding—Seeding into an existing turf (*see also* Winter overseeding).

Pegging sod—Use of pegs to hold sod in place on slopes and waterways until transplant rooting occurs.

Planting bed—A soil area prepared for vegetative propagation or seed germination and establishment of turf.

Plugging—Vegetative propagation of turfgrasses by plugs or small pieces of sod. A method of establishing vegetatively propagated turfgrasses as well as repairing damaged areas.

Poling—Using a long (bamboo) switch or pole to remove dew and exudations from turf by switching the pole in an arc while in contact with the turf surface; also used to break up clumps of clippings and earthworm casts.

Polystand—A turfgrass community composed of two or more cultivars and/or species.

Pregerminated seed—Preconditioning seed prior to planting by placing in a moist, oxygenated environment at optimum temperatures to favor more rapid germination after seeding.

Press rolling—A mechanical planting designed to push sprigs or stolons into the soil followed by firming of the soil around the vegetative propagules.

Pseudo thatch—The upper surface layer above a thatch which is composed of relatively undecomposed leaf remnants and clippings.

Puffiness—Sponge-like condition of turf that results in an irregular surface.

Rebuilding—The practices which result in complete change of a turf area.

Recuperative potential—The ability of turfgrasses to recover from injury.

Reel mower—A mower that cuts turf by means of a rotating reel of helical blades which pass across a stationary blade (bed knife) fixed to the mower frame; this action gives a shearing type of cut.

Reestablishment, turf—A procedure involving (i) complete turf removal, (ii) soil tillage, and (iii) seeding or vegetative establishment of new turf; does not encompass rebuilding.

Release rate, fertilizer—The rate of nutrient release following fertilizer application. Water-soluble fertilizers are termed *fast-release,* while insoluble or coated soluble fertilizers are referred to as *slow-release.*

Renovation, turf—Improvement usually involving weed control and replanting into existing live and/or dead vegetation; does not encompass reestablishment.

Reseeding, turf—To seed again, usually soon after an initial seeding has failed, to achieve satisfactory establishment.

Residual response, fertilizer—Delayed or continued turfgrass response to slow-release fertilizers; lasting longer than the usual response from water-soluble fertilizers.

Resiliency—The capability of a turf to spring back when balls, shoes, or other objects strike the surface; thus, providing a cushioning effect.

Rippling—A wave or washboard pattern on the surface of mowed grass; usually resulting from mower maladjustment, too fast a rate of mower travel; or too low a frequency of clip for the cutting height.

Roller, water ballast—A hollow, cylindrical body, the weight of which can be varied by the amount of water added, used for leveling, smoothing, and firming soil.

Root pruning, trees—Judicious cutting of tree roots to reduce their competition with an associated turf.

Rotary mower—A powered mower that cuts turf by high speed impact of a blade or blades rotating in a horizontal cutting plane.

Row sprigging—Planting of sprigs in rows or furrows.

Scald, turf—The injury of shoots which collapse and turn brown under conditions where intense sunlight heats relatively shallow standing water to lethal temperatures.

Scalping—The removal of an excessive quantity of green shoots at any one mowing that results in a stubbly, brown appearance caused by exposing the stems, stolons, and dead leaves.

Scarifying, turf (*see* Vertical cutting).

Scorching (*see* Scald).

Scum—A layer of algae on the soil surface of thin turf; drying can produce a somewhat impervious layer that impairs subsequent shoot emergence.

Seed mat—A fabricated mat with seed (and possibly fertilizer) applied to one side; the mat serves as the vehicle to (i) apply seed (and fertilizer), (ii) control erosion, and (iii) provide a favorable microenvironment for seed germination and establishment.

Seeding, dormant (*see* Dormant seeding).

Semiarid turfgrass—Turfgrass species adapted to grow and persist in semiarid regions without irrigation, such as buffalograss, blue grama, and sideoats grama.

Settling, soil—A lowering of the soil surface previously loosened by tillage or by excavation and refilling; occurs naturally in time, and can be accelerated mechanically by tamping, rolling, cultipacking, or watering.

Shattering—A method of turf cultivation involving fragmentation of a rigid or brittle soil mass usually by a vibrating mechanical mole device.

Shaving, turf—The cutting and removal of all verdure, thatch, and excess mat by means of a sod cutter followed by turfgrass regrowth from underground lateral stems. Used on bowling greens, especially bermudagrass.
Shoot density—The number of shoots per unit area.
Short-lived perennial—Turfgrasses normally expected to live only 2 to 4 years.
Sickle bar mower—A mower that cuts grass by means of horizontal, rapidly oscillating blades which shear the gathered grass against stationary blades.
Slicing—A method of turf cultivation in which vertically rotating, flat blades slice intermittently through the turf and the soil.
Slit trench drain—A narrow trench (usually 5 to 10 cm wide) backfilled to the surface with a material, such as sand, gravel, or crushed rock, to facilitate surface or subsurface drainage.
Slow-release fertilizer—Designates a rate of dissolution less than is obtained for completely water-soluble fertilizers; may involve compounds which dissolve slowly, materials that must be decomposed by microbial activity, or soluble compounds coated with substances highly impervious to water.
Sod—Plugs, squares, or strips of turfgrass with adhering soil to be used in vegetative planting.
Sod cutter—A device to sever turf from the ground; the length and thickness of the sod being cut is adjustable.
Sod cutting (*see* Sod harvesting).
Sod harvesting—Mechanical cutting of sod, for sale and/or transfer to a planting site, with a minimum of soil to facilitate ease of handling and rooting.
Sod heating—Heat accumulation in tightly stacked sod; may reach lethal temperatures.
Sod knitting—Sod rooting to the extent that newly transplanted sod is held firmly in place.
Sod production—The culture of turf to a quality and maturity which allows harvesting and transplanting.
Sod rooting—The growth of new roots into the underlying soil from nodes in the sod.
Sod strength—The relative ability of sod to resist tearing during harvesting, handling, and transplanting; in research, the mechanical force (kg) required to tear apart a sod when subjected to a uniformly applied force.
Sod transplanting—Transfer to and planting of sod on a new turf area.
Sodding—Planting turf by laying sod.
Sodding, dormant (*see* Dormant sodding).
Soil heating (*see* Soil warming).
Soil mix—A prepared mixture used as a growth medium for turfgrass.
Soil modification—Alteration of soil characteristics by adding soil amendments; commonly used to improve physical conditions of turf soils.
Soil probe—A soil sampling tool usually having a hollow cylinder with a cutting edge at the lower end.
Soil screen—A screen used to remove clods, coarse fragments, and trash from soil; may be stationary, oscillating, or, in the case of cylindrical screens, rotating.
Soil shredder—A machine which crushes or pulverizes large soil aggregates and clods to facilitate uniform soil mixing and topdressing application.
Soil warming—The artificial heating of turf from below the surface, usually by electrical means, to prevent soil freezing and maintain a green turf during winter.
Soiling (*see* Topdressing).
Solid sodding (*see* Sodding).
Spiking—A method of turf cultivation in which solid tines or flat, pointed blades penetrate the turf and soil surface to a shallow depth.

Spongy turf (*see* Puffiness).

Spoon, coring—A method of turf cultivation involving curved, hollow, spoon-like tines that remove small soil cores and leave openings in the sod.

Spot seeding—The seeding of small, usually barren or sparsely covered areas within established turf.

Spot sodding—The repair of small areas of damaged turf using plugs or small pieces of sod.

Sprig—A stolon, rhizome, tiller, or combination used to establish turf.

Sprigging—Vegetative planting by placing sprigs in furrows or small holes.

Spring greenup—The initial seasonal appearance of green shoots as spring temperature and moisture conditions become favorable; thus, breaking winter dormancy.

Spudding—The removal of individual weedy plants with a small spade-like tool which severs the root deep in the soil so the weed can be lifted from the turf manually.

Stolon nursery—An area used for producing stolons for propagation.

Stolonize—Vegetative planting by broadcasting stolons over a prepared soil and covering by topdressing or press rolling.

Strip sodding—Laying of sod strips spaced at intervals, usually across a slope; turf establishment depends on spreading of the grass to form a complete cover; sometimes the area between the strips is interseeded.

Subgrade—The soil elevation constructed at a sufficient depth below the final grade to allow for the desired thickness of topsoil, root zone mix, or other material.

Summer dormancy—The cessation of growth and subsequent death of leaves of perennial plants due to heat and/or moisture stress.

Synthetic turf (*see* Artificial turf).

Syringing—Spraying turf with small amounts of water to: (i) dissipate accumulated energy in the leaves by evaporating free surface water, (ii) prevent or correct a leaf water deficit, particularly wilt, and (iii) remove dew, frost, and exudates from the turf surface.

Temporary grass—Grass species not expected to persist in a turf; and thus are used as temporary cover.

Texture—In turf, refers to the composite leaf width, taper, and arrangement.

Thatch—A loose intermingled organic layer of dead and living shoots, stems, and roots that develops between the zone of green vegetation and the soil surface.

Thatch control—Preventing excessive thatch accumulation by cultural manipulation and/or reducing excess thatch by mechanical or biological means.

Tip burn—Leaf tip necrosis resulting from lethal internal water stress caused by desiccation, salt, or pesticide accumulation.

Topdressing—A prepared soil mix added to the turf surface and worked-in by brushing, matting, raking, and/or irrigation (i) to smooth a green surface, (ii) to firm a turf by working soil in among stolons and thatch forming materials, (iii) to enhance thatch decomposition and, (iv) to cover stolons or sprigs during vegetative planting; also the act of applying topdressing materials to turf.

Topsoil planting—A modification of stolonizing which involves covering the area with soil containing viable rhizomes and/or stolons for the purpose of establishing a turf cover.

Transitional climatic zone—The suboptimal zone between the cool and warm climates where both warm and cool season grasses can be grown.

Trimming—Cutting edges and borders of turf to form clearly defined lines.

Turf—A covering of mowed vegetation, usually a turfgrass, growing intimately with an upper soil stratum of intermingled roots and stems.

Turfgrass—A species or cultivar of grass, usually of spreading habit, which is maintained as a mowed turf.

Turfgrass color—The composite visual color of a turfgrass community perceived by the human eye.

Turfgrass community—An aggregation of individual turfgrass plants that have mutual relationships with the environment as well as among the individual plants.

Turfgrass culture—The composite cultural practices involved in growing turfgrasses for purposes such as lawns, greens, sports facilities, and roadsides.

Turfgrass management—Development of turf standards and goals which are achieved by planning and directing labor, capital, and equipment with the objective of manipulating cultural practices to achieve those standards and goals.

Turfgrass quality—The composite, subjective visual assessment of the degree to which a turf conforms to an agreed standard of uniformity, density, texture, growth habit, smoothness, and color.

Turfgrass uniformity—The visual assessment of the degree to which a turfgrass community is free from variations in color, density, and texture across the surface.

Ureaformaldehyde (UF)—A synthetic slow release N fertilizer known under the generic name, ureaform, and consisting mainly of methylene urea polymers of different lengths and solubilities; formed by reacting urea and formaldehyde.

Vegetative propagation—Asexual propagation using pieces of vegetation, i.e., sprigs or sod pieces.

Verdure—The layer of green living plant tissue remaining above the soil following mowing.

Vertical cutter—A powered mechanical device having vertically rotating blades or tines that cut into the face of a turf below the cutting height for the purpose of controlling thatch and/or grain. The tine type is also referred to as a *power rake*.

Vertical mower—A powered mower that cuts turf by high speed impact of blades moving in a vertical plane; the blades can be of varied shapes and fixed or free swinging (flail).

Warm season turfgrass—Turfgrass species best adapted to growth during the warmer part of the year; usually dormant during cold weather or injured by it; commonly having temperature optimums of 27 to 35°C (80 to 95°F); e.g., bahiagrass, bermudagrass, St. Augustinegrass, and zoysiagrass.

Washboard effect (*see* Rippling).

Watering-in—Watering turf immediately after the application of chemicals to dissolve and/or wash the materials from the plant surface into the soil.

Wear—The collective direct injurious effects of traffic on a turf; is distinct from the indirect effects of traffic caused by soil compaction.

Wet wilt—Wilting of turf in the presence of free soil water when evapotranspiration exceeds water uptake by the roots.

Whipping pole—A bamboo stalk or similar pole used in poling turf.

Wind burn, turf—Death and browning, most commonly occurring on the uppermost leaves of grasses, caused by atmospheric desiccation.

Winter desiccation—The death of leaves or plants by drying during winter dormancy.

Winter discoloration (*see* Low temperature discoloration).

Winter fertilization—A late fall to winter application of fertilizer to turfgrasses at rates which maintain green color without adverse physiological effects; used in regions characterized by moderate winters for the species involved.

Winter overseeding—Seeding cool season turfgrasses over warm season turfgrasses at or near the start of winter dormancy; used in mild climates to provide green, growing turf during the winter period when warm season species are brown and dormant.

Winter protection cover—A barrier placed over a turf to prevent winter desiccation, insulate against low temperature stress, and stimulate early spring green-up.

Winterkill—Any injury to turfgrass plants that occurs during the winter period.

SUBJECT INDEX

C

D

Q

R